Family Planning, Sterility, and Population Growth

FAMILY PLANNING STERILITY AND POPULATION GROWTH

Ronald Freedman

PROFESSOR OF SOCIOLOGY
AND RESEARCH ASSOCIATE
OF THE SURVEY RESEARCH CENTER
THE UNIVERSITY OF MICHIGAN

Pascal K. Whelpton

DIRECTOR, SCRIPPS FOUNDATION FOR RESEARCH
IN POPULATION PROBLEMS, MIAMI UNIVERSITY

Arthur A. Campbell

ASSISTANT PROFESSOR, SCRIPPS FOUNDATION FOR RESEARCH
IN POPULATION PROBLEMS, MIAMI UNIVERSITY

McGRAW-HILL BOOK COMPANY, INC.

1959   New York   Toronto   London

FAMILY PLANNING, STERILITY, AND POPULATION GROWTH

PREFACE

To improve our understanding of American population trends we must learn more than we know now about the factors which determine the number of children that married couples have and the time when they have them. As a beginning we need facts about how many children couples want, and to what extent this differs from the number they expect either because they are physically unable to reach the wanted number or because they exceed the wanted number through unwillingness to adopt family-limitation methods or through failure to use them effectively. This book presents the results of a first study to obtain approximations of these facts on a national scale and shows their implications for family growth and population trends.

These materials are potentially important to many kinds of readers. For the average man and woman, descriptions of how families grow come close to central personal concerns. Most of us are reared in our parents' families and then face a series of crucial decisions in creating new families of our own. Beyond these personal concerns the intelligent citizen needs to be informed about how future family growth will affect population trends, which influence many aspects of our society. Students should find this material helpful as a supplement to general courses in demography, marriage and the family, public health statistics, and modern social problems. It should be especially valuable for students in advanced courses relating to fertility and population projection. Our materials should be of much interest to doctors, public health workers, businessmen, government planners, social scientists, and many others who deal professionally with problems affected by trends in family size and population.

Because the potential audience for the book is so wide and varied, we have attempted to present the results and methods so that they will be clear to the intelligent layman. Obtaining the facts and interpreting them have involved some fairly complex steps; most of the detailed technical explanations have been placed in appendixes, where they are easily available to the scholar but need not concern the general reader.

To simplify the presentation further, some of the statistical materials are excluded entirely. Among them are tables giving the actual numbers of cases on which the rates and percentages of some tables are based. These tables have been mimeographed as Appendix H and may be obtained by sending 25 cents to the Scripps Foundation for Research in Population Problems, Miami University, Oxford, Ohio. Also excluded are tables with cross classifications not considered essential for the general reader. Interested scholars may make arrangements for consulting them.

Acknowledgments. A research project of the magnitude of this study of the fertility of American couples was possible only through the co-operation of several institutions and many individuals. The study was conducted jointly by the Scripps Foundation for Research in Population Problems, Miami University, and the Survey Research Center, University of Michigan. The principal financial support was a grant from the Rockefeller Foundation. Additional funds were provided by the Population Council and the Scripps Foundation. Neither the Rockefeller Foundation nor the Population Council is responsible in any way for the findings and interpretations of the authors.

Two distinguished sponsoring committees endorsed the scientific purposes and auspices of the study in letters distributed to respondents. This undoubtedly contributed to the cordial reception the interviewers received. The general sponsoring committee consisted of persons from several fields. Their names, and their affiliations when the sponsoring letter was used, are as follows:[1]

Mr. Samuel W. Anderson, Assistant Secretary of Commerce for International Affairs

Dr. Detlev W. Bronk, President, The Rockefeller Institute

Dr. Harry J. Carman, Member, Board of Higher Education, New York City

Rev. Harry Emerson Fosdick, Pastor Emeritus, Riverside Church

Mr. Ralph McGill, Editor, *The Atlanta Constitution*

Dr. Lowell J. Reed, President, The Johns Hopkins University

Miss Anna Lord Strauss, Former President, League of Women Voters of the United States

Mr. Charles P. Taft, Former President, Federal Council of Churches of Christ in America; Mayor, Cincinnati, Ohio

Dr. Rufus B. von KleinSmid, Chancellor, University of Southern California

The medical sponsoring committee consisted of the following:[1]

Dr. Russell R. De Alvarez, School of Medicine, University of Washington

Dr. Frank R. Lock, The Bowman Gray School of Medicine, Wake Forest College

[1] The members of the committee served as individuals, and not in any official capacity. Although the committee members endorsed the purposes of the study, they are not responsible for the findings or interpretations.

Dr. Bayard Carter, School of Medicine, Duke University

Dr. Frederick A. Coller, School of Medicine, University of Michigan

Dr. Nicholson J. Eastman, The Johns Hopkins Hospital, Baltimore

Dr. John E. Gordon, School of Public Health, Harvard University

Dr. Alan F. Guttmacher, The Mount Sinai Hospital, New York City

Dr. John Dale Owen, St. Mary's Hospital, Milwaukee

Dr. John Rock, Harvard Medical School, Free Hospital for Women

Dr. Howard C. Taylor, Jr., College of Physicians and Surgeons, Columbia University, The Presbyterian Hospital

Dr. Herbert F. Traut, Medical School, University of California

The interviewing and initial processing of the data were done by the staff of the Survey Research Center. Dr. Charles Cannell directed the field work. His national staff of over 150 field supervisors and interviewers showed enthusiasm and skill in locating and questioning the more than 3,000 eligible women in the sample of households. The high quality of their work was essential to the success of the study.

Many members of the Survey Research Center staff gave valuable assistance. We are especially grateful to Dr. Angus Campbell, Director, and to Dr. Leslie Kish, who was responsible for the design of the sample and counseled us wisely at various stages.

In addition to the three authors, the staff included at various times Dr. Norman Ryder, Scripps Foundation, and Dr. Jeanne Clare Ridley, Dr. David Goldberg, and Mr. Jack Beresford of the Sociology Department of the University of Michigan. Dr. Ryder participated in preparing the questionnaire and in processing the data until leaving the Scripps Foundation for the University of Wisconsin in September, 1956.

Professor David V. Glass of the London School of Economics kindly helped us with interpretations of British materials.

During the early phases of the study we were privileged to have the advice of the Steering Committee for the Development of Plans for New Studies of Factors Affecting Size of Family. The membership of this committee included Frank W. Notestein (Chairman), Ronald Freedman, Philip M. Hauser, Clyde V. Kiser, Frank Lorimer, Donald Marquis, Frederick Osborn, Lowell J. Reed, Pascal K. Whelpton, and the technical staff, Elliot G. Mishler, Charles F. Westoff, and Robert G. Potter, Jr.

Deborah Freedman gave valuable editorial and statistical assistance. Ruth W. Smith of the Scripps Foundation was especially helpful in the statistical work and outlining the figures.

The following persons assisted in developing the special sample of single women in various parts of the country: Dr. T. Stanton Dietrick, Florida State University; Dr. Eleanor Maccoby, Harvard University; Dr. Ruth Riemer, University of California; and Dr. Robert Winch, Northwestern University.

Although we are indebted to many persons and organizations and are deeply grateful for their assistance, we are completely responsible for the design of the study and the interpretation of the data collected.

Ronald Freedman
Pascal K. Whelpton
Arthur A. Campbell

CONTENTS

x   *Contents*

Chapter 1

BACKGROUND AND NATURE OF THE STUDY

This is a report on interviews with 2,713 young married women concerning the past and prospective growth of their families. The interviews covered such vital topics as births and miscarriages, sterility, methods of avoiding pregnancy, and the desired and expected number of children. For many of the women interviewed these topics concern the most important events in their lives. In their cumulative effect these events and expectations in the lives of individual families will have a great impact on the nation's history.

The decisions made by millions of couples about the number of children they will have are now determining the future size of our country's population. Migration, deaths, and births are the vital factors determining the rate at which a country grows. It seems unlikely that immigration will be large enough in the next few decades to affect substantially America's population increase. Our death rate is already low and unlikely to vary greatly in the near future, unless there is a disastrous war or some other catastrophe. The dynamic force in our population growth is the birth rate. This in turn depends in large measure on the decisions of couples about the number and spacing of their children and on the degree of success they have in carrying out these decisions.

From the perspective of history this is a unique situation. Over most of man's existence the size of the population of a tribe or nation has been determined primarily by its death rate or by the rate of migration into or out of its territory, for nearly all groups have had high birth rates. By and large the great *variations* in population size have occurred as the death rate rose with war, epidemics, and famine, or fell in the absence of these scourges. In some periods massive migration also produced large population gains for some areas at the expense of others. Usually such variations in mortality and migration occurred while the number of children borne by the average woman remained fairly constant at a high level. It is true that crude methods of contraception, as well as infanticide and abortion, already were being used long ago to limit family size in some groups and societies. However, there is little

1

evidence that such practices were ever sufficiently widespread or flexible to make possible short-run changes in average family size or in the spacing of children as a response to economic or social changes. Over most of human history neither the number nor the spacing of children has been subject to rational control or individual choice in the population at large.

The Decrease of Family Size in the Western World

In the last 150 years the widespread adoption of family limitation methods in the Western world has produced a radical change in the basis for population growth. In the United States, as in many other countries, there is now a rather general acceptance of the idea of deliberate regulation by each couple of the number and spacing of children in relation to its own needs and resources. Some groups are opposed to some of the motives for family limitation or to some of the methods used, but all major groups in our population now approve of family limitation under some conditions.

This general acceptance of family limitation followed an unprecedented fall in the death rate. These two events have had such profound effects on population trends that in combination they have been called "the vital revolution."

During the period when the idea and practice of family limitation were spreading, the death rate fell greatly in the United States and other Western nations. In most cases the population increased very rapidly in the period after 1750, because the death rate began to fall rapidly before the regulating of conception affected the birth rate. After the birth rate began to decline in the nineteenth century, it fell so sharply that the relative surplus of births over deaths diminished rapidly. Population continued to grow but at a lower rate as time went on. Just before World War II birth rates had fallen so far that in many Western countries the rate of natural increase was very low. In Austria and France there were more deaths than births in some years and the population decreased.[1] The historical trends of the birth and death rates are illustrated in Figures 1–1 and 1–2 for Great Britain and the United States.

The sharp decline occurring before World War II in the birth rates of Western countries resulted chiefly from smaller families rather than

[1] The death rate exceeded the birth rate in Austria during 1935–38 and in France during 1935–39. The population decreased slightly in Austria in these years, and in France from 1934 to 1936 and 1938 to 1939. Immigration prevented a decrease in France from 1936 to 1938. (*Demographic Yearbook, 1948*, United Nations, New York, 1949.)

from fewer or later marriages. In Great Britain, women married in the period 1862–69 had on the average 6.5 children after 25 years of marriage. The number of births within 25 years of marriage declined among

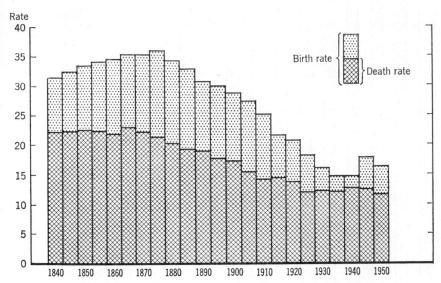

Fig. 1–1. Crude birth and death rates, England and Wales, 1840–1950. (Rates are 5-year averages centering on year indicated.)

the brides of each successive decade; those of 1925 had on the average only about 2.2 children. This downward trend is shown in the following figures:[2]

Date of marriage	Number of births per marriage
1862–69	6.5
1870–79	6.0
1880–86	5.4
1890–99	4.0
1900–09	3.4
1910–19	2.7
1920–24	2.4 (incomplete)
1925	2.2 (incomplete)

[2] D. V. Glass and E. Grebenik, *The Trend and Pattern of Fertility in Great Britain: A Report on the Family Census of 1946* (Papers of the Royal Commission on Population, vol. VI), H.M. Stationery Office, London, 1954, part I, *Report*, p. 131. See Appendix A, Note 1, for a description of these data. Permission to quote these and the other data or statements taken from the Report of the Royal Commission on Population and Papers of the Royal Commission on Population has been granted by the Controller of H.M. Stationery Office.

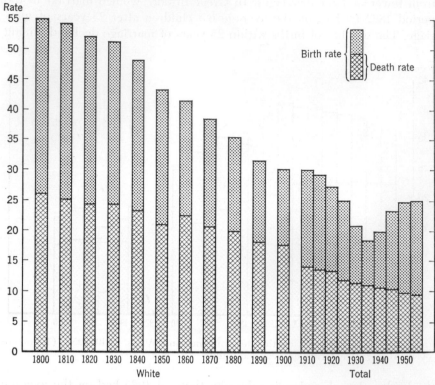

Fɪɢ. 1–2. Crude birth and death rates, United States, 1800–1955. (Rates are 5-year averages centering on year indicated.)

This sharp decline in average family size was accompanied by a radical change in the proportion of families of different sizes as illustrated below:[3]

No. of births	Date of marriage	
	About 1860	1925
Total	100	100
None	9	17
1 or 2	11	50
3 or 4	17	22
5 to 9	47	11
10 or more	16	—

[3] Royal Commission on Population, *Report,* H.M. Stationery Office, London, 1949, p. 26. These data are restricted to women who married under age 45 in the years specified and whose marriage was not broken by death or divorce before age 45.

In the short period of 65 years, Great Britain saw a dramatic shift from large families with five or more children to small families which typically had one or two children.

A roughly similar trend occurred in the United States, but the decline began earlier and from a larger average size of family. This is indicated by the crude birth rate for the white population of the United States, which fell from more than 50 per thousand in 1800 to about 18 during the depression years of the 1930s. It is shown more clearly by changes in the number of children borne by married women who lived to ages 45–49. The average number of births for all ever-married women of these ages in 1910 was about 4.7, but declined steadily to a low of 2.4 for the corresponding group in 1955. At the same time there was a marked shift from larger to smaller families as is shown below:[4]

No. of births	Ever-married women aged 45–49	
	1910	1955
Total	100	100
None	10	16
1 or 2	22	47
3 or 4	22	23
5 or 6	17	8
7 or more	29	6

The American women reaching middle age in 1955 had borne too few children to maintain a stationary population with the death rates of their generation.

There is little doubt that the main factor accounting for these declines in family size is the voluntary use of methods to regulate conception. For Great Britain the increase in the use of these methods is documented in the following figures:[5]

[4] The 1910 figures are from the Sixteenth Census of the United States, 1940, *Population, Differential Fertility 1940 and 1910, Fertility for States and Large Cities,* 1943, pp. 10 and 15. The 1955 figures are from unpublished data of the Scripps Foundation for Research in Population Problems. The decline in family size was larger than the difference between the 1910 and 1955 figures quoted here because the former are not adjusted for the births which were not reported to census enumerators.

[5] E. Lewis-Faning, *Report on an Enquiry into Family Limitation and Its Influence on Human Fertility during the Past Fifty Years* (Papers of the Royal Commission on Population, vol. 1), H.M. Stationery Office, London, 1949, p. 7. These data are for women still alive in 1946 who married before 45 and whose marriage was not broken by death or divorce before 45. Many of those marrying in the later years were younger than 45 when interviewed. For more information about this study see Appendix A, Note 18.

Date of marriage	Percentage using a method of family limitation at some time during married life
Before 1910	15
1910–19	40
1920–24	58
1925–29	61
1930–34	63
1935–39	66

Comparable figures for the United States are not available, but there is no reason to doubt a similar trend. The proportion of couples reporting the use of methods to prevent conception is higher in the present investigation (70 per cent) than that cited for Great Britain in 1935–39. A still higher proportion (89 per cent) was found in an intensive study which was conducted in Indianapolis in 1941, but that study was limited to native white Protestant couples married 12 to 15 years.[6]

The decline in the birth rate was so rapid and family size reached such low levels in many Western countries just before World War II that some of the leading demographers were pointing to the possibility of static or falling population in the last half of this century for several of these countries, including the United States. Most students of the problem expected that family size and the birth rate would continue to decline as more and more people learned to use family limitation methods successfully.

Before World War II a major controversy, carried on among many economists and business analysts, centered on the probable effect on the economy of a stable or a declining population. These issues have not yet been resolved. They receive much less attention now, however, because an increasing population is taken for granted in most projections of economic growth.

The "Baby Boom" after World War II

During or following World War II most Western countries experienced a sharp rise in the birth rate. By 1952, however, birth rates in many of these countries had fallen considerably from postwar peaks. The United States is one of the few countries in which a high postwar birth rate has continued to the present. The extent and duration of the "baby boom" was unanticipated by most population experts. It has led

[6] P. K. Whelpton and Clyde V. Kiser (eds.), *Social and Psychological Factors Affecting Fertility*, Milbank Memorial Fund, New York, 1950, vol. 2, p. 212; or "VI. The Planning of Fertility," *Milbank Memorial Fund Quarterly*, vol. 25, no. 1, p. 66, January, 1947. For further information about this study and its findings see Appendix A, Note 2c.

to a search for new concepts and new methods to use in measuring and analyzing our fertility and population trends. The present investigation is, in part, an attempt to understand the upsurge in the birth rate and to chart its future course by means of data of a type not previously available.

In retrospect, population experts can see that the possibility of a baby boom was implicit earlier in the increased use of methods for deliberately planning family size. Planned families need not be small families. Couples who plan for a small number of children at one time can plan for a larger number at another time. The groups in our population whose birth rates were low in the depression years are usually those whose birth rates rose more after the war, namely, the better educated, the white-collar workers, the urban population, and the higher-income groups. These are also the groups known to use family limitation methods most extensively. Apparently, the groups who effectively planned to have fewer births in the depression also planned to have more births in the favorable postwar years.

Family planning also creates the possibility of shifts in the timing of births even when the total number of children per family remains constant. Changes from favorable to unfavorable economic and social conditions (or the reverse) may bring changes in the spacing of children which produce violent short-run fluctuations in annual birth rates, even though the average size of completed families is stable. Here is an extreme (and unrealistic) example of how this can happen. Suppose that a few prosperous decades are followed by a decade of depression and then a return to prosperity. Suppose also that all couples marrying in any year plan successfully to have three children. Finally, suppose that the couples marrying in the depression postpone having their children until the better times, and those marrying in the prosperous decades have their children as soon as possible while conditions are favorable. The result of such a combination of events would be violent fluctuations in annual birth rates—a sharp drop from the "normal" level to very low birth rates in the depression decade, a larger upsurge to very high rates until the babies postponed during the depression decade are born, and then a return to "normal." The total number of children born, and the average size of completed family for the depression and prosperity marriage groups, would be about the same as with the even spacing of children throughout the entire period.

We know now that such short-run variations in the birth rate without fundamental changes in long-run trends have appeared at some times and places.[7] To a major extent, our high annual birth rate during 1947–57

---

[7] For example, see P. K. Whelpton, *Cohort Fertility: Native White Women in the United States,* Princeton University Press, Princeton, N.J., 1954, chap. 6.

can be explained in this way as a change in the timing of births. Part of the bumper crop of babies during the war and early postwar years were children postponed by couples in the depression decade. Also, the annual marriage rate has been exceptionally high since the war, for couples have been marrying younger. In addition, more couples have been starting their families within 2 years after marrying. As a result many babies have been born to couples relatively early in married life.

What We Need to Know about Fertility Trends

But at this point our factual knowledge ends and speculation begins. The important question on which information is needed may be phrased in different ways: Are today's young married couples going to have much larger families than those of 20 or 30 years earlier, or are they simply having relatively small families more quickly after marriage? Have the basic conditions of family life changed so that the young people now marrying and having children earlier will go on to have larger families and continue the recent upward trend in family size? Is the current baby boom mainly a result of millions of couples having their children in a short period of time while economic conditions are favorable?

Accurate answers to these questions must await the verdict of history. Meanwhile, however, important groups in our country are pressing for the best estimate of the future that social science can give. Many long-range plans depend upon population forecasts in which forecasts of births are a basic ingredient. Almost any long-run strategy for capital outlays, or for training and expansion programs by business or government, must make some assumptions about the future population to be served. Among the activities affected by such forecasts are plans for schools and recreation facilities, public utility construction, social security programs, manpower programs for industry and the armed forces, projections of many types of economic activity (e.g., new home construction and the manufacture of products for children), and training programs for doctors, nurses, and teachers. The importance which the business world attaches to population forecasts is evident in the frequent references to population trends in discussions of the outlook for business.

The official statistics of our country furnish a good beginning for an analysis of the potential or probable trends in births. Every year they supply estimates of how many married women there are, how old they are, where they live, and how many babies are born. Less frequently there is other information for these wives and their husbands, e.g., their education and their occupation in relation to the number of children they have had.

But we do not have other facts of basic importance about our married couples. How many have physical impairments limiting their ability to have children? How many are successfully using methods of family limitation to plan the number and spacing of their children? How are the impairments to reproduction and the attempts to regulate conception related to the present ages of married people and the family growth already achieved? Information on these topics would help us to evaluate population trends more intelligently.

Even more important for future population growth are the expectations and plans of people about having children in coming years. Certainly, for that large proportion of married couples who use family limitation methods we need to know about intentions and expectations for family growth. These couples have the means to realize their expectations. For the minority of couples who do nothing to limit family size or who want as many children as time brings, information is needed about the physiological ability to reproduce. How many can have a child every year or two, and for how many is childbearing unlikely or impossible?

Family growth patterns have not been the same for the different major strata of our population. We know that in 1820 (and probably earlier) the birth rates of the urban population were well below those of the rural population. During most of our history there has been an inverse relationship between social or economic status and fertility. It has seemed strange to many that large families have been most common among the groups who apparently could least afford to raise them—those with lower-status occupations, less education, and smaller income. The general assumption has been that this resulted from the slower rate of adoption of methods to avoid pregnancy in lower-status groups, but we have never had any information for the nation as a whole on differences in family planning between major population strata.

A study of native white Protestant couples in Indianapolis did show that among those using contraception effectively the higher-status groups had more children rather than fewer.[8] Many expect that most of the present differences in family size between major population strata will disappear or be reversed when effective methods of conception control become more widely diffused in the population. Clearly, an analysis of population trends must consider not only what is happening in the total population but in each major segment as well. Various population strata will undoubtedly be affected in different ways by social and economic changes.

[8] Whelpton and Kiser, *op. cit.*, vol. 2, pp. 359–416; or "IX. Fertility Planning and Fertility Rates by Socioeconomic Status," *Milbank Memorial Fund Quarterly*, vol. 27, no. 2, pp. 188–244, April, 1949. For more information about this study see Appendix A, Note 2d.

What is needed for the couples young enough to have children in the major strata of our population is information about how many children they already have, their physiological ability to have more children, their use of family limitation methods, and their plans for additional family growth. These intimate facts of life have not existed in any records or archives. They could be obtained only from the families themselves in personal interviews. This book records the results of such interviews with a representative cross section of young American families. These data from personal interviews can improve our understanding of the current baby boom and the outlook for population growth.

Who Were Interviewed: The Sample

Interviews were conducted with 2,713 white married women between the ages of 18 and 39 (inclusive), living with their husbands or temporarily separated because of the husband's service in the armed forces. These wives were selected in such a way as to constitute a scientific probability sample of the approximately 17 million wives in our national population having the indicated characteristics in March, 1955.

Married women younger than 18 or older than 39 were excluded from our sample. The older wives will not significantly affect the birth rates of future years. The younger wives have distinctive characteristics which might distort our results.[9]

Widows, divorced women, or wives not living with their husbands (for other reasons than military service) were not interviewed, although many of these women will remarry or rejoin their husbands and will bear children. They are a relatively small part of all women in the childbearing ages (approximately 8 per cent of those aged 18–39). Their total contribution to the birth rate will be small; consequently it seemed wiser to omit them from the sample than to try to solve the delicate problem of asking them about their intentions to remarry and have additional children.

Reluctantly, the sample was restricted to white wives. One reason was that important parts of the data needed in the last section of our study were not available for nonwhites. The main reason was that the resources available for field work were limited. White and nonwhite birth rates differ substantially because of differences in socioeconomic status. To have analyzed them separately would have required adequate samples for each. Since white births make up such a large proportion of all births (about 86 per cent in 1950–54) the available resources were used to obtain the largest and best possible sample for this group.

Many of the babies born in the next two decades will be the children

[9] See Appendix A, Note 3.

of women who are now single but who will marry in the next few years. In order to ascertain what ideas young single women have about marriage and desired family size, 254 white single women aged 18–24 were interviewed in connection with this study. Clearly, their attitudes about such matters may change radically, depending on when and whom they marry. We shall present the results of our study of single women in a later report, and state here only that their expectations regarding future childbearing are not directly comparable with those of our young married women.

These various restrictions mean that the 17 million white wives aged 18–39 in 1955 who are represented by our sample constituted about 67 per cent of all American women in this age range, about 75 per cent of all white women, about 91 per cent of all white ever-married women, and practically 100 per cent of those living with their husbands. Of the women not represented, many of those who were single will never marry and many of those who were widowed or divorced will not remarry. Nevertheless, in Chapter 10 an attempt will be made to estimate the future birth rates of these women as well as those represented in our sample.

It would have been desirable to interview husbands as well as wives. Since cost considerations limited the number of persons we could question, we chose about 2,700 wives rather than about half as many wives and their husbands. Many of our factual questions could be answered as accurately by wives as by husbands. In contrast, our few questions about husbands' attitudes no doubt would have been answered more accurately by the husbands themselves than by the wives. In this connection, however, it is worth noting that in an earlier study the expectations about family size expressed by husbands and wives are similar *on the average.*[10] While husbands certainly should be interviewed in later studies, it seemed wise to concentrate our first efforts on wives.

Generalizing from the Sample

While the information obtained from the 2,713 wives is interesting in itself, its value is greatly enhanced because it represents information about the national population of white married women in the childbearing years. Technical details about the sample are given in Appendix C. At this point it may be enough to say that the wives in our sample were selected in such a way that we can be reasonably confident that they represent the larger population *within predictable limits of sampling error.* This means that we can state the probable error resulting from the fact that we interviewed a *sample* of the eligible women rather than

[10] Part of a survey on economic problems conducted by the Survey Research Center in the fall of 1954.

all of them. It does not mean that we can predict "response errors"—whether the respondent told us the "truth." For example, we cannot say whether any significant number of women reported that they had not used contraception when in fact they really had. Such response errors have no intrinsic connection with whether or not a sample is taken, and may occur also when the total population is interviewed.[11] Another way to put this is to say we have a sample of responses which represents the total number of potential responses and which has biases or errors at about the same rate as would be found in the total.

Tables in Appendix C contain estimates of the range of sampling error associated with the sample statistics presented in this book. In estimating sampling error we estimate the chance deviation of a sample statistic from the corresponding value for the total population. For example, we shall state in a later chapter that 75 per cent of the approximately 1,800 Protestant wives in our sample have already tried to regulate conception. The sampling-error tables in Appendix C permit us to state that the proportion of *all* Protestant wives in the United States who have tried to regulate conception is between 73 and 78 per cent, and to add that this statement has at least 95 chances in 100 of being correct.[12]

It is possible to make statements of this kind only because the sample was drawn on a scientific probability basis; that is, all members of the population had a determinate and known chance to enter the sample. This also means that the sample should represent within predictable limits *any* characteristics of the population involved. This is not true of samples drawn on other bases. For example, we might simply have sought accessible and willing respondents who collectively matched the population we are studying on such characteristics as age, number of births, and number of years married. Such a sample would have been easier to find, would have reduced the cost of the study, and *might* have given an approximately correct representation of *some* of the numerous characteristics not used in selecting it. Unfortunately, it is virtually certain that some other characteristics would have been seriously overrepresented and still others would have been seriously underrepresented, and there would be no way of knowing which were in which group.

In short, the usefulness of a probability sample is that it represents (within predictable limits) the population from which it is drawn with respect to *any characteristic whatsoever* of the individual units. This is extremely important for this study, because for many of the characteristics

---

[11] Response errors are somewhat more likely to be made when the total population is interviewed, because the much smaller number of interviewers and field supervisors required for a sample makes possible higher standards for skill and supervision.

[12] Because our sample is restricted to wives aged 18–39 who are living with their husbands or whose husbands are in the armed forces, this statement about all wives in the United States is subject to the same restriction.

investigated there are no data for the total population which can serve
as a check on the sample. We can and do compare figures for our sample
with figures for the total population with respect to such characteristics
as age, number of births, occupation, region of residence, and employment of wife (Appendix C). But with respect to such crucial characteristics as sterility, family limitation practices, and number of children
expected in the future, there are no data for the total population. Confidence in our results must rest on the scientific procedures used to select
a probability sample. Of course, the fact that the sample data correspond
fairly closely to the total population data on items which can be compared does increase our confidence that correct sampling procedures were
followed.

The reader may refer to the tables of sampling errors in Appendix C
to determine the probable chance error for statistics cited in the following
chapters. He may also use these tables to determine whether a difference
between two figures is statistically significant (i.e., greater than is likely
from chance alone). In general, when differences are discussed in the
text they are statistically significant, unless there is an indication to the
contrary.

The size of the sampling error increases as the size of the group
'considered decreases: it varies inversely with the square root of the number of cases in the group. The probable chance errors are relatively small
for statistics based on our total sample, but are larger for statistics
based on smaller subgroups. Consequently, many of the differences
between averages or percentages for pairs of small subgroups may not
be significant. However, when sets of such differences follow a consistent over-all pattern, the pattern may be significant even when the
individual differences are not.

In view of the uniqueness of much of the data in this study, considerable
use is made of such patterns of differences for small subgroups because
of their suggestive value, even where considerable sampling error may
be involved. We shall try to warn the reader when particular differences
discussed are not statistically significant. He may also make his own
evaluation on the basis of the tables of sampling errors.

How the Interview Was Received

No one before had attempted to ask questions about such presumably
sensitive topics as miscarriages, sterility, and family limitation practices
in a scientific sample survey for the entire United States. Lacking previous
experience, there were many doubts regarding the willingness of wives
to talk with our interviewers about such personal topics. These doubts
were greatly reduced during the pretests of our questionnaires and were

completely resolved by the interest shown by most of the wives in the sample.[13]

Ninety-one per cent of the women chosen for the sample cooperated in giving interviews. This is a better response rate than is usually obtained in scientific national sample surveys on presumably less sensitive topics. (An 85 per cent response rate is often considered satisfactory, and 87 per cent is typical for such studies.)

Of the 9 per cent of the eligible wives who were in our sample but were not interviewed, approximately one-half (5 per cent) were women who were seen by an interviewer but refused to cooperate. The others (4 per cent) were women who could not be interviewed because of illness, disability, or prolonged absence, or who were not found at home when three or more visits were made by the interviewer. (In some cases as many as ten visits were made in order to find a respondent.) Most of the women who refused to be interviewed did not object to the particular subject matter of this survey but simply did not want to be bothered with any questions.

Of the 2,713 wives who were interviewed, only 10 (less than one-half of 1 per cent) were unwilling to answer the questions about their attempts to avoid conception. This is less than the refusal rate for our questions about income and the usual refusal rate for income questions in other sample surveys. A few women who were willing to answer all our questions about family growth and family planning said that our questions about income were "too personal"!

The interviewers reported a warm reception in many cases. The wives apparently felt that the problems of family growth were important to them personally. On some surveys dealing with economic or political problems, many women are reluctant to be interviewed because they feel poorly informed on these topics. They may ask an interviewer to go to someone more expert. Very few cases of this kind occurred in our study, probably because the respondents were being asked to talk about matters central in their lives and of obvious day-to-day concern. In this area they might well regard themselves as the real experts—and apparently they did.

The Interview Situation

The respondents were questioned in their homes by about 150 of the trained women interviewers on the national field staff of the Survey Research Center of the University of Michigan. The interviews averaged about 1¼ hours in length, but some ran on for 3 hours. Many of the respondents obviously enjoyed the opportunity to tell a sympathetic

[13] See Appendix A, Note 4.

listener about their childbearing experience, their pride in their family, and their expectations regarding additional children.

Interviews were taken in every part of the country and in all kinds of homes: Tobacco Road shacks, Park Avenue apartments, prosperous farms, small suburban homes, and row houses—a representative range of the situations in which American couples live. The flavor of the interview situation with a 39-year-old woman with nine children in a backwoods rural area may be captured in the following thumbnail sketch:[14]

CASE 1. The respondent lives in a very picturesque primitive cabin on a creek bank with log steps and an old-fashioned loft in the house. She was interested in talking to me and cooperative about answering questions. We had two interruptions during the interview—one of the smallest boys fell in the creek, and one of the oldest nearly shot his sister with a rifle, while shooting at a squirrel back of the house. Her house was very bare, with only two double beds and one single bed for them all to sleep in, but it was spotlessly clean. I asked if either of her married daughters had children, and she said, "Yes, the oldest one [22] has four now and not one of 'em big enough to pull the baby out of the fire."

Of course, this is an extreme case. Most interviews were with mothers in better circumstances and with typically small families.

Many interviewers were asked to stay for coffee, for tea, or for dinner. Family Bibles and albums were brought out occasionally to check or illustrate some point of family history. Details not requested by the interviewers were volunteered in a friendly way by many respondents.

The full list of questions asked in the interview is reproduced in Appendix B. If an answer did not seem to meet the question's objectives the interviewer used nondirective probe questions to help obtain the desired information. The present report utilizes only a part of the material collected. Other information will be presented in later publications.

On the whole, both the interviewers and those reading and analyzing the questionnaires felt that the respondents answered honestly and seriously, indicating respect for both the purposes and auspices of the study. The distribution of the responses to several factual questions can be checked against external sources of information, and many checks for internal consistency can be made. Both types of checks will be referred to as we discuss our results in following chapters. Appendix C also contains comparisons indicating the reliability of certain types of responses.

What women told us about their expected future behavior cannot be

[14] The case material used in this book is taken directly from our questionnaires. However, in many cases minor changes have been made in some of the facts presented about the respondents in order to make identification of any person impossible. The cases are numbered consecutively as they appear in this book; the numbering has no other significance.

checked in the same way as their replies to factual questions. To some extent comparisons can be made with the past behavior of older women. In this way we can estimate whether the expectations reported by younger women are reasonable for particular groups, as will be done in later chapters. Ultimately, it will be possible to check the expectations about future childbearing by comparing our forecasts of births based on them with the actual numbers of births. If studies like this can be repeated every 5 years, it will be possible to develop a series of comparisons between the number of births that are expected and the number that occur during 5- and 10-year periods after the interview. Such a series would show whether various groups tend to overstate or understate intentions regarding family growth, and whether such tendencies are related to socioeconomic and other characteristics and conditions.

It should be noted, however, that even future events cannot serve as a complete check on the validity of present expectations. Expectations honestly held and expressed today may change with changing times or with the personal situation of the individual. It would be unwise to take statements of expectations at face value and predict the future as if each expectation is certain to be realized in action.

Yet when used with due caution, these reports of what young American wives expect and plan for their families, considered jointly with histories of how their families and others have grown in the past, provide a new basis for understanding the trends of family size and population growth in the United States. This is a report of an experimental first study. Additional studies at regular intervals will be needed to assess and develop under changing conditions this new approach to the problem.

Chapter 2

STERILITY AND FECUNDITY OF AMERICAN FAMILIES

Millions of American couples are unable to have children at a normal rate. Many of them are desperately unhappy because they cannot have all the children they want. Sterility is complete for some; they cannot bear *any* children. The poignant feeling of such couples was expressed by a childless respondent, married for 9 years:

CASE 2. "We have both always wanted a child. We've done everything we can to have one. It's our dream and we hope it will come true. My husband wants children—always has. He's very hopeful we'll be able to have one— and whenever it comes—I assure you it will be welcome. We'd like to have three or four children—with the help of God. I can't believe that all our prayers will be unanswered. I think we will have children when God feels we are worthy of them."

Such cases of complete sterility are dramatic and touching, but they are not the most important in the total effect on family growth. Partial sterility—the inability to bear *additional* children after the birth of one or more—is more prevalent. Some couples become sterile after one birth, others after two births, and so on. Still other couples have physiological conditions which make conception improbable, even if it is not definitely impossible. Fecundity varies along a time scale, too. Some couples find that coitus every 2 or 3 days results in conception within a few weeks if contraception is not used. Other couples try to conceive for a long time— years or even decades—before they are successful. Some couples who cannot conceive at one period of married life do so very quickly at another period. Many couples conceive in less than a year if no attempt is made to prevent conception and there are no fecundity impairments, but there is no established standard of what is "normal." Finally, some wives can conceive, but have a miscarriage or stillbirth instead of a living baby.

We shall use the term "fecundity" to refer to the capacity of a couple to have children in the future. The term "subfecundity" will denote the presence of a physical impairment which reduces this capacity substantially. The Subfecund group thus includes couples for whom future childbearing is impossible and couples whose ability to have children

17

appears to be significantly below "normal." The term "fertility" will refer to the number of children actually born, in contrast to "fecundity" —the physiological capacity for bearing children.[1] In populations that control conception effectively, fertility is much below fecundity.

A Summary View

Approximately one-third of all the couples represented by our sample are Subfecund. This means that in the United States about 6 million white couples with the wife aged 18–39 are limited in their ability to have children. By the time the wife is 35–39, more than half of all couples are Subfecund.

Certain facts about this widely prevalent subfecundity stand out as especially significant for the couples now in the childbearing years:

1. *Approximately 10 per cent of all couples are Definitely Sterile;* that is, they cannot have children in the future.

2. *Nine per cent of all couples—1 in 11—have had an operation which makes conception impossible.* Most of the Definitely Sterile couples have had such an operation. Some of these operations are contraceptive in intent; others are performed for health reasons even though the couples very much want more children. Their widespread incidence is startling and important.

3. *Operations which prevent conception are most prevalent in lower-status groups, particularly among poorly educated wives and wives in their late 30s.*

4. *For some couples the problem is not conceiving, but having a child instead of a miscarriage or stillbirth.*

5. *Almost all couples who expect to be childless are Subfecund.* Voluntary childlessness is rare among wives in our sample.

6. *Subfecundity and the use or nonuse of some method of family limitation are closely related.* By the end of the childbearing period substantially all couples are either Subfecund or have tried to regulate conception. Ninety per cent of the Fecund couples with wives aged 30–39 have already used preventive measures. Most of the couples who have not used them are Subfecund and do not need them. Whether intentionally or not, they test their fecundity early in married life and never

---

[1] These definitions of fecundity and fertility were adopted by the Population Association of America in 1934. They are in general agreement with those in Blakiston's *New Gould Medical Dictionary*, Norman L. Hoerr and Arthur Osol (eds.), McGraw-Hill Book Company, Inc., Blakiston Division, New York, 1956. Unfortunately, they are not accepted by all scientists or dictionaries. Many biologists and physicians use fertility to denote the capacity to reproduce and fecundity to denote the amount of reproduction, in accordance with the definitions in Stedman's *Medical Dictionary*, 15th rev. ed., The Williams & Wilkins Company, Baltimore, 1942.

resort to family limitation if they do not conceive easily. For most of them subfecundity makes preventive measures unnecessary.

7. *The concentration of subfecundity among couples who have never tried to regulate conception is true for all major socioeconomic groups in our population.*

8. *Awareness and identification of subfecundity depend in part on family limitation practices.* The couples who use preventive measures most are least likely to realize that they may not be able to have children, and to be classified as Subfecund in this study.

9. *There is no evidence of consistent differences in fecundity between most major social and economic strata of our population.* Low-status groups (as measured by income or education) are more likely than high-status groups to be classified as Subfecund, but it is unlikely that this is due to basic biological differences. Instead, it probably results from the lesser use of family limitation methods early in married life by lower-status groups, which gives them greater opportunity to demonstrate subfecundity. Working wives are more likely than others to be Subfecund, in part because their lower fertility permits them to work. For most other social and economic characteristics, there are no apparent differences in fecundity.

10. *The incidence of subfecundity increases rather rapidly with the age of the wife and the duration of her marriage. It is also affected by the number of children she has borne.*

These general statements indicate that sterility and subfecundity are significant factors in the growth patterns of many American families. They touch the lives of millions of couples who are unable to have as many children as the "normal" or "average" couple. However, we shall see later that in reducing fertility they are much less important than the deliberate limitation of family size.

It is possible for a woman who marries at a young age to have 20 or more children before the end of her childbearing years. Such a case is occasionally reported in our newspapers as an interesting rarity, and is somewhat more frequent in several other countries. Nowhere, however, is the *average* for the women of a whole society as high as 20. According to a "model timetable" prepared by Dr. Alan F. Guttmacher,[2] if women married at age 16, if nothing was done to prevent conception, if the marriage lasted 30 years before either spouse became sterile, if every pregnancy ended with a birth, and if all babies were nursed, the average number of births per couple would be 15. In real life, however, there are few large groups in which the average number of births per couple reaches 7. Among groups whose members marry young and let nature run its course with respect to childbearing, the most prolific known at

[2] See Appendix A, Note 5.

present are the Hutterites, with 10.4 births per couple, and older women who married young in rural Quebec, with 10.0.[3]

In Western societies 2- or 3-child families have been most common in recent decades. The difference between the actual 2- or 3-child families and a theoretical maximum of 15 children is partly the result of involuntary subfecundity but mainly the result of voluntary family limitation practices. There is no evidence that physiological impairments of the reproductive system are more prevalent today than in earlier periods. Instead, control over venereal diseases may well have decreased subfecundity. On the other hand, family limitation practices are now much more prevalent and effective.

In the present chapter we shall be concerned mainly with subfecundity. However, in a country in which most people try to restrict childbearing, the awareness of subfecundity by couples and its identification in an interview study inevitably are affected by birth-regulation practices; consequently these practices must also be considered in our discussion of fecundity.

The 10 sweeping summary statements we have made about fecundity and subfecundity have many implications for American fertility. An examination of the evidence on which they are based is the purpose of this chapter. The initial unqualified statements are intended to focus attention on the high points of our findings, but the evidence does require qualification. To a certain extent, the findings depend on how we collected the data and how we defined such basic concepts as subfecundity and family limitation practices.

No group of researchers can hope to estimate in any exact way the incidence of sterility or subfecundity in the American population in the 1950s. A group of nonmedical researchers must approach such a task with particular humility. Our data on fecundity would have been much better if the interviewing had been more detailed and if our interviewers had had adequate medical training in addition to their other skills. Neither of these conditions could be met. However, even if the couples in our sample could have been examined by a competent medical staff, an accurate determination of the fecundity status of many of them would have been impossible in the current state of medical knowledge. In many cases a doctor is unable to give a physiological explanation for apparent sterility. The only evidence that it exists may be the passage of time during which the couple is unable to have a child.

For the purpose of estimating the fecundity of American couples, the

[3] Joseph W. Eaton and Albert J. Mayer, *Man's Capacity to Reproduce,* The Free Press, Glencoe, Ill., 1954, p. 20; *Census of Canada, 1941,* Ottawa, 1946, vol. 3, p. 701. The Canadian figure is for women aged 45–54 who married before 20. For information about other countries see Appendix A, Note 6.

clinical experience of medical personnel yields biased results because it is not based on a probability sample of all couples or of the Subfecund but is limited to the people who have fecundity problems which are brought to medical attention for health reasons or because a child is wanted. Moreover, there is no national collection of the individual clinical records of doctors on even such biased samples of the population. As demographers, then, we have collected data which are incomplete from a medical standpoint but which do represent a cross section of the population. We present them as a best present approximation to the facts.

Types of Subfecundity and Their Frequency[4]

Couples may be classified as Subfecund with varying degrees of certainty. There is little question if a wife has had her uterus removed —the couple is Definitely Sterile. The evidence is less certain if a wife has failed to conceive for a long period of time but does not know of any physiological condition preventing conception. We have classified all the couples into five fecundity categories based on the extent of their impairment and the certainty of our evidence.

Definitely Sterile couples are those who cannot conceive, that is, couples reporting physical or medical conditions making pregnancy impossible in the future. In the great majority of cases the evidence for definite sterility is an operation on either wife or husband.[5] The few Definitely Sterile couples who have not had such operations reported that other defects in the reproductive system of husband or wife prevented them from having a child (for example, an injury received in an automobile accident). One-fifth of the Definitely Sterile couples had four or more births before the operation or accident which ended fecundity. In contrast, another fifth had never been able to have a child.

The following cases are illustrative of couples classified as Definitely Sterile:

Case 3. This is a Roman Catholic couple of French-Canadian background married for 15 years who have never had any children of their own. One year after marriage the wife had an operation for medical reasons, which made further conceptions impossible. Immediately after the operation, the couple adopted a baby girl. In retrospect the wife believes she would have wanted five or six children if she could have had them. Even now at age 38 she says that she would have three more children if it were possible for her to do so.

---

[4] For further technical details of the fecundity classifications see Appendix D. For those parts of the questionnaire relating most directly to fecundity see questions 19, 20, and 51 in Appendix B.

[5] In most of these operations part of the wife's reproductive system was removed, or the passage of ova through the Fallopian tubes or of sperm through the vas deferens was made impossible.

She says that children "make your home more cheerful and by helping someone else it gives you a good feeling." The couple lives in New England where the husband earns about $3,500 a year in his own business.

CASE 4. This respondent had borne six children; the last three were unwanted "accidents." Her husband was an alcoholic and emotionally unstable. For this reason, her doctor "tied her tubes" after her last delivery.

Probably Sterile couples are those for whom a birth is considered to be improbable (rather than impossible) in the future on the basis of specific medical evidence. For most of this group conception is improbable. However, some couples in the group can conceive easily but pregnancy would be (1) unlikely to result in a birth (e.g., because of a history of repeated fetal deaths), or (2) a serious threat to the wife's health. If another pregnancy is likely to kill the wife, the couple is obviously below "normal" in terms of future reproduction.

The basis for classifying a couple as Definitely Sterile or Probably Sterile is the wife's knowledge and description of physical limitations. Clearly, her statement is not as adequate as medical examinations and records. On the other hand, it represents what she believes to be true and what presumably influences the attitudes and actions of herself and her husband in matters of family growth.

The Probably Sterile group includes the following couples:

CASE 5. This Irish Catholic couple, married for 10 years, lives in New York City where the husband is doing white-collar work at an annual salary of $5,000. The wife, now 34 years old, has a severe rheumatic heart condition. Her first two children were "planned" carefully with the use of the rhythm method. She reports that this required a "dispensation from her priest." Her doctor has warned her that another pregnancy might be fatal to her, so she has been using the rhythm method to avoid another conception. She was very ill with her second child 5 years ago. She reports that "some of my friends say 'you should have your tubes tied,' but that's not permitted by my religion."

CASE 6. The respondent, now 38 years old, has been married twice. Her first marriage ended in a divorce after 12 years of marriage, and her second marriage began 3 years ago. She has never used contraception or a douche, but she has been unable to conceive, although she has always wanted three children and says that "children make a family. I'd love to have them." One year after she was first married her doctor told her that there was only a "slight chance that she could become pregnant." The difficulty, in her words, was "faulty construction of the female organs." The estimate of the doctor was apparently correct since she has tried for 15 years to have children without success. Her second husband is getting started in his own business. She feels that she had bad breaks in her first marriage and wishes she had married her present husband first.

Semifecund couples are those who had not conceived at a "normal" rate, although the wives did not know of any physiological limitation to reproduction. These couples had relatively few births, considering how long they had been married and how little they had done to prevent conception. In addition, they failed to conceive during one or more long periods when preventive measures were not used. (A long period is defined for this purpose as 3 years for wives who have been pregnant and 2 years for other wives.) A couple was classified as Semifecund only if its pregnancy history met both of these requirements.[6] The time intervals used to define semifecundity are obviously arbitrary. The number of Semifecund couples can be increased or decreased by shortening or lengthening the intervals. However, those we used are considerably longer than the average required for a conception, as reported in studies of couples without serious fecundity impairments. They allow for a reasonable time in which fecundity could be tested.

The following cases illustrate our Semifecund group:

CASE 7. The couple had been married for 20 years at the time of the interview. Children were born in 1935 and 1949. The wife—a Catholic—reported that she had never used any family limitation method. Nevertheless, as she put it, "Nature just gave me two children spaced 14 years apart—I had no control over my pregnancies." She did not expect any more children "because we take no precautions and nothing happens. But still it may happen, and if it does I'll accept it."

CASE 8. Another respondent had two children early in her married life, then she was unable to conceive for many years although she never used contraception. She was opposed on principle to the use of contraception. In her own words, "Maybe I would feel differently if I conceived easily. When we wanted a child we prayed. I really don't think I would have become pregnant except for prayer."

Semifecund couples may be able to have several additional children. Indeed, a few of the wives in this group were pregnant at the time of the interview. Many of the Semifecund couples may be able to have all the children they want, although not as quickly as they want them. On the whole, however, the Semifecund couples would have substantially fewer children than Fecund couples if neither group tried to limit family size.

Honesty in reporting efforts to prevent conception affects the accuracy of our classification of couples as Semifecund.[7] Fecund couples would be erroneously labeled Semifecund if, by using contraceptives, they prevented conception for a period of 2 or 3 years (or longer) but failed

---

[6] The requirements are described in more detail in Appendix D.

[7] See Appendix E for a discussion of the accuracy of reporting efforts to prevent conception.

to report having done so. While such errors undoubtedly occurred, it is unlikely that they were numerous.

Another source of error is the failure to report some of the pregnancies which were terminated by illegally induced abortion. No special effort was made to find out about these events because criminal abortion was not one of the main problems being investigated. We believed that probing questions about pregnancies terminated in this manner would be resented by many wives, which might well jeopardize the success of the study and still leave a substantial proportion of criminal abortions unreported. Even if an interviewer suspected that such an abortion was being called a miscarriage, she was supposed to accept the wife's statement. It seems certain that some of the pregnancies stopped illegally were reported (and listed) as ending in miscarriages and that others were not reported and do not appear anywhere on the schedules. Some of the latter no doubt occurred during a 2- or 3-year period with no reported conception or effort to avoid pregnancy, which may have led us to misclassify some couples as Semifecund. There is no basis for estimating accurately how many of the Semifecund couples are involved.

Fecundity Indeterminate is the term designating couples who cannot be classified as to fecundity on the basis of the information we have about them. The difficulty arises because some wives reported using a douche *soon* after intercourse but *for cleanliness only* and said that neither they nor their husbands ever did anything to prevent conception. (We shall use the abbreviation DFCO—douche for cleanliness only—to designate these couples and their practice.) Not all the DFCO couples are affected, because some conceived often enough so that they were classified as Fecund and others had known impairments that relegated them to the Probably Sterile and Definitely Sterile categories. However, a significant number (121) with no known impairment reported one or more long periods during which they might have conceived but did not. It is these couples who have been classified as Fecundity Indeterminate.

The DFCO wives were not asked how regularly they douched after intercourse or what they meant by "soon" after. It is highly probable that some of the 121 in question always douched immediately and thoroughly; for them douching would have a major contraceptive influence regardless of intent. In contrast, for some of the others the douching undoubtedly was so irregular, so careless, and so long after intercourse that it would be unlikely to reduce appreciably the chance of conceiving. If we had adequate information about the thoroughness, promptness, and regularity with which douche was used, the long periods without conception for couples in the first of these two groups would be ascribed to contraception and the couples would be put in the Fecund category according to our definitions. At the other extreme, for those in the second group the long interval would be ascribed to impaired fecundity and the couples included in the Semifecund group. Since such a distinction cannot be made from our data, all these 121 DFCO couples are classified as Fecundity Indeterminate.

Here is an example from the group:

CASE 9. After 14 years of marriage, this 37-year-old school teacher reluctantly has given up hope of having children. She has never used contraception, although she approves of it in principle. She has used a douche for cleanliness. In describing her family history she said: "I have gone to every doctor there is and they don't find anything wrong with me, but I don't get pregnant." She would have liked to have had four children. "I think they would make you happier and bring the family closer together."

It can be argued that couples like this one should be classified as Semifecund because the wife wants children, has not been pregnant, and says that contraception has never been used. On the other hand, her report that doctors "don't find anything wrong with me" gives partial basis for saying that this couple is Fecund, but has not conceived because the wife "has used a douche for cleanliness." (The doctor may not have asked whether the wife douched after intercourse, assuming that because she wanted a child she presumably would not be doing something which would have a strong tendency to prevent conception.) In view of the uncertainty, the couple is classified as Fecundity Indeterminate.

Fecund couples are those for whom there is no evidence of impaired fecundity. They are the cases not included in one of the four Subfecund classes. It is practically certain that some of the couples classified as Fecund are actually Subfecund but are unaware of it. To take an extreme example, a couple always practicing contraception and never conceiving may have an impairment which makes conception impossible but never discover it. On the other hand, the less a couple tries to prevent conception, the more chance it has to demonstrate sterility or to have a semifecund period. In short, classification as Fecund or Subfecund depends not on all the biological facts, but only on those which are not hidden by efforts to avoid pregnancy.

The definitions of fecundity and subfecundity must be functional, not only in this study but also in other studies of nonclinical groups. Even an intensive medical study of a representative sample of all couples in a city or county would have to be satisfied with similar limitations, unless the couples for whom there was no clear-cut proof of fecundity or subfecundity could be required to undergo appropriate tests. Without such tests it would be necessary to classify these couples on the basis of what they or their physicians already know about the presence or absence of impairments, and what could be deduced from histories of their pregnancies and their attempts to prevent conception. Fortunately, dependence on the functional approach is not a serious handicap in a study of the effect of family planning on population growth, because the fecundity impairments not identified in this way have little effect on reproductive histories except to minimize the number of accidental conceptions.

How large is each of the five fecundity groups in the childbearing population? The relative size of each group is shown in Figure 2–1.

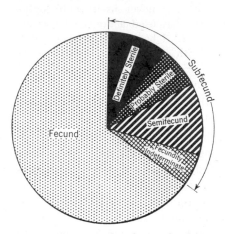

According to our criteria, about 1 couple in 3 has a fecundity impairment. Two out of three couples are Fecund; that is, we have no reason to suspect impaired fecundity. Ten per cent of all the couples—the Definitely Sterile—will have no children in the future. Seven per cent—the Probably Sterile—are unlikely to have children during coming years although a few may do so. Among the 12 per cent who are Semifecund are some who can have one or more children later if they wish to do so, but many in this group will find it difficult to conceive and some will find conception impossible. The 5 per cent whose fecundity is indeterminate include an unknown number of couples who are Semifecund and an unknown number who are Fecund. These estimates of sterility and subfecundity are probably minimal, because (as mentioned above) there are hidden cases of sterility and subfecundity among the Fecund couples who practice contraception regularly.

Fig. 2–1. Per cent distribution by fecundity, for all couples.

The preceding comments relate to the distribution by fecundity of a cross section of couples with wives in the childbearing ages, and do not indicate what proportion of the young couples will develop and discover fecundity impairments before reaching the later years of the childbearing period. By then their situation may resemble that of the older wives in our sample, which will be described later in this chapter.

Operations for Health Reasons or to Prevent Conception, as Fecundity Impairments

Nine per cent of all the wives reported an operation on either the wife or the husband which made another pregnancy impossible. The 245 couples with such an operation constitute 87 per cent of the Definitely

Sterile. Among these 245 couples the operation was on the wife in 220 cases, on the husband in 24 cases, and on husband and wife in 1 case.

That almost 1 out of every 10 couples in the childbearing years had such an operation was considered so startling a finding that all the interviews involving them were carefully reread to make certain that the question was not misunderstood. On the contrary, in most cases the wives volunteered comments about the nature or circumstances of the operation, which strengthened confidence in the validity of the information.

Operations which make childbearing impossible may or may not be performed for that purpose, although all have this effect. We did not ask the questions needed to enable us to determine for each couple whether the reasons were medical or to limit family size. Some wives voluntarily said that they had been sterilized because the doctor believed that their general health or the welfare of their families made further childbearing inadvisable. In contrast, other wives said that the purpose of their operation was to remove a tumor or to correct some other specific abnormality. Unfortunately, we cannot classify the couples for whom such information was not volunteered.

Here are the details for three couples with such operations:

CASE 10. The respondent was very bitter about married life. She felt that she married too young—"before I knew what it was all about." She had four children in rapid succession. The last three were "accidents" conceived despite attempts to prevent conception. With her last pregnancy, she said, "I felt that I was caught in a trap." After her last pregnancy her Fallopian tubes were tied. She said that her life "hasn't worked out at all like I had planned for it to—I was too young to know the difference—I think people should live before they start existing."

CASE 11. Respondent had seven children in 6 years—the last five were "accidents." She reported that her husband had a vasectomy, because she was Roman Catholic and could not be sterilized.

CASE 12. This 39-year-old Jewish mother had her uterus removed for medical reasons after 12 years of marriage. She had previously borne three children although no contraception was ever used. In her own words, "I never conceived easily. Before the last one I prayed and prayed for a girl." She would have liked a fourth child, but she is happy to have three. "The family does everything together," she said. "I never want to be separated from them." She feels that "life has been wonderful. Our children are wonderful. We couldn't ask for more."

There are several kinds of indirect evidence that some of the wives who did not volunteer information about the reasons for an operation were sterilized to prevent further childbearing. For example, the last pregnancy was reported as "unwanted" by either husband or wife (or both) for

20 per cent of the couples who subsequently had an operation, as compared with 14 per cent of the couples who did not have one. Among couples with an operation who had used contraception sometime before the last pregnancy, 37 per cent reported that the last pregnancy occurred despite efforts to prevent it as compared with 22 per cent among couples without an operation. The unwanted and accidental pregnancies of some couples are indirect evidence of motivation for sterilization.

For some couples sterilization is looked upon as a method of family limitation. A few wives volunteered the information that they intended to have such an operation in the future after another child. One indicated that in her social circle a few couples had prevented further family growth by a vasectomy (an operation which makes the passage of sperm impossible). She reported that her friends lacked confidence in the use of other methods than sterilization after a couple had as many children as they wanted, since they knew of accidents involving each of the standard contraceptives.

As a wife grows older the probability increases that she or her husband will have reason for an operation on the reproductive organs. Presumably, this may result either from (1) the longer exposure to health risks, such as the development of a tumor and complications caused by pregnancy, or (2) the occurrence of additional pregnancies which increases the desire to make conception impossible. There is a sharp rise in the incidence of operations with increasing age. In our sample the proportion of couples with operations rises from none among those with wife 18 or 19 years old to 17 per cent among those with wife 35–39 years old (Figure 2–2). Similarly, the percentage rises from 8 for couples with no birth to 16

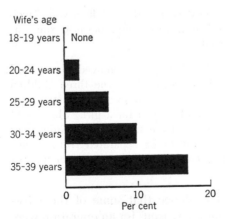

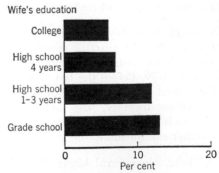

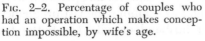

FIG. 2–2. Percentage of couples who had an operation which makes conception impossible, by wife's age.

FIG. 2–3. Percentage of couples who had an operation which makes conception impossible, by wife's education.

for those with 6 or more (Table 2–1). The fact that almost 1 in every 6 wives aged 35–39 has had an operation which prevents childbearing indicates how important this phenomenon is in our population.

TABLE 2–1. PERCENTAGE OF COUPLES WHO HAD AN OPERATION MAKING CONCEPTION IMPOSSIBLE, BY WIFE'S AGE, BY NUMBER OF PREGNANCIES AND BIRTHS

No. of pregnancies and births	Percentage who had an operation			No. of couples in base group		
	Total	Wife's age		Total	Wife's age	
		18–29	30–39		18–29	30–39
Total	9	4	13	2,713	1,270	1,443
No. of pregnancies:						
0	7	3	12	297	175	122
1	5	2	11	517	329	188
2	8	6	11	791	383	408
3	10	3	14	522	213	309
4	13	5	17	285	95	190
5	16	7	20	146	44	102
6 or more	14	13	15	155	31	124
No. of births:						
0	8	3	16	419	259	160
1	5	2	11	603	382	221
2	8	5	10	843	375	468
3	12	4	17	468	165	303
4	15	9	17	190	57	133
5	16	20	15	104	25	79
6 or more	16	*	16	86	7	79

* Less than 20 couples in base group. An asterisk has this meaning in all tables.

Further research is needed to determine to what extent the widespread incidence of "sterilizing" operations is a result of failure to adopt other means of family limitation or of inability to use them successfully. Our data suggest that at least a significant minority of these operations are substitutes for effective contraception. However, their greater prevalence among the older than the younger women in our sample may in part reflect changes in medical practice. It may be that in the past these operations were more commonly performed for health reasons and that more recently other forms of treatment are making such surgery unnecessary.

The incidence of operations which prevent childbearing varies with the socioeconomic status and background of the couples. They are relatively most frequent for poorly educated couples or for older wives in the low-income groups. They are also much more common for Protestants than for Catholics[8] (Table 2–2).

TABLE 2–2. PERCENTAGE OF COUPLES WHO HAD AN OPERATION MAKING CONCEPTION IMPOSSIBLE, BY WIFE'S AGE, BY WIFE'S EDUCATION, HUSBAND'S INCOME, AND WIFE'S RELIGION

Socioeconomic characteristics	Percentage who had an operation			No. of couples in base group		
	Total	Wife's age		Total	Wife's age	
		18–29	30–39		18–29	30–39
Total [a]	9	4	13	2,713	1,270	1,443
Wife's education:						
College	6	3	8	417	191	226
High school, 4	7	3	11	1,236	618	618
High school, 1–3	12	6	19	681	340	341
Grade school	13	6	16	377	119	258
Husband's income:						
$6,000 or more	10	6	12	430	128	302
$5,000–$5,999	10	6	13	393	176	217
$4,000–$4,999	8	5	10	583	261	322
$3,000–$3,999	8	2	16	619	337	282
Under $3,000	10	4	17	581	320	261
Wife's religion:						
Protestant	11	5	16	1,817	855	962
Catholic	5	3	6	787	366	421
Other	8	2	13	109	49	60

[a] In all tables "total" includes couples for whom a particular characteristic is unknown or indeterminate, e.g., in this table couples for whom wife's education or husband's income was not reported.

Operations which prevent childbearing are much less common for wives who are at least high school graduates than for wives with less education (Figure 2–3). We shall see later that the adoption and effectiveness of contraception are directly related to the wife's education. This suggests the possibility that the less well educated couples who are less likely to try to space or limit pregnancies, or to do so effectively, may be more inclined to be sterilized. This is purely a plausible speculation. It may also be that gynecological problems requiring operations are related to

[8] The terms "Catholic" and "Roman Catholic" are used interchangeably in this book.

certain factors associated with educational status and that the explanation is really medical.

The incidence of operations which prevent childbearing is not as closely related to the husband's income as to the wife's education. However, for wives 30–39 years of age, the two lowest-income groups do have relatively many such operations. Income is less indicative of social status among younger couples than among older couples, so that income is a more significant factor for wives 30–39 than for those under 30.

Protestant wives are more than twice as likely as Catholic wives to have had an operation which prevents conception. This undoubtedly reflects the institutional rules in Catholic hospitals that sharply restrict the circumstances under which such operations may be performed. In addition, Catholic religious teaching clearly forbids them where the intent is to stop childbearing and restricts the circumstances under which they may be performed for other reasons. Institutional and cultural factors of this type are likely to account for Catholic-Protestant differences, since there is no obvious reason to expect such marked differences between these groups in the incidence of strictly medical or gynecological problems which might necessitate an operation on the reproductive organs.

Pregnancy Wastage—Fetal Deaths: Miscarriages, Abortions, and Stillbirths

Every year hundreds of thousands of pregnancies are "wasted," because there is a fetal death—a miscarriage, an induced abortion, or a stillbirth.[9] One in four of the wives in our sample who were ever pregnant had at least one fetal death. Approximately 13 per cent of all completed pregnancies[10] were reported to have ended with a fetal death instead of a birth. Since our sample appears to be fairly representative of all women who become pregnant, there are at least 640,000 recognized fetal deaths a year in the United States. Many other fetal deaths occurring early in pregnancy are unrecognized. To put it another way, at least 4,941,000 pregnancies were required to produce the 4,301,000 births that occurred in the United States in 1957.

---

[9] "Miscarriage" is the lay term for what is technically called "spontaneous, or unintentional, abortion" occurring before the end of the seventh or eighth month of pregnancy. "Stillbirth" is the lay term for the spontaneous or unintentional delivery of a dead fetus later in pregnancy. "Induced, or intentional, abortions" are of two types. A "therapeutic abortion" is one performed for health reasons, as distinguished from an "illegal abortion," which is performed to prevent the birth of an unwanted child.

[10] An uncompleted pregnancy is defined as one in progress when the wife was interviewed. All others are defined as completed regardless of whether they lasted a short time or 9 months and regardless of whether they ended with a birth or a fetal death.

In considering the relation between fecundity and fetal deaths we should exclude the fetal deaths due to illegal abortions. A couple may not properly be classed as Subfecund if it could have children but chooses instead to have abortions performed. Under a very strict definition of fecundity, any couple who has had a fetal death (except an illegal abortion) might be described as having a fecundity impairment. We have not chosen to take this extreme position. However, since such fetal deaths do represent a kind of limitation on fecundity (defined as the ability to bear children), it is appropriate that we consider their frequency in the total sample.

In presenting our data on fetal deaths we do not distinguish between miscarriages, therapeutic abortions, and stillbirths, but this is not serious because almost all of them are unwanted. It would be highly desirable to exclude all fetal deaths due to illegal abortions and to present a complete but separate report on them. Unfortunately, we cannot do this. As was mentioned previously, our interviewers made it as easy as possible for a wife to report such an abortion as a miscarriage. A few wives did say voluntarily that an unwanted pregnancy had been ended intentionally, and an unknown number of other wives no doubt reported such an event as a miscarriage. Since we cannot exclude the latter it did not seem worthwhile to deduct the former. Obviously we have no basis for including the fetal deaths due to illegal abortions when neither the pregnancies nor the abortions were mentioned by our respondents.

Although it is generally believed that many illegal abortions are performed each year in the United States, opinions differ widely about the number. A committee appointed to prepare estimates examined the available information and reported: ". . . A plausible estimate of the frequency of induced abortion in the United States could be as low as 200,000 and as high as 1,200,000 per year . . . There is no objective basis for the selection of a particular figure between these two estimates as an approximation of the actual frequency." [11] Since relatively few abortions are induced for medical reasons, this means that there is 1 illegal abortion for every 3 to 20 births. In our discussion of fetal deaths an unknown, but probably minor, proportion of those due to illegal abortion are included.

The probability that a married woman will have at least one fetal death in her reproductive history is quite high. Twenty-one per cent of all wives in the sample reported at least one such death. If we consider only the 2,356 women with at least one completed pregnancy, 25 per

[11] Mary Steichen Calderone (ed.), *Abortion in the United States*, Paul B. Hoeber, Inc., New York, 1958, p. 180. The committee was appointed by the Conference on Abortion at Arden House, New York, in April, 1955, and consisted of Christopher Tietze, M.D., chairman, Carl L. Erhardt, Paul H. Gebhard, Alan F. Guttmacher, M.D., Irene B. Taeuber, and Pascal K. Whelpton.

cent already have had at least one fetal death. Many others will have one by the end of the childbearing period.

Fetal deaths are common in each of our fecundity classes (Table 2-3). Definitely Sterile couples are more likely than other couples to have had at least one fetal death[12] because some of the defects or diseases which made an operation necessary also prevented the normal development of a fetus. The relatively high incidence of fetal deaths among the Probably Sterile couples is due in part to our classifying as Probably Sterile any couple with four or more fetal deaths and a lesser number of births, and also a few others with several fetal deaths who reported being told by a physician that another pregnancy would end with a fetal death. However, even among the Fecund couples almost 1 in 4 with a completed pregnancy has already had at least one fetal death. As mentioned previously some of the fetal deaths occurred because an illegal abortion was performed. But even after allowing for them our data show a widespread incidence of unwanted pregnancy wastage among couples we have classified as having no fecundity impairment, as well as among Subfecund couples.

TABLE 2–3. PERCENTAGE WHO HAD A FETAL DEATH, FOR ALL WIVES AND WIVES WITH AT LEAST ONE COMPLETED PREGNANCY[a], BY FECUNDITY

Fecundity	Percentage who had a fetal death		No. of wives in base group	
	All wives	Wives with at least one completed pregnancy[a]	All wives	Wives with at least one completed pregnancy[a]
Total	21	25	2,713	2,356
Fecund	20	23	1,794	1,599
Definitely Sterile	27	32	283	241
Probably Sterile	35	42	187	156
Semifecund	17	20	328	269
Indeterminate	15	20	121	91

[a] Excludes current pregnancies.

Obviously, the chance that a woman will have at least one fetal death depends on the number of times she will be pregnant. Each pregnancy presents a new risk of a fetal death; hence the proportion of women

[12] We shall, for convenience, occasionally refer to the fetal deaths or fetal death rates of couples, although our data really refer to the pregnancy history (including fetal deaths) of the wife in this and any previous marriages. Only 240 of the wives had been married previously, so for 91 per cent of the couples the fetal death rate for the wife and that for the couple are identical.

who have had at least one fetal death rises with the number of completed pregnancies (Figure 2–4). Almost half of all women with four completed pregnancies have had at least one fetal death, and more than half of those with a larger number of pregnancies. We do not know how much selection such data represent. Some couples who have a strong desire for additional children may have extra pregnancies because one or more result in a fetal death. In other cases a fetal death

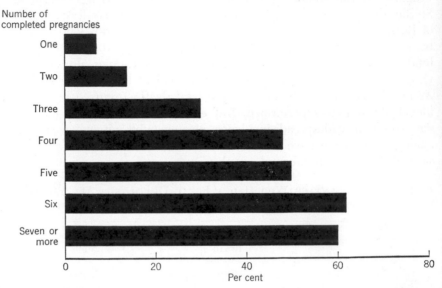

FIG. 2–4. Percentage of wives who had one or more fetal deaths, by number of completed pregnancies.

may lead to a downward revision of desired family size so that the couple does not go on to additional pregnancies.

For comparing the incidence of fetal deaths among groups of women, statisticians use the fetal death rate. This is defined as the number of fetuses dying before or during delivery per 1,000 fetuses resulting from conception. (It is similar to the proportion of completed pregnancies resulting in a fetal death.) For our entire sample, the fetal death rate is 129. This is very close to the rate of 131 reported in the Indianapolis Study, in which questioning about pregnancies and intentional abortions was much more intensive than in our study.[13] Our fetal death rate is far above the rates shown for the United States by the National Office of Vital Statistics, chiefly because many miscarriages and almost all illegal abortions are not reported to registrars.[14] Other studies of selected

[13] See Appendix A, Note 2*b*.
[14] These rates are discussed briefly in Appendix A, Note 7.

groups in the United States show a fetal death rate of between 51 and 123 per 1,000 from unintentional abortions alone.[15] Even after these rates are increased to allow for therapeutic abortions and stillbirths, the majority are below that reported for our sample.

Although our interviewers appear to have been relatively successful in finding out about fetal deaths, one should remember that many of those occurring very early in the gestation period are not recognized and are never reported in any study. It has been estimated that the complete reporting of fetal deaths in the United States might bring the fetal death rate to 150 or even 200 per 1,000.[16]

Table 2–4 shows the fetal death rate for pregnancies of each ordinal number. The rate rises from the first to the fourth pregnancy and is irregularly lower after that.

TABLE 2–4. FETAL DEATH RATE, BY ORDER OF PREGNANCY

Order of pregnancy	No. of fetuses[a]	No. of fetal deaths	Fetal death rate (per 1,000)
Total	6,418	831	129
1st	2,376	253	106
2d	1,857	218	117
3d	1,044	170	163
4th	555	118	213
5th	281	29	103
6th	145	22	152
7th or higher	160	21	131

[a] Includes those born alive and those dying before or during delivery (during miscarriage, abortion, or stillbirth).

Subfecundity and Contraception

The problem of terminology is difficult with respect to "contraception." We shall be discussing, as a group, various ways by which married couples try to avoid conception. They include not only the chemical and appliance contraceptives, but also withdrawal (coitus interruptus), rhythm (periodic continence), and abstinence. They do not include sterilization or illegal abortion. Unfortunately, in English as in other languages, there is no word or short phrase which is commonly

[15] *Foetal, Infant, and Early Child Mortality*, Population Studies, no. 13, United Nations, Department of Social Affairs, Population Division, New York, 1954, vol. 1, p. 15. For a review of information in other studies see other pages of this report.
[16] Cf. Carl L. Erhardt, "Reporting of Fetal Deaths in New York City," *Public Health Reports*, vol. 67, no. 12, pp. 1161–1167, December, 1952.

accepted as having exactly this meaning. "Birth control" and "family limitation" are thought by some to include sterilization and abortion as well as methods associated with sexual intercourse. To others (especially to Catholics) "birth control" and "contraception" may denote the chemical and appliance methods which are forbidden by their Church and are frequently referred to as "artificial birth control." [17] Some three-word phrases, e.g., "regulation of conception," are not entirely satisfactory, because they do not explicitly exclude sterilization.

Under the circumstances the use of some method to space pregnancies or limit their number will usually be called contraception in tables so as to save space. In the text contraception will be interchanged with other terms, e.g., "family limitation," "conception control," and "preventive measures." *In using any of these terms we attach no moral valuation to them.* They have been chosen merely to identify collectively certain specified ways of regulating conception in married life, namely, chemical and appliance methods, withdrawal, periodic continence, and abstinence.[18]

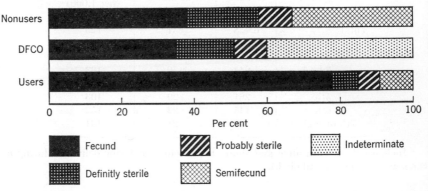

Fig. 2–5. Per cent distribution by fecundity, for Users and Nonusers of contraception.

Couples who have tried at some time to regulate conception are much more likely to be Fecund than those who have not done so. (For the

[17] "By artificial birth control the Church means the use of any mechanical or chemical contraceptives resorted to for the purpose of keeping the male seed from reaching the uterus and thus penetrating to the Fallopian tubes." William J. Gibbons, S.J., "The Catholic Value System in Relation to Human Fertility," in George F. Mair (ed.), *Studies in Population,* Princeton University Press, Princeton, N.J., 1949, p. 119.

[18] Our use of contraception is consistent with the definition in Webster's *New International Dictionary of the English Language:* "The prevention of conception or impregnation." A similar definition is given in several other dictionaries.

In Chapter 6 we shall discuss separately the various methods of avoiding conception, distinguishing those approved and disapproved under Catholic religious doctrine.

sake of brevity, couples of the first type will be referred to as "Users" and other couples as "Nonusers.") The striking relationship between fecundity and family limitation is shown in Figure 2–5 and Table 2–5. Seventy-eight per cent of the Users are Fecund as compared with 38 per cent of the Nonusers (excluding those douching for cleanliness only). Either the Nonusers or the DFCOs have a high proportion in each of the Subfecund categories as compared with the Users.

TABLE 2–5. PER CENT DISTRIBUTION BY FECUNDITY, FOR ALL COUPLES, BY USE OF CONTRACEPTION

Use of contraception	No. of couples	Fecundity					
		Total	Fecund	Definitely Sterile	Probably Sterile	Semi-fecund	Indeter-minate
Total	2,713[a]	100	66	10	7	12	5
Users	1,901	100	78	7	6	9	—
DFCO couples[b]	306	100	35	16	9	—	40
Nonusers	496	100	38	20	9	33	—

The dash indicates a percentage below 0.5 in all tables.

[a] Includes 10 couples for whom information about use of contraception was not ascertained.

[b] In this and subsequent tables DFCO signifies that no attempt was made to prevent conception, but the wife "douched for cleanliness only" soon after intercourse.

The tendency for Users to be Fecund (and vice versa) results chiefly from two facts. First, as explained earlier, Users are less likely than Nonusers to become aware of limitations to fecundity and to be classified as Subfecund. Second, those who begin married life as Nonusers are likely to either remain Nonusers if they discover impairments to fecundity, or adopt contraception if they find that they are able to have children.

The increased chance to demonstrate subfecundity is not the only reason for the high proportion of Nonusers who are Subfecund. More important is the fact that couples who are Fecund are likely to become Users after one, two, or three births. Couples who begin and remain as Nonusers are most likely to be those who have tested their fecundity and have found that they conceive infrequently or not at all. The attitude of such Subfecund couples is indicated by the following statement by a woman who never used contraception: "I might use a method if I had to, but I have never gotten pregnant very easily."

The relationship between fecundity classification and efforts to prevent conception depends on the fact that many couples do not begin such efforts until they have had one or more pregnancies. About half of all Users waited until after at least one pregnancy, and 18 per cent did not begin until after two or more pregnancies. For most of those who find they are sterile or subfecund, contraception is unnecessary. Although few couples test their fecundity deliberately, the process works out this way for many.

Couples who became Users *after* one or more pregnancies were asked whether they wanted as soon as possible after marriage the pregnancies they had before use began. Seventy per cent replied "yes" and 30 per cent "no." Presumably, those who answered "yes" wanted to build their families early and used family limitation methods only after they had one or more of the pregnancies they wanted. Such couples will become very conscious of difficulties in conceiving or in bearing a living child. Couples beginning with this attitude and discovering serious fecundity impairments are likely to never try to prevent conception or to begin such efforts very late. The 30 per cent who did not try to postpone their first pregnancy, although they did not want this pregnancy quickly, probably did not think much about the problem of limiting family size when they were first married but began preventive efforts later under the pressure of circumstances.

There is a far from perfect relationship between fecundity and the use of methods to prevent conception. A significant minority of Users are Subfecund, and a significant minority of Nonusers are Fecund. These exceptions from the selective relationship described above result from a number of offsetting factors:

1. Users who are Subfecund:
   a. Many couples adopt contraception early in their married life and discover a fecundity impairment only when they discontinue contraception to have a child, or when they seek medical treatment because pathology has developed.
   b. Some of the couples who do not begin contraception shortly after marriage find that they conceive slowly. However, their fecundity limitations do not prevent them from having all the children they want. Therefore, after a longer-than-average time, they become Users.
   c. For some of the couples classified as Probably Sterile a pregnancy is so dangerous to the mother's health or so likely to result in a fetal death for other reasons that contraception is used to prevent pregnancy.
   d. Some couples never practice contraception but are sterilized to avoid having more children. They do not "discover" fecundity impairments, but choose a permanent method of contraception. It might be appropriate to classify them as a special type of Fecund User if we could identify them.

2. Nonusers who are Fecund: Some couples from certain cultural backgrounds remain Nonusers even though fecundity impairments are not present and many children are born. Examples are most common among Catholics and farmers in our study.

TABLE 2–6. PERCENTAGE WHO ARE FECUND, FOR USERS AND NONUSERS, BY WIFE'S AGE, BY WIFE'S EDUCATION[a]

Use of contraception[b]	Wife's education				
	Total	College	High school, 4 years	High school, 1–3 years	Grade school
Total					
Total	66	75	69	63	52
Users	78	82	80	76	73
Nonusers	37	39	40	37	31
Difference	41	43	40	39	42
Ages 18–24					
Total	91	95	91	89	86
Users	94	94	95	94	95
Nonusers	82	*	83	81	75
Difference	12	*	12	13	20
Ages 25–29					
Total	73	83	76	67	59
Users	84	90	84	81	83
Nonusers	42	*	47	35	39
Difference	42	*	37	46	44
Ages 30–34					
Total	59	66	63	58	44
Users	74	72	77	70	65
Nonusers	22	*	15	27	25
Difference	52	*	62	43	40
Ages 35–39					
Total	47	63	47	37	45
Users	65	75	62	57	68
Nonusers	13	14	13	3	20
Difference	52	61	49	54	48

[a] Numbers of couples in base groups are shown in mimeographed tables (see Preface).
[b] In this and subsequent tables DFCO couples are classified as Nonusers unless otherwise specified.

These factors tend to minimize the potential relationship between fecundity and contraception. Nevertheless, almost all couples are either Users or Subfecund by the later part of the childbearing period. This is one result of the selective tie between fecundity and contraception, despite the offsetting factors. Almost all Fecund couples eventually become Users. For example, among Fecund couples with wife 35–39 years old, 90 per cent already are Users and an additional 2 per cent still intend to become Users. On the other hand, few older Nonusers are Fecund—only 13 per cent of the Nonusers 35–39 years old.

If the selective process we have described does operate, the *difference* in the proportion Fecund between Users and Nonusers should increase with age. As age rises from 18 to 39, the Fecund should be increasingly concentrated among the Users, and the Nonusers should be increasingly Subfecund. This is true (Table 2–6). The per cent Fecund is higher for Users than for Nonusers in every age group, and the *difference* rises from 12 per cent in the youngest age group to 52 per cent in the oldest.

Nonusers of contraception are much more likely than Users to be Subfecund in all age groups and in all social and economic strata of the population. We show in Table 2–6 the degree to which the proportion Fecund is higher for Users than Nonusers in each subgroup based simultaneously on age of wife and her education—an important socioeconomic characteristic.[19] Furthermore, this fact does not result from the concentration of Nonusers in one of the four Subfecund categories. In each age group the Nonusers have a significantly higher percentage than the Users in *each* of the four Subfecund categories.

To say that almost all couples either become Users or have fecundity impairments is only to confirm with empirical data what we have known must be true. The small families achieved by Americans in recent decades could result only from such a pattern or from a rise in age at marriage. But age at marriage has *declined* since 1940 and was fairly stable during prior decades.

How Subfecundity Increases with Age and Length of Marriage

Both age of wife and duration of marriage affect a couple's fecundity —the percentage Fecund decreases both with the age of the wife and number of years married[20] (Table 2–7 and Figure 2–6). Among wives

[19] Similar results were obtained with a variety of other socioeconomic characteristics.

[20] All references to number of years married are to time since the first marriage of the wife unless indicated otherwise. This differs from the duration of the present marriage only for the 240 women in the sample who had married more than once.

The fecundity classification relates to the couple and not to the wife alone. For convenience, however, we shall frequently use the term "Fecund wives" to mean "wives in Fecund couples."

with similar duration of marriage, relatively fewer of the older wives are Fecund; among wives of similar age, relatively fewer of those married longest are Fecund.

The wife's age affects fecundity to a considerable extent regardless

Wife's age

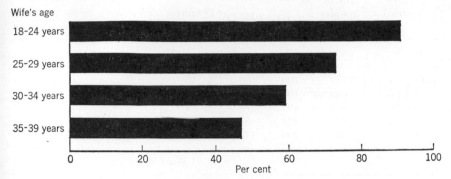

Fig. 2–6. Percentage of couples who are Fecund, by wife's age.

of duration of marriage (Table 2–7). This is consistent with the theory that fecundity decreases after some optimum age for reproduction. But the decrease in fecundity with age undoubtedly is related to the greater length of marital and reproductive experience as age increases. New fecundity impairments may result from the additional pregnancies and births that occur as life continues, and existing impairments may be discovered during the longer period of risk.

The over-all decrease in fecundity with number of years married probably is based on these same factors (Figure 2–7). The influences operating are both the independent effect of advancing age in the longer marriages and the effect of longer marriage periods in giving greater exposure to reproductive risks and in increasing the opportunity for discovering existing impairments.

The proportion of couples in *each* Subfecund category increases with

Duration of marriage

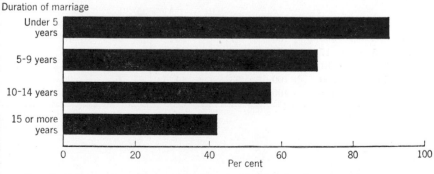

Fig. 2–7. Percentage of couples who are Fecund, by duration of marriage.

TABLE 2–7. PER CENT DISTRIBUTION BY FECUNDITY, FOR ALL COUPLES, BY WIFE'S AGE, BY DURATION OF MARRIAGE

Years married	No. of couples	Fecundity					
		Total	Fecund	Definitely Sterile	Probably Sterile	Semi-fecund	Indeter-minate
Total							
Total	2,713	100	66	10	7	12	5
Under 5	649	100	90	1	4	3	2
5–9	869	100	70	7	6	12	5
10–14	686	100	57	13	9	16	5
15 or more	509	100	42	24	8	19	7
Ages 18–24							
Total	556	100	91	2	4	2	1
Under 5	432	100	93	1	3	2	1
5–9	122	100	84	5	5	4	2
10–14	2	100	*	*	*	*	*
Ages 25–29							
Total	714	100	73	7	6	9	5
Under 5	160	100	86	2	7	4	1
5–9	446	100	72	7	6	10	5
10–14	108	100	59	12	8	14	7
Ages 30–34							
Total	748	100	59	11	9	16	5
Under 5	40	100	82	5	5	5	3
5–9	240	100	64	7	7	18	4
10–14	367	100	58	13	10	15	4
15 or more	101	100	46	18	7	21	8
Ages 35–39							
Total	695	100	47	20	8	18	7
Under 5	17	100	*	*	*	*	*
5–9	61	100	50	12	12	18	8
10–14	209	100	53	14	6	20	7
15 or more	408	100	41	26	9	18	6

either age of wife or length of marriage (Table 2 7). The proportion Definitely Sterile increases consistently with age within length-of-marriage categories and with length of marriage within age groupings. When age of wife and length of marriage are considered simultaneously, there are some erratic fluctuations in the other Subfecund categories, but the general tendency is still for an increase in each Subfecund class as couples become older and are married longer.

Among the oldest wives (35–39) or those married longest (15 or more years) there is a high incidence of subfecundity. Among couples with wife 35–39 years old, 20 per cent are unable to have (more) children (Definitely Sterile) and another 8 per cent probably cannot have (more) children (Probably Sterile). In addition, between 18 and 25 per cent have a history of conceiving at less than the "normal" rate. Only 47 per cent are Fecund couples for whom there is no evidence of a fecundity impairment.

Although our data definitely suggest that the incidence of fecundity impairments rises with age and duration of marriage, they do not represent the changes in the reproductive capacity of any particular group of women as they grow older and their duration of marriage lengthens. For example, although we classify as Subfecund 53 per cent of the women who were 35–39 in 1955, the incidence of subfecundity will be somewhat different among women reaching ages 35–39 in 1970 (who were 20–24 in 1955) and quite possibly will be very different. Changes will occur for several reasons, one of which may be more (or fewer) operations to prevent pregnancy. More important, changes in the extent and effectiveness of methods of contraception, and in the number of times that they are discontinued to have a child, may make it easier (or harder) to recognize the subfecundity that exists, and hence may raise (or lower) the proportion classified as Subfecund.

Each type of subfecundity is more common among the 240 couples with wife married more than once than among the other couples. This would be expected in light of the fact that the 240 wives are older and have been married longer than the others. What may be surprising is that relatively more subfecundity is found among the twice-married wives than the others when the comparisons are restricted to wives of the same age or duration of marriage (Table 2–8). It may be that the incidence of fecundity impairments is high among the twice-married wives because inability to have children was more common among the first marriages that were dissolved than among the others. This explanation seems plausible in view of the strong desire of most couples for two to four children, and the findings of other studies that marriages with few or no children have a higher divorce rate than others.

TABLE 2–8. Percentage of Couples Who Are Fecund, by Number of Times Wife Married, by Wife's Age and Duration of Marriage

No. of times wife married	All couples	Wife's age				Years married			
		18–24	25–29	30–34	35–39	Under 5	5–9	10–14	15 or more
					Per cent				
Once	68	91	74	62	48	90	70	58	43
More than once	49	*	61	44	39	*	70	44	39
				No. of couples in base group					
Once	2,473	539	670	658	606	642	819	600	412
More than once	240	17	44	90	89	7	50	86	97

How Subfecundity Is Related to Number of Pregnancies and Births

How does fecundity vary with the number of pregnancies or births a couple has already had? [21] The answer to this question is of some importance in evaluating the future reproduction of couples who are at different stages of family growth. Demographers use the term "parity" in referring to women grouped by number of children already borne. Zero-parity women have had no birth; first, or one-parity, women have had one birth; etc. We shall frequently use parity, rather than number of births, to simplify our terminology in referring to family building stages.

The incidence of fecundity impairments among couples with wives of different parity is affected by several selective factors. It might be thought that the proportion who are Subfecund would decrease as parity rises, because after couples become Definitely Sterile they no longer can move from a lower to a higher parity, and couples who become Subfecund are less able to do so than are Fecund couples. Since few couples want to be childless or to have only one child, most of those who are not Subfecund would leave the zero- and one-parity groups.

However, other factors modify this simple selective relationship. First,

---

[21] Our tabulations of pregnancies and births are based on those occurring to the wife in this or any previous marriages. The husband's children by previous marriages are not taken into account. Strictly speaking, therefore, we should always refer to the pregnancies or births of the wife, but for convenience in wording we shall occasionally refer, as in this instance, to the pregnancies or births of the couple.

operations which prevent conception tend to increase in frequency as parity rises from 1 to 4. Couples are more likely to "close the book" on family growth for health or other reasons if they have as many children as they want than if they have fewer. Second, the proportion of couples trying to prevent additional pregnancies rises sharply with the birth of the first child, the second, and the third. As has been noted previously, the use of contraception tends to hide fecundity impairments. Consequently, the discovery of subfecundity becomes more difficult as parity rises from 0 to 3, which tends to prevent an increase in the proportion classified as Subfecund. In contrast, couples who go on to have four or more births are increasingly those who do not use contraception and among whom fecundity impairments can be discovered. This tends to raise the proportion classified as Subfecund among wives of higher parity.

The net result is that in each age or duration-of-marriage group the proportion of couples who are Fecund increases as parity rises from 0 to 3 and varies irregularly as parity goes still higher (Table 2–9).

TABLE 2–9. PERCENTAGE OF COUPLES WHO ARE FECUND, BY NUMBER OF BIRTHS, BY WIFE'S AGE AND DURATION OF MARRIAGE[a]

Wife's age and years married	No. of births								
	Total	0	1	2	3	4	5	6	7 or more
Total	66	52	68	69	69	68	71	73	76
Age:									
18–19	95	94	97	*	*	*	*	..	..
20–24	90	87	89	92	91	*	*	*	*
25–29	73	50	66	75	90	88	79	*	*
30–34	59	18	56	65	62	62	85	*	*
35–39	47	13	37	52	52	54	56	54	80
Years married:									
Under 5	90	82	94	95	*	*	*	..	..
5–9	70	21	54	77	85	86	*	*	*
10–14	56	13	41	56	61	72	82	*	*
15 or more	42	4	33	44	50	41	44	62	69

In all tables, two dots indicates a category which is impossible or very improbable.
[a] Numbers of couples in base groups are shown in mimeographed tables (see Preface).

The proportion Fecund decreases very sharply with increasing age among zero- and first-parity wives. By ages 35–39 only 13 per cent of the childless couples and 37 per cent of the couples with one live birth are Fecund. It also decreases with age for wives of second, third, fourth, or fifth parity, but these decreases tend to become slightly smaller with increasing parity. By the time the wife reaches the later childbearing years most of the couples still childless or with only one child are Subfecund.

The proportion of couples who are Fecund in the various parity groups changes with increasing duration of marriage (Table 2–9) in much the same way as with increasing age of wife, since wife's age and duration of marriage are closely related. Within each parity, the proportion Fecund decreases with duration of marriage, as might be expected. Looking at these results in the other direction, within duration-of-marriage groups the proportion Fecund increases with wife's parity until at least the third. In the zero and first parities, there is a very sharp decrease in the proportion Fecund with longer marriage duration. Only 4 per cent of the couples are Fecund among those with a zero-parity wife married 15 years or longer.

In the lower parities the very sharp decreases in the proportion Fecund with length of marriage again reflect the fact that very few couples in the age groups studied voluntarily choose to remain childless or have only one child. With longer marriage durations, those who do not have two or more children are increasingly couples with fecundity impairments.

Childlessness and Subfecundity

Childlessness now results mainly from fecundity impairments. Few of our couples with no fecundity impairment will be voluntarily childless, that is, will deliberately avoid having any children throughout their married life. Some of the couples married more recently have postponed starting their families for various reasons, but definitely plan to have one or more children later. Among the 51 childless couples married 15 years or longer only 4 per cent are Fecund, while 67 per cent are either Definitely or Probably Sterile and 29 per cent are in one of the other Subfecund categories. This contrasts with the situation during 1927–41 which was found in the Indianapolis Study; namely, approximately 40 per cent of the couples with no child had wanted none and had used contraception regularly.[22]

That childlessness has been decreasing in the United States in recent years is shown clearly by fertility tables for the women born in different years who marry and live to middle age. For example, among native white wives aged 45–49 in 1950, 17 per cent had not borne a child. But among native white wives who will be 45–49 in 1965, fewer than 10 per cent were childless in 1955.[23] Late marriages will tend to raise

[22] For more information about this study see Appendix A, Note 2e.

[23] Wilson H. Grabill, Clyde V. Kiser, and Pascal K. Whelpton, *The Fertility of American Women,* John Wiley & Sons, Inc., New York, 1958, p. 345.

slightly the proportion childless for the later group, but this is likely to be balanced by the first births yet to occur. There is little basis for believing that the diminution of *involuntary* childlessness has reduced the percentage from 17 to less than 10, but there are good indications that substantially fewer couples want to have no children. For some couples the existence of fecundity impairments may coincide with the desire for childlessness, but this is not likely to be frequent.

Since almost none of the wives in our sample wishes to be childless, we may focus our attention on involuntary childlessness. Here we ask what proportion of all couples with wives of each age or length of marriage is childless *and* has fecundity impairments of different types (Table 2–10).

TABLE 2–10. PERCENTAGE OF COUPLES WITH NO BIRTH AND ALSO FECUND OR SUBFECUND, BY WIFE'S AGE AND DURATION OF MARRIAGE

Wife's age and years married	No. of couples	Per-centage with no birth	Percentage with no birth and also:				
			Fecund	Subfecund			
				Total	Defi-nitely Sterile	Prob-ably Sterile	Semifecund or Indeterminate
Total	2,713	15	8	7	2	2	3
Age:							
18–19	92	50	47	3	—	1	2
20–24	464	25	22	3	—	1	2
25–29	714	14	7	7	1	2	4
30–34	748	10	2	8	2	2	4
35–39	695	12	2	10	4	2	4
Years married:							
Under 5	649	36	30	6	1	2	3
5–9	869	9	2	7	1	1	5
10–14	686	8	1	7	3	1	3
15 or more	509	10	—	10	5	2	3

The proportion of the childless with a fecundity impairment rises sharply with either age or with length of marriage. If the wife has been married 15 years or longer, practically all childless couples are Subfecund. Approximately 6 per cent of all couples with wife 35–39 years old are childless *and* either Definitely or Probably Sterile. An additional 4 per cent are childless and either Semifecund or Indeterminate. In all, approximately 10 per cent of the couples with wife 35–39 years old are childless *and* have a fecundity impairment.

Relatively few wives *expect* to be childless by the end of their childbearing period, and practically all of them are Subfecund. This is a clue to the very small number who will intentionally avoid having any children. Each wife gave us her estimate of how many children she expects to have when her family is completed (see Chapter 7 for details on "expected family size"). Only 112 couples—or 4 per cent of the entire sample—definitely expect to have no children. Only 8 per cent of these couples are Fecund:

	Per cent
Total	100
Fecund	8
Definitely Sterile	52
Probably Sterile	25
Semifecund	10
Indeterminate	5

Only about nine Fecund couples—less than 1 per cent of the total sample—reported that they definitely intended to have no children. Such a negligible number is consistent with the nationwide decrease in childless families that is now in progress.

Whether the childless couples with fecundity impairments would have children if these impairments did not exist is difficult to determine. Of the 202 wives in this group, 99 expected to have a child; consequently we may assume that they would have at least one if fecundity were "normal." The remaining 103 wives expected to be childless. Our best clue as to how they felt about their situation comes from the answers to the question: "If you could start your married life over again and choose to have just the number of children you would want by the time you were 45, how many would that be?" Only 2 of the 103 replied "no children." In contrast, 6 of the 9 Fecund wives who expected to remain childless said they would want no children if they were to make a fresh start. Obviously, the retrospective picture of an ideal situation does not involve childlessness for any significant number of childless wives. An even smaller proportion of the women with children said that they would want to be childless if they could relive married life.

Is Subfecundity Related to Social and Economic Status?

Are there significant differences in fecundity between major social and economic strata which parallel their differences in fertility? Some theories have attributed to impaired fecundity the lower fertility of such groups as the better educated, the city dwellers, or the persons with larger incomes. Such theories are linked with a variety of subthemes—for example, that urban living or white-collar-job tensions have deteriorating physiological or psychosomatic effects on reproduction. Most students of this problem have discarded the biological hypothesis as factual information has been accumulated. It is now generally believed that the major socioeconomic differentials in fertility do not result from differences in fecundity but rather from differences in social and economic factors which affect age at marriage and the extent and effectiveness of efforts to limit family size.

Our evidence supports the view that major fertility differentials are not the result of fecundity differences. If residents of large cities have fewer children than small-town folk, it is not because they are less fecund. Similarly, the relatively low fertility of the college-educated is not a result of impaired fecundity. For most socioeconomic characteristics there are no significant patterns of fecundity differences. Where fecundity differences do exist, they are generally opposite in direction to fertility differences and therefore cannot explain them.

The best previous evidence on the relationships in a nonclinical population is provided by the Indianapolis Study. In that study, also, it was found that fecundity bears no systematic relationship to such socioeconomic characteristics as income, education, and standard of living.[24] The Indianapolis Study and the present study are alike in that the data on subfecundity do not include *all* cases but only those which the respondents reported or which could be deduced from their reproductive histories during periods when there was no attempt to avoid conception. (However, these are likely to include substantially all the cases which affect the fertility of individual couples in real life.) On the other hand, as pointed out in Appendix A, Note 2, the Indianapolis Study sample differs from that of the present study in several respects affecting the discovery of fecundity. (The most important is that it was limited to Protestant couples in a large city—a group which uses contraception more extensively and from an earlier time in married life than our more general sample and in consequence would be expected to have more "hidden" subfecundity.) Moreover, a different classification by fecundity was used in the Indianapolis Study—one which related to the over-all situation during the preceding 12 to 15 years of married life, rather than primarily to the situation at interview. In spite of these differences the two studies are in agreement in showing no important relationship between fecundity and socioeconomic status.

For our sample, there is some evidence of minor differences in fecundity between different social strata, but in general these differences

[24] P. K. Whelpton and Clyde V. Kiser (eds.), *Social and Psychological Factors Affecting Fertility*, Milbank Memorial Fund, New York, 1950, vol. 2, pp. 359–416; or "IX. Fertility Planning and Fertility Rates by Socioeconomic Status," *Milbank Memorial Fund Quarterly*, vol. 27, no. 2, pp. 188–244, April, 1949.

are not systematic except for a few characteristics. Where consistent fecundity differences are found, they appear to be related to differences in efforts to avoid conception and to be reflecting differences in the *discovery* of subfecundity rather than in its *existence*. Those consistent social differentials in fecundity that appear do not support the hypothesis that major social differentials in fertility result from differences in fecundity impairments. On the contrary, where significant differences are found in our sample, it is generally the social groups characterized by higher fertility which have the higher subfecundity rates. This is consistent with an interpretation that while the physiological conditions determining fecundity vary but little with social status, the discovery of functional sterility is greater for lower-status groups. These groups are less likely to try to avoid conception, which increases the probability that impairments of fecundity will be revealed.

The selective relationship between fecundity and preventive measures discussed earlier in this chapter suggests that we might find that those social strata using contraception least or beginning to use it latest in married life would at least appear to have a higher incidence of subfecundity. This expectation is tempered by several facts: (1) the association between use and fecundity is strong in *all* social strata; (2) various types of fecundity impairments exist in any social stratum irrespective of contraceptive practice; and (3) most couples in all major strata want at least two children and therefore test their fecundity fairly extensively.

For a few variables, the expectation of differences in fecundity is borne out, but in general there are no significant and systematic associations with the social characteristics. We shall discuss in some detail only those few characteristics for which some systematic differences are found.

Educational Level. Fecundity appears to increase with the amount of education of the wife (Table 2–11). This probably is a result of the fact that the proportion attempting to avoid conception and the time such efforts are begun are both related to education. The couples with less education are less likely to use contraception at all and more likely to delay use. Therefore they are more likely to discover fecundity impairments.

When we consider the relationship between wife's education and fecundity for Users and Nonusers separately (Table 2–6), the relationship becomes very irregular or even reversed. This is consistent with the idea that the fecundity differences related to education reflect differences in family limitation practices. It does not minimize the importance of the fact that educational status is associated with functional subfecundity. For the lower educational strata subfecundity is more likely to be rec-

TABLE 2–11. PERCENTAGE OF COUPLES WHO ARE FECUND, BY WIFE'S AGE, BY WIFE'S EDUCATION, HUSBAND'S INCOME, WIFE'S RELIGION, WIFE'S LABOR-FORCE STATUS, AND YEARS WIFE WORKED SINCE MARRIAGE[a]

Socioeconomic characteristics	Wife's age				
	Total	18–24	25–29	30–34	35–39
Total	66	91	73	59	47
Wife's education:					
College	75	95	83	66	63
High school, 4	69	91	76	63	47
High school, 1–3	63	89	67	58	37
Grade school	52	86	59	44	45
Husband's income:					
$6,000 or more	66	88	74	64	58
$5,000–$5,999	64	90	72	59	45
$4,000–$4,999	66	91	75	61	47
$3,000–$3,999	67	90	75	59	39
Under $3,000	67	91	66	52	42
Wife's religion:					
Protestant	66	89	74	59	45
Catholic	66	93	71	59	50
Wife's labor-force status:					
Not in labor force	69	91	76	61	51
In labor force	58	89	62	54	35
Years wife worked since marriage:					
None	69	94	77	57	54
Under 1	79	93	79	71	53
1–4	69	87	75	62	51
5 or more	43	*	48	51	33

[a] Numbers of couples in base groups are shown in mimeographed tables (see Preface).

ognized and to make contraception unnecessary, but this does not mean that the underlying true fecundity distribution is necessarily different for different educational strata.

Husband's Income. Small consistent differences in the fecundity of couples classified by husband's income[25] are found only in one age group (30–34) (Table 2–11). Even this small relationship disappears when we consider separately the Users and Nonusers.

Religion of Wife.[26] Catholics and Protestants do not differ signifi-

[25] This refers to husband's gross income for the year 1954. Total family income was also obtained, but for our purposes it is likely that the husband's income is a better measure of the economic status of the family.

[26] For most purposes we shall use the religion of the wife to classify the sample. In almost every analysis made we found that in the cases where the religion of the wife and husband differed, the wife's religion was the more closely related to fertility variables. This statement will be documented in succeeding chapters.

cantly as to proportion Fecund (Table 2–11), but there are significant differences in specific Subfecund groups. Relatively fewer Catholics are Definitely Sterile, no doubt because of the attitude of the Church toward the performance of operations which make childbearing impossible (Table 2–12). In contrast, relatively more Catholics are Semifecund, because a somewhat smaller proportion attempt to avoid conception and those who do so begin later. This gives more opportunity for Catholic couples to have a period of at least 24 or 36 months with no preventive measures and no conception, which puts them in the Semifecund group according to our definitions. The two types of differ-

TABLE 2–12. PER CENT DISTRIBUTION BY FECUNDITY, FOR ALL COUPLES, BY WIFE'S AGE, BY WIFE'S RELIGION

Wife's religion	No. of couples	Fecundity					
		Total	Fecund	Definitely Sterile	Probably Sterile	Semi-fecund	Indeter-minate
Total							
Total	2,713	100	66	10	7	12	5
Protestant	1,817	100	66	12	7	11	4
Catholic	787	100	66	6	7	16	5
Ages 18–24							
Total	556	100	91	2	4	2	1
Protestant	394	100	90	2	4	2	2
Catholic	146	100	93	2	3	2	—
Ages 25–29							
Total	714	100	73	7	6	9	5
Protestant	461	100	74	8	6	8	4
Catholic	220	100	71	5	8	12	4
Ages 30–34							
Total	748	100	59	11	9	16	5
Protestant	505	100	59	14	9	13	5
Catholic	212	100	59	5	8	24	4
Ages 35–39							
Total	695	100	47	20	8	18	7
Protestant	457	100	45	23	8	18	6
Catholic	209	100	49	12	8	22	9

ences tend to cancel each other, so that the total proportion Subfecund is similar for Catholics and Protestants.

If we compare the percentage Fecund for Catholic and Protestant wives within each age group (Table 2–11), we find no consistent or significant pattern of differences. However, in the three oldest age groups, Catholics do have much lower proportions Definitely Sterile and higher proportions Semifecund than Protestants.[27]

Working Wives. Working wives have a higher incidence of fecundity impairments than those who do not work. Wives who have worked longest since marriage are most likely to be Subfecund.

It is well known that wives who are in the labor force (working wives) have fewer children than those not in the labor force (nonworking wives). In part, this results from the fact that if a couple has fecundity impairments which restrict family growth, the wife can more easily take a job away from home. In every age group, couples with working wives are less likely to be Fecund, and more likely to be Definitely Sterile, than those with wives not working (Table 2–11).[28]

If the wife has worked a long time (5 or more years since marriage), the couple is less likely to be Fecund, and more likely to be Definitely Sterile, than if the wife has never worked since marriage or has worked for a shorter period (Table 2–11). While this is true for wives in every age group, the relationship is strongest for those aged 35–39.

The relationship between fecundity and work experience persists (but is not so close) when Users and Nonusers are considered separately. Within each age group among both Users and Nonusers, the percentage Fecund is lower for those now working than for others, and among the workers is lowest for those who have worked 5 or more years since marriage.

Subfecundity is not the only explanation for the fact that working wives have fewer children. In later chapters we shall see that even among Fecund couples more work experience of wife is associated with lower past fertility, lower expected future fertility, and more effective fertility planning.

It is likely that many women go to work because they are Sterile or Subfecund and want to occupy time they might otherwise give to children. In Chapter 4 we shall see, however, that others who have a strong desire to work try to keep their families small.

[27] Since Catholics marry later than Protestants, fecundity comparisons between Catholics and Protestants were also made within comparable marriage durations. The results are essentially the same as when age of wife is the control. Group differences are also roughly similar when religion of husband is considered rather than religion of wife.

[28] Table 2–11 shows the percentage Fecund by labor-force status; the percentage in each of the Subfecund groups is shown in unpublished tables.

Among the social and economic characteristics which are considered, only three—education, religion, and wife's working status—show any significant pattern of relationship to fecundity. For a variety of other characteristics either the relationships do not exist or are not strong enough or consistent enough to be evident in a sample of the size used in this study. This is apparent in unpublished tables for the following characteristics: region of present residence, size of wife's longest place of residence before marriage, size of couple's longest place of residence, size of present place of residence, husband's occupation, couple's farm background, and couple's Southern farm experience.

In summary, consistent fecundity differences have not been found between most types of social groups considered. The few significant relationships which we have noted appear to be selective in origin, reflecting differences in efforts to limit conception rather than basic biological differences. Differences in fecundity by education and religion probably reflect differences in contraceptive practices and attitudes toward sterilization. The relationship of fecundity to the wife's work history is probably of a different character, reflecting the greater availability for work of wives with fecundity impairments.

Comparisons with Other Studies

Since our study is unique for the national population, there are no comparable data against which we can assess the incidence of fecundity impairments. A comparison is possible for the 86 couples in our sample who are similar in background characteristics to the 1,977 couples studied in Indianapolis.[29] In the Indianapolis Study, 73 per cent of the couples were classified as "relatively fecund." In our comparable subsample, approximately the same proportion can be classified in this way. It should be noted, however, that the couples in our sample made less effort to avoid conception and had more children; hence they were more likely to discover fecundity impairments. We believe, therefore, that the incidence of all impairments—including those not recognized—probably is slightly lower for this part of our sample than for the comparable Indianapolis couples in 1941.

Another interesting comparison is that with the Hutterite group, one of the most fertile for which reproductive records exist. Christopher Tietze has reported that 33 per cent of Hutterite couples have their last

---

[29] The 86 couples were selected to correspond with the Indianapolis Study sample with respect to age of wife, duration of marriage, number of times married, nativity, religion, educational level, and residence in a large city. See Appendix A, Note 2, for more information about the Indianapolis Study.

child before the wife reaches age 40.[30] Since Hutterites presumably do nothing to restrict family size, Tietze assumes that childbearing stops because of sterility. If this assumption is correct, 33 per cent of Hutterite couples become sterile while the wife is under 40. This is not grossly inconsistent with our figure of 28 per cent Definitely or Probably Sterile for couples with wife aged 35–39. However, if we make some allowance for the Semifecund couples in our sample who can bear no (more) children and also make some allowance for other couples who will still become sterile before age 40, the incidence of sterility in our sample probably exceeds slightly that of the Hutterites.

The Effect of Fecundity Impairments on Birth Rates

Fecundity impairments have a minor effect on birth rates in the United States. The major force keeping American families relatively small is contraception rather than subfecundity. Even though a significant number of American couples have fecundity impairments, birth rates would rise substantially if most of the couples who plan to have one, two, or three children wanted one additional child. The detailed analysis to support these generalizations will be presented in Chapter 8.

In a population like ours, most couples want only a small proportion of the children they can have and try more or less successfully to keep from having larger families than desired. Many of the Subfecund couples already have as many children as they wish, and some have more than they want! Still others will be able to have as many as they want, but perhaps not as quickly as they would like or just at the right time. Most of the remainder—about 36 per cent of the entire Subfecund group— will not have as many children as desired but will have some. Relatively few will be unable to have any children. In short, the potential effect of subfecundity in reducing fertility is greatly diminished by efforts to control family size.

The situation would be very different in a population not trying to regulate conception. Under those conditions fecundity impairments like those now present in the United States would reduce actual fertility very considerably below the theoretical level that would be possible if there were no subfecundity.

There is little reason to believe that fecundity impairments are any more widespread today than in earlier periods. In most societies which are thought to have relatively uncontrolled fertility the average woman

[30] Christopher Tietze, "Reproductive Span and Rate of Reproduction among Hutterite Women," *Fertility and Sterility*, vol. 8, no. 1, pp. 89–97, January–February, 1957.

who marries young and lives with her husband until middle age bears only six or seven children.[31] This is indirect evidence of the widespread incidence of impairments in all societies. Today greater medical knowledge and more attention to the individual simply make the existing fecundity impairments in Western countries more visible to physicians and to the general public as well.

In the next four chapters we shall discuss the efforts made to regulate conception—the chief means by which American families are kept small.

[31] See Appendix A, Note 6, for information about six countries.

Chapter 3

THE USE OF METHODS TO REGULATE CONCEPTION

The widespread use of methods to limit family size and to space children has had a profound effect on family growth patterns in Western societies like the United States. Most American couples now can and do plan the size of their families and the spacing of some or all of their children, in response to their socioeconomic situation and their personal desires.

In historical perspective, this is a unique and revolutionary development. While almost all societies have had some control over reproduction, until recent decades most practices have either been ineffective or confined to a relatively small part of the population. Some were in the nature of magic and were useless. More effective methods of contraception,[1] such as coitus interruptus or crude mechanical devices, have been used at various times and places in the past by various segments of the population.[2] Abortion and infanticide have been used much more widely than contraception to limit family growth over most of history.

It is only in recent decades and largely in Western societies that the most dynamic factor in population change has become fertility rather than mortality. Undoubtedly, this is due to the increasing use of effective methods for regulating conception. For at least one Western country (Great Britain) we have substantial direct evidence of the rapid increase in the use of contraception after 1875, in a period when fertility declined rapidly (see Chapter 1). There is also some evidence that the earlier and larger decrease in fertility in urban areas and among better-educated and higher-status groups in Great Britain was associated with earlier, more extensive, and more effective use of contra-

---

[1] As stated in Chapter 2, the term contraception is used to include any method of avoiding conception, except celibacy and sterilization. These methods include periodic continence (rhythm), abstinence for long periods, withdrawal (coitus interruptus), as well as such appliance or chemical methods as condom, diaphragm, jelly, and douche. Abortion is excluded.

[2] Norman E. Himes, *A Medical History of Contraception*, The Williams & Wilkins Company, Baltimore, 1936.

ception in these strata of the population.[3] In the United States the same population strata had the larger fertility declines from the 1850s (or earlier) to the depression decade of the thirties; they have also had the sharper rises in fertility in the postwar baby boom. The long-time decline and the recent rapid rise in annual birth rates are associated with the deliberate planning and timing of births by what has come to be a large majority of married couples. During the depression of the 1930s, contraception presumably was used to limit or postpone family growth in greater degree than during the more favorable 1920s. In the prosperous war and postwar period, millions of couples have had larger families or have had their children earlier, but presumably as part of a plan of some kind. Although these plans vary in their degree of explicitness and stability, we shall see that most couples now have a fairly specific idea of the number of children they want and are using contraception in order to stop when they achieve their goal.

That family limitation is very general in the United States is widely accepted as true even though comprehensive information has been lacking. The two most important previous studies on this topic are for the period preceding World War II and relate to special groups. One study obtained detailed histories of the use of contraception by certain types of white Protestant couples in Indianapolis.[4] Some general information about the use of contraception was obtained in an interview study in 1938–39, but this was restricted to upper-middle-class wives in 30 cities and was not based on a probability sample for the entire country.[5] Most other studies have been restricted to women going to birth control clinics or in maternity wards of hospitals, who obviously are not representative of all married women.[6]

Our data on family planning and on the use of contraception by a cross section of white American couples in the childbearing years are unique. We shall be using them to provide answers to several broad questions: (1) How extensive is the use of methods to avoid conception? (2) How many couples who have not yet used such methods intend to do so in the future? (3) At what stage of family growth does

[3] E. Lewis-Faning, *Report on an Enquiry into Family Limitation and Its Influence on Human Fertility during the Past Fifty Years* (Papers of the Royal Commission on Population, vol. I), H.M. Stationery Office, London, 1949, pp. 55ff. More information about this study is given in Appendix A, Note 18.

[4] See Appendix A, Notes 2c and 2g.

[5] John W. Riley and Matilda White, "The Use of Various Methods of Contraception," *American Sociological Review*, vol. 5, no. 6, pp. 890–903, December, 1940. For more information about the study see Appendix A, Note 8.

[6] For examples of these studies see Regine K. Stix and Frank W. Notestein, *Controlled Fertility: An Evaluation of Clinic Service*, The Williams and Wilkins Company, Baltimore, 1940; Raymond Pearl, *The Natural History of Population*, Oxford University Press, New York, 1939, chap. 4.

contraception begin? (4) To what extent are pregnancies planned, accidental, or unplanned in other ways? (5) How successful are couples in avoiding unwanted conceptions? (6) What are the different patterns of family planning? (7) How are various types of family limitation related to the fecundity of couples and to such basic indicators of different stages of family life as wife's age, duration of marriage, and number of children already born?

How the Information on Family Limitation Practices Was Obtained

Asking questions about contraception in an interview survey obviously poses many problems, because these questions touch an intimate aspect of married life. When this study was planned some experts felt that many wives would be unwilling to answer some of our proposed questions and that their answers to others would not be truthful. The presumed delicacy of the subject is certainly one reason why it had not been dealt with previously in an intensive national sample survey. Because of this concern about problems of rapport with respondents, our schedules contained fewer and less pointed questions than would have been asked if we had realized how interested the wives would be in the interview and how fully they would answer our questions. In retrospect, it seems that certain inadequacies of our data on contraception result more from our not including certain questions than from the unwillingness of the respondents to answer truthfully.

We have already explained in Chapter 1 the efforts that were made to inspire the confidence of the respondents in the purposes and sponsorship of the study. In addition to these general efforts, special care was taken to delay the questions about contraception until about halfway through the interview. Apparently, by this stage most respondents had become convinced that the interviewer was a reliable and sympathetic person. Since the wife had already described her pregnancy history and her expectations for future family growth, it seemed quite natural to discuss the means by which family growth had been or might be planned. Only 10 women refused completely to answer any of the questions about contraception. A few other women were somewhat embarrassed by these questions, but answered them anyway. In the overwhelming majority of cases there was no evidence of hesitancy or embarrassment. The observation of the field supervisors was that whether a respondent was embarrassed depended mainly on whether the interviewer was herself embarrassed about asking the questions and communicated her hesitancy to the respondent.

The first specific question about the couple's family limitation practices was:

43. "Now in your own case, have you or your husband ever done anything to limit the number of your children or to keep from having them at certain times?"

The terms "contraception" and "birth control" were not used because earlier studies and our pretests indicated that some couples used methods which were intended to, or which could, reduce the likelihood of conception, but which they did not consider to be contraception or birth control. In order to have them reported completely, each wife who answered question 43 in the negative was also asked:

44. "Some things couples do may not be considered birth control. Doctors and public health workers are interested in learning how many people use these methods. Have you ever made use of either of the methods on this card—you can tell me by the number on the card."

With this question the wife was shown a card with the following two items:

1. Safe period—rhythm (avoiding those days of the monthly cycle when conception is likely to occur)
2. Douche for cleanliness (soon after intercourse)

A significant number of women who answered question 43 in the negative said they had followed one (or both) of these two practices. Those who mentioned rhythm were classified as Users of a method of avoiding conception.

The women who reported douching for cleanliness only, and no use of contraception, pose a difficult problem of classification here as they did in Chapter 2. If we accept their statements at face value, as we must, they are Nonusers as far as motives are concerned. Some are also Nonusers from the standpoint of their actions, because the douching occurred so long after intercourse and was so perfunctory that it had little if any influence on the conception rate. Others, however, douched thoroughly immediately after intercourse—a practice which reduces substantially the risk of pregnancy.[7] Unfortunately, we did not ask the questions which would be necessary to classify the couples on this basis.

In some of our general tables and discussion we shall show as a separate group the couples with wives who reported douching for cleanliness only (DFCO) and no use of contraception. Occasionally we shall include these couples with other Users in a group called Action Users. For most purposes, however, DFCO couples will be treated as Nonusers and the term User, without further qualification, will refer to Motive Users. An examination of the data indicates that classifying all

---

[7] See Appendix A, Note 2f.

DFCO couples as Nonusers probably is somewhat closer to the truth than classifying all of them as Users.[8] Fortunately, in the many tabulations which were made on an action basis and also on a motive basis, the results are quite similar, chiefly because the number of DFCO couples is small in comparison with the number of Users or other Nonusers. It should be remembered, however, that the inclusion of DFCO couples with Nonusers in most of our analysis understates somewhat the extent of practices which reduce the conception rate.

The Extent of Use of Methods to Regulate Conception

Most of the couples in our sample have already used some type of contraception.[9] Almost all the others either intend to do so in the future or are Subfecund so that contraception is unnecessary or is a less pressing need. Fecund Nonusers who do not intend to become Users include only 6 per cent of all couples on an action basis and 4 per cent on a motive basis.

Seventy per cent of all the couples have at some time used contraception on a motive basis; as many as 81 per cent may have done so on an action basis. Among Fecund couples the past use of contraception is even more prevalent—83 per cent are Motive Users and 89 per cent are Action Users (Figure 3–1).

Many couples who have not yet used contraception intend to do so at some future time. Twenty-nine per cent of the Nonusers reported that they probably would use some method of family limitation in the future. Among the Fecund Nonusers 45 per cent expect to start contraception later on, but the remainder do not. Where a distinction is needed, we shall call these couples "Future Users" and "Never Users," respectively, and designate those who have already used a method as "Past Users."

Between 79 per cent (motive basis) and 86 per cent (action basis) of all couples are either Past or Future Users. For the 1,794 Fecund couples the proportion of Past and Future Users is between 90 per cent (motive basis) and 94 per cent (action basis). Attempts to avoid conception at some time are virtually universal among couples who have no fecundity impairment.

There is, nevertheless, a small minority of couples (6 per cent on an action and 4 per cent on a motive basis) who do not intend to use

---

[8] See Appendix E for a more detailed discussion of the DFCO category. A large number of unpublished tables are available showing Action and Motive Users separately.

[9] See Appendix E for a discussion of the accuracy of reporting use of contraception.

The wife reported on types used in her current marriage and any previous marriages. Therefore we have this information for all the married life of all wives. No questions were asked about methods of contraception during previous marriages of husbands.

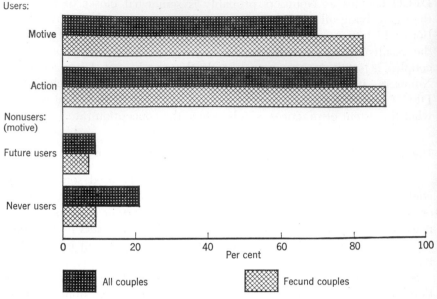

Users:

Motive

Action

Nonusers:
(motive)

Future users

Never users

0   20   40   60   80   100
Per cent

All couples   Fecund couples

Fɪɢ. 3–1. Percentage who have used, will use, and will not use contraception, for all couples and Fecund couples.

any preventive measures at any time although they are Fecund. The following is an example:

Cᴀsᴇ 13. This couple is Catholic. Neither husband nor wife believes in birth control. They have never used it and do not intend to do so. They have six children, and they enjoy them very much. They like big families, and the wife says they will welcome as many as come.

As explained in detail in Chapter 2, however, nearly three-fourths of the Nonusers who do not intend to use contraception are Subfecund. (For examples, see cases 2, 3, 6, 8, and 9 in Chapter 2.)

When Do Efforts to Regulate Conception Begin?

Many couples reported that they did not begin contraception until after one or more pregnancies. This gives credibility to the responses of couples who have not yet used contraception but say they intend to do so in the future. Delay in first use is very common.

About half of all Users began before the first pregnancy. An additional 32 per cent began after the first pregnancy (and before the second), and another 11 per cent began after the second (and before the third) (Table 3–1). The larger the total number of pregnancies, the later the time of first use. While barely one-fourth of the Users with four pregnancies began use before the first pregnancy, three-fifths of those with only one pregnancy did so. The average number of pregnancies before first use rises sharply from 0.82 for all Users to 1.60 for those who have had four or more pregnancies. It is clear that an important pattern of family limitation for many couples is to postpone using contraception until one or more pregnancies have occurred.

TABLE 3–1. PER CENT DISTRIBUTION BY NUMBER OF PREGNANCIES BEFORE FIRST USE OF CONTRACEPTION, FOR USERS, BY TOTAL NUMBER OF PREGNANCIES

Total no. of pregnancies	No. of Users	No. of pregnancies before first use						
		Total	0	1	2	3	4 or more	N.A.
Total	1,901	100	48	32	11	4	3	2
0	127	100	100	..	..	..	..	..
1	351	100	61	37	..	..	..	2
2	591	100	49	36	13	..	..	2
3	404	100	43	30	16	10	..	1
4 or more	428	100	27	31	17	10	12	3

N.A. = not ascertained (for all tables).
Two dots, in all tables, indicates a category which is impossible or very improbable.

Most of the couples who do not begin to use contraception until after one or more pregnancies delay because they want to have children early in marriage. Among the couples who had at least one pregnancy before using contraception 70 per cent answered "yes" to the question: "Did you want all your pregnancies up to that one (the one preceding first use) as soon as possible after marriage?" In contrast, many of the others were not in such a hurry to start their families and were surprised that the first conception occurred so quickly.

The circumstances determining when Users begin to try to regulate conception vary considerably. Some of the richness and variety of the individual case histories behind the statistics are illustrated by the following:

CASE 14. This couple began to use contraception from the beginning of their marriage. The wife worked for 3 years after marriage, then the couple discontinued contraception in order to have a child. After 2 years a second child was planned and conceived in the same way. The wife says that she expects no more children, and she hopes to go back to work to earn money for "extras" when the youngest child is in school.

CASE 15. Married in 1948, the wife is now 25 and the husband 27. They have two children, but the wife did not want the second child. As to an additional child, she says: "I just don't want one. I have all I can handle now without getting skinnier than I am and completely run down." The wife says that contraception was not used until after the second child "because I was just plain ignorant." The husband made $7,000 as a construction worker in 1954. The wife feels that their housing is inadequate.

CASE 16. This couple did not at first believe in using birth control. After the third pregnancy, they began to use the "rhythm" method to avoid additional pregnancies, because they were having serious marital conflicts. Another child then was conceived "accidentally." Since the birth of this child the wife has been using a contraceptive jelly, because she is still unhappy in her marriage, and she doesn't want additional children.

CASE 17. This farm couple, married in 1943, wanted to have a large family from the very beginning of their marriage. After their third child they decided that they wanted eight children. Their eighth child was born last year. No contraception was used until after the eighth child, because a large family was wanted as soon as possible. Contraception is now being used, because they plan to have no more children. The family is in comfortable economic circumstances with a cash income for last year of $7,500.

CASE 18. This couple has 11 children—the last two were twins. The wife says: "I didn't want the first one, but here I've gone along having them until I had 11 before I decided to do something about it." The couple began to use contraception after the twins were born.

Who Uses Contraception: Family Life Stages—Number of Births, Age of Wife, and Duration of Marriage

Although a cross-section view of our sample shows that most couples have used some method of preventing conception, the proportion of Users varies with the stage of the family life cycle. Most of this variation is found in the early years of married life, when most couples have the children they want. Those with the relatively small number considered ideal by most Americans are especially likely to be Users (Table 3–2).

Among Fecund couples with small families (1 to 3 children) the percentage of Users is 85 per cent for those with 1 birth, 89 per cent for those with 2, and 91 per cent for those with 3 (Table 3–2). If we add the Future Users, the proportion of Users rises to between 93 and 95 per cent of the couples with 1 to 3 births. It is clear, then, that nearly all Fecund couples who have had the small number of births generally considered desirable have already used contraception or intend to do so. Among the couples who have had no children the proportion of Users is lower, since many are waiting for a first child before beginning use.

Fecund couples who have had 5 or more births are somewhat less

TABLE 3–2. PERCENTAGE WHO ARE USERS, FOR ALL COUPLES AND FECUND COUPLES, BY NUMBER OF BIRTHS, BY WIFE'S AGE AND DURATION OF MARRIAGE[a]

Wife's age and years married	No. of births							
	Total	0	1	2	3	4	5	6 or more
All couples								
Age:								
Total	70	42	71	77	81	73	67	56
18–24	68	53	77	74	64	*	*	*
25–29	73	48	68	79	86	81	62	*
30–34	73	28	76	80	82	76	73	50
35–39	65	26	56	74	79	66	67	60
Fecund couples								
Age:								
Total	83	63	85	89	91	83	70	59
18–24	71	58	79	78	67	*	*	*
25–29	84	77	85	86	90	81	*	*
30–34	90	*	97	96	96	83	71	54
35–39	90	*	94	97	94	97	77	66
All couples								
Years married:								
Total	70	42	71	77	81	73	67	56
Under 5	65	53	76	66	*	*	*	*
5–9	75	37	69	85	81	77	*	*
10–14	73	30	68	77	86	78	63	62
15 or more	65	20	58	75	79	64	78	56
Fecund couples								
Years married:								
Total	83	63	85	89	91	83	70	59
Under 5	69	60	78	67	*	*	*	*
5–9	88	*	96	93	85	77	*	*
10–14	92	*	97	99	99	85	64	67
15 or more	92	*	100	98	100	100	*	58

* Less than 20 couples in base group. An asterisk has this meaning in all tables.
[a] Numbers of couples in base group are shown in mimeographed tables (see Preface).

likely to be Users than those with smaller families. This is not surprising. Obviously, some of the Fecund couples have large families precisely because they have not used contraception. A small number of such couples intend never to use contraception although they are Fecund and are very prolific by American standards. However, even among the Fecund couples who have had many children the dominant pattern involves the use of contraception at some time. Of those with 6 or more births almost 60 per cent are Past Users and another 10 per cent are Future Users.

Among Fecund couples with a given number of births, the wife's age makes a substantial difference in the proportion who are Past or Future Users. Of those with 3 births, for example, almost all (94 per cent) with wives 35–39 years old are Users, but only 67 per cent of those with wives 18–24 years old. This is a reasonable finding, for the only way that the older Fecund couples who married at the usual ages (wife under 25) could have limited their families to the 2 to 4 children that most of them have is by using contraception. In contrast, many of the younger Fecund couples could not have had many children even if they had not used contraception, simply because they have been married only a short time.

As young Fecund Nonusers grow older they either become Subfecund or have more children and feel greater pressure to control family size. Many of those who remain Fecund will become Users after another birth or two; the others are the "Never Users" who go on to have large families.

Duration of marriage also is related to past use of contraception by Fecund couples. Among those married at least 10 years the proportion of Users is 97 per cent or higher for those who have borne 1, 2, or 3 children (Table 3–2). Again it is clear that the American pattern of small families reflects the use of contraception by almost all Fecund couples. Among those with 1 or 2 births there is a particularly large difference in the proportion of Users between the group married less than 5 years and that married 5–9 years. Other large differences are those between couples married 10–14 years and those married 5–9 years in the group with 3 or 4 births.

Since most couples want and have only a small number of children, the proportion of Fecund couples who are Users is much larger for those married 5–9 years than a shorter period, even when parity is disregarded. Among all Fecund couples married 5–9 years, 88 per cent had already used contraception. The percentage is 92 for Fecund couples married more than 10 years.

It would be a mistake to picture all couples who begin contraception after the birth of the first or second child as having made the decision to do so before or shortly after marriage. It is likely that a significant minority of couples begin married life without having given much thought to contraception and with no explicit intention of using it and decide to begin only after having one or more children. We did not ask directly about such changes in intention, but there is evidence that they were not uncommon. In the first place, the proportion of Fecund couples married a short time who expect to be Users is smaller than the proportion who are in fact Users among those married longer. In addition, the case histories show that some couples did not seriously think about family size problems until successive pregnancies forced them to do so. Others who were at first conscientiously opposed to such practices later changed their minds under similar pressures. Such changes are to be expected in the future; as the younger couples in the sample grow older the proportion who are Users will rise to higher figures.

The following are illustrations of the family histories of couples who changed their attitudes to contraception:

CASE 19. This 33-year-old wife has lived in a small Middle Western town all her life. She had two children within 3 years after marriage, although she didn't want them so soon. She did not begin to use contraception until after her second child because she "hadn't thought much about it." In the 12 years since she began to use contraception she has had two accidental conceptions, both unwanted, and she feels they can't adequately care for so many children.

CASE 20. At first opposed on religious grounds to the use of contraception, this couple quickly had two children. The wife was very sick after each birth, so they reluctantly began to use a diaphragm for contraception, but both of them are unhappy about the moral consequences.

While the most significant variations in the use of contraception can be discussed in relation to number of births, as we have done, variation in relation to age and duration of marriage without reference to parity is also of some interest (Table 3–3). With few exceptions the proportion of Fecund couples who are Users increases substantially with age of wife, duration of marriage, and the two factors combined, regardless of how many children have been born. The most significant fact, however, is that a great majority of Fecund couples are Users among all subgroups based on age and duration of marriage.

The discussion of use of contraception in relation to different stages of family life has concentrated on the Fecund couples to highlight the dynamics of the situation when physiological defects do not introduce a different kind of problem. The relationships for all couples are like those for Fecund couples, but use is at a lower level since the Subfecund couples have less need for contraception. There are some variations determined by the special characteristics of the Subfecund.

To summarize: The majority of Fecund couples have used contraception regardless of whether the stage of family life is measured by the number of children they have had, the number of years they have been married, or the age of the wife. Among the Fecund subgroups we have considered, the variation in use is from a small majority to all members of the subgroup. Even when we consider all couples, including the Subfecund, the only subgroups in which less than half of the couples

TABLE 3–3. PERCENTAGE WHO ARE USERS, FOR ALL COUPLES AND FECUND COUPLES, BY WIFE'S AGE, BY DURATION OF MARRIAGE[a]

Wife's age	Years married				
	Total	Under 5	5–9	10–14	15 or more
All couples					
Total	70	65	75	73	65
18–24	68	65	79	..	..
25–29	73	66	76	72	..
30–34	73	65	76	74	64
35–39	65	*	49	71	65
Fecund couples					
Total	83	69	88	92	92
18–24	71	68	84	..	..
25–29	84	71	90	88	..
30–34	90	79	91	92	87
35–39	90	*	81	94	93

[a] Numbers of couples in base group are shown in mimeographed tables (see Preface).

have already used contraception are (1) the childless couples married more than 5 years or with wife 25 or older, and (2) the couples married 5–9 years with wife aged 35–39.

The Planning Status of Pregnancies

A conception may or may not be planned. Some occur before and some after couples first try to avoid conception. Of those taking place after the first use of contraception, some are carefully "planned" by stopping contraception, some are "accidental" (occurring in spite of attempts at prevention), and the others occur when there is no particular desire to have a pregnancy but no effort is made to avoid one. Some couples completely plan their families by means of contraception. They begin contraception shortly after marriage and have all their children by plan, that is, by discontinuing contraception in order to have a child. These couples are the model of the rational, highly planned family. Here is an illustration:

CASE 21. Married in 1941 and living in one of our great metropolitan centers, this couple has three children, carefully planned and spaced. They were born in 1944, 1948, and 1954. Condom has been the method of birth control. The wife says they approve of birth control, because "most people don't have the income to have as many children as they might want. There are so many opportunities that you want to have your children take advantage of today, and they do cost money." Originally, this couple planned to have only two children, but when the first two were boys, they talked it over and tried for a girl, but they had another boy. They are happy with their family as it is, and they definitely do not plan to have more children. The husband earns about $5,000 a year as a skilled worker. Although he advanced rapidly to his present income, they feel that he has hit a ceiling now and that they must plan to live on this income. The wife does feel that they can plan ahead. In her words, "Things have worked out just fine for me. I wouldn't change any-thing about my life." In 4 or 5 years when her youngest child is in kindergarten she may go back to work to help get "extra things for the family."

The planning efforts of most couples are less rigorous or less successful.

We have classified the 6,639 pregnancies of the couples in our sample by "planning status" as follows:

1. Pregnancies of couples who never used contraception
    a. Wives did not "douche for cleanliness only" soon after intercourse
    b. Wives "douched for cleanliness only" soon after intercourse
2. Pregnancies of couples who used contraception
    a. Pregnancies before use began
    b. Pregnancies after use began
        (1) Planned—contraception was stopped in order to have a child
        (2) Accidental—conception occurred when some method was being used to avoid it
        (3) Other unplanned—conception occurred when contraception was stopped for other reasons than the desire for a child (e.g., the couple was temporarily out of supplies, they could not use the customary method while visiting, they decided to follow the teachings of their church as they understood them)

A majority of pregnancies can be classified easily, because they began when contraception was not used at all during the period in question, or was used regularly. Difficulties arise when a method was occasionally omitted, but not because a child was wanted. In these cases even the wife does not know whether the conception should be classified as "accidental" (the method was used but failed) or as "other unplanned" (the method was temporarily omitted but not to have a child). It is likely that some which we have assigned to one of these groups belong in the other, but there is nothing to indicate that the mistakes of one type greatly outnumber those of the other type.

How are the pregnancies of American couples distributed in these "planning" categories? Table 3–4 and Figure 3–2 show the results of this classification, first for all pregnancies, then for pregnancies of Users, and finally for pregnancies of Users after use was begun.

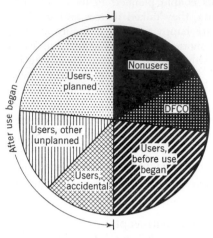

Fɪɢ. 3–2. Per cent distribution by planning status, for all pregnancies.

About one-quarter of all pregnancies were planned by discontinuing contraception in order to have a child. Such planned pregnancies are about one-third of all pregnancies of the couples who tried to regulate conception. They are about one-half of all pregnancies of Users *after* they began preventive measures.

One pregnancy in eight was accidental, occurring in spite of preventive efforts. Obviously, Nonusers cannot have accidental conceptions, nor can Users have them before adopting some method of family limitation. In consequence, the proportion of conceptions that are accidental is higher for Users (16 per cent) than for all couples (12 per cent), and still higher (24 per cent) for the conceptions occurring after some method of control was begun. While the latter proportion gives some idea of the success of the couple's efforts to regulate conception, it is not an accident rate. In order to

TABLE 3–4. PER CENT DISTRIBUTION BY PLANNING STATUS, FOR PREGNANCIES OF ALL COUPLES, OF USERS, AND OF USERS AFTER USE BEGAN

Planning status of pregnancies	Pregnancies of:		
	All couples	Users	Users after use began
Number of pregnancies	6,639	4,850	3,317
Per cent			
Total	100		
Nonusers	17		
DFCO couples	10		
Users	73	100	
Before use began	23	32	
After use began	50	68	100
Planned	24	33	49
Accidental	12	16	24
Other unplanned	12	17	24
Not ascertained	2	2	3

compute such a rate we would need to know not only how many accidental conceptions occurred, but also the length of the periods during which the couples were trying to prevent conception. This information was not obtained.

The planning status of pregnancies varies markedly with their order (i.e., first, second, third, etc.). Among the pregnancies of all couples, about one-sixth of those of the first four orders occurred to couples who never attempted to regulate conception. This proportion increases to about 30 per cent among the pregnancies of sixth or higher order (Table 3–5). At the other end of the continuum, the proportion planned by stopping contraception increases sharply from the first to the second pregnancy and then decreases with succeeding pregnancies. While 33 per cent of all second conceptions were planned in this way, only 10 per cent of those of sixth or higher orders were so planned. The proportion that are accidental rises from 7 per cent for first pregnancies to between 16 and 21 per cent for those of third or higher order. The residual "other unplanned" category increases sharply with pregnancy order from 7 per cent among first pregnancies to about 20 per cent among those of fourth or higher order.

The same general patterns appear at different levels when we consider only the pregnancies of Users or those of Users after first use. Among pregnancies occurring after first use the proportion planned is high (57 or 58 per cent) for first and second pregnancies, and then decreases to 19 per cent for those of sixth and higher order. The proportion that is accidental increases from 19 per cent for first pregnancies to 35 per cent for fifth pregnancies, but is smaller for higher orders (Figure 3–3).

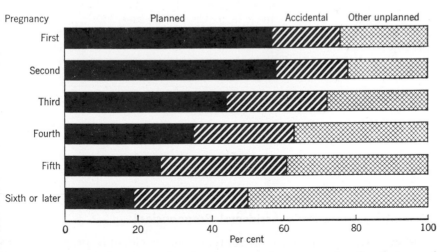

Fig. 3–3. Per cent distribution by planning status, for pregnancies after first use of contraception, by order of pregnancy.

TABLE 3–5. PER CENT DISTRIBUTION BY PLANNING STATUS, FOR PREGNANCIES OF ALL COUPLES, OF USERS, AND OF USERS AFTER USE BEGAN, BY ORDER OF PREGNANCY

Planning status of pregnancies	Order of pregnancy						
	Total	1st	2d	3d	4th	5th	6th or higher
All couples							
Number of pregnancies	6,639	2,416	1,899	1,108	586	301	329
Per cent							
Total	100	100	100	100	100	100	100
Nonusers	17	16	15	15	16	22	29
DFCO couples	10	10	10	10	10	11	11
Users	73	74	75	75	74	67	60
Before use began	23	39	18	12	9	8	8
After use began	50	35	57	63	65	59	52
Planned	24	20	33	28	23	15	10
Accidental	12	7	12	17	20	21	16
Other unplanned	12	7	11	16	20	20	21
Not ascertained	2	1	1	2	2	3	5
Users							
Number of pregnancies	4,850	1,773	1,422	831	428	201	195
Per cent							
Total	100	100	100	100	100	100	100
Before use began	32	53	25	16	12	12	13
After use began	68	47	75	84	88	88	87
Planned	33	27	44	37	31	23	16
Accidental	16	9	15	23	27	31	27
Other unplanned	17	9	14	22	27	30	36
Not ascertained	2	2	2	2	3	4	8
Users after use began							
Number of pregnancies	3,317	825	1,074	695	376	177	170
Per cent							
Total	100	100	100	100	100	100	100
Planned	49	57	58	44	35	26	19
Accidental	24	19	20	28	31	35	31
Other unplanned	24	20	19	25	30	35	41
Not ascertained	3	4	3	3	4	4	9

How Many Users Have Accidental Pregnancies?

Since many Users have more than one accidental pregnancy this question is not answered when we simply know what proportion of their pregnancies is accidental.

About one-fourth of the Users had at least one accidental pregnancy. The proportion having an accident rises rapidly with the number of pregnancies—from 12 per cent for couples with 1 pregnancy to more than 50 per cent for couples with 4 or more (Table 3–6). The increase is particularly abrupt after the second and third pregnancies—the numbers considered ideal by two-thirds of our couples (Figure 3–4). Essentially

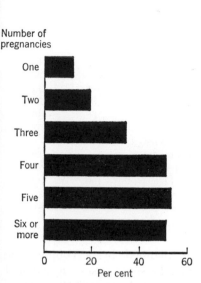

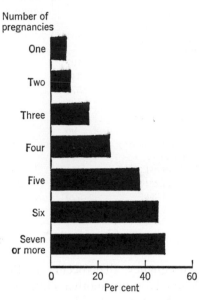

FIG. 3–4. Percentage of Users with at least one accidental conception, by number of pregnancies.

FIG. 3–5. Percentage of couples whose most recent pregnancy was unwanted, by number of pregnancies.

similar results are obtained when births rather than pregnancies are considered.

The proportion of Users with accidental pregnancies rises with length of marriage and age of wife. It increases from 19 per cent for Users married less than 5 years to at least 30 per cent for those married 10 or more years. The major difference is between couples married less than 5 years and all others (Table 3–6). There is also an increase with age from 20 per cent for wives 18–24 years old to 30 per cent for wives aged 35–39. These are simply indications that the incidence of such accidents rises with the length of exposure to the risk.

The number of wives who reported more than one accidental conception was 184, representing 10 per cent of the Users. Of these, 30 wives reported 4 or more accidental conceptions and 1 reported 7.

An accidental pregnancy is not necessarily unwanted. It may simply be

TABLE 3–6. PERCENTAGE OF USERS WHO HAD AT LEAST ONE ACCIDENTAL CONCEPTION, BY NUMBER OF PREGNANCIES, NUMBER OF BIRTHS, WIFE'S AGE, AND DURATION OF MARRIAGE

No. of pregnancies and wife's age	No. of Users	Percentage who had at least one accidental pregnancy	No. of births and years married	No. of Users	Percentage who had at least one accidental pregnancy
Total	1,861[a]	27	Total	1,861[a]	27
No. of pregnancies:			No. of births:		
0	127	0	0	174	3
1	343	12	1	421	15
2	578	19	2	642	22
3	393	34	3	373	43
4	223	51	4	136	51
5	96	53	5	68	46
6 or more	101	51	6 or more	47	57
Wife's age:			Years married:		
18–24	371	20	Under 5	417	19
25–29	519	29	5–9	631	29
30–34	529	27	10–14	490	32
35–39	442	30	15 or more	323	30

[a] Excludes 40 couples for whom information was not complete.

a pregnancy that occurs earlier than is planned by a couple who definitely want another child at some time. In some cases an accident may happen just a few months before the couple would discontinue contraception to have another child. It probably is too harsh to say that couples who have such a pregnancy are ineffective planners, since they may have delayed the pregnancy almost until the time they wanted it. While 18 per cent of the most recent pregnancies of couples in our sample were accidents, two-thirds of these accidental pregnancies were wanted at a later date.

The following are illustrations of two very different types of accidents:

CASE 22. This happy couple has always wanted six or seven children, and they now have five. After the third child, they used contraception to postpone the fourth child for a time. He was conceived accidentally, sooner than wanted, but they were happy to have him. They have since had another child, and they hope to have two more.

CASE 23. The wife was described by the interviewer as a "tragic figure" who had never had a real home, either before or after marriage. She has had six pregnancies in her 10 years of marriage. The first was unplanned but came before the use of contraception began. The next five were all accidents. All were unwanted. She was pregnant at the time of the interview and "furious" about it. She reports that her husband is "no good and runs around." Their income of $2,500 isn't enough to "take care of things. By the time you pay for their clothes you have nothing left for yourself." She described the way her life has worked out as "miserable," and remarked, "I can't plan at all. Do you mean to say that there are people who can?"

Unwanted Pregnancies

What proportion of couples have more pregnancies than they want? An answer to this question is needed when translating into future birth rates the statements of young couples about the number of children they want or expect.

All wives who had ever been pregnant were asked this question:[10]

15. "Before your last pregnancy began did you really want another child (a child) at some time in the future or would you just as soon not have had one?"

They were also asked how they thought their husbands felt about this pregnancy.

Answers to such questions probably provide low estimates of the number of couples who did not want their last pregnancy. Wives who felt this way but were ashamed to say so no doubt outnumber those who wanted their last pregnancy but reported falsely that they did not.

Sixteen per cent of the most recent pregnancies were reported as not wanted by the wife, the husband, or both. Wives more frequently said that they did not want this pregnancy than that they thought their husband was opposed. However, some of the husbands who did not want the last pregnancy may be concealed among the 187 husbands classified as "indifferent" or for whom an answer was not ascertained.[11]

The probability that the most recent pregnancy was unwanted by husband, wife, or both increases rapidly with the number of pregnancies— from 6 per cent for first pregnancies to 62 per cent among ninth or later pregnancies (Figure 3–5). Even among couples who had only four pregnancies, 1 in 4 did not want the last.[12] Once a couple has the two,

---

[10] Asking about attitudes held before the most recent pregnancy was an attempt to minimize the rationalization that may take place after the pregnancy. Some women who reported that they didn't want another pregnancy before the last one occurred indicated when answering a subsequent question that later on they accepted it and were even happy about it.

[11] It would have been preferable to have questioned the husband directly, because reports for the husband by the wife will involve some error. As mentioned earlier, however, it seemed better to interview 2,713 wives than a substantially smaller number of wives and husbands.

[12] The results are essentially the same when a tabulation like that for Figure 3–5 is based on the wife's response for the husband only or for herself only.

three, or four children commonly considered the ideal number, the likelihood that either the husband or the wife will not want another pregnancy increases rapidly. Partly because of the direct relation between number of pregnancies and duration of marriage, the proportion of couples with unwanted last pregnancies rises from 3 per cent for couples married less than 5 years to 22 per cent for those married 15 years or longer.

As measured by the criterion of unwanted last pregnancies, it is clear that there is a substantial minority of couples who do not plan effectively the growth of their families. This does not mean that such couples have many children. From the viewpoint of the biological potential, most of the families with unwanted children are small. But many small families may include an unwanted child when the actual and "ideal" family size is small in the society as a whole. While it is true that unwanted pregnancies are concentrated in the larger families, there are unwanted pregnancies even among the couples who had only one or two.

The contraceptive practice of a society may cause actual fertility to be far below the biological potential, even though many individual couples have unwanted pregnancies by their own standards or by the standards of the society. A massive reduction of fertility for the total population is not inconsistent with the existence of millions of couples who individually are unhappy about having too many children. The reduction of fertility from a potential seven or more children per couple to an actual four per couple is enormously significant from a national point of view. However, from the point of view of the individual couple, having four children instead of seven may be quite unsatisfactory when only two or three are wanted.

In a few interesting cases in our sample the desires and attitudes of the husband and wife were so divergent that one deceived the other in order to have a child that the spouse did not want. For example, one wife reported that she had intentionally failed to use contraception when her husband thought she was using it. Conversely, a few wives reported being tricked by their husbands or suspecting that such a trick was the cause of an accidental pregnancy.[13]

The statistical classification of individual pregnancies as accidental or planned, wanted or unwanted, does not reveal the happiness or the tragedy of many of the individual cases. Some of these situations have been described previously in the notes about individual couples. Other illustrations of interest are the following:

CASE 24. This young Irish Catholic couple has had two pregnancies. They have never tried to avoid conception, and they do not intend ever to do so.

---

[13] It is possible for the deception to be reversed so that a wife secretly uses contraception without telling her husband, but no such case was reported to us.

The wife came from a "wonderful large Irish family." She hopes to have "as many children as the Good Lord will send."

CASE 25. This Southern rural family is living in utter destitution in a tumble-down shack in which many of the windows are broken. The interviewer described the family as "out of Tobacco Road." Married since 1939, they have had eight pregnancies with six live births. The husband is permanently disabled, and the family is dependent on welfare payments. The couple has not used contraception, and they do not expect to do so, although they already have more children than they want. The wife said, "The Good Lord put women here to raise younguns and they oughten to interfere with His business."

CASE 26. This couple had five pregnancies without doing anything to prevent conception, although the wife reported douching for cleanliness. She said that she did not want the last pregnancy, because she hated her husband. When she learned that she was pregnant for the fifth time, she attempted suicide. After the last pregnancy both husband and wife were sterilized. She says she would have left her husband long ago, if it were not for the children.

CASE 27. A white-collar couple. Both husband and wife work. They have two planned children. They have always used contraception except when they stopped to have these two children. They are happy about their family as it is now. They do not want or expect more children, because they believe they can only educate two "properly."

CASE 28. This wife says she wishes she had never married or had children. She is unhappy as a wife and mother. She has borne six children—the last two were accidents. She says she felt trapped when she learned she was pregnant the last time.

Patterns of Family Planning: An Overview

How successful are couples in planning the growth of their families? There is no simple answer to this question, because there are many different ways in which family planning can be described. For example, some couples are unsuccessful in planning their families, because sterility or subfecundity prevents them from having as many children as they want. This situation will be considered in Chapter 8. Here we shall pay little attention to nature's negative role and concentrate on the planning done by couples themselves to space pregnancies and to prevent more than they want.

Couples differ not only in whether they have used or intend to use some method of regulating conception; in addition Users differ in the time when they begin use, the regularity and carefulness of use, and the success of their efforts. Among both Users and Nonusers there are some couples who have already had more pregnancies than they want, some who have had the right number, and some who want more.

In preceding sections we have discussed the planning status of individual pregnancies. Now we are taking a broader view of the couple's fertility history, looking at its *pattern* of contraceptive practice and the success achieved. Whether the most recent pregnancy was planned or unwanted tells only part of the story. Such information needs to be combined with information about earlier pregnancies so as to characterize family planning patterns in terms of general rationality and effectiveness. To cite two examples: At one extreme are couples who wanted a certain number of pregnancies and planned the timing of each of them by stopping contraception. At the other extreme are couples who have had more pregnancies than they want and had them toò close together, but have never done anything to avoid conception and do not intend to do so. Obviously, the various aspects of fertility planning can be combined in a number of ways to classify the many types of situations between these extremes.

As a beginning, let us consider a simple classification into three broad fertility planning types, ignoring the influence of subfecundity:

1. *Completely Planned Fertility.* The couple used contraception regularly and conceived only when they stopped it for that purpose. Nearly all these couples have had one or more planned pregnancies, but a few have used contraception to avoid having any children and have never been pregnant. This is the model of the completely rational family referred to earlier. Such couples have had no accidental or other unplanned pregnancies.

2. *Partially Planned Fertility.* This is a heterogeneous group with a wide variety of histories. Some of the couples have not used contraception, but have had no pregnancy because of subfecundity, short duration of marriage, or both. Most of the couples in the group have had at least one pregnancy, wanted the last pregnancy that occurred, but have not planned all their pregnancies by stopping contraception in order to conceive. Fertility was planned for all these couples in the sense that they have not had more pregnancies than they wanted. Some of them have never used contraception, some have used it intermittently, and some have used it regularly but have had one or more accidental conceptions. Some conceptions occurred long before they were wanted, but every pregnancy was wanted sooner or later.

3. *Excess Fertility.* The couple's most recent pregnancy was unwanted then or later by the husband, the wife, or both. Such couples may or may not have used contraception. The Users in this group may have planned their family growth at earlier stages, but in the end they did not try to prevent an unwanted pregnancy or they tried but were not successful.[14]

---

[14] This classification by fertility planning status is based on pregnancies. For a brief comparison with a classification based on births, see Appendix A, Note 9.

The case descriptions presented earlier in this chapter include examples of couples with Completely Planned fertility (cases 21 and 27) and Excess Fertility (cases 23, 25, and 28). The Partially Planned group includes a wide range of types, from couples who plan to have a small family but temporarily delay using contraception because they want children quickly, to couples who never intend to use contraception because they want as many children as they can have. The following cases illustrate these two extremes:

CASE 29. This young middle-class couple wants three children. Contraception was not begun until after the second child, because they wanted the first two right away. The wife has been using a diaphragm for 2 years now, but she plans to discontinue using it soon to have a third child. Later on she hopes to go back to work when all her children are in school.

CASE 30. This Puerto Rican couple has been in New York for 4 years. They have eight children and are expecting another in 2 months. They expressed great joy in children and appeared to be a very happy family. The husband and wife want as many children as possible. In the wife's words: "There's always room for a baby. They are a big help to you. They make you feel good and busy. My husband's father had 15. We want to beat him with 16. I'm only 35, but we lost 2 years when my husband came to the United States."

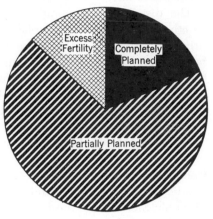

FIG. 3–6. Per cent distribution by fertility planning status, for all couples.

Our sample of American families is distributed among the three broad planning types as shown in Figure 3–6 and by the following:

Fertility planning	All couples	All Fecund couples	All Users	All Fecund Users
Total: Number	2,713	1,794	1,901	1,491
Per cent	100	100	100	100
Completely Planned	19	24	27	29
Partially Planned	66	61	58	56
Excess Fertility	13	13	13	13
Not ascertained	2	2	2	2

These figures give us a cross-section "snapshot" view of the fertility planning status of American families, without regard to differing family life stages. Considering all the couples, about 1 in 5 currently has Completely Planned fertility, 2 in 3 have Partially Planned fertility, and 1 in 8 has Excess Fertility. In the over-all view, then, there is a small but significant minority of couples who have planned so poorly to date that they have had more pregnancies than they want, and a larger group—but still a minority—who have planned all their pregnancies with the use of contraception. Most couples are classified as having Partially Planned fertility: either (1) they have not used contraception and have not conceived because recently married, Subfecund, or both, or (2) they have not had more pregnancies than they wanted eventually but not all their pregnancies have been planned by stopping contraception.

The distribution of families into these three broad types is similar whether we consider all couples, Fecund couples, or Fecund Users. The principal difference is that there are relatively more Completely Planned families and fewer Partially Planned families among Fecund couples than among all couples. This would be expected because Fecund couples have greater need to restrict family size than Subfecund couples, so are more likely to be Users. Only Users can have Completely Planned fertility according to our system of classification.

Fertility planning status differs in significant ways for our five fecundity groups (Table 3–7). Each of the Subfecund groups has relatively fewer Completely Planned families and relatively more Partially Planned families than does the Fecund group. Among the Subfecund couples, the Probably Sterile have the highest proportion Completely Planned, probably, in part, because we classify in this group the couples using contraception to remain childless where there are reasons for thinking that pregnancy might be fatal to the mother. One would expect that relatively fewer of the Subfecund than of the Fecund couples would have

TABLE 3–7. PER CENT DISTRIBUTION BY FERTILITY PLANNING STATUS, FOR ALL COUPLES, BY FECUNDITY

Fecundity	No. of couples	Fertility planning status				
		Total	Completely Planned	Partially Planned	Excess Fertility	N.A.
Total	2,713	100	19	66	13	2
Fecund	1,794	100	24	61	13	2
Subfecund	919	100	9	77	13	1
Definitely Sterile	283	100	7	70	23	—
Probably Sterile	187	100	17	76	5	2
Semifecund	328	100	9	78	11	2
Indeterminate	121	100	—	92	8	—

The dash indicates a percentage below 0.5 in all tables.

Excess Fertility, because many who are Subfecund cannot have as many children as they want. In fact, however, Excess Fertility is equally common in these two broad groups.

The Definitely Sterile couples were not effective planners before further reproduction became impossible. A very small proportion of their families are Completely Planned, and an unusually large proportion are Excess Fertility. The latter is consistent with our earlier interpretation (Chapter 2) that a substantial number of these couples were sterilized to prevent further childbearing rather than because of disease or other defects of the reproductive system. However, the heavy childbearing that produces large Excess Fertility families also makes some wives unable to bear another child.

The rather low proportion of Completely Planned families among the Semifecund can be interpreted to mean that for these couples careful planning is not urgent, if necessary at all. The attitude of many such couples is represented by this one:

CASE 31. This couple has never used any form of contraception but has had only one child in 16 years of marriage. They have never given much thought to birth control, because "too many children were never a problem. We didn't have enough." Their one pregnancy came unexpectedly after 12 years. They had given up hope and thought they were too old. They don't expect any more, because they are "too old, and it's so long since the first one." They do not believe in birth control.

It is apparent that fertility planning status will vary with age, duration of marriage, and number of pregnancies. For example, the longer a couple has been married, the greater the likelihood that they have had more pregnancies than they want and the less the probability that their family is Completely Planned (Table 3–8). Similarly, for Fecund couples and Fecund Users as well as all couples, relatively fewer of the wives in the later 30s than of the younger wives have Completely Planned families (Table 3–9), because as a group they have been married longer and there has been more time in which an accidental conception could occur.

Completely Planned families are small families; large families are likely to represent Excess Fertility. Theoretically, large families could be Completely Planned, but in fact they are not. Not one of the 86 families with 6 or more births is Completely Planned (Figure 3–7 and Table 3–10). Only 1 per cent of the families with 5 births and 3 per cent of those with 4 births are in this category. The proportion of Completely Planned families declines very rapidly as the number of births rises.

The Excess Fertility group includes a larger proportion of couples

Number of births

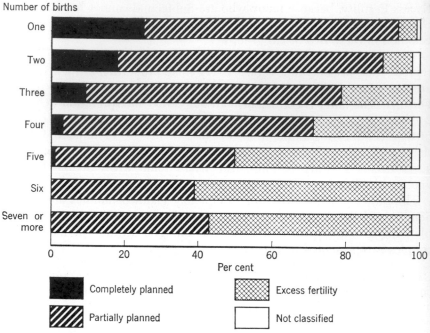

FIG. 3–7. Per cent distribution by fertility planning status, for all couples, by number of births.

at each successively higher parity and takes in more than half of all couples with 6 or more births (Table 3–10 lower deck). After second parity there is a very sharp rise in the proportion classified as Excess Fertility and a very sharp fall in the proportion Completely Planned. Similar statements hold true for wives in each age group. (This is shown in more detail later in Table 3–13.) Couples who have had more than 3 births are unlikely to have planned all of them regardless of the age of the wife. On the other hand, a rather high proportion of the wives of any age with more than 3 children are in the Excess Fertility group and an even higher proportion are in the Partially Planned group. The family with 6 or more children generally is planned less carefully or not planned at all and is larger than the couple wants.

The fertility planning status of our cross section of the population in the spring of 1955 reflects the various life-cycle stages as they were at that time. Many of the couples will move to a different family planning group as they have more children—some planned and some unplanned, some wanted and some unwanted.

In the following pages we shall discuss in more detail subgroupings of our three broad planning categories. The reader who is satisfied with the general picture just presented may wish to skip to the summary at the end of the chapter.

TABLE 3–8. PER CENT DISTRIBUTION BY FERTILITY PLANNING STATUS, FOR ALL COUPLES, BY WIFE'S AGE, BY DURATION OF MARRIAGE

Years married	No. of couples	Fertility planning status				
		Total	Completely Planned	Partially Planned	Excess Fertility	N.A.
		Total				
Total	2,713	100	19	66	13	2
Under 5	649	100	29	67	3	1
5–9	869	100	18	69	11	2
10–14	686	100	16	65	18	1
15 or more	509	100	10	66	22	2
		Ages 18–24				
Total	556	100	25	67	6	2
Under 5	432	100	27	68	3	2
5–9	122	100	21	63	14	2
10–14	2	100	*	*	*	*
		Ages 25–29				
Total	714	100	22	66	11	1
Under 5	160	100	36	60	3	1
5–9	446	100	18	70	10	2
10–14	108	100	10	63	27	—
		Ages 30–34				
Total	748	100	17	66	15	2
Under 5	40	100	25	71	4	—
5–9	240	100	20	69	8	3
10–14	367	100	17	63	18	2
15 or more	101	100	7	60	31	2
		Ages 35–39				
Total	695	100	13	68	17	2
Under 5	17	100	*	*	*	*
5–9	61	100	13	65	17	5
10–14	209	100	17	69	13	1
15 or more	408	100	10	67	21	2

Patterns of Fertility Planning: Nine Important Groups

The preceding three-way classification of fertility planning status oversimplifies the variety of planning patterns used by American families. Except for the Completely Planned group, it does not take into account

TABLE 3–9. PER CENT DISTRIBUTION BY FERTILITY PLANNING STATUS, FOR
ALL COUPLES, FECUND COUPLES, AND FECUND USERS, BY WIFE'S AGE

Wife's age	No. of couples	Fertility planning status				
		Total	Completely Planned	Partially Planned	Excess Fertility	N.A.
All couples						
Total	2,713	100	19	66	13	2
18–24	556	100	25	67	6	2
25–29	714	100	22	66	11	1
30–34	748	100	17	66	15	2
35–39	695	100	13	68	17	2
Fecund couples						
Total	1,794	100	24	61	13	2
18–24	504	100	26	67	5	2
25–29	521	100	26	61	12	1
30–34	445	100	22	58	17	3
35–39	324	100	19	57	21	3
Fecund Users						
Total	1,491	100	29	56	13	2
18–24	358	100	37	54	7	2
25–29	440	100	30	57	12	1
30–34	400	100	25	57	15	3
35–39	293	100	21	56	20	3

whether couples have already used contraception or intend to do so, or
whether the *most recent* pregnancy was planned by stopping contraception. Nor are accidental conceptions taken into account unless they occur
after couples have as many children as they want. Only a more complicated classification can simultaneously consider all these factors. We
shall now work mainly with nine groups obtained by subdividing the
three broad classes. In looking at fertility planning in this more precise
way, we shall be filling in some important elements of the situation which
were neglected in our overview.[15]

In our more detailed fertility planning classification the primary
division separates the couples into those who have used some method of
avoiding conception and those who have not. These groups are then
subdivided according to the planning status of all pregnancies or the

[15] Here as in the overview the classification is based on pregnancies. For a brief
discussion of a classification based on births, see Appendix A, Note 9.

TABLE 3–10. AVERAGE NUMBER OF BIRTHS AND PER CENT DISTRIBUTION FOR ALL COUPLES BY FERTILITY PLANNING STATUS, AND PER CENT DISTRIBUTION BY FERTILITY PLANNING STATUS FOR ALL COUPLES BY NUMBER OF BIRTHS

No. of couples or births	No. of couples	Fertility planning status				
		Total	Completely Planned	Partially Planned	Excess Fertility	N.A.
No. of couples		2,713	508	1,808	347	50
No. of births, average		2.1	1.2	2.0	3.6	2.2

Distribution by number of births

Total		100	100	100	100	100
0		16	31	14	2	16
1		22	30	22	10	14
2		31	30	34	19	36
3		17	8	18	26	18
4		7	1	7	15	6
5		4	—	3	14	4
6 or more		3	—	2	14	6

Distribution by fertility planning status

Total	2,713	100	19	66	13	2
0	419	100	37	59	2	2
1	603	100	25	68	6	1
2	843	100	18	72	8	2
3	468	100	9	70	19	2
4	190	100	3	68	27	2
5	104	100	1	49	48	2
6 or more	86	100	—	41	56	3

most recent pregnancy, whether the couples have had more births than they want and (for Nonusers) whether they expect to begin contraception in the future.[16] The relation between the three-group and the nine-group classification is shown in Figure 3–8.

Essentially this classification orders couples by the extent to which they use contraception and their success in avoiding unwanted pregnancies. At one extreme, the Completely Planned couples have used contraception to plan *all* their pregnancies or to keep from having any. At the other

[16] The fertility-planning-status categories for Users are much the same as those for "relatively fecund" couples which were developed for the Indianapolis Study. Cf. P. K. Whelpton and Clyde V. Kiser (eds.), *Social and Psychological Factors Affecting Fertility*, Milbank Memorial Fund, New York, 1950, vol. 2, pp. 225–230; or *Milbank Memorial Fund Quarterly*, vol. 25, no. 1, pp. 79–85, January, 1947.

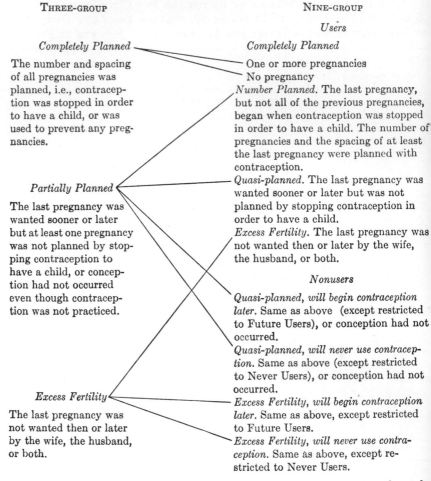

THREE-GROUP

NINE-GROUP

Users

Completely Planned

The number and spacing of all pregnancies was planned, i.e., contraception was stopped in order to have a child, or was used to prevent any pregnancies.

Partially Planned

The last pregnancy was wanted sooner or later but at least one pregnancy was not planned by stopping contraception to have a child, or conception had not occurred even though contraception was not practiced.

Excess Fertility

The last pregnancy was not wanted then or later by the wife, the husband, or both.

Completely Planned

One or more pregnancies
No pregnancy
Number Planned. The last pregnancy, but not all of the previous pregnancies, began when contraception was stopped in order to have a child. The number of pregnancies and the spacing of at least the last pregnancy were planned with contraception.
Quasi-planned. The last pregnancy was wanted sooner or later but was not planned by stopping contraception in order to have a child.
Excess Fertility. The last pregnancy was not wanted then or later by the wife, the husband, or both.

Nonusers

Quasi-planned, will begin contraception later. Same as above (except restricted to Future Users), or conception had not occurred.
Quasi-planned, will never use contraception. Same as above (except restricted to Never Users), or conception had not occurred.
Excess Fertility, will begin contraception later. Same as above, except restricted to Future Users.
Excess Fertility, will never use contraception. Same as above, except restricted to Never Users.

Fig. 3–8. Relationship between three-group and nine-group classification of couples by fertility planning status.

extreme, the Excess Fertility Never Users will have never used contraception and have had at least one more pregnancy than the husband or wife wants.

The Number Planned Users are ranked above the Quasi-planned Users because the most recent pregnancy was planned by discontinuing contraception. Although the Quasi-planned couples reported that they wanted the last pregnancy, it may have begun under a variety of circumstances before contraception was first used, in spite of contraception, or when contraception was stopped for some other purpose than to have a child. As a whole these couples have not demonstrated in their most recent pregnancy the careful planning that is characteristic of the Number Planned group.

Our ordering of the categories of Users is at least partially validated by the incidence of accidental pregnancies:

Fertility planning status of Users	*Per cent of couples with one or more accidental pregnancies*
Completely Planned	..
Number Planned	22
Quasi-planned	37
Excess Fertility	63

Among the Excess Fertility couples 31 per cent have had more than one accidental conception.

Not all Excess Fertility Users have had too many pregnancies because of the failure of some method of contraception. In many cases the unwanted pregnancies began because contraception was not used regularly rather than because it was ineffective. Other couples did not begin use until after having at least one more pregnancy than they wanted. However, as number of children increases, the probability that couples with Excess Fertility have had an accident rises rapidly. Most Excess Fertility Users with more than one birth have had at least one accident.

Another check on the ordering of the classes is based on answers to question 46: "Have you used some method almost always except when you wanted to have a child?"

Fertility planning status of Users	*Per cent of couples who used a method almost always except when they wanted a child*
Completely Planned	87
Number Planned	80
Quasi-planned	63
Excess Fertility	66

The ordering of the first three groups is as expected. The fact that the proportion of couples using a method regularly is somewhat larger for the Excess Fertility Users than the Quasi-planned Users is consistent with the higher accident rate for the former. Apparently they tried to avoid unwanted pregnancies but were not very successful. The Quasi-planned Users are distinguished from the Excess Fertility Users by their success in not exceeding their fertility goals rather than by the extent of their efforts to do so.

"Planning" in this classification scheme has a particular and limited meaning involving mainly the successful use of contraception. A broader definition in terms of the achievement of fertility goals is not unreasonable. For example, it can be argued that only the Excess Fertility couples have unplanned fertility and that all other couples are successful planners in the sense that they have succeeded in avoiding more pregnancies than they want.

From this point of view, several other patterns of planning may be as rational as those we have described. For example, some couples do not begin to use a method of regulating conception until after they have *some* children, because they want to start a family quickly. Then, they successfully use contraception to space one or more additional pregnancies. Other couples want *all* their children quickly after marriage, do not begin contraception until they have them, and then successfully use contraception to avoid additional pregnancies. Together these two groups comprise 13 per cent of all couples and 22 per cent—almost 1 in 4—of all Fecund Users. Those couples might be classified as having Completely Planned fertility because they have acted in a rational manner to meet their goals. In general, these couples have families of moderate size, like the Completely Planned families in the present classification scheme.

In the main, however, we shall rely on a classification which identifies successful planning with successful use of contraception. This procedure is preferred for two reasons. One is that it places more emphasis on reported behavior and less on statements of attitude that may represent ex post facto rationalizations or intentions. Let us consider, for example, the couples with all the children they wanted who had another child because contraception failed. Some of them gradually forget their former attitude regarding family size. It seems more likely that in such cases the wife would report that the last pregnancy was accidental but wanted (and be classified as Quasi-planned) than that she would say that contraception was stopped in order to have a child (and be classified as Number Planned). In these and other cases, a classification based on actions gives more accurate results than one based on remembered attitudes. A second reason for including in the highest planning category only those couples who have used contraception to plan *each* pregnancy is that such couples are acting more rationally from a medical point of view than are those who do not try to space their pregnancies. It is desirable for health reasons not to have one pregnancy begin too soon after the end of the preceding pregnancy. Unless the wife knows that ovulation will be delayed for at least a few months after a pregnancy ends, most Fecund couples need to practice contraception for a time in order to ensure an adequate interpregnancy interval.

Another dimension might have been added to our classification scheme in order to provide for the Subfecund couples who are unable to have as many children as they want. It may be argued that such couples should be taken out of the Completely Planned, Number Planned, and Quasi-planned groups and put in a special group of unsuccessful planners. However, as mentioned at the beginning of this chapter, it seemed advisable not to add this dimension here, but to give these couples special attention in the later chapters dealing with expected size of completed families.

In view of the alternative ways of defining planning, some readers may prefer to think of our fertility-planning-status classification as a set of patterns of behavior rather than an ordered planning scale.

Let us apply our detailed fertility planning classification to all couples first. This gives a cross-section view of the whole population represented by our sample in March, 1955. We are initially disregarding the fact that age, duration of marriage, fecundity, number of births, and other factors affect fertility planning status.

In the total sample, approximately 14 per cent of the couples have had at least one pregnancy and planned all their pregnancies (Table 3–11, left-hand column). An additional 5 per cent have never been pregnant, presumably because of contraception. Together they form the Completely Planned User group. Some of these couples probably are Subfecund but do not know it, because they have not tested their fecundity for many months or years.

An additional 15 per cent of all our couples are Number Planned Users. When they are added to the Completely Planned Users, we find that just about one-third of all couples have planned the *number* of their pregnancies to date by stopping contraception in order to have their most recent pregnancy.

One-quarter of all couples are Quasi-planned Users. They have not had more pregnancies than they want, but they did not deliberately plan the most recent pregnancy. This group no doubt includes some couples who really did not want their last pregnancy but accepted it and rationalized their acceptance.

Excess Fertility Users comprise 9 per cent of all couples—1 in 11 of the total. They clearly are ineffective planners of family size. Despite the fact that they have used contraception they have had at least one pregnancy more than they wanted. We have already seen that almost two-thirds of them had at least one accidental conception; almost one-third had two or more.

About 18 per cent of all couples are Quasi-planned Nonusers who say they do not intend to practice contraception in the future. This group

TABLE 3–11. PER CENT DISTRIBUTION BY FERTILITY PLANNING STATUS, FOR ALL COUPLES, FECUND COUPLES, ALL USERS, AND FECUND USERS

Fertility planning status	All couples	Fecund couples	All Users	Fecund Users
Number of couples	2,713	1,794	1,901	1,491
Per cent				
Total	100	100		
Users	68	82	100	100
Completely Planned	19	24	27	29
Never pregnant	5	6	7	7
Ever pregnant	14	18	20	22
Number Planned	15	18	22	21
Quasi-planned	25	29	36	35
Excess Fertility	9	11	13	13
Nonusers	30	16		
Quasi-planned	26	14		
Future Users	8	6		
Future Nonusers	18	8		
Excess Fertility	4	2		
Future Users	1	1		
Future Nonusers	3	1		
Not ascertained	2	2	2	2

includes many Subfecund couples who do not need to take preventive measures. Another 8 per cent of all couples are Quasi-planned Nonusers who plan to begin use in the future.

The Excess Fertility Nonusers represent a very small part of the total population, and even this small proportion is greatly reduced when the Subfecund are eliminated. If we add together all types of Excess Fertility couples they represent about 1 couple in 8.

Because fecundity is related to the use of contraception it affects in important degree the distribution of couples by fertility planning status. Eliminating the Subfecund couples increases significantly the proportion of Users and decreases sharply the proportion of Nonusers (Table 3–11, second column from left). Fecund couples are more likely than Subfecund couples to be effective Users. Forty-two per cent of the Fecund couples, but only 18 per cent of the Subfecund, planned their most recent pregnancy by means of contraception or used contraception to avoid any pregnancies. The total proportion with Excess Fertility is somewhat larger for Fecund couples than for all couples among the Users, but is somewhat less among the Nonusers. Nevertheless, only 11 per cent of the Fecund couples are Excess Fertility Users, and only 2 per cent are Excess Fertility Nonusers. In other words, couples who are Fecund and have had unwanted pregnancies are very likely to have tried (or to intend to try) to control family size. The proportion who are Quasi-planned Nonusers not intending to use a method is much smaller for Fecund couples than for all couples (8 and 18 per cent, respectively). The physiological condition of most Subfecund couples makes further childbearing unlikely or impossible, and contraception unnecessary.

The over-all distributions shown in Table 3–11 and discussed above give a cross-section picture of the fertility planning status of all couples, Fecund couples, all Users, and Fecund Users. One-third of all the couples and one-half of the Fecund Users have planned the *number* of pregnancies to date by means of contraception—they have Completely Planned or Number Planned fertility. At the other extreme, about 1 in 8 of all couples and of Fecund Users have had more pregnancies than they want. Between these two extremes are many couples—about half of the total sample and one-third of the Fecund Users—who have not had more pregnancies than they want but who did not plan the timing of their most recent pregnancy by stopping contraception.

As was mentioned previously, the fertility planning status of an important proportion of our couples will change in the future as they have additional pregnancies. Some of these changes will occur because couples start contraception and move from a Nonuser to a User group. It is probable that more of the changes will reflect the failure of efforts to regulate conception. For example, some couples with Completely Planned or Number Planned fertility will have an accidental pregnancy and shift to the Quasi-planned or Excess Fertility group. Similarly, some in the Quasi-planned group will have more children than they want and join the others with Excess Fertility.

Changes in the opposite direction will be much less numerous. Most of them will be couples classified as Quasi-planned who stop contraception in order to have another child and thus achieve Number Planned fertility. Moving from the Excess Fertility group to the Quasi-planned or Number Planned group is not impossible, but very few couples who at one time think they have too many children will plan and have still another at a later date. No couple can move to the Completely Planned group by having another child, because to be in that group a couple must plan *each* pregnancy by stopping contraception.

Fertility Planning Status, by Number of Births

Fertility planning status and the number of births a couple has are closely related. Our more detailed classification supports our overview in showing that small families are likely to be planned families and that large families are likely either to be unplanned, unwanted, or both.[17]

[17] The number of births that couples in the various planning groups have and expect to have is discussed in Chapter 8.

Tables 3–12 and 3–13 show how detailed fertility planning status is related to number of births for all couples and Fecund couples and for all couples by age of wife. The following summary of conclusions is based on these tables:

1. The proportion of *all couples* with Completely Planned fertility decreases sharply as the number of births rises for the whole sample and for each age group (Tables 3–12 and 3–13). These couples are concentrated among those with small families but do not include a majority at any parity. The largest Completely Planned family in our sample has 5 children.

2. The *Users* who did not plan all their pregnancies but who wanted all of them (the Number Planned and Quasi-planned Users) also have had moderate numbers of births (averaging 2.5 and 2.2 per couple, respectively). Together they constitute a majority of all couples of second and third parities (Table 3–12). From fourth to sixth parity they decrease rapidly; this is especially true for the Number Planned.

3. Among *Fecund couples* with a moderate number of births—1, 2, 3, or 4—a majority are Users who wanted their last pregnancy (Completely Planned, Number Planned, or Quasi-planned Users). Together these three groups include about 80 per cent of the Fecund couples with 1 or 2 births, 70 per cent of those with 3 births, and 62 per cent of those with 4 births (Table 3–12). Most Fecund couples who have the number of children considered "best" by our society have used contraception more or less successfully to restrict family size. Among these medium-sized families the two largest subgroups are the Number Planned and the Quasi-planned Users—couples who practiced contraception and wanted all their pregnancies but did not plan all of them by stopping contraception.

4. Among *all childless couples* a significant proportion (16 per cent) have never used contraception but intend to start later (Quasi-planned Future Users) (Table 3–12). If they do so and have one or more pregnancies, they will be classified as Number Planned, Quasi-planned, or Excess Fertility Users, depending on the situation when the last pregnancy occurs. With increasing parity the proportion of Quasi-planned Future Users decreases rapidly because the couples originally in this group leave it when they carry out their intention to begin use.

5. As has been said before, a large proportion of the couples who have had up to four pregnancies and do not plan ever to use contraception are Subfecund. As a consequence, Quasi-planned Future Non-users are much less numerous at parities 0 to 4 among Fecund couples than in the total sample (Table 3–12). The differences rapidly become smaller as parity rises above 4.

6. A very small number of Fecund couples who want or will accept

TABLE 3–12. PER CENT DISTRIBUTION BY FERTILITY PLANNING STATUS, FOR ALL COUPLES AND FECUND COUPLES, BY NUMBER OF BIRTHS

Fertility planning status	No. of births								
	Total	0[a]	1	2	3	4	5	6	7 or more
All couples									
No. of couples	2,713	419	603	843	468	190	104	44	42
Per cent									
Total	100	100	100	100	100	100	100	100	100
Users	68	41	70	76	80	71	65	60	50
Completely Planned	19	37	25	18	9	3	1	—	—
Never pregnant	5	30	..	..	..	..	..	..	..
Ever pregnant	14	7	25	18	9	3	1	—	—
No. Planned	15	1	5	26	22	22	11	7	2
Quasi-planned	25	3	36	26	32	26	22	14	19
Excess Fertility	9	—	4	6	17	20	31	39	29
Nonusers	30	57	29	22	18	27	33	36	48
Quasi-planned	26	55	27	20	16	20	16	18	22
Future Users	8	16	10	5	5	5	2	2	—
Future Nonusers	18	39	17	15	11	15	14	16	22
Excess Fertility	4	2	2	2	2	7	17	18	26
Future Users	1	1	1	1	—	1	5	11	2
Future Nonusers	3	1	1	1	2	6	12	7	24
Not ascertained	2	2	1	2	2	2	2	4	2
Fecund couples									
No. of couples	1,794	217	408	579	323	129	74	32	32
Per cent									
Total	100	100	100	100	100	100	100	100	100
Users	82	62	83	88	89	82	67	59	56
Completely Planned	24	56	32	23	12	3	1	—	—
Never pregnant	6	45	..	..	..	..	..	..	..
Ever pregnant	18	11	32	23	12	3	1	—	—
No. Planned	18	1	5	29	24	28	12	9	3
Quasi-planned	29	5	41	28	34	31	26	12	22
Excess Fertility	11	—	5	8	19	20	28	38	31
Nonusers	16	35	15	9	9	16	30	41	41
Quasi-planned	14	34	15	9	8	13	15	16	22
Future Users	6	16	8	4	4	6	3	3	—
Future Nonusers	8	18	7	5	4	7	12	13	22
Excess Fertility	2	1	—	—	1	3	15	25	19
Future Users	1	1	—	—	—	1	7	16	3
Future Nonusers	1	—	—	—	1	2	8	9	16
Not ascertained	2	3	2	3	2	2	3	—	3

[a] Couples who have had no births may have had one or more pregnancies—either pregnancies not yet terminated, or pregnancies which terminated in a fetal death.

TABLE 3–13. PER CENT DISTRIBUTION BY FERTILITY PLANNING STATUS, FOR ALL COUPLES, BY NUMBER OF BIRTHS, BY WIFE'S AGE[a]

No. of births	No. of couples	Total	Users					Nonusers				
			Completely Planned		No. Planned	Quasi-planned	Excess Fertility	Quasi-Planned		Excess Fertility		N.A.
			Never pregnant	Ever pregnant				Future Users	Future Nonusers	Future Users	Future Nonusers	
Ages 18–24												
Total	556	100	11	14	9	28	5	15	15	—	1	2
0	162	100	38	10	—	4	—	23	22	—	1	2
1	211	100	..	22	5	46	3	12	10	1	—	1
2	137	100	..	9	25	28	9	10	14	1	—	4
3	36	100	..	6	16	28	14	19	11	1	6	4
4 or more	10	100	..	*	—	*	*	*	*	*	*	—
Ages 25–29												
Total	714	100	5	17	16	27	8	9	14	1	2	1
0	97	100	36	7	1	4	—	18	29	—	1	4
1	171	100	..	35	5	26	2	15	15	1	1	..
2	238	100	..	18	27	31	3	5	13	1	1	..
3	129	100	..	6	22	35	21	5	8	1	1	1
4	48	100	..	—	19	40	23	8	8	2	1	1
5 or more	31	100	..	—	6	23	33	3	16	3	16	—
Ages 30–34												
Total	748	100	2	15	19	24	11	5	18	1	3	2
0	76	100	21	3	3	—	—	12	58	2	—	1
1	124	100	..	26	6	38	4	3	18	1	2	2
2	247	100	..	24	27	21	6	4	14	—	2	2
3	162	100	..	10	26	28	15	4	9	1	3	2
4	74	100	..	1	24	26	25	4	12	1	6	4
5 or more	65	100	..	—	6	22	31	3	15	9	11	3
Ages 35–39												
Total	695	100	2	11	16	23	12	3	26	1	4	2
0	84	100	17	2	4	4	—	5	66	—	1	1
1	97	100	..	16	5	27	6	4	34	2	4	2
2	221	100	..	18	23	24	8	4	19	1	1	3
3	141	100	..	11	18	35	15	2	16	—	2	1
4	59	100	..	5	27	15	15	—	24	—	10	4
5 or more	93	100	..	1	11	17	34	—	16	4	14	3

[a] For all ages see Table 3–12.

large families, and never start contraception, make up an interesting part of the Quasi-planned Future Nonuser group. At zero parity this group includes an important number of Subfecund couples and recently married Fecund couples who have not faced the problems of a growing family. As parity rises to 3, many of the Subfecund are left behind and many of the Fecund shift to another group because they start contraception or decide to do so in the future. Most of the remaining couples are Fecund Future Nonusers who want large families. They make up 4 per cent of all Fecund couples with 3 live births, but they are a rapidly increasing proportion of couples with more than 3 children (Table 3–12). They compose a significant subgroup—22 per cent—of the couples with 7 or more births, although they are a very small segment of the total American childbearing population. Even among couples with 5 or more births, this type of "wanted" family, permitted to grow naturally, is outnumbered more than 2 to 1 by Excess Fertility families.

7. For both *Users* and *Nonusers* there is a sharp rise in the incidence of Excess Fertility with increasing parity in all age groups (Table 3–13). Among all Fecund couples the percentage of Excess Fertility Users increases from 5 per cent in the first parity to 38 per cent in the sixth (Table 3–12). Similarly there are sharp rises in the proportion of Excess Fertility Nonusers with increasing parity. When we consider the Fecund couples with 5 or more births, between 43 and 63 per cent fall into the Excess Fertility categories.

8. A majority of *all couples* who have had 5 or more births are either Excess Fertility Users or Quasi-planned or Excess Fertility Nonusers. Among *Fecund couples* these groups constitute 58 per cent of those with 5 births, 79 per cent of those with 6 births, and 72 per cent of those with 7 or more births (Table 3–12).

9. Although there are variations in the magnitudes involved, these patterns of relationship of parity to fertility planning status are essentially the same in each age group.

The number of children expected when family growth is completed is related to fecundity and fertility planning status. The expected family size for Fecund couples varies with the use of contraception and the success achieved. The concept of expected family size will be discussed more fully in later chapters. At this point, we shall merely note that the only groups in which a quarter or more of the couples expect to have 5 or more births are the Excess Fertility Users and the two Nonuser groups. These are also the only groups in this classification which expect to have an average of more than 3.5 children.

Together these various patterns of planning for past and future births indicate that among Fecund couples in all age groups small families are likely to be planned families with wanted children. Most large families result from the willing or fatalistic acceptance of pregnancies as they come with no attempt to control their number or spacing, or from ineffective planning which fails to prevent unwanted pregnancies. The latter group is most important numerically among the large families. The data on expected family size support our earlier statements that (1) the Completely Planned large family is practically nonexistent; (2) the wanted large family which is permitted to grow naturally by Non-users is not a numerically important group; and (3) the typical small family is planned either in part or completely with the use of contraception.

Fertility Planning Status, by Duration of Marriage

We have already seen that patterns of family planning depend in part on how many pregnancies have occurred and on wife's age. We have also seen that duration of marriage is closely linked to parity and wife's age. In consequence, when we consider the relationship between fertility planning status and duration of marriage we are on the whole considering from a different point of view the relationships which have already been discussed.

1. The proportion of couples with Completely Planned fertility decreases rapidly with length of marriage. The decrease is especially sharp for the never pregnant, who are less than 1 per cent of the Fecund couples married 15 years or longer. The proportion of Fecund couples who have Completely Planned fertility and at least one pregnancy is rather stable. Between 15 and 20 per cent of the Fecund couples in each duration of marriage are of this type (Table 3–14).

2. The probability that a couple will have more pregnancies than they want (Excess Fertility) increases sharply with duration of marriage. Many of the couples married 15 or more years have been unsuccessful in limiting pregnancies to the wanted number; 22 per cent—more than 1 in 5—are in an Excess Fertility group. Among the Fecund couples married this long the proportion in an Excess Fertility category is even higher—26 per cent, or more than 1 in 4. More than 90 per cent of these Fecund Excess Fertility couples either have used contraception or intend to do so. It should be remembered, however, that our sample is limited to wives under 40; consequently most of those married 15 or more years were married relatively young. In fact, their average age at marriage was only 19. A relatively high proportion of women marrying so young belong to those socioeconomic groups that are less likely to use contraception and, if they use it, do so less effectively.

3. The proportion of couples who have Number Planned fertility increases sharply after 5 years of marriage and then remains fairly stable.

Years married	No. of couples	Total	Completely Planned		No. Planned	Quasi-planned	Excess Fertility	Quasi-planned		Excess Fertility		N.A.
								Users				
								Nonusers				
			Never pregnant	Ever pregnant				Future Users	Future Nonusers	Future Users	Future Nonusers	
All couples												
Total	2,713	100	5	14	15	25	9	8	18	1	3	2
Under 5	649	100	14	15	6	28	2	15	18	—	1	1
5–9	869	100	2	16	19	27	8	8	15	1	2	2
10–14	686	100	2	14	18	24	13	5	18	2	3	1
15 or more	509	100	1	9	18	20	15	2	26	1	6	2
Fecund couples												
Total	1,794	100	6	18	18	29	11	6	8	1	1	2
Under 5	586	100	14	16	6	29	3	15	15	1	—	1
5–9	606	100	2	20	24	30	10	4	5	1	1	3
10–14	388	100	1	20	22	29	17	2	3	2	2	2
15 or more	214	100	1	15	25	26	22	—	3	2	2	4
Fecund Users												
Total	1,459	100	7	22	22	36	13					
Under 5	398	100	20	23	9	44	4					
5–9	522	100	2	24	28	34	12					
10–14	349	100	1	23	24	32	20					
15 or more	190	100	—	18	28	29	25					

Presumably, these are the couples whose earlier planning is more casual but who plan very carefully when they have been married long enough to have two or three children.

4. Quasi-planned Users include an important part of the population in each marriage duration. However, as marriage lengthens they tend to decrease somewhat.

5. Quasi-planned Nonusers expecting to begin contraception later compose a significant group (15 per cent) among Fecund couples married less than 5 years, but diminish rapidly in number to less than 1 per cent among couples married 15 years or longer.

6. Fecund couples who have not had more pregnancies than wanted and say they will never use contraception (Quasi-planned Future Nonusers) are much more numerous among couples married less than 5 years than those married longer. Apparently under the pressure of marital experience and additional pregnancies, such couples change their minds about contraception, have more pregnancies than they want, or become Subfecund.

A Summary View of Fertility Planning and the Use of Contraception

Most American couples have used contraception at some time, but the patterns of fertility planning have many variations. The almost universal use of contraception by Fecund couples is consistent with the fact that most Americans want moderately small families. The variations in the time when contraception is begun and the regularity of its use thereafter are consistent with the fact that different types of couples reach this common goal through different family building patterns. Some couples completely plan small families with the systematic use of contraception, but most plan them only partially. There is a very small minority of Fecund couples who make no use of contraception but are satisfied with the results—they want their large families. But most of the couples not using contraception and planning never to use it are Subfecund and do not need such action to limit family growth.

There is also a significant minority of couples who have more pregnancies than they want. In the early stages of married life, these couples with Excess Fertility are divided fairly equally between those who have and those who have not used contraception, but as length of marriage increases most of them begin use if they are still Fecund. A majority of the couples with six or more children are in one of these Excess Fertility groups. Nevertheless, most of the Excess Fertility couples have only one more child than they want, and very few have three too many.

As we shall see presently (Chapter 7), most Americans want and are having families of two to four children. We have described in this chapter the means by which most couples limit family growth to this moderate size. The extent and patterns of fertility planning vary somewhat with the social, economic, and religious characteristics of the couples. This will be examined in the next chapter. But such variations do not prevent all the major strata in our population from approaching more or less closely the common aspiration for families of two to four children. Instead, they only serve to account for moderate divergences from a generally accepted ideal of what the size of an American family should be.

Chapter 4

FAMILY LIMITATION:
THE SOCIAL AND ECONOMIC CORRELATES

To what extent do the major American socioeconomic and religious groups differ with respect to family limitation? Do the better-educated couples make the most extensive and effective use of methods to regulate conception? What are the differences between Catholics and Protestants, rich and poor, white-collar and blue-collar workers, farm and city families, working wives and housewives? The answers to these questions are important not only for understanding the changing differences in fertility for such groups but also the trends in national birth rates. Since World War II the traditional social and economic differentials in family size apparently have been narrowing.[1] Does this mean that such groups are becoming more alike in their efforts to control conception?

The modern transition from large to small families occurred at different rates in these different socioeconomic and religious groups. The small-family pattern probably was adopted first by the better educated, those in higher-status white-collar occupations, those with higher incomes, some of the Protestant and Jewish groups, and people in large urban centers. The first groups to adopt the small-family pattern were probably also those which first used contraception extensively. Historical data on family limitation are rare, but those available for Great Britain indicate socioeconomic differentials in the use of contraception corresponding to the differentials in fertility for a period going back 75 years.[2]

[1] See, for example, Wilson H. Grabill, Clyde V. Kiser, and Pascal K. Whelpton, *The Fertility of American Women*, John Wiley & Sons, Inc., New York, 1958; Clyde V. Kiser, "Changes in Fertility by Socioeconomic Status during 1940–1950," *Milbank Memorial Fund Quarterly*, vol. 33, no. 4, pp. 394–429, October, 1955; Charles F. Westoff, "Differential Fertility in the United States, 1900–1952," *American Sociological Review*, vol. 19, no. 5, pp. 549–561, October, 1954; "Fertility Trends with Special Attention to Areas of Lower Fertility," in *Proceedings of the World Population Conference, 1954*, United Nations, New York, 1955, vol. I, pp. 563–773.

[2] E. Lewis-Faning, *Report on an Enquiry into Family Limitation and Its Influence on Human Fertility during the Past Fifty Years* (Papers of the Royal Commission on Population, vol. I), H.M. Stationery Office, London, 1949, chap. 1. For more information about this study see Appendix A, Note 18.

For the United States, the data from the 1941 study in Indianapolis indicate that differentials in fertility by socioeconomic status correspond to differences in the effective use of contraception.[3] In that study, different social and economic groups who wanted essentially the same number of children differed in the number they actually had, mainly because some were better able than others to plan and control family growth.

The differences between the rates at which methods of controlling conception have been adopted in different social groups probably are related both to variations in the availability of information about such methods and to differing motivations for family limitation in different social situations. Such population groups as white-collar workers in large cities with easy access to centers of information and communication probably were first to obtain the knowledge and attitudes necessary for practicing family limitation effectively. Those with more education and in white-collar occupations also received training in rational behavior and experience in human relations which may have carried over into their own family planning.

It is likely also that some population groups felt the need to practice family limitation at an earlier period than others, because they were involved earlier in activities that were not centered in the family. Availability of information about contraception is not sufficient to bring about its widespread use. In addition, there must be attitudes which are favorable to family planning and social or economic conditions which make it advantageous. For example, a large family retained its economic value for farmers long after urban white-collar workers found that children were a substantial economic cost. While the daily round of life of the farmer remained family-oriented, the urban dweller—especially the well-educated white-collar worker—gradually was adopting a way of life in which many of his contacts and activities were in new groups and institutions of a nonfamilial character. Similarly, before the development of social welfare programs, poorly paid urban workers found large families with several potential workers to be a kind of social insurance for unemployment and old age, while higher-income groups did not need such safeguards.

The postwar diminishing of fertility differentials between socioeconomic groups may reflect decreasing differences between such groups with respect to the adoption of family limitation. It has seemed plausi-

---

[3] P. K. Whelpton and Clyde V. Kiser (eds.), *Social and Psychological Factors Affecting Fertility*, Milbank Memorial Fund, New York, 1950, vol. 2, pts. VI, VIII, and IX; or "VI. The Planning of Fertility," *Milbank Memorial Fund Quarterly*, vol. 25, no. 1, January, 1947; "VIII. The Comparative Influence on Fertility of Contraception and Impairments of Fecundity," *ibid.*, vol. 26, no. 2, April, 1948; "IX. Fertility Planning and Fertility Rates by Socioeconomic Status," *ibid.*, vol. 27, no. 2, April, 1949. See also Appendix A, Note 2d.

ble as one aspect of the transition from a rural to an urban society that the effective use of methods to regulate conception would spread from higher-status to lower-status groups and from city to country. There is evidence that all major sectors of our population are being drawn toward a single urbanized society in which information and standards of behavior are quickly communicated throughout the social system. The eventual result of such developments may be that all major groups will adopt effective means for limiting family size, which will bring a large reduction of the fertility differentials that have been common in the Western world for more than a century. In the United States as in some European cities traditional fertility differences may be reversed, with higher-income groups having more children than lower-income groups because they can afford more children without sacrificing ·the other amenities of urban life.

The argument that long-standing fertility differentials will diminish as the population becomes more homogeneous culturally has also been applied to the fertility differences between Catholics, Protestants, and Jews. Historically these groups have differed as to social status and rates of urbanization. The higher fertility of Catholics has been interpreted by some as resulting from their more recent urbanization and their lower economic status.[4] According to this interpretation the large Catholic family has been a temporary phenomenon which will disappear as Catholics assume positions in society similar to those of Protestants and Jews. This interpretation has minimized the role of religious ideology in raising Catholic fertility rates by forbidding "artificial birth control" (i.e., all methods of preventing conception except delayed marriage and periodic or longer-term continence). We shall have occasion to test the validity of this theory.

What are the facts today? To what extent do major social and economic groups differ in the use of methods to regulate conception? Do they differ sufficiently to cause major differences in family size? Have increasing education and urbanization reduced traditional differences in control measures as they seem to have done with fertility?

To answer these questions we shall describe in this chapter the family limitation practices of major American social and economic strata defined on the basis of the following characteristics:

1. Religion of wife and husband
2. Education of wife and husband

[4] It may seem incorrect to speak of recent urbanization for Catholics, since in the United States they are much more concentrated in large cities than Protestants. However, this is recent. Most American Catholics are only one or two generations removed from the rural origins of the great wave of migration from eastern and southern Europe about the turn of this century.

3. Economic position of the family as indicated by the husband's income and occupation

4. Wife's participation in the labor force

5. Type of community background as indicated by place of residence

The extent and effectiveness of methods of family limitation will be measured in terms of:

1. The proportion of couples who use a method

2. The time when use of a method is begun

3. The proportion of pregnancies which occur before the first use of a method

4. The proportion of subsequent pregnancies which are accidental

5. Fertility planning status, including a measure of unwanted pregnancies

We shall find that the majority of couples in all important socioeconomic strata have tried to regulate conception. This point is stressed at the outset, because in describing the differences between strata, variation may be given unwarranted emphasis. Some important differences in contraceptive practice do exist between socioeconomic groups, but for most purposes these differences are less important than the fact that a majority of the couples in each major group have used some control method. As we shall see, the only important exception to this generalization is the small group of couples having both little education and low income—a group constituting only 6 per cent of the population under study.

After this word of caution, we can examine the important social differences that exist in family limitation practices. In proper perspective they are large enough to have important consequences. We shall find that among the socioeconomic characteristics considered, religion and education are the two which are now most closely associated with the fertility planning patterns of American couples. The husband's income and occupation, whether the wife works, whether the couple has a farm background, and the type of community in which the couple has lived are less important. But each of these characteristics in the past has had a sufficiently important relation to fertility differentials to merit separate consideration.

The Influence of Religion

More than one-fourth of the white population of the United States is identified with the Roman Catholic Church, which has an explicit set of restrictions about family limitation practices.[5] This is an important

[5] The proportion of white persons aged 14 years or older who are Roman Catholics was 27.8 per cent in March, 1957, according to *Current Population Reports*, U.S. Bureau of the Census, series P-20, no. 79, Feb. 2, 1958, p. 6.

fact in any consideration of American fertility trends, especially since the proportion of Catholics in our population has been increasing.

The religious doctrines of the Catholic Church forbid the use of certain methods of limiting family size and restrict the situations in which other methods may be used. There is no categorical prohibition of all family limitation practices. On the contrary, periodic continence (the rhythm method) or long-continued continence are acceptable in the eyes of the Church, providing that the purpose is not "selfish." Family limitation by those methods is permitted to prevent having more children than the family can care for adequately without serious health risks. The methods forbidden by church doctrine are commonly referred to by Catholics as "artificial birth control" and include any method involving the use of a chemical or mechanical agent, as well as withdrawal (coitus interruptus).[5a]

Some of the major Protestant denominations have encouraged the use of contraception. A few of the minor groups have opposed it. Most of the other groups approve tacitly.

On the one hand, then, Catholics might be expected to have distinctive family planning patterns and to use preventive methods less than other Americans. On the other hand, the long urban experience of the Jews and their high educational and economic status would lead us to expect most of them to use contraception and to do so effectively. Protestants might be expected to be in an intermediate position.

The fact is that a large majority of couples in each of the religious groups has used some method of avoiding conception, but the proportion of Users is lower for Catholics than for Protestants, and lower for Protestants than Jews (Table 4–1). This is true whether we consider the religion of the husband or the wife or both, past or future use, or use from the standpoint of motives or actions.

While Catholic-Protestant differences in the rate of use are consistent and substantial, a large majority of Catholics has used some method. Among Fecund Catholic wives, 70 per cent are Past Users and an additional 10 per cent are Future Users. Many of the Catholic Users have not violated Catholic doctrine but have adopted practices acceptable to the Church, as will be shown in Chapter 6.

Although the proportion of Users is substantially lower among Catholics than among Protestants in all age groups,[6] the differences narrow

---

[5a] For an excellent statement of the Catholic point of view regarding family limitation see William J. Gibbons, S.J., "Fertility Control in the Light of Some Catholic Statements," *Eugenics Quarterly*, vol. 3, nos. 1 and 2, pp. 9–15 and 82–87, March and June, 1956.

For official pronouncements, see Appendix A, Note 10.

[6] See Appendix A, Note 11, for information regarding unpublished tabulations.

TABLE 4–1. PERCENTAGE WHO ARE PAST USERS, OR PAST OR FUTURE USERS, ON A MOTIVE AND ACTION BASIS, FOR ALL COUPLES AND FECUND COUPLES, BY RELIGION OF COUPLE, WIFE, AND HUSBAND

Religion	All couples					Fecund couples				
	No.	Past Users		Past or Future Users		No.	Past Users		Past or Future Users	
		Motive	Action	Motive	Action		Motive	Action	Motive	Action
Total	2,713	70	81	79	86	1,794	83	89	90	94
Couple's religion:										
Both Protestant	1,684	75	86	83	90	1,102	88	93	95	96
Both Catholic	628	57	70	67	77	413	71	79	80	87
Both Jewish	66	86	89	86	89	52	96	98	96	98
Wife Protestant, husband Catholic	91	68	81	79	89	63	81	86	92	94
Wife Catholic, husband Protestant	133	55	73	68	81	89	72	83	82	92
All others	111	74	82	82	86	75	85	91	91	93
Wife's religion:										
Protestant	1,817	75	85	83	89	1,195	88	93	94	96
Catholic	787	57	70	67	77	519	70	79	80	87
Jewish	74	86	89	88	90	57	95	96	96	98
Husband's religion:										
Protestant	1,827	74	85	82	89	1,198	87	92	94	96
Catholic	729	59	71	69	78	481	71	79	81	87
Jewish	75	88	91	88	91	59	96	98	97	98

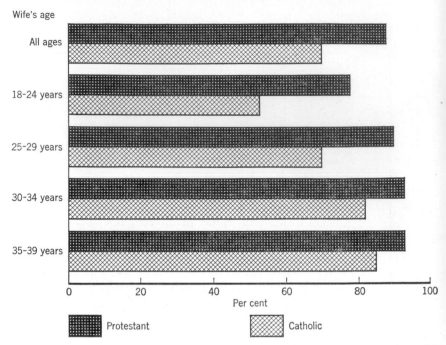

Fɪɢ. 4–1. Percentage of Fecund couples using contraception, by wife's age, by wife's religion.

as age rises (Figure 4–1). This is especially true for Fecund couples. For example, among these couples the difference between the proportion of Catholics and Protestants who are Users declines from 25 percentage points at ages 18–24 to 8 at ages 35–39 (Table 4–2). The narrowing of the difference with advancing age is related to the fact that,

Tᴀʙʟᴇ 4–2. Pᴇʀᴄᴇɴᴛᴀɢᴇ Wʜᴏ Aʀᴇ Uѕᴇʀѕ, ꜰᴏʀ Aʟʟ Cᴏᴜᴘʟᴇѕ ᴀɴᴅ Fᴇᴄᴜɴᴅ Cᴏᴜᴘʟᴇѕ, ʙʏ Wɪꜰᴇ'ѕ Rᴇʟɪɢɪᴏɴ, ʙʏ Wɪꜰᴇ'ѕ Aɢᴇ

| Wife's age | Percentage who are Users | | | | Number of couples in base group | | | |
| | All couples | | Fecund couples | | All couples | | Fecund couples | |
	Wife Prot- estant	Wife Cath- olic	Wife Prot- estant	Wife Cath- olic	Wife Prot- estant	Wife Cath- olic	Wife Prot- estant	Wife Cath- olic
Total	75	57	88	70	1,817	787	1,195	519
18–24	74	51	78	53	394	146	352	136
25–29	80	59	90	70	461	220	341	155
30–34	76	63	93	82	505	212	298	124
35–39	70	55	93	85	457	209	204	104

in general, Catholics who start family limitation begin longer after marriage.

At ages 25–29 and older Catholic-Protestant differentials are smaller for Fecund couples than for all couples. This is consistent with the supposition that many Catholic couples do not use contraception until they have had one or more children and found that they can conceive easily. Catholics are more likely to begin to use contraception only after they are confronted with the problem of a rapidly growing family. The difference between the number of children wanted by Catholics and by Protestants is larger early in married life than after longer periods of marriage (see Chapter 9). Apparently, many Catholics revise downward their ideas about the number of children they want and then begin preventive measures.

When the husband and wife differ as to religious preference, that of the wife is more closely related to whether contraception is begun (Table 4–1). When the wife is Catholic and the husband Protestant, the proportion of Users approaches that for Catholic couples. When the situation is reversed, the proportion of Users is somewhat closer to that for Protestant couples than Catholic couples. In view of this fact, we shall use the wife's religion as an index of the religious affiliation of the couple in most of our analysis.[7]

Close attachment to the Catholic Church, as indicated by frequent church attendance, is associated with a relatively low tendency to try to avoid conception (Table 4–3). This is true despite the fact that both Catholics and Protestants who attend church regularly have relatively high educational and economic status, which tends to increase the proportion restricting family size.

Catholics who seldom or never attend church are more likely to be Users than are other Catholics. Nevertheless, the proportion of Users is lower among these Catholics than among Protestants, regardless of the church attendance of the Protestants. Apparently, efforts to control conception are affected by one's identification with the Catholic Church, even when that identification is not linked to regular attendance at church.

While frequent church attendance is associated with a lower tendency to regulate conception among Catholics, this is not true for Protestants. In fact, for Protestants, frequency of church attendance is directly as-

[7] A study of attitudes toward having a third child, among a sample of residents of large metropolitan areas who recently had a second child, is now being conducted by the Office of Population Research, Princeton University. Preliminary results show that the attitudes of Protestant-Catholic couples married by a Protestant clergyman or a civil official resemble closely those of Protestant couples. In contrast, the attitudes of Protestant-Catholic couples married by a Catholic priest resemble, though not so closely, those of Catholic couples.

TABLE 4–3. PERCENTAGE WHO ARE USERS, FOR COUPLES WITH PROTESTANT OR CATHOLIC WIVES BY WIFE'S AGE, BY CHURCH ATTENDANCE

Wife's religion and church attendance	Percentage who are Users					Number of couples in base group				
	Total	Wife's age				Total	Wife's age			
		18–24	25–29	30–34	35–39		18–24	25–29	30–34	35–39
Protestant:										
Total	75	74	80	76	70	1,817	394	461	505	457
Regular	77	73	83	82	71	603	106	132	160	205
Often	76	74	82	76	74	392	96	105	110	81
Seldom or never	72	75	76	73	64	820	191	224	234	171
Catholic:										
Total	57	51	59	63	55	787	146	220	212	209
Regular	55	50	58	61	50	533	93	144	144	152
Often	58	*	59	67	56	99	18	32	24	25
Seldom or never	61	57	59	61	69	155	35	44	44	32

*Less than 20 couples in base group. An asterisk has this meaning in all tables.

sociated with the proportion of Users. Why should there be this difference? One interpretation is that Catholics who attend church frequently are brought into contact with religious leaders and laymen who often express attitudes unfavorable to family limitation and especially to "artificial birth control." In contrast, Protestants are much less likely to hear this issue discussed in their churches, and the discussions which take place are likely to be favorable to effective family planning. As was mentioned earlier, the wives who attend church tend to have higher educational and economic status than those who do not, and relatively more of the couples in the higher-status groups practice family limitation. These nonreligious-status traits are more likely to have the expected effect of increasing the proportion of Users among the regular churchgoers who are Protestants than among those who are Catholics, because opposing influences are negligible in Protestantism but strong in Catholicism.

The association of regular church attendance with a low tendency to use family limitation methods is less strong for the Fecund Catholic couples than for the Subfecund. Apparently the devout Catholic is more likely to support his religious views with complete nonuse if the pressures of family growth are made less urgent by impaired fecundity. As we shall see in Chapter 5, opposition to the general idea of family limitation is also somewhat greater among Subfecund than Fecund Catholic couples.

The Catholic-Protestant differences in incidence of use are not a result of differences in economic status or education. In every educational group the proportion of couples who are Users is substantially lower for Catholic wives than for Protestant wives, as the following figures show:

Wife's religion	Percentage of couples who are Users			
	College	High school, 4	High school, 1–3	Grade school
Protestant	90	80	70	53
Catholic	62	61	59	41
Difference	28	19	11	12

Similarly, the proportion of Users is substantially lower for Catholics than Protestants regardless of the husband's income:

Wife's religion	Percentage of couples who are Users				
	$6,000 or more	$5,000–$5,999	$4,000–$4,999	$3,000–$3,999	Under $3,000
Protestant	84	81	79	76	63
Catholic	67	68	60	54	46
Difference	17	13	19	22	17

Catholics, like Protestants, are more likely to be Users as economic status or educational status rises, but the religious differentials persist at each income and educational level.

These results contradict the theory that Catholic-Protestant differences in resort to family limitation methods are simply a temporary result of differences in economic status or education, and that they will diminish as the two groups become more alike in these characteristics. Indeed, the *differential* between the proportion of Catholics and Protestants who try to control conception increases substantially as the amount of schooling goes up. It is much larger for the wives who have had at least 4 years of high school than for those with less education, and still larger for college wives.

Neither are Catholic-Protestant differentials in the tendency to restrict fertility a function of such other variables as husband's occupation, or type of community of present or past residence. Under a variety of comparisons for these characteristics the proportion of Users is lower among Catholics than among Protestants in all categories considered. Despite their concentration in large cities, relatively fewer Catholics than Protestants use contraception. The two groups are most alike among wives with extensive work experience after marriage. More will be said about these matters later in this chapter.

There are too few Jewish couples in our sample to permit a detailed analysis by age and church attendance. It is clear, however, that the proportion of Users is highest among Jewish couples. Ninety-five per cent of all Fecund Jewish couples are Users (Table 4–1).

Catholic Users begin preventive measures relatively late in married life, Protestant Users begin earlier, and Jewish Users begin earliest (Figure 4–2 and Table 4–4). Eighty-three per cent of Jewish Users,

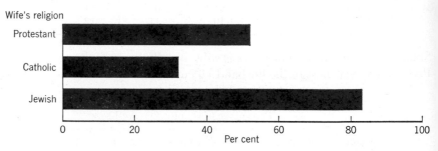

Fig. 4–2. Percentage of Users beginning contraception before first pregnancy, by wife's religion.

52 per cent of Protestant Users, but only 32 per cent of Catholic Users started control measures before the first pregnancy. The religious differences in time of first use persist when number of pregnancies to date is taken into account.

The contraceptive status of pregnancies also varies in relation to religion (Table 4–5). The percentage of all pregnancies of Users which

TABLE 4–4. PER CENT DISTRIBUTION BY NUMBER OF PREGNANCIES BEFORE USE OF CONTRACEPTION BEGAN, FOR USERS, BY WIFE'S RELIGION

Wife's religion	No. of Users	No. of pregnancies before use began						
		Total	0	1	2	3	4 or more	N.A.
Total *a*	1,901	100	48	32	11	4	3	2
Protestant	1,362	100	52	30	10	5	2	1
Catholic	453	100	32	39	16	5	4	4
Jewish	64	100	83	14	3	—	—	—

The dash indicates a percentage below 0.5 in all tables.

N.A. = not ascertained.

a Includes all wives.

occur before they begin contraception is highest for Catholic wives and lowest for Jewish wives. After use is begun the proportion of subsequent pregnancies which are planned is highest for Jewish wives and lowest for Catholic wives, but the Protestant-Catholic differential is small. Accidental and "other unplanned" conceptions are somewhat more common among Catholic than Protestant wives, and least common among Jewish wives. While the Catholic-Protestant differentials in planned, accidental, and other conceptions after preventive measures are begun are consistent in all age groups, they are quite small in size.

TABLE 4–5. PERCENTAGE OF USERS' PREGNANCIES OCCURRING BEFORE USE BEGAN, AND PER CENT DISTRIBUTION BY PLANNING STATUS FOR PREGNANCIES AFTER USE BEGAN, BY WIFE'S RELIGION[a]

| Wife's religion | All pregnancies | | Pregnancies after use began | | | | |
| | Number | Percentage before use began | Number | Per cent distribution by planning status | | | |
				Total	Planned	Accidental	Other unplanned
Total [b]	4,680	32	3,171	100	51	25	24
Protestant	3,359	30	2,345	100	51	25	24
Catholic	1,142	41	677	100	47	28	25
Jewish	135	10	122	100	72	13	15

[a] This and all subsequent tables on planning status of pregnancies exclude *all* pregnancies of those Users for whom the planning status of *any* pregnancy was not ascertained (i.e., 170 pregnancies of Users, of which 24 occurred before and 146 occurred after use began). Therefore the percentages differ slightly from those in Tables 3–4 and 3–5.

[b] Total includes all religions.

Catholics are much less likely than Protestants or Jews to have Completely Planned fertility, that is, to have planned all their pregnancies by stopping contraception.[8] This is the most important religious difference in fertility planning status. Like other contrasts in fertility planning it reflects mainly the above-mentioned differences in the proportion who try to regulate conception and in the time when they begin.

With respect to Fecund Users we see in Table 4–6 that:

1. The proportion of Catholics having Completely Planned fertility is consistently low.

2. Catholics tend to be concentrated in the Number Planned and Quasi-planned categories.

[8] For an explanation of the terms used in referring to the different fertility planning groups, see Figure 3–8.

TABLE 4–6. PER CENT DISTRIBUTION BY FERTILITY PLANNING STATUS, FOR FECUND USERS, BY WIFE'S RELIGION, BY WIFE'S AGE

Wife's religion	No. of couples	Fertility planning status				
		Total	Completely Planned	No. Planned	Quasi-planned	Excess Fertility
				Total			
Total [a]	1,459	100	29	22	36	13
Protestant	1,037	100	32	20	34	14
Catholic	350	100	16	27	45	12
Jewish	53	100	57	17	22	4
				Ages 18–24			
Total	350	100	38	14	41	7
Protestant	269	100	41	15	37	7
Catholic	68	100	21	12	60	7
				Ages 25–29			
Total	437	100	30	21	37	12
Protestant	305	100	31	21	35	13
Catholic	108	100	22	24	44	10
				Ages 30–34			
Total	389	100	25	28	31	16
Protestant	273	100	29	24	29	18
Catholic	96	100	13	38	37	12
				Ages 35–39			
Total	283	100	22	25	33	20
Protestant	190	100	24	23	31	22
Catholic	78	100	10	31	41	18

[a] Excludes 32 couples for whom fertility planning status was not ascertained.

3. Excess Fertility is slightly less common among Catholics than among Protestants. (The opposite was true for the proportion of accidental pregnancies among those of Users after starting contraception. This occurs because relatively more of the accidental pregnancies of Catholics were wanted at a later date and relatively fewer came after the couples had all that they wanted.)

4. Jews are much more likely than others to have Completely Planned

fertility and much less likely to have Quasi-planned or Excess Fertility.

Considering the fertility planning status of *all* couples—including the Subfecund—we see in Table 4–7 that:

1. Among Catholics the proportion with Completely Planned fertility is much lower than among either Protestants or Jews. (Nearly half the Jews are in this group.)

2. Catholics are heavily concentrated among the Quasi-planned Non-users (i.e., Nonusers with no unwanted pregnancies).

3. The proportion of couples with Excess Fertility (considering both Users and Nonusers) is slightly smaller for Catholics than for Protestants, but larger than for Jews. Apparently, Catholics are less likely than Protestants to become Users in order to avoid having more pregnancies than they want, because about 78 per cent of the Excess Fertility Protestants but only 58 per cent of the Excess Fertility Catholics are Users.

4. Catholics are represented among the Number Planned and Quasi-planned Users in approximately the same proportions as Protestants. The really big differences are the concentration of Catholics among Quasi-planned Nonusers and their small representation in the Completely Planned group.[9]

Frequency of church attendance has no consistent relation to fertility planning status for Catholics. For Protestants, more frequent church attendance is associated with a somewhat higher proportion of couples having Completely Planned fertility and a lower proportion having Excess Fertility.

In summary, the fertility planning status of Catholics differs from that of Protestants and Jews chiefly in reflecting a lower proportion of Users and, among Users, a slightly higher proportion of conceptions which are accidental and a lower proportion of couples with Completely Planned fertility. These differences do not result in a higher incidence of couples with Excess Fertility among Catholics than among Protestants. It may be that differences in religious teachings make it less likely that Catholics will report having had more pregnancies than they want than that Protestants will do so, especially when the child resulting from the last pregnancy is several years old.

The differences in fertility planning among the three religious groups should not be exaggerated. The great majority of Fecund couples in each group has used or will use contraception in order to have small or moderate-sized families.

On the other hand, it is certainly true that the family limitation prac-

[9] A classification based on religion of husband gives results which are essentially the same as those for religion of wife in these and the preceding subparagraphs.

TABLE 4–7. PER CENT DISTRIBUTION BY FERTILITY PLANNING STATUS, FOR ALL COUPLES, BY WIFE'S RELIGION, BY WIFE'S AGE

Wife's religion	No. of couples	Total	Fertility planning status								Total Excess Fertility (Users and Nonusers)
			Users				Nonusers		N.A.		
			Completely Planned	No. Planned	Quasi-planned	Excess Fertility	Quasi-planned	Excess Fertility			
Total											
Total[a]	2,713	100	19	15	25	9	26	4	2		13
Protestant	1,817	100	22	16	26	11	21	3	1		14
Catholic	787	100	9	14	25	6	38	5	3		11
Jewish	74	100	48	14	19	4	14	–	1		4
Ages 18–24											
Total[a]	556	100	25	9	28	5	30	1	2		6
Protestant	394	100	30	10	28	5	25	1	1		6
Catholic	146	100	11	6	29	3	46	2	3		6
Ages 25–29											
Total[a]	714	100	22	16	27	8	23	3	1		11
Protestant	461	100	23	17	28	10	18	3	1		12
Catholic	220	100	13	14	25	6	37	3	2		10
Ages 30–34											
Total[a]	748	100	17	19	24	11	23	4	2		15
Protestant	505	100	20	18	24	13	19	4	2		17
Catholic	212	100	7	21	23	8	30	7	4		15
Ages 35–39											
Total[a]	695	100	13	16	23	12	29	5	2		17
Protestant	457	100	15	17	23	14	25	5	1		19
Catholic	209	100	7	14	22	7	39	6	5		13

114

tices of Catholics are consistent with somewhat larger families than the average—the minority of Nonusers is larger for Catholics, Catholics begin control measures later, and more Catholics are in one of the fertility planning categories associated with moderate-sized rather than small families. Nevertheless, these patterns are not consistent with the statements often heard that Catholics have very large families because of uncontrolled fertility and Protestants have very small families because they plan them rationally. In fact, the contraceptive practices of both Protestants and Catholics are consistent with small or moderate-sized families. The proportion of Jews with Completely Planned fertility is so large that it will not be surprising to find in Chapter 9 that average family size is considerably smaller for them than for Protestants or Catholics.

The Influence of Education

The more education a wife or husband has, the more likely it is that the couple has used contraception, that they began early in marriage, and that they have planned their pregnancies and avoided more than they wanted.

While the proportion of couples who are Users rises consistently with education, the difference is particularly great between wives and husbands who did not go beyond grade school and those with more education (Table 4–8). These patterns exist at all ages, among Fecund couples as well as all couples, and for the education of the wife, of the husband, or both.

Among Fecund couples with wives 35–39 the use of contraception is almost universal if the wives had more than grade school education—91 to 97 per cent are Users (Figure 4–3 and Table 4–9). If the wives had only a grade school education, a sizable majority—78 per cent—are Users. The contrast between 78 per cent for those with grade school education and 91 per cent for the better-educated group is illustrative of the basis for our word of caution in the introduction to this chapter. The difference of 13 percentage points is big enough to be significant and noteworthy, but the fact remains that a large majority of wives in each educational group are Users.

The education of both the husband and wife is related to the use of contraception (Table 4–8). There is, for example, a significantly lower proportion of Users when both spouses have a grade school education than when one spouse has a grade school education and the other has more. However, since classifying by wife's education alone gives results which are fairly similar to those based on couple's education, in most

TABLE 4–8. PERCENTAGE WHO ARE PAST USERS, OR PAST OR FUTURE USERS, ON A MOTIVE AND ACTION BASIS, FOR ALL COUPLES AND FECUND COUPLES, BY EDUCATION OF COUPLE, WIFE, AND HUSBAND

Education	All couples					Fecund couples				
	Number	Past Users		Past or Future Users		Number	Past Users		Past or Future Users	
		Motive	Action	Motive	Action		Motive	Action	Motive	Action
Total[a]	2,713	70	81	79	86	1,794	83	89	90	94
Couple's education:										
Both college	291	86	89	90	92	226	93	94	96	96
One high school, other college	428	79	87	84	89	310	89	93	93	95
Both high school, 4	533	76	86	84	90	359	87	92	93	96
One high school, 1–3, other high school, 4	431	72	82	82	90	299	81	87	91	96
Both high school, 1–3	258	63	79	75	84	161	77	87	87	92
One grade school, other more	521	63	77	73	82	309	80	89	89	94
Both grade school	226	45	63	56	69	121	63	71	74	79
Not ascertained	25					9				
Wife's education:										
College	417	84	88	88	90	314	91	93	94	95
High school, 4	1,236	74	84	82	89	855	85	90	92	95
High school, 1–3	681	65	79	75	84	428	79	87	88	92
Grade school	377	48	67	58	72	196	68	78	78	84
Husband's education:										
College	614	81	88	86	90	459	90	94	94	96
High school, 4	841	75	84	82	88	562	86	92	92	95
High school, 1–3	628	66	80	78	87	406	78	86	88	93
Grade school	605	58	73	68	78	358	74	82	84	88

[a] In all tables "total" includes couples for whom a particular characteristic is unknown or indeterminate.

cases we shall take the wife's schooling as our measure of educational attainment.[10]

The relationship between use of contraception and education is less marked on the Action than on the Motive basis, because more of the

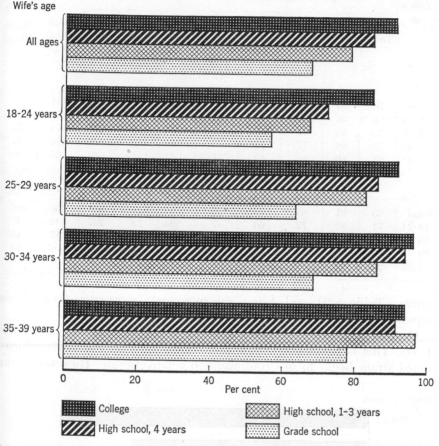

FIG. 4–3. Percentage of Fecund couples using contraception, by wife's age, by wife's education.

wives with less education reported douching for cleanliness only. Motive use increases substantially as educational attainment rises in each age

[10] The use of couple's education with controls for two additional variables, such as age and fecundity, is impractical without a much larger sample than ours.

It seems likely from several tests that a small number of wives with only a grade school education reported incorrectly that they had a high school education while reporting correctly the education of their husbands. This may distort slightly some of the relationships between education of wife and the fertility variables.

TABLE 4–9. PERCENTAGE WHO ARE USERS, FOR ALL COUPLES AND FECUND COUPLES, BY WIFE'S AGE, BY WIFE'S EDUCATION

Wife's age	Percentage who are Users					No. of couples in base group				
	Wife's education					Wife's education				
	Total	Col-lege	High school, 4	High school, 1–3	Grade school	Total	Col-lege	High school, 4	High school, 1–3	Grade school
All couples										
Total	70	84	74	65	48	2,713	417	1,236	681	377
18–24	68	86	70	62	51	556	76	271	166	43
25–29	73	85	78	69	46	714	115	347	174	76
30–34	73	88	77	71	46	748	112	348	176	112
35–39	65	80	68	62	51	695	114	270	165	146
Fecund couples										
Total	83	91	85	79	68	1,794	314	855	428	196
18–24	71	85	72	66	57	504	72	247	148	37
25–29	84	92	86	83	64	521	96	262	117	45
30–34	90	96	94	86	69	445	74	220	102	49
35–39	90	94	91	97	78	324	72	126	61	65

group (Table 4–9), and Action use increases consistently, though less rapidly.[11]

Couples with less education are more likely than others to be Future Users. This is consistent with the fact that those in the lower educational strata begin to use contraception relatively late. However, even

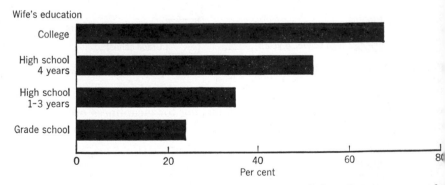

FIG. 4–4. Percentage of Users beginning contraception before first pregnancy, by wife's education.

[11] Data on Action use for each age group are in unpublished tables.

if we consider both Past and Future Users, the higher rate of use in upper educational strata persists.

Better-educated couples are more likely than others to start controlling conception early in their reproductive history (Figure 4-4 and Table 4-10). For example, 68 per cent of the Users with college-educated

TABLE 4-10. PER CENT DISTRIBUTION BY NUMBER OF PREGNANCIES BEFORE USE OF CONTRACEPTION BEGAN, FOR USERS, BY WIFE'S EDUCATION

Wife's education	No. of Users	No. of pregnancies before use began						
		Total	0	1	2	3	4 or more	N.A.
Total	1,901	100	48	32	11	4	3	2
College	353	100	68	22	7	1	2	—
High school, 4	912	100	52	31	10	3	2	2
High school, 1-3	451	100	35	42	11	6	3	3
Grade school	184	100	24	29	23	11	10	3

wives began preventive measures before the first pregnancy as compared with 24 per cent of those with wives having only a grade school education. These large differences persist when couples with the same number of pregnancies are compared.

Once use is begun, the couples with better-educated wives are more likely to be successful in planning their pregnancies and less likely to have accidental or other unplanned pregnancies. For example, couples with college wives planned 59 per cent of all pregnancies after first use, but those with wives having no more than a grade school education planned only 34 per cent (Table 4-11).

TABLE 4-11. PERCENTAGE OF USERS' PREGNANCIES OCCURRING BEFORE USE BEGAN, AND PER CENT DISTRIBUTION BY PLANNING STATUS FOR PREGNANCIES AFTER USE BEGAN, BY WIFE'S EDUCATION

Wife's education	All pregnancies		Pregnancies after use began				
	Number	Percentage before use began	Number	Per cent distribution by planinng status			
				Total	Planned	Accidental	Other unplanned
Total	4,680	32	3,171	100	51	25	24
College	811	20	646	100	59	22	19
High school, 4	2,090	30	1,459	100	54	22	24
High school, 1-3	1,172	36	774	100	45	31	24
Grade school	605	47	321	100	34	29	37

TABLE 4–12. PER CENT DISTRIBUTION BY FERTILITY PLANNING STATUS, FOR FECUND USERS, BY WIFE'S EDUCATION, BY WIFE'S AGE

Wife's education	No. of Fecund Users	Fertility planning status				
		Total	Completely Planned	No. Planned	Quasi-planned	Excess Fertility
Total						
Total	1,459	100	29	22	36	13
College	288	100	39	20	33	8
High school, 4	714	100	33	20	36	11
High school, 1–3	327	100	18	29	37	16
Grade school	130	100	10	19	39	32
Ages 18–24						
Total	350	100	38	14	41	7
College	61	100	52	13	33	2
High school, 4	178	100	42	11	42	5
High school, 1–3	91	100	22	21	43	14
Grade school	20	100	20	15	50	15
Ages 25–29						
Total	437	100	30	21	37	12
College	88	100	38	20	35	7
High school, 4	223	100	37	20	33	10
High school, 1–3	97	100	15	27	40	18
Grade school	29	100	7	10	59	24
Ages 30–34						
Total	389	100	25	28	31	16
College	71	100	41	21	31	7
High school, 4	204	100	26	27	33	14
High school, 1–3	83	100	19	35	31	15
Grade school	31	100	7	29	16	48
Ages 35–39						
Total	283	100	22	25	33	20
College	68	100	29	25	31	15
High school, 4	109	100	26	21	34	19
High school, 1–3	56	100	16	36	30	18
Grade school	50	100	8	20	38	34

Fertility planning status is also consistently associated with educational level. The better educated the couple, the more probable it is that they will be in one of the effective planning categories and the less likely that they will have more pregnancies than they want.

Let us consider the Fecund Users (Table 4–12). For these couples:

1. The proportion having Completely Planned fertility increases with education.

2. The proportion with too many pregnancies (Excess Fertility) decreases with education.

3. Quasi-planned families (last pregnancy wanted but not planned) tend to be relatively more numerous in groups with lower education.

4. Number Planned families are most common relatively in the high school 1–3 group.

The preceding generalizations hold for all age groups and are valid for all couples as well as for Fecund Users. The proportion of couples with Excess Fertility decreases as education rises for both Users and Nonusers when all couples are considered.

When husband's and wife's education are considered jointly (Table 4–13), the fertility planning patterns found are essentially the same as those for the wife's education alone, but the differences are increased by considering the education of both spouses.

TABLE 4–13. PER CENT DISTRIBUTION BY FERTILITY PLANNING STATUS, FOR FECUND USERS, BY COUPLE'S EDUCATION

Couple's education	No. of Fecund Users	Fertility planning status					
		Total	Completely Planned	No. Planned	Quasi-planned	Excess Fertility
Total	1,459	100	29	22	36	13
Both college	210	100	43	20	30	7
One high school, other college	272	100	36	17	37	10
Both high school, 4	310	100	35	24	32	9
One high school, 1–3 other high school, 4	234	100	24	22	40	14
Both high school, 1–3	118	100	20	30	36	14
One grade school, other more	235	100	17	25	38	20
Both grade school	75	100	11	15	41	33
Not ascertained	5	100	*	*	*	*

In summary, then, increasing education is associated with fertility planning patterns involving more couples using contraception, more starting use earlier, and more planning their fertility effectively. However, before we interpret the significance of the relationship between education and family planning, let us consider another important indicator of status in our society—income—which is, of course, related to education.

The Influence of Income

While a substantial majority of couples in all income groups are Users, the size of this majority increases with the husband's annual income[12] (Table 4–14). As we shall see later, however, once use is begun, the association with fertility planning status is smaller and much less consistent for income than for education. While fertility planning status varies with income for the total sample, there is no significant relationship when only Fecund Users are considered.

In considering the relationships of income to resort to contraception, it is important to take age into account, since income increases with age for the couples in our sample and age is also related to the adoption of preventive measures. In each age group, there is a marked and generally consistent increase in the use of contraception by all couples and Fecund couples as income rises, although in some age groups there are minor reversals in position for adjacent income classes[13] (Table 4–15).

The large differentials in the proportion of Users are between the lowest-income group (under $3,000) and the next-higher groups. The lowest-income group is distinctive at all ages. In each case the difference between it and the next-higher group equals or exceeds the largest difference between any other successive income groups. However, even for the lowest-income group a majority of couples of each age are Users. The smallest proportion (52 per cent) is in the 35–39 age group with incomes under $3,000.

Among Fecund couples the relationship between income and use of contraception is similar to that for all couples, but the proportions adopting control measures are larger. Again, the lowest-income group is distinctive, though somewhat less so than among all couples. Users are relatively least numerous (64 per cent) among couples with young wives and low incomes. In the oldest age group (35–39) the percentage of couples who are Users varies from 81 in the next-to-lowest income group to 98 in the next-to-highest.

As age advances, there is a smaller increase in the proportion of Users

---

[12] See Appendix A, Note 12, for information regarding the relation between family income and the proportion of couples who are Users.

[13] The User differential between income classes is much smaller on an action basis than on a motive basis, because the proportion of DFCO wives is higher in the lower-income groups. Nevertheless, even on an action basis there is a regular, but smaller, rise in the proportion of Users as income increases.

TABLE 4–14. PERCENTAGE WHO ARE PAST USERS, OR PAST OR FUTURE USERS, ON A MOTIVE AND ACTION BASIS, FOR ALL COUPLES AND FECUND COUPLES, BY HUSBAND'S INCOME

Husband's income	All couples					Fecund couples				
		Percentage who are:					Percentage who are:			
		Past Users		Past or Future Users			Past Users		Past or Future Users	
	Number	Motive	Action	Motive	Action	Number	Motive	Action	Motive	Action
Total	2,713	70	81	79	86	1,794	83	89	90	94
$6,000 or more	430	79	86	83	88	283	93	96	95	97
$5,000–$5,999	393	76	86	85	89	252	90	94	95	97
$4,000–$4,999	583	72	83	80	87	388	85	91	92	95
$3,000–$3,999	619	69	82	78	87	413	83	90	90	94
Under $3,000	581	58	76	73	84	387	71	79	84	88

as income rises among Fecund couples. The differentials by income among Fecund Users are largest in the youngest age group and become progressively smaller in succeeding age groups, because with increasing age all Fecund couples, regardless of such characteristics as income, have to face the problems of rapidly growing families if they are not Users.

TABLE 4–15. PERCENTAGE WHO ARE USERS, FOR ALL COUPLES AND FECUND COUPLES, BY WIFE'S AGE, BY HUSBAND'S INCOME[a]

Wife's age	Husband's income					
	Total	$6,000 or more	$5,000– $5,999	$4,000– $4,999	$3,000– $3,999	Under $3,000
All couples						
Total	70	79	76	72	69	58
18–24	68	82	78	72	73	62
25–29	73	84	79	72	74	59
30–34	73	82	77	78	70	59
35–39	65	75	72	68	60	52
Fecund couples						
Total	83	93	90	85	83	71
18–24	71	87	82	75	76	64
25–29	84	93	90	83	86	73
30–34	90	94	92	94	91	79
35–39	90	95	98	93	81	86

[a] Numbers of couples in base groups are shown in mimeographed tables (see Preface).

Higher income is also associated with earlier first use of contraception (Table 4–16). This is true with only minor variations within subgroups classified by number of pregnancies to date. In fact, the relationship is strengthened when number of pregnancies is held constant. For example, among Users with two pregnancies, 38 per cent of those with incomes of less than $3,000 but 67 per cent of those with incomes above $6,000 began use before the first pregnancy.

Once use is begun, higher income is associated with a somewhat lower proportion of pregnancies that are accidental or "other unplanned," and a somewhat higher proportion that are planned (Table 4–17). These relationships to income are similar to those found for education. However, the association is less regular and consistent for income than for education within specific age groups.[14]

[14] See Appendix A, Note 13, for additional information on this topic.

The fertility planning status of all couples is related to income, because income is directly related to both fecundity and use of contraception. The more significant relationships in Table 4–18 are:

1. The proportion of couples with Completely Planned fertility tends to increase with income at all age levels, but especially among wives 35–39.

TABLE 4–16. PER CENT DISTRIBUTION BY NUMBER OF PREGNANCIES BEFORE USE OF CONTRACEPTION BEGAN, FOR USERS, BY HUSBAND'S INCOME, HUSBAND'S OCCUPATION, AND YEARS WIFE HAS WORKED SINCE MARRIAGE

Socioeconomic characteristics	No. of Users	No. of pregnancies before use began						
		Total	0	1	2	3	4 or more	N.A.
Total	1,901	100	48	32	11	4	3	2
Husband's income:								
$6,000 or more	343	100	58	28	8	2	2	2
$5,000–$5,999	302	100	48	33	11	4	2	2
$4,000–$4,999	423	100	49	30	12	4	2	3
$3,000–$3,999	430	100	44	34	11	6	4	1
Under $3,000	340	100	44	33	13	6	3	1
Husband's occupation:[a]								
Upper white collar	504	100	63	25	6	3	2	1
Lower white collar	217	100	54	29	12	3	1	1
Upper blue collar	443	100	43	37	10	5	3	2
Lower blue collar	476	100	38	36	15	5	4	2
Farm	152	100	38	28	16	9	7	2
Years wife worked since marriage:								
None	551	100	39	35	15	5	3	3
Less than 1	346	100	47	34	11	3	3	2
1–4	704	100	55	30	8	5	2	—
5 or more	281	100	54	29	10	3	3	1

[a] Does not include men with indeterminate occupations or not in civilian labor force (e.g., students, members of armed forces).

2. The proportion of couples who are Nonusers with more pregnancies than they want (Excess Fertility) is small, but tends to decrease with rising income at ages 25–29 and older. The total proportion with Excess Fertility is not as closely or consistently related to income as it is to education.

3. The proportion of couples who are Nonusers but have wanted all their pregnancies (Quasi-planned Nonusers) decreases fairly consistently with rising income at all ages.

Among Fecund Users fertility planning is not related to income in

TABLE 4–17. PERCENTAGE OF USERS' PREGNANCIES OCCURRING BEFORE USE BEGAN, AND PER CENT DISTRIBUTION BY PLANNING STATUS FOR PREGNANCIES AFTER USE BEGAN, BY HUSBAND'S INCOME, HUSBAND'S OCCUPATION, AND YEARS WIFE WORKED SINCE MARRIAGE

Socioeconomic characteristics	All pregnancies		Pregnancies after use began				
	Number	Percentage before use began	Number	Per cent distribution by planning status			
				Total	Planned	Accidental	Other unplanned
Total	4,680	32	3,171	100	51	25	24
Husband's income:							
$6,000 or more	953	22	741	100	56	20	24
$5,000–$5,999	747	31	515	100	54	25	21
$4,000–$4,999	1,050	30	725	100	51	29	20
$3,000–$3,999	1,021	37	633	100	50	26	24
Under $3,000	739	41	429	100	41	26	33
Husband's occupation:							
Upper white collar	1,202	22	933	100	58	21	21
Lower white collar	501	28	358	100	56	26	18
Upper blue collar	1,142	34	756	100	46	25	29
Lower blue collar	1,171	40	709	100	41	32	27
Farm	459	40	275	100	57	20	23
Years wife worked since marriage:							
None	1,541	34	1,021	100	49	26	25
Less than 1	788	34	519	100	49	27	24
1–4	1,672	30	1,173	100	51	25	24
5 or more	620	33	417	100	54	23	23

any consistent way as it is to education.[15] Income has some relation to whether Fecund couples will be Users, but among Fecund Users it is not closely associated with fertility planning status. This suggests that, as effective contraception diffuses throughout the population, there may be even less relation between income and family limitation.

The Joint Influence of Education and Income

Education and income together are two of the most important indicators of status in our society. They are, of course, correlated with each other. We have already seen that family limitation practices are consistently related to education and that their relationship with income is significant but less close. What results are obtained if income and education are considered simultaneously?

[15] Data supporting this statement are in unpublished tables.

TABLE 4–18. Per Cent Distribution by Fertility Planning Status, for All Couples, by Husband's Income, by Wife's Age

Husband's income	No. of couples	Fertility planning status								
		Users					Nonusers		N.A.	Total Excess Fertility (Users and Nonusers)
		Total	Completely Planned	No. Planned	Quasi-planned	Excess Fertility	Quasi-planned	Excess Fertility		
						Total				
Total	2,713	100	19	15	25	9	26	4	2	13
$6,000 or more	430	100	24	19	26	9	18	2	2	11
$5,000–$5,999	393	100	19	20	27	10	20	2	2	12
$4,000–$4,999	584	100	18	17	27	9	25	2	2	12
$3,000–$3,999	619	100	18	14	26	10	27	4	1	13
Under $3,000	581	100	16	10	22	9	34	7	2	16
						Ages 18–24				
Total	556	100	25	9	28	5	30	1	2	6
$6,000 or more	34	100	35	12	29	6	18	—	—	6
$5,000–$5,999	50	100	22	20	30	6	20	2	—	8
$4,000–$4,999	93	100	25	12	31	3	26	1	2	4
$3,000–$3,999	151	100	29	9	30	4	26	1	1	5
Under $3,000	206	100	23	5	26	4	37	2	3	6
						Ages 25–29				
Total	714	100	22	16	27	8	23	3	1	11
$6,000 or more	94	100	29	17	29	9	16	—	—	9
$5,000–$5,999	126	100	23	21	27	7	19	2	1	9
$4,000–$4,999	168	100	21	16	26	9	26	1	1	10
$3,000–$3,999	186	100	16	16	31	10	23	2	2	12
Under $3,000	114	100	18	13	19	8	32	9	1	17
						Ages 30–34				
Total	748	100	17	19	24	11	23	4	2	15
$6,000 or more	141	100	21	24	27	9	17	1	1	10
$5,000–$5,999	128	100	18	20	26	9	18	3	6	12
$4,000–$4,999	174	100	17	20	29	11	19	3	1	14
$3,000–$3,999	134	100	19	19	19	13	25	4	1	17
Under $3,000	143	100	11	12	20	15	30	10	2	25
						Ages 35–39				
Total	695	100	13	16	23	12	29	5	2	17
$6,000 or more	161	100	23	17	22	11	20	4	3	15
$5,000–$5,999	89	100	10	18	27	17	25	3	—	20
$4,000–$4,999	148	100	14	18	20	11	29	4	4	14
$3,000–$3,999	148	100	7	13	25	13	34	7	1	20
Under $3,000	118	100	7	13	19	12	38	9	2	21

127

While income and education are both related to contraceptive practice, the relationship of education is much more important. The increase in the proportion of couples who are Users as education rises within income classes is much greater than the increase as income rises within education classes. This is true for both the younger and older wives (Table 4–19).

TABLE 4–19. PERCENTAGE OF ALL COUPLES WHO ARE USERS, BY WIFE'S EDUCATION, BY HUSBAND'S INCOME, BY WIFE'S AGE[a]

Wife's education		Husband's income			
	Total	$6,000 or more	$5,000–$5,999	$3,000–$4,999	Under $3,000
Total					
Total	70	79	76	71	58
College	84	86	87	85	78
High school, 4	74	79	80	73	66
High school, 1–3	65	77	63	67	60
Grade school	48	50	69	54	39
Ages 18–29					
Total	71	84	79	73	61
College	85	90	93	82	80
High school, 4	74	83	81	75	64
High school, 1–3	66	*	68	68	61
Grade school	48	*	*	56	36
Ages 30–39					
Total	69	78	76	69	56
College	84	85	82	89	*
High school, 4	73	77	80	71	68
High school, 1–3	67	71	60	66	60
Grade school	49	*	*	54	40

[a] Numbers of couples in base groups are shown in mimeographed tables (see Preface).

When *both* education and income are very low the proportion of Users is also notably low—40 per cent or less among the couples with wife having a grade school education and husband having an income of less than $3,000. This is one of the few subgroups found in which less than half of the couples are Users. Their resort to contraception contrasts sharply with that of couples having incomes of $6,000 or more and a college education, among whom 85 to 90 per cent are Users. This distinctive low-income–low-education group is a relatively small part of the total sample—approximately 6 per cent. (Case 34 cited on page 131 is illustrative of the poor planners among this depressed group.)

Income and education are related to fertility planning status in much the same way as to the adoption of family limitation.[16] The variation with education is more pronounced by far than that with income. Again, it is true that the combination of low education and low income is especially distinctive. For example, in this group only 5 per cent of the couples have Completely Planned fertility while 32 per cent have Excess Fertility (Table 4–20). At the opposite extreme, among couples with a college education and an income of $6,000 or more, 33 per cent have Completely Planned fertility while only 8 per cent have Excess Fertility. The proportion of families that are Completely Planned increases sharply with education in the income classes, but the variations with income in the education groups are small and irregular. Similarly, the very sharp decline in Excess Fertility as education rises within income categories is not matched by declines with income in the education groups. These statements apply both to the younger wives (18–29) and the older wives (30–39).

In general, this analysis confirms the importance of wife's education, independent of income, in relation to certain aspects of family limitation.[17] It seems likely that higher education gives the wife a wider range of contacts and information which are likely to make her treat her problem more rationally (in the sense of self-consciously analyzing her situation and the possible courses of action). It may cause her to aspire to a style of life and a variety of personal relationships which require careful planning, including the planning of family growth.

The following cases illustrate both the patterns typically associated with differing educational backgrounds and the exceptions which are quite frequent, since after all, education and fertility planning status are only moderately related.

The following is an example of the "rational" urban, college-educated couple with a Completely Planned family:

CASE 32. This doctor's family has an income of more than $10,000 a year. They had five planned pregnancies, but one child died shortly after birth. They now feel that four children is the right size family and won't have any more, because they have "four to put through college and nowadays they get married early and need a little more help." The wife says: "Children are a joy and fun. We learned a lot by having a family."

[16] To simplify the presentation the comparisons in this section are restricted to the percentage of couples with Completely Planned fertility and the percentage with Excess Fertility.

[17] Unpublished data also show that education is more closely related than income to the planning status of pregnancies.

TABLE 4–20. PERCENTAGE OF ALL COUPLES WHO HAVE COMPLETELY PLANNED FERTILITY, AND EXCESS FERTILITY, BY WIFE'S EDUCATION, BY HUSBAND'S INCOME, BY WIFE'S AGE[a]

Wife's education		Husband's income			
	Total	$6,000 or more	$5,000–$5,999	$3,000–$4,999	Under $3,000
Completely Planned Fertility					
Total					
Total	19	24	18	18	16
College	33	33	34	28	40
High school, 4	23	24	20	24	22
High school, 1–3	11	14	10	9	12
Grade school	4	4	*	6	5
Ages 18–29					
Total	23	31	23	22	22
College	37	44	29	31	42
High school, 4	28	32	28	28	28
High school, 1–3	12	*	12	9	14
Grade school	5	*	*	7	6
Ages 30–39					
Total	15	22	15	14	9
College	29	29	41	25	*
High school, 4	17	20	14	18	13
High school, 1–3	10	13	8	9	10
Grade school	4	*	*	6	4
Excess Fertility					
Total					
Total	13	11	12	12	16
College	8	8	7	9	4
High school, 4	10	10	10	10	8
High school, 1–3	15	16	19	15	14
Grade school	24	27	17	19	32
Ages 18–29					
Total	9	9	9	9	10
College	4	5	7	4	*
High school, 4	6	5	7	7	3
High school, 1–3	12	*	15	10	11
Grade school	19	*	*	16	29
Ages 30–39					
Total	16	13	16	16	23
College	11	9	7	15	*
High school, 4	13	12	13	14	15
High school, 1–3	18	13	23	19	19
Grade school	27	*	*	20	33

[a] Numbers of couples in base groups are shown in mimeographed tables (see Preface).

That the planning of family size has penetrated all educational levels is clear. Here is an example of a rather unusual couple with only a grade school education whose plans are not too dissimilar from those of the preceding couple:

CASE 33. This couple migrated to a Middle Western city from a Southwestern state where both were reared on farms. Neither had more than 8 years of schooling, but they want their children to have more. They have had three planned pregnancies. They really wanted only two children, and the third pregnancy was to replace a stillbirth. They definitely want no more than the two, the wife says, because "two is enough to raise and educate. More would make both of us have to work too hard to bring them up the way we want to. I don't think you should have too many kids. You ought to be able to bring them up right without hardship on anybody." The family income last year was $4,000—all from the husband's wages as a semiskilled worker.

We have seen that Excess Fertility is relatively frequently found among couples with a grade school education. Here is an example of one of the less happy couples with little education and several unwanted pregnancies:

CASE 34. This couple already has seven children, although the wife is only 26, and they have been married for only 8 years. Since their marriage began, the only year in which she did not bear a child was the one in which they separated for 11 months after a quarrel. She really wanted only two children, but she says her husband doesn't care and doesn't cooperate with her efforts to prevent further pregnancies. She didn't want the last pregnancy, and when it came, she felt "tired and crushed." She says that "children are a pleasure to have. I wouldn't be without them, but I have too many." She is pregnant again now, but she believes that her tubes will be tied after this birth because, in her words, "I keep having them every year, and I can't go on this way. We can't afford what we have, and I'm ruining my health. The doctor says he never saw anyone so fertile. My marriage started off wrong. We were too young and didn't know anything about responsibility." The husband made $2,500 last year as a semiskilled worker. Neither husband nor wife finished grade school.

Some college-educated couples, too, have more children than they want and are not unlike the preceding grade school couple:

CASE 35. This small-town couple, both college graduates, live in a small community where the husband, a businessman, made about $5,000 in his own business last year. Though they wanted only two children, they have had four. The last two were accidents and were definitely not planned for. She felt "furious" when she learned she was pregnant the last time, but just had to accept it. She says, "I like to guide children and watch them grow up, but I don't like to have to stay home all the time and not be able to work."

Finally, lest it be supposed from the foregoing examples that only the couples with rational Completely Planned families are happy, consider the following case—a poorly educated couple never using contraception but enjoying its large family. (This couple is classified among the Quasi-planned Nonusers and represents a type which is fairly common among the less well educated.)

CASE 36. This Catholic family has seven children after 16 years of married life. Neither the wife nor the husband went to high school. The 3-year period during the war when the husband was away in the army was their longest without the birth of a child. Both of them come from large families, and they love a lot of children. The wife says, "They make a home a home, give a stronger feeling between the wife and the husband. They are lots of enjoyment." The husband makes about $5,000 as a skilled worker, in the small town in which they have always lived. She doesn't believe in limiting family size unless there are special health conditions or the parents aren't getting along. "In our religion we don't believe in it. We are taught that it is normal to have children." She says, "I certainly am happy in my marriage and family. I couldn't ask for anything more."

The Influence of Occupational Status

Variations in prestige and in style of life are associated with occupation in a way not adequately measured by income. Studying the size of families of men with specific occupations (e.g., accountants, carpenters, doctors, etc.) would be the ideal way to analyze the unique influences of the social situations associated with different occupations. Our sample, however, is too small for this purpose.

For our analysis, the husbands are grouped into the following occupational categories:

Upper-white-collar workers: Proprietors, managers, officials, and professional workers

Lower-white-collar workers: Salesmen, and clerical and kindred workers

Upper-blue-collar workers: Craftsmen, foremen, and kindred workers

Lower-blue-collar workers: Operatives and kindred workers, service workers, and laborers (nonfarm)

Farm workers: Farmers, farm managers, and farm laborers

The first four categories have been used as a crude status ranking for nonfarm occupations in a number of studies. The farm group is arbitrarily placed last, because it does not fit into this urban hierarchy. The economic and social status of farm workers varies widely. Unfortunately, our sample is too small to permit us to separate them into subgroups. Even if this were possible, it would be difficult to fit the subgroups into an urban ranking.

In general, the foregoing ranking of the four nonfarm occupational groups corresponds to their ranking with respect to various measures of contraceptive practice: the proportion of couples who are Users, the time of beginning use, and the effectiveness of planning as indicated by either fertility planning status or the planning status of pregnancies. In these respects farm workers rank either below all workers with non-farm occupations, or, in some cases, between the two blue-collar groups.

More specifically, the proportion of couples who are Users tends to decrease with decreasing nonfarm occupational status at all ages (Table 4–21). Farm workers consistently have a lower proportion of Users than the three highest nonfarm occupational groups, but are not consistently different from lower-blue-collar workers. Among Fecund couples the difference between upper- and lower-white-collar workers is neither large nor consistent within age groups.

TABLE 4–21. PERCENTAGE WHO ARE USERS, FOR ALL COUPLES AND FECUND COUPLES, BY WIFE'S AGE, BY HUSBAND'S OCCUPATION[a]

Wife's age		Husband's occupation					
	Total	Upper white collar	Lower white collar	Upper blue collar	Lower blue collar	Farm	Others
				All couples			
Total	70	81	76	69	62	63	70
18–24	68	81	72	68	66	58	64
25–29	73	87	82	69	65	67	71
30–34	73	82	86	70	64	64	83
35–39	65	76	60	68	53	60	*
				Fecund couples			
Total	83	92	90	84	77	73	75
18–24	71	81	76	74	67	58	69
25–29	84	94	92	81	77	78	80
30–34	90	93	98	91	84	83	*
35–39	90	95	97	93	86	74	*

[a] Numbers of couples in base groups are shown in mimeographed tables (see Preface).

The time when contraceptive practice is begun is related to the occupational groups in a similar manner, upper-white-collar workers starting use earliest and farm workers starting latest (Table 4–16). For example, while 63 per cent of the upper-white-collar couples began contraception before the first pregnancy, only 38 per cent of either the lower-blue-collar couples or the farm couples did so.

Similarly, once use is begun, the higher the occupational status of nonfarm couples, the greater the proportion of pregnancies which are planned and the smaller the proportion which are accidental or "other unplanned" (Table 4–17). In this respect the farm-worker group deviates rather widely from its usual rank position, having a low proportion of accidental pregnancies and a high proportion planned among pregnancies after first use. However, since most of the pregnancies of farm couples occur either to Users before first use or to couples who have never used a method, this statement relates only to about three-eighths of the pregnancies of the farm-worker group.

Fertility planning status also varies in relation to occupational rankings, with an occasional reversal of adjacent occupational groups. In general, higher occupational status and effective planning go together. For Fecund Users, Table 4–22 shows that:

1. The proportion of couples having Completely Planned fertility increases, and the proportion having Excess Fertility decreases, with higher occupational status for nonfarm occupations.

2. Farm workers tend to have a relatively low proportion at both extremes—Completely Planned and Excess Fertility—and to be concentrated among the Number Planned and Quasi-planned. However, the position of this group varies considerably with age of wife.

Similar relationships to fertility planning are found when all couples are considered instead of Fecund Users.[18] The most important additional conclusion is that the proportion of couples that are Nonusers wanting all their pregnancies (Quasi-planned Nonusers) is higher in the lower occupational ranks and is uniformly high in the farm-worker group.

In summary, high nonfarm occupational status is associated with much Completely Planned fertility, little Excess Fertility, and few Nonusers. Farm workers are scarce at either extreme—relatively few have either Completely Planned fertility or too many pregnancies. They are concentrated among the Nonusers who want all their pregnancies and the Users in the intermediate planning categories. While these occupational differences are fairly consistent within each age group, there are rather frequent reversals between adjacent occupational groups. The differences are not as large or as stable as those for education.

Education is more closely related than occupation to the use of family limitation methods and apparently accounts for much of the difference by occupation. When several measures of contraception are considered we find that they vary in much greater degree with education within occupational groups than with occupation within educational groups (Table 4–23). So far as fertility planning is concerned, it is true at each educational level (with one exception) that each of the two white-collar

---

[18] This statement is based on data in an unpublished tabulation.

TABLE 4–22. PER CENT DISTRIBUTION BY FERTILITY PLANNING STATUS, FOR FECUND USERS, BY HUSBAND'S OCCUPATION, BY WIFE'S AGE

Husband's occupation	No. of couples	Fertility planning status				
		Total	Completely Planned	No. Planned	Quasi-planned	Excess Fertility
			Total			
Total	1,459	100	29	22	36	13
Upper white collar	392	100	39	19	31	11
Lower white collar	179	100	33	24	32	11
Upper blue collar	313	100	23	25	37	15
Lower blue collar	372	100	21	21	40	18
Farm	113	100	23	29	38	10
			Ages 18–24			
Total	350	100	38	14	41	7
Upper white collar	66	100	39	14	41	6
Lower white collar	37	100	43	19	38	—
Upper blue collar	71	100	37	22	35	6
Lower blue collar	99	100	31	10	45	14
Farm	24	100	37	13	42	8
			Ages 25–29			
Total	437	100	30	21	37	12
Upper white collar	119	100	39	17	32	12
Lower white collar	60	100	37	23	35	5
Upper blue collar	94	100	26	21	40	13
Lower blue collar	108	100	22	18	43	17
Farm	40	100	20	37	35	8
			Ages 30–34			
Total	389	100	25	28	31	16
Upper white collar	103	100	46	21	23	10
Lower white collar	53	100	25	30	28	17
Upper blue collar	86	100	13	29	42	16
Lower blue collar	105	100	16	30	34	20
Farm	40	100	20	37	35	8
			Ages 35–39			
Total	283	100	22	25	33	20
Upper white collar	104	100	32	23	31	14
Lower white collar	29	100	27	24	25	24
Upper blue collar	62	100	17	28	28	27
Lower blue collar	60	100	16	30	34	20
Farm	22	100	9	18	55	18

TABLE 4–23. PERCENTAGE OF ALL COUPLES WHO ARE USERS, WHO HAVE COMPLETELY PLANNED FERTILITY, OR WHO HAVE EXCESS FERTILITY, BY HUSBAND'S OCCUPATION, BY WIFE'S EDUCATION[a]

Husband's occupation	Wife's education				
	Total	College	High school, 4	High school, 1–3	Grade school
Percentage who are Users					
Total	70	85	74	66	49
Upper white collar	81	84	83	71	58
Lower white collar	76	90	74	67	*
Upper blue collar	69	71	76	63	57
Lower blue collar	62	82	69	67	40
Farm	63	100	59	68	52
Percentage who have Completely Planned fertility					
Total	19	33	23	11	4
Upper white collar	29	33	28	23	8
Lower white collar	24	35	29	10	*
Upper blue collar	15	20	21	9	8
Lower blue collar	12	18	19	9	2
Farm	13	38	14	11	5
Percentage who have Excess Fertility					
Total	13	8	10	15	24
Upper white collar	10	7	10	13	15
Lower white collar	9	10	6	12	*
Upper blue collar	13	9	10	17	19
Lower blue collar	18	7	11	18	32
Farm	10	5	8	9	15

[a] Numbers of couples in base groups are shown in mimeographed tables (see Preface).

groups has a higher proportion of Completely Planned families than either blue-collar group, but variation with education is more important.

The Influence of the Working Wife

One of the paradoxes of the postwar period is that more and more wives and mothers are working for pay, although the country has had an unprecedented upsurge in the marriage rate and a so-called baby boom. The working wife is no longer a rarity. The proportion of wives who are in the labor force increased rapidly in the postwar period from 21 per cent in 1947 to 30 per cent in 1956. Equally spectacular is the increase (from 11 to 16 per cent) in the proportion with jobs among mothers of preschool children (younger than 6). Thirty-six per cent of the mothers of school age children (ages 6–17) were at work in 1956.[19]

How can the increased participation in the labor force by wives and mothers be consistent with the postwar marriage pattern and baby boom? In part it reflects the taking of jobs by a high proportion of wives least able to have children, of those whose families are complete, and of those whose youngest child has started school. We have already seen that the wives most likely to be employed are the Subfecund whose smaller families leave them free for more outside activity. But this is not the whole story. If the wife wishes to work, many Fecund couples plan their family growth to make this possible. The family limitation practices of couples with working wives are consistent with the wife's participation in the nation's labor force.

Among Fecund couples, working wives are much more likely than nonworking wives to have Completely Planned fertility. Among Fecund Users, 42 per cent of the working wives but only 25 per cent of the nonworking wives have Completely Planned fertility (Table 4–24). The proportion with such fertility also increases with the number of years the wife has worked since marriage (Table 4–25). Working wives are somewhat less likely than others to have Excess Fertility.

Couples with working wives are particularly likely to be in the Completely Planned never-pregnant group. For example, among Fecund Users with young wives, 48 per cent of those with wife working but only 5 per cent of those with wife not working are classified in this way (Table 4–24). Among wives 35–39, 7 per cent of those working but only 1 per cent of those not working are so classified. The proportion of couples with Completely Planned fertility and no pregnancies is directly related to length of wife's work since marriage among Fecund Users with wives 25–39 years old.

The fact that Fecund couples with working wives are much more likely to have Completely Planned fertility is not a function of such other characteristics as the wife's education, husband's income, or wife's religion. This is shown in a separate analysis for Fecund couples by Jeanne Clare Ridley, who examined the relation of wife's labor-force history to the proportion of Completely Planned families.[20] She found the strong association with wife's current labor-force status and number of years worked to be sustained among Fecund couples regardless of their socioeconomic characteristics. Apparently, a significant minority

[19] For recent data on the employment status of married women see "Marital Status and Family Status of Workers: 1956," *Current Population Reports, Labor Force, U.S. Bureau of the Census*, series P-50, no. 73, April, 1957.

[20] Jeanne Clare Ridley, *The Relationship of Non-familial Activities to Fertility Behavior*, Ph.D. dissertation in sociology, University of Michigan, 1957.

TABLE 4–24. PER CENT DISTRIBUTION BY FERTILITY PLANNING STATUS, FOR FECUND USERS, BY WIFE'S LABOR-FORCE STATUS, BY WIFE'S AGE

Wife's labor-force status	No. of Fecund Users	Fertility planning status					
		Total	Completely Planned		Partially Planned		Excess Fertility
			Never pregnant	Ever pregnant	No. Planned	Quasi-planned	
Total							
Total	1,459	100	7	22	22	36	13
Not in labor force	1,135	100	2	23	24	37	14
In labor force	324	100	23	19	15	33	10
Ages 18–24							
Total	350	100	17	21	14	41	7
Not in labor force	257	100	5	24	17	45	9
In labor force	93	100	48	13	8	29	2
Ages 25–29							
Total	437	100	5	25	21	37	12
Not in labor force	352	100	2	27	22	37	12
In labor force	85	100	22	13	16	38	11
Ages 30–34							
Total	389	100	2	23	28	31	16
Not in labor force	301	100	1	23	30	30	16
In labor force	88	100	8	23	21	33	15
Ages 35–39							
Total	283	100	2	20	25	33	20
Not in labor force	225	100	1	17	27	33	22
In labor force	58	100	7	29	14	34	16

of Fecund couples in all strata have avoided pregnancy to date because a child would interfere with the wife's work.

The fact that Fecund couples with working wives are at a given time disproportionately concentrated in the Completely Planned never-pregnant category does not mean that large numbers of them expect to remain childless. On the contrary, as will be brought out in Chapter 9, most of the never-pregnant working wives are young women who are merely delaying the first child.

TABLE 4–25. PER CENT DISTRIBUTION BY FERTILITY PLANNING STATUS, FOR FECUND USERS, BY YEARS WIFE WORKED SINCE MARRIAGE, BY WIFE'S AGE

Years wife worked since marriage	No. of Fecund Users	Total	Fertility planning status				
			Completely Planned		Partially Planned		Excess Fertility
			Never pregnant	Ever pregnant	No. Planned	Quasi-planned	
Total							
Total	1,459	100	7	22	22	36	13
None	428	100	2	18	27	36	17
Less than 1	284	100	11	16	22	40	11
1–4	562	100	8	27	19	35	11
5 or more	174	100	8	27	19	30	16
Ages 18–24							
Total	350	100	17	21	14	41	7
None	107	100	6	18	24	44	8
Less than 1	105	100	25	16	11	43	5
1–4	134	100	19	27	9	37	8
5 or more	3	100	*	*	*	*	*
Ages 25–29							
Total	437	100	5	25	21	37	12
None	123	100	2	24	24	35	15
Less than 1	86	100	3	12	27	46	12
1–4	186	100	8	32	18	36	6
5 or more	37	100	13	27	11	22	27
Ages 30–34							
Total	389	100	2	23	28	31	16
None	98	100	—	13	38	31	18
Less than 1	68	100	2	18	29	32	19
1–4	151	100	3	28	23	31	15
5 or more	70	100	7	30	22	30	11
Ages 35–39							
Total	283	100	2	20	25	33	20
None	100	100	—	16	25	33	26
Less than 1	25	100	—	24	28	28	20
1–4	91	100	2	19	25	34	20
5 or more	64	100	5	25	22	34	14

The relationship of wife's work history to fertility planning status for all couples is roughly similar to that for Fecund Users, but the comparison is complicated by the higher subfecundity of the nonworking wives which reduces their need for careful planning. The statistical results are not presented, and we shall only point out here that even for the total sample, working wives are more likely than others to have Completely Planned fertility and to be in the never-pregnant subgroup.

If the wife places a high value on working, the couple is likely to be especially careful in using contraception. Several wives reported that they were taking pains to limit the number of their children, or to have none, because they enjoyed their work or being active outside of the home, or because they wanted extra income.

Fertility planning status has been emphasized in this discussion because it differentiates most clearly the working wives from the others. However, it is also true that among Fecund couples, those with working wives—particularly wives who have worked a long time—are more likely to be Users (Table 4–26), to begin use early, and once use is begun to be slightly more successful in planning their pregnancies. Some of these relationships are rather small and in specific cases are not statistically significant, but they are consistent in each age group. As we shall see in Chapter 6, it is also true that if the wife has worked a long time the couple is likely to be using an effective method of contraception.

TABLE 4–26. PERCENTAGE OF FECUND COUPLES WHO ARE USERS, BY WIFE'S AGE, BY WIFE'S LABOR-FORCE STATUS AND YEARS WIFE WORKED SINCE MARRIAGE[a]

Wife's age	Wife's labor-force status			Years wife worked since marriage			
	Total	Not in labor force	In labor force	None	Less than 1	1–4	5 or more
Total	83	83	85	78	79	87	94
18–24	71	71	72	67	68	78	*
25–29	84	84	86	81	85	85	95
30–34	90	89	95	83	91	94	93
35–39	90	90	93	86	94	93	97

[a] Numbers of couples in base groups are shown in mimeographed tables (see Preface).

The association between the wife's working and the effectiveness of the couple's fertility planning has several explanations. One is simply negative selection: many of the couples not planning effectively have too many children to permit the wife to work easily. Unless forced to work by sheer economic necessity, these women tend to be excluded from the labor force by the lack of fertility planning or the ineffectiveness of the efforts made. More positively, if the wife wants to work and the husband wants her to do so, the couple has a strong motivation to plan family growth so as to make work possible. Moreover, it is likely that the wife's working contacts will put her in touch with other wives whose attitudes are favorable to contraception and who have information to communicate about effective practices.

In this connection it is very significant that among Fecund wives 35–39 years old who have been in the labor force for a long time, Catholics are rather similar to Protestants with respect to the proportion trying to limit family size, the success of their efforts, and their ideas about the expected number of children.[21] The wife's work experience is the one influence which virtually eliminates the difference in proportion of Users between Catholic and Protestant wives in their 30s (Figure 4–5).

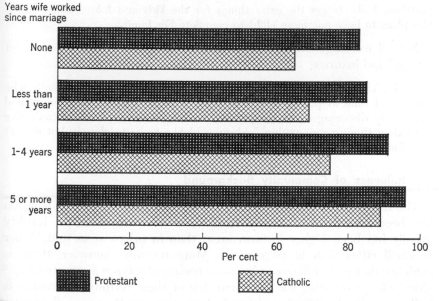

FIG. 4–5. Percentage of Fecund couples using contraception, by years wife worked since marriage, by wife's religion.

We interpret this to mean that the common experiences and contacts in the working situation outside the family minimize the effects of religious differences.

Here are several cases illustrating the attitudes of some working wives:

CASE 37. This 37-year-old mother has two children. The first was planned; the second was an accident. She says, "If it is in my power, we won't have

[21] *Ibid.*, chap. 4. Ridley also shows that among older women who have worked at least 5 years since marriage the proportion having Completely Planned families is the same for Catholic as for Protestant couples.

any more. I'm very active. I like business, and I want to participate in community affairs. With more than two to bring up and educate, I wouldn't be free to do outside things. . . . If we had more children, we might find it difficult to give them a college education and other things they need." The father in this family has a good managerial post in which he makes a salary of $8,000.

CASE 38. This couple has had two planned pregnancies. They plan to have another one, carefully spaced and planned. She wants to get out to work as soon as possible, because "it does you good to get out and you take better care of yourself. If you work, you go to the beauty shop, you look better, and you keep yourself up with the times."

CASE 39. This mother of two likes to work. She worked for 5 years before the birth of her second planned child. She wants to work again because she feels that "working is in my blood. When my children are all in school I will work parttime. I like to get the extra things for the kids and I love office work." She plans to have one more child to complete her family.

Not all working wives have planned families, nor are all working for "extras" and luxuries:

CASE 40. This wife has had eight children. The husband is an alcoholic who has served time in prison. The wife must work to support the family, and she is very discouraged. As she put it, "I work all the time, but I can't give the kids nothin' or save nothin'." She would like to go to church, but doesn't feel that she has the proper clothes for church.

The Influence of Community Background

The relation between community background and number of children has been considered in many studies. In Western countries fertility usually has been higher in farm areas than in urban areas and higher in small cities than in large cities. More recently, however, there is evidence that such differences between community types are narrowing.[22] One factor accounting for the narrowing of these fertility differences is believed to be the diffusion of family limitation practices from the larger urban centers where they were first adopted by large numbers of people. Another factor is the great mobility of our population, which mixes together in the same communities people who have lived in very different types of communities at earlier periods of their lives. Such explanations have been based on indirect evidence, since data have not been available on resort to contraception in different types of communities.

The big differences in efforts to control pregnancy that must have existed formerly no longer are found when we classify couples according to their residential histories. The only important consistent differences

[22] See the references cited in footnote 1 of this chapter.

today are those separating the relatively small farm population from the various urban groups. Even these differences are mainly the result of the educational differences between farm and nonfarm people. These generalizations summarize the results of examining the relationship between contraceptive practice and four different classifications of community backgrounds: (1) the farm background of the couple, (2) the type of community in which the husband and wife lived longest before and after marriage, (3) the type of community in which the couple is living now, and (4) the type of community of couples whose life experience has all been in places of a single type.[23]

To analyze the relationship of farm background to use of contraception all couples were classified as:

No farm background
Some farm background (either wife or husband lived on a farm for some
    time, usually while growing up)
Now on a farm

On the basis of this classification, there is a consistent pattern of differences in the efforts of couples to control conception. As compared with couples never on a farm, fewer of the couples *now* on a farm are Users (Table 4–27), more of the Users began use later, and once use was begun, somewhat fewer had planned pregnancies and more had accidental and other unplanned pregnancies. The couples now on a farm are also less likely than the other couples to have Completely Planned fertility (Table 4–28). This is true for all couples and for Fecund Users. Among Fecund Users, present farm residence or farm background is also associated with Excess Fertility.

The influence of farm life is apparently carried into the urban setting by farm-to-city migrants. At least it is true that the family limitation practices of the couples with some farm background tend to be intermediate between those of the couples with no such background and the couples now living on a farm.

The community backgrounds of Catholics and Protestants are so different that it is necessary to take religion into account when assessing the relationship between community background and efforts to regulate conception. Catholics are concentrated in very large cities, and relatively few of them have a farm background. Only 13 per cent of the couples in our sample now on a farm are Catholic, but 42 per cent of those never on a farm and 51 per cent of those in the 12 largest cities are Catholic.

[23] Since most of the results of this analysis are negative only a few illustrative statistical tables are presented here. However, unpublished data measuring the use of contraception in various ways are available for all the community-background classifications.

TABLE 4–27. PERCENTAGE OF ALL COUPLES WHO ARE USERS, BY COUPLE'S FARM BACKGROUND, BY WIFE'S RELIGION, BY WIFE'S AGE[a]

Couple's farm background	Wife's age				
	Total	18–24	25–29	30–34	35–39
Total					
Total	70	68	73	73	65
None	72	70	76	76	66
Some	70	70	72	71	68
Now on a farm	63	55	68	71	54
Protestant					
Total	75	74	80	76	70
None	79	77	87	79	73
Some	75	76	77	76	71
Now on a farm	66	57	74	73	58
Catholic					
Total	57	51	59	63	55
None	61	56	61	70	57
Some	53	46	58	51	55
Now on a farm	42	*	*	*	*

[a] Numbers of couples in base groups are shown in mimeographed tables (see Preface).

Despite these differences in the location of Catholics and Protestants, the relationship between farm background and family limitation practices is essentially the same for both religious groups. However, these practices are much more closely related to religion than to farm background. For example, even among Catholic couples *never* on a farm there are relatively fewer who are Users, and relatively fewer with Completely Planned fertility, than there are among Protestant couples *now* on a farm (Tables 4–27 and 4–28).

The variations of family limitation practices that do exist in both religious groups in relation to farm background are closely related to, and may be mainly a result of, differences in education. If the educational background is the same, farm couples are about as likely to have used contraception and to have used it effectively as are indigenous urban couples (Table 4–29).

Among farm couples there are relatively four times as many grade school wives and only one-third as many college wives as among couples never on a farm. The fact that farm-nonfarm differences in family

TABLE 4–28. PER CENT DISTRIBUTION BY FERTILITY PLANNING STATUS, FOR ALL COUPLES, BY COUPLE'S FARM BACKGROUND, BY WIFE'S RELIGION, BY WIFE'S AGE

Fertility planning status	Total			Protestant			Catholic		
	Couple's farm background								
	None	Some	Now on farm	None	Some	Now on farm	None	Some	Now on farm
Total									
Number of couples	1,136	1,262	300	574	978	258	481	261	40
Per cent									
Total	100	100	100	100	100	100	100	100	100
Completely Planned	22	17	12	27	20	14	12	6	2
Partially Planned	66	66	74	60	64	71	74	76	90
Excess Fertility	10	15	13	12	15	14	9	15	5
Not ascertained	2	2	1	1	1	1	5	3	3
Ages 18–29									
Number of couples	541	587	135	291	446	116	215	131	17
Per cent									
Total	100	100	100	100	100	100	100	100	100
Completely Planned	27	21	16	31	25	19	16	8	*
Partially Planned	66	66	74	62	63	71	77	77	*
Excess Fertility	5	12	10	7	11	10	4	13	*
Not ascertained	2	1	—	—	1	—	3	2	*
Ages 30–39									
Number of couples	595	675	165	283	532	142	266	130	23
Per cent									
Total	100	100	100	100	100	100	100	100	100
Completely Planned	18	14	8	23	17	9	9	4	4
Partially Planned	63	67	75	58	64	72	72	76	87
Excess Fertility	15	18	15	17	18	17	14	16	4
Not ascertained	4	1	2	2	1	2	5	4	5

imitation practices disappear when education is held constant suggests that they will diminish with the progressive narrowing of educational differences which is expected for the future. For the present, however, it remains true that the influence of older farm traditions may affect a substantial part of our population—the 11 per cent living on a farm and the 47 per cent with a farm background of some type. Although perhaps resulting from differences in educational standards, the dif-

TABLE 4–29. PERCENTAGE OF ALL COUPLES WHO ARE USERS, WHO HAVE COMPLETELY PLANNED FERTILITY, OR WHO HAVE EXCESS FERTILITY, BY COUPLE'S FARM BACKGROUND, BY WIFE'S EDUCATION

Farm background	Wife's education				
	Total	College	High school, 4	High school, 1–3	Grade school
Percentage who are Users					
Total	70	85	74	66	49
None	72	84	75	65	39
Some	70	84	75	67	53
Now on a farm	63	100	64	65	49
Percentage who have Completely Planned fertility					
Total	19	33	23	11	4
None	22	34	25	11	5
Some	17	31	22	11	5
Now on a farm	12	33	15	10	4
Percentage who have Excess Fertility					
Total	13	8	10	15	24
None	10	8	8	14	23
Some	15	7	11	17	27
Now on a farm	13	—	12	12	19
Number of couples in base group					
Total	2,713	417	1,236	681	377
None	1,136	219	573	269	75
Some	1,262	176	530	341	215
Now on a farm	300	21	128	68	83
Not ascertained	15	1	5	3	4

ferences associated with farm background are real and affect a large part of the population.

A second way of looking at community backgrounds is to consider the longest place of residence of the wife and husband both before and after marriage on the basis of the following community types: (1) large city (over 50,000), (2) small city (under 50,000), (3) rural nonfarm, and (4) farm. Various combinations of these categories were analyzed with age and religion controls.

The most important and consistent differences found are those between the farm group and the other community types, but these differences are more fully apparent in the farm-background classification, already discussed. The distinctions between the three other categories yield differences for the use of contraception, but with respect to planning status and other aspects of contraception, most differences are either not significantly large or are inconsistent. The distinction between small city and large city is not significant in most comparisons.

A third principle of classification of community background is the present place of residence of the couples. Although many Americans do not live in communities of the type in which they grew up, there is considerable interest in knowing how family limitation practices differ from one type of community to another. These differences affect the current population increase of different types of communities.

The following seven types of communities are used to classify the present residence of the couples:[24]

Metropolitan areas	*Nonmetropolitan areas*
12 largest cities	Small cities (2,500–50,000)
Other large cities (50,000 or more)	Rural nonfarm
Suburbs of 12 largest cities	Farm
Suburbs of other large cities	

This classification recognizes the increasing tendency for our society to be organized around a system of great metropolitan communities. It also distinguishes between the 12 largest metropolitan communities from New York to San Francisco and the other cities of 50,000 or more which vary in size from Nashville, Tennessee, to Waterloo, Iowa. The inclusion of two types of suburban areas recognizes both the presumed distinctiveness of suburban life and the differences between the suburbia of very large cities and other large cities.

Where people are living now is not closely related to differences in efforts to avoid conception. The important exception is that people living on farms have relatively fewer Users and less effective fertility planning by Users than people living in various nonfarm settings. When age and religion are held constant, the other differences are inconsistent or too small to be significant.

It is true that, as a whole, metropolitan areas are consistently different from nonmetropolitan areas, but these differences are small and are due almost entirely to the distinctiveness of the rural couples—and especially the farm couples—of the nonmetropolitan areas. The family limitation practices of residents of small nonmetropolitan cities resemble those of residents of metropolitan areas. As compared with couples living in nonmetropolitan areas, those in metropolitan areas are more likely to be Users (Table 4–30), to begin use early, and to have Completely Planned fertility, and are less likely to have Excess Fertility. While these dif-

[24] See Appendix A, Note 14, for more information about the classification.

ferences are consistent in all age groups, they are not large and reflect mainly the influence of the farm couples in the nonmetropolitan areas.

We had expected to find distinctive patterns of family limitation among the Protestants in the suburbs of the 12 largest cities, because these suburbanites are generally described as an especially rational and well-informed group. It is true that the proportion of couples who are Users is higher for the Protestant wives of each age who live in the suburbs of the 12 largest cities than for those living elsewhere (Table 4–30). However, this consistent pattern of difference in use does not extend to the

TABLE 4–30. PERCENTAGE OF ALL COUPLES WHO ARE USERS, BY PLACE OF RESIDENCE, BY WIFE'S RELIGION, BY WIFE'S AGE[a]

Wife's age	Total	Place of residence						
		Metropolitan areas				Nonmetropolitan areas		
		12 largest cities	Other cities of 50,000 or more	Suburbs of:		Small cities (2,500–50,000)	Rural non-farm	Farm
				12 largest cities	Other large cities			
				Total				
Total	70	69	69	79	72	72	67	62
18–24	68	72	67	77	75	68	64	55
25–29	73	72	66	83	78	80	70	68
30–34	73	73	75	81	69	72	69	71
35–39	65	61	69	74	66	69	63	52
				Protestant				
Total	75	79	76	89	77	77	70	66
18–24	74	67	78	87	79	79	66	56
25–29	80	83	74	94	80	85	74	75
30–34	76	69	82	89	75	76	71	73
35–39	70	56	72	86	74	71	67	56
				Catholic				
Total	57	63	57	65	54	52	54	42
18–24	51	68	43	57	*	35	*	*
25–29	59	58	54	71	65	60	53	*
30–34	63	72	64	69	48	54	60	*
35–39	55	55	64	56	47	62	*	*

[a] Numbers of couples in base groups are shown in mimeographed tables (see Preface).

other aspects of efforts to control conception, such as the time of first use of contraception or fertility planning status.

The farm group is the only one based on present residence that appears to be distinctive in relation to efforts to avoid conception, but we have already seen that this distinction is closely associated with educational attainment. It does not persist when years of school completed is held constant.

The population of the United States is so mobile that the community-background group for many couples will differ widely if we consider only the couple's history since marriage instead of including the pre-marital history of one or both spouses. The number of different combinations of community backgrounds is so great that we were unable to construct a simple scale with which we could classify all the couples. We suspect that this explains why none of the single classifications proved to be very highly correlated with most aspects of fertility planning. The fact is that in most American families at least one spouse has not lived under homogeneous community influences for a lifetime.

The best that we could do was to select couples whose community backgrounds were reasonably homogeneous. For this purpose we defined "reasonably homogeneous" as meaning that the couples were presently living in the type of place in which both husband and wife had lived longest both before and after marriage. These couples are subdivided into four groups, each of which represents a "pure" community type.[25]

Large city (above 50,000)   Rural nonfarm
Small city (below 50,000)   Farm

Only 38 per cent of the couples in the sample met the criteria for inclusion in one of these four homogeneous groups. The fact that 62 per cent of the couples did *not* fall into these groups testifies to the heterogeneous backgrounds of American couples.

For this select group of couples with homogeneous backgrounds, there is a more consistent increase in the extent and effectiveness of contraception with increasing urbanization, but even for them the variation is mainly associated with differing educational levels. Among either Fecund couples or all couples in this group, the proportion of Users tends to increase with urbanization (Figure 4–6). Every one of the Fecund couples with Protestant wife 30–39 and only large city experience is a User, and 94 per cent of the comparable couples with a Catholic wife are Users (Table 4–31).

With respect to other ways of measuring efforts to regulate conception, the two urban groups are not consistently different from each other.

---

[25] See Appendix A, Note 15, for more information about this classification.

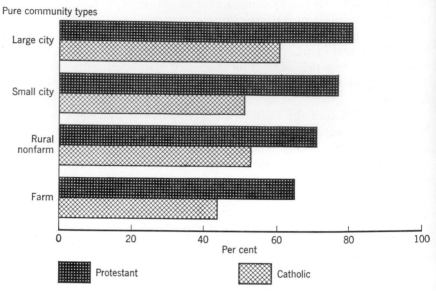

Pure community types

Fig. 4–6. Percentage of couples using contraception, by pure community types, by wife's religion.

TABLE 4–31. Percentage Who Are Users, for All Couples and Fecund Couples, by Pure Community Types, by Wife's Religion, by Wife's Age[a]

Pure community types	Wife's religion and age					
	Protestant			Catholic		
	Total	18–29	30–39	Total	18–29	30–39
All couples						
Total	75	77	74	57	56	59
Large city	82	81	83	61	54	66
Small city	77	80	75	51	56	47
Rural nonfarm	71	70	73	53	52	*
Farm	65	66	64	45	*	*
Fecund couples						
Total	88	84	94	70	63	83
Large city	90	84	100	77	61	94
Small city	90	88	92	68	66	*
Rural nonfarm	84	78	94	59	52	*
Farm	77	72	83	*	*	*

[a] Numbers of couples in base groups are shown in mimeographed tables (see Preface).

TABLE 4–32. PER CENT DISTRIBUTION BY FERTILITY PLANNING STATUS, FOR COUPLES WITH PROTESTANT AND CATHOLIC WIVES, BY PURE COMMUNITY TYPES, BY WIFE'S AGE

Pure community types	Fertility planning status and wife's religion											
	Protestant						Catholic					
	No. of couples	Total	Completely Planned	Partially Planned	Excess Fertility	N.A.	No. of couples	Total	Completely Planned	Partially Planned	Excess Fertility	N.A.
Ages 18–29												
Total	855	100	26	63	10	1	366	100	12	78	8	2
Large city	84	100	32	62	5	1	95	100	13	85	1	1
Small city	69	100	35	56	9	—	27	100	8	74	7	11
Rural nonfarm	79	100	20	63	13	4	25	100	4	76	12	8
Farm	65	100	15	73	12	—	11	100	*	*	*	*
Ages 30–39												
Total	962	100	17	64	18	1	421	100	7	75	14	4
Large city	86	100	26	49	21	4	135	100	8	75	13	4
Small city	81	100	28	57	12	3	38	100	3	82	13	2
Rural nonfarm	56	100	14	55	28	3	13	100	*	*	*	*
Farm	92	100	9	73	16	2	9	100	*	*	*	*

151

There is, in general, an ordering with the farm group at one extreme and the two urban groups at the other. Thus the farm group began use latest, has the smallest proportion of pregnancies which are planned, and has the smallest proportion of couples with Completely Planned fertility (Table 4–32). While the proportion of couples having Excess Fertility decreases with urbanization among wives under 30, whether Protestant or Catholic, there is no consistent relationship at ages over 30. In general, the rural nonfarm couples tend to be intermediate between the farm couples and the two urban types, but this is not always so. For some of the measures, the pure community types serve mainly to differentiate the farm couples from the others. Among the indigenous nonfarm population, size of community seems to be less important than it was in the past.

Educational levels are far more important than community types when these are considered jointly (Table 4–33). There is no consistent relation between use of contraception and community type within educational groups. On the other hand, use increases sharply as education rises within each pure community type. The rural group does have the lowest proportion of couples with Completely Planned fertility at each educational level, but whether a family is Completely Planned is related

TABLE 4–33. PERCENTAGE OF ALL COUPLES WHO ARE USERS OR WHO HAVE COMPLETELY PLANNED FERTILITY, BY PURE COMMUNITY TYPES, BY WIFE'S EDUCATION[a]

Pure community types	Wife's education			
	College	High school, 4	High school, 1–3	Grade school
Percentage who are Users				
Total	84	74	65	48
Large city	83	75	66	58
Small city	97	71	64	32
Rural nonfarm	*	73	69	46
Farm	*	65	67	50
Percentage who have Completely Planned fertility				
Total	33	23	11	4
Large city	38	25	11	8
Small city	44	26	13	8
Rural nonfarm	*	22	12	4
Farm	*	12	10	2

[a] Numbers of couples in base groups are shown in mimeographed tables (see Preface).

much more closely to education than to community type. The differences persisting under controls for educational level are mainly those separating the rural farm group from the other three.

The virtual elimination of major differences in family limitation practice between different types of nonfarm communities is probably a result of a double process. On the one hand, the tremendous mobility of the American population has thoroughly mixed together people of very different backgrounds in communities of different size and type. On the other hand, the influence of the metropolitan community has been reaching out to every section of the country, imbuing all our people with common standards and aspirations that affect not only what they consume and produce but also the number of children they want and how they plan family growth. As farm-nonfarm educational differences disappear, even the farm couples apparently are adopting these common standards for planning fertility.

Chapter 5

ATTITUDES TOWARD FAMILY LIMITATION

Basic to the widespread use of some method of contraception by American married couples is a strong consensus of opinion supporting the general idea of spacing children and preventing excessively large families. The use of contraception is, in itself, indirect behavioral evidence of the existence of these underlying attitudes. To measure them directly all wives were asked the following question:

41. "Many married couples do something to limit the size of their families and to control when their children come. How do you feel about that?"

Those respondents who opposed efforts to control the number and spacing of children were then asked a second question:

41b. "Are there any conditions under which you think it is all right for a married couple to limit family size or control when children come?"

The words birth control and contraception were avoided in these questions, since we were interested in attitudes toward the general idea of family limitation and child spacing rather than attitudes toward specific methods. Nevertheless, it is likely that some respondents, especially Catholics, identified the phrase "family limitation" with particular disapproved methods and expressed less favorable attitudes than they would have done in answer to a separate question about the use of rhythm (periodic continence). In consequence, the results to be presented in this chapter probably understate the degree of approval of family limitation practices as defined in this report (i.e., including rhythm).

On the basis of their answers to the foregoing questions, all wives were classified with respect to their attitudes toward the general idea of controlling the number and spacing of children, as follows:

Unqualified approval. Approved without any qualification

Qualified approval. Approved, but qualified their response with respect to some special circumstance

Pro-con. Answer was ambivalent, neither clearly approving nor disapproving

Qualified disapproval. Disapproved in answer to the first question, but in answer to the second question indicated circumstances under which they approved of control measures

Unqualified disapproval. Disapproved under all circumstances.

The Influence of Religion

An overwhelming majority of all wives approved of the general idea of family limitation under some conditions (Figure 5–1). Only 5 per cent of them expressed unqualified opposition.

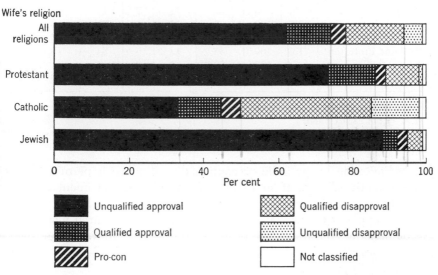

FIG. 5–1. Per cent distribution by attitude toward family limitation, for all wives, by wife's religion.

The *degree* of general approval is very different for Catholics and Protestants. While both Catholic and Protestant wives overwhelmingly approved of some control methods under some conditions, many more Catholics than Protestants disapproved either completely or with qualifications. Only 1 per cent of the Protestants but 13 per cent of the Catholics expressed unqualified disapproval (Table 5–1). At the other extreme 72 per cent of the Protestants but only 33 per cent of the Catholics approved completely.

The attitude toward the general idea of regulating conception which is most consistent with the teachings of the Catholic Church probably is qualified approval. Although the Church definitely condemns coitus interruptus and "artificial birth control," it does not condemn family limitation in general. Indeed, its representatives have pointed out that

TABLE 5–1. PER CENT DISTRIBUTION BY ATTITUDE TOWARD FAMILY LIMITA-
TION, FOR ALL WIVES, BY RELIGION OF WIFE AND HUSBAND

Religion of wife and husband	No. of wives	Wife's attitude toward family limitation						
		Total	Unqualified approval	Qualified approval	Procon	Qualified disapproval	Unqualified disapproval	N.A.
Total	2,713	100	62	12	4	16	5	1
Wife Protestant:ᵃ	1,817	100	72	13	4	9	1	1
Husband Protestant	1,684	100	73	13	3	9	1	1
Husband Catholic	91	100	62	11	7	14	2	4
Wife Catholic:ᵃ	787	100	33	12	5	35	13	2
Husband Catholic	628	100	32	12	6	35	13	2
Husband Protestant	133	100	35	12	5	34	13	1
Wife Jewish	74	100	88	4	3	4	–	1
Wife other	35	100	69	11	6	–	9	5

The dash indicates a percentage below 0.5 in all tables.

N.A. = not ascertained.

ᵃ Includes wives with husband of other religious preference than Protestant or Catholic.

family limitation by periodic or continued continence is permissible for "serious motives," e.g., if more children would be detrimental to the support and care of those already born, or to the mother's health.

For example, after presenting the position of the Church against the use of periodic continence for selfish reasons—"to achieve the gratifications of marriage, while avoiding its major responsibility"—Rev. William J. Gibbons, S.J., writes:[1]

On the other hand, it is unjustifiable to belittle or condemn the use of periodic continence, as some have done, on the grounds that rarely if ever, is the motivation legitimate. The precarious health of a mother, or a well grounded fear that an additional child cannot be cared for properly, are valid reasons for having recourse to such continence. Nor is the motivation of those to be condemned who look ahead and try to foresee how they will care for future offspring. Such an approach to fertility is rational and legitimate, provided of course the parents avoid the opposite error of thinking the fewer the children the better.

The Catholic wives who said they disapproved of every kind of deliberate action "to limit family size or control when children come"

[1] William J. Gibbons, S.J., "The Catholic Value System in Relation to Human Fertility," in George F. Mair (ed.), *Studies in Population,* Princeton University Press, Princeton, N.J., 1949, p. 121.

For additional information regarding the attitude of the Catholic Church toward family limitation see Appendix A, Note 10.

apparently misinterpreted our question or do not understand the position of the Church regarding the use of periodic or long-term continence. These wives were not asked about the reasons for their extreme position, but the attitudes of some can be gleaned from interviewers' notes. There we find such statements as the following:

"I'm against it, because God didn't intend us to be that way."

"Absolutely no—I'm against it. It's against God's will. We are put here to create—if God wanted us to control it he would have made us like animals—only possible a couple of times a year."

Most of the Catholics who voiced qualified approval or disapproval of family limitation appeared to be expressing in behavior and attitude a point of view more consistent with Church doctrine. For example:

CASE 41. This 33-year-old middle-class Italian Catholic wife attends church regularly. Her family of three children was completely planned with the use of the rhythm method. She and her husband feel that they have just the number of children they have always wanted. They don't feel that she should have more children, because she had a very hard time delivering the last baby. She feels that family limitation is all right "if circumstances require it. Couples should have enough money and good health to provide for their children, but if they control they should use rhythm."

However, some Catholics who thought that it is all right under certain conditions to use a Church-approved method to limit family size were not well informed as to what these conditions are. For example, one wife said that according to Catholic doctrine the rhythm method is forbidden until after the seventh child.

Many of the Catholics who made no effort to limit family size or who used only the rhythm method wanted all the children they had and appeared to be satisfied to have the additional children that they expected would come as a consequence of their conformance to their religious beliefs.

Some Catholic wives who disapprove of family limitation had more children than they wanted but accepted these children without serious regret. For example, one mother of four children said that she only wanted one. She and her husband have never used any method of family limitation and do not intend to do so. She expressed her attitude as follows:

"If people can afford them, they should have as many as God wills them. I think this business of stopping them does more harm than good. I just hope God doesn't want us to have any more."

The strength of conviction of some Catholics is exemplified by cases in which another pregnancy might be a serious hazard to the mother's health, and a physician had recommended an appliance method of contraception but the mother was unwilling to use it. It is clear that with some couples this is an issue troubling conscience. For example:

CASE 42. This couple was married in 1940. They have had six children, including three in the first 3 years of marriage. Her last three children were diabetic and her last two were "accidentally" conceived while using the rhythm method. She has had one kidney removed. Her doctor strongly recommends that she should not have any additional children. She is "scared to death" about having another baby, but she is unconditionally opposed to any method other than rhythm, although she is disturbed because it hasn't worked for her.

CASE 43. This Catholic respondent's doctor had prescribed the use of a diaphragm to prevent another pregnancy which he regarded as a serious health risk. In her words, "I couldn't go for it. I'd be outside the Church, and I think the soul is more important."

In some cases there is considerable marital conflict, because one Catholic spouse is guided by Church doctrine while the other opposes it. For example:

CASE 44. Both husband and wife are Catholic. He attends church regularly, but she does not. At the time of the interview she was pregnant for the second time. For health reasons, she believed that this should be the last child. She had never used any method of contraception. In her own words, "He [the husband] doesn't believe in it. He is a strict Catholic. I am strict, too, but in my case it's different. We still have to come to an understanding about this. I won't have more than two, and he has to be convinced—that's all. I'll use something unless the doctor can do something for me after my second baby."

A significant number of Catholic wives frankly disapproved of the position of the Church. Some of them are estranged from the Church, but others are regular churchgoers. For example:

CASE 45. This 31-year-old Catholic wife attends church regularly. She has had five children and is now pregnant again, although she says she wanted only one child, because she is not happily married. She has used several different appliance methods ineffectively. Her last four pregnancies were "accidents." She expresses her attitude as follows: "I believe in it [an appliance method] and use it although it is against my religion. I believe it's more of a sin to bring children into the world and not be able to care for them properly."

Catholic wives who approved of family limitation and used methods not approved by the Church were not asked whether they thought that they were in conflict with Church doctrine. The supplementary remarks volunteered by the wife and recorded by the interviewer indicated a feeling of conflict in relatively few cases. On the whole, the attitudes and behavior reported by these Catholic wives are very much like those of Protestants.

Some Catholic wives reported a change in attitude after several pregnancies. The following is the view of one of them:

Case 46. This Catholic respondent was married in 1951 and had children in 1952, 1953, and 1954. Since her last child was born she and her husband have agreed that he will use a condom. In her own words, "A year ago I would have been against it, but now I'm not. I just can't have them every year. I just can't take it even if I wanted to, but it was hard to go against my religion." This respondent may have been trying to rationalize her position when she indicated her belief that the attitude of the Church was growing more lenient on this issue.

In Protestant-Catholic marriages the husband's religion appears to have little influence on the wife's attitude (Table 5-1). The attitudes of Catholic wives with Protestant husbands are very similar to those of wives in Catholic marriages. On the other hand, Protestant wives with Catholic husbands expressed attitudes which are somewhat less favorable than those of wives in Protestant marriages. That the wife's attitude is more closely related to her own religion than to her husband's in mixed marriages is consistent with our earlier finding (Chapter 4) that in mixed marriages the use of contraception is more closely related to the wife's religion than to the husband's. Similar relations with regard to expected family size will be discussed in Chapter 9.

In most mixed marriages one spouse had apparently accommodated to the view of the other. In some cases, however, the issues of whether to limit family size and what methods to use were a source of serious marital conflict. For example:

Case 47. The wife is a staunch Catholic, and the husband is a Protestant. He and his family disapprove of large families and believe in birth control. Disagreements on this issue have produced two temporary separations. They use the rhythm method, but he believes in the use of appliance methods. They have not resolved the problem, but they no longer discuss it.

Case 48. The husband is a Catholic and does not believe in birth control. The Protestant wife does. She explains that she plans to use a diaphragm. This will involve no action on his part, so they believe that he will not be committing a sin.

Catholic wives who attend church regularly expressed unqualified disapproval in just about twice the proportion for those attending seldom or never (Figure 5-2). Thus it appears that the more devout Catholics are more likely than the less devout to exaggerate the Church's opposition to family limitation. In a few instances, nominal Catholics reported estrangement from the Church on the issue of contraception, indicating that they did not attend church because of guilt feelings or disagreement with the position of the Church. However, even the Catholic wives who reported seldom or never attending church are considerably less favorable

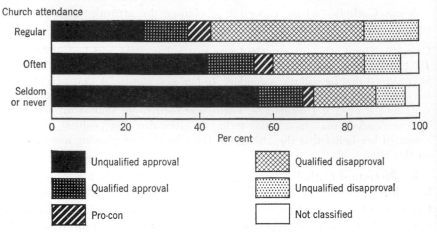

Fig. 5-2. Per cent distribution by attitude toward family limitation, for Catholic wives, by church attendance.

to family limitation than are Protestants. Many Catholics who seldom attend church endorsed the position of the Church. One former Catholic, converted at marriage to her husband's Protestant denomination, indicated that her early Catholic training still affected her beliefs:

"I suppose birth control is all right. I don't object to it, but I just never have used it. Somehow I can't bring myself to do it. I still think it's wrong for me. I think it's all right for other people."

On the other hand, some Catholics who attend church regularly resemble the Protestants who expressed unqualified approval of family limitation in that they used methods not approved by the Church:

CASE 49. This 37-year-old Catholic wife—a regular church attendant—has been married for 14 years. She has the two children she always wanted. They were carefully planned and spaced by discontinuing temporarily the use of the diaphragm, which she has otherwise used almost always since marriage. Her opinion is that family limitation is "perfectly all right. I can't see the right in bringing children into the world that you can't take care of properly with money and good health." When her two children are older, she plans to work to save money for travel and other extras.

For Protestant wives, regularity of church attendance has little relation to family limitation attitudes (Table 5-2). This is not surprising since the issue is not of any doctrinal importance for most Protestant groups. Only a small number of Protestant wives expressed attitudes of disapproval similar to those of Catholics. There is no significant difference in the attitudes of members of the major Protestant denominations. Even wives belonging to fundamentalist sects approved strongly, 74 per cent expressing unqualified approval and only 4 per cent unqualified disapproval.

TABLE 5–2. PER CENT DISTRIBUTION BY ATTITUDE TOWARD FAMILY LIMITATION, FOR PROTESTANT AND CATHOLIC WIVES, BY CHURCH ATTENDANCE

Wife's church attendance	No. of wives	Total	Wife's attitude toward family limitation					
			Unqualified approval	Qualified approval	Pro-con	Qualified disapproval	Unqualified disapproval	N.A.
Protestant								
Total	1,817	100	72	13	4	9	1	1
Attends regularly	603	100	74	13	5	7	1	–
Attends often	392	100	75	10	3	10	1	1
Attends seldom or never	820	100	70	14	3	10	1	2
Catholic								
Total	787	100	33	12	5	35	13	2
Attends regularly	533	100	25	12	6	42	15	–
Attends often	99	100	42	13	5	25	10	5
Attends seldom or never	155	100	56	12	3	17	8	4

Jewish wives are extremely favorable to the ideas of family limitation, 88 per cent of them approving without qualification. These results are consistent with our earlier findings that Jewish couples use contraception most extensively and effectively.

The Influence of the Couple's Use of Contraception, and of Their Fecundity

In each religious group, behavior and attitudes are consistent, in that Users expressed much stronger approval of family limitation than Nonusers[2] (Table 5–3). However, Catholic Users are much less likely than Protestant Users to approve completely and much more likely to express qualified disapproval. In fact, the attitudes of Catholic Users are distributed in about the same way as those of Protestant Nonusers. Being a Protestant and a User is associated with complete approval of family

[2] Although we are discussing the wife's attitudes toward family limitation, our data on fecundity and contraception refer to the couple, as we have explained in earlier chapters.

limitation for 82 per cent of the couples. At the opposite extreme, only 14 per cent of Catholic Nonusers expressed unqualified approval. Among both Protestant and Catholic wives, the attitudes of those who reported douching for cleanliness only resemble the attitudes of Nonusers more closely than the attitudes of Users.

TABLE 5–3. PER CENT DISTRIBUTION BY ATTITUDE TOWARD FAMILY LIMITATION, FOR ALL WIVES, BY COUPLE'S USE OF CONTRACEPTION, BY WIFE'S RELIGION

Use of contraception	No. of wives	Wife's attitude toward family limitation						
		Total	Unqual-ified ap-proval	Qual-ified ap-proval	Pro-con	Qual-ified disap-proval	Unqual-ified disap-proval	N.A.
Total								
Total	2,713	100	62	12	4	16	5	1
Users	1,901	100	73	11	3	10	2	1
DFCO	306	100	42	16	8	25	7	2
Nonusers	496	100	29	16	4	33	15	3
Protestant								
Total	1,817	100	72	13	4	9	1	1
Users	1,362	100	82	10	3	4	–	1
DFCO	193	100	51	19	6	21	1	2
Nonusers	256	100	42	19	4	24	7	4
Catholic								
Total	787	100	33	12	5	35	13	2
Users	453	100	45	13	5	30	6	1
DFCO	107	100	25	9	11	35	19	1
Nonusers	223	100	14	11	3	45	24	3

An individual's actions do not always correspond to his moral values. While almost all wives classified as Users supported the idea of family limitation under some conditions, a very small number (28 out of 1,901) disapproved of it under any conditions. Most of this small group (21 out of 28) were Catholic wives who used only a Church-approved method, but some were using methods forbidden by Church doctrine. A few of the latter expressed strong feelings of conflict and guilt, indicating that they believed that family limitation was morally wrong but that they were impelled to such behavior by the pressure of their personal situation. While many Catholic Users do not favor wholeheartedly the idea of family limitation, a large majority of the Catholic wives who approved of family limitation are Users. It is not too surprising that the proportion of Users is much the same for Catholics and Protestants when both express favorable attitudes (Table 5–4). But it may be surprising that there are relatively more Users among Catholics who disapprove (with or without qualification) than among Protestants expressing similar attitudes. This does not mean that Catholic Users who disapprove are violating the doctrines of their Church, for most of them practice only the

TABLE 5–4. PERCENTAGE WHO ARE USERS, FOR ALL COUPLES AND FECUND COUPLES, BY WIFE'S ATTITUDE TOWARD FAMILY LIMITATION, BY WIFE'S RELIGION[a]

Fecundity and wife's religion	Total	Wife's attitude toward family limitation				
		Unqualified approval	Qualified approval	Pro-con	Qualified disapproval	Unqualified disapproval
All couples:						
Total [b]	70	84	62	59	45	23
Protestant	75	84	62	62	36	13
Catholic	57	78	64	55	50	26
Fecund couples:						
Total [b]	83	92	82	79	62	29
Protestant	88	93	81	80	59	*
Catholic	70	88	82	70	62	29

* Less than 20 couples in base group. An asterisk has this meaning in all tables.
[a] Numbers of couples in base group are shown in mimeographed tables (see Preface).
[b] Includes all wives.

Church-approved rhythm method. This is clear in the following figures for wives who disapproved of the idea of family limitation (with or without qualification):

Religion of wife	Number disapproving	Percentage		
		Not using a method	Using only rhythm	Using other methods
Protestant	184	67	13	20
Catholic	376	56	33	11

Presumably, most Protestants have less reason than Catholics for developing attitudes regarding contraception which are incompatible with their practice, since they are not members of an organized group opposing certain methods of contraception. If incompatibility of practice and attitude does develop, most Protestants have less reason for permitting a personal conflict between behavior and attitude to persist. On the other hand, many Catholics who adopt family limitation practices they believe to be wrong continue to hold religious values opposing family limitation, because their affiliation to the Church continually reinforces this attitude. It is possible, however, that the rather high rate of use by Catholics who said they disapproved of the idea of family limitation results from the fact that they practice periodic continence and really disapprove only of the methods condemned by the Church.

The fecundity of a couple affects both the wife's attitude toward family limitation and the way these attitudes are expressed in the actual use of preventive methods. Wives who favor family limitation are more numerous relatively among Fecund couples than among Subfecund couples[3] (Table 5-5). Apparently, a woman's attitudes on this issue are related to her known risk of having additional pregnancies. As we have seen, the proportion of Users is higher for Fecund couples than for the Subfecund at each attitudinal level for each religious group (Table 5-4). Apparently, for the Fecund the possibility of additional pregnancies increases the probability of use among those who disapprove of family limitation. Even among the 56 Fecund Catholics who expressed unqualified disapproval of family limitation, 29 per cent are past Users and an additional 9 per cent are Future Users.

The Influence of Socioeconomic Factors

The attitudes of wives toward family limitation are not significantly associated with such demographic characteristics as age or duration of marriage. In view of the overriding importance of the Catholic-Protestant dichotomy for these attitudes, religion rather than a demographic characteristic is used as the primary control in the remainder of this chapter.

Attitudes of Protestant wives toward family limitation are related in varying degrees to such socioeconomic characteristics as wife's education, husband's occupation, husband's income, and farm background. This is not true for Catholic wives. Among Catholics there is no consistent pattern of relationship between these general characteristics and the attitudes expressed toward family limitation. Apparently, being Catholic has more weight than these differing socioeconomic characteristics in determining the attitudes which Catholic women express on this issue.

---

[3] Relatively more wives are favorable to family limitation among Fecund couples than among couples in any of the four Subfecund groups. However, it is significant that the proportion favorable is almost as large for the Definitely Sterile as for the Fecund. This is consistent with the interpretation that some of the Definitely Sterile had chosen an extreme method of family limitation; i.e., they had been sterilized to prevent further childbearing.

TABLE 5–5. PER CENT DISTRIBUTION BY ATTITUDE TOWARD FAMILY LIMITA-TION, FOR ALL WIVES, BY COUPLE'S FECUNDITY, BY WIFE'S RELIGION

Fecundity	No. of wives	Wife's attitude toward family limitation						
		Total	Unqual-ified ap-proval	Qual-ified ap-proval	Pro-con	Qual-ified disap-proval	Unqual-ified disap-proval	N.A.
					Total			
Total	2,713[a]	100	62	12	4	16	5	1
Fecund	1,794	100	67	11	3	14	4	1
Subfecund	919	100	51	15	5	21	6	2
					Protestant			
Total	1,817	100	72	13	4	9	1	1
Fecund	1,195	100	78	11	3	6	1	1
Subfecund	622	100	62	16	5	14	2	1
					Catholic			
Total	787	100	33	12	5	35	13	2
Fecund	519	100	37	12	6	33	11	1
Subfecund	268	100	25	13	4	39	17	2

[a] Includes all wives.

Education is strongly related to the degree of approval of family limitation for Protestants (Table 5–6). Eighty-five per cent of college-educated Protestant wives approved wholeheartedly, and none disapproved under all circumstances. On the other hand, only 50 per cent of the Protestant women with a grade school education approved com-pletely, and 4 per cent were strongly opposed. These results are con-sistent with our earlier findings (Chapter 4) that wife's education is related more closely and consistently than other socioeconomic variables (except religion) to the adoption and effective use of contraception.

Husband's income and occupational status are also consistently re-lated to the family limitation attitudes of Protestant wives (Table 5–6). The relationship for income is less regular than those for education and occupation, although there is less approval of family limitation in the lowest-income group than in any higher group (Table 5–6). More of the Protestant wives of couples who never lived on a farm than of those now living on a farm strongly approved of family limitation. Those not now on a farm but with some farm background are in the middle position on the attitude continuum. For Protestants, then, the four selected back-

TABLE 5–6. PER CENT DISTRIBUTION BY ATTITUDE TOWARD FAMILY LIMITA-
TION, FOR PROTESTANT WIVES, BY WIFE'S EDUCATION, HUSBAND'S INCOME,
HUSBAND'S OCCUPATION, AND COUPLE'S FARM BACKGROUND

Socioeconomic characteristics	No. of Protestant wives	Wife's attitude toward family limitation						
		Total	Unqualified approval	Qualified approval	Pro-con	Qualified disapproval	Unqualified disapproval	N.A.
Total	1,817	100	72	13	4	9	1	1
Wife's education:								
College	306	100	85	8	4	2	–	1
High school, 4	794	100	76	13	4	5	1	1
High school, 1–3	457	100	71	13	2	11	2	1
Grade school	260	100	50	16	4	22	4	4
Husband's income:								
$7,000 or more	167	100	77	10	6	5	1	1
$6,000–$6,999	133	100	78	14	5	3	–	–
$5,000–$5,999	248	100	74	15	4	7	–	–
$4,000–$4,999	368	100	79	11	2	6	1	1
$3,000–$3,999	417	100	70	14	4	11	–	1
Under $3,000	422	100	67	11	3	14	3	2
Husband's occupation:								
Upper white collar	427	100	80	11	4	4	–	1
Lower white collar	191	100	81	9	2	6	1	1
Upper blue collar	415	100	72	14	2	10	1	1
Lower blue collar	486	100	66	14	4	12	2	2
Farm	194	100	61	14	4	16	4	1
Couple's farm background:								
None	837	100	79	10	3	7	–	1
Some	720	100	70	15	4	8	1	2
Now on farm	258	100	59	14	4	18	4	1

ground variables considered are related to attitudes toward family limitation in much the same way as to the actual use of some method.

While there are no clear-cut relationships between socioeconomic
status and attitudes toward family limitation among Catholic wives, there
is some indication that higher socioeconomic status means greater disapproval in expressed attitudes. Among Catholic wives more of the
college-educated than of those with less education disapproved of family
limitation (Table 5–7). Similarly, relatively fewer of the Catholic wives
of white-collar workers than of blue-collar workers approved completely. With respect to the influence of farm background, Catholic and
Protestant wives are alike; fewer of those with some farm background or
now on a farm than of those with no farm background completely approve

of family limitation. In general, however, the patterns of relationship with socioeconomic variables are not as consistent or as strong for Catholic wives as for Protestant wives.

TABLE 5–7. PER CENT DISTRIBUTION BY ATTITUDE TOWARD FAMILY LIMITA-
TION, FOR CATHOLIC WIVES, BY WIFE'S EDUCATION, HUSBAND'S INCOME, HUS-
BAND'S OCCUPATION, AND COUPLE'S FARM BACKGROUND

Socioeconomic characteristics	No. of Catholic wives	Wife's attitude toward family limitation						
		Total	Unqual-ified ap-proval	Qual-ified ap-proval	Pro-con	Qual-ified disap-proval	Unqual-ified disap-proval	N.A.
Total	787	100	33	12	5	35	13	2
Wife's education:								
College	73	100	23	15	6	40	15	1
High school, 4	396	100	32	13	5	37	12	1
High school, 1–3	208	100	41	9	7	32	9	2
Grade school	110	100	31	12	4	29	20	4
Husband's income:								
$7,000 or more	49	100	33	14	4	31	18	–
$6,000–$6,999	44	100	30	16	2	41	9	2
$5,000–$5,999	133	100	34	12	6	38	8	2
$4,000–$4,999	195	100	33	12	6	35	13	1
$3,000–$3,999	183	100	32	11	4	38	13	2
Under $3,000	151	100	35	12	5	31	15	2
Husband's occupation:								
Upper white collar	137	100	29	16	4	40	11	–
Lower white collar	82	100	23	19	10	33	15	–
Upper blue collar	214	100	33	9	6	36	14	2
Lower blue collar	263	100	37	11	5	33	11	3
Farm	46	100	33	13	2	28	22	2
Couple's farm background:								
None	583	100	35	10	6	35	12	2
Some	160	100	27	18	5	36	13	1
Now on farm	40	100	30	17	3	25	22	3

Our findings that for Catholics the socioeconomic characteristics affect the *practice* of family limitation (Chapter 4) more than the general attitude toward the idea raise interesting questions. Is there a certain amount of compartmentalization of belief and action so that, for example, college-educated Catholics can differ in action but not in attitude from those with a grade school education? Does the greater variation in action than in belief create special problems of conscience and conflict for some groups of Catholics?

It is possible that these discrepancies between action and attitudes are not real, but reflect inadequacies in our research instrument. For example, better-educated Catholics may be more self-conscious about family limitation and therefore may be more impelled to express disapproval when asked questions about things which have some relation to "artificial birth control."

Reasons for Attitudes toward Family Limitation

In probing for reasons for a wife's attitude toward family limitation we did not present her with a fixed list from which to choose. Our information was obtained in answers to "open" questions, asking why she felt as she did. The reasons given are presumably those that are pertinent to her own situation; as many as three were mentioned by some respondents.

The reasons for approving the idea of family limitation tend to cluster about four major themes:

1. *Economic and financial.* The number of children should be limited so that financial resources will permit adequate care, education, and other advantages for those that are born.

2. *Health.* The health of the wife should be protected by preventing too many or too frequent conceptions, or preventing any if she is not physically fit. Some references were also made to protecting the health of the children or the family as a whole.

3. *Adequate child care.* A mother can give adequate time to her children only by limiting their number and spacing them.

4. *Happy family life.* Families are "happier" if children are limited to the number wanted and are spaced correctly. Having more children than are wanted makes for unhappy families.

While a variety of other reasons for approval were also given, 86 per cent of all the favorable reasons can be placed under these four major headings. They are listed above in the order of the frequency with which they were mentioned.

Economic reasons for favoring family limitation are most important for those expressing either complete or qualified approval. Forty-five per cent of all wives and 60 per cent of the wives strongly supporting control measures mentioned economic reasons (Table 5–8).

Among those expressing unqualified approval, there is very little difference between Protestants and Catholics in the distribution of reasons.[4] Economic reasons clearly are most important for both groups. However, among those approving with qualifications, Catholics were more likely than Protestants to mention health reasons as the basis for

[4] Data for Protestant wives and for Catholic wives, like those for all couples in Table 5–8, are in unpublished tables.

TABLE 5–8. PERCENTAGE OF WIVES MENTIONING (AFTER GENERAL QUESTION) SPECIFIED REASONS FOR FAVORABLE AND UNFAVORABLE ATTITUDE TOWARD FAMILY LIMITATION, BY WIFE'S ATTITUDE TOWARD FAMILY LIMITATION[a]

Attitude and reasons	Total	Unqualified approval	Qualified approval	Pro-con	Qualified disapproval	Unqualified disapproval	N.A.
Number of wives	2,713	1,668	330	109	439	127	40
Percentage giving reasons for:							
Favorable attitudes							
Economic and financial	45	60	48	30	4	..	
Health	24	29	30	21	5	..	
Adequate child care	16	22	15	8	1	..	
Happy family life	14	20	13	6	–	..	
General social problems	2	2	2	1	–	..	
Avoid too many pregnancies	7	10	8	5	1	..	
Up to individual beliefs	7	4	15	48	3	..	
Unfavorable attitudes							
Religious	20	..	8	65	76	84	
Health	1	..	1	8	2	–	
Aesthetic	–	..	–	–	1	–	
Other	1	..	2	3	5	7	
Percentage not giving reasons	6	3	9	7	7	9	

Two dots, in all tables, indicates a category which is impossible or very improbable.
[a] The general questions are 41 and 41a, Appendix B.
The percentages in each column are based on the number of wives expressing the attitude indicated. The sum of the percentages exceeds 100 in five of the six columns because some wives gave more than one reason.

approval and less likely to mention economic reasons, the adequacy of child care, or the quality of family life.

Very few wives, either Protestant or Catholic, mentioned general social problems (e.g., overpopulation or juvenile delinquency) as a basis for favoring family limitation. The reasons given are almost entirely oriented to personal problems and needs.

Some of the wives found it difficult to place themselves clearly for or against the general idea of family limitation. Among those whose attitudes were classified as pro-con (neither for nor against, or with mixed feelings) approximately half made the neutral statement that whether family limitation is all right depends on the belief of the individual couple. However, a large proportion (65 per cent) of these ambivalent wives mentioned religious reasons for being against family limitation, although they felt unable to place themselves as opposing the general idea.

The reasons for opposing family limitation are almost entirely religious, 90 per cent being of this type. No other type was mentioned by a significant number of wives. A very few said "birth control" measures are injurious to health, and a very few opposed them on aesthetic grounds. But for both Protestants and Catholics the only substantial basis for opposition is religious belief.

About three-fourths of the wives who initially opposed the idea of family limitation qualified their opposition later when asked if there are any conditions under which they thought it would be all right. Fifty-eight per cent of those who expressed qualified disapproval said they would approve if there are health problems, and 27 per cent would approve if there are economic problems (Table 5–9). While health problems were mentioned by a somewhat larger proportion and economic conditions by a somewhat smaller proportion of Catholic than Protestant wives, the differences between the two religious groups in reasons given are not great. Nine per cent of the Protestants but only 1 per cent of the Catholics who were partially opposed mentioned "adequate child care" as a possible reason for approving. It is clear that for those who approve of family limitation only under special conditions, health is the most important special condition, and economic factors are second, but of decidedly less importance. No other reason has much influence.

TABLE 5–9. PERCENTAGE MENTIONING (AFTER PROBING QUESTION) SPECIFIED CONDITIONS UNDER WHICH FAMILY LIMITATION WOULD BE ALL RIGHT, FOR WIVES WHO EXPRESSED QUALIFIED DISAPPROVAL, BY RELIGION[a]

Conditions	Total	Protestant	Catholic
Number of wives	439	161	275
Per cent			
Total	100	100	100
Ill health	58	54	61
Poor economic situation	27	29	25
Inadequate child care	4	9	1
Too many pregnancies	1	3	–
Other	5	1	7
Not specified	5	4	6

[a] The probing question is 41c, Appendix B.

In summary, the great majority of wives of every socioeconomic status, regardless of religion, approve of the idea of controlling the number or spacing of children under some circumstances. The degree of approval is very different for Catholics and Protestants, with Catholics much less likely to approve without reservations. Higher status and an urban background are associated with greater approval of family limitation for

Protestants but not for Catholics. In fact, the proportion of wives approving is larger for Protestants with low socioeconomic status or with a farm background than it is for any Catholic group considered. Behavior and attitude tend to be consistent for both Catholics and Protestants, with relatively more Users than Nonusers approving.

Economic reasons clearly provide the most important expressed motivation for approval of family limitation; health and the adequacy of family care are the other important reasons. Opposition to family limitation, whether by Protestants or Catholics, is almost entirely on religious grounds. But even most of the couples disapproving family limitation in general, favor it to cope with serious health or economic problems.

Chapter 6

THE METHODS OF FAMILY LIMITATION
USED BY AMERICAN COUPLES

Although family limitation has come to be practiced by a large majority of couples in our society, we have known little about what methods are used, who adopts them, and how effective they are. There is practical need for information on these topics, since the size of American families and the growth of the American population depend so much on the degree of control exercised through contraception.[1] Previous studies of the use of various methods in the United States were confined to certain cities or to selected groups and were done prior to World War II. They refer to conditions before correct information about the rhythm method was widely diffused and before millions of men in the armed forces had been exposed to a massive educational program about the value of condom for prophylactic purposes.

In a study of Indianapolis couples covering their married life from 1927 to 1941 it was found that each of the methods of contraception commonly used had reduced the average birth rate of the Users to far below its biological potential.[2] We have already noted, however, that a method which is effective for a substantial proportion of couples may be considered quite ineffective by a particular couple that has the two or three children desired, uses the method, and then has accidental and unwanted conceptions. Methods that have considerable average effectiveness from a statistical point of view may be quite unsatisfactory to couples having more children than they want, even if their families are relatively small. For example, the two common nonappliance methods—

---

[1] Readers are reminded that we are using the terms "contraception" and "family limitation" interchangeably, and without moral connotation, in referring to all methods of avoiding conception (except sterilization). The various methods are grouped together on the basis of their final objective—regulating conception or limiting family growth. (For a more detailed discussion, see Chapter 2, pp. 35–36.)

[2] Charles F. Westoff, Lee F. Herrera, and P. K. Whelpton, "XX. The Use, Effectiveness, and Acceptability of Methods of Fertility Control," *Milbank Memorial Fund Quarterly*, vol. 31, no. 3, pp. 291–357, July, 1953; or *Social and Psychological Factors Affecting Fertility*, vol. 4, pp. 885–951. See also Appendix A, Note 2g.

withdrawal and rhythm—as used during 1927–41 by couples in the Indianapolis Study reduced the likelihood of conception by 90 per cent and 63 per cent, respectively. Similarly, a postwar study in Great Britain shows that a high proportion of British couples were using nonappliance methods with enough success to restrict family size to a low average level.[3] Nevertheless, for some couples the failure of these methods at times had serious consequences.

In the present chapter we shall be concerned with answering three questions about the married couples we have sampled:

1. What proportion have used each method of contraception?
2. How do socioeconomic characteristics—especially religion—affect the choice of methods?
3. How effective are the different methods of contraception, as used?

The General Popularity of Various Methods

Information about the kinds of methods used comes from two questions Appendix B, questions 44 and 45). If a wife said that she or her husband had tried to regulate conception she was handed Card 1 listing 11 different methods:

Card 1

1. Safe period—rhythm
   (Avoiding those days of monthly cycle when conception is likely to occur)
2. Douche
   (Soon after intercourse)
3. Withdrawal
   (By husband before completion)
4. Abstinence
   (Abstaining for more than a month)
5. Rubber condom
   (Prophylactic)
6. Diaphragm
7. Jelly
8. Vaginal suppository
9. Foam tablet
10. Tampon, vaginal cap, or stem pessary
11. Lactation
    (Continuing to nurse a baby because you wanted to postpone pregnancy)

To help a wife who might be embarrassed about naming the contraceptives the interviewer told her: "You can tell me by the numbers on the card, if you wish." The respondents seemed to understand the terms on the card, although it is possible that incorrect answers were given by some wives who knew only a colloquial name for the method used.

If a wife said that nothing had been done to regulate conception, she was asked question 44: "Some things couples do may not be considered

[3] E. Lewis-Faning, *Report on an Enquiry into Family Limitation and Its Influence in Human Fertility during the Past Fifty Years* (Papers of the Royal Commission on Population, vol. I), H.M. Stationery Office, London, 1949. See also Appendix A, Note 18.

birth control. Doctors and public health workers are interested in learning how many people use these methods. Have you ever made use of either of the methods on this card?" and handed Card 2:

Card 2

1. Safe period—rhythm
   (Avoiding those days of monthly
   cycle when conception is likely to
   occur)

2. Douche—for cleanliness
   (Soon after intercourse)

A substantial number then replied that they had used the rhythm method. Those who reported that they douched for cleanliness only are classified as Users on an action basis in certain sections of this book, but as Non-users on a motive basis in this chapter.

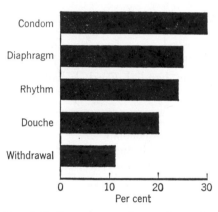

FIG. 6–1. Percentage of couples who have used specified methods of contraception.

Many wives reported that more than one method had been used, so the number of reports of methods is greater than the number of wives reporting. For example, some couples utilized different methods in the periods between different pregnancies. Other couples combined two methods for greater protection, e.g., condom and lysol douche (However, diaphragm and jelly or cream used together are counted as a single method in this report.) Still other couples alternated between two methods, e.g., using douche at certain times and condom at other times. Another type of alternate practice is diaphragm and rhythm; i.e., the couples used diaphragm during the period just before and after expected ovulation and trusted nature at other times.

Considering all reports of methods of control, the five mentioned by the largest proportion of wives are those shown in Figure 6–1 and listed below:

Method	Percentage of wives reporting method
Condom	30
Diaphragm (and jelly)	25
Rhythm	24
Douche	20
Withdrawal (coitus interruptus)	11

Added together, the reports of these five methods account for 92 per cent of all reports. Other methods of family limitation, obviously, are unimportant.

In 46 per cent of all *reports* of methods used, condom or diaphragm is mentioned. When we classify as appliance methods all those involving a mechanical or chemical agent we find that reports of condom and diaphragm make up 67 per cent of the appliance reports. Since these methods are generally regarded as the two most effective, it is significant that they are so important in contraceptive practice.

The number of couples using douche for contraception may be understated somewhat in this chapter since the discussion is on a motive basis and douching for cleanliness only is not considered to be a contraceptive practice. If all the DFCO wives were included, reports of douche would lead the list. However, we are certain that for some of these wives douching was not contraceptive in either intent or effect (see Appendix E).

When we confine our attention to couples who have ever used some method of contraception (and whom we refer to as Users) we find that about half reported having tried two or more different methods and that about 1 in 6 reported three or more. Numerous Users indicated that if one method failed they changed to another method. One wife reported that she had accidental conceptions with seven different methods. The couples who used more than one method are, in general, those who had more accidental pregnancies than others. Many of the changes from one method to another were motivated by such accidents, but we do not know how many because we did not ask about the reasons for change.

A few wives volunteered comments about folk practices and beliefs. One reported trying a carbonated soft drink as a contraceptive douche and one a pickle-juice douche. Another reported her belief that "short women don't become pregnant easily," but was beginning to doubt it, since she had conceived accidentally and she was short! A newly married woman said she thought that contraception was unnecessary in her case because her husband worked near radium and was "radioactive." Such reports are exceptional.

Changes in Popularity between 1938–39 and 1955

Since 1938–39 there have been significant changes in the popularity of the various methods used by urban couples to prevent conception. This is shown by comparisons between the results of the present study and those of the only previous study of a national sample of the population.[4] By far the most important shift is a large decrease in the proportion of urban Users relying on douche—from 44 to 11 per cent (Table 6–1). The biggest increase is that in rhythm—from 11 to 24 per cent. Smaller gains are shown by condom and by diaphragm. In both years about five-sixths of the urban couples trying to limit family size were relying on these four methods.

TABLE 6–1. PERCENTAGE REPORTING SPECIFIED METHOD OF CONTRACEPTION FOR URBAN USERS IN 1938–39 STUDY AND IN PRESENT STUDY, BY RELIGION OF WIFE

Method	Current Users, current method, in 1938–39 study[a]			All Users, last method, in present study		
	Total	Protestant	Catholic	Total	Protestant	Catholic
Number of Users	2,005	1,421	365	1,236	791	366
Percentage reporting:[b]						
Condom	20	19	12	29	32	18
Diaphragm	21	22	13	26	31	12
Rhythm	11	5	38	24	11	54
Douche	44	47	38	11	13	8
Withdrawal	5	5	7	6	6	8
Jelly (alone)	4	4[c]	2[c]	4	6	1
All other	6	7	3	7	7	5

[a] John W. Riley and Matilda White, "The Use of Various Methods of Contraception," *American Sociological Review*, vol. 5, no. 6, pp. 896, 899, December, 1940.

[b] The sum of the percentages exceeds 100 because some couples reported two (or more) methods used in combination (e.g., condom and douche) or alternately (e.g., condom or withdrawal).

[c] Estimated from data in the published tables, for comparison with present study in which reports of jelly used with diaphragm or condom were not tabulated.

The large gain made by rhythm since 1938–39 no doubt reflects the considerable increase in the amount of published material about the way to use rhythm successfully. Not many years ago few people thought that the likelihood of conceiving was much different in one part of the menstrual cycle than another, and most of those few had the notion that the middle of the cycle was "safest." Even during the 1930s a substantial minority of the couples in the Indianapolis Study who resorted to rhythm believed that coitus should be avoided during a few days before and

[4] John W. Riley and Matilda White, "The Use of Various Methods of Contraception," *American Sociological Review*, vol. 5, no. 6, pp. 890–903, December, 1940. The results from this study which are presented here are not completely comparable with those from the present study, in part because they are restricted to "upper class married women" and to the current method of current Users. For further information about this study see Appendix A, Note 8.

after menstruation. Since then much has been written about the actual situation, and various calendars and other devices which make it easy to identify the relatively "safe" and "dangerous" days have been advertised and sold widely. The influence of religious teaching no doubt explains the bigger shift to rhythm among Catholics than Protestants.

The greater popularity of condom probably results chiefly from the large-scale campaign for protection against venereal disease in the greatly expanded armed forces during World War II. Among Catholics the proportion relying on condom rose by 50 per cent; among Protestants it rose by nearly 70 per cent (Table 6–1 and Figure 6–2).

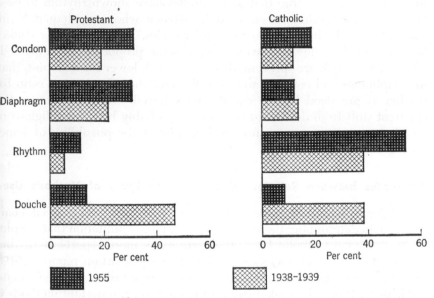

FIG. 6–2. Percentage practicing specified methods of contraception, for urban Users with Protestant and Catholic wives, in 1955 and 1938–39.

The proportion using diaphragm increased by 40 per cent among Protestants but remained practically stationary among Catholics. One explanation of the rise in the Protestant group may be a change in medical education; the proportion of physicians taught about diaphragm in medical schools has risen greatly in recent years. Another factor may be the expansion of Planned Parenthood clinics, which commonly recommend this method.

Little is known about the reasons why reliance on douching for contraception has fallen off so greatly. It is obvious, of course, that since rhythm, condom, and diaphragm have been adopted much more widely, some other methods must have lost in popularity. Douche was the only other method in common use; hence the reasons which have led more couples to choose rhythm, condom, and diaphragm have been important in leading fewer to depend on douche. One would have expected, however, that these reasons would have reduced the popularity of withdrawal and the other minor methods, which has not been the case.

Differences in the effectiveness of methods may be a partial explanation of the changes noted. More couples probably have come to realize that medical opinion and numerous studies rank diaphragm and condom above douche from the standpoint of protection and changed their practices accordingly. In contrast, there is no conclusive evidence to show that rhythm is superior to douching from the standpoint of preventing conception. It is true that some studies have shown rhythm to be a fairly effective method when used by women who are adequately instructed and who have had fairly regular cycles.[5] However, other studies have shown that the "effectiveness ratio"—the proportion of "expected" pregnancies which are "prevented"—is not much lower for douching than for diaphragm and condom and is well above the effectiveness ratio for rhythm as practiced by the couples interviewed.[6] In consequence, the apparent shift from douche to rhythm has probably been for religious or moral reasons in large measure, and in spite of the possibility of somewhat greater risk.

Differences between Religious Groups in the Types of Methods Used

Religious preference is more important than any other social characteristic in determining the specific types of family limitation that couples choose.[7] Among Catholic Users there are many more reports of rhythm than of the next three methods combined; the proportion reporting it is more than twice as large for Catholics as for Protestants (Figure 6–3 and Table 6–2). While the rank order for the other four important methods is about the same for Catholics and Protestants, the proportion using each method other than rhythm is much lower for Catholics than for Protestants.

The methods reported by the small Jewish sample again indicate that this group is distinctive. A very high proportion relied on condom or diaphragm; a very low proportion ever practiced rhythm or withdrawal. Reports of condom or diaphragm constitute 81 per cent of the reports of the 64 Jewish Users.

[5] Christopher Tietze, Samuel R. Poliakoff, and John Rock, "The Clinical Effectiveness of the Rhythm Method of Contraception," *Fertility and Sterility*, vol. 2, no. 5, pp. 444–450, September-October, 1951. For more information see Appendix A, note 16.

[6] See Appendix A, Note 2g.

[7] The discussion of religious differences in this chapter relates to religion of wife unless otherwise indicated.

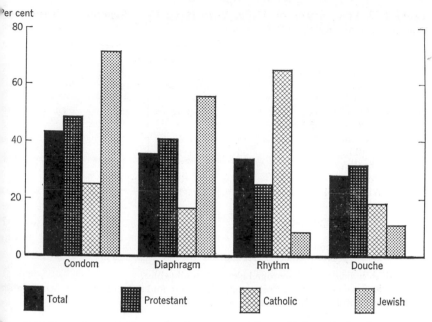

Fig. 6–3. Percentage of Users who have practiced specified methods of contraception, by wife's religion.

To provide a simple classification to follow in describing the relationship of family limitation methods to socioeconomic characteristics, we have grouped all the methods into three basic types:

1. *Rhythm* (periodic continence)[8]
2. *Withdrawal* (coitus interruptus)
3. *Appliance methods* (all methods involving the use of a chemical or mechanical agent, including condom, diaphragm, douche, jelly, tampon, pessary, or suppository)

The two nonappliance groups are treated separately, since rhythm is accepted by the Catholic Church but withdrawal is not. We shall be considering how many couples have *ever* used and how many have used *only* each basic type, in relation first to religion and then to other socioeconomic characteristics.

The use of appliance methods is very extensive. Approximately 79 per cent of all Users have tried such methods, and approximately half have restricted themselves to such methods (Table 6–3). Appliance methods are even more important for Protestants and Jews. Eighty-nine

---

[8] We have included in this category (rhythm) the very few cases of prolonged abstinence and prolonged lactation for the purpose of preventing conception, because these methods also have Catholic approval when the intent is moral. This category might logically be termed "natural methods" from a Catholic standpoint, but is here called "rhythm" because of the overwhelming predominance of this method.

TABLE 6–2. PERCENTAGE OF USERS WHO HAVE USED SPECIFIED METHODS OF CONTRACEPTION, BY WIFE'S RELIGION

Method	Religion			
	Total *a*	Protestant	Catholic	Jewish
Number of Users	1,901	1,362	453	64
Percentage reporting:				
Condom	43	48	25	72
Diaphragm	36	41	17	56
Rhythm	34	25	65	8
Douche	28	32	18	11
Withdrawal	15	17	13	6
Jelly	6	8	2	2
Suppository	4	5	2	3
Abstinence	2	4	1	—
Other methods	2	3	1	—

The dash indicates a percentage below 0.5 in all tables.

a Includes Users other than Protestants, Catholics, and Jews. The same principle applies to the "Total" columns of other tables.

per cent of the Protestant Users have adopted appliance methods, and 6 per cent have tried *only* appliance methods. Among Jewish Users 9 per cent have used appliance methods, and 85 per cent have limited themselves to this type.

The use of appliance methods by Catholics is considerably less common, but still very significant. Forty-seven per cent of Catholic Users have adopted such methods, and 24 per cent have tried only such methods.

The practice of rhythm by more than one-third of all Users indicates that this method has become important; nevertheless it is much less popular than appliance methods in the general population. It is reported by a much larger proportion of Catholic Users than of others, but it is not at all uncommon among Protestants. One-quarter of all Protestant Users reported having utilized it at some time.

Protestants who have tried rhythm usually have also tried other methods. Seventy per cent of the Protestants who had practiced rhythm had also used withdrawal or an appliance method. On the other hand Catholics are much more likely to have restricted themselves to rhythm. Only 29 per cent of the Catholics who had used rhythm had also used one of the other methods. Catholics who have ever used either withdrawal or an appliance method are more likely than Protestants to have used rhythm also.

Withdrawal was reported by 15 per cent of all Users. The proportions are slightly higher for Protestants and slightly lower for Catholics. With

TABLE 6–3. PERCENTAGE EVER USING AND MOST RECENTLY USING SPECIFIED TYPES OF CONTRACEPTION, FOR ALL COUPLES AND USERS, BY WIFE'S RELIGION

Type	Type ever used, by wife's religion				Type used most recently, by wife's religion			
	Total	Prot-estant	Cath-olic	Jew-ish	Total	Prot-estant	Cath-olic	Jew-ish
All couples								
Number of couples	2,713	1,817	787	74	2,713	1,817	787	74
Per cent								
Total	100	100	100	100	100	100	100	100
Nonusers	30	25	43	13	30	25	43	13
Users	70	75	57	87	70	75	57	87
Rhythm only	12	6	27	1	15	9	31	1
Withdrawal only	2	2	2	2	5	5	4	3
Appliance methods only	36	45	14	73	46	56	19	80
Rhythm and withdrawal	–	–	1	–	–	–	–	–
Rhythm and appliance	11	12	9	5	2	2	2	–
Withdrawal and appliance	7	8	3	4	–	–	–	–
Rhythm, withdrawal, and appliance	2	2	1	–	–	1	–	–
Not ascertained	–	–	–	2	2	2	1	3
Any use of:								
Rhythm	25	20	38	6	17	12	33	1
Withdrawal	11	12	7	6	5	6	4	3
Appliance methods	56	67	27	82	48	59	21	80
Users								
Number of Users	1,901	1,362	453	64	1,901	1,362	453	64
Per cent								
Total	100	100	100	100	100	100	100	100
Rhythm only	17	8	47	1	21	12	53	2
Withdrawal only	3	3	3	1	7	7	7	3
Appliance methods only	52	60	24	85	66	75	33	92
Rhythm and withdrawal	1	–	2	–	–	–	1	–
Rhythm and appliance	15	15	15	6	3	3	4	–
Withdrawal and appliance	9	11	6	5	–	1	–	–
Rhythm, withdrawal, and appliance	3	3	2	–	–	–	–	–
Not ascertained	–	–	1	2	3	2	2	3
Any use of:								
Rhythm	36	26	66	8	24	15	58	2
Withdrawal	15	17	13	6	8	8	8	3
Appliance methods	79	89	47	96	69	79	37	92

drawal is not, however, a method that is reported by many couples as the *only* method ever used. Only 23 per cent of the couples ever using withdrawal restricted themselves to this method. On the other hand, 66 per cent of the couples ever using appliance methods and 47 per cent of those ever using rhythm had used only those methods.

A small proportion of Users (3 per cent) reported trying all three basic types. The most frequent combination is rhythm and appliance, reported by 15 per cent of both Catholic and Protestant Users.

When we consider the type of method used most recently, the popularity of appliance methods is even more striking. Among all couples who have ever tried appliance methods approximately 7 out of 8 report them as the latest method (Table 6–3). For rhythm the corresponding proportion is 2 out of 3; for withdrawal it is 1 out of 2. Here again there are important differences between religious groups. Among Protestants the likelihood that a method ever used was being used most recently is greatest for appliance methods, but among Catholics it is greatest for rhythm (about 8 out of 9 in both cases).

Couples who used both rhythm and appliance methods are more likely to have tried rhythm first and appliance methods subsequently than to have done the opposite. This is true for both Protestants and Catholics. Of all couples who adopted both rhythm and appliance methods, 54 per cent reported using appliance methods most recently, 27 per cent reported using rhythm most recently, and 19 per cent reported using both in combination or alternately.[9] Apparently, Catholics tend to rely on rhythm only, but *if* they also utilize another method, they are more likely to shift from rhythm to appliance methods than to make the opposite shift.

Catholic Conformity to Church Doctrine Regarding Methods

For Catholics, a crucial test of conformity to Church doctrine about family limitation is whether they do not try to regulate conception, or, if they try, whether they restrict themselves to rhythm. Many more Catholics reported using only rhythm than was the case for Protestants or Jews. Nevertheless, 30 per cent of all Catholics and more than 50 per cent of Catholic Users had adopted either withdrawal or appliance methods, that is, methods unacceptable to the Church (Table 6–3). Among Users 47 per cent of the Catholics had restricted themselves to rhythm compared with 8 per cent of the Protestants. This is one indication of the adherence of Catholics to Church doctrine. Altogether, 70 per cent of the Catholics had *so far* met the conformity test under discussion, either by making no effort to control family size or by using only an acceptable method.

[9] These per cents are based on unpublished data.

The 30 per cent of the Catholics in the sample who had already departed from Church doctrine do not include a substantial proportion of those who will eventually do so, since many of the other Catholics were interviewed when in the early stages of married life. Catholics who use contraception tend to begin somewhat later in married life than Protestants and to turn to appliance methods only after trying rhythm and having accidental conceptions.

Among the Fecund Catholic couples married at least 10 years, 50 per cent have used a method other than rhythm. This figure indicates the extent of deviation from Church doctrine by Catholics who cannot depend on low fecundity to limit family size and who have been married long enough to face the problems of a growing family. It is almost certain, however, that some of the couples who used a method which the Church condemns as sinful did so in order to have no more children than they could care for properly—a motive which is endorsed by the Church.[10]

Catholic Users with wives who demonstrate close attachment to the Church by regular church attendance are more likely than the less regular churchgoers to restrict themselves to rhythm (Table 6–4). If the wife attended church regularly, 40 per cent of the Catholic Users had tried a method other than rhythm, but if the wife attended church "seldom or never" the percentage is 83. Smaller differences are found when we consider all Catholics rather than Users. For Protestants, in contrast, there is no significant relationship between church attendance and type of contraception.

In mixed marriages the religion of the wife is likely to be dominant in determining whether any method is used and, if one is used, the type chosen. When both husband and wife are Catholic, the proportion of Users restricting themselves to rhythm is highest, but when the wife is Catholic and the husband Protestant, the proportion using only rhythm is also considerably above average (Table 6–5). When the wife is Protestant and the husband Catholic, the choice of methods resembles the pattern for Protestant couples.

Since some Catholics are in mental conflict about the issue of contraception (Chapter 5), we should expect that the proportion adopting forbidden methods would be higher for the Fecund than for the Subfecund. Presumably, the Fecund Catholics have more need for family limitation; hence we should expect fewer of them to feel impelled to utilize only methods not violating the moral norms of their religion. This expectation is correct, but the difference found is not very large. The proportion of Catholic Users restricting themselves to rhythm is only a little smaller for the Fecund (46 per cent) than for the Subfecund (53 per cent) (Table 6–6). We saw earlier that the proportion of all Catholic

[10] See Appendix A, Note 10.

TABLE 6–4. PERCENTAGE EVER USING SPECIFIED TYPES OF CONTRACEPTION, FOR ALL COUPLES AND USERS WITH CATHOLIC WIVES, BY FREQUENCY OF WIFE'S CHURCH ATTENDANCE

Type	Church attendance			
	Total	Regular	Often	Seldom or never
All couples				
Number of couples	787	533	99	155
Per cent				
Total	100	100	100	100
Nonusers	43	45	42	39
Users	57	55	58	61
Rhythm only	27	33	18	10
Withdrawal only	2	1	2	2
Appliance methods only	14	8	20	30
Rhythm and withdrawal	1	2	–	–
Rhythm and appliance	9	7	11	14
Withdrawal and appliance	3	3	4	4
Rhythm, withdrawal, and appliance	1	1	1	1
Not ascertained	–	–	2	–
Any use of:				
Rhythm	38	43	30	25
Withdrawal	7	7	7	7
Appliance methods	27	19	36	49
Users				
Number of Users	453	299	59	95
Per cent				
Total	100	100	100	100
Rhythm only	47	60	32	17
Withdrawal only	3	2	3	3
Appliance methods only	24	15	34	49
Rhythm and withdrawal	2	3	–	–
Rhythm and appliance	15	12	19	23
Withdrawal and appliance	6	5	7	6
Rhythm, withdrawal, and appliance	2	3	2	2
Not ascertained	1	–	3	–
Any use of:				
Rhythm	67	78	52	42
Withdrawal	13	13	12	12
Appliance methods	48	35	61	80

couples who are Users is substantially larger for the Fecund (70 per cent) than for the Subfecund (31 per cent). It is clear, therefore, that fecundity is more important in determining whether Catholics will adopt some family limitation practice than in determining whether those who do so will restrict themselves to a Church-approved method.

TABLE 6–5. PERCENTAGE OF USERS ADOPTING SPECIFIED TYPES OF CONTRA-
CEPTION, BY COUPLE'S RELIGION

Type		Couple's religion					
	Total	Both Prot-estant	Both Cath-olic	Both Jew-ish	Wife Prot-estant, husband Catholic	Wife Catholic, husband Protestant	Other
Number of Users	1,901	1,268	359	57	62	73	82
Per cent							
Total	100	100	100	100	100	100	100
Rhythm only	17	7	50	2	14	37	16
Withdrawal only	3	3	3	2	2	1	1
Appliance methods only	52	60	23	84	52	30	50
Rhythm and withdrawal	1	1	2	–	–	3	1
Rhythm and appliance	15	15	13	5	21	21	20
Withdrawal and appliance	9	11	5	5	6	7	11
Rhythm, withdrawal, and appliance	3	3	3	–	3	1	–
Not ascertained	–	–	1	2	2	–	1
Any use of:							
Rhythm	36	26	68	7	39	62	36
Withdrawal	13	17	13	7	11	12	13
Appliance methods	79	89	45	95	82	59	80

It is incorrect to assert either that Catholics rigidly conform to religious doctrine about types of contraception or that they ignore it. Our data show clearly that religious affiliation is a very powerful determinant of behavior in this area. On the other hand, they also show clearly that many Catholics—even those who attend Church regularly—do use types of contraception which are unacceptable to the Church.

The fact that there are such large differences between Catholics and Protestants with respect to whether the regulation of conception is attempted and the methods which are adopted has led us to use religion of wife rather than a demographic factor as the major control in the following sections of this chapter.

TABLE 6–6. PER CENT DISTRIBUTION BY TYPE OF CONTRACEPTION USED, FOR USERS, BY WIFE'S RELIGION, BY COUPLE'S FECUNDITY

Type of contraception	Religion and fecundity					
	Total [a]		Protestant		Catholic	
	Fecund	Sub-fecund	Fecund	Sub-fecund	Fecund	Sub-fecund
Number of Users	1,491	410	1,048	314	371	82
Per cent						
Total	100	100	100	100	100	100
Rhythm only	17	17	8	8	46	53
Withdrawal only	2	4	2	4	2	5
Appliance methods only	52	55	59	62	25	22
Rhythm and withdrawal	1	–	1	–	2	1
Rhythm and appliance	16	13	16	13	16	13
Withdrawal and appliance	9	9	11	11	6	5
Rhythm, withdrawal, and appliance	3	1	3	2	3	–
Not ascertained	–	1	–	–	–	1
Any use of:						
Rhythm	37	31	28	23	67	67
Withdrawal	15	14	17	17	13	11
Appliance methods	80	77	89	88	50	40

[a] Includes all Users.

Attitude toward Family Limitation and Type of Methods Used

The type of contraception that a couple adopts is related to the wife's attitude toward the general idea of family limitation. Greater approval of the idea is associated with more reports of appliance methods and fewer reports of rhythm, for both Catholics and Protestants. The contrasts between those who approve and those who disapprove are considerable for either Protestants or Catholics, but for Protestants the number who disapprove is small.

Among the Catholic Users with wife disapproving of family limitation (either with or without qualification), approximately 3 out of 4 have practiced only rhythm, while among those with wife expressing unqualified approval only 1 in 4 has done so (Table 6–7). While the relationship between attitudes and type of contraception chosen exists for both Protestants and Catholics, it is still true that at each attitude level the Catholic Users are much more likely to have restricted themselves to rhythm and much less likely to have tried an appliance method.

TABLE 6–7. PERCENTAGE OF USERS ADOPTING SPECIFIED TYPES OF CONTRACEPTION, BY WIFE'S ATTITUDE TOWARD FAMILY LIMITATION, BY WIFE'S RELIGION

Wife's attitude toward family limitation	No. of Users	Type of contraception[a]							
		Total	Rhythm only	Withdrawal only	Appliance methods only	2 or more types	Any use of:		
							Rhythm	Withdrawal	Appliance methods
Total [b]									
Total	1,901	100	17	3	52	28	36	13	79
Unqualified approval	1,393	100	7	2	61	30	27	16	90
Qualified approval	205	100	26	3	41	30	49	14	69
Pro-con	64	100	31	5	39	22	44	16	61
Qualified disapproval	196	100	63	5	16	11	74	13	30
Unqualified disapproval	29	100	76	3	–	21	96	7	17
Protestant									
Total	1,362	100	8	3	60	29	26	17	89
Unqualified approval	1,111	100	5	2	62	31	24	17	92
Qualified approval	142	100	17	4	51	28	39	11	80
Pro-con	39	100	20	5	51	21	28	18	72
Qualified disapproval	58	100	36	5	38	21	46	19	58
Unqualified disapproval	3	100*	*	*	*	*	*	*	*
Catholic									
Total	453	100	47	3	24	26	67	13	48
Unqualified approval	204	100	25	1	44	30	48	11	74
Qualified approval	60	100	48	2	15	35	73	22	45
Pro-con	23	100	52	4	13	26	74	13	39
Qualified disapproval	137	100	75	4	6	12	87	11	17
Unqualified disapproval	26	100	73	4	–	23	96	8	19

* Less than 20 couples in base group. An asterisk has this meaning in all tables.

[a] The type was ascertained for all Users in most subgroups and for at least 95 per cent in all subgroups.

[b] Includes all Users.

187

Very few of the couples with wife who opposed (with or without qualification) the general idea of family limitation had ever used any method other than rhythm. Among all the wives expressing qualified opposition, 83 per cent reported either no method or only rhythm. Among those who expressed unqualified opposition 94 per cent reported either no method ever used or the use of rhythm only. The results are roughly at this level for both Protestants and Catholics. In contrast, among all couples (including Nonusers) 74 per cent of those with the wife unqualifiedly approving contraception had tried an appliance method as compared with only 4 per cent of those with the wife expressing unqualified disapproval.

For Catholics the relationship between attitudes toward family limitation and the type of contraception used may in part result from a misunderstanding of one of our questions. As mentioned earlier, general terms were used in asking the wife about her attitude toward the idea of family limitation. Nevertheless, some Catholic wives may have thought that the question referred to methods forbidden by the Church and answered on that basis. However, the similarity of the relationship for Catholics to that for Protestants leads us to believe that misunderstanding by Catholics was not important. We are more inclined to the interpretation that for Catholics, as for others, persons disapproving of the general idea of family limitation are less likely than others to go so far as to purchase the materials for appliance methods, keep them on hand, and use them. To persons with such values, rhythm probably seems more natural and therefore a less serious violation of basic beliefs.

Type of Methods Used and Duration of Marriage

Differences in the type of family limitation with duration of marriage may reflect the effects of either historical change in choice of methods or longer marital experience. One of the important differences for both Protestant and Catholic Users is the larger proportion who have tried rhythm among those married shorter periods of time (Table 6–8). This suggests a general increase in recent years in knowledge about rhythm or in motivation to adopt it.

Among Protestant Users, the proportion resorting to appliance methods is high (86 to 91 per cent) for each marriage-duration group. For Catholic Users there are significant differences: both the proportions *ever* using and using *only* appliance methods are larger among wives married longer. These differences undoubtedly result in part from the fact that Catholics are more likely to turn to appliance methods after an initial use of rhythm than to do the reverse. In addition, however, the tendency to avoid appliance methods may be stronger for younger Catholics than for

TABLE 6–8. PERCENTAGE OF USERS ADOPTING SPECIFIED TYPES OF CONTRACEPTION, BY DURATION OF MARRIAGE, BY WIFE'S RELIGION

Years married	No. of Users	Type of contraception[a]					Any use of:		
		Total	Rhythm only	Withdrawal only	Appliance methods only	2 or more types	Rhythm	Withdrawal	Appliance methods
		Total [b]							
Total	1,901	100	17	3	52	28	36	13	79
Under 5	422	100	20	2	52	26	40	10	77
5–9	648	100	17	2	50	31	38	16	79
10–14	499	100	16	3	54	26	32	16	79
15 or more	332	100	14	4	54	28	30	19	81
		Protestant							
Total	1,362	100	8	3	60	29	26	17	89
Under 5	302	100	9	2	59	30	32	11	89
5–9	431	100	6	2	60	32	26	17	91
10–14	370	100	9	2	60	28	25	18	88
15 or more	259	100	8	5	58	28	24	22	86
		Catholic							
Total	453	100	47	3	24	26	67	13	48
Under 5	95	100	59	2	22	16	74	6	37
5–9	186	100	45	3	23	29	68	14	50
10–14	110	100	45	5	26	24	63	14	49
15 or more	62	100	42	–	29	29	61	13	55

[a] The type was ascertained for all Users in most subgroups and for at least 99 per cent in all subgroups.　[b] Includes all Users.

those who are older. This possibility is suggested by the larger proportion of women with shorter marriage durations who report some use of rhythm. It may reflect success of Church efforts to induce the younger generation of Catholic couples to adopt approved methods, or it may reflect the spread of information about how to use the rhythm method successfully. If there is such a tendency, it contradicts the assertions occasionally made that Catholics are increasingly adopting appliance methods.

Among both Protestant and Catholic Users the proportion that has tried withdrawal is relatively small among those married less than 5 years. Probably this reflects a basic decrease in the proportion that will ever adopt this method, since withdrawal is most common among the less educated and the educational level has been rising steadily.

Type of Methods Chosen by Users with Different Socioeconomic Characteristics

The type of contraception utilized by both Protestants and Catholics depends to some extent on their socioeconomic characteristics. But the important Catholic-Protestant differences in methods adopted cannot be explained by differences in nonreligious background characteristics. The religious differences persist when we compare couples who are similar with respect to any one of the following criteria: wife's education, husband's income, husband's occupation, number of years wife has worked, couple's farm background, and size of present place of residence. Among Users in each stratum defined by these criteria, Catholics are more likely than Protestants to adopt rhythm and less likely to try appliance methods. Nevertheless, for both Catholics and Protestants the type of family limitation practice chosen by Users varies with the socioeconomic characteristics and residential history of the couples. Despite some similarities, the relationships differ in certain crucial respects for the two religious groups. We shall consider first the characteristics which measure in various ways the socioeconomic status of the couple, namely, wife's education, husband's income, and husband's occupation.

In one respect Catholics and Protestants are similar; namely, resort to withdrawal is most prevalent among the lower-status Users, whether status is measured in terms of education, income, or occupation. Education is more closely related to the adoption of withdrawal than are the other measures of socioeconomic status. This method is reported by about twice as high a proportion of wives with a grade school education as of those with a college education. The inverse association between the use of withdrawal and socioeconomic status, together with the low proportion of recently married couples adopting this method, point to less use of it in

TABLE 6-9. PERCENTAGE OF USERS ADOPTING SPECIFIED TYPES OF CONTRACEPTION, BY WIFE'S EDUCATION, BY WIFE'S RELIGION

Wife's education	No. of Users	Type of contraception[a]					Any use of:		
		Total	Rhythm only	Withdrawal only	Appliance methods only	2 or more types	Rhythm	Withdrawal	Appliance methods
					Total [b]				
Total	1,901	100	17	3	52	28	36	13	79
College	353	100	12	2	56	29	36	10	85
High school, 4	912	100	20	2	50	28	39	14	78
High school, 1–3	451	100	15	3	53	28	31	19	80
Grade school	184	100	20	7	49	24	32	21	72
					Protestant				
Total	1,362	100	8	3	60	29	26	17	89
College	274	100	5	2	60	33	32	12	93
High school, 4	632	100	8	2	60	30	27	16	89
High school, 1–3	319	100	8	3	58	30	24	21	87
Grade school	137	100	13	7	59	21	22	20	80
					Catholic				
Total	453	100	47	3	24	26	67	13	48
College	45	100	67	–	18	15	80	4	31
High school, 4	241	100	52	1	20	27	74	11	44
High school, 1–3	122	100	34	4	36	24	51	14	60
Grade school	45	100	38	9	20	33	62	24	49

[a] The type was ascertained for all Users in most subgroups and for at least 98 per cent in all subgroups.

[b] Includes all Users.

the future as more young people finish high school and go on to college.

In the relationship of socioeconomic status to the adoption of rhythm, there is both an important similarity and an important difference between the two religious groups. This is clearest if we consider wife's education. For both groups the proportion of Users *ever* practicing rhythm tends to increase with educational level; in contrast, the proportion practicing *only* rhythm decreases with education for Protestants, but generally increases for Catholics (Table 6-9; the high school 1–3 group is an exception for Catholics).

One possible explanation of the direct relationship between education and the proportion of Catholic Users ever relying on rhythm is that its successful use requires not only careful calculation but also self-discipline and the control of impulsive behavior by rational criteria. This may make the method less attractive to persons with little education, or to blue-collar workers whose occupational experience is unlikely to stress the planning and calculation required of many white-collar workers.

Why does the proportion of Catholic Users who restrict themselves to rhythm increase with education? Our interpretation is that rhythm is most likely to be used as an *exclusive* method by couples who have both the sophistication to understand it and the special religious motivation that will compensate for the self-denial and risk involved in depending on it. The better-educated Catholics have both of these qualifications. They have not only the mental characteristics but also the religious values and sanctions which compensate for the necessary self-discipline and for the greater likelihood of accidental conception. The less-educated Catholics may have the same religious motivation as the better-educated Catholics, but are likely to lack the self-control and rationality. While the better-educated Protestants may have the knowledge to use rhythm successfully, they have no special motivation to restrict themselves to this method instead of using the appliance methods which are more effective and involve less self-denial. This seems a reasonable explanation of the fact that among Protestant Users the proportion relying entirely on rhythm decreases with education. The opposite tendency with respect to the adoption of rhythm at some time probably reflects in part its use as an alternate method, i.e., depending on rhythm during the safe parts of the menstrual cycle and on appliance methods at other times. It seems likely that better-educated couples have more confidence than others in their ability to do this without having an accidental conception; this would tend to cause a direct relation between education and the proportion ever using rhythm.

It is conceivable that the proportion of better-educated Catholics actually using rhythm is not as high as reported. One might argue that these couples simply are more likely than the less educated to say that they use rhythm and not another method because they are more aware that Catholic doctrine is a controversial issue and wish to give an interviewer a picture of themselves as good Catholics. This interpretation does not seem plausible in view of the relatively more numerous reports of rhythm by better-educated Protestants who do not have the same motivation for misreporting. It seems more plausible that the similar relationships for the two groups result from the greater sophistication required for the use of this method.

Resort to rhythm is less closely related to income or occupation than to education. For both Protestants and Catholics the two groups with highest income are those with the largest proportion ever using rhythm, but a middle-income group rather than the two lower groups has the smallest proportion (Table 6–10). The two white-collar groups are significantly different from the two blue-collar groups with respect to the proportion ever using rhythm, but the upper and lower strata within each of them are not consistently different (Table 6–11).

Among Catholic Users conformity to Church doctrine about contraceptive methods tends to increase with education and urban occupational rank, although not with income. This is contrary to a popular view that the better-educated and higher-status Catholics are more likely to deviate from this aspect of Church doctrine.

A large majority of Protestant Users in each status group has tried appliance methods, so the proportion of Protestants making use of these methods does not vary much with any of the three measures of status. For example, although the proportion of Protestant Users reporting appliance methods increases with education, it is no less than 80 per cent for Protestant Users with only a grade school education.

For Catholic Users, the situation is quite different. Appliance methods are reported by more than half of the wives of lower blue-collar workers and wives with 1 to 3 years of high school education, but by barely one-third of the wives of white-collar workers and less than one-third of the wives with a college education. This is consistent with our earlier interpretation that, while blue-collar and less-educated Catholics may have the religious motivation to avoid appliance methods, they are less likely to have the education and character traits probably associated with the exclusive use of the Church-approved methods.

Protestant-Catholic differences in type of contraception adopted exist in communities of every size. A large majority of Protestant Users in every size group report having tried appliance methods. Even for the farm couples the figure is 76 per cent (Table 6–12). On the other hand, in every type of nonfarm community, close to half of the Catholic Users report appliance methods—the range is from 41 to 57 per cent.[11] The

[11] Data for all couples are available in unpublished tables.

TABLE 6–10. PERCENTAGE OF USERS ADOPTING SPECIFIED TYPES OF CONTRACEPTION, BY HUSBAND'S INCOME, BY WIFE'S RELIGION

Husband's income	No. of Users	Type of contraception[a]					Any use of:		
		Total	Rhythm only	Withdrawal only	Appliance methods only	2 or more types	Rhythm	Withdrawal	Appliance methods
		Total[b]							
Total	1,901	100	17	3	52	28	36	13	79
$7,000 or more	193	100	18	2	55	25	37	11	80
$6,000–$6,999	150	100	12	1	53	34	39	11	85
$5,000–$5,999	302	100	17	2	49	32	39	15	80
$4,000–$4,999	423	100	19	2	54	25	34	15	78
$3,000–$3,999	430	100	19	4	50	27	37	16	76
Under $3,000	340	100	15	4	51	30	33	20	80
		Protestant							
Total	1,362	100	8	3	60	29	26	17	89
$7,000 or more	137	100	8	3	61	28	29	14	89
$6,000–$6,999	114	100	5	—	60	34	32	10	93
$5,000–$5,999	202	100	4	1	60	35	27	16	93
$4,000–$4,999	290	100	7	2	63	28	24	17	90
$3,000–$3,999	315	100	10	4	57	29	28	17	86
Under $3,000	266	100	10	4	57	29	25	21	86
		Catholic							
Total	453	100	47	3	24	26	67	13	48
$7,000 or more	34	100	62	—	18	20	82	6	35
$6,000–$6,999	28	100	43	—	25	32	71	11	54
$5,000–$5,999	91	100	45	5	25	25	67	13	48
$4,000–$4,999	117	100	50	3	27	20	62	12	47
$3,000–$3,999	99	100	53	3	23	21	68	11	43
Under $3,000	69	100	39	2	23	36	69	16	56

[a] The type was ascertained for all Users in most subgroups, and for at least 99 per cent in all subgroups.   [b] Includes all Users.

TABLE 6-11. PERCENTAGE OF USERS ADOPTING SPECIFIED TYPES OF CONTRACEPTION, BY HUSBAND'S OCCUPATION, BY WIFE'S RELIGION

Husband's occupation	No. of Users	Type of contraception[a]					Any use of:		
		Total	Rhythm only	Withdrawal only	Appliance methods only	2 or more types	Rhythm	Withdrawal	Appliance methods
		Total[b]							
Total	1,901	100	17	3	52	28	36	13	79
Upper white collar	504	100	15	2	55	28	34	12	83
Lower white collar	217	100	20	1	55	24	37	12	78
Upper blue collar	443	100	19	4	50	27	36	17	76
Lower blue collar	476	100	16	3	51	29	33	19	80
Farm	152	100	26	4	46	24	41	17	69
Other	109	100	9	-	49	40	45	9	88
		Protestant							
Total	1,362	100	8	3	60	29	26	17	89
Upper white collar	366	100	5	2	62	31	27	14	92
Lower white collar	157	100	10	1	62	27	27	14	89
Upper blue collar	307	100	8	3	61	28	23	20	88
Lower blue collar	323	100	6	3	59	31	23	21	89
Farm	132	100	20	4	52	24	34	17	75
Other	77	100	3	-	57	40	39	9	96
		Catholic							
Total	453	100	47	3	24	26	67	13	48
Upper white collar	90	100	61	1	17	21	74	10	38
Lower white collar	48	100	60	2	21	17	77	4	35
Upper blue collar	126	100	45	5	25	25	67	13	47
Lower blue collar	143	100	37	2	32	28	56	16	57
Farm	19	100	63	5	5	27	89	21	32
Other	27	100	29	-	26	41	67	11	67

[a] The type was ascertained for all Users in most subgroups, and for at least 96 per cent in all subgroups.   [b] Includes all Users.

TABLE 6–12. PERCENTAGE OF USERS ADOPTING SPECIFIED TYPES OF CONTRACEPTION, FOR PROTESTANT AND CATHOLIC WIVES, BY PLACE OF RESIDENCE

Place of residence[b]	No. of Users	Type of contraception[a]							
		Total	Rhythm only	Withdrawal only	Appliance methods only	2 or more types	Any use of:		
							Rhythm	Withdrawal	Appliance methods
						Protestant			
Total	1,362	100	8	3	60	29	26	17	89
Metropolitan areas:									
12 largest cities	73	100	3	1	71	25	19	15	94
Other large cities	241	100	7	2	62	29	27	15	90
Suburbs of 12 largest cities	166	100	7	3	66	24	25	12	90
Other suburbs	228	100	6	2	62	30	23	17	91
Nonmetropolitan areas:									
Small cities	255	100	7	1	60	32	26	18	90
Rural nonfarm	240	100	7	4	53	36	28	22	88
Farm	159	100	18	6	51	25	34	17	76
						Catholic.			
Total	453	100	47	3	24	26	67	13	48
Metropolitan areas:									
12 largest cities	109	100	37	2	34	25	56	11	57
Other large cities	108	100	47	5	21	27	68	16	44
Suburbs of 12 largest cities	79	100	48	—	25	27	71	9	51
Other suburbs	49	100	57	2	16	25	75	10	41
Nonmetropolitan areas:									
Small cities	47	100	47	—	19	34	70	13	53
Rural nonfarm	44	100	45	7	27	21	63	20	43
Farm	17	100	*	*	*	*	*	*	*

[a] The type was ascertained for all Users in most subgroups, and for at least 98 per cent in all subgroups.   [b] The groups are explained in Appendix A, Note 14.

TABLE 6–13. PERCENTAGE OF USERS ADOPTING SPECIFIED TYPES OF CONTRACEPTION, BY YEARS WIFE WORKED SINCE MARRIAGE, BY WIFE'S RELIGION

Years wife worked since marriage	No. of Users	Type of contraception[a]					Any use of:		
		Total	Rhythm only	Withdrawal only	Appliance methods only	2 or more types	Rhythm	Withdrawal	Appliance methods
Total[b]									
Total	1,901	100	17	3	52	28	36	13	79
None	551	100	23	3	48	26	39	16	73
Less than 1	346	100	19	2	50	29	41	12	79
1–4	704	100	15	2	54	29	34	15	81
5 or more	281	100	10	3	57	29	25	20	85
Protestant									
Total	1,362	100	8	3	60	29	26	17	89
None	397	100	13	4	54	29	30	19	83
Less than 1	234	100	6	1	61	32	29	13	93
1–4	509	100	6	3	62	29	25	16	90
5 or more	209	100	4	3	61	31	20	21	91
Catholic									
Total	453	100	47	3	24	26	67	13	48
None	132	100	54	2	23	20	69	9	42
Less than 1	99	100	53	3	22	22	74	10	44
1–4	158	100	44	3	22	31	69	14	49
5 or more	60	100	33	3	37	27	47	20	62

[a] The type was ascertained for all Users in most subgroups and for at least 99 per cent in all subgroups.   [b] Includes all Users.

differences between the two religious groups in communities of the same size are more important than the differences between size groups. Nevertheless, two significant, if small, differences do exist by community type:

1. Both Protestant and Catholic Users living in metropolitan areas are slightly more likely than those living elsewhere to have adopted appliance methods, and slightly less likely to have adopted either rhythm or withdrawal.

2. For both Catholic and Protestant Users, the proportions that have *ever* tried appliance methods or tried *only* appliance methods are highest, and the proportions that have *ever* tried rhythm or tried *only* rhythm are lowest, for couples living in the 12 largest cities.

The methods of contraception chosen are related to the wife's work history since marriage (Table 6–13). Protestant Users whose wives have had work experience are more likely than other Protestant Users to try appliance methods and to use them exclusively. They are less likely to rely exclusively on rhythm.

Catholic Users whose wives have worked a long time are more likely than other Catholic Users to have adopted methods not approved by the Church—either appliance methods or withdrawal—and to rely exclusively on appliance methods. Similar relationships are found when duration of marriage is taken into account.

These results are consistent with the expectation that working wives have both greater motivation to choose efficient methods and more opportunity to learn about the appliance methods which are most effective. Their work usually lessens their dependence on home, family, and Church, and brings them into contact with women having different religious affiliations and points of view. Catholic wives who work have more opportunity to learn about methods forbidden by their Church but used by non-Catholics. It is likely that family problems, including methods of spacing and limiting the number of children, are a subject for conversation in informal work groups which include Catholic women and that attitudes toward conception control are changed in consequence.

The Choice of Methods by All Couples in Different Socioeconomic Groups

In the preceding section the analysis for education, income, and occupation was concerned with the choice of methods *once use is begun.* That involves comparisons among Users. Here, in contrast, we shall discuss certain questions about the influence of socioeconomic char-

acteristics which require the consideration of all couples, including
Nonusers.

Among all Protestant couples there is a sharp rise in the proportion
using appliance methods as education rises and a moderate increase as income and urban occupational status increase. While we found earlier that
Protestants of differing status do not differ greatly in the adoption of
appliance methods *once use is begun*, those in the higher-status groups
are much more likely to be using appliance methods, because more of
them are Users. When we take both use and method into account, we
find that the average college-educated Protestant is twice as likely to
have tried appliance methods as the average Protestant with a grade
school education (Table 6–14). The contrasts are not so striking when
income or occupation is the criterion of status.

The rise with higher status in the proportion of Protestants ever using
rhythm is also much more striking for all couples than for Users. Thus,
only 12 per cent of all Protestants with a grade school education, but
29 per cent of all those with a college education, have tried rhythm. There
are smaller but similar relationships between income or occupation and
the adoption of rhythm.

The effects of including Nonusers in the analysis are more complex
for Catholics, because for Catholics the use of *some* method is *directly*
associated with status, but there is some tendency for the use of appliance methods or withdrawal to be *inversely* correlated with status.
These relationships in opposite directions partially cancel each other.

For example, let us consider this question: To what extent is socioeconomic status associated with the use by Catholics of a method forbidden by the Church? When we considered only Users we found that
the proportion of Catholics restricting themselves to the Church-approved
rhythm method increases significantly with education or urban occupational status (though not with income). But Catholics can also conform
to Church doctrine by not using *any* method of family limitation, and
lower-status Catholics are more likely than those of higher status to
follow this latter course. Since these alternatives are related to the status
measures in opposite directions, the result of considering both together
is to conceal the relationships between socioeconomic status and conformance to Church doctrine.

Considering all Catholics instead of Users, it is still true that white-
collar workers are more likely than blue-collar workers to follow Church
precepts regarding family limitation, but the differences are greatly
reduced (Table 6–15). In the case of education the greatest conformity
is still among college-educated women, but the least conformity is among
high school rather than grade school women (Figure 6–4). There is no

TABLE 6–14. PERCENTAGE NOT USING CONTRACEPTION, OR USING SPECIFIED TYPES, FOR COUPLES WITH PROTESTANT WIVES, BY WIFE'S EDUCATION, HUSBAND'S INCOME, AND HUSBAND'S OCCUPATION

Socioeconomic characteristics	No. of couples	Type of contraception[a]				Any use of:		
		Total	None	Rhythm only	Other methods	Rhythm	Withdrawal	Appliance methods
Total	1,817	100	25	6	69	19	13	67
Wife's education:								
College	306	100	10	4	86	29	11	84
High school, 4	794	100	20	6	74	22	13	71
High school, 1–3	457	100	30	6	63	17	15	61
Grade school	260	100	47	7	46	12	11	42
Husband's income:								
$7,000 or more	167	100	18	7	75	24	11	73
$6,000–$6,999	133	100	14	4	81	28	9	80
$5,000–$5,999	248	100	19	3	78	22	13	75
$4,000–$4,999	368	100	21	6	73	19	13	71
$3,000–$3,999	417	100	24	8	68	21	13	65
Under $3,000	422	100	37	6	57	16	13	54
Husband's occupation:								
Upper white collar	427	100	14	4	82	24	12	79
Lower white collar	191	100	18	8	74	22	11	73
Upper blue collar	415	100	26	6	68	17	15	65
Lower blue collar	486	100	34	4	62	15	14	59
Farm	194	100	32	14	54	23	12	51
Other	104	100	26	2	72	29	7	71

[a] The type was ascertained for all couples in most subgroups, and for at least 99 per cent in all subgroups.

TABLE 6–15. PERCENTAGE NOT USING CONTRACEPTION, USING SPECIFIED TYPES, AND CONFORMING TO CATHOLIC DOCTRINE, FOR COUPLES WITH CATHOLIC WIVES, BY WIFE'S EDUCATION, HUSBAND'S INCOME, AND HUSBAND'S OCCUPATION

| Socioeconomic characteristics | No. of couples | Type of contraception[a] | | | | Any use of: | | | Conforming to Catholic doctrine[c] |
		Total	None	Rhythm only	Other methods[b]	Rhythm	Withdrawal	Appliance methods	
Total	787	100	41	28	31	41	8	27	69
Wife's education:									
College	73	100	38	42	20	50	2	19	80
High school, 4	396	100	39	32	29	45	7	27	71
High school, 1–3	208	100	41	20	38	30	8	35	61
Grade school	110	100	59	16	25	25	10	20	75
Husband's income:									
$7,000 or more	49	100	31	43	26	56	4	24	74
$6,000–$6,999	44	100	36	28	36	45	7	35	64
$5,000–$5,999	133	100	32	31	37	46	9	33	63
$4,000–$4,999	195	100	40	30	30	37	7	28	70
$3,000–$3,999	183	100	46	28	26	37	6	23	74
Under $3,000	151	100	54	18	28	32	7	26	72
Husband's occupation:									
Upper white collar	137	100	34	40	26	49	7	25	74
Lower white collar	82	100	42	35	23	45	2	20	77
Upper blue collar	214	100	41	26	33	40	8	28	67
Lower blue collar	263	100	46	20	34	30	9	31	66
Farm	46	100	59	26	15	37	9	13	85
Other	45	100	40	18	42	40	7	40	58

[a] The type was ascertained for all Users in most subgroups, and for at least 99 per cent in all subgroups.

[b] Includes couples who have used rhythm *and* other methods.
[c] Nonusers or Users of rhythm only.

significant difference in this respect between grade school– and college
educated wives, although the *method* of conformity is very different—
a large proportion of grade school women reporting nonuse but a large
proportion of college women reporting rhythm only.

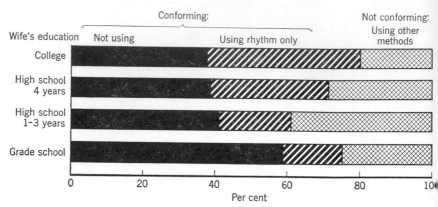

F𝐈𝐆. 6–4. Percentage distribution by conformity to Church doctrine, for couples with
Catholic wives, by wife's education.

In short, among all Catholics those in the lower-status group are more
likely to meet Church standards by not trying to regulate conception
(Table 6–15), but among Catholic Users those with lower status are less
likely to restrict themselves to Church-approved methods (Tables 6–9
to 6–11).

How does farm background affect the type of contraception chosen?
For Protestants, the couples now on farms have the lowest proportion
using any method, the lowest proportion adopting appliance methods, and
the highest proportion adopting withdrawal. The couples never on farms
are at the opposite pole in these comparisons.[12] There are so few
Catholics on farms that a sample the size of ours does not permit a
significant analysis of the type of method they use.

Socioeconomic Characteristics Related to the Use of Specific Methods

At the beginning of this chapter we saw that for Protestants the five
methods most frequently reported are (in order of importance) condom,
diaphragm, douche, rhythm, and withdrawal (Table 6–2). For Catholic
couples the corresponding methods are rhythm, condom, douche, diaphragm, and withdrawal. Our question now is: To what extent does
the popularity of these methods vary with socioeconomic status? Do
groups with dissimilar backgrounds have dissimilar preferences? We

[12] The statements about farm background are supported by unpublished data.

shall see that for both Protestant and Catholic there are important differences between socioeconomic groups in the proportion adopting each
of these five methods. We shall also see that the Protestant-Catholic
differences in preferences are not the result of distinctive status with
respect to education, income, and place of residence, but are found at
various levels.

Let us first consider Protestants. In every group the method adopted
by the largest proportion of couples (and Users) is either condom or
diaphragm. Condom is an important method in all strata, ranking first
in most cases. When it is second choice, diaphragm ranks first. This
occurs in certain upper-status or metropolitan groups, namely, couples
with college-educated wives, with husbands in upper-white-collar occupations, with husbands' income $5,000 or more, or living in two types
of metropolitan communities. Among other types of couples diaphragm
commonly is second. However, diaphragm is used relatively little by
two groups, ranking fourth among farm couples and fifth among grade
school wives.

The association between education and method chosen by Protestant
Users is particularly striking for diaphragm. Fifty-seven per cent of all
Users with college wives have adopted diaphragm, as compared with

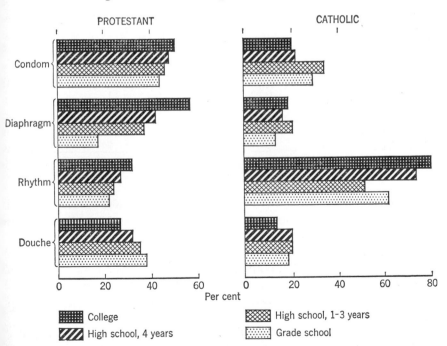

Fig. 6–5. Percentage practicing specified methods of contraception, for Users with
Protestant and Catholic wives, by wife's education.

only 17 per cent of those with grade school wives (Table 6–16 and Figure 6–5). As between the various community types, the selection of diaphragm by Users is most common (51 per cent) in the suburbs of the largest cities and least common (29 per cent) among farm wives.

TABLE 6–16. PERCENTAGE OF USERS ADOPTING CONDOM, DIAPHRAGM, OR DOUCHE, BY WIFE'S RELIGION, BY SELECTED SOCIOECONOMIC CHARACTERISTICS[a]

Socioeconomic characteristics	Condom			Diaphragm			Douche		
	Total[b]	Protestant	Catholic	Total[b]	Protestant	Catholic	Total[b]	Protestant	Catholic
Total	44	48	25	36	41	17	28	32	18
Wife's education:									
College	48	51	20	52	57	18	23	27	13
High school, 4	42	48	21	35	42	16	28	32	19
High school, 1–3	43	46	34	33	37	20	31	35	19
Grade school	41	44	29	16	17	13	32	37	18
Husband's income:									
$7,000 or more	40	42	12	51	57	23	24	30	9
$6,000–$6,999	47	52	29	47	53	14	30	32	29
$5,000–$5,999	41	48	24	40	51	15	25	27	23
$4,000–$4,999	47	53	27	37	46	15	25	30	14
$3,000–$3,999	39	43	22	27	31	13	29	33	18
Under $3,000	46	49	30	28	29	25	35	39	22
Husband's occupation:									
Upper white collar	46	49	21	45	52	13	24	28	14
Lower white collar	42	47	19	38	44	12	22	26	8
Upper blue collar	43	49	24	32	39	17	30	35	17
Lower blue collar	44	50	30	29	32	20	32	36	24
Farm	33	36	–	28	33	–	24	24	–
Other	48	49	41	44	48	37	42	47	26
Couple's farm background:									
None	42	50	25	35	45	16	24	30	18
One has some	48	53	29	40	45	20	30	34	17
Both have some	44	45	33	37	38	28	34	35	20
Now on farm	33	36	–	27	29	–	27	29	–
Place of residence:									
Metropolitan areas	44	50	26	38	47	17	24	29	18
12 largest cities	48	57	34	31	45	14	19	29	17
Other large cities	36	44	18	38	47	18	23	27	16
Suburbs 12 largest cities	43	48	29	42	51	19	28	31	24
Other suburbs	50	55	20	40	44	18	27	30	14
Nonmetropolitan areas	43	46	23	33	35	18	33	36	19
Small cities	46	49	30	36	38	23	37	38	28
Rural nonfarm	45	49	25	34	37	18	33	37	14
Farm	32	35	–	26	29	–	28	30	–

[a] Numbers of couples in base groups are shown in mimeographed tables (see Preface).
[b] Includes all Users.

The choice of condom by Protestant couples is less closely related to measures of socioeconomic status and urbanization. The higher status and the urbanized Protestants are somewhat more likely than others to have tried condom, chiefly because they are more likely to be Users. Among Users, condom is about as likely to be adopted by the lower-status as by the higher-status couples (Table 6–16). It is reported by fewer farm couples than others, but there is no consistent relationship among the nonfarm groups.

Douche commonly ranks third in importance among Protestant couples (and Users) in the various strata. However, it is second to condom for some low-status groups, namely, couples with grade school wives, husband's income below $4,000, and husbands who are lower-blue-collar workers. There is little relation between socioeconomic status and the proportion of couples adopting douche as a preventive measure, partly because the groups whose Users are most likely to try douche also have a high proportion of Nonusers. Among Users, the proportion reporting douche for contraception is somewhat larger among lower-status than upper-status groups and outside metropolitan areas than within them (Table 6–16).

Rhythm is the fourth most popular method among Protestant couples (and Users) in a majority of the groups. However, it ranks second (to condom) among farm couples. There is a marked tendency for the proportion of Users who practice rhythm to be larger in the upper-status than in the lower-status group and among farm couples than other couples (Tables 6–9 to 6–12).

Withdrawal is the least important of the five methods for couples with Protestant wives. In every stratum but one it ranks fifth; the exception is couples with grade school wives, among whom it ranks fourth (ahead of diaphragm). But even in this group it is reported by barely one-tenth of the couples (Table 6–14).

For Protestants, then, the adoption of one or more of the five most common methods does show certain associations with socioeconomic characteristics. Condom is the most popular method, reported by a relatively large proportion of Users in most groups. Diaphragm ranks second on the whole and is preferred by the Users in higher-status groups. Douche for contraception tends to be adopted by relatively more of the lower-status Users and by Users outside of metropolitan areas.

Among Catholics, the most important fact is the predominance of the rhythm method, which ranks first in every group considered. Furthermore, there is considerable difference between the proportion of Users adopting rhythm and the proportion adopting the second method in every stratum. The smallest margin is that for Users with wives going partly through high school, among whom 51 per cent reported rhythm and 34 per cent reported condom (Figure 6–5). As was shown earlier, the proportion of Users choosing rhythm is much larger in the upper than in the lower socioeconomic groups, and somewhat larger among rural and suburban couples than those in cities.

Condom is the method reported by the second-largest proportion of Catholic couples (and Users) in every stratum except one—husbands with incomes of $7,000 or more (among whom diaphragm ranks second). Many Catholics may choose condom rather than diaphragm because condoms can be purchased relatively anonymously, whereas the adoption of diaphragm usually involves a visit to a physician or a clinic.

If it is true (as many believe) that Catholic men are less influenced than Catholic women by the teachings of the Church, another reason for the more widespread use of condom than diaphragm by Catholics may be the fact that it involves initiative by the husband rather than the wife. There is some tendency for condom to be preferred by relatively more of the Users in the lower-status than the upper-status groups, and by more of the Users in cities than in suburban or rural areas (Table 6–16).

Diaphragm and douche usually are in third or fourth place. Choice of diaphragm is not associated with high socioeconomic status for Catholics as it is for Protestants. In fact, among all Catholics and Catholic Users there is no consistent relation between status and the proportion of couples resorting to diaphragm (Table 6–16). Similar statements can be made for douche. However, there is a slight tendency for diaphragm and douche to be adopted by relatively more blue-collar than white-collar Users, and by more Users in small cities than elsewhere.

Withdrawal ranks lowest among the five methods for Catholics in most strata as it does for Protestants. The only exceptions are couples with grade school wives, with a farm background, or living in rural nonfarm places. Among these groups it ranks third or fourth (compare Table 6–16 with Tables 6–9 to 6–12).

The Effectiveness of Different Methods of Contraception

How effective are different methods of contraception? In order to answer this question precisely we should be able to compute the number of accidental conceptions per year of exposure with each method. Unfortunately, the questions which would have permitted us to do this were omitted from our schedules in an effort to keep the interviews from being too long. The best we can do with our data is to take the couples who ever used (or used only) a given method and compute for them the proportion of accidental conceptions among all conceptions occurring after first use of *any* method. This is not a satisfactory yardstick because it understates the effectiveness of all efforts to regulate conception, and the superiority of the more effective specific methods over those which are less effective. We use it because our data do not provide a better measure for evaluating the success achieved with various types of contraception.[13]

If couples have an accident with one method of contraception, there is a strong tendency for them to shift to another method. The proportion of accidental pregnancies among those after first use rises from 19

[13] For additional discussion of "percentage accidental" as a measure of effectiveness see Appendix A, Note 17.

er cent for couples reporting only one method to 42 per cent for those reporting four or more different methods. On the other hand, the proportion of planned pregnancies among those after first use decreases from 57 per cent for couples who have used only one method to 32 per cent for couples who have used four or more.

The selective principle probably is at work for the Users of each method. If we compare couples who have tried only one method with couples who have used that method and at least one other, we find in every case that the former have a smaller proportion of accidental pregnancies and a larger proportion of planned pregnancies after use began. For example, the "percentage accidental" is 25 for all couples that have ever used appliance methods but is 20 for those that have used *only* appliance methods (Table 6–17). Couples are more likely to restrict themselves to a particular method if they are successful with it than if it fails.

It is significant that this selective principle apparently operates least among couples who have used rhythm. The difference in the "percentage accidental" between those using only a particular method and those using that method and another is only 2 percentage points for rhythm —much less than for any of the other six leading methods. This no doubt reflects a tendency for Catholics to continue to rely on rhythm even though it fails, because it is the Church-approved method.

Now that the shortcomings of "percentage accidental" have been pointed out, let us see what it indicates about the comparative effectiveness of different methods. The most important fact is that couples have more success with appliance methods than with rhythm. For both Catholic and Protestant couples who have ever used appliance methods, accidental conceptions after the first use of any method amount to about 25 per cent of all conceptions after first use (Table 6–17). For those who have *ever* used rhythm the corresponding proportion of accidents is 31 for Catholics and 34 for Protestants. A lower "percentage accidental" for appliance methods than for rhythm is found also for couples using *only* each type of method. This too is true for both Protestants and Catholics. It appears, however, that the superiority of appliance methods over rhythm with respect to preventing accidents is less for Catholics than for Protestants. This may reflect a greater desire of Catholics to be successful with rhythm because it is approved by their Church.

We can also make comparisons for each specific type of contraception (Table 6–18). The "percentage accidental" is relatively low for condom, diaphragm, and jelly. This is true for couples who utilized only one of these methods and for those who tried any one of them and other methods also. Rhythm, douche, and withdrawal appear to have been

TABLE 6–17. PER CENT DISTRIBUTION BY PLANNING STATUS, FOR ALL PREG NANCIES OF USERS AFTER FIRST USE, BY TYPE OF CONTRACEPTION EVER USED BY WIFE'S RELIGION[a]

Type of contraception ever used	No. of pregnancies after first use	Planning status of all pregnancies after first use			
		Total	Planned	Accidents	Other unplanned
Total					
Total	3,171	100	51	25	24
Rhythm only	441	100	44	30	26
Withdrawal only	71	100	49	13	38
Appliance methods only	1,634	100	58	20	22
Any use of rhythm	1,134	100	43	32	25
Any use of withdrawal	557	100	39	32	29
Any use of appliance methods	2,617	100	52	25	23
Protestant					
Total	2,345	100	51	25	24
Rhythm only	135	100	38	30	32
Withdrawal only	62	100	45	13	42
Appliance methods only	1,380	100	57	21	22
Any use of rhythm	637	100	42	34	24
Any use of withdrawal	437	100	40	30	30
Any use of appliance methods	2,131	100	52	25	23
Catholic					
Total	677	100	47	28	25
Rhythm only	303	100	46	30	24
Withdrawal only	9	*	*	*	*
Appliance methods only	135	100	61	14	25
Any use of rhythm	477	100	44	31	25
Any use of withdrawal	112	100	35	38	27
Any use of appliance methods	342	100	47	25	28

[a] The 146 pregnancies after first use, among Users for whom the planning status of *any* pregnancy was not ascertained, are excluded from this table.

equally effective among couples who tried more than one method. In contrast, among couples who tried *only* one method, the "percentage accidental" is much higher for rhythm than for douche or withdrawal.

Most couples are more interested in regulating the size of their families than in preventing accidental pregnancies *before* they have as many children as they want. For this reason it is helpful to consider the fertility planning status of Users who tried different control methods.

TABLE 6–18. PER CENT DISTRIBUTION BY PLANNING STATUS, FOR ALL PREG-
NANCIES OF USERS AFTER FIRST USE, BY SPECIFIED METHOD OF CONTRACEP-
TION, BY WHETHER COUPLE USED ONLY THIS METHOD

Method	No. of pregnancies after first use	Planning status of all pregnancies after first use			
		Total	Planned	Accidents	Other unplanned
All methods[a]	3,171	100	51	25	24

		Using only this method			
Condom	334	100	67	14	19
Diaphragm	420	100	66	15	19
Rhythm	441	100	44	30	26
Douche	95	100	46	17	37
Withdrawal	71	100	49	13	38
Jelly	27	100	52	11	37

		Ever using this method			
Condom	1,489	100	52	26	22
Diaphragm	1,337	100	53	26	21
Rhythm	1,134	100	43	32	25
Douche	960	100	39	32	29
Withdrawal	557	100	39	32	29
Jelly	205	100	52	25	23

[a] Excludes the pregnancies after first use among Users for whom the planning status of *any* pregnancy was not ascertained (see also Table 6–17).

Among Protestants who adopted only one type of method the proportion with Completely Planned fertility is highest for appliance
methods (33 per cent) and lowest for rhythm (19 per cent) (Table
6–19). Similarly, in the Number Planned group reports of appliance
methods are more numerous than those of rhythm. This relationship
probably reflects in part the effect of selective motivation—the couples
who are most interested in planning their families are most likely to
rely on the most effective type of method, i.e., appliance methods.

At the other extreme of the planning scale, the proportion of couples
with Excess Fertility is equally high (13 per cent) for couples who
have used only rhythm or only appliance methods. In trying to account
for this similarity it would be helpful to know more about the couples
concerned. It is possible that the number of Excess Fertility couples
who have used only appliance methods is so large because it includes
couples in the lower socioeconomic groups who do not try to control

TABLE 6–19. PER CENT DISTRIBUTION BY FERTILITY PLANNING STATUS, FOR USERS, BY WIFE'S RELIGION, BY TYPES OF CONTRACEPTION ADOPTED

Fertility planning status	Types of contraception							Any use of:		
	Total[a]	Rhythm only	With-drawal only	Appliance methods only	Rhythm and appliance only	With-drawal and appliance only	Rhythm, with-drawal and appliance	Rhythm	With-drawal	Appliance methods
	All Users									
Number	1,901	325	49	987	288	178	50	679	293	1,503
Per cent										
Total	100	100	100	100	100	100	100	100	100	100
Completely Planned	27	16	27	33	23	22	14	19	21	29
Number Planned	22	22	20	23	23	16	14	22	16	22
Quasi-planned	36	46	43	30	39	39	50	43	43	33
Excess Fertility	13	9	8	13	13	22	22	12	19	15
Not ascertained	2	7	2	1	2	1	–	4	1	1
	Protestant Users									
Number	1,362	107	36	812	209	148	39	362	230	1,208
Per cent										
Total	100	100	100	100	100	100	100	100	100	100
Completely Planned	29	19	25	33	24	24	18	21	22	30
Number Planned	21	21	22	23	21	15	8	19	15	21
Quasi-planned	35	41	47	30	39	38	49	42	43	33
Excess Fertility	14	13	6	13	14	22	25	15	19	15
Not ascertained	1	6	–	1	2	1	–	3	1	1
	Catholic Users									
Number	453	214	12	110	70	25	11	304	57	216
Per cent										
Total	100	100	100	100	100	100	100	100	100	100
Completely Planned	16	14	*	19	17	16	*	15	16	17
Number Planned	25	24	*	26	30	16	*	25	19	27
Quasi-planned	43	47	*	36	36	44	*	45	46	38
Excess Fertility	11	7	*	16	13	24	*	9	17	15
Not ascertained		6						6	3	3

amily size until excessive childbearing leads the wife to attend a 'lanned Parenthood clinic at which she is taught to use a diaphragm.

Among Protestant couples *ever* using one of the three types of meth •ds the proportion having Completely Planned and Number Planned ertility is highest for those reporting appliance methods. In contrast, Excess Fertility is equally common among Users of appliance methods nd of rhythm and less common than among Users of withdrawal. Quasi-planned families are considerably less numerous relatively among •ouples who have used appliance methods (only or ever) than among hose using either of the other two types.

Among Catholics who restricted themselves to one type of method, he proportion with Completely Planned or Number Planned fertility s highest for those who adopted appliance methods. In contrast to 'rotestants, Excess Fertility is more common for Catholics who used •nly appliance methods than for those who used only rhythm.

Additional evidence of a tendency for the less successful Users of •ne type of method to shift to other types is provided by the Fertility 'lanning classification. Among all Users and Protestant Users the pro-)ortion with Completely Planned or Number Planned fertility is lowest ind the proportion with Excess Fertility is highest, for the couples who ried all three types of methods. For the Catholic Users in our sample he only important change is from rhythm to appliance methods. The •ouples who tried rhythm and appliance methods were about as suc-:essful in planning their family growth as those who relied on appli-ince methods only. In comparison with those restricting themselves to •hythm, more have Number Planned fertility and fewer have Quasi-)lanned fertility.

In summary, our measures of effectiveness indicate that couples have ;reater success with appliance methods than with withdrawal or rhythm, ind among appliance methods have greater success with condom, dia-)hragm, or jelly than with douche. Although more precise measures)robably would yield larger differentials, it should be emphasized that he *actual* differences are not large in relation to the *potential* differ-:nces. Neither are they inconsistent with the view that most couples •an restrict their children to a relatively small number by using any)f these six methods regularly and carefully. This view is supported lirectly by the small proportion of the Users of most methods who have .arger families than they want.

Comparison of British and American Use of Appliance and Nonappliance Methods

In 1946–47 the Royal Commission on Population collected information about the use and effectiveness of contraception in Great Britain.[14] Reports were obtained from women under 45 whose first marriage had not been terminated, and from older women whose first marriage had lasted at least until age 45.[15] There is some reason to believe that the British report may have understated the proportion of couples who were Users. It is likely also that the use of appliance methods increased in Great Britain during the 8 or 9 years that elapsed between the British survey (in 1946–47) and the present study (in 1955). Nevertheless, certain comparisons between the two studies seem worthwhile, especially in view of the fact that this is the first time that comparisons of the types of methods used in two major countries can be made on the basis of national samples. The experience of all our wives (who were first married during 1928–55) will be compared with that of the British wives first married during 1920–47.

The proportion who tried to regulate conception appears to be somewhat smaller for the British couples than for the American couples. For example, 66 per cent of the British wives married 7–12 years reported control measures compared with 75 per cent of the American wives married 5–9 years (Table 6–20). However, these differences in the proportion of Users may be due mainly to underreporting in the British study or to changes between 1946–47 and 1955.

There are some rather striking differences in choice of methods between the two groups, which appear too large to have resulted from sampling or reporting biases or from the difference in years.

First, reliance on appliance methods has been far more prevalent in the United States than in Great Britain. Among the recently married couples who tried to control conception the proportion that used appliance methods is 57 per cent for the British and 77 per cent for the Americans. The differential formerly was substantially larger, but has been reduced by the tendency for more of the younger British couples to adopt appliance methods.

Second, among the appliance methods there has been more use of condom and vaginal tablets in Britain than in the United States and less use of diaphragm.

---

[14] E. Lewis-Faning, *Report on an Enquiry into Family Limitation and Its Influence on Human Fertility during the Past Fifty Years* (Papers of the Royal Commission on Population, vol. I), H.M. Stationery Office, London, 1949, pp. 81 and 160. More information about this study is given in Appendix A, Note 18.

[15] *Ibid.*, p. 3.

| Years married | Married during | No. of couples | All couples | | | | Users | | |
| | | | Ever using | | Using only | | Ever using appliance methods | Using only | |
			Any method	Appliance methods	Withdrawal	Rhythm		Withdrawal	Rhythm
					British couples[a]				
Less than 7	1940–47	974	55	31	24		57	43	
7–12	1935–39	617	66	37	29		56	44	
12–17	1930–34	440	63	30	33		47	52	
17–22	1925–29	339	61	22	39		36	64	
22–27	1920–24	342	58	18	40		31	69	
					American couples[b]				
Under 5	1950–55	680	65	50	1	13	77	2	20
5–9	1945–50	878	75	59	1	13	79	2	17
10–14	1940–45	675	73	58	2	12	79	3	16
15–27	1928–40	480	65	53	3	9	81	4	14

[a] E. Lewis-Faning, *Report on an Enquiry into Family Limitation and Its Influence on Human Fertility during the Past Fifty Years* (Papers of the Royal Commission on Population, vol. I), H.M. Stationery Office, London, 1949, pp. 7, 8, 56. The British report presents data for nonappliance methods as a group, but not for withdrawal or rhythm. In the text, however, it is stated that "the amount of reported use of abstinence and 'safe period' was trivial and nonappliance methods may be taken throughout to refer to Coitus Interruptus" (p. 8). In consequence, the British data for nonappliance methods are shown here for withdrawal. The British couples are classified by the year in which they were married. Since they were interviewed during August, 1946, through June, 1947, there is overlapping in the groupings in the left-hand column. (This column is not shown in the report.)

[b] The American couples are classified by duration of marriage. Since they were interviewed in March and April, 1955, there is overlapping in the groupings shown in the second column from the left. For most (395) of the 480 wives on the bottom line the number of years since first marriage is 15–19.9.

Third, the use of rhythm "was trivial" among the British couples, but was reported by 20 per cent of the recently married American Users. However, this difference would be somewhat smaller if the American data were for 1946–47 instead of 1955.

Fourth, withdrawal has been far more important in Great Britain than the United States. Among the recently married couples who had adopted contraception 43 per cent of the British had used only withdrawal, compared with 2 per cent of the Americans. This differential has been decreasing substantially as more British couples have taken up appliance methods.

The British data, like our data, indicate no significant difference in the effectiveness of fertility planning between couples using appliance methods and those using withdrawal. Among the British couples married 12 years or more the percentage whose most recent conception was accidental is about the same for those who ever used appliance methods as for those who used withdrawal only:

| Method used | Wives first married before 1935[a] | | | |
| | No. of wives | Average no. of births | Percentage with: | |
			An unwanted child	Last conception accidental
Total	823	2.7	24	20
Appliance (at some time)	292	2.6	28	21
Nonappliance (withdrawal) only	531	2.7	22	19

[a] E. Lewis-Faning, *Report on an Enquiry into Family Limitation and Its Influence on Human Fertility during the Past Fifty Years* (Papers of the Royal Commission on Population, vol. I), H.M. Stationery Office, London, 1949, pp. 70 and 160.

Unwanted children appear to be somewhat more numerous relatively among the appliance users. However, this may merely reflect one aspect of the analytical procedure, namely, the inclusion among couples ever using appliance methods of those who previously were unsuccessful users of withdrawal.

The British couples marrying before 1935 and using withdrawal were successful in keeping their family size quite small—approximately 2.7 births per couple by 1946–47 after more than 10 years of marriage. This is additional evidence in support of the statement that if it chooses to do so, a population can restrict its birth rate to a low level by the widespread use of one of the earliest methods known to man as well as by the modern methods which are commonly thought to be much more effective.

Chapter 7

EXPECTED FAMILY SIZE:
PRINCIPAL FINDINGS AND TRENDS

Following the demobilization of the armed forces after World War II, the crude birth rate in the United States climbed to 25.8 births per 1,000 persons in 1947, the highest level achieved for over 25 years.[1] Many people who were familiar with the long-time downward trend in fertility, which had continued with only minor interruptions for over a century, thought that this rise was temporary and that the birth rate would start to fall in 3 or 4 years. Instead, it has remained at a high level ever since, never being much below 24. In 1957, the most recent year for which information is available, the birth rate was 25.0. At no time in the postwar period has it come close to the low of 16.6 recorded in 1933.

The fact that the crude birth rate has been higher in the postwar period than in the 1930s is due primarily to the operation of two factors: a larger proportion of women have been marrying at younger ages, and more of those marrying have started their families relatively soon after marriage. These factors may have only a minor effect on the final average number of children that women will have borne by the end of the childbearing period, however. Of greater importance to the long-run trend in fertility is the average number of children that wives will bear. The attention of the present chapter and of the two following is focused on this factor. How much has average family size been changing? Will completed families be much larger in the future than they have been in the past? What are the factors governing family size? To what extent have the various socioeconomic classes participated in the changes in family size?

---

[1] All birth rates cited are based on registered births and on the population without adjustment for incomplete enumeration. 1915–55: National Office of Vital Statistics, *Vital Statistics of the United States, 1955*, vol. I, p. LXVIII; 1956–57: *Monthly Vital Statistics Report*, vol. 6, no. 13, p. 2.

Number of Births Expected

In order to investigate these problems, the wives in our sample were asked how many children they had already borne and how many they expected to bear in the future. In some cases a range was given in response to the questions on expected births, so that it is convenient to present the most likely, minimum, and maximum numbers of births or children expected.[2] No allowance was made for the children who may die in future years; consequently there is no difference between the expected number of births and of children unless a child had already died. The average numbers of births and children expected are as follows:

	Births	Children
Most likely	3.0	2.9
Minimum	2.7	2.7
Maximum	3.3	3.2

Of the total number expected, 2.1 births had already occurred by the time of the interview in early 1955, and 2.0 children were living (Figure 7–1).

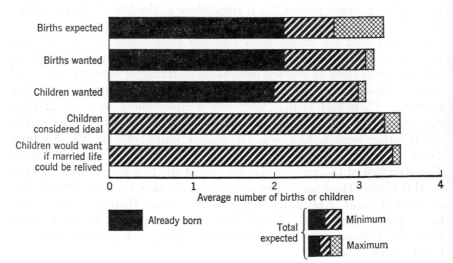

Fig. 7–1. Average number of births wife expects and wants, and average number of children wife wants and considers ideal.

[2] A detailed description of the method of obtaining numbers of births expected is presented in Appendix F.

Almost all the wives interviewed gave a numerical reply to the questions on how many children they expected altogether. Only a few refused to mention a number because it was "in God's hands," "up to fate," or unknown for other reasons. Such answers are most numerous (59 responses, or 2 per cent of the total sample) for the question on the largest number of children thought likely.

A large majority (74 per cent) of the wives expected 2, 3, or 4 births. Only 13 per cent expected fewer than 2, and only the same proportion expected more than 4 (Table 7–1). Most of the women who expected no births or only 1 are Subfecund. A substantial proportion (40 per cent) of those expecting 5 or more said that they would rather have fewer births than they expected. It is apparent from such results that most American wives relate their fertility expectations to a common and widespread standard—2 to 4 children. Those who have fewer children do so largely because they are Subfecund, and many of those who have

TABLE 7–1. PER CENT DISTRIBUTION BY FINAL NUMBER OF BIRTHS EXPECTED, FOR ALL WIVES, BY COHORT

Cohort	No. reporting	No. of births expected							
		Total	None	1	2	3	4	5	6 or more
		Most likely expected							
Total	2,693	100	5	8	28	26	20	6	7
1931–37	502	100	1	5	28	28	28	5	5
1926–30	716	100	4	6	28	25	25	6	6
1921–25	752	100	5	9	27	28	18	6	7
1916–20	723	100	8	13	28	22	12	7	10
		Minimum expected							
Total	2,697	100	7	11	31	24	16	5	6
1931–37	502	100	2	11	33	25	22	4	3
1926–30	717	100	6	9	32	25	20	4	4
1921–25	753	100	8	10	31	25	15	5	6
1916–20	725	100	11	13	29	22	10	7	8
		Maximum expected							
Total	2,654	100	3	5	26	25	24	8	9
1931–37	501	100	1	2	25	28	30	7	7
1926–30	705	100	2	3	25	25	29	8	8
1921–25	741	100	4	5	24	27	23	8	9
1916–20	707	100	6	10	29	22	15	8	10

more than 4 do so unintentionally. That the *preferred* number of children is 2, 3, or 4 is emphasized by the finding that 85 per cent of the women said they would have a number in this range if they could live their married lives over again.

Are these expectations realistic? We can ask this question about the expectations of each wife interviewed and get one answer, or we can ask it about the average expectations of groups of wives and get a different answer. If we consider each woman interviewed, we can be sure that many will not have the same number of births that they expect. This statement is supported by a study of the family size preferences of a small group of engaged couples who were first interviewed in the middle 1930s. The correlation coefficient between the number of children the bride-to-be said she wanted and the number she actually bore in the 20 years following marriage is only .27, which indicates very poor agreement between the desires and the actual experience of an individual.[3] The relationship between the husband's desires and the couple's performance is no closer, as indicated by a correlation coefficient of .26. However, the average numbers of children wanted just before marriage (2.8 for the women and 2.6 for the men) are very close to the average number born (2.6). Many of these couples had fewer births than they originally wanted, and many others had more. On the whole, these deviations very nearly canceled each other.

We have reason to believe that the same principle applies to the present study. Many wives will not bear all the children they expect, because they will become Subfecund or because they will change their minds about how many they want. Many others will bear more than they expect, because they will have accidental pregnancies or will decide to have more children. On the average, these opposite tendencies probably will very nearly cancel each other. As we proceed through the analysis of the data on expectations by socioeconomic and other variables, however, we shall find certain groups of wives who appear to expect unrealistically high or unrealistically low numbers of births if we judge what is "realistic" from the behavior of wives a few years older. The young wives who have not gone beyond grade school, for example, expect fewer births than it seems probable that they will have. On the other side of the picture, the young and well-educated Catholic wives as a group expect record-breaking high numbers of births. These and other deviations will be treated in detail later in the analysis. For the time being we simply note that they do exist.

    [3] Charles F. Westoff, Elliot G. Mishler, and E. Lowell Kelly, "Preferences in Size of Family and Eventual Fertility Twenty Years After," *The American Journal of Sociology*, vol. 42, no. 5, pp. 491–497, March, 1957.

There are two previous large-scale studies in which married people were questioned about the expected size of their own families. One covered a national sample of 500 husbands and wives under 45 who were interviewed in October, 1954.[4] The average number of children expected by these persons is 2.8, which is about the same as the 2.9 in the present study. No significant difference is found between the average numbers expected by the men and the women interviewed in the 1954 study. From this we may tentatively conclude that however wives may differ from their own husbands in their attitudes toward family size, the average expectations of all wives and all husbands are approximately the same and, presumably, equally realistic.

The other large-scale survey that included a question on expected family size is the Detroit Area Study of 1955,[5] in which married women under 40 were interviewed. The average number of children expected by the respondents is 2.9, which is virtually the same as the corresponding number for the 12 largest cities covered in our study (2.8). Thus, for both of these independent studies, in which questions about future childbearing were asked in very different contexts, the average expectations are very similar to those we are presenting.

Other considerations support the reasonable character of the expectations reported in this study. One is that many of the wives have already borne some or all of the children they expect to have, and their opinions as to future childbearing are based on considerable experience as mothers. Altogether, about two-thirds of the children expected have already been born. Even the younger wives with less experience on which to base their expectations give answers that seem reasonable in the light of the experience of older women. Each wife was asked to state her expectations only after answering questions about her general attitudes toward family size and, when there were previous pregnancies, after reviewing in detail her own pregnancy history. Furthermore, experience with contraception provides most of the wives with a realistic basis for judging their ability to keep from having more pregnancies than they want.

Virtually all the births expected in the years following the interview will occur to about half of the wives included in our sample, according to their statements. Since the couple's fecundity has an important bearing on the wife's fertility expectations, we present below the distribution of the total sample with respect both to fecundity and to whether or not additional births are expected:

[4] The 1954 October Interim Economic Survey of the Survey Research Center of the University of Michigan.
[5] The Detroit Area Study of the University of Michigan.

	Per cent
Total	100
Fecund, Semifecund, and Indeterminate	
Expect more births	48
Uncertain whether will have more births	9
Do not expect more births	26
Probably Sterile	
Will have more births if can	5
Would not have more births even if could	2
Definitely Sterile, cannot have more births	10

To allow for the probability that some of the uncertain wives in the first broad group will have additional children, it was assumed for them that the most likely total number expected is the average of (1) the number already borne and (2) the maximum number that they said they would have altogether if they bear additional children.

If the uncertain wives declined to state such a maximum, it was assumed that they will have 0.5 additional births, on the average. A small allowance was also made for additional births to the Probably Sterile who said they would have more births if they could. In order to obtain their most likely expectations, it was assumed that those for whom a pregnancy involves no special health risk or likelihood of fetal death will have an average of 0.3 more births. Further details on the method of determining expected numbers of births are presented in Appendix F.

Of the wives who expect more children, 82 per cent are Fecund and probably capable of achieving their expectations. Only 18 per cent are classified as Semifecund or Fecundity Indeterminate, for whom there is some doubt about ability to bear the number of children expected. One in five of those expecting more children was pregnant at the time of the interview. At least for these wives, future expectations have a substantial basis.

Attitudes toward Family Size

In addition to the questions on expected number of children, the wives were asked questions designed to elicit their more generalized attitudes toward ideal family size and the number of children they would like to have, as contrasted with their personal expectations. Such questions were asked because it is clear that attitudes and desires are major determinants of family size. With the widespread use of family limitation methods, which has been described in previous chapters, most couples need not exceed the number of children they want. It is true that some couples cannot have as many children as they would like because of sterility, late age at marriage, and other conditions that they cannot change, but most couples are not subject to such restrictions. For the majority, the number of children born will depend on their own wishes, as determined by such factors as liking for children, economic circumstances, and the prevailing attitudes toward family size.

The question "What do you consider is the ideal number of children for the average American family?" was not designed to discover the wife's personal ideal, but sought a picture of her more stereotyped impressions of what family size should be. Here we find an overwhelming emphasis on the 2-, 3-, or 4-child family, 94 per cent of the wives considering one of these numbers as ideal (Table 7–2). The most popular numbers are 3 and 4, chosen by almost three-quarters of the wives. Often in replying to these questions the women gave a range, such as "two or three,"

TABLE 7–2. PER CENT DISTRIBUTION OF ALL WIVES BY NUMBER OF CHILDREN CONSIDERED IDEAL, WANTED IF MARRIED LIFE COULD BEGIN ANEW, AND WANTED AT TIME OF INTERVIEW AND BY NUMBER OF BIRTHS WANTED AT TIME OF INTERVIEW

Type of reply	No. reporting	No. of children or births							
		Total	None	1	2	3	4	5	6 or more
Children considered ideal									
Minimum	2,684	100	–	–	21	34	39	3	3
Maximum	2,684	100	–	–	17	30	44	5	4
Children wanted if married life could begin anew									
Minimum	2,638	100	1	2	24	26	35	4	8
Maximum	2,638	100	1	1	23	24	36	5	10
Children wanted at time of interview[a]									
Minimum	2,646	100	1	6	33	26	25	4	5
Maximum	2,646	100	1	6	31	26	26	4	6
Births wanted at time of interview[a]									
Minimum	2,646	100	1	6	32	25	25	5	6
Maximum	2,646	100	1	5	30	25	26	6	7

The dash indicates a percentage below 0.5 in all tables.

[a] The difference between the distributions of women by children and births wanted at time of interview is due to the inclusion of children who died among births wanted and their exclusion from children wanted.

rather than a single number. In presenting their replies, therefore, it is convenient to show the average minimum and average maximum numbers. In general, the replies indicate that the stereotyped "ideal" number of children is larger than the number expected:

No. of children	Minimum	Maximum
Ideal	3.3	3.5
Expected	2.7	3.2

This seems reasonable, because it simply means that for many couples the realities and limitations of their situation tend to prevent them from having as many children as they consider ideal for the average couple. Similar discrepancies between realities and ideals occur in many areas of life.

It is interesting to compare the results of our study with earlier findings of the American Institute of Public Opinion. In 1941 and 1945 that organization asked a national sample of single and married women 21 to 34 years old how many children they considered ideal.[6] In both years, about nine-tenths of the women interviewed gave 2, 3, or 4 children as their ideal—in other words, about the same proportion as in our study. Within this range, however, the proportions preferring particular numbers have shifted significantly in the 14 years between 1941 and 1955, as shown by the percentage distributions below and in Figure 7–2. In this period the most popular ideal rose from 2 to 4 children, and the average from 3.0 to 3.4.

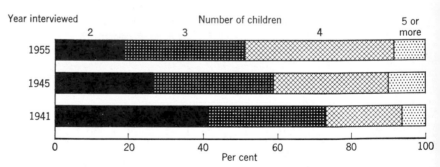

Fig. 7–2. Per cent distribution of women by number of children considered ideal: 1941, 1945, and 1955.

[6] *Public Opinion Quarterly*, Fall, 1945, p. 372. The inclusion of single women in these samples should not affect greatly their comparability with our sample of married women. This opinion is based on the close agreement between average ideal family size found for our sample of single women 18–24 years old and that found for our sample of married women in this age group.

Ideal number of children	Percentage of women stating specified ideal		
	1941	1945	1955
All replies	100	100	100
None	–	–	–
1	1	1	–
2	40	25	19
3	32	33	32
4	21	31	41
5	3	7	4
6 or more	3	3	4
Average number	3.0	3.3	3.4

Thus, there do not appear to be fixed ideals around which fertility varies. On the contrary, the ideals themselves seem to fluctuate, perhaps in response to economic conditions, perhaps in response to such intangibles as "fashion." Among the women who bore the majority of their children in the 1930s, the two-child family was probably the most popular ideal. Now the four-child family is the most popular ideal. What caused this shift? We might speculate about the relative roles of such factors as the greater need for the feeling of security that a family may provide (brought about in part, perhaps, by the unsettled state of international affairs), the greater prosperity of the postwar period that makes easier the support of larger families, and many other influences. But we cannot identify with certainty all the causes of the changes in attitudes toward family size, nor can we measure precisely the influence of any cause. We simply note that changes in attitudes have occurred and emphasize that they will probably occur again. It is hoped that the present study and subsequent studies will throw light on the factors underlying such changes in attitudes and improve our ability to predict the number of births that will occur.

In order to come closer to their personal attitudes toward family size, each wife in our sample was asked how large her family would be "if you could start your married life over again and choose to have just the number of children you would want." This is a hypothetical question, of course, but it is much less impersonal than the question about the number of children considered ideal for the average American family. We might consider the replies to it as expressing "personal" rather than "general" ideals. Again, we find a strong preference for 2 to 4 children, for 85 per cent of the wives gave a number in this range (Table 7–2). Very few (1.1 per cent) said they would want to have no children if they could live their married lives over again, and only 1.5 per cent said they would want to have only 1 child. Whatever advantages the one-child family may have for parents and children, for most wives they are greatly outweighed by the disadvantages. Approximately one-eighth of the wives interviewed said they would have 5 or more children if they could. It is interesting to note, however, that slightly over half of the women who said they would like to have 5 or more children actually expected fewer than 5. It seems quite possible that the replies of such women exaggerate the number who really prefer large families.

The average number of children the wives would want if they could relive their married lives is, of course, substantially above the number they expect:

	Minimum	Maximum
Number of children would want if married life could be relived	3.4	3.5
Final number of children expected	2.7	3.2

Not all the excess of personal ideals over expectations comes from Subfecund couples who cannot have as many children as the wives wish; a considerable amount of it is from wives who expect to have about as many children as they want *in their present circumstances*. Evidently the personal ideal family size of many women is greater than the number of children they and their husbands feel it is prudent to have.

The most realistic question about *desired* (as contrasted with *expected*) family size is that regarding the number of children wanted at the time of the interview. The averages of these numbers (3.0 and 3.1 for the minimum and maximum replies, respectively) are in the upper part of the range between the minimum and maximum numbers expected (2.7 and 3.2). This indicates a tendency for women to say they want more children than they expect, even within the limits set by their economic circumstances. However, over half of the wives interviewed said that they want about the same number of children as they expect:

Comparison of children wanted and expected	*Percentage of respondents*
All replies	100
Most likely expected is larger than maximum wanted	15
Most likely expected is smaller than minimum wanted	23
Most likely expected is equal to maximum or minimum wanted or between these numbers	59
Number expected or wanted not reported	3

The most common kind of discontent with expected family size—wanting more children than expected—is due primarily to subfecundity.

Nearly half of the Subfecund wives said they want more children than they expect, as compared with only one-tenth of the Fecund. As we shall see in the next chapter, however, the desires of the Subfecund wives appear to be slightly exaggerated and probably represent some wishful thinking.

Almost one-seventh of the wives interviewed regard their prospective families as too large. A higher proportion of the older wives than of the younger wives gave evidence of this kind of dissatisfaction, partly because they had been married longer and had more children, but partly because they did not want quite as many children as the younger wives. Dissatisfaction was also expressed by a higher proportion of Nonusers than of Users of contraception. In addition, accidental conceptions helped to swell the number of Users who considered their expected family size too large, especially among the older women.

The number of children a wife wants should not be regarded as a fixed quantity which does not vary throughout the reproductive period of her married life. Indeed, numerous wives reported fluctuations in their desires, as evidenced by their replies to the following questions:

38. "Just before you were married, how many children did you think you would want during your married life?"
39. "A year after your first child was born, how many children did you want altogether?"

The minimum and maximum replies to the first of these questions averaged, respectively, 3.1 and 3.2, or slightly more than the number of children wanted at the time of the interview (3.0 and 3.1). The average number of children wanted one year after the birth of the first child, however, is substantially lower (2.6 and 2.7). Evidently the introduction to the cares of motherhood at first reduces the number of children many women would like to have. Later, however, their desires return to the higher levels reported for the time of marriage. The answers to these retrospective questions cannot be accepted with a high degree of confidence, but it seems reasonable to suppose that they do reflect, though somewhat inaccurately, real fluctuations in attitudes toward family size.

In the brief description of some of our findings given above, we have treated the sample as a whole. It must not be supposed, however, that the description applies to all women, regardless of age, length of time married, fecundity, religion, and other important characteristics. In some cases there are very substantial differences in expectations, desires, and attitudes between different groups. These differences will be described in the remainder of this chapter and in the following two chapters. The next section of the present chapter describes recent and prospective trends in size of completed family. Chapter 8 describes the effects of fecundity, contraception, and fertility planning status on the number of children born up to the time of the interview, the number of additional children expected, and the size of completed families. Chapter 9 describes the relationships between fertility and socioeconomic status (education, income, occupation, religion, size of residence, etc.). In later portions of the book the information described in these chapters will be used as a basis for making projections of future birth rates and numbers of births in the United States.

Trends in Past and Expected Family Size by Birth Cohort

Among the white population of the United States there has been a steady fall in the average number of children borne by married women who live to the end of the childbearing period. Apparently the lowest point in this trend will be an average of about 2.4 births to married women reaching age 45 during 1955–65. The recent high birth rates observed among somewhat younger wives, however, have halted this downward trend. The wives in their 20s expect to have substantially larger families than women of their mothers' generation, though not as large as their grandmothers had two generations earlier. If these expectations materialize, it will mean a reversal of the long-time downward trend in fertility.

In order to facilitate our discussion of trends in completed family size (i.e., the average number of children borne by a group of married women living to the end of the childbearing period), the wives included in our study have been classified according to their year of birth. This provides a convenient designation that does not change from one year to the next, as does identification by age. For example, when we say that the married women in our sample who reached ages 20–24 in 1950 had then had an average of 0.9 children and that those who reached ages 25–29 in 1955 had then had an average of 1.9 children, we do not make clear the fact that both of these statistics relate to women born in the same years. By referring to such groups of women by their year of birth rather than by their age at different times, as in the example above, we facilitate our discussion of trends in completed fertility or in cumulative fertility by specified ages. The women born in a specified year make up the "cohort" of that year. For methodological reasons the cohorts are classified according to the fiscal year of birth, rather than the calendar year.[7] For example, the cohort of 1920 is composed of

---

[7] The reasons for using fiscal years are summarized in Wilson H. Grabill, Clyde V. Kiser, and Pascal K. Whelpton, *The Fertility of American Women*, John Wiley & Sons, Inc., New York, 1958, pp. 420–425.

women born in the 12-month period from July 1, 1919 to June 30, 1920.

Average family size has stopped decreasing. That it is in the process of rising is shown on page 228 and in Figure 7–3, where the expected fertility of the wives represented by the present study (cohorts of 1916–

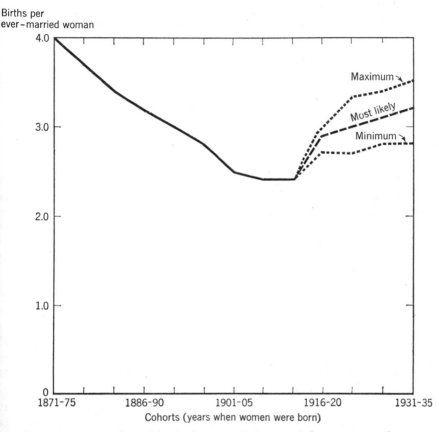

Fig. 7–3. Average number of births by ages 45–49: actual for ever-married women in cohorts of 1871–75 to 1911–15 and expected by wives in cohorts of 1916–20 to 1931–35.

37) is compared with the actual completed (or nearly completed) fertility of the cohorts of 1871–1915.

A low of 2.4 births per woman who had married before 45 and lived to that age was reached by women who were born in the 10-year period 1906–15. These women became 15–24 years old in 1930 and 25–34 years old in 1940, thus passing a substantial portion of what are usually the most fertile childbearing years in a period of economic depression. It seems reasonable to suppose that poor economic conditions influenced them to keep the average size of their families relatively small. The

Woman's year of birth (cohort)	Average no. of births per married woman living to age 45[a]		
	Minimum	Most likely	Maximum
1931–37	2.8	3.2	3.4
1926–30	2.8	3.1	3.4
1921–25	2.7	3.0	3.3
1916–20	2.7	2.9	3.0
1911–15		2.4[b]	
1906–10		2.4[b]	
1901–05		2.5	
1896–1900		2.8	
1891–95		3.0	
1886–90		3.2	
1881–85		3.4	
1876–80		3.7	
1871–75		4.0	

[a] The figures shown for the cohorts of 1916–37 are the average numbers of births expected by the wives interviewed in our study (white, husband present). Those for the cohorts of 1871–1915 are from fertility tables of the Scripps Foundation for all native white women who married before age 45 and lived to that age. For a discussion of the very slight effect of the differences in nativity and marital status, see Appendix A, Note 19, and Appendix G.

[b] Partially estimated.

women born in 1916–20 will have more births than the cohorts immediately preceding them, and the more recent cohorts of 1921–37 anticipate even higher fertility. The women of the 1931–37 cohorts who had married before 1955 and are represented in our sample expect to have an average of 3.2 births, which is almost as many as their grandmothers had 50 years, or nearly two generations, earlier.

In general, then, the expectations of the wives interviewed in this study suggest that the average size of completed families is in the process of rising substantially. It would be a mistake, however, to assume, as is often done, that such a rise in fertility will bring about an increase in the proportion of large families. In fact, the opposite seems to be the case; this study suggests that the expected rise in average family size will be accompanied by a continuation of the decline in the proportion of families with six or more children. As a result, the distribution of modern families by size will be quite different from that for families of a generation earlier, even though their average size may be nearly the same. The radical change in the proportions of wives having differing numbers of children is illustrated by the comparison of two groups of cohorts 30 years apart, shown below and in Figure 7–4. The figures shown for the older cohort group, that of 1891–95, relate, of course

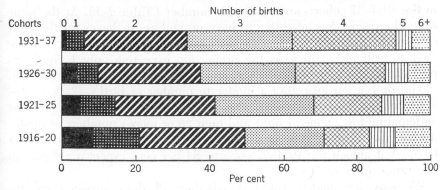

FIG. 7–4. Per cent distribution by most likely number of births expected, for wives, by cohorts.

to the number of children actually borne, whereas those shown for the 1921–25 cohort group represent expectations. Nevertheless, the comparison is instructive:

	\multicolumn{7}{c}{Percentage of wives having or expecting}					
Cohort	None	1	2	3	4	5	6 or more
Cohorts of 1921–25	5	9	27	28	18	6	7
Cohorts of 1891–95	13	21	20	15	10	6	15

Even though both groups of cohorts may have very nearly the same completed fertility (an average of 3.0 births) the distributions of wives by number of children borne differ considerably. For the younger cohorts, a high level of fertility will be achieved by a large decrease in the proportion of childless and 1-child couples and a large increase in the proportion with 2, 3, or 4 children (73 per cent expected for the 1921–25 cohorts and only 45 per cent occurring for the 1891–95 cohorts). At the same time, the proportion of wives who have 6 or more births will be much lower for the 1921–25 cohorts than for the 1891–95 cohorts (7 per cent as compared with 15 per cent).

It is not necessary to go back as far as the cohorts of 1891–95 to see that large families are becoming less common. Even within the relatively few cohorts covered in our study, the proportion of wives who have 6 or more births will decline from the earlier to the more recent cohorts unless the younger couples are much less successful in controlling family size than they think they will be. Whereas one-tenth of the wives of the 1916–20 cohorts expect 6 or more births, only one-twentieth of those in the 1931–37 cohorts anticipate this number (Table 7–1). At the same time, the proportion intending to have no children is lower for the later cohorts (8 per cent for the 1916–20 cohorts and 1 per cent for the 1931–37 cohorts), and so is the proportion expecting only 1 child (13 per cent for the cohorts of 1916–20 and 5 per cent for those of 1931–37).

The proportion expecting a moderate number of births—2, 3, or 4— is higher for the later cohorts. This is a result of their low proportions anticipating low (none or one) and high (6 or more) numbers of births. Among the 1916–20 cohorts, 62 per cent think they will have 2 to 4 births, but among the 1931–37 cohorts, 84 per cent expect a number in this range (Figure 7–4).

We may legitimately question whether all these expectations are realistic. It does not seem at all likely, for example, that only 1 per cent of the wives in the 1931–37 cohorts will be childless, in view of the information in Chapter 2 on the rising incidence of sterility with age.[8] Neither does it seem probable that only 10 per cent of these women will have 5 or more births, in view of our findings on the frequency of accidental conceptions among the older wives, presented in Chapter 3.[9] Whether the net tendency is for the expectations to understate or overstate actual family size will be discussed in Chapter 8. Here we simply conclude that the data on expectations do reflect an ongoing trend toward families of moderate size and away from childless, one-child, and relatively large families.

In considering the cohort trends in fertility expectations, it must be remembered that our sample does not represent all the women born in a given span of years but only those who had married by early 1955 and were living with their husbands at that time (or were separated because the husband was in the armed forces). This limitation has little effect on the analysis for the women aged 35–39 (cohorts of 1916–20) because a large majority (over 80 per cent) of all the women in these cohorts were married and living with their husbands at the time of the interview. For these older cohorts our sample of presently married women gives a good picture of childbearing history and expectations. The women born in 1916–20 who marry after 1955 are almost sure to have lower fertility than those who married earlier, but because of their small number they will depress only slightly the fertility of the whole group (see Chapter 10 and Appendix G, Note 1).

The situation is quite different for the younger women in the 1936–37 cohorts. A much smaller proportion (less than one-third) of them had married by 1955, so the responses of the wives interviewed are less

[8] For example, 12 per cent of the wives in the 1916–20 cohorts (aged 35–39 in 1955) are childless, and a large majority of them are Subfecund.

[9] For example, 30 per cent of the Users 35–39 years of age had at least one accidental pregnancy.

applicable to all the women belonging to these cohorts who will eventually marry. The differences in marital status between the cohorts represented by the sample are indicated by the following percentages for the total population of the United States in April 1955:

Age	Approximate cohort group	Per cent married, husband present or in armed forces[a]
18–19	1936–37	29.4
20–24	1931–35	64.7
25–29	1926–30	80.2
30–34	1921–25	83.8
35–44	1911–20	80.8

[a] *Current Population Reports, Population Characteristics,* "Marital Status and Family Status: April 1955," U.S. Bureau of the Census, series P-20, no. 62, Oct. 31, 1955, p. 8. Figures were not given for age groups 35–39 and 40–44 separately nor for the white population alone. Comparable percentages for the white population alone, which our sample represents, probably are only slightly higher (less than 2 percentage points).

Another way of stating the bias that should be kept in mind when using the cohort data collected in the present study is that although our sample of wives living with their husbands represents the women in the earlier cohorts (1916–20) who married at any age up to 39, it represents only those women in the latest cohorts (1936–37) who married before age 20. These cohort differences in age at marriage cannot be ignored completely because variations in age at marriage influence fertility in three ways. First of all, the women who marry young are more likely to belong to those socioeconomic groups with traditionally high fertility rates. Secondly, younger age at marriage allows women to spend more of their married years in the childbearing period than would otherwise be the case, thus increasing the number of years in which they can bear children. Thirdly, the younger the age at marriage, the less the risk that the onset of subfecundity at a relatively early age will stop reproduction before the couple has all the children they want. However, as we shall see later, the extent to which younger age at marriage results in larger families depends chiefly on the number of children wanted and the efforts made to prevent more births than are wanted.

Fertility comparisons for wives married at different ages are shown in Table 7–3. Expected family size varies substantially with age at marriage only for women marrying early in the childbearing ages (under 18) or relatively late (30 or over). For the women marrying during ages 18–24, when most women do marry, the number of births anticipated varies within a narrow range. Even women marrying at ages 25–29

TABLE 7–3. AVERAGE NUMBER OF BIRTHS BY 1955, AND OF MOST LIKELY EXPECTED ADDITIONAL AND TOTAL BIRTHS, FOR ALL WIVES, BY COHORT, BY AGE AT MARRIAGE[a]

Cohort	Age at marriage						
	Total	Under 18	18–19	20–21	22–24	25–29	30–39
Births by 1955							
Total	2.1	2.5	2.1	2.0	1.9	1.6	0.9
1931–37	1.1	1.5	1.0	0.8	0.3	..	..
1926–30	1.9	2.6	2.3	1.7	1.4	0.6	..
1921–25	2.3	3.0	2.8	2.3	2.1	1.3	*
1916–20	2.6	3.4	2.7	2.6	2.4	2.1	1.0
Most likely expected additional births							
Total	1.0	0.9	1.0	1.0	1.0	1.0	1.0
1931–37	2.0	1.5	2.2	2.4	3.1	..	..
1926–30	1.2	0.8	0.9	1.2	1.7	2.1	..
1921–25	0.6	0.4	0.4	0.5	0.8	1.2	*
1916–20	0.3	0.2	0.2	0.3	0.4	0.5	0.7
Most likely expected total births							
Total	3.0	3.3	3.1	2.9	2.9	2.6	1.8
1931–37	3.2	3.0	3.2	3.2	3.4	..	..
1926–30	3.1	3.5	3.2	2.9	3.0	2.7	..
1921–25	3.0	3.4	3.2	2.8	2.9	2.5	*
1916–20	2.9	3.6	2.8	2.9	2.8	2.6	1.7

Two dots, in all tables, indicates a category which is impossible or very improbable.
* Less than 20 couples in base group. An asterisk has this meaning in all tables.
[a] Number of couples in base group are shown in mimeographed tables (see Preface).

think they will have families that are not much smaller than those of women who marry during ages 18–24.

These data suggest that couples who marry later than average can have the number of children they want, provided they do not wait too long. This is an important finding because it means that the fluctuations in age at marriage of the type that has occurred in response to changing economic conditions need not strongly affect average family size. Most couples are aiming for relatively small families (2–4 children) that can easily be completed in 5 to 10 years. Consequently, most of the women marrying as late as age 35 have enough time to bear all the children they want.[10]

[10] See Appendix A, Note 20.

Age at marriage apparently has some effect on expected family size within the age range 18–24, however, for the women marrying at ages 22–24 expect slightly fewer births than those marrying at 18 or 19. As the gap between the ages being compared widens, the relationship between age at marriage and fertility becomes more pronounced. The wives who married when they were younger than 18 expect an average of 3.3 births, which is 83 per cent more than the 1.8 expected by the few women marrying after age 30. Even such differences are not extreme, however. The wives marrying young do not, after all, expect very large families, and those marrying in their 30s still expect an average of nearly two children.

When we look at the data for the separate birth cohorts we find some deviations from the general pattern. Among the 1931–37 cohorts, the women who married at ages 22–24 expect more births than do those who married when they were younger. This reversal of the usual relationship is found only for the Catholic wives, however. Among these members of the 1931–37 cohorts, the college educated tend to marry later and to expect more children than do those with less education, thus raising the anticipated fertility of the older marriages. (See Chapter 9 for socioeconomic differences in fertility.) This finding emphasizes the importance of socioeconomic factors in mediating the influence of age at marriage on fertility. The mere fact that some women will spend more childbearing years in marriage than will others does not necessarily mean that they will have more children.

The cohort differences in expected births for the various age-at-marriage groups show conflicting trends. The expectations of wives married when 18 or older appear to be increasing, but those of wives married before 18 appear to be decreasing. These differences are due largely to the contrast between the 1931–37 cohorts, on the one hand, and the remaining cohorts on the other. If we restrict comparisons to the three earlier groups, 1916–20 to 1926–30, we find small cohort differences in numbers of births expected, regardless of age at marriage. These differences are not statistically significant, nor do they follow a consistent pattern. Our conclusion about cohort trends in expectations, then, depends largely on our evaluation of the expectations of the 1931–37 cohorts.

It is our opinion that the women of these cohorts who married at ages 20 and over are not likely to have as many children as they expect. This belief is based on our evaluation of the unusually high fertility anticipated by the college-educated Catholic women, mentioned above, which is chiefly responsible for the high expectations of those marrying later in the 1931–37 cohorts. Secondly, we think that the women of the 1931–37 cohorts who married before they were 18 years old are likely to have more births than they expect. This opinion is based on two facts: a high proportion of these women have not gone beyond grade school, and this educational group has had many ineffective family planners in the past. Such wives may think while they are young that they will be able to control family size successfully, but the experience of older women of similar educational attainment makes it appear doubtful that they will restrict themselves to an average of only 3.0 births.

In summary, the expectations of the 1931–37 cohorts appear to be somewhat unrealistic from at least two points of view, and therefore we cannot say with assurance that there is a definite trend upward or downward in expected family size, *when age at marriage is held constant*. As we shall see in Chapter 10, however, even after allowances are made for births to the additional women in each cohort who will marry before age 45, there appears to be a slight upward trend in the expected fertility of all wives in successive cohorts up to 1926–30, which is associated with a desire for larger families. On the basis of this and other evidence, it appears that among the cohorts included in our study, average family size is more likely to rise slightly than to decline or remain constant. Moreover, all these cohorts will have larger families than did the preceding cohorts of 1901–15.

The total numbers of births expected by the wives in our study are made up of two components: the children born by the time of the interview in early 1955 and those expected in the years following. It is useful to analyze total expectations in terms of these components because we can see to what extent total expectations are based on actual past experience and on predictions about the future. We find, of course, that the wives in the earlier cohorts had more children at the time of the interview and expected fewer afterward than those in the more recent cohorts. This is true regardless of age at marriage (Table 7–3). The 1916–20 cohorts, for example, already had nine-tenths of all the children they expected, whereas the 1931–37 cohorts had only a third of their probable total.

The number of births by 1955 is influenced substantially by length of time married (Table 7–4). The data in this table demonstrate the important role of duration of marriage in accounting for cohort differences in past births, for we see that within each duration group these differences are much smaller than the cohort differences for the combination of all duration groups. For example, the women who had been married less than 5 years had borne an average of about 1 child, regardless of the cohort to which they belong. We do find, however, that within each duration group for which a comparison is possible, the 1916–20 cohorts had slightly fewer children than the more recent cohorts.

TABLE 7–4. AVERAGE NUMBER OF BIRTHS BY 1955, AND OF MOST LIKELY EXPECTED ADDITIONAL AND TOTAL BIRTHS, FOR ALL WIVES, BY COHORT, BY DURATION OF MARRIAGE[a]

Cohort	Years married					
	Total	Under 5	5–9	10–14	15–19	20 or more
Births by 1955						
Total	2.1	0.9	2.1	2.6	2.8	3.5
1931–37	1.1	0.9	2.1	. .	. .	. .
1926–30	1.9	1.1	2.1	2.7	. .	. .
1921–25	2.3	0.9	2.0	2.7	2.9	. .
1916–20	2.6	*	1.7	2.4	2.7	3.5
Most likely expected additional births						
Total	1.0	2.0	0.9	0.5	0.3	0.2
1931–37	2.0	2.2	1.2	. .	. .	. .
1926–30	1.2	1.8	1.0	0.7	. .	. .
1921–25	0.6	1.7	0.8	0.5	0.3	. .
1916–20	0.3	*	0.5	0.4	0.2	0.2
Most likely expected total births						
Total	3.0	3.0	3.0	3.1	3.0	3.6
1931–37	3.2	3.1	3.4	. .	. .	. .
1926–30	3.1	2.9	3.1	3.4	. .	. .
1921–25	3.0	2.5	2.8	3.2	3.2	. .
1916–20	2.9	*	2.2	2.8	3.0	3.7

[a] Numbers of couples in base group are shown in mimeographed tables (see Preface).

The number of births expected in the years following the interview is smaller for the older women than for the younger within each duration group. For example, among the women married 5 to 9 years, those in the 1916–20 cohorts expect an average of only 0.5 more births, but those in the 1931–37 cohorts expect to bear 1.2 additional children. This is due in part to the fact that the older women have fewer years left in the childbearing period than the younger women, but also reflects the fact that they want fewer children.

The number of additional births expected varies greatly with the number of children already born and decreases rapidly as women approach the 3-child average desired by so many wives (Table 7–5). Among the wives who have had four or more births, however, the average number of additional births expected rises as the number of children already born increases. This is because the couples who have relatively large numbers of births are increasingly those who do not believe in planning or who have tried to plan family size and have failed, as was noted in Chapter 3. For example, among the 64 Fecund couples with 6 or more children, there were none who had planned both the number and the spacing of their pregnancies and only 4 who had deliberately planned their most recent birth by temporarily dis-

TABLE 7–5. AVERAGE NUMBER OF MOST LIKELY EXPECTED ADDITIONAL AND TOTAL BIRTHS, FOR ALL WIVES, BY COHORT, BY PARITY[a]

Cohort	Parity							
	Total	0	1	2	3	4	5	6 or more
Most likely expected additional births								
Total	1.0	1.8	1.3	0.8	0.5	0.6	0.6	0.6
1931–37	2.0	3.0	1.9	1.4	1.1	*	. .	. .
1926–30	1.2	1.7	1.5	1.0	0.8	0.8	1.2	*
1921–25	0.6	1.0	0.8	0.6	0.4	0.5	0.6	0.8
1916–20	0.3	0.4	0.3	0.3	0.3	0.3	0.4	0.5
Most likely expected total births								
Total	3.0	1.8	2.3	2.8	3.5	4.6	5.6	7.6
1931–37	3.2	3.0	2.9	3.4	4.1	*	. .	. .
1926–30	3.1	1.7	2.5	3.0	3.8	4.8	6.2	*
1921–25	3.0	1.0	1.8	2.6	3.4	4.5	5.6	7.5
1916–20	2.9	0.4	1.3	2.3	3.3	4.3	5.4	7.6

[a] Numbers of couples in base group are shown in mimeographed tables (see Preface).

continuing the use of contraception. In contrast, among the Fecund couples with 3 children, 12 per cent had planned the timing of all of their pregnancies and 24 per cent had planned the timing of the last. Thus, as parity (i.e., the number of children already born) rises, the proportion of successful planners declines and the average number of additional births expected goes up.

When parity is the same, younger wives expect more additional children than do older wives. For example, a young wife with one child expects more additional births than an older wife with one child. There are several reasons for such relationships: first, young women may want more children than older women; second, young women will have more years in which to bear additional children; third, the younger the age at which a given number of children has been attained, the higher the proportion of nonplanners or unsuccessful planners (Chapter 3).

The extent and effectiveness of family planning and the incidence of fecundity impairments influence fertility considerably. Variations in these factors account for many of the fertility differences described here. In the next chapter we shall see how family planning, fecundity, and certain demographic variables (birth cohort and duration of marriage) interact to affect family size.

Chapter 8

THE INFLUENCE OF FECUNDITY IMPAIRMENTS
AND FAMILY PLANNING ON NUMBER OF CHILDREN

In the last chapter we saw how past and expected average numbers of births differ according to the wife's birth cohort and other demographic variables. To a major extent these differences are the result of variations in the incidence of fecundity impairments and in the use of contraception among different groups of couples, which were discussed in Chapters 2 to 4. The fact that most births come relatively early in married life, for example, is due partly to deliberate planning and partly to the rising incidence of fecundity impairments as married life progresses. In this chapter we shall see how fecundity impairments and family planning combine to produce the past and expected average numbers of births that we have observed. To do this we shall seek the answers to three broad questions:

1. How far do fecundity impairments and the use of contraception reduce actual family size below potential?

2. How do the Fecund and the Subfecund couples differ in the way they control fertility and in the number of children the wife expects to have?

3. To what extent do subfecundity and unplanned conceptions cause expected fertility to deviate from the number of children desired?

Although we cannot hope to get exact answers to any of these questions from the limited data available, this study enables us to make the first approximations based on the actual experience and thinking of a national sample of wives in the childbearing period.

The Reduction of Actual Family Size Below Potential Due to Fecundity Impairments and Contraception

As was pointed out in Chapter 3, nearly all couples either try to regulate conception, intend to do so if they have not yet begun, or are Subfecund and have little or no need to limit family size. This description applies to 94 per cent of the couples in our sample. The questions we are trying to answer here are: How much do contraception and subfecundity reduce fertility below the hypothetical maximum, and what is the relative effect of each factor?

To answer these questions we first need to find out how many children would have been born if all the couples in our sample had been Fecund and if none of them had practiced contraception. Although we know that fertility under these hypothetical conditions would be high, we cannot say exactly how high it would be. The best we can do is to estimate hypothetical maximum fertility on the basis of what we know about the average length of time it takes Fecund couples to conceive while they are not using contraception and the average length of pregnancies. The total of these items is the average number of months between the end of one pregnancy (or the beginning of marriage) and the end of the next pregnancy. We can then divide the average number of months married for the wives in our sample (minus time lost because of separations and periods between marriages) by the average interpregnancy interval and find the number of pregnancies that would result in the absence of fecundity impairments and any attempt to limit fertility.

According to the results of the Indianapolis Study, the average number of months per pregnancy between marriage and the termination of the tenth pregnancy would vary between 16 and 18 for "relatively fecund" couples if they did not practice contraception.[1] Guttmacher has estimated that the average interval would be 19 months for women who do not nurse their babies.[2] As a rough approximation, let us assume an average interpregnancy interval of 17 months. Since the wives in our sample had been married an average of 96.4 months (not counting time lost because of separation from husband or intervals between marriages), they could have had 5.67 pregnancies at the rate of one every 17 months. Not all these pregnancies would have resulted in a birth, however. Applying the fetal death rate of 129 per 1,000 pregnancies found for our sample yields an average of 4.94 births per couple. The actual number of births per couple in our sample (2.06) falls short of this hypothetical maximum by 58 per cent. This reduction below potential fertility represents the combined effects of subfecundity and contraception.

Most of the younger and recently married couples are Fecund, and many have not yet begun preventive measures; consequently, the reduc-

---

[1] P. K. Whelpton and Clyde V. Kiser (eds.), *Social and Psychological Factors Affecting Fertility*, Milbank Memorial Fund, New York, 1950, vol. II, p. 315; or "VIII. The Comparative Influence on Fertility of Contraception and Impairments of Fecundity," *Milbank Memorial Fund Quarterly*, vol. 26, no. 2, p. 194, April, 1948. For additional information about the Indianapolis Study, see Appendix A, Note 2.

[2] See Appendix A, Note 5.

tion of actual fertility below potential is considerably smaller for them than for the whole sample. According to Table 8–1, which compares actual and potential fertility for wives of varying durations of marriage, the reduction below potential fertility for wives married less than 5 years is about 36 per cent. For those married 15 years or more, however, the reduction below potential is about 68 per cent. These older women would have had three children for every one they had actually borne if they had all remained Fecund and if contraception had not been used.

TABLE 8–1. ESTIMATED REDUCTION OF ACTUAL BELOW POTENTIAL BIRTHS PER COUPLE DUE TO CONTRACEPTION AND TO SUBFECUNDITY AND CONTRACEPTION COMBINED, BY DURATION OF MARRIAGE

Type of data	Years married [a]			
	Under 5	5–9	10–14	15 or more
Number of couples	649	869	686	509
Average number of births by interview:				
Potential [b]	1.43	3.99	6.32	9.16
Observed, Fecund couples[c]	1.00	2.34	2.98	3.52
Observed, all couples	0.91	2.03	2.54	2.91
Percentage reduction below potential due to:				
Contraception	30	41	53	62
Contraception and subfecundity combined	36	49	60	68

[a] Of the tables on duration of marriage in Chapters 7 to 9, only this is based on the number of days between marriage and interview. The others (e.g., Tables 8–2, 8–3, and 9–3) are based on classifications by marriage cohort of wife (i.e., by calendar year of marriage). The results differ slightly because, for example, duration of marriage in the latter classification scheme is given as 5 to 9 years (inclusive) for wives married during 1945–49, whereas the true limits are approximately from 5 years and 2 months to 10 years and 4 months.

[b] Assuming that couples of "normal" fecundity not using contraception could have one pregnancy every 17 months and that 87.1 per cent of these pregnancies would result in a birth.

[c] Numbers of Fecund couples in base group are shown in mimeographed tables (see Preface).

To what extent is this reduction below potential due to fecundity impairments, and to what extent is it due to family limitation? We can obtain an approximate answer to this question from the experience of the Fecund couples. If none of them had used contraception, the average number of births by the time of interview presumably would have been around 9.16 for those married 15 years or longer (Table 8–1 and Figure 8–1). Actually, however, the average is only 3.52 births, a reduction below potential of 62 per cent. All this reduction is due to the

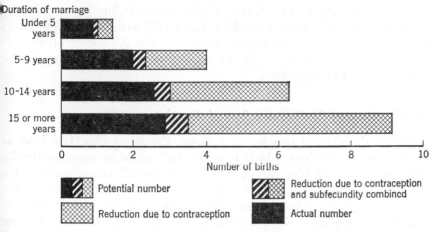

Fig. 8–1. Average number of births by 1955, estimated potential number, and reduction due to contraception and subfecundity, for wives by duration of marriage.

use of contraception, assuming that there is no hidden subfecundity among the Fecund couples. Since there probably is some undiscovered subfecundity among the Fecund, the reduction of fertility that is due to the practice of contraception is probably somewhat less than estimated.

The fact that the reduction below potential fertility for Fecund and Subfecund combined is larger than that for the Fecund alone (68 per cent as compared with 62 per cent for those married 15 or more years) is due to the additional loss from subfecundity. Our estimates suggest, then, that fecundity impairments alone reduce fertility by a much smaller amount than does contraception alone.[3] This conclusion appears to be valid regardless of duration of marriage. Even though the proportion using contraception is lowest for the group married less than 5 years, preventive measures still account for the major part of their reduction of actual below potential fertility.

Such findings are consistent with the view, held by most demographers, that the transition from large to small families in the Western world during the past century was due to the increased desire for small families, implemented by family limitation practices, and not to any rise in the incidence of fecundity impairments. In fact, there is no evidence that fecundity impairments have increased in frequency in the United States or in any other industrial country. The British Royal Commission, for example, came to the conclusion that as far as Great

[3] It is not possible with the data gathered in the present study to estimate the reduction in fertility that is due to subfecundity alone. We know only that it is much smaller than the reduction due to contraception alone. For a more detailed analysis in support of this finding see Appendix A, Note 21.

Britain is concerned, "the theory of substantial decline in reproductive capacity is not only unsupported by direct evidence, it is not even very plausible *a priori*. The alternative view, that the decline in family size has been brought about wholly or mainly by deliberate family limitation, is far better supported." [4]

The Planning of Fertility by Fecund Couples

Among the Fecund couples as a group, the wives expect to bear an average of 3.4 children, which is nearly half again as many as the 2.8 expected by the Subfecund. As is the case for all wives, most of the Fecund expect to have 2, 3, or 4 births. Altogether, 79 per cent of the Fecund expect a number in this range. In contrast, less than 1 per cent of these women said they expected no children. The childless Fecund couple is now such a rarity in the United States that we cite the following case simply as a curiosity:

CASE 50. This 28-year-old wife, married for 6 years, says, "We just haven't wanted to bother with children." She has a part-time job so that she can have "pretty clothes and a good time." Her general attitude is frankly expressed in these words: "If I had children I'd have to stay home nights, and they cost a lot of money."

It hardly needs to be said that such women have only a negligible influence on the birth rate in the United States.

Family Size, by Use of Contraception. As was pointed out in Chapter 3, very nearly all the Fecund couples make some effort to limit the number of their children. Only 8 per cent of those married 15 or more years had never used contraception. As a result, by the time of the interview this small group had an average of nearly 7 children. Such high fertility is now very rare; the widespread use of various control measures keeps it from being more common.

Among the Fecund couples, 83 per cent had used contraception by the time of the interview, and an additional 7 per cent (mostly young couples) plan to begin some time in the future. Only 9 per cent of the Fecund couples intend never to regulate family size. These groups differ considerably with respect to both past fertility and future expectations as is shown below and in Figure 8–2.

These summary results are misleading if we forget that the groups differ with respect to age and length of time married. The Future Users of contraception, for example, are mostly young, recently married couples and consequently had fewer children by 1955 than those in any other

[4] Royal Commission on Population, *Report*, H.M. Stationery Office, London, 1949, p. 32.

Use of contraception	No. of wives	Average no. of births			
		By 1955	Expected total		
			Most likely	Minimum	Maximum
All Fecund couples	1,794	2.2	3.4	3.1	3.5
Have used contraception	1,491	2.2	3.2	2.9	3.3
Have not used contraception	296	2.2	4.3	3.7	4.5
Will use contraception	133	1.8	3.8	3.4	4.0
Won't use contraception	162	2.5	4.7	4.0	4.9

category. When we classify the Future Users by wife's birth cohort and duration of marriage, as in Table 8–2, we find that within the separate cohorts and durations the Future Users have generally had more children than the Users, though not as many as those who will never use contraception.

The expectations of the Fecund are remarkably stable with respect to wife's birth cohort. In no case does the average number of births expected deviate significantly from 3.4. This stability is due to the uniform expectations of the Users. The Nonusers (Future Users and those who will not use contraception) show higher expectations for the earlier than for the more recent cohorts, but the proportion of Nonusers becomes so small by ages 35–39 (cohorts of 1916–20) that variations in their

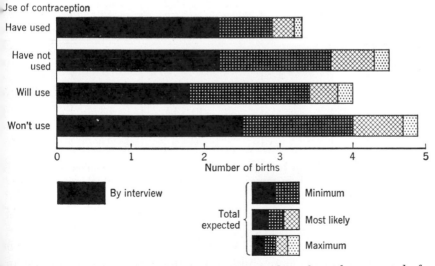

FIG. 8–2. Average number of births by 1955, and total number expected, for Fecund couples, by use of and intention to use contraception.

TABLE 8–2. AVERAGE NUMBER OF BIRTHS BY 1955, AND OF MOST LIKELY EX-
PECTED TOTAL BIRTHS, FOR FECUND COUPLES, BY USE OF AND INTENTION TO
USE CONTRACEPTION, BY WIFE'S COHORT, AND DURATION OF MARRIAGE[a]

Cohort and years married	Total Fecund	Users	Nonusers		
			Total	Will use	Won't use
Births by 1955					
Cohort:					
Total	2.2	2.2	2.2	1.8	2.5
1931–37	1.1	1.2	1.0	1.1	1.0
1926–30	2.1	2.1	2.4	2.2	2.6
1921–25	2.6	2.5	3.6	3.3	3.9
1916–20	3.0	2.9	4.6	*	4.8
Most likely expected total births					
Cohort:					
Total	3.4	3.2	4.3	3.8	4.7
1931–37	3.3	3.1	3.8	3.5	4.1
1926–30	3.4	3.3	4.4	3.8	4.8
1921–25	3.4	3.2	4.9	4.4	5.2
1916–20	3.4	3.2	5.4	*	5.6
Births by 1955					
Years married:					
Under 5	1.0	1.0	0.9	0.9	0.9
5–9	2.4	2.2	3.2	3.2	3.2
10–14	3.0	2.8	5.2	*	5.4
15 or more	3.5	3.2	*	*	*
Most likely expected total births					
Years married:					
Under 5	3.1	2.9	3.7	3.4	4.0
5–9	3.3	3.2	4.5	4.3	4.7
10–14	3.6	3.3	6.2	*	6.5
15 or more	3.7	3.5	*	*	*

* Less than 20 couples in base group. An asterisk has this meaning in all tables
[a] Numbers of couples in base groups are shown in mimeographed tables (see Preface)

expectations have a negligible effect on the cohort differences in the
expectations of all use categories combined.

The couples who intend to use preventive measures but had not yet
done so expect to have more children than those who had already begun
(3.8 births as compared with 3.2). The extent to which the expectations

of Future Users exceed those of Past Users varies with wife's birth cohort and duration of marriage. For the recent cohorts and shorter durations, the expectations of the two groups are quite close; for the earlier cohorts and longer durations they are far apart (Table 8–2). This is, of course, a reasonable result. Many young couples who have not yet begun using contraception do not want large families. Instead, they simply want to have one, two, or three children relatively early in marriage (wives in the 1931–37 cohorts had actually borne an average of 1.1) and then begin contraception either in order to prevent any future pregnancies or to space the occurrence of those desired. In contrast, many of the older Future Users had not yet begun using contraception because they want relatively large families.

One of the most interesting groups included in the study is composed of the 162 Fecund couples (6 per cent of the total sample) who (according to the wife) will never try to limit the size of their families. They are the exceptions to one of the most important generalizations about modern family building patterns: that nearly all couples are Users or Subfecund. These few couples are neither. The expectations of the young wives in this group are quite unrealistic. Those in the 1931–37 cohorts said that they expected an average of only 4.1 births altogether, and over two-thirds of them expected to have only 2, 3, or 4 children. If they remain Fecund and make no attempt to prevent conception, almost all of them will bear at least 10 children. Why, then, do they say they expect so few? Apparently because they are not well informed about the reproductive potential of young married couples. As these wives grow older and have a pregnancy every other year or so, it is probable that in many cases the wife or husband will modify their intention never to limit the sizes of their families.[5]

Among the Fecund couples who do not intend to use contraception, the few older wives (1916–20 cohorts) expect to bear an average of 5.6 children, most of whom had already been born by 1955. One reason that the expected fertility of such women is not higher is that they married at later ages than most of the other women in these cohorts.

Family Size, by Fertility Planning Status. It was pointed out in Chapter 3 that couples differ considerably in the way they plan their fertility. Three broad groups were distinguished: Completely Planned, Partially Planned, and Excess Fertility. As would be expected, they differ significantly with respect to past and expected fertility. In general, the more careful planners have and expect the smaller families. A major

---

[5] The questions about future use of some method of regulating conception was worded carefully so that Catholics would not interpret it as applying only to methods not approved by their Church (see question 44*b* in Appendix B). It is possible, however, that some of the Nonusers did interpret the question this way and gave a negative answer, even though they expect to practice periodic continence.

TABLE 8–3. Average Number of Births by 1955, and of Most Likely Expected Total Births, for Fecund Couples, by Fertility Planning Status, by Wife's Cohort, and Duration of Marriage[a]

Cohort and years married	Total Fecund	Completely Planned	Partially Planned		Quasi-planned		Excess Fertility		
			Total	Number Planned	Users	Non-users	Total	Users	Non-users
Births by 1955									
Cohort:									
Total	2.2	1.2	2.2	2.5	2.2	1.8	3.6	3.4	4.8
1931–37	1.1	0.6	1.3	1.9	1.4	1.0	1.9	2.0	*
1926–30	2.1	1.1	2.3	2.5	2.3	2.1	3.2	3.1	*
1921–25	2.6	1.7	2.6	2.6	2.5	3.2	3.8	3.6 }	5.3
1916–20	3.0	2.0	2.9	2.9	2.8	*	4.3	4.0 }	
Most likely expected total births									
Cohort:									
Total	3.4	2.6	3.5	3.4	3.3	4.1	4.1	3.8	5.8
1931–37	3.3	2.9	3.5	3.4	3.1	3.8	3.1	3.0	*
1926–30	3.4	2.8	3.6	3.5	3.5	4.1	3.9	3.5	*
1921–25	3.4	2.4	3.5	3.4	3.3	4.7	4.1	3.9 }	5.9
1916–20	3.4	2.3	3.3	3.3	3.1	*	4.6	4.2 }	
Births by 1955									
Years married:									
Under 5	1.0	0.5	1.2	1.7	1.4	0.9	1.5	*	*
5–9	2.4	1.5	2.5	2.4	2.4	3.0	3.1	2.9	*
10–14	3.0	2.0	3.0	2.8	2.9 }	5.6	4.0	3.7 }	5.8
15 or more	3.5	2.3	3.3	3.0	3.1 }		4.5	4.2 }	
Most likely expected total births									
Years married:									
Under 5	3.1	2.7	3.3	3.3	3.1	3.7	2.9	*	*
5–9	3.3	2.6	3.6	3.4	3.4	4.3	3.6	3.3	*
10–14	3.6	2.4	3.7	3.3	3.5 }	6.5	4.4	4.1 }	6.4
15 or more	3.7	2.5	3.5	3.4	3.2 }		4.8	4.4 }	

[a] Numbers of couples in base groups are shown in mimeographed tables (see Preface)

difference is between the Completely Planned (who expect an average o
2.6 births) and the Partially Planned (3.5 births). The Excess Fertility
couples expect an average of 4.1 births, which is about one-sixth above
the number expected by the Partially Planned (Table 8–3 and Figure
8–3).

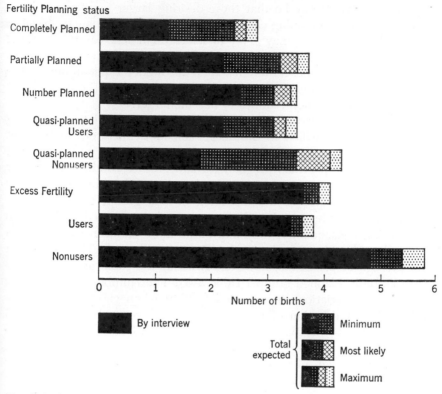

Fig. 8–3. Average number of births by 1955, and total number expected, for Fecund couples, by fertility planning status. (Most likely and maximum are the same for Excess Fertility couples.)

It is apparent that the Completely Planned constitute a special group. Not only do they try to time the occurrence of each pregnancy, but they also limit themselves to a relatively small number. Being Fecund, they could easily have as many children as the Partially Planned, but they deliberately choose not to. Their most popular family size is 2 children, expected by 43 per cent of them; 28 per cent expect 3, and 18 per cent 4. Only 2 per cent of the Completely Planned expect to have 5 or more children.

The expected fertility of the Completely Planned is higher among the more recent than among the earlier cohorts. This may be the result of one or both of two tendencies. It may represent a real rise from earlier to later cohorts in the number of births desired by the strict family planners. On the other hand, it may simply result from the tendency for the more prolific to be eliminated from the Completely Planned group as time passes. For example, a couple may have Completely Planned fertility for the first few years of their married life, but then have an accidental pregnancy, which changes their classification to Partially Planned or

Excess Fertility. It may be that those desiring larger families are more likely to have their planning classification change in this manner, because wanting more children may tend to make them less careful in using contraception than other couples with Completely Planned fertility. In sum, we cannot yet be certain whether the higher expectations of the more recent cohorts among the Completely Planned represent a tendency for the carefully planned families to become larger.

The Partially Planned group includes couples with a variety of planning patterns. Those classified as Number Planned deliberately interrupted their use of contraception so as to have their most recent pregnancy, but had one or more previous pregnancies under other conditions (usually before beginning contraception, or accidentally while contraception was being used). Because of the definition of this group, all the women included in it had begun, though not necessarily completed, at least two pregnancies; consequently, they had borne more children by 1955 than any of the other couples classified as Partially Planned. Their expected final average of 3.4 births, however, is about the same as that for the entire Partially Planned group (Table 8–3). The Number Planned show no significant variations in expected fertility when classified either by birth cohort or duration of marriage. (The difference between the 3.3 births expected by the 1916–20 cohorts and the 3.5 births expected by the more recent cohorts is not statistically significant.)

The other broad planning category included among the Partially Planned is the Quasi-planned. The Users in this group did not have their most recent pregnancy by deliberately interrupting contraception in order to conceive. It was not regarded as an unwanted pregnancy, however, even though it occurred somewhat earlier than desired. The Quasi-planned Users expect to have slightly fewer births than the other groups included among the Partially Planned. Their expectations vary with wife's birth cohort and duration of marriage but do so irregularly. Were it not for the low expectations of the wives in the most recent cohorts and those married most recently, the trend in the fertility of couples in this less rigorous planning category would appear to be upward.

Some of the couples with Partially Planned fertility are Nonusers who want all the pregnancies they have had. This group—the Quasi-planned Nonusers—is composed largely of young, recently married couples. Many of them will doubtless begin contraception later in married life, but at the time of the interview they were not yet trying to limit family size and had willingly accepted all the children that came. As a group, they expect more children (4.1) than do the wives in any other planning category except the Excess Fertility Nonusers (Table 8–3). The Quasi-planned Nonusers married 10 years or more expect considerably more births than do those married less than 5 years (6.5 as compared with

3.7). Needless to say, very few couples remain in this planning category for 10 years.

The couples who failed in their efforts to prevent unwanted conceptions, or who had not tried to limit their families to the number they consider desirable (the Excess Fertility group), expect as many children (4.1) as the least careful of the successful planners (the Quasi-planned Nonusers). This emphasizes the importance of the couple's point of view in determining their planning status: the Excess Fertility families are not necessarily larger than the planned families. In fact, 62 per cent of the Excess Fertility wives expect no more than the 2, 3, or 4 births wanted by the large majority of the wives interviewed. The expected fertility of the group is high only because a relatively large proportion—one-third —expect 5 or more births.

The expectations of the Excess Fertility couples are considerably higher for the earlier cohorts and the longer durations of marriage than for the more recent cohorts and the shorter durations. This is because the older wives have already borne more children than the younger; neither the younger nor the older expect to have many more.

The Users included in the Excess Fertility group expect significantly fewer births than do the Nonusers (3.8 compared with 5.8) (Table 8-3). The Users have made some attempt to limit their family size, but have not succeeded in preventing more pregnancies than they wanted. Their *desired* number of births average 2.8, which is only slightly above the 2.6 desired and expected by the most diligent planning group (Completely Planned). The Excess Fertility Nonusers not only expect more births than the Excess Fertility Users, but they also want more (3.7 on the average). Still, this is well below the 5.8 they expect. Such high fertility has little effect on the birth rate in the United States because so few couples— only 2 per cent of our sample—are in this group.

In summary, we can say that the number of births expected and fertility planning status are closely related for Fecund couples. Whether expected family size determines planning status or whether the opposite is true varies from couple to couple. Certainly the planning pattern many couples adopt is determined chiefly by the number of children they want. This is true of virtually all the Completely Planned and a majority of the Partially Planned (particularly the Number Planned and the Quasi-planned Nonusers). In other cases, a couple's fertility planning status is the unintentional result of the pregnancies that occur. This is true of all the Excess Fertility and some of the Partially Planned (especially the Quasi-planned Users). Regardless of which is cause and which effect, expected family size and fertility planning status are closely related.

The Planning of Fertility by Subfecund Couples

Wives of Subfecund couples expect to bear an average of 2.3 children, which is about one-third below the 3.4 births expected by the Fecund. In spite of their fecundity impairments, 63 per cent of the Subfecund wives expect to have normal-size families of 2, 3, or 4 children. However, a significant minority (13 per cent) think that they will have no children. In fact, the large majority (92 per cent) of the couples definitely expecting never to have any children are classified as Subfecund. Thus, as was pointed out in Chapter 2, childlessness among the couples in our sample is due almost entirely to fecundity impairments.

The fact that the Subfecund wives as a group are older and have been married longer than the Fecund accounts for the relatively small difference between the average numbers of children already borne by the Subfecund and Fecund (1.9 and 2.2, respectively, which represent a difference of only one-sixth). Within each group of cohorts except the most recent (1931–37), the average number of births for the Subfecund is one-quarter to one-third below that for the Fecund. (Compare Tables 8–2 and 8–4.) Similar differences between the past fertility of the Fecund and Subfecund are also revealed among women married approximately the same length of time.

It is virtually impossible to make any statements about intercohort trends in family size for the Subfecund. We cannot tell if family size is increasing or decreasing from cohort to cohort, because the expectations of the Subfecund are so closely related to the stage of family building at which impaired fecundity first becomes apparent. Since the different cohorts were at different stages of family building when they were interviewed (the latest cohorts were just beginning their families, and the earliest cohorts had completed theirs or were in the process of doing so), the Subfecund couples in each cohort naturally had different average numbers of births to date, and consequently the wives had different expectations about the size of their completed families. Those in the latest cohorts (1931–37) had 0.9 births and expected a total of 1.9, while those in the earliest cohorts (1916–20) had 2.2 and expected 2.4 altogether (Table 8–4). However, this does *not* mean that the family size of the Subfecund is declining.

Family Size, by Type of Subfecundity. The Subfecund do not constitute a homogeneous group. The couples in this category range from the Definitely Sterile, for whom no births are possible in the future, to the Indeterminate, whose long periods without conception may be due either to fecundity impairments or the use of "douche for cleanliness only." Between these two extremes are two intermediate groups, the Probably Sterile and the Semifecund. (All four groups are defined in detail in

TABLE 8–4. AVERAGE NUMBER OF BIRTHS BY 1955, AND OF MOST LIKELY EXPECTED TOTAL BIRTHS, FOR THE FOUR GROUPS OF SUBFECUND COUPLES, BY WIFE'S COHORT[a]

Cohort	Total Subfecund	Definitely Sterile	Probably Sterile	Semifecund	Indeterminate
			Births by 1955		
Total	1.9	2.4	1.4	1.8	1.5
1931–37	0.9	*	*	*	*
1926–30	1.4	2.1	1.2	1.3	1.1
1921–25	1.9	2.4	1.8	1.7	1.6
1916–20	2.2	2.5	1.4	2.2	2.0
			Most likely expected total births		
Total	2.3	2.4	1.5	2.8	2.5
1931–37	1.9	*	*	*	*
1926–30	2.2	2.1	1.3	2.9	2.4
1921–25	2.4	2.4	1.9	2.7	2.4
1916–20	2.4	2.5	1.4	2.8	2.6

[a] Numbers of couples in base groups are shown in mimeographed tables (see Preface).

Chapter 2 and Appendix D.) They differ considerably with respect to past and expected fertility, as indicated below and in Figure 8–4:

Fecundity	No. of wives	Average no. of births			
		By 1955	Expected total		
			Most likely	Minimum	Maximum
Subfecund	919	1.9	2.3	2.1	2.8
Definitely Sterile	283	2.4	2.4	2.4	2.4
Probably Sterile	187	1.4	1.5	1.4	2.9
Semifecund	328	1.8	2.8	2.3	3.0
Indeterminate	121	1.5	2.5	2.0	2.9

Among the Subfecund, those classified as Semifecund expect the largest number of births. Such couples had experienced long periods during which conception did not occur, even though no preventive measures were taken. Apparently their ability to conceive is subnormal but not entirely lacking.

As pointed out in Chapter 2, couples classified as Indeterminate are similar to the Semifecund in that they, too, had long periods with no conception. On the average, the Fecundity Indeterminate expect to bear

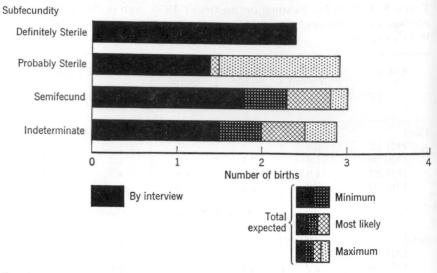

Fɪɢ. 8–4. Average number of births by 1955, and total number expected, for Subfecund couples, by type of subfecundity.

one more child, which would bring their completed fertility to 2.5 births.

The number of births expected is lowest (1.5 on the average) for the Probably Sterile couples. The wives were not certain that having children was impossible in the future, but it seemed improbable because of known physical impairments, because pregnancy would be a serious threat to the mother's health, or in view of a history of repeated fetal deaths. Their *minimum* expected number of births is the same as the number of children born by the date of the interview. Slightly over one-quarter of the Probably Sterile couples will have an additional child if they can do so; these wives indicated that this would involve no serious threat to their health and no abnormal likelihood of a fetal death. Because of the conditions which might prevent pregnancy, it was assumed, in tabulating the *most likely* expectations of these couples, that only 30 per cent would be able to have another child. In tabulating the *maximum* expectations of the Probably Sterile, it was assumed that they would have all the additional children they wanted; consequently, their maximum expectations are nearly twice as great as their most likely expectations (2.9 births compared with 1.5 births). (See Appendix F for a detailed description of the method of determining expected numbers of births.)

The expectations of the Definitely Sterile are, of course, the number of children born by the time of the interview, because additional births are impossible. These couples had an average of 2.4 births, which is larger than the average for the Fecund couples as well as for the couples in the other Subfecund groups. The fact that the Definitely Sterile are older helps to explain their higher fertility but does not do so completely, for within each birth cohort we find that the Definitely Sterile had more births by 1955 than the remainder of the Subfecund (Table 8–4). The high past fertility of the Definitely Sterile can be explained partly by the fact that as more children are borne there is more chance that the wife will become unable to bear another child, or that the couple will want an operation for the purpose of preventing additional conceptions. This is illustrated by the following data:

No. of births	Per cent of couples who are Definitely Sterile
Total	10
None	14
1	6
2	8
3	12
4	16
5 or more	17

Thus, the Definitely Sterile couples tend to include many who have had several births, which may be regarded as a partial cause of their complete inability to have more.

Family Size, by Use of Contraception and Fertility Planning Status. A majority (55 per cent) of the Subfecund couples are Nonusers, presumably because they have not needed to limit their fertility. The 45 per cent who are Users actually had more children by 1955 and expected to have more altogether than the Nonusers; this is true regardless of age or duration of marriage. It is probably safe to assume that more of the Subfecund Nonusers either knew at marriage that they might not be able to have children, or became aware of it relatively early in married life and, consequently, had few if any births and never needed to adopt preventive measures.

Although among the Subfecund the Nonusers had fewer children up to the time of the interview and expect smaller completed families than the Users, yet they expect slightly more additional births than do the Users (0.6 instead of 0.4) (Table 8–5). This finding appears at first to be inconsistent with the lower past and expected completed fertility of the Nonusers. However, the Nonusers contain all the Indeterminate couples and about half of the Semifecund. The couples in both of these categories have higher *future* expectations than do those classified as Definitely Sterile or Probably Sterile; hence the Nonusers have higher *future* expectations than do the Users, even though their total expectations are lower.

The regulation of conception was of vital concern to some of the

TABLE 8–5. AVERAGE NUMBER OF BIRTHS BY 1955, AND OF MOST LIKELY EXPECTED TOTAL BIRTHS, FOR SUBFECUND COUPLES, BY USE OF CONTRACEPTION, BY WIFE'S COHORT, AND DURATION OF MARRIAGE[a]

Cohort and years married	Total Subfecund	Users	Nonusers
Births by 1955			
Cohort:			
Total	1.9	2.2	1.6
1931–37	0.9	*	0.9
1926–30	1.4	1.9	1.1
1921–25	1.9	2.3	1.5
1916–20	2.2	2.5	1.9
Most likely expected total births			
Cohort:			
Total	2.3	2.6	2.2
1931–37	1.9	*	2.2
1926–30	2.2	2.5	2.0
1921–25	2.4	2.6	2.1
1916–20	2.4	2.7	2.2
Births by 1955			
Years married:			
Under 5	0.5	0.7	0.4
5–9	1.4	1.8	1.1
10–14	2.0	2.3	1.7
15 or more	2.5	2.7	2.2
Most likely expected total births			
Years married:			
Under 5	1.6	1.3	1.7
5–9	2.1	2.4	2.0
10–14	2.4	2.6	2.2
15 or more	2.7	2.9	2.5

[a] Numbers of couples in base groups are shown in mimeographed tables (see Preface).

Subfecund before their fecundity impairments became apparent. Variations in the manner of planning families have left their mark on the fertility of such couples. However, the categories used to describe the various ways in which couples plan their families are not entirely satisfactory when applied to the planning efforts of the Subfecund. For example, the term Completely Planned implies that the couple ha succeeded, so far, in having the number of births wanted. This is true for nearly all Fecund couples, but it is not true for many of the Sub-fecund couples whose family planning efforts have caused them to be classified in this group. Although all the latter had used contraception, and either had no pregnancies or had all their pregnancies while contraception was interrupted in order to conceive, many of them had not succeeded in having as many children as they want. This is also true of many of the Subfecund couples with Partially Planned fertility. In a very real sense, the Subfecund couples who have not had as many children as they would like are unsuccessful planners, even though they were able to plan the timing of all their pregnancies, or at least the latest that occurred. There are good reasons for creating one or more special planning categories for such couples, whose fertility might be called "underplanned." Rather than introduce new terms or change definitions, however, we have used the same planning classification for the Subfecund couples that we used for the Fecund couples. We can thus see how fecundity differences cause fertility to vary when planning practices up to the most recent pregnancy are the same.

The most effective users of contraception among the Subfecund—those with Completely Planned fertility—had an average of only 1 child by the time of the interview and expected an average total of only 1.6 [6] (Table 8–6). One-third had no births prior to the interview, and most

TABLE 8–6. AVERAGE NUMBER OF BIRTHS BY 1955, AND OF MOST LIKELY EX-PECTED TOTAL BIRTHS, FOR SUBFECUND COUPLES, BY FERTILITY PLANNING STATUS[a]

Fertility measure	Total Sub-fecund	Com-pletely Planned	Partially Planned					Excess Fertility		
			Total	Num-ber Planned	Quasi-planned			Total	Users	Non-users
					Users	Non-users				
Births by 1955	1.9	1.0	1.7	2.3	2.2	1.4		3.5	3.8	3.2
Most likely expected total births	2.3	1.6	2.2	2.8	2.5	2.0		3.6	3.9	3.4

[a] Numbers of couples in base groups are shown in mimeographed tables (see Preface).

of these childless couples expect to have no children in the years to follow. A substantial proportion of these couples tried to avoid having

[6] Wife's birth cohort and duration of marriage have not been used as control variables along with planning status for the Subfecund because the resulting tables would contain too many cells with too few cases for significant averages.

the first pregnancy too soon after marriage, later discontinued their preventive measures in order to have a child, and then discovered that they were unable to do so. Thus, the extensive and effective use of contraception and the occurrence of fecundity impairments have combined to keep the fertility of the Subfecund Completely Planned very low.

Over three-quarters of the Subfecund are classified as Partially Planned. As a group, they expect an average of 2.2 children, or substantially more than the 1.6 expected by the Completely Planned. This difference is due in only minor degree to variations in the severity of the fecundity impairments exhibited by the couples in these planning categories. For the most part, the nonuse of contraception or its less regular or less effective use by the Partially Planned permitted them to have families that are more nearly "normal" in size than are the families of the Completely Planned.

The highest fertility noted for any of the groups included among the Partially Planned is for the Number Planned. This is due largely to the fact that a couple must have had at least two pregnancies to qualify for this category. (See the definition which is given in Chapter 3, Figure 3–8.)

Quasi-planned couples constitute the largest group among the Subfecund, two-thirds of whom qualify for it. The Users among the Quasi-planned have had more births and expect more altogether, for the reasons cited previously for the higher fertility of Users among the Subfecund.

About one-eighth of the Subfecund couples had more pregnancies than they wanted and are therefore classified as Excess Fertility; they are equally divided between Users and Nonusers. Most of the Excess Fertility Users are Definitely Sterile and had a relatively large number of births by the time of interview. This finding is, of course, consistent with the relatively high past fertility of the Definitely Sterile noted previously. The Nonusers among the Subfecund Excess Fertility couples had fewer births by interview than the Users and expect fewer altogether. This is consistent with the lower fertility of Nonusers than of Users among the Subfecund noted previously.

The number of births expected varies with fertility planning status in much the same way for Subfecund as for Fecund couples. Expectations are smallest for the Completely Planned, intermediate for the Partially Planned, and largest for those with Excess Fertility. Thus, in spite of their limited ability to have children, the fertility of the Subfecund is partially related to family planning practices.

Success in Achieving Desired Family Size

The major determinant of family size in the United States is the number of children that couples want to have. Contraception makes it possible for couples who conceive easily to avoid unwanted pregnancies, and advances in medical treatment make it possible for many couples with fecundity impairments to reach their desired goal. A substantial majority (59 per cent) of the wives in our sample expect to have the number of children that they want, but a significant minority (38 per cent) think they will not be satisfied. Fifteen per cent of the wives said that they expect more children than they want, and 23 per cent said that they expect fewer than they want.

A number of factors may be responsible for a couple's failure to achieve desired family size. For example, some couples feel that their economic position is too precarious to support all the children they would like to have, and stop with a smaller number. Others feel compelled for religious reasons to have more children than the number that would satisfy their personal preferences. The chief causes of failure to have the number of children wanted, however, are fecundity impairments and unplanned conceptions. To what extent do these two opposing forces, one tending to reduce fertility below the desired level and the other tending to raise it above this level, offset each other?

We can obtain only an approximate answer to this question, partly because we cannot identify all couples with fecundity impairments and unplanned conceptions, but also because it is difficult to determine precisely how many children a couple really desires. In order to estimate this number, the wives who thought that they and their husbands could have more births, and the wives who were uncertain about their ability to have more, were questioned intensively about the number wanted. They were asked how many they wanted at different times in their married life, whether they had changed their minds about the preferred number, and how many they wanted after their most recent change in preference (see questions 38 to 40 in Appendix B). It was thought that asking several questions about desired family size would focus the wife's attention more closely on the problem and its various implications than would posing only one question.

For these couples, the reply to the question about the most recent attitude is utilized in this section. The number of *births* wanted at the time of interview is obtained by adding the number of children who had died to the number of children wanted. This is done in order to make number of births wanted comparable with number of births expected.

Wives who knew or thought that they were *not* able to have additional births were asked only how many children they would like to have altogether, counting those they already had (see question 19*i* in Appendix B). (Again, the number of births wanted is determined by adding the number of children who had died to the number wanted.) Unfortunately, when the questionnaire was being prepared it did not seem desirable to ask the wives who thought they could not have more children (and did not want more) whether they already had more than they wanted. We know, however, that some of these wives did have more than wanted—particularly some of the Definitely Sterile who had had accidental conceptions and underwent operations in order to prevent further childbearing (see Chapter 2). Nevertheless, because we cannot identify all these wives or determine for others the extent of the excess over the number wanted, we were forced to assume that the number of births the wife wants is the same as the number she has. This overstates the number of children wanted and the proportions expecting to have the number of births that they want and understates the proportions expecting more births than wanted. (The proportion expecting fewer births than wanted is not affected, since the wording of question 19*i* did not prevent the wife from saying that she wanted a *larger* number of children than she already had.) This bias affects the replies of an important proportion of the wives of couples classified as Definitely Sterile and of a few of those in the other Subfecund groups. It does not affect the replies of the Fecund. We estimate that it overstates the average number of births wanted by 15 to 20 per cent for the Definitely Sterile, 5 or 6 per cent for the Subfecund as a group, and about 2 per cent for all couples. However, it appears not to have affected significantly the average number wanted by the Probably Sterile as a group. (See Appendix A, Note 22, for an explanation of the bias and the method of estimating its size.)

In addition to this bias, which relates only to women who thought they could not have more children, there may be a tendency for other wives to give as the number wanted the same number that they already have, even though they would not have had that number of children if they and their husbands had used contraception effectively. This tendency would also overstate the number of children wanted and the proportion expecting the number wanted and understate the proportion expecting more than wanted. The effect of such a bias might be estimated by interviewing the same wives every few years and noting how the number of children they want changes with their reproductive experience. Lacking such studies, we can only call attention to the possibility that this bias exists; we cannot estimate its size. Judging from the replies of the wives in our sample, however, we think that it is not great—particularly in view of the large number who wanted more or fewer children than they expected.

Still another bias may arise from a tendency for wives to give as the number of children wanted the number they would want under ideal conditions. This would also raise the number wanted unduly. We tried to avoid this bias by concentrating the wife's attention on the number of children wanted most recently in her present circumstances (see questions 38 to 40 in Appendix B), but this attempt may not have been entirely successful.

Obviously, our measure of "births wanted at interview" is not perfect, but it allows us to give some suggestive answers about the relationship of expected to desired family size. In view of the importance of this topic, we have used the number wanted, as defined above, and have drawn attention to portions of the text where our analysis could be significantly affected by the tendency of our procedure to overstate the number of births wanted.

In comparing the number of births expected with the number wanted, we have used the following operational definitions:

Expects more than wants. The most likely expected number of births (defined in Appendix F) is above the *maximum* number wanted.

Expects fewer than wants. The most likely expected number is below the *minimum* number wanted.

Expects number wanted. The most likely expected number is equal to the *minimum* or *maximum* number wanted or is between them.

The eventual agreement or disagreement between the actual number of births and the number a wife wants is, in part, a matter of conjecture. In the large group whose expectations and desires are equal, for example, the wives who already have the number of births wanted may later have accidental conceptions and exceed the number wanted. Among those who have not yet had the number wanted, some may not be able to have all that they want and others may have too many.

The attitudes of some of the wives who expect more births than they want are also conjectural in part. Fewer than half of them already have too many, and the others expect to exceed the wanted number in the future (Table 8–7). This may seem rather surprising. What influences a wife to expect more children than she wants? Several factors may be responsible. One is that past efforts to prevent conception have been so ineffective that she thinks that future efforts will also fail. Another is that her husband wants more children than she does, and she expects her family size to be influenced more by his wishes than her own.

Whatever the reasons for the discrepancy or agreement between the wife's expectations and desires, it should be remembered that the com-

TABLE 8–7. PER CENT DISTRIBUTION BY COMPARISON BETWEEN PAST, EXPECTED, AND WANTED NUMBERS OF BIRTHS, FOR ALL WIVES, BY COHORT

Comparison of past, expected, and wanted births	Cohort				
	Total	1931–37	1926–30	1921–25	1916–20
Number of wives	2,713	506	722	754	731
Per cent					
Total	100	100	100	100	100
Expects more than wants	15	10	16	19	15
Has more than wants	6	2	5	8	8
Has number wanted	7	3	8	10	6
Has fewer than wanted	2	5	3	1	1
Expects number wanted	59	76	64	52	49
Has number wanted	25	8	19	29	39
Has fewer than wanted	34	68	45	23	10
Expects and has fewer than wants	23	12	19	27	32
Not ascertained	3	2	1	2	4

parisons of expected and desired fertility shown here are not final. Like comparisons at the end of the childbearing period undoubtedly would show somewhat different proportions satisfied or dissatisfied with the size of their families. In general, we should probably find a greater proportion dissatisfied with their actual completed family size than we now find dissatisfied with what they expect completed family size will be. This is suggested by the data for wives of the 1916–20 cohorts, most of whom considered their families completed by the time of the interview. Among these wives, 47 per cent expected that their families would be too large or too small, in contrast to 38 per cent for all wives.

That almost half of the older women in our sample indicate some dissatisfaction with their prospective family size is a surprising finding. The most common type of dissatisfaction expressed is that they won't have enough children. Altogether, 32 per cent of the wives in the 1916–20 cohorts expect fewer children than wanted. The proportion expecting more than wanted among these cohorts is only about half as great even after allowing for the bias mentioned earlier.

The Effect of Differences in Fecundity. Expecting fewer children than wanted is the most common type of dissatisfaction for members of all cohorts. It appears to be due largely to fecundity impairments, for we find that among the wives who expect their families to be smaller than they would like them to be, 71 per cent of the couples are Subfecund.

The opposite kind of dissatisfaction—expecting too many children—is concentrated among the Fecund couples, as would be anticipated.

This group includes a large majority (83 per cent) of the wives expressing this kind of dissatisfaction.

It is apparent from these findings that fecundity has an important influence on satisfaction with prospective family size. Fecund couples are much more likely than Subfecund couples to be satisfied with the number of children they expect to have. For 68 per cent of the Fecund, but less than 42 per cent of the Subfecund, the wives expect to have the number of births that they want (Table 8–8). The proportion sat-

TABLE 8–8. PER CENT DISTRIBUTION BY COMPARISON BETWEEN NUMBERS OF BIRTHS EXPECTED AND WANTED BY WIFE, FOR ALL COUPLES, BY FECUNDITY

Fecundity	No. of couples	Per cent distribution				
		Total	Wife expects more births than wanted	Wife expects number of births wanted	Wife expects fewer births than wanted	N.A.
Total	2,713	100	15	59	23	3
Fecund	1,794	100	19	68	10	3
Subfecund	919	100	8	42	48	2
Definitely Sterile[a]	283	100	34		65	1
Probably Sterile[a]	187	100	29		69	2
Semifecund	328	100	15	55	27	3
Indeterminate	121	100	14	51	33	2

N.A. = not ascertained.

[a] Because of the biased replies of many of the wives of Definitely Sterile and Probably Sterile couples (mentioned in the text and in Appendix A, Note 22), the proportion of wives expecting more births than wanted is understated for these groups and the proportion expecting the number wanted is overstated. The proportion expecting at least the number wanted (the sum of the two proportions mentioned above) is not affected, however, because in this respect the biases cancel each other. Hence, this combination is shown rather than the separate proportions.

isfied with prospective family size is somewhat less than 42 per cent for the Subfecund, because (as mentioned earlier) it includes some wives who already have *too many* children. The proportion of the Subfecund who expect to have *at least* the number wanted (50 per cent) is not affected by the biased replies of some of the wives in this group.

It is significant that half of the wives of Subfecund couples expect to have all the children they want or more than they want in spite of impaired reproductive ability. As is pointed out in Chapter 2 and Appendix A, Note 21, however, the fecundity classification is based on the couple's ability to have children in the future and not on their past ability. As a result, the Subfecund group contains many couples who would have been regarded as Fecund at some earlier date. Among them are some who had all the children they wanted and a few who had more than they wanted. For such couples, fecundity impairments cannot be said to have caused actual fertility to deviate from desired fertility.

Among the Subfecund, the couples who are least likely to have as many children as they want are those with the most severe fecundity impairments—the Definitely and Probably Sterile. About two-thirds of the wives in these categories expect fewer births than they want (Table 8–8). On the other hand, among the other two Subfecund groups (Semifecund and Indeterminate), only 29 per cent think that they will have fewer births than wanted. Thus, satisfaction with prospective family size is closely related to the degree to which fecundity is impaired.

Some of the Subfecund couples who regard their prospective families as too small could have more children if the wife or husband took medical treatment or had an operation. Altogether, 5 per cent of the Subfecund couples were given this information by a physician. Very few of these couples intend to take advantage of such medical aid, however. This suggests that most of the Subfecund couples with small families do not want additional children sufficiently to take the action which would permit having them. It also strengthens our suspicion that if the Subfecund couples were Fecund, they would not as a group have as many children as the wife says they would.

Where the numbers of births expected and wanted disagree, how large is the discrepancy between them? Considering all dissatisfied couples, it usually amounts to only 1 or 2 births. Wives who think their families will be too large expect an average of 4.2 births but want not more than 2.8—a difference of 1.4 (Table 8–9). Those who think their families will be too small expect an average of 2.0 births but want at least 3.6—a difference of 1.6. Thus, where discrepancies exist between expectations and desires, they are seldom very large. Of course, such a finding would be anticipated in a population such as ours, which is reproducing well below the biological potential. Where most couples want and have only 2, 3, or 4 births, the discrepancy between the number expected and the number wanted cannot be large for many couples.

Throughout this discussion, we must remember that a couple's satisfaction with family size cannot always be measured appropriately in terms of numbers. Probably the greatest degree of dissatisfaction exists among those couples who are unable to have any children. The birth of only one child would very likely mean more to them than would two

TABLE 8–9. AVERAGE NUMBER OF BIRTHS WIFE EXPECTS AND WANTS, FOR
ALL COUPLES, BY COMPARISON BETWEEN NUMBER EXPECTED AND WANTED,
BY FECUNDITY, BY WIFE'S COHORT[a]

Cohort	Wife expects more births than wanted		Wife expects number of births wanted	Wife expects fewer births than wanted	
	Most likely expected	Maximum wanted	Most likely expected	Most likely expected	Minimum wanted
Total					
Total	4.2	2.8	3.0	2.0	3.6
1926–37	3.9	2.6	3.2	2.0	3.5
1916–25	4.4	2.9	2.9	2.0	3.6
Fecund					
Total	4.3	2.8	3.1	2.7	3.7
1926–37	3.9	2.6	3.2	2.9	3.7
1916–25	4.6	3.0	2.9	2.6	3.7
Subfecund					
Total	3.7	2.6	2.8	1.7	3.5
1926–37	*	*	2.8	1.4	3.4
1916–25	3.8	2.6	2.8	1.8	3.6

[a] Numbers of couples in base groups are shown in mimeographed tables (see Preface).

additional births to a couple who would like to have four children but
expect only two. Fortunately, the proportion of wives who expect never
to have any children is very small—only 5 per cent of all wives and 8
per cent of the wives in the 1916–20 cohorts.

Both the average number of births expected and wanted vary with
the wife's satisfaction with her prospective family size. Those who think
their families will be too large expect more births than the satisfied
wives (4.2 as against 3.0) and want fewer (2.8 as against 3.0) (Table
8–9). Conversely, those who regard their prospective families as too
small expect fewer births than the satisfied wives (2.0 as against 3.0)
and want more (3.6 as against 3.0). It may be that the desires of both
dissatisfied groups are exaggerated and that neither would have just the
number of births that they say they want if they were able or willing
to have as many as they would like. The possibility also exists, of course,
that some of the women whose expectations and desires agree would

TABLE 8–10. PER CENT DISTRIBUTION BY COMPARISON OF NUMBERS OF BIRTHS WIFE EXPECTS AND WANTS, FOR ALL COUPLES, BY FECUNDITY, BY FERTILITY PLANNING STATUS

Fertility planning status	No. of couples	Per cent distribution				
		Total	Wife expects more births than wanted	Wife expects number of births wanted	Wife expects fewer births than wanted	N.A.
Total						
Total	2,713	100	15	59	23	3
Completely Planned	508	100	8	71	20	1
Partially Planned	1,808	100	12	59	26	3
Number Planned	417	100	16	62	21	1
Quasi-planned	1,391	100	11	58	28	3
Users	683	100	14	65	19	2
Nonusers	708	100	9	50	37	4
Excess Fertility	347	100	41	45	12	2
Users	253	100	41	48	10	1
Nonusers	94	100	41	37	17	5
Fecund						
Total	1,794	100	19	68	10	3
Completely Planned	424	100	9	79	11	1
Partially Planned	1,097	100	17	69	11	3
Number Planned	319	100	18	67	13	2
Quasi-planned	778	100	16	70	10	4
Users	520	100	17	69	12	2
Nonusers	258	100	14	71	9	6
Excess Fertility	234	100	52	42	3	3
Users	196	100	50	45	4	1
Nonusers	38	100	66	24		10
Subfecund [a]						
Total	919	100	8	42	48	2
Completely Planned	84	100	30		69	1
Partially Planned	711	100	49		49	2
Number Planned	98	100	54		45	1
Quasi-planned	613	100	47		50	3
Users	163	100	58		41	1
Nonusers	450	100	44		53	3
Excess Fertility	113	100	70		29	1
Users	57	100	70		30	
Nonusers	56	100	69		29	2

N.A. = not ascertained.

[a] Because of the overstatement of the proportion expecting the number of births wanted and the understatement of the proportion expecting too many births among the Subfecund (see text and Appendix A, Note 22), these two proportions are combined.

have had more or fewer births than they expect if fecundity had not been impaired or if they had not had any unplanned conceptions. However, it is not possible with the available data to evaluate the accuracy of the desires stated.

Among the wives who consider their prospective families too small, the amount by which expectations fall short of desires is greater for Subfecund couples (1.8 births) than for Fecund couples (1.0 birth). In this group, the wives of Subfecund couples want twice as many children as they expect.

The Effect of Fertility Planning. The proportion of wives who are satisfied or dissatisfied with their prospective family size varies considerably with fertility planning status. However, the relationship of satisfaction to fertility planning differs for the two broad fecundity groups. Among Fecund couples the wives are most likely to be satisfied with prospective family size if fertility is Completely Planned; 79 per cent of the wives in this group expect the number of births wanted (Table 8–10). Among Subfecund couples, however, the Completely Planned apparently are the *least* successful in achieving desired family size.

Most (69 per cent) of the Subfecund with Completely Planned fertility expect to have fewer births than they want. This is partly because the Completely Planned typically delay starting their families for a somewhat longer period after marriage than do all other couples, which increases their risk of becoming Subfecund before they complete their families. It is chiefly because our definition of Completely Planned fertility excludes those couples who have had more pregnancies than wanted. Thus, the careful control exercised by couples with Completely Planned fertility is more likely to lead to the wife's satisfaction with expected family size if they remain Fecund. If they become Subfecund they run a somewhat greater risk than other couples of having fewer children than they want. Thirty-five per cent of the Subfecund couples with Completely Planned fertility had never had a conception. This should not be interpreted as meaning that the use of family limitation measures causes sterility. Most of these couples could not have had a child even though contraception had never been adopted.

Couples with Excess Fertility are the least successful in achieving desired family size among the Fecund. A majority (52 per cent) of the wives in this group expect to have more births than they want. That this should be the typical complaint of the Excess Fertility group is understandable, for it includes only those couples for whom the most recent *pregnancy* was not wanted—by wife, husband, or both. It is surprising, however, that a substantial minority (42 per cent of the wives) expect to have as many *births* as wanted, and 3 per cent expect fewer births than wanted. That so large a proportion of the Fecund wives in the Excess Fertility group expect no more births than they want may seem inconsistent with our definition of the group. It may be explained as follows:

1. A couple's classification as to fertility planning status depends on the attitude of *either* wife or husband toward the most recent pregnancy, but the comparison of births wanted and expected depends only on the *wife's* desires and expectations. Thus, a couple could be classified as Excess Fertility because the husband did not want the most recent pregnancy even though the wife wanted it and may have wanted more.

2. When the last pregnancy began it may have been unwanted by both wife and husband because it involved some risk to the wife's health, and not because it might increase family size. Thus, the couple may have regarded their family as too small, but still have not wanted additional pregnancies.

3. The wife may have been satisfied with the number of children already born, but then became pregnant and had a miscarriage. She would still consider family size satisfactory, but the couple would be classified as Excess Fertility according to our definitions.

4. There may be a few cases of inconsistency in a wife's reply to various portions of the questionnaire. For example, a wife with five pregnancies may have said in question 15 that her most recent pregnancy was not wanted, possibly for reasons of health or economic hardship, and in question 40c that she wanted to have six children. In answering the latter question, she may have been thinking in terms of ideal conditions in which the limitations of health or income were not important. As was pointed out earlier, we tried to avoid such misinterpretation, but probably were not entirely successful.

For the Subfecund, we cannot be sure how successful the wives in the Excess Fertility group expect to be in achieving desired family size. Our uncertainty is due mostly to the upward bias in the proportion expecting the number of births wanted, which is particularly great among the Definitely Sterile (Appendix A, Note 22). Since a relatively large proportion of Subfecund couples with Excess Fertility are Definitely Sterile, this bias may affect comparisons of births expected and wanted for the Excess Fertility group even more than it affects the comparisons for other planning groups among the Subfecund. According to our definition, 51 per cent of the wives in the Subfecund Excess Fertility group expect the number of births wanted. This proportion is undoubtedly too high, but we cannot estimate how much it should be reduced.

What we can say with some assurance about the expected success of the Subfecund with Excess Fertility is that they are the most successful among the Subfecund in avoiding too *few* births. Less than one-third of them expect fewer births than wanted. Thus, their less careful use of contraception, or their lack of any attempt to prevent pregnancy, helped them avoid the typical failure of the Subfecund—not having enough births.

The couples with Partially Planned fertility occupy an intermediate position with respect to agreement between expected and wanted births. Among the Fecund, the Partially Planned resemble most closely the Completely Planned, with a high proportion (69 per cent) of the wives expecting to have the number of births wanted.

Among the Subfecund, a smaller proportion of the Partially Planned than of the Completely Planned expect to have fewer births than wanted (49 and 69 per cent, respectively). Some of the Partially Planned had never tried to limit family size, and others had unplanned conceptions which enabled more of them to avoid having families that are too small.

In general, our data show that fertility planning status and expected success in achieving desired family size are closely related. The relationship differs for the two broad fecundity groups, however. Among the Fecund, the Completely Planned expect to be most successful and the Excess Fertility expect to be least successful. Among the Subfecund, in contrast, the opposite is true, using as a criterion of success the proportion expecting too few births. (This is the only criterion we can use for the Subfecund in view of our lack of information regarding some of the wives in this group.) This draws attention to an important feature of fertility planning, namely, that in most cases fecundity impairments are unpredictable. Few, if any, couples foresee the help or hindrance that fecundity impairments will provide in having just the family size desired. As a consequence, couples who set out to plan carefully the spacing of their children may become subfecund before they consider their families completed. On the other hand, couples who do not plan carefully or whose attempts to prevent conception are ineffective may become subfecund and for this reason have no more children than they want. Examples of each situation include a significant proportion of couples.

The Resulting Family Size. What does the discrepancy between the wives' expected and desired fertility mean in terms of average family size for all groups combined? For the sample as a whole, the average number of births expected (3.02) is only 2 to 4 per cent below the number wanted (3.09 to 3.14)[7] (Table 8–11). This small difference results from two opposite and partially compensating tendencies: (1) the excessively high fertility of Fecund couples with one or more births

[7] Throughout this discussion (and in Table 8–11), we cite two figures for the number wanted by all wives and by those in the Subfecund group. The higher figure is the number wanted as defined earlier in this chapter. The lower figure incorporates an allowance for the overstatement of number wanted by the wives in the Definitely Sterile group. See Appendix A, Note 22, for method of estimating the latter figure.

than they wanted (about half of the Excess Fertility group), and (2) the low fertility of the Subfecund couples.

TABLE 8–11. AVERAGE NUMBER OF BIRTHS WIFE EXPECTS AND WANTS, AND PERCENTAGE EXCESS OF EXPECTED BIRTHS, FOR ALL COUPLES AND COUPLES WITH WIVES IN THE 1916–20 COHORTS, BY FECUNDITY, BY PLANNING STATUS FOR FECUND[a]

| Type of data | Total [b] | Fecund | | | Subfecund [b] |
		Total	Completely and Partially Planned	Excess Fertility	
			Total		
Births expected	3.02	3.36	3.25	4.10	2.34
Births wanted	3.09 to 3.14	3.12	3.15	2.94	3.03 to 3.18
Per cent expected over wanted	−2 to −4	8	3	39	−23 to −26
			1916–20 cohorts		
Births expected	2.88	3.40	3.05	4.63	2.42
Births wanted	3.01 to 3.13	3.04	2.95	3.28	2.98 to 3.21
Per cent expected over wanted	−4 to −8	12	3	41	−19 to −25

[a] Numbers of couples in base groups are shown in mimeographed tables (see Preface).
[b] See footnote 7 on page 267.

The above findings do not tell the whole story because they relate to all couples, including many who have not yet had an adequate opportunity to test their fecundity. It is natural that such couples will expect to have approximately the same number of births that they want. In order to exclude such couples we have analyzed the 1916–20 cohorts separately. Among these wives, expected family size is 4 to 8 per cent below desired, which is somewhat greater than the 2 to 4 per cent for wives in all cohorts combined. Again, the excess above wives' desires among the Fecund Excess Fertility couples fails to compensate completely for the deficit below desires among the Subfecund (Table 8–11 and Figure 8–5). This is partly because the Subfecund are approximately five times as numerous as the Fecund Excess Fertility by the time wives have reached ages 35–39.

The net effect of subfecundity and excess fertility on numbers of births among the older women can be better appreciated if we consider that for every 1,000 babies wanted by wives in the 1916–20 cohorts 99 to 134 will fail to be born because of fecundity impairments, an excess of 12 or 13 births over the number desired will occur to Fecund couples with Completely or Partially Planned fertility, and an excess of 44 to 46 such births will occur to Fecund Excess Fertility couples. The balance is a deficit of 40 to 78 births below the 1,000 desired.

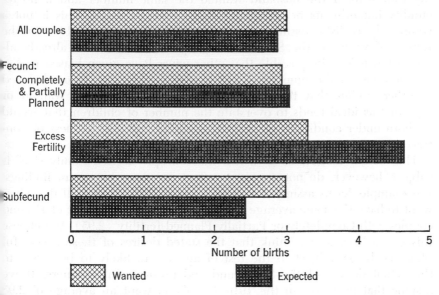

FIG. 8–5. Average number of births wanted and expected (most likely) by wives in 1916–20 cohorts, for all couples by fecundity, by planning status of Fecund.

An important implication of this analysis is that fertility will tend to decline as couples become more effective in their use of the methods of contraception which are now known, or as more efficient methods are developed. If, for example, all but the Subfecund couples in the 1916–20 cohorts had limited their births to the number wanted, the average number of births expected by all wives would be about 6 per cent lower than it now is. This assumes, of course, that the incidence of fecundity impairments would remain constant, which may not be a realistic conjecture. However, it seems likely that the effectiveness of methods of family limitation will improve more rapidly than will the treatment of fecundity impairments, for several reasons. (1) The need for simple and effective contraception is widely recognized, and considerable research is being done to meet this need. (2) Information about effective methods of contraception is reaching low-income, poorly educated groups that have in the past contained high proportions of Nonusers and unsuccessful Users. (3) Some of the physical conditions impairing fecundity that were prevalent in the past (largely venereal diseases) have been nearly eliminated, so that there is little room for improvement here, and many of the remaining conditions are difficult to diagnose and treat.

Thus far in the analysis we have assumed (for all groups but the Definitely Sterile) that the wives would have the number of births they say they want if the husband wanted the same number and if no fecundity impairments or accidental conceptions occurred. This is not a completely realistic assumption. Aside from the upward bias in the replies of wives in the Subfecund group, which we have already allowed for, it is quite possible that other wives have given biased replies to questions on the number of children wanted. It has been observed in other studies that the number of children reported as wanted or regarded as ideal tends to overstate the number of children that would be born under conditions of perfect fecundity and effectiveness of contraception.[8]

The various distortions to which the concept "desired family size" is subject, however, do not appear to affect our more important findings. For example, let us assume for the cohorts of 1916–20 that all the wives want to have the same average number of births as the wives of Fecund couples with Completely or Partially Planned fertility (2.95). We choose this group because we think that the stated desires of these successful planners, being subject to the test of action, are likely to be closer to the actual desires of the Subfecund and unsuccessful planners. If we assume that all wives in the 1916–20 cohorts want an average of 2.95 births, the following results are obtained:

Group	*Percentage by which expected births deviate from wanted births*
Total	− 2
Fecund	15
Completely or Partially Planned	3
Excess Fertility	57
Subfecund	−18

The discrepancies between expected and wanted births are still in the same direction as when the stated desires of the group are the basis of comparison (compare with bottom line of Table 8–11). Thus, while the exact quantification of the deviations of expected from desired births may not be possible, our main conclusions remain intact: (1) expected family size is slightly below desired; and (2) the deficit below desired due to subfecundity is almost made up by the excess above desired of those who have unwanted pregnancies.

[8] Cf. Robert G. Potter, Jr., "A Critique of the Glass-Grebenik Model for Indirectly Estimating Desired Family Size," *Population Studies,* vol. 9, no. 3, pp. 251–270 March, 1956.

Summary

Were it not for contraception and fecundity impairments, the wives in our sample who were married 15 or more years would have borne about 9 children. Contraception is much more important than are fecundity impairments in keeping fertility at about 3 births per wife—far below this high potential.

Among Fecund couples, the wives expect an average of 3.4 children. Most of these couples try to plan their families, although only a minority (24 per cent) have planned every pregnancy by interrupting the use of contraception. Wives in this group expect relatively few births—an average of 2.6. A majority of the Fecund couples have Partially Planned fertility and are less careful in their attempts to limit family size; the wives in this group expect substantially more births—3.5. A few Fecund couples (13 per cent) have had more conceptions than they wanted; these wives expect an average of 4.1 births. Among Fecund couples about 7 out of 10 of the wives expect to have as many births as they want, 2 out of 10 expect more births than they want, and 1 out of 10 expects fewer than wanted. Generally, the deviation of expected from wanted births amounts to one or two.

Among the Subfecund couples the wives expect an average of 2.3 births, or 1.1 fewer than do the Fecund. Slightly over half of the Subfecund couples have never used contraception. The fecundity impairments of the Nonusers appeared so early in the childbearing period that the wives expect fewer births altogether (2.2) than do the Subfecund who are Users (2.6). Almost half of the Subfecund couples expect fewer births than they would like to have.

More than half of the couples expect to have the number of children that they want. Fecundity impairments reduce the fertility of some couples below the desired level, however, while unwanted conceptions raise the fertility of other couples above the desired level. On balance, these two opposite tendencies yield a net number of births only slightly below the number desired. In other words, the deficit below the number wanted caused by subfecundity is not quite balanced by the excess over the number wanted caused by accidental or other unplanned conceptions.

Chapter 9

FAMILY SIZE IN DIFFERENT
SOCIAL AND ECONOMIC GROUPS

The development of wide differences between the fertility rates of the various social and economic groups of the population in Western countries was associated with the vast changes in conditions of life wrought by the expansion of commerce, the spread of the factory system of production, and the development of medical science. The growth of cities imposed crowded living conditions; the family tended to lose the characteristics of a productive economic unit in which children added to income; the improvement of health conditions allowed more children to survive birth and infancy so that families had more living children; and lower death rates brought about a more rapid increase in population, which increased population density both on farms and in cities. These changes influenced most people to want fewer births, but different groups were affected in different ways. Apparently the better-educated city dwellers were the first to reduce their fertility by a substantial margin. Eventually, other segments of the population followed their lead, but at different rates. Farm families, for example, are now much smaller than they were 100 years ago, but their average size has not yet declined to the levels characteristic of urban areas.

The existence of fertility differentials between various socioeconomic groups has had some good and some unfortunate consequences. Certainly the more rapid decline in the size of moderate-income white-collar urban families than in the size of poorer families has enabled parents in this group to attend more adequately to the health and education of their children. On the other hand, some would argue that it is probably fortunate for the economic development of the United States that the fertility of all people did not decline as rapidly as did the fertility of the moderate-income urban groups; otherwise the population might have declined and we might have lost an important impetus for economic expansion. A fertility differential that is often regarded as harmful is the higher reproductivity of the less educated groups; another is the higher fertility of low-income people. It is argued by some that such differentials tend to reduce the quality of the population, in part because they believe that low education and low income are associated with low mental capacity, and in part because the lower education and income groups obviously are less able to take proper care of children. Some fertility differentials, such as those between couples living in cities of different size, may have no particular implications either for economic well-being or for the quality of the population.

In the United States we now seem to have reached a phase of demographic evolution where fertility differentials are smaller than they were a few decades ago. Some of the differentials, such as those associated with income, education, and place of residence, even show signs of disappearing. The trend toward uniformity in fertility probably is due in part to changing attitudes toward family size. As we shall see, there are indications that the family size desired by the higher-income, better-educated, and urban groups has increased, while that desired by the lower-income, less educated, and rural groups has declined. It is not yet certain that such changes in attitudes are permanent, but there is substantial evidence that they have occurred. Another reason for the narrowing of fertility differentials is the spread of information about effective methods of contraception to additional segments of the population. This has reduced the fertility of groups whose relatively large families have resulted from lack of knowledge about effective methods of contraception and the failure of their efforts to use the less effective methods that they knew about.

Evidence relating to the current and probable future fertility differences between certain socioeconomic groups is presented in the present chapter. The characteristics used to define these groups are considered to be the most significant, from the point of view of population analysis, of those for which we obtained information. They include religion, education, income, occupation, wife's work experience, type of residence, and region of residence. Differences between the fertility of groups defined by these criteria will have an important influence on their contributions to our future population.

Religion

As was pointed out in Chapter 4, the two major religious groups in the United States—the Protestants and the Roman Catholics—differ with respect to attitudes concerning both family size and methods of limiting it. The Catholic Church teaches that the primary purpose of marriage is reproduction; other aims are regarded as secondary. Moreover, the Church teaches that fertility should be restricted only for "serious motives." The most important consideration in deciding whether or not to

have additional children is the welfare of the prospective children. The
wife's health and the economic burden imposed by additional children
are legitimate but secondary considerations.[1] When it does seem advisable for married couples to limit their fertility, either temporarily or

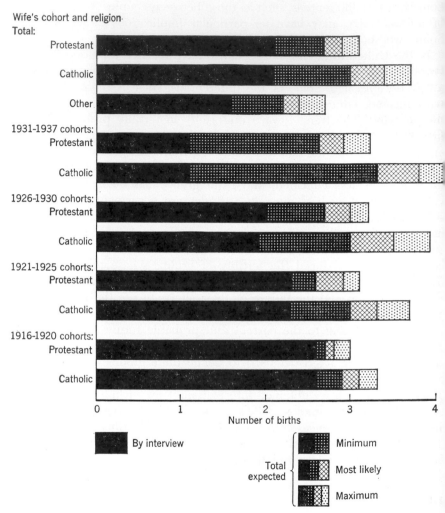

Fig. 9–1. Average number of births by 1955, and total number expected, for wives
by religion, by cohort.

permanently, the only means considered by the Catholic Church to be
morally acceptable are periodic continence and complete abstinence
from sexual intercourse. Thus, although the Church cannot be said to
advocate unrestrained childbearing, the net effect of its widely pub-

[1] See Appendix A, Note 10.

licized teaching is to discourage small families.[2] The major Protestant denominations, on the other hand, either have no explicit and uniform policy regarding family size and the use of contraception, or else advocate family planning with the use of medically approved methods. Are these attitudinal differences between the two religious groups translated into differences in reproductive behavior?

According to the information collected in the present study, the average numbers of births to Protestant and Catholic wives by the time of the interviews are approximately equal (Figure 9–1). This is true regardless of age. Even among the women 35–39 years old (in the cohorts of 1916–20) who had very nearly completed their families, there are no differences in the average number of children already borne by Catholics and Protestants (2.6 for each group) (Table 9–1).

TABLE 9–1. AVERAGE NUMBER OF BIRTHS BY 1955, AND OF MOST LIKELY EXPECTED TOTAL BIRTHS, FOR ALL WIVES, BY RELIGION, BY COHORT[a]

Cohort	Religion			
	Total	Protestant	Catholic	Other
Births by 1955				
Total	2.1	2.1	2.1	1.6
1931–37	1.1	1.1	1.1	*
1926–30	1.9	2.0	1.9	1.3
1921–25	2.3	2.3	2.3	2.2
1916–20	2.6	2.6	2.6	1.7
Most likely expected total births				
Total	3.0	2.9	3.4	2.4
1931 37	3.2	2.9	3.8	*
1926–30	3.1	3.0	3.5	2.5
1921–25	3.0	2.9	3.3	2.6
1916–20	2.9	2.8	3.1	2.0

* Less than 20 couples in base group. An asterisk has this meaning in all tables.
[a] Numbers of couples in base groups of all tables in this chapter are shown in mimeographed tables (see Preface).

The fact that the Catholic wives had borne no more children than the Protestant wives by the time of the interview is due primarily to the higher age at marriage of the Catholics. Because the Catholics had married when they were an average of 1.5 years older than the Prot-

[2] It should not be supposed, however, that the leaders of the Catholic Church feel that couples should be advised as to how many children they should have. See Appendix A, Note 10.

TABLE 9–2. AVERAGE NUMBER OF BIRTHS BY 1955, AND OF MOST LIKELY EX-
PECTED TOTAL BIRTHS, FOR ALL WIVES, BY RELIGION, BY COHORT, BY AGE AT
MARRIAGE

Cohort and religion	Age at marriage					
	Total	Under 18	18–19	20–21	22–24	25 and over
	Births by 1955					
Total:						
All religions	2.1	2.5	2.1	2.0	1.9	1.5
Protestant	2.1	2.5	2.1	1.9	1.8	1.4
Catholic	2.1	2.7	2.2	2.2	2.0	1.6
1931–37 cohorts:						
All religions	1.1	1.5	1.0	0.8	0.3	..
Protestant	1.1	1.5	0.9	0.8	*	..
Catholic	1.1	1.6	1.1	1.0	*	..
1926–30 cohorts:						
All religions	1.9	2.6	2.3	1.7	1.4	0.6
Protestant	2.0	2.5	2.3	1.7	1.2	*
Catholic	1.9	*	2.4	1.8	1.6	*
1921–25 cohorts:						
All religions	2.3	3.0	2.8	2.3	2.1	1.2
Protestant	2.3	3.0	2.7	2.2	2.1	0.8
Catholic	2.3	*	2.8	2.8	2.1	1.5
1916–20 cohorts:						
All religions	2.6	3.4	2.7	2.6	2.4	1.9
Protestant	2.6	3.5	2.6	2.5	2.3	1.9
Catholic	2.6	3.1	2.9	3.3	2.7	1.9
	Most likely expected total births					
Total:						
All religions	3.0	3.3	3.1	2.9	2.9	2.5
Protestant	2.9	3.3	3.0	2.7	2.7	2.1
Catholic	3.4	3.7	3.6	3.5	3.4	2.8
1931–37 cohorts:						
All religions	3.2	3.0	3.2	3.2	3.4	..
Protestant	2.9	3.0	2.9	2.9	*	..
Catholic	3.8	3.0	4.0	3.9	*	..
1926–30 cohorts:						
All religions	3.1	3.5	3.2	2.9	3.0	2.7
Protestant	3.0	3.3	3.1	2.8	2.7	*
Catholic	3.5	*	3.6	3.1	3.5	*
1921–25 cohorts:						
All religions	3.0	3.4	3.2	2.8	2.9	2.5
Protestant	2.9	3.4	3.1	2.7	2.7	1.8
Catholic	3.3	*	3.4	3.5	3.2	3.1
1916–20 cohorts:						
All religions	2.9	3.6	2.8	2.9	2.8	2.4
Protestant	2.8	3.6	2.8	2.7	2.6	2.3
Catholic	3.1	3.7	3.2	3.6	3.1	2.5

Two dots, in all tables, indicates a category which is impossible or very improbable.

estants, they had spent fewer years in marriage by the time of the interview and consequently had fewer years in which to bear children. If we compare the average number of children borne by Protestant and Catholic women in each cohort who married at the same age, we find that the Catholics have generally been more fertile than the Protestants (Table 9–2).

The somewhat higher fertility of Catholic wives is also reflected in comparisons of average numbers of births to women who have been married approximately the same length of time (Table 9–3).

TABLE 9–3. AVERAGE NUMBER OF BIRTHS BY 1955, AND OF MOST LIKELY EXPECTED TOTAL BIRTHS, FOR ALL WIVES, BY RELIGION, BY DURATION OF MARRIAGE

Years married	Religion			
	Total	Protestant	Catholic	Other
Births by 1955				
Total	2.1	2.1	2.1	1.6
Under 5	0.9	0.9	1.0	0.8
5–9	2.1	2.0	2.2	1.9
10–14	2.6	2.6	2.7	2.0
15 or more	2.9	2.9	3.1	*
Most likely expected total births				
Total	3.0	2.9	3.4	2.4
Under 5	3.0	2.8	3.5	2.7
5–9	3.0	2.8	3.3	2.5
10–14	3.1	3.0	3.3	2.1
15 or more	3.1	3.0	3.5	*

The relatively small difference between the fertility of Protestants and Catholics in the present study is supported by the results obtained in a Census Bureau survey conducted in March, 1957, which included questions on marital status and number of births.[3] The Bureau's data relate to the number of children ever born per 1,000 ever-married women of all races, 15–44 years old. It is not feasible to adjust these rates so that they are comparable with ours in all respects, but we have used them as a basis for estimating rates for white women. In order to increase still further the comparability of our rates and those of the Bureau, both are standardized for age. The Census Bureau rates are slightly higher than ours for both religious groups (Table 9–4). This

[3] *Statistical Abstract of the United States, 1958,* U.S. Bureau of the Census, 1958, p. 41.

is due chiefly to the inclusion of women 40–44 years old (and their births) in the census rates and their exclusion from our rates. However, both sets of rates are alike in showing that the difference between the fertility of Protestants and Catholics is very small. Our rates indicate no difference, whereas the census rates show slightly higher fertility for the Catholics. This discrepancy is well within the range of sampling error.

TABLE 9–4. NUMBER OF BIRTHS PER 1,000 WOMEN (STANDARDIZED FOR AGE),[a] BY RELIGION, ACCORDING TO PRESENT STUDY AND A CENSUS BUREAU SURVEY

Religion	Present study (1955): children ever born per 1,000 white wives, 18–39, husband present	Census Bureau survey (1957): children ever born per 1,000 ever-married women, 15–44	
		All races[b]	White[c]
Protestant	2,060	2,206	2,130
Catholic	2,060	2,210	2,198
Per cent excess of Catholic	–	–	3

The dash indicates a percentage below 0.5 in all tables.

[a] The standard is the distribution by age of ever-married women in the United States in 1950.

[b] *Statistical Abstract of the United States: 1958*, U.S. Bureau of the Census, 1958, p. 41.

[c] Based on the assumption that the rates for *nonwhite* women are the same in each religious group.

Although the number of births by interview for the wives in our study is virtually the same for the two religious groups, the average total number of births expected differs. The most likely expected number of births for the Catholic women is 17 per cent more than that for the Protestant women. The range between minimum and maximum expectations is wider for the Catholics than for the Protestants, however, suggesting greater uncertainty about future childbearing on the part of the Catholics:

Wife's religion	No. of wives	Average no. of births			
		By 1955	Expected total		
			Most likely	Minimum	Maximum
Protestant	1,817	2.1	2.9	2.7	3.1
Catholic	787	2.1	3.4	3.0	3.7

If the Protestant wives were to reach their maximum expectations of 3.1 births and the Catholic wives were to attain only their minimum expectations of 3.0 births, the customary fertility differences between the two religious groups would be reversed. But this is not likely to occur.

In general, the religious differences we find with respect to expected size of completed families agrees with information obtained from two other studies. In a nationwide survey of 500 married couples conducted by the Survey Research Center, University of Michigan, in October, 1954, it was found that Catholic respondents expected to have an average of 3.0 children and Protestants an average of 2.8, a difference of 7 per cent. In the Detroit Area Survey of 1955, Catholic couples expected 5 per cent more births than Protestant couples (2.95 as compared to 2.80), although when they were interviewed they had had 5 per cent fewer births than the Protestants (1.96 as compared with 2.06).

Will the Catholics in our study surpass the Protestants in average completed family size? Evidently they expect to, but because they were older when married they will have to bear their additional children at later ages than the Protestants. Among the oldest wives interviewed (in the 1916–20 cohorts), the Catholics expect to have an average of 0.5 additional births, as compared with a Protestant average of 0.2. These additions would bring the Catholic average up to a total of 3.1 births, or about 11 per cent above the Protestant average of 2.8.

Although we cannot be sure that the completed fertility of the Catholic wives represented by our sample will exceed that of the Protestant wives, there are several reasons for expecting that it will. In the first place, a higher proportion of the Catholic wives than of the Protestant wives were pregnant at the time of interview (13.0 per cent as compared with 9.5 per cent). Among the women married less than 5 years, 1 in 4 of the Catholics but only 1 in 6 of the Protestants was pregnant. Secondly, the Catholic wives space their births more closely than the Protestant wives, as the following comparisons indicate:

Wife's religion	Average no. of months between	
	Marriage and first birth	First and second births
Protestant	27	36
Catholic	23	33

In other words, although Catholics marry a little later in life than Protestants, after marriage they bear children somewhat more rapidly than do Protestants. The net result should be more births for Catholic wives by the end of the childbearing period. Another factor is the lower divorce rate among Catholics. Even though most divorced women remarry, as a group they bear fewer children than those who remain married. Consequently, the higher divorce rate among Protestants than among Catholics tends to widen the religious differences in the fertility of those who have ever married.

Apparently the attitudes of Catholic brides favor relatively large families but are modified later. The Catholic women in the 1916–20 cohorts, for example, said that when they married they wanted an average of 3.5 children, but that at the time of the interview (roughly 15 years later) they wanted an average of 3.1 children. This suggests that the influence of Catholic teaching on attitudes toward family size is somewhat stronger at the time of marriage than it is later in married life. The following example illustrates a rather drastic downward revision in the number of children wanted:

CASE 51. At the time of her marriage, this young Catholic mother wanted six children but after the first was born she decided that four would be enough because she and her husband began to realize "how much work babies are and how much they cost." After the birth of her third child, she and her husband decided not to have any more "because we decided it cost too much and we couldn't give more than three all we want them to have." The husband is a professional man with an annual income of about $7,000.

In contrast, the average number of children desired by the Protestant wives does not decline after marriage. Among the Protestant women in the 1916–20 cohorts, for example, the number of children wanted at the time of marriage and the number wanted at the time of the interview both average 2.9.

The decline in the number of children wanted by the Catholics in the course of married life may help to account for the age differences in their expectations. The oldest Catholics interviewed (1916–20 cohorts) expect to have a final average of 3.1 births, as compared with 3.8 births for the latest cohorts (1931–37). The average number of births expected by the Protestant wives in the different cohorts, on the other hand, varies within a relatively narrow range—between 2.8 and 3.0. If the expectations of both Catholics and Protestants are considered to be equally good indices of future reproductive behavior, then the different cohort trends in expected births suggest that the Catholic-Protestant fertility differentials will widen. However, it seems more likely, in view of the reports of the older Catholic women, that the expectations of the younger Catholics will be reduced as they have more experience with bearing and raising children.

The difference between the expectations of the Catholics and Protestants is concentrated among the Fecund couples, who make up about two-thirds of each group. Among the Subfecund, the two religious groups show no differences in expected numbers of births:

Fecundity	Most likely total number of births expected	
	Protestant	Catholic
Fecund couples	3.2	3.9
Subfecund couples	2.4	2.4

Among the Fecund, the two religious groups differ in the proportion adopting contraception. Eighty-eight per cent of the Fecund Protestants reported having used some method of control, as compared with only 70 per cent of the Fecund Catholics (Chapter 4). Whether contraception is used or not, however, the Catholic wives expect more births than do the Protestant:

Use of contraception	Most likely total number of births expected	
	Protestant	Catholic
Fecund Users	3.1	3.6
Fecund Nonusers	4.0	4.7

The fertility expectations of Catholic wives also exceed those of Protestant wives when allowances are made for differences in the way families are planned. Among the Fecund couples who have controlled both the number and the spacing of their children, for example, Catholic wives expect a total of 2.9 births on the average whereas Protestant wives expect only 2.6 (Table 9–5). The religious differentials for the other planning categories are in the same direction. Even among those women who regard their number of pregnancies as excessive, the Catholics expect more births than the Protestants.

Inasmuch as religious affiliation affects fertility expectations in important degree, it would seem reasonable that the degree of attachment to the church would also exercise some influence. Among the Protestants, church attendance makes little difference in average number of births expected. Among the Catholics, however, substantial differences were reported, especially by the younger wives. The Catholic wives of the 1931–37 cohorts who said that they attend church regularly expect 50 per cent more births than do those who said that they seldom go to church (an average of 4.2 births as compared with an average of 2.8 births) (Table 9–6). The attitude of the young regular church-goers is typified by the following example:

CASE 52. This 24-year-old Catholic mother of four children expects to have two or three more. She feels that "a marriage isn't a marriage unless there are children. That is the main purpose of marriage—to create a family. Two people don't make a family. Children do. I want a big family. I love children." Her husband has a parttime job in addition to his regular job and makes about $6,000 a year.

TABLE 9–5. AVERAGE NUMBER OF BIRTHS BY 1955, AND OF MOST LIKELY EXPECTED TOTAL BIRTHS, FOR FECUND COUPLES, BY WIFE'S RELIGION, BY FERTILITY PLANNING STATUS

| Wife's religion | Total | Fertility planning status | | | | | |
| | | Users | | | | Nonusers | |
		Completely Planned	Number Planned	Quasi-planned	Excess Fertility	Quasi-planned	Excess Fertility
Births by 1955							
Total	2.2	1.2	2.5	2.2	3.4	1.8	4.8
Protestant	2.1	1.2	2.4	2.1	3.4	1.9	*
Catholic	2.3	1.2	2.7	2.5	3.3	1.7	4.7
Other	1.8	1.3	*	*	*	*	*
Most likely expected total births							
Total	3.4	2.6	3.4	3.3	3.8	4.1	5.8
Protestant	3.2	2.6	3.2	3.1	3.8	3.8	*
Catholic	3.9	2.9	3.8	3.8	3.9	4.4	6.0
Other	2.8	2.6	*	*	*	*	*

Among Catholic wives, the expectations of the regular churchgoers are lower for the earlier than for more recent cohorts, while those of the less devout are higher for the earlier cohorts (Table 9–6). What are the reasons for this reversal? We think it is due primarily to age differences in attitudes toward family size. For the young regular churchgoers, the official position of the Church may be a very important influence on their thinking about family planning. Such women have not yet had to face the many problems encountered in raising relatively large families. These problems may have modified the influence of the Church on the thinking of the older wives who attend regularly, however, and may have caused them to reduce the number of children

TABLE 9–6. AVERAGE NUMBER OF BIRTHS BY 1955, AND OF MOST LIKELY EX-
PECTED TOTAL BIRTHS, FOR PROTESTANT AND CATHOLIC WIVES, BY REGULARITY
OF CHURCH ATTENDANCE, BY COHORT

| Cohort | Total [a] | Religion and church attendance | | | | | |
| | | Protestant | | | Catholic | | |
		Regularly	Often	Seldom	Regularly	Often	Seldom
				Births by 1955			
Total	2.1	2.2	2.0	2.0	2.0	2.4	2.3
1931–37	1.1	1.0	0.9	1.2	1.0	*	1.4
1926–30	1.9	1.9	2.0	2.0	1.8	2.1	2.1
1921–25	2.3	2.3	2.3	2.4	2.2	2.6	2.6
1916–20	2.6	2.7	2.5	2.5	2.5	3.1	2.9
			Most likely expected total births				
Total	3.0	2.9	2.9	2.9	3.4	3.5	3.2
1931–37	3.2	3.0	2.9	2.9	4.2	*	2.8
1926–30	3.1	2.9	3.1	3.0	3.6	3.5	3.1
1921–25	3.0	2.8	2.8	2.9	3.3	3.3	3.2
1916–20	2.9	2.9	2.9	2.7	3.0	3.6	3.5

[a] Includes all wives.

that they want. This explanation is consistent with the decline in the
number of children wanted by Catholic wives in the course of married
life, which was inferred from the reports of the older Catholic wives
mentioned previously.

Among the Catholic wives who seldom attend church, the effect of
Catholic doctrine on family planning should be considerably less than
it is among the regular churchgoers. On this basis alone, we would
expect the prospective fertility of the less devout to be lower than that
of the more devout. This is true for all but the women 35–39 (cohorts
of 1916–20), among whom the family size expected by the wives who
seldom attend church exceeds by one-sixth that of those who attend
regularly. It seems likely that the less devout Catholic women in the
earlier cohorts have less education than the more devout, and therefore
are less effective users of contraception. Not all the data needed to support this explanation are available, but it seems reasonable on the basis
of what we know about the association between church attendance and
education and that between education and family planning.

One of the important factors associated with the Protestant-Catholic differences in fertility expectations is the divergence in attitudes toward family limitation. In general, those who approve of efforts to control the number or the spacing of pregnancies expect fewer births than those who disapprove of such efforts. As we saw in Chapter 5, the proportion who approve of family limitation is almost twice as high among Protestants as among Catholics. In both religious groups the expected fertility of those who approve is about 20 per cent below that of those who disapprove (Table 9–7). If each group were like the total population in the distribution of wives by attitude toward family limitation, the average number of births expected by Protestant wives would rise a fraction above 2.9, but that for Catholics would fall from 3.4 to 3.2. Catholics would still anticipate higher fertility than Protestants, but the excess would fall from the observed level of 17 per cent to 10 per cent.

TABLE 9–7. PER CENT DISTRIBUTION BY ATTITUDE TOWARD FAMILY LIMITATION, AND AVERAGE NUMBER OF MOST LIKELY EXPECTED TOTAL BIRTHS, FOR ALL WIVES, BY RELIGION, BY ATTITUDE TOWARD FAMILY LIMITATION

Attitude toward family limitation	Per cent distribution			Most likely expected total births		
	Total [a]	Protestant	Catholic	Total [a]	Protestant	Catholic
Total	100	100	100	3.0	2.9	3.4
Approve	74	85	45	2.9	2.8	3.1
Mixed feelings	5	5	7	3.1	3.0	3.2
Disapprove	21	10	48	3.6	3.4	3.7

[a] Includes all wives.

It is clear from these results that differences in attitudes toward family limitation cannot completely account for the differences in the fertility expectations of the two religious groups. Whether they approve of the practice of family limitation or not, Catholic wives still expect more births than Protestant wives.

Most of the women interviewed were married to men of the same religious faith as their own, but a small proportion (8 per cent) were members of "mixed" marriages in which one partner was Protestant and the other Catholic. Such couples are of interest because they give us some idea of the relative importance of the wife's and husband's attitudes in determining current fertility and completed family size. The total numbers of births to date and expected for the four possible marriage combinations of Catholics and Protestants are as follows:

Religion	No. of wives	Average no. of births			
		By 1955	Expected total		
			Most likely	Minimum	Maximum
Both Protestant	1,684	2.1	2.9	2.7	3.1
Both Catholic	628	2.1	3.4	3.0	3.8
Wife Protestant, husband Catholic	91	1.8	2.9	2.6	3.1
Wife Catholic, husband Protestant	133	2.1	3.2	2.9	3.7

The wife's religion seems to be more important than the husband's in determining completed family size. Among the "mixed" marriages, the Catholic wives expect more births than do the Protestant wives. If their expectations are realized, the Catholic husbands in such marriages will have fewer children than the Protestant husbands. The greater importance of the wife's religion is also demonstrated in attitudes toward family limitation practices as noted in Chapter 6.

In some cases, such as the following, the different family sizes desired by wife and husband in a Catholic-Protestant marriage have been a matter of controversy:

CASE 53. This young Catholic mother of four children doesn't have any upper limit on her desired family size. She just "wants children." Her Protestant husband, however, wanted to have no more than three children. He earns about $5,000 a year as a semiskilled worker. He feels very strongly that they should have limited their family size to a small number and that they should have used contraception to prevent unwanted pregnancies. They have separated for short periods as a result of disagreement on these issues, but couldn't stay apart because, in the wife's words, they "love each other so much." Now they are using rhythm to postpone additional births. The wife is uncertain about whether they will have more children because she isn't sure that rhythm will work.

Catholic women consistently reported higher fertility expectations than Protestant women within virtually all the socioeconomic groups differentiated in the present study. In other words, the religious differences in expected births cannot be explained by variations in educational attainment, income, farm background, or size of place of longest residence or of residence at the time of the interview. A minor but significant exception is found when the religious groups are subdivided according to educational attainment. Among wives whose education proceeded no further than grade school, there is very little difference between Catholics and Protestants with respect to the total number of births expected. As educational level rises, however, the differentials between the two groups widen substantially. This result resembles the finding of the study conducted in Indianapolis in 1941, which showed that the relative excess of Catholic over Protestant completed fertility was larger for the college wives than for those with a grade school education.[4]

Among the college-educated women in the present study, the expectations of Catholics exceed those of Protestants by 44 per cent (3.9 births as compared with 2.7) (Table 9–8). In fact, among Catholics, the

TABLE 9–8. AVERAGE NUMBER OF BIRTHS BY 1955, AND OF MOST LIKELY EXPECTED TOTAL BIRTHS, FOR ALL WIVES, BY RELIGION, BY EDUCATION

Religion	Education				
	Total	College	High school, 4	High school, 1–3	Grade school
Births by 1955					
Total	2.1	1.8	1.8	2.1	2.9
Protestant	2.1	1.8	1.8	2.1	3.0
Catholic	2.1	1.9	1.9	2.1	2.8
Other	1.6	1.4	1.6	*	*
Most likely expected total births					
Total	3.0	2.9	2.9	3.0	3.6
Protestant	2.9	2.7	2.7	2.9	3.6
Catholic	3.4	3.9	3.3	3.1	3.7
Other	2.4	2.5	2.3	*	*

college-educated wives expect to have larger families than do the wives with only a grade school education (Figure 9–2). This is the opposite of the educational differences in expected fertility found among the Protestants. Evidently the attitude favoring moderately large families among Catholics is more influential among the better educated than among the less educated. One factor that helps to explain the higher expectations of the college-educated Catholic wives is their younger age. At the time of the interview, their average age was 3 or 4 years lower than that of the women who terminated their education in grade school. (This is because higher proportions of Catholic wives in the later cohorts than in

[4] P. K. Whelpton and Clyde V. Kiser (eds.), *Social and Psychological Factors Affecting Fertility*, Milbank Memorial Fund, New York, 1946, vol. I, p. 80; or "II. Variations in the Size of Completed Families of 6,551 Native-White Couples in Indianapolis," *Milbank Memorial Fund Quarterly*, vol. 22, no. 1, p. 91, January, 1944.

the earlier cohorts have attended college. It is not related to differences in age at marriage between the education groups.) As we have seen, the younger Catholic women have considerably higher expectations than do the older.

As mentioned earlier (page 280), the number of children expected by many of the young Catholics will probably be reduced later in married life. The reductions may be particularly great for the college-educated wives whose expectations are so high. Several cases of such modifications were reported. For example:

CASE 54. This young Catholic college-educated mother was pregnant when interviewed. This will be her third planned child. At the time of her marriage she and her husband wanted five children, but after the first they decided that three would be enough because they "didn't know how much babies would cost until then. We knew we couldn't take care of more than three."

Another exception to the consistency of the Catholic-Protestant differential in expected births is found among Fecund wives in their 30s who have been employed for 5 or more years. Both the Protestant and Catholic wives in this group expect to have an average of 2.5 births altogether. However, the religious differences in expectations are maintained for Fecund wives who have worked for less than 5 years. Apparently the relationship between prolonged work experience and fertility is similar for both Protestants and Catholics.

In summary, the data collected in the present study show very little difference in the fertility to date of the Catholic and Protestant wives, but suggest that as these wives grow older the differences will widen and the completed families of Catholics will be somewhat larger than those of Protestants. It is apparent that Catholics, despite their generally less careful control of conception, expect to have moderate-sized families not greatly different from those of Protestants. Furthermore, the proportion who did not want their last pregnancy (Excess Fertility) is not significantly different for Protestants and Catholics (14 and 12 per cent, respectively). It would seem that in general Catholics can adhere to the teachings of their Church about contraception and also heed the Church's counsel of "moderation," so that families do not overburden a couple's resources.

The Jewish couples covered in the present study expect significantly fewer children (2.4) than either Catholics (3.4) or Protestants (2.9). Unfortunately, the small size of the Jewish sample (74 respondents) makes detailed comparisons impossible. The low fertility of the Jews in the United States as a whole is apparently attributable in large measure to their concentration in large cities where the fertility of all groups is low. In the 12 largest cities included in the sample, the Jews and the Protestants expect the same average number of births (2.3), but the

Catholics expect 3.1.[5] In the large cities the Jews and Protestants are alike in wanting fewer children than do the Catholics and in using more effective methods of preventing conception (as noted in Chapter 6).

Education

The different rates at which people of varying educational attainment reproduce has long been regarded as one of the more important aspects of fertility analysis. If there is a direct association between educational attainment and inheritable mental ability, higher fertility among the less educated would be expected to decrease the average mental capacity of the population. The significance of educational differences in fertility lies not only in their possible dysgenic consequences, however, but also in the kinds of environment for child growth provided by people of differing educational background. Better educated parents are likely to provide a more stimulating and more constructively oriented environment for their children than are the less educated. Furthermore, the better educated are more likely to encourage their children to extend their education to college or professional school. In view of these considerations, it is reasonable to assume that regardless of whether higher fertility among the better educated tends to raise the average mental ability of the population, it does help to raise educational attainment. Higher fertility among the less educated, on the other hand, promotes an opposite tendency.

The present study indicates that wives of lower educational attainment expect to bear the larger number of children:

Wife's education	No. of wives	Average no. of births			
		By 1955	Expected total		
			Most likely	Minimum	Maximum
College	417	1.8	2.9	2.6	3.2
High school, 4	1,236	1.8	2.9	2.6	3.2
High school, 1–3	681	2.1	3.0	2.7	3.2
Grade school	377	2.9	3.6	3.3	3.8

The greatest difference in expected completed fertility is found between women who did not go beyond grade school and those who went to high school. The differences between the fertility expectations of

[5] The wives who are neither Roman Catholic, Protestant, nor Jewish number only 35 and are about evenly divided among those who have no church preference and those who belong to Eastern Orthodox congregations. Their expected total fertility of 2.6 births is close to that of the Jewish group with whom they are combined in most of the tabulations.

wives with varying amounts of high school and college education are very small. Thus, among the wives whose education extended beyond grade school, who make up a large majority (86 per cent) of the wives interviewed, the number of years spent in school has little effect on expected fertility (Figure 9–2).

These variations in expectations are consistent with the differences in births to date. Not only do the better-educated women expect fewer children altogether, but they had borne fewer by the time of the interview.

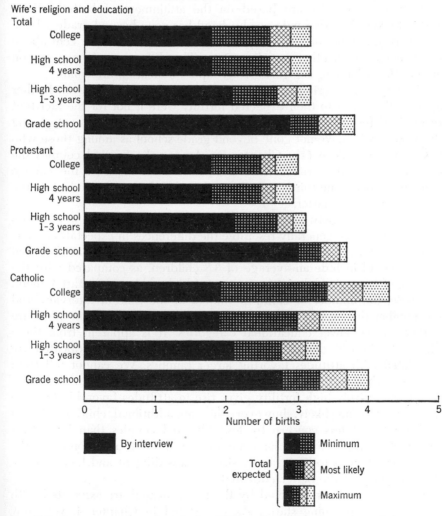

FIG. 9–2. Average number of births by 1955, and total number expected, for wives, by education, by religion.

When the couples are classified by the educational attainment of the husband, rather than of the wife, the differences in prospective family size become smaller. Women whose husbands went no further than grade school expect to have an average of 3.4 births, which is 17 per cent above the average of 2.9 expected by the higher educational categories. This compares with an excess for the grade school group of 24 per cent (3.6 over 2.9 births) when the basis of the classification is the wife's education. The contrast emphasizes the greater influence on family size of the wife's educational attainment than the husband's.

The sharpest differences in fertility expectations are found when the educational categories are based on the attainment of both husband and wife. When neither wife nor husband has gone beyond grade school, the average number of births expected is 4.0, which is 38 per cent above the average of all other couples (2.9). The differences in expectation among the remaining categories for couple's education are small.

The wives of differing educational background would be even further apart with respect to their expected fertility were it not for the fact that recognized fecundity impairments are almost twice as frequent among the women who have not gone beyond grade school as among those who have gone to college (see Chapter 2). Among the Fecund couples the expectations of the grade school women exceed those of the college women by over one-third. For Fecund and Subfecund combined, the excess is only one-quarter.

The differences between the various educational categories in attitudes toward family size generally resemble the differences in expectations. The women who went no further than grade school thought that the ideal family should include an average of 3.8 children, as compared with the average of approximately 3.4 for women of higher educational attainment. Likewise, the number of children wanted at the time of interview and the number that would be wanted if married life could begin anew are higher for the lower educational categories. It is apparent from these differences in attitudes that the larger families of the less educated are associated with attitudes favoring larger families. We cannot tell from our data whether these attitudes influence actual numbers of births or whether relatively high fertility gives rise to attitudes favorable to large families. It seems likely, however, that an additional child is viewed with somewhat less concern by less educated couples than by better-educated couples with the same number of children and, consequently, that their attempts to limit family size are less diligent and less effective than are those of the better educated.

The larger families expected by the less educated are associated with differences in planning status. As was stated in Chapter 4, very few (6 per cent) of the Fecund couples with grade school wives successfully plan both the number and the spacing of their children, whereas over one-third of those with college-educated wives do so. At the other extreme, almost one-third of the Fecund grade school wives have had unplanned and unwanted pregnancies, as compared with only 8 per cent of the Fecund college wives. Furthermore, nearly a third of the less educated wives reported no use of contraception, as compared with only 8 per cent of the college wives. It is clear from these statistics that among the Fecund couples the less educated wives are less interested and less successful than the better educated in limiting their families. This fact accounts for a large portion of the fertility differentials between the educational groups.

Even within the separate planning groups, however, we generally find that the grade school women expect more children than do the others. We cannot be certain about the educational differences in expectations among those classified as Completely Planned, inasmuch as there are too few grade school women in this group to provide a statistically significant average. Among the Fecund high school and college women in this group, however, we find a slight *direct* association between educational attainment and expected fertility (Table 9–9). Another planning group that fails to show the customary inverse relationship between education and average number of births consists of the Fecund couples who have not used contraception and have not yet had what they consider too many pregnancies (Quasi-planned Nonusers). The college wives in this group expect an exceptionally high average number of births (5.3), as compared with 4.8 for women who terminated their education in grade school. The expectations of both groups exceed those of the high school women (3.8 births) by considerable margins. The high expectations of the college wives in this category may be associated with religion. Many of the young well-educated Catholic women qualified for this particular planning category, and their high expectations, noted in a previous section, may bring the average of the college group up to a high level.

The educational differences in expected fertility vary with husband's income. Among couples with low incomes, the wives who have not gone beyond grade school expect almost 30 per cent more births than do the wives who have gone to college (Table 9–10). The relative difference between the educational levels decreases as income rises, however. Among the couples with husband's income $6,000 or more the expectations of the grade school women exceed those of college-educated women by only 18 per cent.

Better-educated wives soon will be having more children than the less educated, if the fertility expectations of the recently married wives are realized. The wives married 10 or more years ago exhibit the historical association between low educational attainment and high fertility, but the more recently married do not do so because of a distinct rise in the expectations of the college-educated women. Among wives married in the 5 years preceding the interview, those with a college education anticipate bearing substantially more children than do those with only a grade school education (3.2 as compared with 2.7 births) (Table 9–11). Although the foundation for such a reversal of the customary differentials may have been laid, whether it occurs will depend on future action. By

TABLE 9–9. AVERAGE NUMBER OF BIRTHS BY 1955, AND OF MOST LIKELY EXPECTED TOTAL BIRTHS, FOR FECUND COUPLES, BY WIFE'S EDUCATION, BY FERTILITY PLANNING STATUS

Fertility planning status	Education				
	Total	College	High school, 4	High school, 1–3	Grade school
Births by 1955					
Total	2.2	1.9	1.9	2.2	3.5
Users:					
Completely Planned	1.2	1.3	1.2	1.3	*
Number Planned	2.5	2.4	2.5	2.5	3.2
Quasi-planned	2.2	2.1	2.1	2.4	2.7
Excess Fertility	3.4	3.4	3.0	2.9	4.8
Nonusers:					
Quasi-planned	1.8	1.4	1.5	1.7	3.2
Excess Fertility	4.8	*	*	*	*
Most likely expected total births					
Total	3.4	3.2	3.2	3.3	4.4
Users:					
Completely Planned	2.6	2.7	2.6	2.4	*
Number Planned	3.4	3.2	3.4	3.4	3.8
Quasi-planned	3.3	3.2	3.3	3.3	3.6
Excess Fertility	3.8	3.7	3.4	3.5	4.9
Nonusers:					
Quasi-planned	4.1	5.3	3.9	3.6	4.8
Excess Fertility	5.8	*	*	*	*

1955, the wives who had not gone beyond grade school had borne more children than those in any other educational category. The number of additional births expected is higher for the better-educated groups, however, and in the case of the wives married for less than 5 years the additional births expected by the college-educated women are enough to bring their expected total slightly above that of the grade school wives. This is due largely to the high expectations of the college-educated

Catholic wives (Figure 9–2). Probably the two most important areas of doubt are (1) whether the young college-educated Catholic wives will actually have the relatively large families that they expect, and (2) whether the young grade school wives will be able to avoid exceeding their relatively low expectations. On the latter point, it should be remembered that the proportion of unintentional conceptions is higher among the less well educated groups (see Chapter 4).

TABLE 9–10. AVERAGE NUMBER OF BIRTHS BY 1955, AND OF MOST LIKELY EXPECTED TOTAL BIRTHS, FOR ALL WIVES, BY EDUCATION, BY HUSBAND'S INCOME

Husband's income	Education				
	Total	College	High school, 4	High school, 1–3	Grade school
Births by 1955					
Total	2.1	1.8	1.8	2.1	2.9
$7,000 or more	2.3	2.1	2.4	3.0 ⎫	2.7
$6,000–$6,999	2.2	1.9	2.1	2.4 ⎭	
$5,000–$5,999	2.0	2.0	2.0	2.1	2.4
$4,000–$4,999	2.1	2.0	1.9	2.3	2.9
$3,000–$3,999	2.0	1.7	1.8	2.1	2.9
Under $3,000	2.0	1.0	1.4	1.9	3.0
Most likely expected total births					
Total	3.0	2.9	2.9	3.0	3.6
$7,000 or more	2.9	2.7	3.1	3.2 ⎫	3.3
$6,000–$6,999	3.0	2.9	2.9	3.1 ⎭	
$5,000–$5,999	2.9	3.0	2.9	2.8	3.0
$4,000–$4,999	3.0	3.0	2.8	3.1	3.5
$3,000–$3,999	3.0	3.0	3.0	2.9	3.5
Under $3,000	3.2	3.0	2.9	3.0	3.9

The possibility of a reversal of the customary educational differences in fertility is also suggested, though not as strongly, when the women are grouped by birth cohort, as in Table 9–12. The grade school wives of the 1931–37 cohorts had already borne more children by interview than the college women, but the college women expect to bear more children altogether.

The prospective narrowing of educational differences in fertility suggested by our data is consistent with the past trend documented by Census Bureau figures. According to data on number of births to women of different ages, collected in the census of 1950, the fertility of married

TABLE 9–11. AVERAGE NUMBER OF BIRTHS BY 1955, AND OF MOST LIKELY EXPECTED TOTAL BIRTHS, FOR ALL WIVES, BY EDUCATION, BY DURATION OF MARRIAGE

Years married	Education				
	Total	College	High school, 4	High school, 1–3	Grade school
Births by 1955					
Total	2.1	1.8	1.8	2.1	2.9
Under 5	0.9	0.8	0.9	1.1	1.2
5–9	2.1	2.1	1.9	2.1	2.5
10–14	2.6	2.4	2.5	2.6	3.1
15 or more	2.9	2.2	2.5	2.7	3.8
Most likely expected total births					
Total	3.0	2.9	2.9	3.0	3.6
Under 5	3.0	3.2	3.0	2.8	2.7
5–9	3.0	3.0	2.8	3.0	3.3
10–14	3.1	2.7	3.0	3.1	3.7
15 or more	3.1	2.4	2.7	3.0	4.1

grade school women in the cohorts of 1890–1905 exceeded that of college women in the same cohorts by approximately 80 per cent.[6] This excess declined to about 65 per cent for the 1905–10 cohorts, and data for younger women suggest a further narrowing to slightly over 55 per cent for the 1910–15 cohorts.

In addition, the proportion of persons in the childbearing ages who have not gone beyond grade school becomes smaller every year. This trend will also contribute to the decline in the proportion of births occurring to parents with low educational status.

The higher expectations of the college wives in the recent than in the earlier cohorts may represent a fundamental change in the attitudes of the better educated toward family size. There are several possible explanations for such a change, for example, the diminishing value of a small family (obtained by contraception) as a status symbol, the increased emphasis in higher education on the psychological advantages of family living, and the upward trend in the incomes of college graduates. In addition, for several decades college students have been coming from a widening range of socioeconomic backgrounds. This trend may increase the proportion of

[6] *United States Census of Population: 1950,* vol. IV, *Special Reports,* pt. 5, chap. C, "Fertility," U.S. Bureau of the Census, 1955, table 21, p. 70. For additional information see Wilson H. Grabill, Clyde V. Kiser, and Pascal K. Whelpton, *Fertility of American Women,* John Wiley & Sons, Inc., New York, 1958.

TABLE 9–12. AVERAGE NUMBER OF BIRTHS BY 1955, AND OF MOST LIKELY EXPECTED TOTAL BIRTHS, FOR ALL WIVES, BY EDUCATION, BY COHORT

Cohort	Education				
	Total	College	High school, 4	High school, 1–3	Grade school
Births by 1955					
Total	2.1	1.8	1.8	2.1	2.9
1931–37	1.1	0.8	0.9	1.4	1.6
1926–30	1.9	1.6	1.7	2.3	2.5
1921–25	2.3	2.0	2.2	2.3	3.1
1916–20	2.6	2.4	2.3	2.4	3.4
Most likely expected total births					
Total	3.0	2.9	2.9	3.0	3.6
1931–37	3.2	3.5	3.1	3.0	3.3
1926–30	3.1	3.0	2.9	3.3	3.5
1921–25	3.0	2.6	3.0	2.9	3.6
1916–20	2.9	2.7	2.6	2.7	3.7

college-educated women from those segments of the population wanting relatively many children. We cannot tell from the information collected in the present study what explanation is the most important, but all the four mentioned seem to have been operating. It is a matter of common observation that today's college graduates have immensely better immediate economic prospects than did the graduates of the 1930s. As a result, they are marrying and beginning their families at an earlier age than did the college graduates of a generation earlier. A substantial number even have a child before they have completed their education, a practice that was very uncommon in the 1930s. Furthermore, many more of today's college men and women have been exposed to courses on marriage and the family, so may be better prepared to rear children and more confident of their ability to do so successfully than were the college graduates of 20 to 30 years ago. Regardless of the causes behind the apparent shift in the attitudes of the college-trained women toward family size, it is a healthy sign for the quality of the American population.

Income and Occupation

The significance of economic differences in fertility is similar to that of educational differences. If inheritable mental ability is associated with income, as may be the case, higher fertility among people with low incomes tends to reduce the average intelligence of the population. Whether such a relationship exists or not, it is certain that people with lower incomes are less able to provide their children with good medical attention, a healthy environment in which to develop, and advanced education. Historically, the people with the higher incomes were probably among the first to reduce fertility significantly. Such people have been better informed about methods of contraception and more highly motivated to limit the size of their families than the lower-income groups. There are several possible factors that may have led the higher-income groups to have fewer children. One important cause may have been the fact that children represent an economic burden impeding social mobility. Another possible reason is the location of many of the couples with higher incomes in large cities where fertility is usually low. Still another factor may be the less familistic orientation of the economically advantaged classes. It must not be supposed that they have been uninterested in their children, but they have had other cultural interests, probably resulting from their better education, that may have reduced the importance of large families. Whatever the reasons for the development of economic class differences in fertility, they have long been observed in the industrialized nations of the West, among them the United States.

The present study indicates that even though there are still differences in the fertility of the various income groups, they are very small:

Current annual income of husband	No. of wives	Average no. of births			
		By 1955	Expected total		
			Most likely	Minimum	Maximum
$7,000 or more	244	2.3	2.9	2.7	3.2
$6,000–$6,999	186	2.2	3.0	2.8	3.1
$5,000–$5,999	393	2.0	2.9	2.6	3.1
$4,000–$4,999	583	2.1	3.0	2.7	3.2
$3,000–$3,999	619	2.0	3.0	2.7	3.3
Under $3,000	581	2.0	3.2	2.9	3.5

The women whose husbands were currently making less than $3,000 per year expect to have significantly higher fertility than do the wives of husbands with greater incomes, but the difference is not large (Figure 9–3). The average number of children born by 1955 was actually larger for the high-income groups than for those with low incomes, but this differential is due to the influence of age—the higher-income couples are

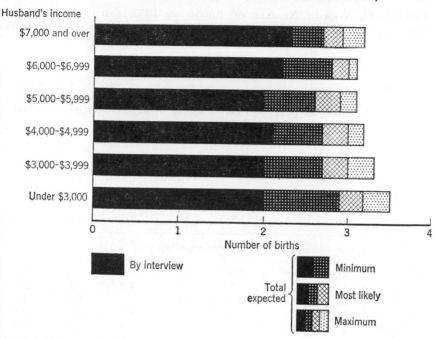

Husband's income

$7,000 and over
$6,000-$6,999
$5,000-$5,999
$4,000-$4,999
$3,000-$3,999
Under $3,000

0   1   2   3   4

Number of births

By interview

Total expected { Minimum / Most likely / Maximum }

FIG. 9–3. Average number of births by 1955, and total number expected, for wives, by husband's income.

older, and so the wives had an opportunity to bear more children by the time of the interview.

Small differences between the expected fertility of the various income groups are also found when the wives are grouped by cohorts (Table 9–13). These differences are slightly larger and more consistent for the earlier cohorts (1916–20) than for the later cohorts, but the variations do not warrant any clear-cut statements about intercohort changes in the relationship of income to fertility.

Similarly, the differences in expected fertility by income groups are larger for wives who have been married longer (10 years or more) than for those married fewer years (Table 9–14). Moreover, while the relationship between income and expected size of completed family is inverse among women married 5 years or more, it appears U-shaped for shorter durations; i.e., the larger families are expected by those with low and high incomes and the smaller families by those with middle incomes.

The economic differences in expected births are concentrated largely among the Fecund, who constitute about two-thirds of each income group. No significant differences in expectations among the income classes are found for couples whose fecundity is impaired.

TABLE 9–13. AVERAGE NUMBER OF BIRTHS BY 1955, AND OF MOST LIKELY EXPECTED TOTAL BIRTHS, FOR ALL WIVES, BY COHORT, BY HUSBAND'S INCOME

| Cohort | Husband's income | | | | | | |
	Total	$7,000 or more	$6,000– $6,999	$5,000– $5,999	$4,000– $4,999	$3,000– $3,999	Under $3,000
	Births by 1955						
Total	2.1	2.3	2.2	2.0	2.1	2.0	2.0
1931–37	1.1	*	*	1.2	1.4	1.1	1.0
1926–30	1.9	2.2	1.6	1.9	1.8	2.0	2.0
1921–25	2.3	2.3	2.6	2.2	2.3	2.4	2.5
1916–20	2.6	2.5	2.5	2.4	2.6	2.5	2.9
	Most likely expected total births						
Total	3.0	2.9	3.0	2.9	3.0	3.0	3.2
1931–37	3.2	*	*	3.1	3.2	3.1	3.2
1926–30	3.1	3.5	2.8	3.0	3.0	3.2	3.3
1921–25	3.0	2.9	3.1	2.9	3.0	2.9	3.1
1916–20	2.9	2.8	3.0	2.7	2.8	2.8	3.2

TABLE 9–14. AVERAGE NUMBER OF BIRTHS BY 1955, AND OF MOST LIKELY EXPECTED TOTAL BIRTHS, FOR ALL WIVES, BY DURATION OF MARRIAGE, BY HUSBAND'S INCOME

| Years married | Husband's income | | | | | | |
	Total	$7,000 or more	$6,000– $6,999	$5,000– $5,999	$4,000– $4,999	$3,000– $3,999	Under $3,000
	Births by 1955						
Total	2.1	2.3	2.2	2.0	2.1	2.0	2.0
Under 5	0.9	1.1	1.1	1.0	0.9	1.0	0.8
5–9	2.1	2.0	2.1	1.9	2.1	2.1	2.1
10–14	2.6	2.6	2.7	2.6	2.4	2.6	2.8
15 or more	2.9	2.7	2.5	2.6	3.1	3.0	3.0
	Most likely expected total births						
Total	3.0	2.9	3.0	2.9	3.0	3.0	3.2
Under 5	3.0	3.3	3.0	2.9	2.8	3.0	3.1
5–9	3.0	2.8	2.9	2.8	3.1	3.0	3.1
10–14	3.1	3.0	3.1	3.0	2.9	3.1	3.4
15 or more	3.1	2.8	2.9	2.8	3.3	3.1	3.3

Differences in the extent to which families are planned are closely associated with economic differentials in expected numbers of births. Nearly one-third of the Fecund couples with husbands making $7,000 or more per year have planned both the number and the spacing of their pregnancies, as contrasted with only one-fifth of the Fecund couples in the lowest-income group. Similarly, a quarter of the high-income couples but only one-eighth of the low-income couples among the Fecund have Number Planned fertility (see Chapter 3). Within the separate planning categories, the income differentials in expected fertility virtually disappear (Table 9–15). Clearly, the small income differentials that do exist are related to the differences in the extent and effectiveness of family limitation practices, and not to differences in number of children wanted.

Replies to the questions on attitudes toward family size indicate that among the older wives, relatively more of those in the low-income group

TABLE 9–15. AVERAGE NUMBER OF BIRTHS BY 1955, AND OF MOST LIKELY EXPECTED TOTAL BIRTHS, FOR FECUND COUPLES, BY HUSBAND'S INCOME, BY FERTILITY PLANNING STATUS

Fertility planning status		Husband's income					
	Total	$7,000 or more	$6,000–$6,999	$5,000–$5,999	$4,000–$4,999	$3,000–$3,999	Under $3,000
Births by 1955							
Total	2.2	2.6	2.3	2.1	2.3	2.1	2.0
Users:							
Completely Planned	1.2	1.8	1.5	1.3	1.3	1.1	0.8
Number Planned	2.5	3.1	2.5	2.4	2.4	2.5	2.3
Quasi-planned	2.2	2.6	2.2	2.3	2.4	2.2	1.8
Excess Fertility	3.4	3.7		2.7	3.5	3.2	3.6
Nonusers:							
Quasi-planned	1.8	*	*	*	2.1	1.9	1.6
Excess Fertility	4.8	*	*	*	*	5.0	
Most likely expected total births							
Total	3.4	3.4	3.2	3.2	3.4	3.3	3.6
Users:							
Completely Planned	2.6	2.6	2.5	2.5	2.5	2.7	2.8
Number Planned	3.4	3.8	3.2	3.4	3.3	3.4	3.5
Quasi-planned	3.3	3.5	3.3	3.1	3.4	3.4	3.1
Excess Fertility	3.8	4.0		3.2	3.9	3.4	4.1
Nonusers:							
Quasi-planned	4.1	*	*	*	4.2	3.9	4.2
Excess Fertility	5.8	*	*	*	*	6.1	

favor larger families than of those with higher incomes. Among the
women of the 1916–20 cohorts—the oldest interviewed—those whose
husbands make less than $3,000 per year stated an average of 3.8 children
as the number they considered ideal, and those with husbands in the
higher-income groups stated 3.3. In contrast, the average number of
births wanted at the time of interview does not differ significantly between the economic groups. The average wanted by the lowest-income
group is 3.3, a figure well below their ideal of 3.8, whereas the average
wanted by women with higher incomes is 3.1. Evidently many of the
poorer women in the 1916–20 cohorts wanted for themselves smaller
families than they considered as ideal for others.

The income differentials in expected numbers of births are greater
among Catholics than Protestants. Protestant wives in the low-income
group (under $3,000 per year) expect only slightly more births than
do those in the higher-income group (3.0 as compared with 2.8), but the
poorer Catholic wives expect a substantially larger average number of
births than do those with higher incomes (3.7 as compared with 3.3)
(Table 9–16). This difference between the two major religious groups is
very probably due to differences in their attitudes toward, and use of,
family limitation measures.

TABLE 9–16. AVERAGE NUMBER OF BIRTHS BY 1955, AND OF MOST LIKELY
EXPECTED TOTAL BIRTHS, FOR ALL WIVES, BY RELIGION, BY HUSBAND'S IN-
COME

Religion	Total	Husband's income					
		$7,000 or more	$6,000–$6,999	$5,000–$5,999	$4,000–$4,999	$3,000–$3,999	Under $3,000
Births by 1955							
Total	2.1	2.3	2.2	2.0	2.1	2.0	2.0
Protestant	2.1	2.3	2.2	2.0	2.1	2.1	2.0
Catholic	2.1	2.6	2.2	2.2	2.2	2.0	2.0
Other	1.6	1.8	1.5		1.6	1.6	
Most likely expected total births							
Total	3.0	2.9	3.0	2.9	3.0	3.0	3.2
Protestant	2.9	2.9	2.8	2.7	2.8	2.9	3.0
Catholic	3.4	3.4	3.6	3.2	3.4	3.3	3.7
Other	2.4	2.4	2.5		*	2.8	

Even though the Catholic wives in the lower-income groups *expect*
more births than do those in the higher-income groups, they would *prefer*

to have fewer births than would those with higher incomes. Catholic women married to husbands with incomes under $3,000 per year said that they would like to have an average of 3.4 to 3.6 births (compared with 3.7 expected); those married to husbands with incomes of $7,000 or more said that they wanted an average of 3.9 to 4.1 births (compared with 3.4 expected). Apparently the desires of the Catholics with higher incomes are more consistent with the Church's attitudes in favor of relatively large families than are the desires of the poorer Catholics. In spite of their stated desire for more children, however, Catholic wives in high-income groups expect fewer births than do those in low-income groups. Similar differences between expectations and desires are not found for Protestants.

In a prior section we saw that the extent of educational differences in fertility is related to economic status. Conversely, the economic differences in fertility change with educational status. Such differences in expected fertility are greater among wives whose education did not extend beyond grade school than they are for those who have more education (Table 9–10). Apparently, higher income encourages members of the grade school group to want fewer children, find out about contraception, and limit their fertility. Income does not appear to influence very strongly the expected fertility of women who have gone to high school or college. This may reflect the more nearly equal aspirations and access to birth control information for all women who have gone beyond grade school.

Thus far in the discussion of economic differences in fertility we have used the husband's income as an index of economic position. When we consider family income,[7] rather than husband's income only, we find a somewhat stronger relationship between income and fertility:

Annual income of family	No. of wives	Average most likely expected total births
$7,000 or more	405	2.7
$6,000–$6,999	271	2.8
$5,000–$5,999	444	2.9
$4,000–$4,999	544	3.1
$3,000–$3,999	532	3.2
Under $3,000	429	3.4

When family income is used as an index of economic status, the difference in fertility expectations between the highest- and lowest-income

[7] In the large majority of cases, family income consists of husband's income, or husband's income plus wife's income. In only a few cases in this study were other members of the family reported as contributing to its support.

groups considered is 0.7 births. When husband's income is used, the difference is only 0.3 births.

Using family income, we find the traditional fertility differences: the high-income families have fewer children than the low-income families. This relationship holds good with only minor inconsistencies when wives are classified according to their birth cohort (Table 9–17), although it is strongest for the oldest cohorts. The apparent reversal of the relationship for the 1931–37 cohorts, which show the highest-income group to have the highest expectations, is not statistically significant because our sample contains only 27 couples in these cohorts with incomes of $7,000 or more. Nevertheless, the weakness of the relationship between family income and fertility expectations for the younger cohorts does suggest that even this differential is destined to disappear.

TABLE 9–17. AVERAGE NUMBER OF BIRTHS BY 1955, AND OF MOST LIKELY EXPECTED TOTAL BIRTHS, FOR ALL WIVES, BY COHORT, BY FAMILY INCOME

Cohort	Family income						
	Total	$7,000 or more	$6,000–$6,999	$5,000–$5,999	$4,000–$4,999	$3,000–$3,999	Under $3,000
	Births by 1955						
Total	2.1	1.8	2.0	2.0	2.1	2.2	2.2
1931–37	1.1	0.8	1.0	0.9	1.2	1.2	1.2
1926–30	1.9	1.4	1.4	1.9	1.9	2.3	2.3
1921–25	2.3	1.9	2.3	2.2	2.4	2.5	2.8
1916–20	2.6	2.2	2.6	2.3	2.7	2.7	3.1
	Most likely expected total births						
Total	3.0	2.7	2.8	2.9	3.1	3.2	3.4
1931–37	3.2	3.6	3.0	3.0	3.1	3.1	3.2
1926–30	3.1	2.9	2.4	3.0	3.0	3.4	3.5
1921–25	3.0	2.5	2.9	2.8	3.1	3.1	3.4
1916–20	2.9	2.5	3.1	2.7	3.0	3.0	3.4

Why is the relationship of fertility to income somewhat stronger when family income rather than husband's income is used as the basis of classification? It is because the couples with low family incomes are more likely to be those in which the wife does not work and has relatively many births, while the couples with high family incomes are more heavily weighted with those that include working wives who have relatively few children.

Because the strong relationship of fertility to family income is due primarily to the influence of the wife's employment status and not to the family income *per se,* we cannot say that family income alone has much influence on fertility.

One-quarter of the wives were gainfully employed at the time of the interview, and three-quarters of these working wives had full-time jobs. These figures, however, do not describe the full extent to which a job and marriage have been combined, for we find that over two-thirds of the wives in each cohort have been gainfully employed at some time since marriage. Of course, the length of time they have worked varies considerably. The youngest women (1931–37 cohorts) have been married too recently to have worked very long while married—68 per cent of them have worked, but few have worked as long as five years. In contrast, among the oldest women interviewed (1916–20 cohorts), a majority (58 per cent) have worked for at least 1 year during their married life, and nearly one-third of them have worked 5 or more years.

The causal relationship between wife's work experience and fertility can be viewed in two ways. Among the Subfecund, it seems likely that a small family leaves the wife free to take a job that she might not otherwise have sought. Among the Fecund, on the other hand, the advantages of gainful employment may motivate working wives to keep their families small. The fertility expectations of both the Fecund and the Subfecund support these conjectures, for in each group we find that the wives who have never worked have had more births and expect more births than those who have. In addition, the wives who have worked for longer periods of time have generally had fewer births and expect fewer than those who have worked for shorter periods (Table 9–18 and Figure 9–4).

TABLE 9–18. AVERAGE NUMBER OF BIRTHS BY 1955, AND OF MOST LIKELY EXPECTED TOTAL BIRTHS, FOR ALL WIVES, BY NUMBER OF YEARS WIFE WORKED SINCE MARRIAGE, BY FECUNDITY OF COUPLE

Fecundity	Years wife worked since marriage				
	Total	None	Less than 1	1–4	5 or more
Births by 1955					
Total	2.1	2.5	1.9	1.9	1.6
Fecund	2.2	2.6	1.8	2.0	2.0
Subfecund	1.9	2.3	2.1	1.8	1.3
Most likely expected total births					
Total	3.0	3.5	3.2	3.0	2.1
Fecund	3.4	3.7	3.4	3.2	2.6
Subfecund	2.3	2.8	2.3	2.4	1.8

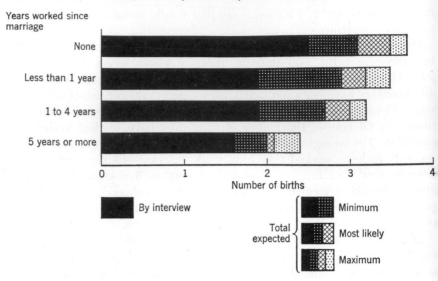

Fɪɢ. 9–4. Average number of births by 1955, and total number expected, for wives, by years worked since marriage.

The following case illustrates the attitudes of many Fecund working wives:

Cᴀsᴇ 55. This mother worked until 3 months before the birth of her first child, which occurred 2 months before the interview. She plans to return to work in a year and then have only one more child a little later. She doesn't want more than two children because she wants to work to help provide for her family. "I want them to have things nice. I don't believe in having children and not being able to support them right. My own family was too big. I want a career. I like to work. I don't sew and do those things like other women do at home." In the previous year she earned $3,000 and her husband earned $5,000.

The relationship between expected fertility and the length of time the wife has worked is similar for women of all birth cohorts but the most recent (1931–37). Among these young women, those who have worked expect to have very nearly the same average number of births as those who have not (3.1 as compared with 3.2), and there is no difference between the expectations of those who have worked less than a year and those who have worked for longer periods (Table 9–19). As these women become older, however, the wider differentials found for the older women may develop.

Longer work experience of the wife is related to lower fertility for Fecund couples in virtually all segments of the population, for we continue to find the relationship when these couples are classified by such

TABLE 9–19. AVERAGE NUMBER OF BIRTHS BY 1955, AND OF MOST LIKELY EXPECTED TOTAL BIRTHS, FOR ALL WIVES, BY COHORT, BY NUMBER OF YEARS WIFE WORKED SINCE MARRIAGE

Cohort	Years wife worked since marriage				
	Total	None	Less than 1	1–4	5 or more
	Births by 1955				
Total	2.1	2.5	1.9	1.9	1.6
1931–37	1.1	1.4	0.9	1.1	*
1926–30	1.9	2.4	2.0	1.7	1.2
1921–25	2.3	2.7	2.6	2,3	1.6
1916–20	2.6	3.2	3.1	2.5	1.8
	Most likely expected total births				
Total	3.0	3.5	3.2	3.0	2.1
1931–37	3.2	3.2	3.1	3.1	*
1926–30	3.1	3.6	3.1	3.0	2.2
1921–25	3.0	3.4	3.3	2.9	2.2
1916–20	2.9	3.6	3.3	2.8	2.1

variables as duration of marriage, educational attainment and religion of wife, and husband's income.[8] It is clear, then, that the wife's employment history is of fundamental importance in the analysis of fertility.

Another economic variable associated with fertility is husband's occupation. In some respects, occupation differentiates social groups more sharply than does income. For example, there are probably greater differences in the ways of life of mechanics and lawyers in the same income class than between lawyers in different income classes (except when the very high- and very low-income groups are compared). For the purposes of fertility analysis, it is especially important to isolate farmers in view of their comparatively high reproductivity. The wives of farmers and farm laborers included in the present study expect a substantially larger average number of births than do the wives of husbands having other occupations, as is shown at the top of page 306.

Among the nonfarm groups, there is a slight relationship between occupation and expected fertility, but it is not great (Figure 9–5).

The occupational differences in expected fertility are much greater for the earlier cohorts than for the more recent cohorts, which suggests that a definite narrowing of the occupational differences in fertility is

[8] Jeanne Clare Ridley, *The Relationship of Non-familial Activities to Fertility Behavior,* Ph.D. dissertation in sociology, University of Michigan, Ann Arbor, Mich., 1957.

Husband's occupation	No. of wives	Average no. of births			
		By 1955	Expected total		
			Most likely	Minimum	Maximum
Upper white collar	620	1.9	2.8	2.6	3.1
Lower white collar	286	1.9	2.8	2.6	3.1
Upper blue collar	644	2.1	2.9	2.7	3.2
Lower blue collar	765	2.2	3.1	2.8	3.3
Farm	242	2.7	3.7	3.3	3.9
Armed forces	124	1.4	2.9	2.7	3.2
Other	32	1.2	3.5	3.0	3.8

under way. This narrowing is being brought about by the operation of two opposite trends: a rise in the expected fertility of the higher-status nonfarm occupations (white collar) and a lowering of the expectations of the wives of farmers and farm laborers. The expectations of the lower-status nonfarm occupations (blue collar) show no significant upward or downward trend. The prospective rise in the fertility of the higher-status

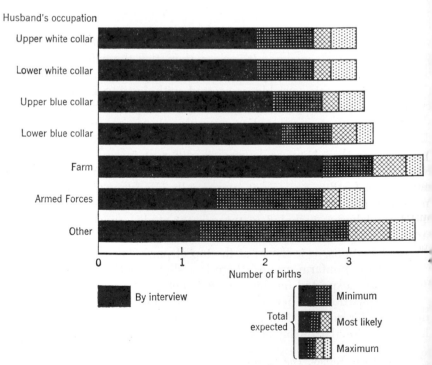

Fig. 9–5. Average number of births by 1955, and total number expected, for wives by husband's occupation.

nonfarm occupations is illustrated by the cohort trend in the number of births expected by wives of men in the upper-white-collar occupations (professional men, proprietors, managers, and officials). The expectations of such women rise from 2.5 births for the 1916–20 cohorts to 3.4 births for the 1931–37 cohorts (Table 9–20). The expectations of the lower-

TABLE 9–20. AVERAGE NUMBER OF BIRTHS BY 1955, AND OF MOST LIKELY EXPECTED TOTAL BIRTHS, FOR ALL WIVES, BY COHORT, BY HUSBAND'S OCCUPATION

Cohort		Husband's occupation					
	Total	Upper white collar	Lower white collar	Upper blue collar	Lower blue collar	Farm	Other
			Births by 1955				
Total	2.1	1.9	1.9	2.1	2.2	2.7	1.4
1931–37	1.1	1.2	1.1	1.2	1.2	1.4	0.7
1926–30	1.9	1.7	1.7	1.9	2.1	2.5	1.9
1921–25	2.3	2.0	2.3	2.4	2.5	2.4	2.3
1916–20	2.6	2.3	2.2	2.4	2.7	3.8	*
			Most likely expected total births				
Total	3.0	2.8	2.8	2.9	3.1	3.7	3.1
1931–37	3.2	3.4	3.1	2.9	3.1	3.6	3.2
1926–30	3.1	3.0	2.8	3.1	3.1	3.7	2.9
1921–25	3.0	2.7	2.9	3.1	3.1	3.1	2.8
1916–20	2.9	2.5	2.7	2.7	3.0	4.2	*

white-collar and skilled occupations also rise, but not as sharply. Such trends probably reflect an increasing emphasis on family-oriented values among the higher-status nonfarm occupations. The expectations of the wives of farmers and farm laborers, in contrast, fall from 4.2 births for women in the 1916–20 cohorts to 3.6 births for those in the 1931–37 cohorts.[9] This trend suggests that the increasing adoption of urban values on the part of the farm population has affected attitudes favoring smaller families. There are even examples of young farm couples in "backward" rural areas who expect to have small families:

CASE 56. The husband is a sharecropper in a poor Southern farm area. In 1954 the family's income was $1,500, about $1,000 of which was earned by

[9] This decline is irregular, being interrupted by a sharp drop to 3.1 for the 1921–25 cohorts and a rise to 3.7 for the 1926–30 cohorts. It is believed that the low average expectation for the 1921–25 cohorts is an anomaly due to sampling variability. This opinion is supported by the regular intercohort trends in expectations for couples living on farms (Table 9–23).

the husband and the rest by the wife. They had been married for two years at the time of the interview and as yet had no children, although the wife had had a miscarriage the previous year. They would like to have three children and expect to use contraception after having one or two. They want to limit their family size because, according to the wife, "Three's aplenty. We don't want no big families like we came from. Life is too hard for the kids that way." She had 11 brothers and sisters.

Apparently, income has little effect on occupational differences in expected fertility, except among upper-white-collar workers where there appears to be a direct relationship. Within each income category we find that the farm wives expect the highest average number of births and that income has little influence on expectations of other broad occupational categories (Table 9–21).

TABLE 9–21. AVERAGE NUMBER OF BIRTHS BY 1955, AND OF MOST LIKELY EXPECTED TOTAL BIRTHS, FOR ALL WIVES, BY HUSBAND'S INCOME, BY HUSBAND'S OCCUPATION

Husband's income	Husband's occupation						
	Total	Upper white collar	Lower white collar	Upper blue collar	Lower blue collar	Farm	Other
Births by 1955							
Total	2.1	1.9	1.9	2.1	2.2	2.7	1.4
$7,000 or more	2.3	2.3	*	2.0	*	2.9	*
$6,000–$6,999	2.2	1.8	*	2.3	2.2	*	*
$5,000–$5,999	2.0	1.8	2.0	2.1	2.1	2.4	*
$4,000–$4,999	2.1	1.9	1.8	2.1	2.1	3.4	*
$3,000–$3,999	2.0	1.6	1.6	2.1	2.1	3.0	1.5
Under $3,000	2.0	1.7	2.0	1.9	2.3	2.3	1.0
Most likely expected total births							
Total	3.0	2.8	2.8	2.9	3.1	3.7	3.1
$7,000 or more	2.9	3.0	*	2.4	*	3.7	*
$6,000–$6,999	3.0	2.8	*	2.8	3.0	*	*
$5,000–$5,999	2.9	2.8	2.8	3.0	2.8	3.1	*
$4,000–$4,999	3.0	2.8	2.7	3.0	3.1	4.0	*
$3,000–$3,999	3.0	2.9	2.8	3.0	3.0	3.8	2.8
Under $3,000	3.2	2.8	3.1	2.9	3.3	3.6	3.2

When the broad occupation groups are subdivided into smaller and more homogeneous categories, a few additional differences in expected fertility emerge. One is within the farm group, the wives of farm laborers expecting more births than the wives of farmers (4.0 as compared with 3.6 births). A breakdown of the nonfarm occupations shows that the wives of unskilled laborers expect more births (3.6 on the average) than do the women in other groups, but the differences in expectation between wives of professional men, proprietors, clerks, salesmen, craftsmen, service employees, etc., are all very small and of doubtful significance. Even the wives of men in the professional category, often regarded as the highest-status group, reported an expected average of 2.9 births, which is almost the same as the 3.0 births expected by the total sample. It must be remembered, however, that these comparisons relate to women of all ages. A classification of the expectations of detailed occupational classes for each cohort might reveal some interesting differences. Unfortunately, the small size of the sample makes it impossible to obtain statistically significant averages for such small groups.

Economic differentials in fertility have become very small. This may be a temporary condition brought about by the relative prosperity of the postwar period, but it seems more probable that it represents the culmination of the long-time trend in the dissemination of knowledge about methods of controlling conception to additional segments of the population—particularly those with low incomes. Certainly it can be said that the distribution of children by income groups is now more "rational" than it was formerly when the differentials between the various economic classes were much wider. Perhaps the further spread of information about contraception will eventually bring about a reversal of the income differences in fertility.

Residence

Place of residence is associated, in varying degree, with many of the socioeconomic variables discussed in the preceding sections of this chapter. For example, Catholics tend to live in the larger cities where millions of Catholic immigrants settled early in the present century. Farmers reside in the open country, and college graduates are drawn to towns and cities. Because of such relationships alone, significant differences would be expected in the fertility of couples living in cities, towns, and rural areas. In addition, the different ways of life associated with residence in different kinds of areas affect family size. Rural-urban differences in fertility are, of course, familiar to most people. Not only statistics but informal observation continually verifies the impression that farm families are larger than city families. In the past, this differential was associated in part with the different roles of farm and city children. For farmers, until more recently than for men in most other occupations, children represented not only a source of much-needed labor but also the assurance of an economically secure old age. The business ventures of most people living in towns and cities, in contrast, tended less and less to be family enterprises; consequently, large families came to be regarded less as assets than as burdens. Certainly economic considerations were not the only factors that lowered the size of urban families, but they were undoubtedly of great importance. Even among people living in urban areas there has been an association between city size and fertility, with smaller communities having larger families, on the average.

The social and economic differences between farm and city are now much less distinct than they once were. Urban areas, too, have become culturally and economically more homogeneous than they were in the past. Greatly increased communication between city and town has brought people closer together not only physically and economically, but also with respect to their values and attitudes. Such changes might be expected to have a significant effect on residential differences in fertility.

The present study indicates that wives who live on farms still expect substantially larger families than those living elsewhere:

Residence[a]	No. of wives	Average no. of births			
		By 1955	Expected total		
			Most likely	Minimum	Maximum
Metropolitan areas:					
12 largest cities	337	1.7	2.8	2.5	3.0
Other large cities	517	1.9	2.9	2.6	3.2
Suburbs of largest cities	318	2.1	3.0	2.8	3.2
Other suburbs	397	2.1	2.9	2.6	3.1
Nonmetropolitan areas:					
Small cities	429	1.9	2.9	2.7	3.1
Rural nonfarm	431	2.3	3.1	2.9	3.4
Farm	284	2.8	3.7	3.4	4.0

[a] For definitions see Appendix A, Note 14.

The women who live in rural areas but not on farms expect slightly more births than those living in towns and cities, but the difference is not great (Figure 9–6).

Wives living in the 12 largest cities of the United States expect to have fewer children than those living elsewhere, but their expectations do not differ greatly from those of wives living in other cities or in suburban areas. One of the reasons for this small difference is the high proportion of Catholics in the 12 largest cities, where they account for slightly more than half of all white wives aged 18–39. Among Catholic women, those

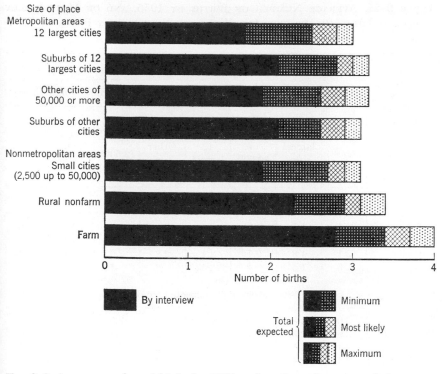

Fɪɢ. 9–6. Average number of births by 1955, and total number expected, for wives, by size of place of present residence.

in the 12 largest cities expect 3.1 births, or only one-sixteenth below the 3.3 births expected by those in other urban or suburban areas (Table 9–22). Protestant women in the 12 largest cities, however, expect an average of only 2.3 births, which is about one-sixth lower than the 2.8 births expected by Protestant women in other urban or suburban areas. Clearly, city size is more closely related to the fertility of Protestants than to that of Catholics.

The development of suburbs has aroused a great deal of interest in recent decades because more and more Americans are moving to them. Suburbs offer many advantages for family living that are not usually found in large cities: they are less densely populated, many families can afford to live in detached houses or in relatively large apartments, and often there is more room for children to play and more adequate schools than are available in cities. In view of these features, it would seem reasonable to expect suburban couples to have somewhat larger families than couples located in large cities. The present study indicates that wives living in the suburbs of the 12 largest cities expect slightly more births than do wives living in the central cities themselves, but the

TABLE 9–22. AVERAGE NUMBER OF BIRTHS BY 1955, AND OF MOST LIKELY EXPECTED TOTAL BIRTHS, FOR ALL WIVES, BY RELIGION, BY PLACE OF RESIDENCE

Religion	Total	Metropolitan areas				Nonmetropolitan areas		
		12 largest cities	Other cities of 50,000 or more	Suburbs of:		Small cities (2,500– 50,000)	Rural non- farm	Farm
				12 largest cities	Other large cities			
Births by 1955								
Total	2.1	1.7	1.9	2.1	2.1	1.9	2.3	2.8
Protestant	2.1	1.6	1.8	2.0	2.1	1.8	2.2	2.8
Catholic	2.1	1.8	2.1	2.1	2.2	2.0	2.4	2.9
Other	1.6	1.5	*	*	*	*	*	*
Most likely expected total births								
Total	3.0	2.8	2.9	3.0	2.9	2.9	3.1	3.7
Protestant	2.9	2.3	2.7	2.9	2.8	2.8	2.9	3.6
Catholic	3.4	3.1	3.3	3.3	3.2	3.4	3.9	4.4
Other	2.4	2.4	*	*	*	*	*	*

difference between these two groups is surprisingly small (3.0 births expected by the suburban women, as compared with 2.8 expected by those living in the central cities). Again, part of this difference is due to the relatively small influence of city residence on the expected fertility of Catholics. Among Protestants, however, residence in the suburbs of the 12 largest cities, rather than in the cities themselves, has a pronounced association with expected fertility, as is shown in Table 9–22. There is little evidence as yet regarding the cause-effect aspects of this association —whether Protestant couples move to the suburbs because they want more children, or whether living in the suburbs leads them to want more. Each probably is important.

If we exclude the 12 largest cities and compare the women living in other cities of 50,000 or more with the women living in the suburbs of these smaller cities, we find no significant difference in the fertility expectations of the city and suburban groups, either for Protestants or Catholics. Apparently the relative advantages provided for families by suburban living are greater in the larger than in the smaller metropolitan areas.

The residential differences in expected fertility, like the differences for the various educational and economic categories, appear to be narrowing. This narrowing is being accomplished by a rising trend in the expected fertility of wives living in urban and suburban areas and a downward trend in the expected fertility of farm wives. The intermediate group—rural nonfarm—shows no definite upward or downward trend. These tendencies are inferred from the replies of women belonging to the different cohorts (Table 9–23). Among the oldest women interviewed (1916–20 cohorts), the rural-urban differences in expected births are quite wide, although the differences between women in the various urban categories are small. Among the youngest women (1931–37 cohorts), however, the rural-urban differences in expected fertility are neither consistent nor statistically significant. In fact, the women of the 1931–37 cohorts who live in the 12 largest cities expect more births (3.3) than those in other urban and suburban categories (3.1). This reflects in part the influence of the young Catholic women. As was noted earlier, these women are concentrated in the largest cities and expect more births than are likely to occur, judging from the reports of older Catholic women.

TABLE 9–23. AVERAGE NUMBER OF BIRTHS BY 1955, AND OF MOST LIKELY EXPECTED TOTAL BIRTHS, FOR ALL WIVES, BY COHORT, BY PLACE OF RESIDENCE

Cohort		Place of residence						
		Metropolitan areas				Nonmetropolitan areas		
	Total	12 largest cities	Other cities of 50,000 or more	Suburbs of:		Small cities (2,500–50,000)	Rural non-farm	Farm
				12 largest cities	Other large cities			
Births by 1955								
Total	2.1	1.7	1.9	2.1	2.1	1.9	2.3	2.8
1931–37	1.1	1.0	1.0	1.1	1.4	0.8	1.2	1.2
1926–30	1.9	1.3	1.6	2.0	2.2	1.8	2.2	2.4
1921–25	2.3	2.0	2.3	2.3	2.2	2.1	2.7	2.9
1916–20	2.6	2.1	2.4	2.4	2.3	2.5	2.7	4.0
Most likely expected total births								
Total	3.0	2.8	2.9	3.0	2.9	2.9	3.1	3.7
1931–37	3.2	3.3	3.1	3.1	3.2	3.1	3.0	3.3
1926–30	3.1	2.8	2.9	3.2	3.1	3.2	3.1	3.5
1921–25	3.0	2.6	2.9	3.0	2.7	2.8	3.3	3.6
1916–20	2.9	2.5	2.7	2.7	2.5	2.7	3.1	4.2

The influence of type of place of residence on fertility might be more adequately investigated with the use of a residential classification based on the place of longest residence since marriage, rather than on the place of residence at the time of the interview. The latter basis is used in the foregoing discussion because the various urban and suburban classes can be defined more easily than if place of longest residence after marriage is used. It is possible, however, to classify place of longest residence for two broad groups of cities (those having populations of 50,000 or more and those having populations of 2,500 up to 50,000) as well as for farm and rural nonfarm residence. When this is done, we find that the differentials in expected fertility are much the same as those based on place of present residence:

Place of residence after marriage	Average most likely expected total number of births for wives classified by:	
	Present residence	Longest residence
Cities of 50,000 or more	2.9	2.7
Cities of 2,500–49,999	2.9	3.0
Rural nonfarm	3.1	3.1
Farm	3.7	3.7

The greatest difference between the two systems of classification is found for cities having 50,000 or more people. Apparently the expected fertility of women living in cities of 50,000 or more at the time of the interview is as high as 2.9, in part because of the comparatively recent migration of people who have, or expect to have, relatively large families.

The influence of farm residence on fertility is strong, as is shown by the data for both place of residence at the time of interview and place of longest residence since marriage. Does the influence of farm residence on fertility extend to people who have *ever* lived on farms, regardless of their present residence? Apparently it does, but not to any great extent:

Farm experience of husband and wife	No. of wives	Average no. of births			
		By 1955	Expected total		
			Most likely	Minimum	Maximum
None	1,136	1.8	2.8	2.6	3.1
Wife some, husband none	312	1.8	2.8	2.5	3.1
Husband some, wife none	373	2.1	2.9	2.7	3.2
Both some, but not on farm at interview	577	2.2	3.1	2.8	3.3
Both on farm at interview	300	2.8	3.7	3.4	4.0

Where both husband and wife have had some farm experience, expected fertility is higher than if only one partner has ever lived on a farm, but not a great deal higher. If only the husband or the wife has lived on a farm, the effect of farm residence on expected fertility is virtually nil (Figure 9–7).

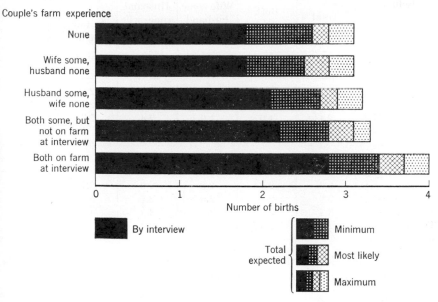

Fig. 9–7. Average number of births by 1955, and total number expected, for wives, by couple's farm experience.

Among Catholics the influence of previous farm residence is much stronger than has been described above for all religious groups combined. When the wife or the husband or both partners in a Catholic marriage have had some farm experience, expected fertility is significantly higher than when neither spouse has had farm experience (Table 9–24). When both husband and wife reported some farm background, but were not living on a farm at the time of interview, the average number of births expected by Catholic wives is 4.0, which is 25 per cent above the 3.2 births expected by Catholic wives if the couple has no farm background. When the wife, but not the husband, has had some farm experience, the average expected number of births is much the same as when the husband but not the wife has lived on a farm (3.5 and 3.4).

The widest differences in the fertility expectations of couples living in different environments are found when we focus attention on those who spent the greater part of their lives, both before and after marriage, in specific kinds of areas. The following data, which relate to 1,036 such

TABLE 9–24. AVERAGE NUMBER OF BIRTHS BY 1955, AND OF MOST LIKELY EXPECTED TOTAL BIRTHS, FOR ALL WIVES, BY RELIGION, BY COUPLE'S FARM EXPERIENCE

Religion	Couple's farm experience					
	Total	Both none	Wife some, husband none	Husband some, wife none	Both some	
					Not on farm now	On farm now
Births by 1955						
Total	2.1	1.8	1.8	2.1	2.2	2.8
Protestant	2.1	1.8	1.8	2.0	2.2	2.8
Catholic	2.1	1.9	1.9	2.4	2.7	2.9
Other	1.6	1.6	*	*	*	*
Most likely expected total births						
Total	3.0	2.8	2.8	2.9	3.1	3.7
Protestant	2.9	2.7	2.6	2.7	3.0	3.6
Catholic	3.4	3.2	3.5	3.4	4.0	4.4
Other	2.4	2.4	*	*	*	*

couples, show clearly the effects of different environments on family size for two broad groups of birth cohorts:

Place of longest residence before *and* after marriage	Most likely expected total births		
	All couples	Wife in cohorts of:	
		1926–37	1916–25
Large city[a]	2.8	3.0	2.7
Small city[b]	2.9	3.2	2.8
Rural nonfarm	3.2	3.2	3.1
Farm	3.8	3.4	4.1

[a] Includes couples living in cities of 50,000 or more, or in suburbs of such cities, who spent most of their lives in such areas.
[b] Includes couples living in cities of 2,500 up to 50,000, or in suburbs of such cities, who spent most of their lives in such areas.

Thus, when couples are classified according to "pure" community type, fertility differences are greater than when the basis of classification is place of present residence or place of longest residence since marriage.

The influence of community background on fertility appears to be diminishing even when we consider this relatively stable group that has been subject to the same or similar residential environments since childhood. As the above table shows, the differences in fertility expectations are considerably narrower for the more recent cohorts (1926–37) than for the earlier (1916–25).

Wives living in different regions of the United States differ little with respect to the number of births they think they will have:

Region of residence	No. of wives	Average no. of births			
		By 1955	Expected total		
			Most likely	Minimum	Maximum
Northeast	669	1.9	3.0	2.7	3.3
North Central	853	2.1	3.1	2.8	3.3
South	758	2.2	3.0	2.7	3.2
West	433	2.0	3.0	2.7	3.2

None of these regional differences in expectations is large enough to be statistically significant. When the regional variations in expected fertility are analyzed by wife's cohort, however, some interesting differences emerge. Among the oldest women interviewed (1916–20 cohorts), those living in the Northeast report significantly lower expected fertility (an average of 2.5 births) than those living in other regions (2.9, 3.1, and 3.0 births for North Central, South, and West, respectively) (Table 9–25). Indeed, such a differential might well be expected for all cohorts, in view of the urban-industrial character of the Northeast. As we proceed from the earlier to the more recent cohorts, however, the expected fertility of women living in the Northeast rises substantially to a high of 3.3 births per wife in the 1931–37 cohorts. This is the same as the average number of births expected by the young wives living in the North Central region, but higher than the number expected by those in the South and West (2.9 and 3.1, respectively). Wives in the North Central region also show a rise in expected fertility from earlier to more recent cohorts, although it is not as great as the rise noted for women in the Northeast. These trends again highlight the changing nature of fertility differentials in the United States: women in the urban-industrial sections are having more children, whereas those living in the more rural areas are either having fewer children or show little change in their expected fertility.

TABLE 9–25. AVERAGE NUMBER OF BIRTHS BY 1955, AND OF MOST LIKELY EXPECTED TOTAL BIRTHS, FOR ALL WIVES, BY COHORT, BY REGION OF RESIDENCE

Cohort	Region of residence				
	Total	Northeast	North Central	South	West
Births by 1955					
Total	2.1	1.9	2.1	2.2	2.0
1931–37	1.1	1.0	1.2	1.1	1.1
1926–30	1.9	1.7	2.0	2.0	2.0
1921–25	2.3	2.3	2.3	2.4	2.3
1916–20	2.6	2.3	2.5	2.9	2.7
Most likely expected total births					
Total	3.0	3.0	3.1	3.0	3.0
1931–37	3.2	3.3	3.3	2.9	3.1
1926–30	3.1	3.2	3.1	3.0	3.1
1921–25	3.0	3.1	3.0	3.0	2.9
1916–20	2.9	2.5	2.9	3.1	3.0

Summary

Americans are becoming more uniform with respect to family size. Many of the long-observed variations in the fertility of people belonging to different socioeconomic groups are disappearing. This seems to be true of people with different educational backgrounds, different incomes and occupations, and different places of residence. The disappearance of the traditional fertility variations is the result of two opposite trends: (1) a rise in the fertility of groups with higher status and of urban people generally, and (2) a decline in the fertility of groups with lower status and of people living on farms. The rise in the fertility of the higher-status and urban groups appears to be associated with a change in their attitudes, which are now favorable to somewhat larger families than was the case 20 or 30 years ago. The decline in the fertility of the lower-status and rural groups seems due to their increasing preference for moderate-sized families implemented by their increasingly extensive and successful use of contraception.

One socioeconomic difference that seems likely to be maintained is that between the wives who work for several years after marriage and those who do not. The wives with longer work histories are more likely to have small families either because they want to work or because they are Subfecund and work to occupy their time.

We cannot yet state with any certainty what will happen to the Protestant-Catholic difference in family size. One of the chief sources of our uncertainty is that there are no historical data to give perspective regarding the current situation. The cohort data suggest at first glance that the Protestant-Catholic differences in fertility may widen in the future, because of the very high expectations of young Catholic wives in the most recent cohorts. However, further examination shows that in the earlier cohorts the number of children borne by Catholic wives was substantially smaller than the number they say they expected when they were married. Such a shrinkage may occur among the more recent cohorts also. Nevertheless, it does seem probable that Catholics will continue to have somewhat higher fertility than Protestants because the Catholic Church opposes the use of the more effective methods of control now available and places much emphasis on childbearing as the primary purpose of marriage.

Chapter 10

FUTURE TRENDS IN FAMILY SIZE:
A LONGER AND BROADER VIEW

The preceding sections of this book have dealt almost entirely with the information collected from the wives who were interviewed. In Chapter 2 attention centered on the physiological ability of couples to have children in future years. Chapters 3 to 6 dealt with the efforts of married couples to regulate conception and control family size. The discussion of these topics provided the background for Chapters 7 to 9, in which information about expected size of completed families was analyzed.

So far, then, we have tried to achieve two of the three main goals of the study, namely, to provide better information regarding (1) the influence of impaired fecundity and contraception on family size, and (2) the number of births wanted and expected by married couples of childbearing age. The third main goal is to provide better forecasts of numbers of births in coming years. This is one of the prime requisites for improving the forecasts of national population which are needed for so many purposes.

The Importance of Forecasts of Fertility

Although population growth is influenced by changes in immigration, emigration, and deaths, as well as by changes in births, the extent to which actual population growth has departed from the forecasts made in recent decades has depended chiefly on the changes in fertility. This is illustrated by the first population forecasts for the United States which were made by the component method, that is, by projecting sex-age specific rates (or numbers) for births, deaths, and net immigration and applying them to the actual population in the base year and the computed population in subsequent years, classified by sex and age.[1] These forecasts, which were made in 1927, came within 0.5 per cent of the population of January 1, 1930, were 4.7 per cent above the 1940 figure, were

[1] P. K. Whelpton, "Population of the United States, 1925 to 1975," *American Journal of Sociology*, vol. 34, pp. 253–270, September, 1928. Rates are commonly used for births and deaths, and numbers for net immigration.

almost exactly right for 1950, and were 4.3 per cent below the estimated population of 1955 (Table 10–1). Not only is the over-all agreement fairly good, but in general the projected numbers are close to the actual numbers for the cohorts that had been born *prior* to the time when the forecasts were prepared (shown below the horizontal lines in Table 10–1). For example, the forecast of the number of persons 30–34 years old in 1955 (born in 1920–24) is within 0.6 per cent of the actual 1955 figure. At older ages the differences are somewhat larger because death rates declined more rapidly than was expected by Whelpton in 1927.

TABLE 10–1. FORECASTS OF THE POPULATION OF THE UNITED STATES MADE IN 1927 (IN THOUSANDS) AND PER CENT DEVIATION FROM ACTUAL POPULATION[a]

Age	January 1, 1930		January 1, 1940		January 1, 1950		January 1, 1955	
	Population	Per cent deviation	Population	Per cent deviation	Population	Per cent deviation	Population	Per cent deviation
Total	122,977	0.5	137,611	4.7	150,967	0.5	156,786	−4.3
0–4	12,152	6.1	12,705	21.0	13,185	−17.8	13,151	−27.2
5–9	12,846	2.0	12,791	19.3	13,430	1.1	13,600	−18.8
10–14	11,841	−1.2	12,415	5.2	13,010	16.9	13,363	1.9
15–19	11,389	−1.0	12,748	3.4	12,716	19.3	13,010	17.0
20–24	10,842	0.0	11,871	2.6	12,461	7.3	12,759	17.8
25–29	9,725	−1.0	11,372	2.7	12,698	4.0	12,396	4.9
30–34	9,257	1.7	10,554	3.3	11,578	1.0	12,449	0.6
35–44	16,296	−4.1	17,922	−2.0	20,772	−2.1	21,786	−4.0
45–64	22,015	3.2	26,172	0.7	29,478	−3.8	31,583	−4.8
65 & over	6,615	0.3	9,061	1.4	11,639	−2.5	12,689	−8.6

[a] The forecasts are from P. K. Whelpton, "Population of the United States, 1925 to 1975," *American Journal of Sociology*, vol. 34, no. 2, pp. 253–270, September, 1928. The totals shown here are slightly smaller than the published figures because the allowance for incomplete reporting of children under 5 has been deducted in order to make the forecasts comparable with the census. The numbers in age groups above the horizontal lines relate to persons born after the forecasts were made. The totals relate to persons born before and after.

In contrast, the forecasts for persons born *after* 1925 are substantially too large for some periods and too small for others. For example, the projected number of persons under 10 years of age in 1940 (born in 1930–39) is approximately 20 per cent above the actual figure. The chief reason for this divergence is that in 1927 it was not thought that there would be a severe depression during the 1930s which would cause a large drop in annual birth rates and numbers of births. For this reason, also, the forecasts of the number of persons aged 10–19 in 1950 and 15–24 in 1955 are too high in about the same degree. At the other extreme, the forecasts of the population under 5 years of age in 1950 and under 10 in 1955 are far too small because World War II and the upsurge in the birth rate after it ended were not foreseen in 1927. For 1950 the deficits of the forecasts at ages under 5 and over 35 are approximately equal to the surpluses at the intermediate ages. For 1955 the deficits exceed the surpluses by a small amount; they will do so on a larger scale for 1960.

If information of the type collected in this study had been available to Whelpton in 1927, there is no certainty that he would have made better forecasts of births during the 1930s than those which were published. This is because in 1927 most married couples, as well as many economists, were expecting economic conditions to continue much as they were. Even those who thought that a recession was coming did not anticipate that it would be so severe. In consequence, it is probable that even the minimum fertility expectations which married couples would have reported in 1927 would have led to forecasts of births during the 1930s that would have been substantially larger than the number which actually occurred. Similarly, the minimum number of expected births reported by the wives in our study may prove to be somewhat too high if a severe depression should begin in the near future.

In contrast, if the results of a study like this had been available in 1945, they undoubtedly would have improved substantially the forecasts of births which were made in that year.[2] Even the high forecast in that series is about 18 per cent too small for births during 1945–49 and 27 per cent too small for those during 1950–54. In 1945 there was little information on the extent to which births had been postponed during the depression years of the 1930s and the war years of the 1940s. Then it was believed that continuation of the long-time trend toward smaller families was the major reason why annual rates were as low as they were in the 1930s. Now it appears that large-scale postponement of marriage and childbearing had more influence. A study of the attitudes of young people in 1945 probably would have given at least partial evidence of this situation, and of the intention to make up hundreds of thousands of postponed marriages and births. Furthermore, in 1945 there was little indication that so many people were going to marry younger and start families with less delay after marriage—the two developments which contributed the major part of the baby boom during 1946–55. A study like this might have provided substantial information about the change that was in process. However, the high expectations about future marriage

---

[2] P. K. Whelpton, assisted by Hope Tisdale Eldridge and Jacob S. Siegel, *Forecasts of the Population of the United States, 1945–1975*, U.S. Bureau of the Census, 1947.

and childbearing that would have been reported in 1945 probably would have understated the number of births during 1946–55, because in 1945 it was not certain that the nation would be so prosperous during the next 10 years. In short, in order to improve forecasts of births as much as is desirable, information about expected size of family must be supplemented by sound forecasts of economic conditions and by more knowledge about the relationships between economic conditions and fertility.[3]

The Cohort Approach to Forecasts of Fertility

In this chapter and the next the information collected about expected size of completed families will be utilized in the preparation of what is hoped will be better forecasts of fertility and of population growth than are now available for the remainder of this century. The cohort approach will be followed, which means that forecasts of age-specific birth rates and death rates will be made for groups of people as they live through successive ages. The death rates are needed for all cohorts represented at any time during the period to be considered, and the birth rates for the cohorts with women of childbearing age. Finally, an allowance must be made for the movement of people into or out of the United States during this period.

The cohort approach is especially helpful in connection with forecasts of fertility. By focusing attention on the childbearing of real groups of people as they live through the reproductive ages, statements can be made which are understandable in terms of the behavior of individuals and married couples. For example, one can readily comprehend what is meant by the assumptions that 95 per cent of the women born in 1931–35 and living to age 45 will have married before age 45 and that the average number of births to those who marry will be 3. In contrast, it is difficult to interpret in terms of the behavior of individuals or married couples the assumptions that during 1956–65 the birth rate will remain at 24 per 1,000 (the 1955 figure) and that it will then decline to 20 per 1,000 in 1980.

If the cohort approach is not used in forecasting fertility one is forced to rely on information about past trends in the crude birth rate (the number of births per 1,000 persons) or in more specific rates (e.g., births per 1,000 women aged 15–19, 20–24, etc.). These trends must be extrapolated by mathematical formulas or on the basis of the judgment of the forecaster. The forecasts of births prepared by Whelpton, Eldridge, and Siegel in 1946 were influenced greatly by the fact that the age-specific

[3] A study of these relationships has been begun by the Scripps Foundation for Research in Population Problems.

birth rates of native white women were only about three-fourths as large during 1935–44 as during 1918–21. Other data indicated that the 1918–21 rates were only about half as large as those of the early 1800s. In view of this rapid downward trend it seemed reasonable in the high series to continue the 1935–44 age-specific rates unchanged and to assume in the medium and low series that age-specific birth rates would decline about 15 and 30 per cent, respectively, between 1935–44 and 1975. Actually they rose sharply during the last half of 1946, and in 1950–54 were about 55 per cent larger than in 1935–44.

The cohort approach permits the use not only of information about the past, but also of the expectations of a sample of the population such as the wives interviewed in this study. These people, rather than the demographers, the sociologists, or the statisticians making the forecasts, will have practically all the births that occur. It is certain that many of the specific couples in our sample will *not* have in the future the exact number of births that they expected to have when they were interviewed. Nevertheless, as mentioned in Chapter 7, there are valid reasons for thinking that the difference between actual and expected average numbers of births will not be large for the group as a whole unless economic conditions change substantially from what they were in 1955, or there is atomic war or other major catastrophe.

Our forecasts of fertility will be based on actual past rates and the future expectations of the wives in our study. We shall use as a starting point the actual birth rates of cohorts of women during several past decades, which are now provided by cohort fertility tables.[4] These tables are based on the annual birth rates for the members of a cohort who are living at each age. Adding these annual rates gives cumulative birth rates, that is, the total number of births per 1,000 women surviving to a given age. The cumulative rate by the end of the childbearing period (ages 45–49) is the final birth rate of the cohort. These rates are available for the women who have married by the age in question, and also for all women (ever-married plus single); both types are available for native white women and for total women. Forecasts of final rates for cohorts now in the childbearing ages will be made by combining the actual past rates and the future rates implied by the wives' expectations. Let us see how these expectations are used.

Past and Expected Future Birth Rates for Cohorts, Estimated from Study Data

From our study we have information about past and expected future birth rates for the white women in the cohorts of 1916–35, who in 1955

[4] Pascal K. Whelpton and Arthur A. Campbell, *Fertility Tables for Birth Cohorts of American Women,* to be published by the National Office of Vital Statistics.

were married and living with husband, or separated from him because of his military service.[5] From the cohort fertility tables we have the past birth rates of all the white women in the cohorts of 1871–1937 who had married by ages 45–49, or by 1955 if they had not yet reached these ages. In order to use both types of rates together in making our projections we must adjust one or the other so that they will be comparable. The best way to do this is to estimate the past or expected future birth rates for the members of the cohorts of 1916–35 who were not included in our sample. These are the women who had married before 1955 but were widowed, divorced, or legally separated from husband when our interviewing was done, and those who were single in 1955 but will marry before ages 45–49—the end of the childbearing period.

In order to simplify our discussion we shall consider groups of cohorts —for example, the cohorts of 1931–35—rather than the individual cohorts of each year. As a consequence our references to age groups need a word of explanation. When we say that nearly 17 per cent of the white women in the cohorts of 1931–35 had married by ages 15–19 (or by July 1, 1950), we are referring to the percentage on the sixth line of the third column of the following table, which is obtained by averaging the percentages on the first five lines:

Cohort	July 1, 1950		July 1, 1955		Interval between July 1, 1950, and July 1,1955	
	Age	Percentage married	Age	Percentage married	Between ages	Increase in percentage married
1931	19	37.9	24	82.0	19 & 24	44.1
1932	18	24.4	23	77.7	18 & 23	53.3
1933	17	13.0	22	72.2	17 & 22	59.2
1934	16	6.1	21	65.2	16 & 21	59.1
1935	15	2.1	20	56.5	15 & 20	54.4
1931–35	15–19	16.7	20–24	70.7	15–19 & 20–24	54.0

Similarly, when we say that 54 per cent of the women in the cohorts of 1931–35 married between ages 15–19 and 20–24, we are referring to

[5] The cohorts of 1936 and 1937 will be omitted from this discussion because the 70 wives who were interviewed had married before age 20 and represent only about 32 per cent of all the members of these cohorts who will marry before the end of the childbearing period. Moreover, as was pointed out in Chapter 7, the women in the cohorts of 1916–35 who married before age 20 have expectations regarding family size which differ significantly from those of women who married somewhat older.

the average of the percentages shown above on the first five lines in the right-hand column.

The wives interviewed in the cohorts of 1916–20 represent a very large majority (90 per cent) of all the women in these cohorts who will have married by ages 45–49 in 1965; consequently, it is a relatively simple matter to estimate the size of completed family for the entire group. Even for the cohorts of 1931–35, the wives aged 20–24 living with husband in 1955 constitute approximately 65 per cent of all the women who will have married by ages 45–49 in 1980. The procedure followed in estimating actual birth rates by 1955 and expected final rates for the women in these cohorts who will have married by ages 45–49 but who in 1955 were not married with husband present (or in armed forces) is outlined briefly here. Readers who want more details about the procedure are referred to Appendix G, Note 1.

Information about the current marital status of ever-married women is available from census reports. They show for the cohorts we are discussing that a high proportion (over 90 per cent) of the women who had married prior to 1955 were living with husband at the time of our field work or were temporarily separated from him by his military service. In other words, the wives in our sample represent most of the cohort members who have married.

Census data also provide information on the extent to which cumulative birth rates vary with marital history. Among ever-married women 20–39 years old, widows have had about as many births as wives with husband present, but divorcees have had substantially fewer. Women who are separated from their husbands for reasons other than death, divorce, or military service have cumulative birth rates which are intermediate between those of widows and divorcees but closer to the former than the latter. Because these differences are not large relatively and because such a high proportion of the women who have ever married by ages 20–39 are currently married, the fertility of all ever-married women is less than 3 per cent below that of the currently married women living with husband. Consequently, our information about the cumulative fertility rates of wives living with husbands provides the basis for trustworthy estimates about the rates of all members of the cohorts of 1916–35 who had married by 1955.

For the women who were single in 1955 but will marry by the end of the childbearing period, the first step is to estimate the relative size of the group. Because of the trend toward early marriages it includes only about 2 per cent of the women in the cohorts of 1916–20 but about 30 per cent of those in the cohorts of 1931–35. (The basis for the forecast of marriage expectations is discussed in a later section of this chapter.) In estimating the probable future childbearing of the brides-to-be we can use the experience and expectations of the wives in our study who married at the ages in question. For example, the numbers of births anticipated by the wives in the cohorts of 1926–30 who married at ages from 20–24 to 25–29 provide a basis for the estimate for the women in the cohorts of 1931–35 who will marry at these ages. Similarly, the expectations of the women in the cohorts of 1921–25 who married at ages from 25–29 up to ages 30–34 provide a basis for the estimate for the corresponding women in the cohorts of 1926–30 and 1931–35. Finally, the birth rates for the women who will marry after ages 35–39 can be estimated in part from census data regarding the experience of women in the cohorts of 1900–05 who married after ages 35–39.

Are the results biased if the estimates of expected future birth rates for the single women in one group of cohorts who will marry at given ages are based on the reported expectations of the wives in a preceding group of cohorts who married at these ages? The answer would be yes if there was an upward or downward trend in the size of completed family expected among the cohorts we are considering. Fortunately, as indicated in Appendix G, Note 1, there does not appear to be such a trend; hence our procedure is acceptable.

On the whole, there is excellent agreement between the estimated past and expected future rates based on study data (as explained above) and the past rates from cohort tables. (Compare the upper and lower decks of Table 10–2.) For three of the four groups of cohorts in question the cumulative rates by the ages reached in 1955 differ by less than 3 per cent. The closest agreement is for the cohorts of 1926–30, the birth rate per 1,000 ever-married women living to ages 25–29 being 1,961 according to the cohort tables and 1,930 according to the estimates based on the study data. The largest difference (8 per cent) is for the cohorts of 1931–35 at ages 20–24 in 1955; the cohort tables show a cumulative birth rate of 1,280 per 1,000, and the estimates from study data show 1,185.

Fairly close agreement between the two series of rates is found also for ages reached in 1950, 1945, 1940, and 1935. In the 10 comparisons which are possible from Table 10–2, 5 of the differences are smaller than 5 per cent, and 4 are between 5 and 12 per cent. In general, however, the estimated rates based chiefly on the actual and expected births of the women in our study tend to be slightly smaller than the rates from the cohort tables. While this may merely reflect sampling variability, it could also result from biases in the estimates for the women who were not interviewed—the widows, divorcees, and certain other married women not living with husband at the time of the study. The fact that the cohort-table birth rates do tend to be slightly larger needs to be kept in mind later in evaluating the forecasts of fertility.

Before considering the estimated future rates for the cohorts of 1916–

TABLE 10–2. CUMULATIVE BIRTH RATES BY SPECIFIED AGES, AND INCREASES DURING AGE INTERVALS, FOR WHITE OR NATIVE WHITE EVER-MARRIED WOMEN IN GROUPS OF COHORTS FROM 1881–85 TO 1931–35, ESTIMATED FROM PRESENT STUDY OR SHOWN BY COHORT TABLES[a]

Cohorts	Ages 15–19	Increase	Ages 20–24	Increase	Ages 25–29	Increase	Ages 30–34	Increase	Ages 35–39	Increase	Ages 45–49	Estimated rates by 45–49 Low	High
Estimates based on present study													
1931–35	555	630	1,185	1,160	2,345	530	2,875	121	2,996	6	3,002	2,613	3,338
1926–30	535	480	1,015	915	1,930	845	2,775	178	2,953	19	2,972	2,645	3,264
1921–25	350	578	928	722	1,650	660	2,310	530	2,840	48	2,888	2,637	3,176
1916–20	535	345	880	585	1,465	655	2,120	423	2,543	274	2,817	2,620	2,996
Cohort tables													
1931–35	601	679	1,280										
1926–30	557	523	1,080	881	1,961								
1921–25	604	366	970	724	1,694	658	2,352						
1916–20	590	414	1,004	521	1,525	580	2,105	373	2,478	152	2,630(est.)		
1911–15	620	395	1,015	447	1,462	473	1,935	329	2,264	136	2,400(est.)		
1906–10	647	488	1,135	453	1,588	389	1,977	277	2,254	127	2,381		
1901–05	603	597	1,200	531	1,731	428	2,159	256	2,415	106	2,521		
1896–1900			1,218	625	1,843	482	2,325	328	2,653	124	2,777		
1891–95					1,929	542	2,471	375	2,846	189	3,035		
1886–90							2,593	426	3,019	247	3,266		
1881–85									3,190	265	3,455		

[a] The estimated rates based on the present study are for white women. The rates from cohort tables are for native white women. They are similar to the rates in Pascal K. Whelpton, *Cohort Fertility: Native White Women*, Princeton University Press, Princeton, N.J., 1954, but have been revised on the basis of additional data. However, the rates in this table are for current ages (e.g., ages 15–19 include women who have reached their fifteenth birthday but *not* their twentieth), while rates in that book and in Appendix Table G-4 are for exact ages.

[b] The rates and increases below the horizontal lines are actual; those above the horizontal lines are estimates based in part on expectations of wives in present study. For an explanation of the meaning of the "increase" columns see Appendix G, Note 2.

20 to 1931–35 let us think how we might have forecast the final rates if the study had not been made. How would we have filled in the blank spaces in the upper right-hand triangle of the lower deck of Table 10–2? We see from the cohort tables that the final birth rate per 1,000 ever-married women living to ages 45–49 declined from 3,455 for the cohorts of 1881–85 to about 2,400 for the cohorts of 1906–10 and 1911–15. This is a drop of about 30 per cent. We see also that the decline has stopped and that at least a temporary rise has begun. This is shown by the similarity of the final rates for the 1906–10 and 1911–15 cohorts (about 2,380 and 2,400, respectively) and also by the somewhat larger rate for the 1916–20 cohorts by ages 35–39 than for the two preceding groups by 45–49. Finally, we see that the ever-married women in the more recent cohorts have substantially higher rates at younger ages than those in preceding cohorts. Thus the rate by ages 30–34 for the cohorts of 1921–25 is more than 20 per cent larger than the low for the 1911–15 group; a gain of nearly 35 per cent has been made by the 1926–30 cohorts at ages 25–29; and there is a slightly smaller gain by the 1931–35 cohorts at ages 20–24. However, rates for ever-married women aged 15–19 have fluctuated irregularly with no significant upward or downward trend.

One method of forecasting the final rate of the cohorts of 1916–20 to 1931–35 would be to assume that the ratio between (1) the rate of these cohorts by the ages reached in 1955 and (2) the rate of the 1906–10 cohorts by the corresponding ages could be applied to the final rate of the 1906–10 group. This procedure gives the following forecasts of final rates:

Cohort	Age in 1955	Rate by these ages	Ratio to corresponding rate of 1906–10 cohorts	Forecast of final rate based on these ratios
1916–20	35–39	2,478	1.10	2,619
1921–25	30–34	2,352	1.19	2,833
1926–30	25–29	1,961	1.23	2,929
1931–35	20–24	1,280	1.13	2,690

The results show the final rate rising to 2,929 for the cohorts of 1926–30, which seems reasonable, and past experience shows that the rate might decline to 2,690 for the cohorts of 1931–35 if a severe depression should develop in the early 1960s.

Another procedure that might be followed would utilize ratios between successive groups of cohorts. We could start with the final rate of 2,619 for the 1916–20 cohorts (shown above) and assume that the final rate for the 1921–25 group would exceed it by 12 per cent (the difference between the cumulative rates by ages 30–34). This would give a final rate of 2,933 for the 1921–25 cohorts. Continuing the process would give the results shown below:

Cohort	Age in 1955	Rate by these ages	Ratio to corresponding rate of preceding group of cohorts	Forecast of final rate based on these ratios
1916–20	35–39	2,478	1.10	2,619
1921–25	30–34	2,352	1.12	2,933
1926–30	25–29	1,961	1.16	3,402
1931–35	20–24	1,280	1.19	4,048

The method is justified from a statistical standpoint, and a final rate of 4,048 births per 1,000 women is not high from a biological standpoint—in fact it is about the same as that of the cohorts of the 1860s. While these projections might be used if our study information were not available, they are clearly too high according to the statements of the wives in our sample.

Many other methods of extrapolation could be applied. Some would give lower rates than the first described above, others would give higher rates than the second, and others would lie between the two extremes. In choosing between the various methods the forecaster would be compelled to rely entirely on his own judgment and that of his colleagues. Fortunately, our study has been conducted, and we can utilize the composite opinions of a probability sample of married couples. This does not mean that we shall accept unchanged the estimates based on their reported expectations. Instead, we shall now evaluate and modify the estimates of future fertility in Table 10–2 which are based on wives' statements.

The Estimates of Future Fertility Rates

Let us consider first the estimated number of births per completed family obtained by using the most likely expectations of the women in our study. They show substantially larger families for the cohorts of 1916–20 than for those of 1911–15 according to the fertility tables and then a slight upward trend to the cohorts of 1931–35 (Table 10–2). The ever-married women in the cohorts of 1906–10 had a birth rate of 2,381 per 1,000 by the time they reached ages 45–49 in 1955, and those in the cohorts of 1911–15 are certain to have a rate very close to 2,400 in 1960. In contrast the most likely expectations of the wives in the cohorts of 1916–20 indicate a final rate of 2,817 in 1965. This would be an increase of about 400 (or 17 per cent) from the two preceding groups and would mean that families would be slightly larger than those of the cohorts of 1896–1900. Still larger families are indicated by the most likely expectations of women in the later cohorts studied, the estimated final birth rate rising to 3,002 for the cohorts of 1931–35.

It should be remembered, of course, that some of the wives in the study were uncertain as to whether they could have children in the future, and that many of those who thought they could do so were not sure about how many they would have. Instead of saying that they definitely expected to have a certain number of children, some of them gave a range, for example, "two or three," or "at least one but not more than three." In some cases the range reflected doubts about the number wanted, perhaps because of health or for economic reasons. For others it reflected uncertainty about ability to stop family growth when all the children wanted are born. The attitudes of these women are indicated by replies like "We have the four we want. If we're lucky we won't have any more." In general, the most likely expectations reflect the middle of the range given (see Appendix F).

It is to take account of these uncertainties that low and high estimates of the final number of children have been made for the four groups of cohorts, based on the minimum and maximum expectations of the wives interviewed. The low estimates for these groups are quite similar. If performance agrees with minimum expectations, the average number of births per completed family will rise from about 2.4 in the cohorts of 1906–15 to a little over 2.6 in the cohorts of 1916–20 and stay at that level among subsequent cohorts (Table 10–2). This would be an increase of about 8 per cent from the lowest point yet reached in the United States, but would mean that families would be somewhat smaller than those of wives in the 1896–1900 cohorts and still smaller than among earlier groups. In contrast, if actual fertility follows the maximum expectations, the average number of births per completed family will jump from about 2.4 in the cohorts that have recently finished childbearing to 3.0 for the cohorts of 1916–20, and then rise slowly to 3.3 for the 1931–35 group. This is about equal to the number of children per ever-married woman reaching ages 45–49 in the 1920s.

As would be expected, the range between the low and high estimated final rates is larger for the younger than for the older women. It decreases from 725 for the cohorts of 1931–35 whose members were 20–24 years old when the interviewing was done to 376 for the cohorts of 1916–20 whose members were 35–39. On the whole, the low rates are about as much below the medium rates as the high are above them.

Comparisons between the estimated completed fertility rates for the cohorts of 1916–20 to 1931–35 and the actual rates of earlier cohorts indicate that the low and high estimates very probably will bracket the trend which will develop. As will be brought out in Chapter 11, however, the future population of the United States would be very much larger if the increase in number of children per family were to follow the wives' maximum expectations than if it were to follow the minimum. It is highly important, therefore, to try to narrow the range between our low- and high-fertility projections as much as seems reasonable.

Projected Birth Rates for Ever-married White Women

For the cohorts of 1916–20, the expectations of the wives in our study indicate a birth rate by ages 45–49 of between 2,620 and 2,996 per 1,000 women who have married (Table 10–2). The estimated rate by ages 35–39 (by 1955) is 2,543; consequently, between ages 35–39 and 45–49 the rate must rise by between 77 and 453 points in order to reach the final figure. Actually, the increase during these ages for the previous cohorts included in the fertility tables has varied from a low of 106 (cohorts of 1901–05) to 265 (cohorts of 1881–85). In view of these facts, the high estimate—calling for an increase of more than 450—appears very improbable. Even the estimate based on the most likely expectations seems decidedly too large, for it would require the rate to rise 274 points after ages 35–39, which is more than double the actual increase for the cohorts of 1896 to 1915. The low series—with a rise of about 77 points—seems to understate the births that are likely to occur.

Because the women in the cohorts of 1916–20 have few years in the childbearing period after 1955, it is very probable that the increase in their birth rate will be closer to the actual increases for preceding cohorts than is indicated by their expectations. On the basis of trends in cohort birth rates up to 1957 and in crude rates up to 1958, it seems desirable to assume a rise between ages 35–39 and 45–49 of not less than 132 points or more than 172, with 152 as a medium figure. The low assumption is about the same as the actual figure for the cohorts of 1906–15, and the high assumption is somewhat smaller than the change for the 1891–95 group. Adding these numbers to the rate of 2,478 by ages 35–39 (shown by the cohort tables) gives our final projected rates, namely, medium 2,630, low 2,610, and high 2,650. We have thus reduced the range between low and high from 376 to 40 for the cohorts of 1916–20.

In the medium fertility projections for ever-married white women we shall use as the final rate for the cohorts of 1921–25 to 1931–35 the estimates based on the most likely expectations of the wives in our study, rounded to the nearest 50 or 100.

In the low and high series we shall narrow the range between the low and high estimates in major degree for the cohorts of 1921–25 and in minor degree for those of 1931–35. The first justification for this step is the fact that we are considering rates per 1,000, while the wives interviewed were considering individual children. For example, those who were not sure about the final number of children that they expected to have usually expressed their uncertainty in such terms as three or four, at least two but not more than four, etc. This tends to give a relatively wide range—the maximum expectation commonly exceeds the minimum by 25 to 50 per cent and occasionally exceeds it by 100 per cent. If it had been possible to develop a system which would have allowed wives to reply in fractions instead of whole numbers, it is highly probable that on the whole their minimum and maximum expectations would have been closer together.

The second justification for narrowing the range is the improbability that all the couples represented in our sample will try to have the minimum numbers expected by the wives, or that all will try to have the maximum numbers expected. Even if conditions during future years are unfavorable to family growth in general, it seems much more likely that some couples will try to reach the maximum expectations expressed in 1955 than that all will try to stop at the minimum. Conversely, even though conditions favor family growth, it is unlikely that they will lead all couples to try to have the maximum numbers of births expected by the wives. Our adjustments are arbitrary in size, because as yet there is no information about the relationship between wives' expectations regarding future childbearing as expressed at a given time and the number of births that occur during subsequent years. A guiding principle is that the relative narrowing of the range should be larger for members of the earlier than of the later cohorts, because the former already have more of the children they expect and have fewer years left in the childbearing period. Thus for white women in the cohorts of 1921–25, the final rates estimated from the wives' expectations vary from 2,637 to 3,176—a difference of 539—but the rates for the projections vary from 2,800 to 3,000—a difference of only 200. (The modified rates are shown later in the left-hand panel of Table 10–4.) In contrast, for the cohorts of 1931–35 the range is changed from 725 to 400—a reduction which is substantially smaller relatively.

The cohorts of 1936–40 could not be adequately represented in our sample, because their members were only 15–19 years old at the time our field work was done, and relatively few (about 17 to 19 per cent) of those who will marry had done so. For these cohorts our projected final rates for white women are based on the most likely, minimum, and maximum expectations of the cohorts of 1931–35, rounded to the nearest 50 or 100. Subsequent cohorts have the same final rates in our medium and high series. In the low series, however, it seems wise to remember that the final birth rate of the ever-married white women reaching ages 45–49 during 1955–60 is about 2,400 per 1,000 and to project a return close to that situation for the cohorts of 1946–50 and later years.

Next, let us consider briefly what the wives in our study said about the timing of their expected future births. This information will be analyzed in detail in a later report. Here, however, it is helpful to look at the over-all picture for groups of cohorts during 5-year periods.

It is apparent that the wives' expectations overstate on the whole the number of children that they will bear during the first 5 years after the interview. We have already concluded that the most likely and maximum expectations of the wives in the 1916–20 cohorts exaggerate their total childbearing during coming years. These women were 35–39 years old when interviewed in 1955 and will be too old to have many births during 1960–65.[6] Consequently, we must conclude that their most likely and maximum numbers of births expected during 1955–59 also are too large.

When we consider the cohorts of 1921–25 we find a similar tendency for wives to overstate the number of children that they will bear during the first 5 years after the interview. Their most likely expectations indicate that the cumulative birth rate of all the ever-married cohort members will increase by 530 per 1,000 from ages 30–34 to 35–39 (Table 10–2). This is well above the actual increase shown by the tables for previous groups of cohorts since 1886–90, which has varied between about 256 and 426. Unlike the older women, however, the wives in the 1921–25 cohorts apparently understated the births that they will have 5 or more years after the interview. Thus their expectations indicate a rise in the cumulative birth rate of only 48 between ages 35–39 and 45–49, which is less than half of the smallest increase on record (Table 10–2). These two biases appear to balance each other, for the estimated increase in the cumulative rate after ages 30–34, based on the wives' replies, is between 327 and 866, with 578 as most likely (Table 10–3). The most likely figure is completely in line with past performance, for the actual increase after ages 30–34 has varied from 362 for the cohorts of 1901–05 to 673 for those of 1886–90. For these cohorts, therefore, we must discount the short-term birth expectations, even though we accept unchanged the medium expectations about size of completed families.

---

[6] The reference to 1955–60 is to the 5-year period beginning on July 1, 1955. The 5-year period beginning January 1, 1955, would be referred to as 1955–59. This principle is followed in all references to time periods.

TABLE 10-3. INCREASE OF CUMULATIVE BIRTH RATES DURING SPECIFIED AGE INTERVALS, FOR EVER-MARRIED WHITE OR NATIVE WHITE WOMEN IN GROUPS OF COHORTS FROM 1881-85 TO 1931-35, ESTIMATED FROM PRESENT STUDY OR SHOWN BY COHORT TABLES[a]

Cohorts	Increase to ages 45-49 from current ages											
	20-24			25-29			30-34			35-39		
	Medium or actual	Low	High	Medium or actual	Low	High	Medium or actual	Low	High	Medium or actual	Low	High
	Estimates based on present study											
1931-35	1,817	1,428	2,153									
1926-30	1,957	1,630	2,249	1,042	715	1,334						
1921-25	1,960	1,709	2,248	1,238	987	1,526	578	327	866			
1916-20	1,937	1,740	2,116	1,352	1,155	1,531	697	500	876	274	77	453
	Cohort tables[b]											
1916-20	1,626 (1940)			1,105 (1945)			525 (1950)			152 (1955)		
1911-15	1,385 (1935)			938 (1940)			465 (1945)			136 (1950)		
1906-10	1,246 (1930)			793 (1935)			404 (1940)			127 (1945)		
1901-05	1,321 (1925)			790 (1930)			362 (1935)			106 (1940)		
1896-1900	1,559 (1920)			934 (1925)			452 (1930)			124 (1935)		
1891-95				1,106 (1920)			564 (1925)			189 (1930)		
1886-90							673 (1920)			247 (1925)		
1881-85										265 (1920)		

[a] Computed from Table 10-2. For a discussion of the meaning of these "increases," see Appendix G, Note 2.

[b] The year when the cohort group reached the ages in question is shown in parentheses. The increases for the cohorts of 1916-20 and 1911-15 are based partly on estimates of rates after ages 35-39 and 40-44, respectively.

335

For the next group of cohorts, as for those of 1921–25, the future birth rates estimated from study data appear to be unreasonably high for 1955–60 and unreasonably low for later years, but the final rate by ages 45–49 appears to need only relatively minor modifications. The most likely expectations of the wives in the 1926–30 group indicate that the birth rate of the ever-married women will rise 845 points from ages 25–29 to ages 30–34 (during 1955–60), which exceeds by 25 to 120 per cent the actual rise during this age interval for preceding groups as far back as 1891–95 (Table 10–2). In contrast, the expected rise from ages 30–34 to 45–49 is only 197, which is about half of the smallest figure for any previous cohort. These two apparent biases come close to canceling each other as far as completed fertility is concerned. The most likely expectations indicate a rise of 1,042 from ages 25–29 to 45–49, which is only 11 per cent larger than the actual increase for the cohorts of 1911–15 and is somewhat smaller than that of the 1891–95 group (Table 10–3). However, the range between final low and high expected rates can be narrowed as indicated earlier in this section.

For the youngest 5-year group in our study (cohorts of 1931–35) it is the rise in the birth rate from ages 20–24 to 25–29 (again during 1955–60) which appears to be substantially overstated by the wives expectations, and the subsequent increases which appear to be under-stated. The study data indicate an increase of 1,160 from ages 20–24 to 25–29, which is from 30 to 160 per cent larger than the actual increases for earlier cohorts at the same ages (Table 10–2). But the indicated increase after ages 25–29 is only 657 according to the most likely figures which is well below the actual change of prior groups (between 790 and 1,106 in Table 10–3). Here again, one apparent distortion at least partially balances the other, for the total increase after ages 20–24 and the final rate by ages 45–49 according to the minimum and most likely expectations do not appear out of line with previous experience.

Can we accept with little or no change the expectations of the wives in our sample regarding final family size if we believe that large-scale modifications are needed in their statements as to when the additional children will be born? In forming an opinion we need to consider whether there are reasonable explanations for an upward bias in wives short-run expectations regarding future childbearing, which is approximately balanced by a downward bias in their subsequent expectations. First, however, it should be emphasized that the estimated increases in birth rates during 1955–60 ought to be (and are) larger than the increases in the actual rates of preceding cohorts during the same age periods (but in earlier years), in part because real changes in family formation are under way. These changes include a substantial increase in the proportion of couples having two to four children instead of fewer or more and a marked tendency to have them younger than formerly and then stop childbearing. They are quite likely to continue for at least a few more years unless there is a substantial recession.

But after an ample allowance is made for the real tendency to concentrate childbearing at younger ages, there remain biases in the reported timing of additional births. One reason why the number of births expected by a wife during the next 5 years is likely to exceed the actual number is that most of the couples who will become sterile, and hence cannot have the additional children they want, will not have much advance notice that this is going to happen. A second reason is that certain other couples will be like the foregoing in having fewer births than they expect in the short run, although unlike them in having more than they expect to have later. These are the couples who will develop less serious fecundity impairments. Many of them will eventually be able to have as many children as they want, but family formation will take longer than anticipated. This is illustrated by the past experience of numerous couples in our sample, who told the interviewer that after trying for several years they finally had one or more children that were wanted earlier.

A third group may have as many births as expected in the short run, but certainly will have more than expected later, namely, the couples who are unable to stop family growth when they wish to do so. For example, about 90 per cent of the wives in the cohorts of 1931–35 expect to stop with four or fewer children, and only 10 per cent expect to have five or more. Since nearly 14 per cent of the ever-married women in the cohorts of 1906–10 had at least five births, the expectations of the later group envisage a drop of well over one-fourth in the proportion of "large" families. So rapid a decline is not impossible but it is questionable. More important here is the fact that among Users in the cohorts of 1916–20 accidental conceptions made up about one-sixth of all conceptions. Some of these accidental conceptions merely meant that a wanted child came earlier than planned, but others added one or more children to a family that had already reached the size desired.

It is true that the proportion of couples who know about rhythm and other control methods and can use them effectively has increased substantially in past years and is likely to continue to increase in the future. Moreover, some of the research now in progress undoubtedly will lead to the improvement of present methods, and to the development of new methods which will be easier to use and more acceptable to married couples. For example, it is probable that a simpler test of oncoming ovulation will be developed which will reduce the risk involved in depending on periodic continence. It is also quite possible that a pill will be perfected which will give protection (and have no undesirable side effects) as long as taken according to directions. We should expect, therefore, that efforts to regulate conception will become more widespread and effective in the future.

Looking ahead, it is likely that the above-mentioned biases in the reported timing of expected births will diminish. Research in the causes and treatment of partial and complete sterility will enable more couples to have the children that they want as quickly as they want them. At the same time, the improvement of methods of control will allow more couples to prevent accidental pregnancies after their families reach the size desired. Both developments will help to narrow the apparent gap between expected and actual birth rates during subsequent years.

Little is known as yet about what may be the most important bias in wives' reports of when additional children will be born. Do those who want one or more children and conceive easily actually have these children as soon as they say they expect to have them, or do they tend to put them off somewhat longer? Our data suggest that such women do understate the time to the next child, but as yet it is not possible to say this with assurance, nor to suggest how large the bias is. What is needed first is a study in 1960 to see to what extent the expectations for 1955–60, which were reported in 1955, are carried out. It would provide answers about the relationship between expectations and performance under the economic conditions of 1955–60. Later, similar studies should be made for subsequent periods to provide information for other types of conditions. This will improve our ability to interpret reported expectations about future childbearing and make more reliable forecasts of numbers of births in coming years.

Although there clearly are valid reasons for believing that wives say that their future births will occur earlier than will actually be the case, we do not find valid reasons for believing that wives, as a group, either substantially understate or exaggerate the total number of future births. While some wives certainly will be unable to have as many as they expect, others certainly will be unable to avoid having more than they expect. Moreover, while some couples will reduce their expectations as they have more experience with child care, others will enjoy their children more than they anticipated and will "raise their sights." It now appears that changes in one direction will approximately balance those in the other direction and that wives' expectations give the best indication now available regarding future trends of completed fertility.

Fertility Projections for All Ever-married Women

The fertility projections for ever-married white women which we have been discussing are needed here to provide a basis for comparable projections for all ever-married women. For reasons explained in Chapter 1 only white women were interviewed in our study. However, in the forecasts of future population of the United States, to be presented in Chapter 11, we shall consider the total population rather than the white population.[7] For various reasons there is much more interest in information about the size, growth, and composition of the total population than of the major groups that compose it. Distinctions between the native and foreign-born groups, which were so important during the first two or three decades of this century, have largely disappeared. Some of those relating to race are weakening as the educational differences become smaller and as restrictions on employment are removed. Accordingly, we shall now widen our consideration of fertility trends so as to include all women.

Projections of final fertility rates for *all* ever-married women are made from those for *white* ever-married women on the basis of the past trend in the differential between the two groups. For ever-married women living to ages 45–49 in the cohorts of 1871–75 the cumulative birth rate is 4,372 for all women and 3,967 for native white women, a difference of 405 (Table 10–4). The differential declined rapidly among subsequent cohorts; for those of 1906–10 and 1911–15 the rate for all ever-married women exceeds those for white women and native white women by only about 60 points (or 2½ per cent). For subsequent cohorts the difference is assumed to be 50. The projected rates for all ever-married women in the right-hand panel of Table 10–4 are obtained from those for white ever-married women in the left-hand panel by adding 50 to the latter. In view of the general tendency of fertility differentials to narrow, it may well be that adding 50 gives a slight upward bias to the fertility projections. However, this addition increases the rates in the medium series by less than 2 per cent.

From the cohorts of 1871–75 to those of 1906–10 the average number of births to all ever-married women living to middle age was cut almost in half. The medium projections assume that one-third of this reduction will be regained, the high assume the regaining of half, and the low assume that what has been regained will be lost once more.

In the medium projections there is a substantial rise from the low mark of about 2,450 births per 1,000 women for the cohorts of 1906–10 and 1911–15 to 2,950 for the 1921–25 group, and then a small increase to 3,050 for the cohorts of 1931–35 and subsequent years (Figure 10–1). Since the fall in the final birth rate from the cohorts of 1871–75 and earlier to those of 1906–10 was steeper for all women than for native white women, this represents a more striking reversal of the former trend than is the case for the native white group discussed above.

[7] Projections for the white population will be published in a subsequent report.

TABLE 10–4. ACTUAL BIRTH RATES, AND MEDIUM, LOW, AND HIGH PROJECTED BIRTH RATES, BY AGES 45–49, FOR WHITE AND TOTAL EVER-MARRIED WOMEN IN GROUPS OF COHORTS FROM 1871–75 TO 1946–50

| Cohort | Year when reach ages 45–49 | Actual or projected rates[a] | | | | | | Excess of rates for total women |
| | | White or native white women[b] | | | Total women | | | |
		Medium	Low	High	Medium	Low	High	
1946–50	1995	3,000	2,450	3,300	3,050	2,500	3,350	50
1941–45	1990	3,000	2,550	3,300	3,050	2,600	3,350	50
1936–40	1985	3,000	2,700	3,300	3,050	2,750	3,350	50
1931–35	1980	3,000	2,800	3,200	3,050	2,850	3,250	50
1926–30	1975	2,950	2,800	3,100	3,000	2,850	3,150	50
1921–25	1970	2,900	2,800	3,000	2,950	2,850	3,050	50
1916–20	1965	2,630	2,610	2,650	2,680	2,660	2,700	50
1911–15	1960	2,400	2,400	2,400	2,460	2,460	2,460	60
1906–10	1955	2,381			2,442			61
1901–05	1950	2,521			2,627			106
1896–1900	1945	2,777			2,925			148
1891–95	1940	3,035			3,244			209
1886–90	1935	3,266			3,486			220
1881–85	1930	3,455			3,731			276
1876–80	1925	3,693			4,026			333
1871–75	1920	3,967			4,372			405

[a] The cohorts of 1951–55 and later are assumed to have the same rates by ages 45–49 as the cohorts of 1946–50. Rates for the cohorts of 1911–15 to 1941–45 are partially or wholly projected; those for earlier cohorts are actual, from cohort fertility tables prepared by the Scripps Foundation for Research in Population Problems.

[b] Rates for the cohorts of 1916–20 to 1931–35 are based on the expectations of the white wives in our sample (Table 10–2). Rates for earlier cohorts are for native white women.

In the low fertility projections the final rate reaches its maximum at 2,850 for the cohorts of 1921–35 and then declines gradually to 2,500 for the cohorts of 1946–50 and later. This is not quite as low as the actual rate for the cohorts of 1906–15. In the high series the rise in average size of completed families is somewhat more rapid than in the medium—the rate goes up to 3,350 for the cohorts of 1936–40 and remains at that level. This is about the same as the actual rate for the cohort of 1890, but is well below the rate for the 1871–75 group.

The Timing of Future Births

Having accepted the foregoing estimates of final birth rates of ever-married women, our next problem is to estimate the course that will be followed in reaching these final rates. We have already noted that

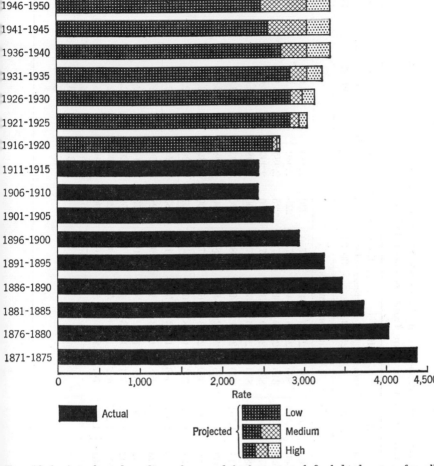

FIG. 10–1. Actual, and medium, low, and high projected final *birth* rates, for all *ever-married women* living to middle age, by groups of cohorts.

there appears to have been a marked tendency for the wives in our sample to overstate the number of children they will bear in the next few years and to understate the number they will bear subsequently. In consequence, we shall use with caution the wives' expectations regarding the timing of births, and select timing patterns which take into account the intercohort trends in the actual experience of earlier cohorts in preceding years.

Let us look first at the intercohort changes which have occurred in the past. The birth rate by ages 15–19 fluctuated somewhat irregularly between 650 and 740 among the cohorts of 1891–95 to 1931–35 and then rose sharply to about 850 for the 1936–40 group in 1955 (Table 10–5 and Figure 10–2). On the whole, however, intercohort differences

TABLE 10–5. ACTUAL AND PROJECTED CUMULATIVE BIRTH RATES BY SPECIFIED AGES, AND INCREASES DURING AGE INTERVALS, FOR ALL EVER-MARRIED WOMEN IN GROUPS OF COHORTS FROM 1871–75 TO 1961–65[a]

Cohorts	Year reach 15–19	Rate by 15–19	Increase	Rate by 20–24	Increase	Rate by 25–29	Increase	Rate by 30–34	Increase	Rate by 35–39	Increase	Rate by 40–44	Increase	Rate by 45–49
						Medium assumptions								
1961–65	1980	840	660	1,500	800	2,300	450	2,750	230	2,980	68	3,048	2	3,050
1956–60	1975	850	660	1,510	805	2,315	440	2,755	225	2,980	68	3,048	2	3,050
1951–55	1970	865	665	1,530	810	2,340	420	2,760	225	2,985	63	3,048	2	3,050
1946–50	1965	880	670	1,550	830	2,380	390	2,770	220	2,990	58	3,048	2	3,050
1941–45	1960	916	680	1,596	830	2,426	372	2,798	200	2,998	50	3,048	2	3,050
1936–40	1955	847	714	1,561	850	2,411	402	2,813	190	3,003	45	3,048	2	3,050
1931–35	1950	737	639	1,376	976	2,352	476	2,828	180	3,008	40	3,048	2	3,050
1926–30	1945	682	481	1,163	880	2,043	696	2,739	200	2,939	59	2,998	2	3,000
1921–25	1940	714	338	1,052	706	1,758	661	2,419	407	2,826	122	2,948	2	2,950
1916–20	1935	651	416	1,067	506	1,573	568	2,141	383	2,524	154	2,678	2	2,680
1911–15	1930	672	423	1,095	428	1,523	457	1,980	328	2,308	147	2,455	5	2,460
1906–10	1925	699	492	1,191	461	1,652	386	2,038	273	2,311	129	2,440	2	2,442
1901–05	1920	660	642	1,302	531	1,833	428	2,261	259	2,520	104	2,624	3	2,627
1896–1900	1915	661	616	1,277	682	1,959	505	2,464	329	2,793	128	2,921	4	2,925
1891–95	1910	701	661	1,362	707	2,069	584	2,653	396	3,049	181	3,230	14	3,244
1886–90	1905							2,768	467	3,235	229	3,464	22	3,486
1881–85	1900									3,436	262	3,698	33	3,731
1876–80	1895											3,987	39	4,026
1871–75	1890													4,372

Cohorts	Year reach 15–19	Rate by 15–19	Increase	Rate by 20–24	Increase	Rate by 25–29	Increase	Rate by 30–34	Increase	Rate by 35–39	Increase	Rate by 40–44	Increase	Rate by 45–49
						Low assumptions								
1961–65	1980	690	440	1,130	500	1,630	470	2,100	300	2,400	98	2,498	2	2,500
1956–60	1975	690	460	1,150	520	1,670	450	2,120	280	2,400	98	2,498	2	2,500
1951–55	1970	700	480	1,180	530	1,710	430	2,140	260	2,400	98	2,498	2	2,500
1946–50	1965	720	510	1,230	570	1,800	400	2,200	220	2,420	78	2,498	2	2,500
1941–45	1960	889	550	1,439	600	2,039	349	2,388	160	2,548	50	2,598	2	2,600
1936–40	1955	847	693	1,540	700	2,240	348	2,588	120	2,708	40	2,748	2	2,750
1931–35	1950	737	639	1,376	947	2,323	380	2,703	110	2,813	35	2,848	2	2,850
1926–30	1945	682	481	1,163	880	2,043	625	2,668	140	2,808	40	2,848	2	2,850
1921–25	1940	714	338	1,052	706	1,758	661	2,419	349	2,768	80	2,848	2	2,850
1916–20	1935	651	416	1,067	506	1,573	568	2,141	383	2,524	134	2,658	2	2,660
						High assumptions								
1961–65	1980	1,000	800	1,800	950	2,750	410	3,160	160	3,320	28	3,348	2	3,350
1956–60	1975	1,000	800	1,800	950	2,750	410	3,160	160	3,320	28	3,348	2	3,350
1951–55	1970	1,000	800	1,800	950	2,750	410	3,160	160	3,320	28	3,348	2	3,350
1946–50	1965	990	800	1,790	950	2,740	390	3,130	180	3,310	38	3,348	2	3,350
1941–45	1960	967	780	1,747	951	2,698	400	3,098	200	3,298	50	3,348	2	3,350
1936–40	1955	847	754	1,601	980	2,581	517	3,098	200	3,298	50	3,348	2	3,350
1931–35	1950	737	639	1,376	1,031	2,407	580	2,987	200	3,187	61	3,248	2	3,250
1926–30	1945	682	481	1,163	880	2,043	736	2,799	269	3,048	100	3,148	2	3,150
1921–25	1940	714	338	1,052	706	1,758	661	2,419	444	2,863	185	3,048	2	3,050
1916–20	1935	651	416	1,067	506	1,573	568	2,141	383	2,524	174	2,698	2	2,700

[a] Rates above the horizontal lines are projected. Rates for subsequent cohorts are the same as those for the 1961–65 cohorts.

343

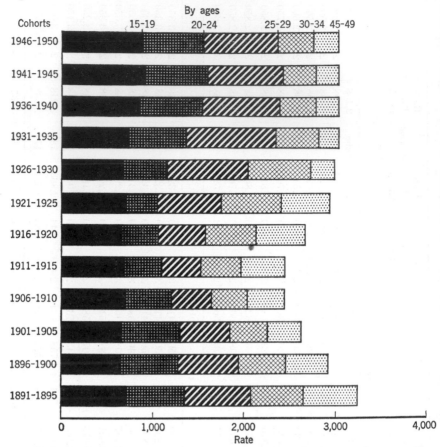

Fig. 10–2. Actual, and medium projected cumulative *birth* rates by ages from 15–19 to 45–49, for all *ever-married women,* by groups of cohorts.

in the birth performance of these quite young married women have been small.

The increases in the cumulative birth rate of ever-married women during the intervals between ages 15–19 and 30–34 have had a decidedly U-shaped trend. In each case the increase was first reduced by more than one-third in one or two decades. Moreover, in each case the subsequent rise was enough more rapid than the preceding decline so that the increases during 1950–55 exceeded those at the same ages for the cohorts of a generation earlier. For example, the increase of the cumulative birth rate from ages 20–24 to 25–29 was 707 for the cohorts of 1891–95, fell to 428 for the 1911–15 group, and then jumped to 880 for the 1926–30 cohorts.[8]

[8] For information about the significance of the increases in the cumulative birth rate of ever-married women in a cohort as age rises, see Appendix G, Note 2.

One cause of the larger increases of cumulative birth rates of more recent cohorts during the younger ages is the larger families which they are having. This is not the whole story, however. A second cause is the tendency to marry at younger ages, which is only partially taken into account in this table. For example, if equal numbers of women in a cohort married during each year of age from 17 to 24 (and no marriages were broken during these ages), by the time these wives reached age 25 the average duration of marriage would be 4.5 years. In contrast, if twice as many married at 17, 18, 19, and 20 as at the next four older ages, the average duration of marriage by age 25 would be 5.17 years. This change is too extreme to be realistic, but it illustrates the way in which a reduction in age at marriage does increase the duration of marriage of ever-married women of a given age and tends to increase their birth rate.

Finally, the intercohort rise in the fertility of young ever-married women is due in part to the fact that more wives are starting childbearing with less delay after marriage than was formerly the case. The interval between marriage and the first birth (or subsequent births) tended to be long for couples marrying during the depression years of the 1930s, in part because the effect of unemployment, low income, etc., was only partially offset by the various relief programs. A large-scale delay in family formation occurred also during World War II, when many husbands were temporarily separated from their wives because of military service.

At age intervals between 30–34 and 45–49 the past intercohort trend of increases in cumulative birth rates of ever-married women has also been U-shaped, but the rise from the low mark is smaller compared with the previous decline than is the case at younger age intervals. For example, the rise between ages 30–34 and 35–39 was 383 points for the cohorts of 1916–20—nearly half again as much as for the 1901–05 group but much less than the increase for the cohorts of the 1880s. Moreover, the explanation of the recent upward trend is very different at these ages than at the younger ages. Here it is the making up of births that were postponed earlier.

To help us evaluate the importance of changes in the timing of births by ever-married women let us look at the cohorts of 1921–25. By ages 15–19 (by 1940) the birth rate of the members who had married was relatively high—714 per 1,000. During 1941–45 these cohorts were seriously affected by World War II, large numbers of husbands being away from their wives for many months. In consequence, many births were postponed and the increase in the cumulative rate from ages 15–19 (in 1940) to ages 20–24 (in 1945) was only 338 per 1,000—much the smallest on record. Many of these postponed births were made up in the postwar decade. Partly for this reason (but partly because of an increase in average size of completed families) the rise in the cumulative rate from ages 20–24 to 25–29 and then to 30–34 is much larger for the cohorts of 1921–25 than for any of the five (or more) preceding groups.

We noted above that the final birth rate of ever-married women living to ages 45–49 probably will be much the same for the cohorts of 1921–25 (projected between 2,850 and 3,050) as for those of 1896–1900 (actual 2,925). In spite of this similarity there are large differences in the way that the final rate is distributed by age intervals, as is shown below:

Cohorts	Rate by ages 15–19	Increase in cumulative rate between ages:					Cumulative rate by ages 45–49
		15–19 and 20–24	20–24 and 25–29	25–29 and 30–34	30–34 and 35–39	35–39 and 45–49	
1921–1925	714	338	706	661	407[a]	124[a]	2,950[a]
1896–1900	661	616	682	505	329	132	2,925
Difference	53	−278	24	150	78	−8	25

[a] Medium projections after 1955.

If the timing pattern of the earlier cohorts is taken as a standard, a substantial proportion of the births to women in the later group were postponed between ages 15–19 and 20–24 (during 1940–45) and were made up between ages 25–29 and 30–34 (during 1950–55) or are being made up between ages 30–34 and 35–39. This is shown by the relatively small increase for the 1921–25 cohorts between ages 15–19 and 20–24 and by their larger increase between ages 25–29 and 30–34 and (almost certainly) between ages 30–34 and 35–39. During the interval between ages 20–24 and 25–29 large numbers of lower-order births were being made up by this group, but large numbers of higher-order births were being postponed as a consequence of the postponement of lower-order births during the war.

The foregoing comparison understates the magnitude of the change in the timing pattern of childbearing because it does not allow for the influence of another factor. This is the increase in the proportion of wives having two, three, or four children and the decrease in the proportion having no child or only one, or having large families (six or more children). Fewer childless and one-child wives means higher cohort rates for first and second births; fewer large families means lower rates for sixth and subsequent births. Since first and second births usually occur during younger ages and sixth and higher-order births during older ages, these changes in the distribution of families by size should have made the rate for all births during ages under 25–29 larger for the cohorts of 1921–25 than for those of 1896–1900, and the rate from ages 25–29 to 45–49 smaller for the more recent group. In fact, however, the rate by ages 25–29 is smaller for the cohorts of 1921–25 (1,758) than for those of 1896–1900 (1,959), while the increase from 25–29 to 45–49 will be larger for the more recent group (about 1,192) than for the earlier group (966).

If wives bear most of their children relatively early in the childbearing period, the population will increase at a more rapid rate than if they bear the same number of children relatively late in the childbearing period. This is true because the oncoming generation will reach the childbearing ages at an earlier date. Consequently, it is appropriate to allow in our high fertility projections not only for more births per woman marrying by 45–49, but also for an increase in the proportion of births occurring at younger ages. Similarly, in the low fertility series a decrease in size of completed families is combined with a decrease in the proportion of births occurring at younger ages. The medium fertility series is intermediate in both respects.

The Medium Fertility Projections. The medium projections of cumulative birth rates of all ever-married women assume a slight reversal in the recent tendency for married women to bear more of their babies at younger ages. Thus the birth rate of women married by ages 15–19 declines about 8 per cent from the high mark that apparently is being reached by the cohorts of 1941–45 during 1955–60; nevertheless the rate assumed for the 1961–65 and later groups exceeds the highest rate on record for any cohorts prior to those of 1936–40. Similar statements hold true for the increases in the cumulative birth rate between ages 15–19 and 20–24 and ages 20–24 and 25–29.

Between 1955–60 and 1970–75 the birth rate of ever-married women at age intervals above 25–29 is assumed to decline much more rapidly than at younger ages. The chief reason for these larger decreases is the simple fact that if women are going to bear a given number of children, the more they bear at younger ages the fewer are left to come at older ages. For example, in the preceding section the final rate for the cohorts of 1931–35 was set at 3,050 births per 1,000 women marrying by middle age. The younger childbearing of the cohort members who married by ages 20–24 (by July 1, 1955) had already given them a cumulative rate of 1,376. This is assumed to increase to 2,352 by ages 25–29 in the medium series. If from ages 25–29 to 30–34 the projected increase for this group were as large as that for the preceding group, the rate by ages 30–34 would be within two points of the final figure. This would not allow for the few births that are almost certain to occur after ages 30–34. In consequence, the increase in rate from ages 25–29 to 30–34 is reduced considerably from the cohorts of 1926–30 to those of 1941–45.

It is the cohorts of 1936–40 and 1941–45 in which the tendency for ever-married women to have their children while relatively young is assumed to reach a peak in the medium series. It is these cohorts in which the ever-married women actually have, or are assumed to have, the highest cumulative birth rates by ages 15–19, 20–24, and 25–29. Since the final rates by ages 45–49 have already been set, it is these cohorts that must have comparatively small additions to the cumulative birth rate during the latter part of the childbearing period.

At age intervals over 30–34 there is another reason for the large drop in the medium fertility rates from 1955–60 to 1965–70 or 1970–75. The cohorts of 1921–25 and earlier are having relatively more births at these older ages (during 1955–60) than several preceding groups of cohorts because they are still making up some of the births postponed as a consequence of the depression of the 1930s or of the absence of men during World War II. Subsequent cohorts will not have large numbers of postponed births to make up at these ages according to our medium series. (This contingency is provided for in the low series.)

It should be noted that there are three types of controls for the projected increases in the cumulative birth rates in the medium fertility series. First, for each group of cohorts the sum of the increases during the various age intervals must equal the medium final rate by ages 45–49 that was selected earlier. Second, the intercohort changes must allow for a slight reversal of the tendency for married women to have their children at younger ages. Third, the increases for different cohorts during 1955–60 (the numbers just above the horizontal lines in the "increase" columns of Table 10–5) must be consistent with an independent estimate of the total number of births during this period. As explained in Appendix G, Note 3, when these projections were made in June, 1958, it appeared that there would be between 19,400,000 and 22,000,000 births during the 5 years beginning on July 1, 1955, with 20,700,000 as a medium estimate. The medium birth rates (in combination with the medium projected marriage rates discussed later in this chapter) give the latter number. Later developments between June, 1958, and February, 1959, indicated that the low and medium estimates probably should be raised to 20,500,000 and 21,000,000, respectively, and the high estimate reduced to 21,500,000.

The Low Fertility Projections for All Ever-married Women. When the computations for the low series were made in June, 1958, it appeared highly desirable to allow for the possibility that the recession which began in 1957 might develop into a severe depression. Accordingly, it is assumed in this series that the previous tendency for wives to bear more of their children at younger ages was reversed in late 1958 or in 1959.

The reversal is rather abrupt like that from 1925–30 to 1930–35, but does not go so far as a return to the delayed-timing pattern of the cohorts of 1911–15.

After dropping sharply from 1955–60 to 1965–70, the birth rates at younger ages are assumed to decline slowly until 1975–80 or later. For example, the increase in the cumulative rate of ever-married women between ages 15–19 and 20–24 is 693 for the cohorts of 1936–40 (during 1955–60) in the low series but is assumed to drop to 510 for the 1946–50 group during 1965–70 and then decrease gradually to 440 for the cohorts of 1961–65 (Table 10–5). Even so, it is somewhat above the corresponding rates for the cohorts of 1911–15 and 1916–20 during the 1930s. Similar statements hold for the cumulative birth rate by ages 15–19 and the increase from ages 20–24 to 25–29.

Partly balancing the declines in birth rates of younger wives in the low fertility projections are the increases at older ages. (There is not a complete balancing because of the decrease assumed in average size of completed family.) For example, the rise of the cumulative birth rate between ages 30–34 and 35–39 is 349 for the cohorts of 1921–25 (during 1955–60), drops abruptly among the next three groups, but then goes up to 300 for the cohorts of 1961–65. This is nearly as high as for the cohorts of 1896–1900. The increase in the rate between ages 35–39 and 40–44 also drops sharply during the 1960s and rises later on.

The low projected rates for 1955–60 are in line with the low estimate of 19,400,000 births that was made in June, 1958. In view of the rapid improvement in economic conditions during the last half of 1958, a more reasonable low estimate for 1955–60 would be 20,500,000 births. For the same reason, it is probable that the low estimate for 1960–65 should be increased somewhat.

The High Fertility Projections for All Ever-married Women. In the high series we have allowed for a substantial continuation of the trend toward concentrating childbearing during younger ages. The birth rate of ever-married women by ages 15–19 is assumed to rise from 847 for the cohorts of 1936–40 (during 1950–55) to 1,000 for those of 1951–55 and later. Similarly, the increase in the rate between ages 15–19 and 20–24 is assumed to rise from 639 for the cohorts of 1931–35 to 800 for the cohorts of 1946–50 and later. In both cases the new increase exceeds by a substantial margin the largest in the cohort tables now available.

The upward trend in birth rates of wives during younger age intervals is partially balanced by a downward trend at older age intervals. (The balance is not complete because of the allowance for larger families.) Thus the increase in the cumulative birth rate between ages 30–34 and 35–39 is assumed to fall nearly 60 per cent from the cohorts of 1916–20 (during 1950–55) to those of 1951–55 and later. Similarly, the increase between ages 35–39 and 40–44 drops more than 80 per cent from the cohorts of 1911–15 to those of 1951–55. (Fertility at these older ages is high for the earlier cohorts during 1955–60, however, because of the making up of births postponed in earlier years, discussed above.) The rates for 1955–60 in the high projections give 22,100,000 births during these years, which is consistent with the high estimate mentioned earlier. In February, 1959, with data available on numbers of births up to November, 1958, it appeared that a more reasonable high estimate of births during 1955–60 is 21,500,000.

The shift to younger childbearing that is assumed in the high fertility projections cannot go on indefinitely, of course, because of the limits set by nature and by our customs. Unless our customs change, very few girls will marry before 15, and most wives will not have their first baby until at least nine months after the wedding. And unless nature changes, at least one year will usually elapse between births (except for twins or triplets). The trend toward younger childbearing in our high fertility projections does not come close to these limits, but does narrow the gap significantly.

Projections of Marriage Rates for All Women

In the preceding section we discussed the projections of birth rates of ever-married women. Next, we must consider projections of marriage rates. This is obvious, because the number of children born in future years will depend not only on the birth rates of married women but also on the number of women who marry. We need to project for the cohorts in question the proportion of women that will have married by various ages and their marriage rate during age intervals.

Here we are dependent primarily on census data. Fortunately, questions on marital status have been included in each census since 1890, and tabulations show the number of women of each age who have married. Similar information has been obtained in the Current Population Survey for selected years during 1947–55. Adding the proportions currently married, widowed, divorced, or legally separated, and allowing for the failure of marital status to be reported in some cases, gives the proportion ever married—the proportion who married for the first time prior to the age under consideration. Only first marriages are considered because birth rates of ever-married women in cohort fertility tables are for all women who have married by a given age, regardless of whether their first marriage has been broken.

Fairly accurate estimates of the total number of marriages performed in each year are available as far back as the 1880s. For our purpose, however, they are much less useful than the census data on marital status, because until recent years the marriages were not classified by age of bride or by whether the bride had been married previously. Even for 1957 this information is available only for 19 of the 29 states in the newly established Marriage Registration Area.

The proportion of the women of a given age who have ever married (shown by the census) is the equivalent of the cumulative marriage rate by that age. Similarly, the increase in the proportion ever married from a given age in one census to a 10-year-older age in the census 10 years later is approximately equal to the sum of the central first marriage rates for the cohort in question during the intervening years. Estimates of cumulative marriage rates at mid-points between censuses have been prepared by the Scripps Foundation, using as a partial guide the available information on annual numbers of marriages and (with an appropriate lag) the trends in rates for first births.

The marriage rates in question have one minor bias, namely, a tendency to be slightly too high at the younger ages. It occurs because some of the single women who have an illegitimate child are reported as married. Fortunately, this bias has no appreciable effect on the birth projections which we shall make, for reasons which will be brought out in the next section.

The outstanding intercohort change in cumulative marriage rates during recent years has been the striking tendency to marry at younger ages. For example, slightly over half of the women in the cohorts of 1886–90 to 1916–20 had married by ages 20–24, but over 70 per cent of those in the cohorts of 1931–35 had been brides by these ages (Table 10–6 and Figure 10–3). A slightly steeper upward intercohort trend is found in the proportion married by 15–19, but it has much less impact on the over-all picture because of the much smaller numbers of women involved. At each age from 25–29 to 45–49 the intercohort change in the cumulative marriage rate has been successively smaller; the rise from the cohorts of 1871–75 to those of 1911–15 amounts to about 4 per cent at ages 45–49.

The tendency for more women to marry younger shows up strikingly in the marriage rate between 15–19 and 20–24 (in the "increase" columns of Table 10–6).[9] This rate was fairly stable (between 380 and 420) from the cohorts of 1891–95 to 1916–20, but then shot up to around 550 for the 1926–30 and following groups. At older ages the recent tendency has been for the marriage rate to decline. Obviously, when many more

---

[9] These increases are real rates and are not subject to the restrictions that apply to the increases in cumulative birth rates for ever-married women discussed in Appendix G, Note 2.

TABLE 10-6. ACTUAL AND PROJECTED CUMULATIVE MARRIAGE RATES BY SPECIFIED AGES, AND INCREASES DURING AGE INTERVALS, FOR ALL WOMEN IN GROUPS OF COHORTS FROM 1871-75 TO 1946-50[a]

Cohorts	Year reach 15-19	Rate by 15-19	Increase	Rate by 20-24	Increase	Rate by 25-29	Increase	Rate by 30-34	Increase	Rate by 35-39	Increase	Rate by 40-44	Increase	Rate by 45-49
						Medium assumptions								
1946-50	1965	150	485	635	200	835	65	900	25	925	10	935	5	940
1941-45	1960	152	483	635	200	835	65	900	25	925	10	935	5	940
1936-40	1955	169	477	646	200	846	64	910	20	930	10	940	5	945
1931-35	1950	171	538	709	184	893	41	934	9	943	5	948	2	950
1926-30	1945	125	552	677	207	884	55	939	9	948	5	953	2	955
1921-25	1940	119	485	604	263	867	62	929	13	942	8	950	5	955
1916-20	1935	119	409	528	297	825	82	907	23	930	11	941	7	948
1911-15	1930	131	380	511	261	772	104	876	42	930	13	931	9	940
1906-10	1925	134	405	539	227	766	87	853	44	897	22	919	12	931
1901-05	1920	129	409	538	245	783	73	856	32	888	22	910	11	921
1896-1900	1915	124	420	544	239	783	85	868	22	890	15	905	10	915
1891-95	1910	117	403	520	249	769	98	867	29	896	10	906	8	914
1886-90	1905			515	242	757	94	851	39	890	15	905	9	914
1881-85	1900					750	99	849	31	880	10	900	10	910
1876-80	1895							838	35	873	17	890	12	902
1871-75	1890									880	11	891	9	900

Low assumptions

Cohorts	Year reach 15–19	Rate by 15–19	Increase	Rate of 20–24	Increase	Rate by 25–29	Increase	Rate by 30–34	Increase	Rate by 35–39	Increase	Rate by 40–44	Increase	Rate by 45–49
1946–50	1965	120	430	550	200	750	95	845	35	880	13	893	7	900
1941–45	1960	147	453	600	180	780	75	855	25	880	13	893	7	900
1936–40	1955	169	471	640	170	810	65	875	20	895	13	908	7	915
1931–35	1950	171	538	709	181	890	30	920	5	925	3	928	2	930
1926–30	1945	125	552	677	207	884	54	938	6	944	4	948	2	950
1921–25	1940	119	485	604	263	867	62	929	13	942	8	950	5	955
1916–20	1935	119	409	528	297	825	82	907	23	930	11	941	7	948
1911–15	1930	131	380	511	261	772	104	876	42	918	13	931	9	940

High assumptions

Cohorts	Year reach 15–19	Rate by 15–19	Increase	Rate of 20–24	Increase	Rate by 25–29	Increase	Rate by 30–34	Increase	Rate by 35–39	Increase	Rate by 40–44	Increase	Rate by 45–49
1946–50	1965	175	558	733	190	923	40	963	10	973	5	978	2	980
1941–45	1960	157	536	693	220	913	50	963	10	973	5	978	2	980
1936–40	1955	169	499	668	230	898	60	958	10	968	5	973	2	975
1931–35	1950	171	538	709	192	901	52	953	10	963	5	968	2	970
1926–30	1945	125	552	677	207	884	58	942	10	952	6	958	2	960
1921–25	1940	119	485	604	263	867	62	929	13	942	8	950	5	955
1916–20	1935	119	409	528	297	825	82	907	23	930	11	941	7	948
1911–15	1930	131	380	511	261	772	104	876	42	918	13	931	9	940

a Rates above the horizontal lines are projected. Rates for subsequent cohorts are the same as those for the 1946–50 cohorts.

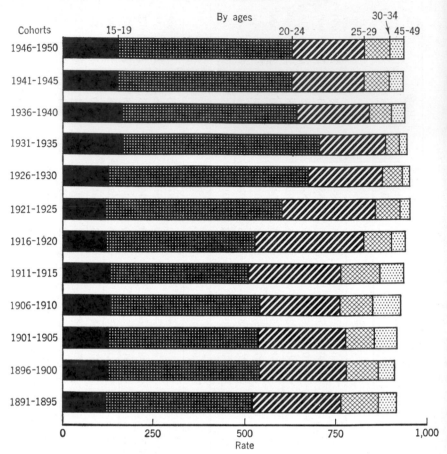

Fɪɢ. 10–3. Actual, and medium projected cumulative *marriage* rates by ages from 15–19 to 45–49, for *all women,* by groups of cohorts.

women married at young ages fewer were left to marry for the first time at subsequent ages, because the total proportion marrying by middle age has risen only slightly.

Projections of cumulative marriage rates and rates during age intervals must be based mainly on judgment and past trends, supplemented by the information on marriage expectations collected from the single women aged 18–24 who were included in our sample.[10] In our medium marriage projections it is assumed that the tendency to marry younger reached a peak among the cohorts of the 1930s and that subsequently there will be a slight tendency in the other direction. The proportion married by ages 15–19 apparently is slightly smaller for the cohorts of

[10] The information collected from single women will be analyzed in a subsequent report.

1936–40 (by 1955) than for those of 1931–35 (by 1950). The decrease in annual marriage rates from 1946 to 1954, the low level from 1954 to 1956, and the further decrease from 1956 to 1958 also suggest that the trend toward younger marriage has at least stopped, if not reversed.

The proportion marrying by middle age is assumed to reach a peak at 955 per 1,000 for the cohorts of 1921–30, whose members will reach age 45 between 1965 and 1975, and then decline gradually to 940 for the cohorts of 1941–45 and later.

In the low marriage projections there is a more abrupt reversal of the recent tendencies for more women to marry by younger ages and for fewer to remain permanently single. The proportion married by middle age is assumed to rise to 955 for the cohorts of 1921–25, as in the medium series, and then to decline to 900 for the cohorts of 1941–45 and later. This represents a return to the situation of the cohorts of the 1870s, whose members reached middle age in the 1920s. Marriage rates at younger ages are assumed to decline rapidly after 1955–60 and approximate the rates of the cohorts of 1916–20 at ages under 20–24. Such an abrupt change is not likely to occur unless the country is in the throes of a severe depression during the early 1960s.

The high marriage projections assume a renewal of the tendency for fewer women to remain single and for more to become brides before or during the early 20s. The proportion marrying by middle age rises from 940 for the cohorts of 1911–15 to 980 for those of 1941–45 and later. Increases of about the same relative size occur in the cumulative marriage rates by younger ages. Rates by all ages will exceed the highest yet recorded.

In each series the marriage rates projected for the current period (1955–60) were selected so that when applied to the numbers of women in the cohorts concerned they yield numbers of marriages which seem reasonable. When the projections were made (in June, 1958), available information about first marriages since July 1, 1955, indicated that from July 1, 1955, to June 30, 1960, there would be between 5,210,000 and 5,520,000, with 5,370,000 as a medium figure. Subsequent developments (by February, 1959) indicated that more probable low and medium estimates are 5,350,000 and 5,440,000.

Projections of Birth Rates for All Women—Single and Ever-married

In the two preceding sections we have described the projections of marriage rates and of birth rates of ever-married women. Multiplying the cumulative first marriage rate by a given age by the cumulative birth rate of ever-married women by this age gives the cumulative birth rate of all women regardless of marital status. For example, Table 10–6

Table 10–7. Actual and Projected Cumulative Birth Rates by Specified Ages, and Increases during Age Intervals, for All Women in Groups of Cohorts from 1871–75 to 1961–65[a]

Cohorts	Year reach 15–19	Rate by 15–19	Increase	Rate by 20–24	Increase	Rate by 25–29	Increase	Rate by 30–34	Increase	Rate by 35–39	Increase	Rate by 40–44	Increase	Rate by 45–49
						Medium assumptions								
1961–65	1980	126	826	952	968	1,920	555	2,475	281	2,756	94	2,850	17	2,867
1956–60	1975	128	831	959	974	1,933	547	2,480	276	2,756	94	2,850	17	2,867
1951–55	1970	130	842	972	982	1,954	530	2,484	277	2,761	89	2,850	17	2,867
1946–50	1965	132	852	984	1,003	1,987	506	2,493	273	2,766	84	2,850	17	2,867
1941–45	1960	139	874	1,013	1,013	2,026	492	2,518	255	2,773	77	2,850	17	2,867
1936–40	1955	143	865	1,008	1,032	2,040	520	2,560	233	2,793	72	2,865	17	2,882
1931–35	1950	126	849	975	1,125	2,100	541	2,641	196	2,837	53	2,890	8	2,898
1926–30	1945	85	703	788	1,017	1,805	767	2,572	214	2,786	71	2,857	8	2,865
1921–25	1940	85	550	635	888	1,523	723	2,246	416	2,662	139	2,801	16	2,817
1916–20	1935	77	487	564	734	1,298	644	1,942	404	2,346	174	2,520	21	2,541
1911–15	1930	88	472	560	617	1,177	557	1,734	385	2,119	166	2,285	27	2,312
1906–10	1925	94	548	642	624	1,266	472	1,738	335	2,073	169	2,242	30	2,272
1901–05	1920	85	615	700	735	1,435	501	1,936	301	2,237	151	2,388	32	2,420
1896–1900	1915	82	613	695	839	1,534	605	2,139	347	2,486	157	2,643	33	2,676
1891–95	1910	82	626	708	883	1,591	709	2,300	432	2,732	195	2,927	38	2,965
1886–90	1905							2,356	523	2,890	256	3,135	51	3,186
1881–85	1900									3,024	304	3,328	67	3,395
1876–80	1895											3,548	83	3,631
1871–75	1890													3,935

Cohorts	Year reach 15–19	Rate by 15–19	Increase	Rate by 20–24	Increase	Rate by 25–29	Increase	Rate by 30–34	Increase	Rate by 35–39	Increase	Rate by 40–44	Increase	Rate by 45–49
					Low assumptions									
1961–65	1980	83	539	622	600	1,222	552	1,774	338	2,112	119	2,231	19	2,250
1956–60	1975	83	549	632	620	1,252	539	1,791	321	2,112	119	2,231	19	2,250
1951–55	1970	84	565	649	633	1,282	526	1,808	304	2,112	119	2,231	19	2,250
1946–50	1965	86	590	676	674	1,350	509	1,859	271	2,130	101	2,231	19	2,250
1941–45	1960	131	732	863	727	1,590	452	2,042	200	2,242	78	2,320	20	2,340
1936–40	1955	143	843	986	828	1,814	450	2,264	160	2,424	71	2,495	21	2,516
1931–35	1950	126	849	975	1,092	2,067	420	2,487	115	2,602	41	2,643	7	2,650
1926–30	1945	85	703	788	1,017	1,805	698	2,530	148	2,651	49	2,700	8	2,708
1921–25	1940	85	550	635	888	1,523	723	2,246	361	2,607	99	2,706	16	2,722
1916–20	1935	77	487	564	734	1,298	644	1,942	404	2,346	155	2,501	21	2,522
					High assumptions									
1961–65	1980	175	1,144	1,319	1,219	2,538	505	3,043	187	3,230	44	3,274	9	3,283
1956–60	1975	175	1,144	1,319	1,219	2,538	505	3,043	187	3,230	44	3,274	9	3,283
1951–55	1970	175	1,144	1,319	1,219	2,538	505	3,043	187	3,230	44	3,274	9	3,283
1946–50	1965	173	1,139	1,312	1,217	2,529	485	3,014	207	3,221	53	3,274	9	3,283
1941–45	1960	152	1,059	1,211	1,252	2,463	520	2,983	226	3,209	65	3,274	9	3,283
1936–40	1955	143	926	1,069	1,249	2,318	650	2,968	224	3,192	66	3,258	8	3,266
1931–35	1950	126	849	975	1,194	2,169	678	2,847	222	3,069	75	3,144	8	3,152
1926–30	1945	85	703	788	1,017	1,805	813	2,618	284	2,902	114	3,016	8	3,024
1921–25	1940	85	550	635	888	1,523	723	2,246	451	2,697	199	2,896	17	2,913
1916–20	1935	77	487	564	734	1,298	644	1,942	404	2,346	193	2,539	21	2,560

a Rates above the horizontal lines are projected. Rates for subsequent cohorts are the same as those for the 1961–65 cohorts.

shows that the cumulative marriage rate of the women in the cohorts of 1926–30 was 677 by ages 20–24 and 884 by ages 25–29. Similarly, Table 10–5 shows that the cumulative birth rates of these ever-married women were 1,163 and 2,043. Multiplying the appropriate pairs of rates gives 788 and 1,805 as the cumulative birth rate of all members of the cohorts of 1926–30 by ages 20–24 and 25–29. The difference—1,017—is the current birth rate of all cohort members during the age interval from 20–24 to 25–29. If the numbers of women in these cohorts aged 20–24 on July 1, 1950, and 25–29 on July 1, 1955, are averaged and multiplied by the rate of 1,017 per 1,000, the result is the number of births that occurred to these women during the 5-year period 1950–55.[11]

The actual past rates and the future projected rates thus obtained are shown in Table 10–7 and Figure 10–4. By examining the rates by ages 45–49 we can see the combined influence of the assumptions about final proportion marrying and size of completed family which were made in the two preceding sections. In the medium series the projected final rate rises to approximately 2,900 births per 1,000 members of the cohorts of 1931–35 who live to ages 45–49 and declines only very slightly among subsequent cohorts. In the low series the final birth rate declines to 2,250 per 1,000 for the cohorts of 1946 and later. This would mean a situation similar to that of the cohorts of 1906–10. In the high series the final rate rises to very close to 3,300, or an average of about 3.3 children for all women in the cohorts of 1941–45 and later who live to middle age. This is approximately the rate for women in the cohorts of the 1880s who became 45–49 during the 1930s.

The combined influence of the assumptions regarding the changes in the timing pattern of marriages and of births to married women may be seen clearly by looking at rates for younger ages. In the medium series there is a slight reversal of the tendency for cohort members to marry and have children at the younger ages. Nevertheless, the cumulative birth rates at various ages under 30–34 remain substantially higher than they were for the women in the cohorts of 1890–1925. In most cases the high mark is set by the cohorts of the 1930s.

In the low projections there is an abrupt reversal after 1958 or thereabouts in the tendency to marry and concentrate childbearing in the younger ages. However, it does not go so far as to return to the low marks set by the cohorts of 1911–15. As indicated earlier, such an extreme trend is not to be expected unless a severe depression develops and lasts for a few years.

In the high series the recent trend toward childbearing at younger

---

[11] It is the sum of the numbers of births to the women in each of these cohorts during each year of the period. These numbers were used in computing the birth rates in the cohort tables.

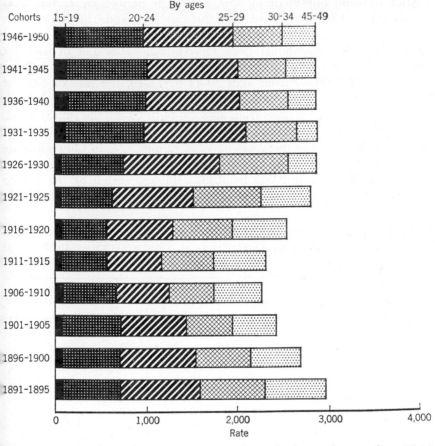

FIG. 10–4. Actual, and medium projected cumulative *birth* rates by ages from 15–19 to 45–49, for *all women,* by groups of cohorts.

ages continues at a rapid pace up to the cohorts of the 1950s. If performance should be in line with the high fertility projections, the women in these cohorts would have approximately 77 per cent of all births before age 27, which is more than half again as large as the actual proportion (51 per cent) for the cohorts of 1911–15.

Period Birth Rates during Coming Years

Cohort fertility is a relatively new concept in population studies. In fact it is so new that many demographers have not as yet used cohort fertility rates enough to be able to interpret them accurately and easily. It is desirable, therefore, to see what our projections of cohort fertility rates signify in terms of birth rates like those used commonly in the past.

After showing our medium, low, and high projections of the total population in Chapter 11 we shall present the crude birth rates for each of these series. Here we can serve our purpose more easily and accurately with conventional gross reproduction rates. Let us consider 1950–55. If we refer to Table 10–7 and add the birth rate of 143 for the cohorts of 1936–40 from ages 10–14 to 15–19, the rate of 849 for the 1931–35 cohorts from ages 15–19 to 20–24, and so on up to the rate of 30 for the 1906–10 cohorts from ages 40–44 to 45–49, the sum is 3,332, and may be termed the cumulative or final birth rate of a hypothetical group of cohorts whose members have, at various ages in the childbearing period, the 1950–55 birth rates of members of actual cohorts at these ages. Multiplying 3,332 by 0.487 (the proportion of the babies that were girls) gives 1,623 per 1,000—the conventional gross female

TABLE 10–8. ACTUAL AND PROJECTED FEMALE GROSS REPRODUCTION RATES (1) FOR FIVE-YEAR PERIODS (HYPOTHETICAL COHORTS) FROM 1920–25 TO 1975–80 AND (2) FOR ACTUAL COHORTS FROM 1871–75 TO 1961–65[a]

Period (July 1 through June 30)	Rates for 5-year periods (hypothetical cohorts)			Actual cohorts	Rates for actual cohorts		
	Actual or medium	Low	High		Actual or medium	Low	High
1975–80	1,353	999	1,618	1961–65	1,396	1,096	1,599
1970–75	1,344	966	1,638	1956–60	1,396	1,096	1,599
1965–70	1,363	989	1,738	1951–55	1,396	1,096	1,599
1960–65	1,438	1,137	1,784	1946–50	1,396	1,096	1,599
1955–60	1,711	1,611	1,829	1941–45	1,396	1,140	1,599
1950–55	1,623			1936–40	1,404	1,225	1,591
1945–50	1,435			1931–35	1,411	1,291	1,535
1940–45	1,191			1926–30	1,395	1,319	1,473
1935–40	1,051			1921–25	1,372	1,326	1,419
1930–35	1,104			1916–20	1,237	1,228	1,247
1925–30	1,330			1911–15	1,126		
1920–25	1,543			1906–10	1,106		
				1901–05	1,179		
				1896–1900	1,303		
				1891–95	1,444		
				1886–90	1,552		
				1881–85	1,653		
				1876–80	1,768		
				1871–75	1,916		

[a] The rates are in thousands. Those below the horizontal lines are actual; those above these lines are partly or entirely projected.

reproduction rate for 1950–55. For convenience, such a rate will be referred to as a period rate, and the gross reproduction rate for an actual cohort will be referred to as a cohort rate.

The period gross reproduction rate for 1950–55 is 1,623. For 1955–60 our fertility projections give rates which vary from 1,611 in the low series to 1,829 in the high series, with 1,711 as a medium figure (Table 10–8). In each of the three series the period gross reproduction rate declines from the high mark reached during 1950–55 or 1955–60. In the medium series the decrease amounts to more than 20 per cent, in the low series it is nearly 40 per cent, while in the high it is about 10 per cent. At first glance it may seem unreasonable to have a decline in the period rate computed from the high projected cohort rates for marriages and for births to ever-married women, which assume not only an increase in the proportion of women marrying and in the size of family of those who marry, but also more marriages and childbearing at younger ages. It should be noted, however, that the gross reproduction rate of 1,623 for 1950–55, which is computed from actual age-specific rates, exceeds the final rate for any real cohorts since those of the early 1880s (Figure 10–5). Moreover, it exceeds by a substantial margin the fertility expectations of the women who were bearing most

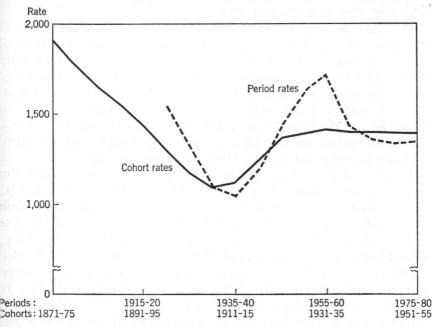

Fɪɢ. 10–5. Actual and projected female gross reproduction rates, for time periods and actual groups of cohorts.

of the children born during 1950–55, namely, the members of the cohorts of 1921–25 to 1931–35 whose *maximum* expectations indicate a cohort gross reproduction rate of between 1,420 and 1,535. It is clear, therefore, that age-specific rates could not remain for several years as high as they were during 1950–55 unless the average size of completed family were to increase substantially more than is anticipated by the wives in our study. Since the gross reproduction rate for 1955–60 very probably will exceed that for 1950–55, a reduction after 1955–60 is almost inevitable rather than unreasonable.

The medium series envisages that declines in cohort age–specific birth rates will lower the period gross reproduction rate to about where it was during 1925–30. In the low series a new trough would be reached, somewhat under that of 1935–40. The high series assumes a gradual decline, with the rate after 1980 somewhat smaller than it was during 1950–55.

The fluctuations in period gross reproduction rates have a substantially wider amplitude than the fluctuations in the gross reproduction rates of actual cohorts. For example, the period rate dropped 32 per cent from 1920–25 to 1935–40 (in 15 years) and then jumped 54 per cent from 1935–40 to 1950–55 (also in 15 years). In contrast, the most rapid 15-year change in the rate for actual cohorts is the 23 per cent decline from the cohorts of 1891–95 to those of 1906–10.

The wider fluctuations of the period gross reproduction rates than of the cohort rates, and the extremely low and high rates for periods of a few years, reflect primarily the changes in the timing of marriages and births which have been pointed out. Many people postponed marriage during the 1930s, and many of the couples who married delayed starting their families; it was in these years that period birth rates reached record lows in the United States. After the end of the war there was a substantial making up of births postponed previously and a marked tendency to marry and start childbearing at younger ages.

The effect of these changes in timing is spread over several years. For example, young couples who postponed the first baby from 1942 to 1947 and expected to have four children are likely to have postponed their second baby from 1944 to 1949 and their fourth from 1948 (or later) to 1953 (or later). The consequence is that during 1945–57 (or later) annual birth rates and numbers of births are swelled by the births that would have occurred during earlier years if the depression and recovery and the mobilization and demobilization associated with World War II had not caused such large changes in the timing patterns of marriage and childbearing. They have also been swelled by the births that would have occurred later if there had not been a substantial reduction in average age at marriage and childbearing.

Changes in Timing Patterns and in Numbers of Births

As married couples become fairly successful in regulating conception, not only can they avoid having more children than they want, but they can have those they want *when* they want them. They can postpone pregnancy when unemployment is high and incomes are low, as was the case during the depression of the 1930s, and try to conceive later when conditions improve. Conversely, when business is booming couples can have their children sooner than they would otherwise. Formerly, such changes in economic conditions influenced annual births and birth rates only indirectly, by discouraging or encouraging marriage. Now they can operate in two ways, changing the ages at which married couples have their children as well as the ages at which single persons marry. In consequence, large-scale shiftings of births from one period to another have taken place in the United States in recent decades. They have been responsible in major degree for the ups and downs of annual birth rates.

Measuring the number of births involved in these changes was very difficult before the development of cohort fertility tables and still can be only approximate. A major problem is how to "unscramble" the two important factors that influence fertility in each year, namely, changes in size of completed families and changes in the timing of the births that make up these families.

The best procedure developed as yet has two important steps. The first is the selection of some timing pattern as a standard. For the United States a reasonable standard is the actual timing pattern of some of the cohorts whose members have reached the end of the childbearing period. The percentage distribution by age periods of the final cumulative birth rates for all women living to middle age in these cohorts is then applied to the final rates of preceding or subsequent cohorts in order to obtain the rates which would have been in effect during each age period with the standard timing pattern. Next, applying these hypothetical rates to the numbers of women in the appropriate cohorts gives the "standard-pattern" numbers of births, i.e., the numbers that would have occurred if the standard timing pattern had been in effect. The differences between these hypothetical numbers and the actual numbers show the effect of the change in the timing pattern.

This brings us to the second step, namely, what to use as the final rates of the cohorts whose members are still young enough to bear children. For example, if we wish to measure the extent to which the number of births during 1950–54 was influenced by intercohort changes in the timing of births, as distinguished from intercohort changes in size of completed families, we must consider (among others) the cohorts of 1931–35 whose members were 15–19 years old in 1950. For such cohorts it is necessary to use projected final rates, like those developed earlier in this chapter.

Our end product, therefore, will be a series of estimates. Each set in the series will show how much the number of births in a given period of years has been increased or decreased by changes in the timing of births from a pattern chosen as a standard, in conjunction with actual and/or projected changes in size of completed families. By comparing different sets of estimates it is possible to draw useful conclusions regarding the relative impact on annual fertility of changes in timing and changes in family size.

It is important to note that the procedure must be followed separately for births of each order, because intercohort changes in timing and in final rates vary greatly with order of birth. Moreover (as has been mentioned earlier), the postponement of first births during one year tends to mean the postponement of second births a year (or more) later and the postponement of higher-order births with an increasing lag. This means that many of the postponed first births may be made up 2 years later when many second births are being postponed. To simplify the present discussion we shall not refer to numbers of births of particular orders, but only to totals obtained by combining such numbers. The more detailed analysis will be published later.

The best timing pattern to use as a standard for the United States at present probably is the actual distribution of the final rates for births of each order to women in the cohorts of 1891–1900 as a group. On the one hand, these are the earliest cohorts for which we have a complete (or nearly complete) history of first marriage and childbearing. On the other hand, they are the latest cohorts whose fertility was not influenced in major degree by the depression of the 1930s or by World War II. World War I influenced their marriage and childbearing patterns more than those of most of the preceding or subsequent cohorts, but it was a much less powerful force than the other two events. The 1891–1900 cohorts have been chosen as the standard in a study (by Whelpton) from which partial results are now available.

The cohorts of 1906–10 and later, whose women have borne most of the children since 1930, have timing patterns which differ substantially from those of the cohorts of 1891–1900. For some of these cohorts the tendency has been to marry and bear children at older ages. In contrast, more of the women in certain other cohorts have married and had more of their children at younger ages. In order to understand the effect of these dissimilar patterns we shall examine two groups of cohorts, namely, those of 1911–15 and of 1931–35. For the earlier group the final fertility rate is approximately 2,310 births per 1,000 women living to middle age; for the later group our projected final rate is between 2,650 and 3,150. Here we shall focus our attention on the medium figure of 2,900 (Table 10–7). For both groups we shall contrast the actual number of births during age and time periods with the number that would have occurred if the final rates for births of each order had been distributed among age intervals in the same proportion as for the cohorts of 1891–1900.

Cohorts of 1911–15. The women in these cohorts began to marry in the late 1920s. By ages 15–19 (by 1930) they had borne nearly 60,000 more children than if they had observed the standard timing pattern we have chosen. Then came the depression. So many single people postponed marriage and so many married couples put off having children during 1930–34 that the number of births was reduced more than 500,000 below the standard-pattern number (Table 10–9, column *G*, and Figure 10–6). In addition, the actual number during 1930–34 was depressed because nearly 60,000 births had occurred earlier in 1925–29. An additional 820,000 births were postponed during 1935–39. This means the actual number of births fell below the standard-pattern number by 18 per cent during 1930–34 and also during 1935–39 (columns *C* and *D*).

At the beginning of 1940 these women were 25–29 years old and had a "deficit" of more than 1,300,000 births. Fortunately, their husbands or prospective husbands were still older; hence a large proportion were not drafted in World War II. As unemployment dropped sharply and wages rose during 1940–44 many postponed marriages were solemnized and nearly 400,000 postponed babies were born (Table 10–9, column *H*). Nearly all of them were the first or second in the family. But while these postponed births were being made up, nearly 200,000 third to sixth births were being postponed as a consequence of the putting off of first and second births during the 1930s.

After the end of the war these cohorts had much higher fertility than if the timing pattern of the earlier group had prevailed. More than 700,000 postponed births were made up during 1945–49, and about 360,000 during 1950–54. In consequence, the actual number of births during 1945–49 and 1950–54 exceeded the standard-pattern number by about 42 and 51 per cent, respectively. Only about 65,000 postponed babies remained to be born during 1955 or later. Nearly all of them have made their appearance.[12]

Cohorts of 1931–35. The experience of these women also differs from that of the 1891–1900 group and is even more unlike that of the 1911–15 cohorts. These women began to marry and bear children in the late

---

[12] One of the provisions of the procedure is that by the end of the childbearing period the number of births made up equals the number postponed earlier except for a relatively slight deficit due to the death of some women.

TABLE 10–9. NUMBERS OF BIRTHS ADVANCED, "HAD OCCURRED EARLIER," POSTPONED, OR MADE UP, FOR WOMEN IN THE COHORTS OF 1911–15 AND 1931–35 DURING SUCCESSIVE FIVE-YEAR AGE INTERVALS, USING MEDIUM PROJECTIONS OF FINAL FERTILITY RATES, AND THE TIMING PATTERNS OF THE COHORTS OF 1891–1900 AS A STANDARD (IN THOUSANDS)[a]

Interval between exact ages	Period (calendar years)	Number of births		Difference due to changes in timing patterns		Number of births			
		(A) With timing patterns of cohorts of 1891–1900	(B) Actual	(C) Number (B − A)	(D) Per cent (C ÷ A)	(E) Advanced	(F) Had occurred earlier	(G) Postponed	(H) Made up
Cohorts of 1911–15									
10–14 and 15–19	1925–29	297	355	58	19.5	58	0	0	0
15–19 and 20–24	1930–34	3,156	2,598	−558	−17.7	6	−58	−506	0
20–24 and 25–29	1935–39	4,481	3,655	−826	−18.4	0	−6	−820	0
25–29 and 30–34	1940–44	3,124	3,332	208	6.7	6	0	−190	392
30–34 and 35–39	1945–49	1,664	2,364	700	42.1	0	0	−18	718
35–39 and 40–44	1950–54	711	1,076	365	51.3	5	0	0	360
40–44 and 45–49[b]	1955–59	155	194	39	25.2	0	−11	0	50
Cohorts of 1931–35									
10–14 and 15–19	1945–49	330	480	150	45.5	150	0	0	0
15–19 and 20–24	1950–54	3,529	4,187	658	18.6	658	0	0	0
20–24 and 25–29[b]	1955–59	5,419	6,250	831	15.3	1,031	−200	0	0

[a] From study being conducted by P. K. Whelpton, Scripps Foundation for Research in Population Problems.　[b] Preliminary estimates.

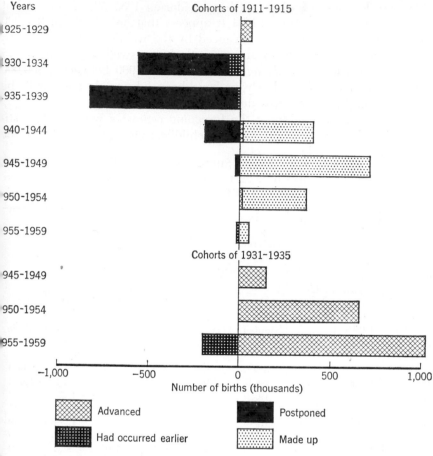

Fɪɢ. 10–6. Numbers of births advanced, "had occurred earlier," postponed, or made up, for women in cohorts of 1911–15 and 1931–35.

940s and set new records for these actions. By 1950 their births exceeded he standard-pattern number by between 145,000 and 166,000 (between 3 and 53 per cent), depending on whether the high or low fertility projections are used (Table 10–9 and Figure 10–6). (In this connection it should be noted that the *high* fertility projections mean *larger* standard-pattern birth rates at each age interval, which *decreases* the estimated number of births advanced as a result of earlier marriage and childbearing.) The new timing pattern advanced a much larger number of births to 1950–54. The relative change is smaller, however, because the women were living from ages 15–19 to 20–24 during this period, and birth rates of all women are much higher at these ages than at younger ages.

We are less sure of what will happen during 1955–59, of course, but as this is written (in July, 1958) it appears that an additional 800,000 to 1 million births are being advanced by the women in these cohorts. This means that their births are currently being swelled by roughly 15 per cent because of the changes in timing. By 1960 between 1,300,000 and 2 million births are likely to have been advanced. There will be correspondingly fewer births during the 1960s.

All Cohorts. By combining the foregoing estimates with similar estimates for the other cohorts in the childbearing ages we obtain the

TABLE 10–10. NUMBERS OF BIRTHS SHIFTED FROM ONE FIVE-YEAR PERIOD TO ANOTHER AS RESULT OF CHANGES IN TIMING PATTERNS FOR MARRIAGE AND CHILDBEARING FROM THOSE OF THE COHORTS OF 1891–1900 (IN THOUSANDS)[a]

Period (calendar years)	Number of births		Difference due to changes in timing patterns		Number of births			
	(A) With timing patterns of cohorts of 1891–1900	(B) Actual	(C) Number (B − A)	(D) Percent (C ÷ A)	(E) Advanced	(F) Had occurred earlier	(G) Postponed	(H) Made up
1955–59[b]	16,700	20,300	3,600	21.6	2,950	−300	−50	1,000
1950–54	16,584	19,411	2,827	17.0	1,284	−6	−124	1,673
1945–49	16,313	17,372	1,059	6.5	528	0	−1,231	1,762
1940–44	15,142	14,294	−848	−5.6	22	−23	−1,674	827
1935–39	14,056	12,107	−1,949	−13.9	18	−50	−1,986	69
1930–34	13,597	12,267	−1,330	−9.8	38	−198	−1,170	0
1925–29	13,855	13,806	−49	−0.4	154	−191	−12	0
1920–24	14,518	14,776	258	1.8	258	0	0	0
1915–19	14,546	14,561	15	0.1	15	0	0	0

[a] From study being conducted by P. K. Whelpton, Scripps Foundation for Research in Population Problems.

[b] Preliminary estimates.

over-all picture for various periods of years. Changes in the timing of marriage and childbearing shifted approximately 2,800,000 births to 1950–54, so that the actual number exceeded the standard-pattern number by about 17 per cent (Table 10–10 and Figure 10–7). Somewhat more than half of the increase represents the making up of births postponed earlier, while nearly half represents the advancing of births because of the tendency to marry and have children at younger ages. During 1945–49 the changes in timing pattern swelled the number of births by over 1 million. In this period some cohorts were postponing

ubstantial numbers of births, others were making up large numbers
postponed earlier, and still others (those in the early childbearing ages)
were advancing births.

The situation during the years just mentioned is in striking contrast
o that of World War II and the depression decade of the 1930s. During
World War II women in the young childbearing ages were postponing
arge numbers of births while older women were making up some of

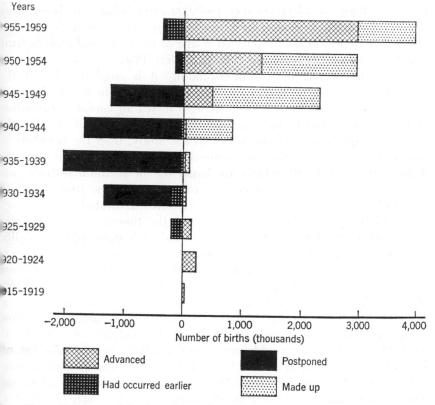

Years

FIG. 10–7. Numbers of births advanced, "had occurred earlier," postponed, or
 made up, during 5-year periods from 1915–19 to 1955–59.

those postponed during the depression. The net deficit in this period
mounted to about 850,000 births. During the 1930 decade there was
 net postponement of over 3 million births, presumably because the
depression kept many single people from marrying and led many of
those who married to delay children longer than had been customary
formerly.

The magnitude of these fluctuations is emphasized at the close of
this chapter because, if it is not realized, one's judgment of future

fertility is likely to be distorted seriously by the large number of birth and the high birth rate in each year during 1947–58. At the beginning of 1955 there were still approximately 1 million postponed births according to our standard pattern, most of which will be made up before 1960. A much larger shift to 1955–59 is the advancing of between 2,500,000 and 3,500,000 births that would have occurred in 1960 or later if such unusually large numbers of women had not gone to the altar, and subsequently to the maternity ward, before 1960. It is probable, therefore, that between 3,500,000 and 4,500,000 extra babies are being born during the current period. This raises by about 22 per cent the number of births that would have occurred if age at marriage and childbearing had remained as it was for the cohorts of 1891–1900.

To lessen the risk of misunderstanding, it is emphasized that the foregoing estimates represent the effect of changes in the timing pattern *over and above the effect of changes in size of completed families.* If couples are going to have as many children as are indicated by the minimum expectations of the wives in our study, then the numbers of births shifted to the 1950s are somewhat larger than the estimates in Tables 10–9 and 10–10, which are based on the medium fertility projections. Conversely, if the maximum expectations come true, the shifting of births is on a somewhat smaller scale than indicated.

Would the picture be much different if the timing pattern of somewhat earlier or later cohorts had been used as a standard? A detailed answer cannot be given as yet, but in general the answer is no. Women in the cohorts of the 1880s bore a slightly larger proportion of their babies at older ages than did those of the 1890s. If the timing pattern of the earlier group were used as the standard, the estimated number of births advanced to the 1950s would be slightly larger than those shown in Tables 10–9 and 10–10. Using the cohorts of 1906–10 or 1911–15 as a standard would increase substantially the estimated numbers of births advanced to the 1950s and decrease the estimated numbers postponed before or during World War II and made up afterward. The timing pattern for the 1901–05 cohorts is very much like that of the 1891–1900 cohorts; using it would give essentially the results discussed above.

What do the past and current shifts imply regarding births in coming years? The answer depends in large measure on whether the new timing pattern will be followed or whether there will be further changes. If the new timing pattern is followed without change there will be a decrease in annual birth rates and numbers of births until it becomes firmly established. This will happen with the increase in the size of completed families which is assumed in the medium projections. However, the decrease will be larger if family size shrinks in line with the low fertility projections, and smaller if family size goes up as assumed in the high projections. The fact to be emphasized is that *a tendency to have children at younger ages increases annual birth rates and numbers of births only while it is in progress.* Once the new pattern is established there is a return to the base corresponding to the numbers of persons of childbearing age and to the size of completed families. The situation is similar to the effect on manufacturers' orders which is exerted when wholesalers and retailers build up inventories. If consumer demand remains constant, manufacturers' orders are raised while inventories are being increased, or lowered while inventories are being decreased. But once the desired higher (or lower) inventory level is reached, manufacturers' orders return to the base provided by customer demand. If age at marriage and childbearing and the size of completed families were to stabilize at about where they are for the cohorts of 1926–30, we would expect a decrease of approximately 2 million births from 1955–59 to 1960–64. This is the medium fertility projection.

One should remember, however, that the timing patterns of recent cohorts are more extreme than those of earlier cohorts in the extent to which marriage and childbearing are concentrated in the younger ages. In consequence, a severe depression like that of the 1930s might cause a more extreme postponement of marriage and childbearing than occurred in that decade. The resulting drop in annual birth rates and numbers of births might be more abrupt than that from the 1920s to the 1930s. This contingency, together with a decrease in family size, is taken into account in the low fertility projections.

Finally, if there are the continuation of the tendency to have children younger and the increase in family size which are assumed in the high fertility projections, there will be only a small decrease in annual birth rates from 1955–59 to 1960–64 and the number of births will increase slightly.

Summary

The usefulness of population projections for the United States depends largely on the assumptions regarding future fertility. The fertility projections presented here are the first to utilize the expectations of a national probability sample of wives in the childbearing ages and the experience of actual cohorts of women, as well as the forecaster's interpretation of past trends in annual birth rates.

Our medium, low, and high projections of the average size of completed families—the number of births per 1,000 ever-married women living to middle age—are based on cohort fertility tables, carried forward according to the most likely, minimum, and maximum expectations of the wives in our study. Our assumptions about "timing"—the ages at which women marry and have their babies—are based on the cohort fertility tables, supplemented by study data. The tables indicate how timing patterns have varied in the past under the influence of depression, prosperity, war, and peace.

The medium fertility projections for ever-married women assume a rise in family size to about 3 births per woman, with a timing pattern similar to that being developed by the cohorts of the 1930s. The low series is based on a return to the small families (averaging about 2.5 births) of the cohorts of 1906–15 and a partial return to their older ages at marriage and childbearing. The high series allows for births per ever-married woman to rise to 3.3 (the maximum expectation of the wives interviewed) and for some continuation of the recent tendency to marry and have babies at younger ages.

Population growth depends not only on family size but also on the proportion of women who marry. Our medium marriage projections envisage that 94 per cent of the women who live to middle age will have married, but at slightly older ages than in recent years. The low series assumes that 90 per cent will marry (as was the case for women aged 45–49 in 1920) and that age at marriage will be raised much as it was by the depression of the 1930s. The high forecast is that 98 per cent will marry and that the recent tendency to marry younger will continue for a time.

Multiplying the projected cumulative birth rates for ever-married women by the projected marriage rates gives the birth rates for all women which are used in computing numbers of births in future years.

The annual birth rates and numbers of births which have occurred in past years, and which would occur if fertility were to follow our projections, are influenced greatly by changes in the timing of childbearing. Several hundred thousand babies were postponed from the 1930s to the 1940s, and other hundreds of thousands from World War II to the postwar period. Moreover, the number of births during 1947–57 has been swelled by the millions advanced from later years as a result of younger marriage and childbearing. As a consequence, annual birth rates almost certainly will fall for at least a few years, and numbers of births may decline. Widely different, but possible, changes in future years are shown by the medium, low, and high fertility projections.

It is quite unlikely that actual fertility trends will follow closely any of our projections. The low and high series are designed to represent extremes which are rather unlikely to be reached. The medium series represents a central trend around which actual rates may fluctuate. We believe that actual fertility is likely to be below the medium projections more often than above them.

Chapter 11

POPULATION GROWTH, 1955 TO 2000

In the first half of the twentieth century the population of the United States doubled. Will growth in the last half of the century be this rapid? Between 1900 and 1950 the median age rose from 23 to 30 years and the number of males per 100 females dropped from 104 to 99. What kind of changes can we expect in the next 50 years? To get approximate answers to these and more specific questions about the size and composition of the population, we prepared forecasts extending from 1955 to the end of the century.

These projections are unique in several respects. First, they are based on marriage rates and on birth rates for ever-married women. Second, the marriage and birth assumptions are on a cohort basis. As explained in Chapter 10, this permits us to make explicit assumptions about final marriage and birth rates for each cohort and about the timing of marriages and births within each cohort. Third, the assumptions made about size of completed family are based largely on the expectations of a nationwide probability sample of wives in the childbearing period. These distinctive features should permit us to prepare better projections than those based on less adequate techniques and information. It must be remembered, however, that no one can be certain of predicting future population with accuracy. The best we can hope to do is give a range within which future population seems likely to vary during the next 25 years, and beyond that period to give a central trend that now seems reasonable but is by no means certain.

Method of Preparing the Population Forecasts

The forecasts were prepared by the "cohort-component" method; that is, allowances were made for each component of population growth (births, deaths, and international migrants) separately for groups of cohorts. (In this context, as previously, we are using the word cohort to designate a group of persons born in the same year, but are referring to males as well as females.) We started with a 1955 population, classified

373

by age and sex, and for each succeeding 5-year period subtracted deaths from each age group and added births and immigrants. The numbers of births were obtained by applying the fertility assumptions described in Chapter 10 to numbers of women classified by age for 1955 and every fifth year thereafter. The numbers of deaths and immigrants were obtained by applying the mortality and migration assumptions described below to successive age-sex distributions.

Base Population, 1955. In order to prepare forecasts for future years we must begin with reliable figures for the population, classified by age and sex in the base year. We could use the official estimate for 1955, prepared by the Bureau of the Census, but we prefer not to do this, because the official estimate is lower than the actual population and contains biases in age distribution. These shortcomings reflect similar biases in the 1950 census, on which the 1955 population estimate was partially based. The 1950 census is too low because some people were missed by the enumerators; its age distribution is slightly in error because the proportion missed varied from age to age and because the ages of some people were reported incorrectly. The Census Bureau is, of course, aware of these biases, but it continues to publish estimates containing them so that the estimates will be consistent with the most recent census count.

As a basis for our forecasts, we estimated a corrected population for July 1, 1955, as follows: (1) the official estimate of numbers by sex and age for July 1, 1950,[1] was adjusted to allow for underreporting and misstatement of age, with the use of correction factors estimated by Ansley Coale;[2] (2) the corrected population for 1950 was brought forward to July 1, 1955, with the use of estimated births for the population under 5 years old and deaths and immigrants for all age-sex groups. These components of change were estimated by the Census Bureau.

Because a corrected estimate of the population, classified by age and sex, was used as the base, the forecasts are not strictly comparable with the 1950 census. They will probably not be comparable with the 1960 census either, because it will also be subject to errors of omission and misstatement of age. As of July 1, 1950, the corrected population, which is consistent with the forecasts, exceeds the Census Bureau estimate by 5.5 million, or 3.6 per cent. As of July 1, 1955, the population base for our forecasts exceeds the Bureau estimate by the same absolute amount as

---

[1] "Estimates of the Population of the United States, by Age, Color, and Sex: July 1, 1950 to 1956," *Current Population Reports,* U.S. Bureau of the Census, series P-25, no. 146, Nov. 12, 1956.

[2] Ansley J. Coale, "The Population of the United States in 1950 Classified by Age Sex, and Color: A Revision of Census Figures," *Journal of the American Statistical Association,* vol. 50, no. 269, pp. 16–54, March, 1955.

in 1950, which is 3.3 per cent of the 1955 total.[3] We cannot now say how large the difference between census counts or estimates and our forecasts will be in 1960 or later years, but we are sure that our forecasts of the total population (and of virtually all age groups) will need to be lowered or the census counts or estimates raised before the two series are comparable.

Mortality Assumptions. Next, we must make assumptions about what proportion of the population in each age group will be living at older ages. For this purpose we use survival rates—the proportion of persons who survive from one age to another. The medium survival rates used to project the population are averages of high and low forecasts of future survival rates prepared by Greville.[4] First, he made high and low forecasts for the year 2000 for age-specific death rates separately for 10 groups of causes of death; these forecasts were based on informed opinions of public health specialists in the National Office of Vital Statistics and the National Institutes of Health as to how far mortality from each group of causes would be reduced below the level observed in 1953. Second, he derived survival rates for the year 2000 from these death rates. Third, he obtained survival rates for intervening years by mathematical interpolation between those for 1949–51, 1953–55, and 2000.

Of the mortality rates forecast for the year 2000, Greville writes:[5]

Needless to say, they are highly conjectural; in general terms, the low-mortality projection is intended to reflect a definitely optimistic view as to the future course of mortality rates, while the high-mortality projection is intended to reflect a pessimistic view, particularly with regard to the possibility of reduction in death rates for the diseases typical of old age. However, the high-mortality projection does contemplate some future improvement in mortality.

The expectation of life at birth computed from the medium forecasts of survival rates is presented on page 376 for each 5-year period between 1955 and 2000 (1949–51 values are shown for comparison).[6]

Migration Assumptions. We adopted the migration assumptions developed by the Census Bureau, namely, a net immigration of 1.4 million persons in the 5-year period July 1, 1955–60, and 1.2 million in every

[3] In the comparisons both for 1950 and 1955 we are using the Census Bureau estimates that are comparable with the 1950 census, not the estimates that include a corrected population under 5 years of age.

[4] T. N. E. Greville, *Illustrative United States Population Projections,* Actuarial Study no. 46, U.S. Department of Health, Education and Welfare, Social Security Administration, Division of the Actuary, pp. 18–21, May, 1957.

[5] *Ibid.,* p. 10.

[6] The expectation of life at birth is the average number of years that persons born in a specified period (such as 1955–60) would live if they were subject to the age-specific mortality rates of that period throughout their lives.

Period	Male	Female
1949–51	65.5	71.0
1955–60	66.9	73.1
1960–65	67.7	74.0
1965–70	68.5	74.8
1970–75	69.2	75.5
1975–80	69.8	76.0
1980–85	70.4	76.5
1985–90	70.8	76.8
1990–95	71.1	77.0
1995–2000	71.3	77.1

subsequent 5-year period, with an age-sex distribution like that in 1950–55.[7] These assumptions are consistent with the volume and composition of the movement into the country during 1950–55. Whether such migration will continue in future years is a matter of conjecture; these assumptions should be considered as arbitrary.

Future Trends in the Total Population

The population of the United States may double in the last half of this century, just as it did in the first half. According to our medium projections, the number of inhabitants will reach 300 million shortly before the end of the century and 312 million by 2000, as compared with 157 million in 1950. Looking a little less far into the future, it seems fairly certain that our population will surpass the 200 million mark by 1980 unless atomic war occurs. The medium series shows 239 million for this year, and the low and high series show 215 million and 262 million, respectively (Table 11–1 and Figure 11–1).

In spite of the outlook for large future growth, the tendency for larger numbers of persons to be added to our population every 5 years seems likely to be temporarily reversed in the near future. Between 1950 and 1955, the population grew by 13.6 million. Our medium forecast for the current 5 years is 13.8 million, but for 1960–65 it is only 11.1 million (Table 11–1). In the latter half of the 1960s, the addition to our population rises to 12.3 million and continues rising to 20 million in the last 5 years of the century.

If actual fertility trends follow the low projections, the number of people added to our population every 5 years will drop drastically from 12.6 million in 1955–60 to 6.8 million in 1965–70, but will then rise to 9.3 million in 1975–80.

[7] "Revised Projections of the Population of the United States, by Age and Sex: 1960 to 1975," *Current Population Reports,* U.S. Bureau of the Census, series P-25, no. 123, Oct. 20, 1955.

Our high forecast is the only one that does not show a fall in our population increment in the next few years. Instead, it indicates the possibility of a relatively constant increase of over 15 million for both 1960–65 and 1965–70. After that, the high increment rises to 23 million in 1975–80. It is certain that actual population growth will not follow closely any

TABLE 11–1. PROJECTED POPULATION, 1955–2000, AND ABSOLUTE AND PERCENTAGE INCREASE IN POPULATION DURING FIVE-YEAR PERIODS

July 1	Total population (thousands)	Increase in preceding 5 years	
		Absolute (thousands)	Per cent
1955	170,739	13,587	8.6
Medium			
1960	184,582	13,843	8.1
1965	195,643	11,061	6.0
1970	207,953	12,310	6.3
1975	222,533	14,580	7.0
1980	239,000	16,467	7.4
1985	256,049	17,049	7.1
1990	273,265	17,216	6.7
1995	291,677	18,412	6.7
2000	311,997	20,320	7.0
Low			
1960	183,361	12,622	7.4
1965	190,631	7,270	4.0
1970	197,421	6,790	3.6
1975	205,418	7,997	4.1
1980	214,673	9,255	4.5
High			
1960	185,985	15,246	8.9
1965	201,397	15,412	8.3
1970	219,272	17,875	8.9
1975	239,267	19,995	9.1
1980	262,149	22,882	9.6

of our projections, particularly in view of the cyclical pattern of fertility trends that has replaced the steadily downward movement observed before 1940. *Such forecasts show only what would happen if immigration, mortality, and fertility were to follow specified trends which seem reasonable in the light of current knowledge.* Our best guess is that future

Population (millions)

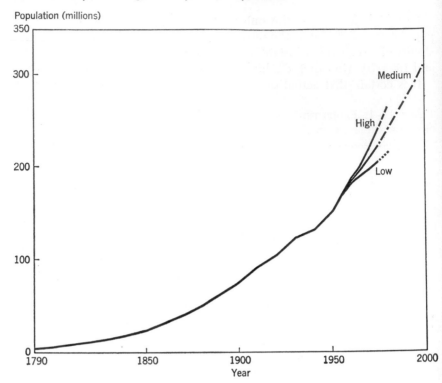

Fig. 11–1. Actual and projected population, 1790 to 2000.

waves of population growth will occur around a central trend somewhat below the medium series, but this is by no means certain.

The effects of different possible fertility trends are reflected in our medium, low, and high projections, each of which is based on the same assumptions about mortality and immigration. The low and high series extend only to 1980 because that is as far into the future as we think it reasonable to project the extreme marriage and family building patterns incorporated into the assumptions on which these forecasts are based. According to the low and high forecasts, the 1980 population may be as much as one-tenth below or above our medium forecast of 239 million. If such a wide departure from our medium series of marriage and birth rates actually occurs by 1980, however, it probably will be followed by at least a partial return to "normal" (or what now seem to be normal) family building patterns. Consequently, low and high forecasts should not differ from the medium forecast in much greater degree after 1980 than is shown here for 1980. It would be interesting to construct a series of forecasts assuming fluctuating marriage and fertility rates rather than the stabilized rates we have used for later cohorts in preparing the series presented here. Such forecasts would, in one sense, be more realistic representations of what we expect to happen, in that we do expect family building patterns to vary. The difficulty in preparing them is that we have no basis for predicting the size, direction, or dates of the future variations which may occur in the timing patterns of marriage and childbearing.

What would be the difference between the actual population and our medium forecasts if the actual trends in mortality and migration should differ from those we have assumed? To answer this question, we prepared several additional population projections, using the medium fertility assumptions but allowing the mortality and migration assumptions to vary within what now seem "reasonable" limits. As we know from past experience, however, conditions affecting these variables sometimes change in greater degree than appeared "reasonable" a few years earlier. The discovery of means of controlling cancer or of postponing heart attacks or strokes, for example, would lower our death rates well below the levels postulated by Greville's low assumptions. On the other hand, atomic war could raise our death rates to fantastic heights. With respect to migration, the government could stop admitting immigrants, or allow many more to come to the United States than we have assumed it would. These extreme contingencies do not now seem likely, however, and therefore we are making more moderate assumptions in trying to determine the extent to which future population may be raised or lowered by changes in mortality and immigration.

If there is no immigration after 1960 but our medium fertility and mortality assumptions prove correct, the actual population in the year 2000 will be 14.3 million (or 4.6 per cent) below our medium forecast of 312 million. Conversely, if the number of immigrants is double that assumed, the population in 2000 will be 14.3 million (or 4.6 per cent) above the medium forecast.

Changing from Greville's medium mortality assumptions to his low or high assumptions has less effect on the size of our future population than the changes in immigration just mentioned.[8] If mortality is as high as Greville's high assumption, the actual population in 2000 will be 4.7 million (or 1.5 per cent) below the medium forecast of 312 million; if

[8] Some idea of the extent to which Greville's low and high mortality assumptions differ from his medium assumptions may be obtained by the following comparisons of expectation of life in 1995–2000 derived from the three assumptions.

	Medium	Low	High
Male	71.3	73.9	68.9
Female	77.1	78.8	75.4

mortality is as low as his low assumption, the actual population will exceed our medium forecast by 6.1 million, or 2.0 per cent.

Thus we can say that the largest variations in mortality that now seem reasonable to actuaries and public health officials would not cause the actual population to deviate as much from our forecasts as the variations in immigration that may occur. However, neither mortality nor immigration has as much influence on future population as fertility. This is partly because births constitute the largest component of population change (in 1950–54 there were 2.6 times as many births as deaths and 14 times as many births as immigrants) and partly because birth rates are subject to wider fluctuations than death rates. (Numbers of immigrants may show greater *percentage* variations than numbers of births, but inasmuch as immigrants are so much less numerous than births, these variations are much smaller absolutely than are variations in births.)

Fertility trends different from the one chosen for our medium forecasts could easily cause the population to be 10 per cent larger or smaller in 2000. This is about the same as the deviation of our high and low forecasts from the medium series in 1980. By 2000, such a wide proportionate deviation would represent a difference of approximately 30 million between actual and predicted population. This is over twice as much as the difference of 14.3 million obtained by varying immigration within what now seems a reasonable range, and five to six times greater than the difference of 4.7 to 6.1 million due to possible variations in mortality. Such comparisons emphasize again the overwhelming importance of fertility in determining future population trends.

Not only has fertility become our most important component of population growth, but rather small changes in fertility can have a profound effect on our future population. For example, if family size increased to 3.35 births per ever-married woman instead of 3.05, as assumed for our medium forecasts, if the proportion marrying by 45–49 increased to 98 per cent instead of 94 per cent, and if median age at childbirth declined to 23.7 instead of 24.9, the population in the year 2000 would be 381 million, or 69 million above our medium forecasts. In contrast, if average family size were to decline to 2.5, the proportion marrying by 45–49 were to decline to 90 per cent, and median age at childbirth were to rise to 26.7 years, the population at the end of the century would be only 246 million—66 million below our medium forecasts. Neither 2.5 nor 3.35 births per family seems impossible—they differ by less than one child per family. Both averages are relatively low in the perspective of history. Likewise, we can easily imagine the proportion of women marrying to be as low as 90 per cent (as it was for the middle-aged women in the 1920s) or as high as 98 per cent, although the latter figure seems less probable than the former. Similarly, the high and low assumptions about median age at childbirth (23.7 and 26.7) are only 3 years apart, and each seems quite possible. The main point we wish to emphasize is that neither our low nor high fertility assumptions appear to differ greatly from our medium assumptions, yet they lead to very different population forecasts. There are two main reasons for this: first, the effect of changes in fertility on population is cumulative—more births now means more parents later, and so on, generation after generation. Second, decreasing or increasing the length of a generation (measured here by median age at childbirth) affects population growth by speeding up or retarding the birth of successive generations. For example, the population will grow more rapidly if the number of years between a generation is 24 years than if it is 27 years—even if average family size is the same in both cases. Few people realize the great impact on population growth of what appear to be small changes in average family size, proportions ever marrying, and median age at childbirth continued for several decades.

Future Trends in Births, Deaths, and Natural Increase

In the process of computing the population projections, future numbers of births and deaths were obtained. Let us see what they imply about crude period rates in future years.[9]

Viewed from the long-range perspective of history, our current crude birth and death rates (about 24 and 9, respectively) are low, even though the birth rate is higher than it was 20 to 25 years ago. Two centuries ago, birth and death rates in the Western world were much higher and very nearly equal (probably 40 to 45 per 1,000). Then, with advances in sanitation and medicine, the death rate began to fall but the birth rate lagged behind. This lag brought about a relatively large gap between births and deaths, which meant very rapid population growth. Gradually, however, the gap began to close as the birth rate also declined, and population growth slowed down. For a time, many persons thought that in the more advanced countries the birth rate would decrease to the level of the death rate during the twentieth century, causing population growth to cease altogether. This broad pattern of a decline in mortality followed by a decline in fertility has been called the demographic transition.

Until recently, the population of Western countries conformed closely with the general trend described by the demographic transition. Since

[9] Period rates are rates that relate to events (births and deaths in this context) that occur in a single year or short period of years. Examples of period rates are the widely used annual crude birth, death, and marriage rates, age-specific birth and death rates, expectation of life, and the gross and net reproduction rates as commonly defined.

the latter half of the 1940s, however, the United States and many other technically advanced countries have not continued to show the declines in birth rates expected by hypothesis, but instead have had a marked upswing in fertility.

It is clear from the decline of fertility in the United States during the depression of the 1930s and its increase afterward that if family size is to a large extent voluntarily controlled as it is here, annual birth rates can be expected to show cyclical trends, or "waves." The birth rate may eventually descend to the level of the death rate, as expected according to the theory of the demographic transition, but there is no evidence this will occur in the near future. Meanwhile, the timing of marriages and births, and the number of children couples want, probably will fluctuate in response to changing economic and political conditions and changing attitudes toward family life. This will alternately depress and elevate the crude birth rate for many years to come.

In 1955, when the data presented in this book were collected, the United States was riding the crest of a wave of births that started rising in the late 1930s with the recovery from the depression. As was pointed out in Chapter 10, the upward movement of this wave was caused not so much by changes in average family size as by a lowering of age at marriage and childbearing, and the making up of births postponed during World War II and the depression that preceded it. When all the postponed births are made up, and the tendency to marry and have the first birth at progressively younger ages stops, age-specific birth rates will decline and the crest of the wave will have passed. This may occur even though the average size of completed families becomes substantially larger than it is now.

The expectation that the present wave of population growth will eventually subside is brought out by Table 11–2, which shows actual average annual crude rates for births, deaths, and natural increase for 5-year periods from 1915–19 to 1950–54 and projected rates from 1955–60 to the end of the century. Here we see a drop in the crude birth rate from 24.3 in 1915–19 to 17.1 in 1935–39 and a subsequent rise of about the same magnitude to 24.5 in 1950–54. According to our medium forecast this rate will decline slightly from 1950–54 to 1955–60 and then drop substantially to an average of 19 or 20 in the 1960s.[10] This decline is not due to any decrease in average family size; on the contrary, this factor is assumed to increase slightly. It is due solely to our assumptions about the timing of marriages and births. The medium assumptions are that proportions marrying and starting their families at the younger ages will

---

[10] The prospective crude birth rates cited in this chapter are not precisely comparable with current rates published by the National Office of Vital Statistics for reasons explained in Appendix A, Note 23.

Table 11–2. Actual and Projected Births, Deaths, and Excess of Births over Deaths, Numbers and Rates, 1915–2000, by Five-year Periods

Period[a]	Absolute numbers (in thousands)			Rate per 1,000 population		
	Births[b]	Deaths[c]	Births minus deaths	Birth[d]	Death[e]	Natural increase
Actual						
1915–19	14,561	7,396	7,165	24.3	14.4	9.9
1920–24	14,776	6,598	8,178	22.9	12.0	10.9
1925–29	13,806	7,016	6,790	20.2	11.8	8.4
1930–34	12,267	6,867	5,400	17.6	11.0	6.6
1935–39	12,107	7,092	5,015	17.1	11.0	6.1
1940–44	14,294	7,071	7,223	19.8	10.6	9.2
1945–49	17,372	7,131	10,241	23.3	10.1	13.2
1950–54	19,411	7,430	11,981	24.5	9.5	15.0
Medium						
1955–60	20,696	8,253	12,443	23.3	9.3	14.0
1960–65	18,465	8,604	9,861	19.4	9.1	10.3
1965–70	20,201	9,091	11,110	20.0	9.0	11.0
1970–75	23,030	9,650	13,380	21.4	9.0	12.4
1975–80	25,469	10,202	15,267	22.1	8.8	13.3
1980–85	26,615	10,766	15,849	21.5	8.7	12.8
1985–90	27,404	11,388	16,016	20.7	8.6	12.1
1990–95	29,311	12,099	17,212	20.8	8.6	12.2
1995–2000	32,022	12,902	19,120	21.2	8.5	12.7
Low						
1955–60	19,442	8,220	11,222	22.0	9.3	12.7
1960–65	14,579	8,509	6,070	15.6	9.1	6.5
1965–70	14,548	8,958	5,590	15.0	9.2	5.8
1970–75	16,308	9,511	6,797	16.2	9.4	6.8
1975–80	18,079	10,024	8,055	17.2	9.5	7.7
High						
1955–60	22,136	8,290	13,846	24.8	9.3	15.5
1960–65	22,924	8,712	14,212	23.7	9.0	14.7
1965–70	25,904	9,229	16,675	24.6	8.8	15.8
1970–75	28,583	9,788	18,795	24.9	8.5	16.4
1975–80	32,049	10,367	21,682	25.6	8.3	17.3

[a] For actual numbers and rates, January 1 of initial year through December 31 of terminal year. For projected numbers and rates, July 1 of initial year through June 30 of terminal year.

[b] Actual numbers of births have been adjusted for incomplete registration.

[c] For 1915–32, estimated by assuming that the crude death rate in the entire United States was the same as that in the Death Registration Area. For 1933–54, registered deaths unadjusted for incomplete registration.

[d] Actual birth rates are based on registered births because such rates are more comparable with projected rates than are rates based on corrected births. See Appendix A, Note 23, for explanation.

[e] Actual rates shown for Death Registration Area.

decline somewhat and then stabilize. The low assumptions, which reverse the timing patterns more radically than the medium assumptions and also allow average family size to decline, imply a sharp drop in the crude birth rate: from 22.0 in 1955–60 to 15.0 in 1965–70. Only if fertility is like the high assumptions, which extend recent trends in timing patterns and allow family size to increase, can the crude birth rate remain relatively stable in the next 10 years at 24 or 25—approximately the 1950–55 level. Thus current indications point toward a drop in the crude birth rate sometime between 1957 and 1970, as explained in more detail in Chapter 10. It would require a substantial change in family building patterns, such as incorporated in our high assumptions, to prevent such a decline.

What the trend in the crude birth rate will be after 1970 is less certain, but it will probably rise for 10 years or so. An increase is anticipated not because of fluctuations in the timing of marriages and births or in average family size—factors which we assumed would be virtually stable by 1970 —but simply because of a rapid increase in the number of young adults available to marry and start their families. Actually, the number of people in the high-fertility age groups (approximately 18–29 years old) will rise continuously from 1960 until about 1980 as a direct result of the upswing in numbers of births between the late 1930s and the late 1950s. (See discussion of trends in the 18–29 age group later in this chapter.) But this increase in the number of potential parents is not likely to raise the crude birth rate in the 1960s, because the expected stabilization of marriage and fertility timing patterns during that decade will reduce the period age-specific birth rates. After stabilization has been reached, however, the rapid increase in the number of young people should be sufficient to cause crude birth rates to rise during the 1970s.

This prospective rise should be considered only as a tendency, however; it is by no means certain. If timing patterns change radically in response to unforeseen political or economic events, as they have in the past, they may offset the foregoing tendency toward a moderate increase in birth rates during the 1970s. The accumulation of additional information on factors affecting family size, such as that gathered in the present study, together with reliable forecasts of economic conditions, would enable us to improve forecasts of fertility 10 to 20 years in advance.

After 1980 our medium forecasts imply that the crude birth rate will be virtually constant at about 21 per 1,000. In fact, however, it is likely to fluctuate in view of the wide swings to which it has been subject in the past. In presenting the long-range medium forecasts we are merely suggesting a possible central trend around which deviations may occur. This central trend seems likely now, but it may not seem so in another 10 or 20 years.

What will happen to our future death rates? In all probability the crude rate will stabilize at a level close to 8 or 9 per 1,000 population. This stabilization is expected to result from two opposing tendencies—the continued lowering of death rates at each age and the continued increase in the proportion of old people, among whom death rates are high. It makes little difference what assumptions we use regarding future mortality. If age-specific death rates follow Greville's high mortality assumptions the crude death rate may reach 10 per 1,000. In contrast, if they follow his low mortality assumptions the death rate may decline to 7.

Because of the prospective stability of the annual crude death rate, the annual crude rate of natural increase (birth rate minus death rate) will vary in the same direction and by approximately the same absolute amount as will the annual crude birth rate. According to the medium projections, the rate of natural increase will decline from 14.0 in 1955–60 to 10 or 11 in 1960–70 and fluctuate in a narrow range between 12 and 13 thereafter. The high assumptions show a rise from about 15 in 1955–65 to 17.3 in 1975–80. The low assumptions indicate the possibility of a fall to a rate as low as 6 in the 1960s, followed by a slight upturn to 7 or 8 in the 1970s. The rates derived from the high and low assumptions are regarded as extremes, but they are extremes that could occur. However, it seems more likely that the moderate trend suggested by the medium assumptions will be followed, at least until 1980.

Even though the medium projections imply a "moderate" rate of population increase—about 1.3 per cent per year in the last quarter of this century—the continuation of this rate of growth for another half century would produce a population of about 600 million by 2050. Such a large population could be reached without any increase in family size above that expected by the wives in our study or any great reduction in mortality. A population of this size would probably require fundamental changes in the American society and economy. Again, we wish to emphasize that such huge numbers of people can result from comparatively moderate marriage and fertility rates for cohorts. Thus the assumed moderate rise in proportion marrying and in average family size and the lowering of median age at childbirth have profound implications if continued indefinitely.

Prospective Changes in Sex and Age Structure

In this section we shall see what the base population and the assumptions we have made about the components of population growth imply about the future sex and age composition of the population.

Sex Ratio. There will probably continue to be more females than males in our population. The sex ratio (number of males per 100 females) of the total population will probably vary within a narrow range during the last half of the century—between 97 and 99 according to our medium forecast. The projections show a drop from 99.2 in 1955 to 97.5 in 1975, followed by a slow rise to 98.5 by the year 2000 (Table 11–3).

TABLE 11–3. SEX RATIOS OF PROJECTED POPULATION BY SELECTED AGE GROUPS, 1955–2000, BY FIVE-YEAR PERIODS, MEDIUM PROJECTIONS

July 1	Age				
	Total	Under 18	18–44	45–64	65 and over
1955	99.2	104.3	100.2	95.4	86.0
1960	98.5	104.4	100.2	94.6	80.8
1965	97.9	-104.4	100.5	94.0	76.9
1970	97.6	104.4	101.0	93.8	74.0
1975	97.5	104.5	101.3	94.0	72.6
1980	97.5	104.6	101.4	94.2	72.2
1985	97.7	104.6	101.6	94.4	72.3
1990	97.9	104.7	101.7	95.3	72.7
1995	98.2	104.7	101.9	96.1	73.3
2000	98.5	104.7	102.1	96.4	73.6

Such small changes in the sex ratio are characteristic of the age groups that form the bulk of the population. At ages under 18, the projected sex ratio, which is governed largely by the sex ratio at birth and the sex differences in infant mortality rates, is virtually constant at 104. At ages 18–44, the medium forecasts show a slow rise from 100 to 102 in the last half of the century, which is due to the narrowing absolute difference between male and female death rates. At ages 45–64 there are variations in a narrow range between 94 and 96 (Table 11–3).

At ages 65 and over, however, our forecasts show rather wide shifts in the sex ratio; from 86 in 1955 it drops to the low 70s in 1975 and later years.

Broad Changes in Age Structure. The medium projections do not imply any radical changes in the broad age structure of our population during the last half of the century. According to this series, the proportion of children and young people under 18 years of age will vary in a narrow range between 33 and 35 per cent, the proportion of adults of working age will be between 55 and 57 per cent, and the proportion of persons 65 and over will rise slightly from 9 to 10 or 11 per cent (Table 11–4).

Somewhat different broad age distributions by 1980 result from the other fertility projections, however. By 1980, the low and high forecasts show the following percentages in each broad age group:

Age	Low	High
All ages	100	100
Under 18	26	38
18–64	62	53
65 and over	12	9

Within the next quarter of a century, as in the past, age structure will depend chiefly on the trend in fertility. The higher the annual birth rates, the higher the proportion of children and young people under 18 and the lower the proportion of adults. Radical changes in mortality and immigration could have an important effect on age structure, but as mentioned earlier we cannot now foresee trends in these variables very different from those assumed.

TABLE 11–4. PER CENT DISTRIBUTION BY BROAD AGE GROUPS, AND MEDIAN AGE, FOR PROJECTED POPULATION, 1955–2000, BY FIVE-YEAR PERIODS

July 1	Per cent				Median age
	Total	Under 18	18–64	65 and over	
Medium					
1955	100	33	58	9	30.2
1960	100	35	56	9	29.5
1965	100	35	56	9	28.9
1970	100	34	56	10	28.2
1975	100	33	57	10	28.1
1980	100	33	57	10	28.4
1985	100	34	55	11	28.8
1990	100	34	55	11	29.1
1995	100	33	56	11	28.8
2000	100	33	57	10	28.6
Low					
1960	100	35	56	9	29.8
1965	100	33	57	10	29.9
1970	100	30	60	10	30.1
1975	100	27	62	11	30.7
1980	100	26	62	12	31.7
High					
1960	100	36	55	9	29.2
1965	100	37	54	9	27.6
1970	100	37	54	9	26.2
1975	100	37	53	10	25.7
1980	100	38	53	9	25.4

The broad changes expected in age structure can also be seen from the median age of the projected population. The medium series shows a slight decline in median age, from 30.2 in 1955 to 28.1 in 1975, and fluctuations within a narrow range between 28 and 29 thereafter (Table 11–4). If people have as many children by as young ages as shown by the high fertility series, however, median age by 1980 will be as low as 25 years, which is what it was in 1920. If fertility falls and age at childbearing rises as much as shown by our low assumptions, on the other hand, median age in 1980 will be as high as 32 years. Neither extreme seems probable now.

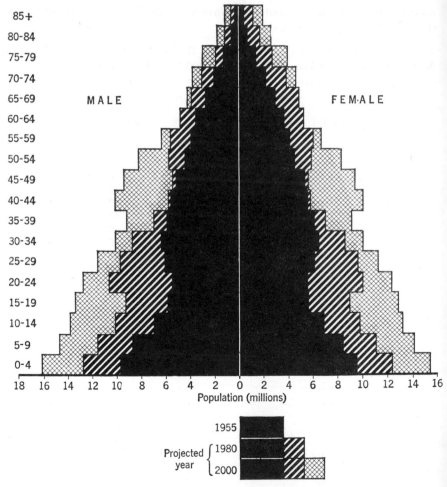

FIG. 11–2. Projected population, by age and sex, 1955, 1980, and 2000 (medium series).

Although we do not now foresee any radical changes in broad age structure, there will be rather wide fluctuations in numbers of people in more narrowly defined age groups (Figure 11-2). The recent postwar wave of high birth rates and rapid population growth will be clearly reflected in the changing numbers of people at specific ages. The sharp increase in birth rates soon after World War II has already increased the number of children of elementary school age, causing a crisis in public education. Soon the postwar baby boom will affect enrollments in high school and college, and later the numbers entering the labor force, marrying, and having children. In short, the high birth rates of the late 1940s and the 1950s will affect our population for years to come. Let us see to what extent numbers of persons in particular age groups will change as a result of recorded past and prospective future fertility rates.

Preschool Children, under 6 Years. We are less certain about forecasts of preschool children than about those for any other major age category, because none of those who will be in this group in 1965 or later years were born when this was written. According to our medium fertility projections, the number of children under 6 years of age will continue to increase to 24 million in 1960, and then decline to about 22 million in 1965 (Table 11-5). This decline follows the reduction in numbers of births during the late 1950s and the 1960s (Table 11-2), which is the result of the fact that most of the births postponed before 1955 will have been made up by 1960, and our medium assumption that the proportions of women marrying and having children at younger ages will decline slightly in the next few years and then stabilize.

After 1970, however, the number of preschool children will increase markedly, reflecting rising numbers of births in the late 1960s and 1970s. This will not be due to larger families, but to an increase in the number of potential parents. Most of the young men and women who will marry and start their families in the late 1960s and the 1970s were born in the prosperous high-fertility years of the postwar period. Unless annual fertility rates drop after 1965, we can expect the number of births to increase markedly and the number of preschool children to follow this trend. This secondary wave of population growth, resulting from a wave that occurred a generation earlier, demonstrates the long-lasting effects on age structure that can result from changes in annual fertility.

Even the low fertility projections show an increase in the number of children under 6 years of age between 1970 and 1980. Only a substantially larger reduction in fertility and change in timing could prevent it. This series also shows the considerable reduction in the number of preschool children that would occur from 1960 to 1965 if fertility were sharply reduced in the next few years. From 23 million children under 6 in 1960 the low series shows a reduction to 18 million in 1965 (Table 11-6).

Age	1955	1960	1965	1970	1975	1980	1990	2000
					Total			
Total	170,739	184,582	195,643	207,953	222,533	239,000	273,265	311,997
Under 6	22,770	24,232	22,189	23,452	26,934	29,925	32,430	37,668
6-13	24,802	29,193	31,721	30,898	30,139	34,126	41,292	44,782
14-17	9,507	11,904	14,386	15,770	15,923	14,607	18,886	21,250
18-21	8,800	9,972	12,528	14,713	16,125	15,437	17,113	20,756
22-29	18,982	18,036	19,645	24,163	28,737	31,750	30,149	37,883
30-44	36,234	37,089	36,354	35,235	37,127	43,181	57,114	58,925
45-64	34,946	37,417	40,288	43,334	44,815	44,848	46,185	58,861
65-69	5,685	6,348	6,570	7,100	8,071	8,658	9,985	9,015
70 and over	9,013	10,391	11,962	13,288	14,662	16,468	20,111	22,857
Broad groups:								
Under 18	57,079	65,329	68,296	70,120	72,996	78,658	92,608	103,700
18-29	27,782	28,008	32,173	38,876	44,862	47,187	47,262	58,639
18-44	64,016	65,097	68,527	74,111	81,989	90,368	104,376	117,564
18-64	98,962	102,514	108,815	117,445	126,804	135,216	150,561	176,425
65 and over	14,698	16,739	18,532	20,388	22,733	25,126	30,096	31,872
					Males			
Total	85,034	91,602	96,804	102,704	109,833	117,997	135,196	154,838
Under 6	11,632	12,382	11,343	11,993	13,777	15,310	16,596	19,278
6-13	12,672	14,909	16,196	15,783	15,402	17,444	21,117	22,906
14-17	4,834	6,072	7,337	8,039	8,122	7,454	9,645	10,855
18-21	4,455	5,043	6,361	7,470	8,189	7,843	8,703	10,569
22-29	9,535	9,055	9,854	12,174	14,497	16,024	15,231	19,180
30-44	18,049	18,476	18,139	17,598	18,569	21,632	28,700	29,636
45-64	17,062	18,185	19,519	20,973	21,718	21,756	22,531	28,897
65-69	2,686	2,914	2,984	3,189	3,616	3,907	4,533	4,156
70 and over	4,109	4,566	5,071	5,485	5,943	6,627	8,140	9,361
Broad groups:								
Under 18	29,138	33,363	34,876	35,815	37,301	40,208	47,358	53,039
18-29	13,990	14,098	16,215	19,644	22,686	23,867	23,934	29,749
18-44	32,039	32,574	34,354	37,242	41,255	45,499	52,634	59,385
18-64	49,101	50,759	53,873	58,215	62,973	67,255	75,165	88,282
65 and over	6,795	7,480	8,055	8,674	9,559	10,534	12,673	13,517
					Females			
Total	85,705	92,980	98,839	105,249	112,700	121,003	138,069	157,159
Under 6	11,138	11,850	10,846	11,459	13,157	14,615	15,834	18,390
6-13	12,130	14,284	15,525	15,115	14,737	16,682	20,175	21,876
14-17	4,673	5,832	7,049	7,731	7,801	7,153	9,241	10,395
18-21	4,345	4,929	6,167	7,243	7,936	7,594	8,410	10,187
22-29	9,447	8,981	9,791	11,989	14,240	15,726	14,918	18,703
30-44	18,185	18,613	18,215	17,637	18,558	21,549	28,414	29,289
45-64	17,884	19,232	20,769	22,361	23,097	23,092	23,654	29,964
65-69	2,999	3,434	3,586	3,911	4,455	4,751	5,452	4,859
70 and over	4,904	5,825	6,891	7,803	8,719	9,841	11,971	13,496
Broad groups:								
Under 18	27,941	31,966	33,420	34,305	35,695	38,450	45,250	50,661
18-29	13,792	13,910	15,958	19,232	22,176	23,320	23,328	28,890
18-44	31,977	32,523	34,173	36,869	40,734	44,869	51,742	58,179
18-64	49,861	51,755	54,942	59,230	63,831	67,961	75,396	88,143
65 and over	7,903	9,259	10,477	11,714	13,174	14,592	17,423	18,355

[a] Projections for age groups not affected by variations in the fertility assumptions are shown below the horizontal lines.

The high series shows a continuing rise in the number of preschool children between 1955 and 1980. The rate of increase slows down between 1960 and 1970, as annual marriage and fertility rates approach the high levels postulated, but gathers speed between 1970 and 1980 with the increase in the numbers of young people who can become parents.

TABLE 11–6. PROJECTED POPULATION BY AGE AND SEX, 1960–1980, LOW AND HIGH SERIES (IN THOUSANDS)[a]

Age	Low				
	1960	1965	1970	1975	1980
Total					
Total	183,361	190,631	197,421	205,418	214,673
Under 6	23,011	17,989	16,960	19,130	21,282
6–13	29,193	30,909	26,959	22,588	24,412
14–17	11,904	14,386	15,669	14,407	11,062
18–21	9,972	12,528	14,713	15,881	13,478
22–29	18,036	19,645	24,163	28,737	31,284
Broad groups:					
Under 18	64,108	63,284	59,588	56,125	56,756
18–29	28,008	32,173	38,876	44,618	44,762
18–44	65,097	68,527	74,111	81,745	87,942
18–64	102,514	108,815	117,445	126,560	132,791
Males					
Total	90,978	94,243	97,322	101,095	105,575
Under 6	11,758	9,197	8,674	9,784	10,888
6–13	14,909	15,781	13,772	11,553	12,478
14–17	6,072	7,337	7,987	7,351	5,651
18–21	5,043	6,361	7,470	8,064	6,852
22–29	9,055	9,854	12,174	14,497	15,784
Broad groups:					
Under 18	32,739	32,315	30,433	28,688	29,017
18–29	14,098	16,215	19,644	22,561	22,636
18–44	32,574	34,354	37,242	41,130	44,268
18–64	50,759	53,873	58,215	62,848	66,024
Females					
Total	92,383	96,388	100,099	104,323	109,098
Under 6	11,253	8,792	8,286	9,346	10,394
6–13	14,284	15,128	13,187	11,035	11,934
14–17	5,832	7,049	7,682	7,056	5,411
18–21	4,929	6,167	7,243	7,817	6,626
22–29	8,981	9,791	11,989	14,240	15,500
Broad groups:					
Under 18	31,369	30,969	29,155	27,437	27,739
18–29	13,910	15,958	19,232	22,057	22,126
18–44	32,523	34,173	36,869	40,615	43,675
18–64	51,755	54,942	59,230	63,712	66,767

[a] Projections for age groups not affected by variations in the fertility assumptions are shown below the horizontal lines. They are the same as those in Table 11–5.

Table 11–6. Projected Population by Age and Sex, 1960–1980, Low and High Series (in Thousands)[a] (*Continued*)

Age	High				
	1960	1965	1970	1975	1980
			Total		
Total	185,985	201,397	219,272	239,267	262,149
Under 6	25,635	27,010	30,106	33,525	37,488
6–13	29,193	32,654	35,449	38,248	42,948
14–17	11,904	14,386	15,884	17,679	18,564
18–21	9,972	12,528	14,713	16,403	17,726
22–29	18,036	19,645	24,163	28,737	32,268
Broad groups:					
Under 18	66,732	74,050	81,439	89,452	99,000
18–29	28,008	32,173	38,876	45,140	49,994
18–44	65,097	68,527	74,111	82,267	93,175
18–64	102,514	108,815	117,445	127,082	138,023
			Males		
Total	92,319	99,746	108,491	118,387	129,827
Under 6	13,099	13,808	15,396	17,149	19,180
6–13	14,909	16,673	18,109	19,546	21,954
14–17	6,072	7,337	8,097	9,019	9,475
18–21	5,043	6,361	7,470	8,330	9,009
22–29	9,055	9,854	12,174	14,497	16,287
Broad groups:					
Under 18	34,080	37,818	41,602	45,714	50,609
18–29	14,098	16,215	19,644	22,827	25,296
18–44	32,574	34,354	37,242	41,396	46,928
18–64	50,759	53,873	58,215	63,114	68,684
			Females		
Total	93,666	101,651	110,781	120,880	132,322
Under 6	12,536	13,202	14,710	16,376	18,308
6–13	14,284	15,981	17,340	18,702	20,994
14–17	5,832	7,049	7,787	8,660	9,089
18–21	4,929	6,167	7,243	8,073	8,717
22–29	8,981	9,791	11,989	14,240	15,981
Broad groups:					
Under 18	32,652	36,232	39,837	43,738	48,391
18–29	13,910	15,958	19,232	22,313	24,698
18–44	32,523	34,173	36,869	40,871	46,247
18–64	51,755	54,942	59,230	63,968	69,339

The wide range between our high and low series of projections of young children by 1980 is a result of uncertainty about the course fertility will take. The low series shows 21 million children under 6, whereas the high series shows 37 million. Both figures result from our most extreme assumptions about the timing of marriages and births and about eventual family size. If actual marriage and birth rates do follow one of these assumed trends, they will probably not remain at the high or low level postulated for many years.

If the trends assumed for our medium series extend to the end of the century, the number of children under 6 will then be about 38 million, an increase of almost two-thirds over the 23 million in 1955.

Children 6–13 Years Old. The number of children eligible to attend elementary school (grades 1 through 8) is now increasing rapidly and will continue to increase up to 1965. At that time the age group 6–13, which includes the large bulk of those enrolled in elementary schools, will contain approximately 32 million children, as compared with only 25 million in 1955 (Table 11–5). Thus the problem of how to increase the capacity of our elementary school system as rapidly as the number of school-age children rises will continue for several more years.

After 1965, however, the elementary schools should enjoy a respite from the pressure of a rapidly increasing child population. If our medium fertility assumptions prove to be approximately correct, the number of children 6–13 years old will change little between 1965 and 1975. Actually, the medium series shows a slight decline in this 10-year period.

After 1975, however, the pressure on the elementary schools will again rise, as the result of an increase in births expected to begin in the late 1960s. This rise, as explained earlier, is expected as a result of an increase in numbers of young parents. The medium series shows the number of children 6–13 years old constantly rising to 45 million by the end of the century—80 per cent more than in 1955. Such a long-range forecast is, of course, highly speculative.

The rise in the population of elementary school age could be much greater after 1955 than described above. If family size increases and if people continue to marry and have babies at earlier ages, as is assumed in the high fertility projections, the number of children 6–13 years old will reach 43 million by 1980 (Table 11–6). This seems highly unlikely, however. On the other hand, if our low fertility assumptions should prove to be correct, the population of elementary school age would decrease sharply after 1965 and reach a low of 23 million by 1975. This trend also seems unlikely.

Children 14–17 Years Old. Children of high school age, taken here as 14–17 years, will continue to increase until 1975. By the latter year there will be 16 million such children surviving from babies already born, or two-thirds more than the 9.5 million in 1955 (Table 11–5). Present high school facilities will have to expand considerably to handle this increase.

Between 1975 and 1980 the population of high school age will decline by about 1.3 million, if marriage and fertility patterns stabilize during the next few years, as postulated in our medium projections. After 1980, the medium assumptions yield a steadily rising number in the age range 14–17, reaching 21 million by the end of the century. This is over two times the 1955 population in this age group.

The high fertility projections indicate that the population of high school age could reach 19 million by 1980, whereas the low assumptions show only 11 million by that time (Table 11–6). Both forecasts are regarded as unlikely extremes.

Ages 18–21. This age group is critical for several institutions in our society. It includes the bulk of college students and a large proportion of the people looking for their first job and starting new households. The number of persons in this age range is virtually certain to increase— from 9 million to about 16 million between 1955 and 1975, a rise of over 80 per cent in only 20 years (Table 11–5).

This rise will certainly tax the colleges and will very likely strain the ability of our economy to absorb new workers. At the same time, however, the increasing numbers marrying and entering the labor market will mean more new consumers for important products. They will want houses, automobiles, and the many other goods and services on which our economy depends. Whether the rising number of young men and women will stimulate the economy by creating more consumer demand or depress it by glutting the labor market remains to be seen. All we can say now is that a very large increase in the population 18–21 years old will occur and will very probably have an important effect on the economy. The most rapid rise is expected from 1965 to 1970, when the number of such persons jumps from 12.5 to 14.7 million, or by 17 per cent in only 5 years.

The high and low forecasts indicate that there could be as many as 18 million in the age range 18–21 in 1980, or as few as 13 million (Table 11–6). Both extremes are unlikely.

After the rise to a high of 16 million in 1975, the medium series shows a decline to 15 million in 1980, reflecting the decline in annual numbers of births during the late 1950s and/or the 1960s. After 1980, the increase is resumed, and the number in the age range 18–21 reaches 21 million by the end of the century.

Ages 18–29. From some points of view, the trend in the number of young adults 18–29 years old is more significant than the trend in the narrower group 18–21 years of age. Between ages 18 and 29, the large majority of people marry and have more than half of their children. In the United States, where age at marriage and childbirth is relatively low, these are the high-fertility ages. Therefore, we may think of this group as constituted primarily of young parents. Trends in the number of such people will have an important effect on future numbers of births.

The number of young adults 18–29 years old will remain stationary a about 28 million until 1960, reflecting the relative stability in numbers of births during the 1930s (Tables 11–5 and 11–2). After 1960 the number of young adults rises rapidly as persons born during and after World War II enter the group. By 1975, it should include about 45 million men and women. This 60 per cent increase will lead inevitably to increasing numbers of births after 1965, regardless of which fertility assumption we choose. Even the low series indicates a rise of 24 per cent in the average annual number of births between 1965–70 and 1975–80 (Table 11–2).

During the 1980s, the number in the 18–29 age group stabilizes at 47 million, according to our medium series. This reflects the decline in numbers of births during the late 1950s and/or the 1960s that is likely to occur. The recovery from this decline yields increasing numbers 18–29 years old in the last decade of the century.

Ages 18–64. People in this broad age group constitute the bulk of the labor force. In the spring of 1958, 92 per cent of both the men and the women in the labor force were 18–64 years old. Therefore trends in the population in this age range indicate roughly the trends in the size of the labor force. Neither total numbers in the labor force nor the absolute changes in the size of the labor force correspond exactly to changes in the 18–64 group, however, because some of the people in this broad age range do not work. In early 1958, for example, 93 per cent of the men 18–64 years old and 41 per cent of the women in this age group were in the labor force. It is possible, and highly worthwhile, for certain purposes, to make projections of the size of the labor force. However, such an endeavor is outside the scope of the present book, which relates primarily to fertility and its impact on the size and age-sex structure of the population.

In 1955 there were 99 million people 18–64 years old. By 1975 the number in this age group is virtually certain to increase to about 127 million (Figure 11–3). We can be relatively sure of this increase because all the persons who will be 18–64 years old in 1975 were born before 1958, when our fertility projections begin.

The most rapid gain in the 18–64 age group will occur in the 10 years between 1965 and 1975, when the number increases by 18 million, or 17 per cent. This rise is due primarily to the much larger number of births during 1947–57 than during previous years (Tables 11–5 and 11–2).

After 1975, the trend in the number of persons in the working ages becomes less certain. By 1980, it could be as small as 133 million or as large as 138 million, according to our low and high projections. If fertility in future years follows the trend described by our medium assumptions, the number in the 18–64 age group will continue to increase fairly rapidly in the last quarter of the century. The medium forecast for the year 2000 is 176 million, which is 78 per cent above the 1955 figure.

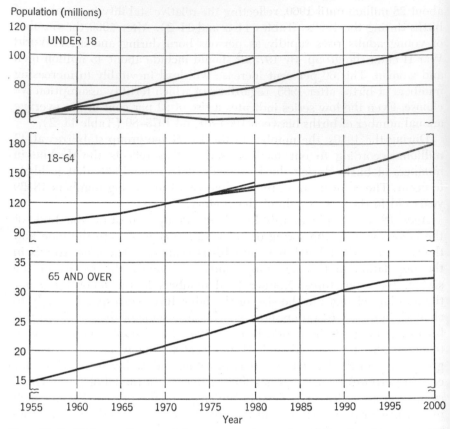

Population (millions)

UNDER 18

18-64

65 AND OVER

1955 1960 1965 1970 1975 1980 1985 1990 1995 2000
Year

Fig. 11–3. High, medium, and low projected population, by broad age groups, 1955 to 2000.

Our medium series suggests a very slight tendency for the proportion of the population in the 18–64 group to decline. From 58 per cent in 1955, this proportion varies irregularly between 55 and 57 per cent in later years. Such changes are too small to have a significant effect on our economy.

If fertility follows our high projections, however, the number and proportion of children will increase so rapidly that by 1980 persons 18–64 years old will include only 53 per cent of the population. Such a trend would undoubtedly increase the ratio of dependents (mainly children under 18, nonworking wives, and retired persons) to producers (mainly the men and women 18–64 years old in the labor force). On the other hand, if fertility follows the low projections the percentage who are 18–64 years old will increase to 62 per cent by 1980 and the ratio of dependents to producers will fall from its current level.

The number of men in the group 18–64 years old is expected to increase somewhat more rapidly than the number of women. This results from Greville's assumptions of larger absolute declines in male than in female mortality and is reflected in the rising sex ratio of this age group. From 98.5 males per 100 females in 1955, it at first declines slightly and then increases to 100.2 by the end of the century, according to our medium forecasts. These implied changes are very small; basically they mean that the sex composition of the population in the working ages is very nearly stable.

Changes in age composition within the 18–64 group are expected to be small. Although there will be some variation in the relative size of narrowly defined age groups (such as ages 18–21), the proportions under and over 45 years old change but little. In 1955, 65 per cent of the persons 18–64 were in the younger portion of this range, arbitrarily defined here as 18–44 years. The medium series shows a decline to 63 per cent by 1970, a rise to 69 per cent by 1990, and a decline to 67 per cent by 2000. In the long run there may be a tendency for the age of the labor force to increase gradually as declining death rates allow larger proportions to survive to the older ages. However, changes in numbers of births exercise such a strong influence on age distribution that they could easily cause significant departures from such a trend.

Ages 65 and Over. People of retirement age, taken here as 65 years old and over, constitute one of the most rapidly and steadily growing age groups in our population. Between 1955 and the end of the century their number will more than double, increasing from 14.7 million to 31.9 million (Figure 11–3). This is a rise of 117 per cent, which is considerably above the rise of 83 per cent expected for the total population according to the medium series.

The more rapid increase of the elderly than of the total population is reflected in the increasing proportion of persons over 65 in our population projections. In 1955 this age group was 8.6 per cent of the total. By 1990 our medium forecast implies that it will be 11 per cent. By the year 2000 it will decline to 10.2 per cent (for reasons that will be explained later), but this will be a temporary setback.

The proportion of the total population that is in a particular age group is influenced not only by the number of persons in that age group but also by the numbers in other age groups. If fertility follows the high projections, the resulting numbers of young people will be large and the proportion of persons who are 65 and over will not increase as rapidly as shown by our medium series. On the other hand, if fertility follows the low projections, the proportion past 65 will be higher than implied by our medium series. For example, our medium series for 1980 shows 10.5

per cent in this age group, but our high and low series show 9.6 and 11.7 per cent, respectively, even though the age-specific death rates are the same in each case.

Two factors are responsible for the upward trend from 1955 to 2000 in the proportion of persons who are 65 and over. The most important is the much smaller number of births during 1855–90 (when the people 65 and over in 1955 were born) than during 1900–35. Of lesser importance, but usually receiving most of the credit, is the steady decline of mortality rates which permits more and more people to survive to the older ages.

The effect of variations in past births on the population 65 years old and over can be seen in the decline in the rate of growth of this age group after 1990. During 1955–90 the rate of growth averages 2.1 per cent a year; during 1990–95 it goes down to 1 per cent a year; and during 1995–2000 to 0.2 per cent a year. This drop in the rate of growth is due to the entrance into this age group of persons born during 1925–34, a period when the annual number of births was declining rapidly (Table 11–2). Actually, the number of persons 65–69 years old does decrease during 1990–2000 (Table 11–5). The only reason the entire age group 65 and over does not also decline is that the group 70 and over continues to rise.

Although our projections do not extend beyond the year 2000, we can be virtually certain that, barring any widespread disasters, the population 65 and over will again show rapid gains when the people born in the high-fertility years of 1947–57 enter this age group. This will be during 2012–22. Thus the drop in the growth rate of our population of retirement age in the last decade of this century will be only temporary.

The rapid increase in the number of elderly persons during the next half century will have repercussions in many areas of our national life. It will affect our social security and old-age-assistance systems and the retirement plans of private industries. In a society such as ours, in which many old persons live separately from their children, housing accommodations and recreational facilities for such people will have to be increased rapidly and additional provisions made for the care of the infirm among them.

Summary

Forecasts of the size and age-sex composition of the population bebetween 1955 and 2000 were prepared by using the fertility projections described in Chapter 10 and the projections about mortality and migration described in the present chapter. The medium series indicates a population of 239 million people by 1980. If fertility were to follow the course described by our low or high projections, however, we would have as few as 215 million or as many as 262 million by 1980. The medium series shows our population doubling in size between 1950 and 2000 and reaching 312 million in the latter year.

With respect to the age-sex composition of the population, our medium series implies no radical changes by the end of the century. There will continue to be an excess of women over men. The ratio of males to females will decline rapidly at the older ages (65 and over) until 1980 and then stabilize or rise slowly. At the younger ages, no significant changes in sex ratio are expected.

The medium series indicates a slightly younger population in future years than we now have. This is due to increases in the proportion of children and young adults. The high and low projections yield trends in age distribution that do not seem likely to occur, but are nonetheless possible. They indicate that by 1980 the proportion of children under 18 in the population could be as low as 26 per cent or as high as 38 per cent; the medium forecast shows 33 per cent. The extreme forecasts are extended only to 1980 because it seems quite unlikely that the conditions they represent will be maintained for a longer period. In general, we expect the future population to vary around a central trend somewhat below our medium forecasts.

Chapter 12

WHAT IT ALL MEANS: AN OVERVIEW

At the beginning we emphasized the fact that the decisions made in millions of individual American families are determining the changing size and composition of our national population. We have now described in some detail what these decisions are, what values about family size lie behind them, and what success families have in achieving their values. We have also described the implications of these facts for population growth when combined with current trends in marriage, mortality, and immigration. From the detailed descriptions of family and population growth patterns many ideas emerge which have important implications for our national life. Different observers emphasize different emergent generalizations, depending on the problems in which they are interested. We have chosen to emphasize in conclusion five major ideas and to speculate about some of their implications. Although our statements about fecundity, family planning, and desired size of family are based on our study of white couples, they apply quite well to all American couples because the nonwhite minority is relatively small. Unfortunately, comparable information is not yet available for nonwhites.

1. *Fecundity impairments are very widespread in the American population, but they are not very important in determining the course of population trends.* Fecundity impairments are very common in the American population, but we have no reason to believe that they are more prevalent than in other contemporary or earlier populations. They do represent serious personal and family problems for many people. Progress in eliminating such fecundity impairments is important to reduce the unhappiness of millions of couples unable to have as many children as they want.

Medical progress in correcting such fecundity impairments probably would affect the distribution of family size, but is not likely to have an important effect on population growth. It might cut in half the small proportion of couples unable to have children and make a similar cut in the proportion unable to have a second child. However, the over-all increase in the total number of births would be small. Even if all fecundity impairments were eliminated, the number of births would be increased

y only 10 to 15 per cent. It is most unlikely that all the various causes of
ubfecundity can be eliminated in the foreseeable future. The fact is
hat about half of the Subfecund couples now are able to have as many
hildren as they want. The elimination of fecundity impairments un-
oubtedly would increase the number of unwanted children, since the
npairments now serve as a form of family limitation for some couples. On
he whole, reducing fecundity impairment is much more important in
elping couples meet a personal problem than in changing population
rends.

2. *Family limitation is now almost universally approved and is practiced
idely and effectively by the white couples who need it.* The extent and
ffectiveness of control measures vary between major groups, but the
imilarities are more impressive than the differences. Although an impor-
int proportion of pregnancies come earlier than desired, a majority of
vhite couples in all social strata do not have larger families than they
vant.

It is true that a significant minority of couples have more children
han they want. For most of them the fact that most other couples plan
amily size successfully is only likely to accentuate their own dissatisfac-
ion and unhappiness. The fact that most of them have only one or two
nore children than they want as compared with a potential of six or more
mwanted children is not much comfort to the couples themselves. It
eems probable that the number of couples in this unhappy position will
lecrease in future years, in part because research will improve methods
f family limitation, but also in part because a rising general level of
ducation will provide more couples with the personal qualifications
nd the information required for effective family planning. Education is
low one of the most important factors associated with differences in
amily planning. The minority of couples who have more children than
hey want still number in the millions. They are apparently becoming
nore conscious about family problems, so they may express an in-
reasing demand for clinical advice and counseling even while changing
onditions reduce their number.

As the number of such couples decreases, the effect will be to further
ccelerate the decline in the number of really large families. A rather large
roportion of the couples who are having more than the commonly ac-
epted goal of two to four children do not want the larger number. If
nany of them become successful planners, we may expect further con-
entration on families of moderate size.

The very widespread use of family limitation means also that we may
xpect an increased variability of the birth rate in relation to social and
conomic changes. As more and more of the population practice family
imitation effectively, changes both in the number of children couples

have and in the timing of childbearing may be greater and occur more rapidly. We have already explained how such changes have been affect ing our population growth. As research and education decrease the num ber of couples who have fewer or more children than they want, the annual birth rate may be more volatile than in recent decades unles economic conditions are stable.

More family planning may also mean less variation in the marriage rate Couples who feel they cannot afford to have children need not postpon marriage for that reason, if they are confident that they can postpon pregnancies until their economic position improves. Part of the ex planation for the low average age at marriage in the United States n doubt is that couples feel that they can marry young but postpon children, if necessary. The attraction of the idea that "two can live a cheaply as one" is enhanced if the couple is confident the numbers wil not quickly grow to three or four.

3. *All classes of the American population are coming to share a commor set of values about family size.* The consensus among different socia strata about how many children are wanted and expected is surprisingly great. We do not know for how long a time this consensus has existed but its strength at present is undeniable. The traditionally high fertility o the farm population and of urban couples with low socioeconomic statu is no longer supported—if it ever was—by a desire for large families Lack of knowledge about effective means of preventing conception may always have been the most important reason for the extra children. Now that more or less effective family planning is diffused so widely through out the society, all the major sectors of the population have the *means* to reach the family building goals they share. The expected family size of different social strata is more similar than actual fertility in the past, and the official record of family building now indicates that traditional dif ferentials are being greatly narrowed if not eliminated.

The rapidity with which new standards of family size have spread throughout the whole society since World War II indicates how quickly a population may now adjust its values about such vital matters as reproduction. Apparently our population is now so closely linked together in a single system of communication and interdependence that even or such a basic matter as how many children a couple should have, new values can be developed, diffused, and put into action on a massive scale very quickly. This is also true for values about the ages at which couples should marry and how they should space their children. To the extent that changes in opinions about such matters can occur quickly throughout the society, there is further support for the idea that fluctuations in annua birth rates will be great in the future, unless there is peace and economic stability.

The narrowing of traditional fertility differentials has important implications for our society. Many observers have feared that the relatively high birth rates of lower-status families in the past would have a harmful effect on the quality of our population either because of the poorer heredity or the poorer social environment bestowed on their children by parents with low incomes and little education. Whatever merit this view had, its pertinence is reduced as the fertility differentials between social classes are narrowed. Furthermore, the differences in standard of living between social classes should be reduced in the future since differences in per capita income will decrease if couples with low incomes have no more children than those with high incomes.

Some observers believe that the chances to move upward on the social and economic ladder have been enhanced in the United States in the past by the fact that upper-status parents have not produced enough children to take over the higher positions in society to which their family advantages may have given them easy access. To the extent that this has been true, a relative increase in the fertility of the upper-income group may be a factor in reducing upward social mobility.

Religious differences in fertility values still exist, although they, too, seem to be yielding to the process of standardization of norms. Catholics do want and expect more children than Protestants, but the difference now lies within the range of variation prescribed by the common norm of two to four children. Few Catholics want really large families. Most Catholics approve of the idea of family limitation. Some are using the more effective methods disapproved by the Church, but the majority are loyal to the standards of the Church. As a group they are successful in restricting their families to the commonly accepted goal. It is possible that the effectiveness of the rhythm method may be enhanced by the discovery of some simple method of determining whether ovulation will soon take place. If this occurs, Protestant-Catholic differences may be further reduced. However, the fact is that Protestant-Catholic differences exist now in all major sectors of the population and the better-educated Catholics seem to be most loyal to Catholic values. This may mean that religious differences will persist long after other traditional differences disappear.

The disappearance of traditional fertility differentials may only mean that traditional social distinctions are less important than formerly. It seems likely that such a fundamental matter as family growth will be related more or less closely to whatever major social distinctions develop in American life. For example, in the age of the "organization man" it may be necessary to look for new dimensions in a man's place in the economy and society in order to understand why couples have a certain number of children and why they plan them more or less effectively.

4. *The consensus on the two-to-four-child family may be an important indication of a more familistic orientation in American life.* The content of the new consensus may be as important as the fact that it exists. The long-time decline in family size from the 1800s or earlier to the decade of the 1930s has been explained by some as a result of the declining importance of the family as compared with other social institutions. The same argument should lead to the conclusion that the present increase in family size is associated with the increasing importance of the family. The mass migration to single-family suburban homes, the increase of leisure spent in family activities, and the growing emphasis on the family as the source of personal emotional security in an insecure world are among the signs to which observers of the contemporary scene point in emphasizing the resurgence of a familistic orientation in American life. The almost complete rejection of childlessness by American couples and their strong disavowal of the one-child family are proof of the seriousness with which they hold the view that a couple needs at least one or two children for a satisfying marriage.

The wide agreement that very small families are undesirable does not portend any return to the big family of an earlier day. The rejection of childlessness or the one-child family is matched by the rejection of families of five or more children. Even among those who are having such larger families, half or more are doing so unwillingly. Americans want a moderate-sized family—neither too small nor too big.

Even if the new family norm implies a new emphasis on family values, it apparently does not mean a return to a completely traditional role for mothers. At least there is no indication that it will reverse the trend for larger numbers of mothers to be gainfully employed. The working wife either is unable to have as many children or wants fewer than her friend who is a full-time homemaker. But this does not mean that she rejects her role as a mother. The working wife who prefers to be childless in order to pursue a career is a rarity. The emerging pattern for working wives is to combine the role of worker with that of mother-wife in a somewhat smaller family than the average.

5. *If present family growth plans are continued and realized, the American population will grow rapidly, although there may be important troughs and crests in the growth curve.* The moderate families Americans expect will produce substantial population growth if present marriage and childbearing patterns persist. This growth will occur even if there is no significant reduction in mortality and little or no immigration. That large families are not required for large population increases may be one of the most important conclusions to be drawn from the projections prepared for this study. With little change in mortality, marriage patterns, or immigration, the three-child family would lead to a population of

312 million by 2000 and of 600 million by 2050. Projecting the same assumptions for another century would lead to astronomically large population figures. Even the forecast for the year 2000 means a population so large as to imply a fundamental change in many aspects of our society. Americans may soon have to choose between the consequences of a very large population or a revision of their present values about marriage and childbearing.

Changes in the timing pattern of marriage and family growth are more important than changes in family size in determining some population trends. For example, it seems very likely that the number of births will dip between 1958 and 1965 and then rise to a greater or lesser extent after 1965, even if there is no further change in family size or in age at marriage and childbearing. This important change will occur as a consequence of previous changes in the timing patterns of family growth. With the increasing rational control by individuals of their own fertility, an understanding of population trends will require knowledge not only about causes of changes in completed size of family but also of causes of changes in the timing of marriage and reproduction.

The projections of *total population* prepared for this volume do not differ radically from those issued by the Bureau of the Census with more conventional and limited data. They do differ for specific *age groups*. Despite the similarity of over-all results, we believe that the present forecasts are more useful than those prepared by more conventional procedures. One reason is that they take into account the final family size expected by the married couples who are doing the childbearing, instead of depending entirely on past trends of birth rates and the forecaster's judgment of how these trends will change. Another reason is that they make the meaning of more assumptions explicit in such human terms as when people marry, how many marry, how many children they have, and when they have them. This means that when parts of the actual population trends deviate from parts of the projections —as they inevitably will—it will be easier to recognize the specific changes in marriage and family building patterns that have produced the deviations.

It is true that at present we lack factual information regarding the extent to which wives will bear the number of children they say they expect to have. Arrangements to obtain such information need to be made. As we learn more about the relation between expected and actual childbearing and the reasons why changes in specific family building habits occur, we shall be able to make better forecasts of the growth of the American population.

Appendix A

Technical Notes

NOTE 1. *Fertility trends in Great Britain*

D. V. Glass and E. Grebenik, *The Trend and Pattern of Fertility in Great Britain: A Report on the Family Census of 1946* (Papers of the Royal Commission on Population, vol. VI), H.M. Stationery Office, London, 1954, part I, *Report.* The data for marriages during 1862–1919 are from page 131; those for 1920–24 and for 1925 are from page 162. Marriages of brides 45 or older are excluded. Marriages of 1862–86 are restricted to those for which wife and husband were enumerated together in the census of 1911. (In most cases it was the first marriage of the wife.) Marriages of 1890–1925 are restricted to first marriages (of wife) which were (*a*) still in existence in 1946, or (*b*) broken before 1946 but not before the wife reached age 45. If fertility of marriages which last many years differs from that of marriages which are broken earlier, this would bias the trend which is shown by these data. There probably is such a bias, but it probably is small. The average number of births per marriage is slightly too low for the marriages of 1920–24 and 1925 because some of the wives who married while young bore children after the data were collected in 1946.

NOTE 2. *The Indianapolis Study*

P. K. Whelpton and Clyde V. Kiser (eds.), *Social and Psychological Factors Affecting Fertility,* Milbank Memorial Fund, New York, 5 vols., 1946, 1950, 1952, 1954, and 1958. The 33 reports brought together in these volumes were published originally in various issues of the *Milbank Memorial Fund Quarterly* from July, 1943, to July, 1958. The study was conducted in Indianapolis in 1941. It was based on a stratified random sample of all Indianapolis couples with the following characteristics: married in 1927–29, lived in a large city most of their married life, each spouse a native white Protestant who had completed at least the eighth grade and married only once, and wife under 30 when married.

406

a. The 1,977 couples in the inflated sample were classified by fecundity into two groups.

(1) The "relatively fecund" group consists of 1,444 couples, or 73 per cent of the total. It includes (*a*) all couples with four or more births and (*b*) all couples with three or fewer births unless they knew or had good reason to believe that they had been unable to conceive during a period of at least 24 months (if never pregnant) or 36 months (if pregnant one or more times). Failure to conceive during periods of these durations when living together and not trying to prevent conception was considered "good reason."

(2) The "relatively sterile" group includes the remaining 533 couples —27 per cent of the total. (Vol. 2, p. 212; or *Milbank Memorial Fund Quarterly*, vol. 25, p. 66, January, 1947.)

b. The wives reported 3,829 completed pregnancies with 3,865 fetuses, of which 3,358 were alive on delivery and 507 were dead. This gives a fetal death rate of 131. Probing questions were asked when the interviewers suspected that an illegal abortion might have occurred but was not being reported or was being called a miscarriage. In spite of such efforts only 84 illegal abortions were reported. They amounted to 2.2 per cent of the pregnancies and 16.6 per cent of the fetal deaths. (Vol. 2, p. 312; or *Milbank Memorial Fund Quarterly*, vol. 26, p. 192, April, 1948.)

c. Contraception had been used by 89 per cent of all couples in the study, by 98 per cent of the "relatively fecund" couples, and by 64 per cent of the "relatively sterile." (Vol. 2, p. 212; or *Milbank Memorial Fund Quarterly*, vol. 25, p. 66, January, 1947.)

d. Among the 1,444 relatively fecund couples, 403 were classified as having completely planned fertility; i.e., these couples used contraception "always" and had no conceptions, or conceived only when contraception was discontinued because a child was wanted. In this group the average number of births per couple is 1.39 for the 109 couples with the highest index of socioeconomic status and between 0.91 and 1.00 for the 294 couples in the four groups with a lower index of socioeconomic status. (Vol. 2, p. 409; or *Milbank Memorial Fund Quarterly*, vol. 27, p. 238, April, 1949.)

e. Among the 1,977 couples there were 382 who did not have a birth. Some of these couples wanted at least one child but were unable to have any for physiological reasons. For the remaining couples it is not possible to determine with assurance whether childlessness was voluntary or involuntary. However, it presumably was voluntary for most of those who did not want a child and practiced contraception "always" or "usually."

Three series of estimates were made of the comparative importance of voluntary and involuntary childlessness, each series involving a different distribution of the couples for whom both factors may have operated. In the high series for impaired fecundity it was assumed that this was the sole cause of the childlessness of a high proportion of the couples for whom contraception may also have had some effect, and the childlessness of the remaining couples in the questionable group was ascribed to control measures. The reverse was done in the high series for control measures. (In each case the size of the proportion was based on the extent to which the couples who practiced contraception and then stopped to have a child were able to have one.) The medium series is midway between the high and low.

Cause	Assumption regarding joint causation		
	High	Medium	Low
Control measures	47.6	40.2	32.7
Impaired fecundity	67.3	59.8	52.4

It appears that between one-third and one-half of the childless couples in the Indianapolis Study were childless from choice and that between one-half and two-thirds were unable to have a child. (Vol. 2, p. 336; or *Milbank Memorial Fund Quarterly*, vol. 26, p. 215, April, 1948.)

f. Effect on time required for conception of (1) contraception and (2) "douching for cleanliness only" soon after intercourse. That DFCO delayed conception to an important degree is shown by the following data for the "relatively fecund" couples who had conceptions of the order specified (see page 409).

On the whole, the intervals from marriage or the end of one pregnancy to the next conception were more than twice as long for the DFCO couples as for those who did nothing to prevent conception. Moreover, the intervals for the DFCO couples were about as long as those of the couples who practiced contraception but had an unplanned pregnancy; i.e., they did not stop contraception in order to have a child.

Some couples practiced contraception, or douched for cleanliness only, during the entire 12- to 15-year period from marriage to interview and had no pregnancy. Such couples are omitted from the following table. Other couples used these practices throughout the period beginning with the end of the first pregnancy, had no subsequent pregnancy, and are omitted from the second and third decks of the table. Including such couples would lengthen the periods in the three right-hand columns—the months during which there was no conception presumably because of the effect of the practices in question.

On the other hand, the table does not include the "relatively sterile"

No. of couples and months in interval	Couples not practicing contraception		Couples practicing contraception	
	Not using "douche for cleanliness only"	Using "douche for cleanliness only"	Not stopping because baby wanted	Stopping because baby wanted
First conception				
Number of couples	373	61	508	381
Months from marriage to first conception	7	26	21	47
Second conception				
Number of couples	108	28	562	313
Months from end of first pregnancy to second conception[a]	12	22	33	44
Third conception				
Number of couples	49	23	347	96
Months from end of second pregnancy to third conception[a]	12	31	32	43

[a] These intervals include the puerperium (the first month after the end of a pregnancy) and the months (if any) when DFCO and/or contraception was used.

SOURCE: Computed from Table 5 of P. K. Whelpton and Clyde V. Kiser (eds.), *Social and Psychological Factors Affecting Fertility*, Milbank Memorial Fund, New York, 1950, vol. 2, p. 224; or "VI. The Planning of Fertility," *Milbank Memorial Fund Quarterly*, vol. 25, p. 78, January, 1947.

couples—those who had fewer than four births and did not conceive during a 2- or 3-year period when neither contraception nor DFCO was practiced. If they could be added it would tend to lengthen the intervals shown in the left-hand column more than those in the other three columns. This omission tends to balance the foregoing.

On the whole, the data indicate that DFCO tends to reduce significantly the likelihood of conception, but to do so in lesser degree than douching when used for contraception instead of cleanliness only, or than the various methods of contraception (as a group) as they were used by the couples studied.

g. *The effectiveness of specified methods of contraception.* Estimates of the proportion of the "expected" conceptions of "relatively fecund" couples which were prevented by using specified methods of contraception "always" and "always, usually, or sometimes" are given below:

Method	Per cent using method	Per cent of expected conceptions prevented[a]			
		Contraception used "always"		Contraception used "always, usually, sometimes"[b]	
		1st	2d and higher order	1st	2d and higher order
Condom	28.7	97.6	94.7	96.7	93.2
Diaphragm and jelly	15.3	99.5	96.0	99.5	95.7
Douche:					
Lysol[c]	15.1	85.5	82.4	83.5	78.3
water[c]	14.0	88.3	79.2	84.9	77.6
Vaginal suppository	8.3	94.0	85.1	91.8	84.4
Withdrawal	6.3	96.5	94.2	95.3	90.2
Condom and water douche	6.1	97.1	93.8	95.7	92.8
Safe period[d]	2.2	*	64.8	*	62.5

* Less than 20 couples in base group. An asterisk has this meaning in all tables.

[a] The number of "expected" conceptions was estimated by dividing the number of months during which the specified method was used by the average number of months required for conception among "relatively fecund" couples when no preventive method was used. Dividing the actual number of conceptions when the method was used by the "expected" number and multiplying by 100 gave the "ineffectiveness ratios" published in the reports on the study. Subtracting these ratios from 100 gives the percentages shown here.

[b] The small differences between the percentages when the method was used "always" and "always, usually, or sometimes" merely mean that most of the time when the method was used it was used "always."

[c] Includes douching for cleanliness only soon after coitus as well as douching for contraception.

[d] Periodic continence, or rhythm. Some of the couples using this method thought incorrectly that the "safe" period for most women was midway between successive menstrual periods.

SOURCE: P. K. Whelpton and Clyde V. Kiser, *Social and Psychological Factors Affecting Fertility*, Milbank Memorial Fund, New York, 1950, vol. 4, pp. 905, 936–937; or *Milbank Memorial Fund Quarterly*, vol. 31, pp. 311, 342–343, July, 1953.

NOTE 3. *The exclusion of wives younger than 18 or older than 39*

Comparatively few women marry before their eighteenth birthday, and very few before their seventeenth. Those who do marry at ages 15–17 differ in important ways from those who marry at ages 18–24, the ages at which a large majority of the first marriages occur. For example, the very young wives are concentrated in the lower socioeconomic groups, and a high proportion have had a premarital conception.

If our budget had been several times as large we might have endeavored to interview enough of these extremely young wives so that we could have analyzed them separately. Our real choice was between omitting them or combining them with the other young wives in our study. The information that was available indicated that the wives who were 18 and 19 in 1955 are more representative of the wives who will be 20–24 in 1960 than are those who were 15–17 in 1955. Similarly, there is less bias if data for wives aged 20–24 in 1955 are compared with data for those 18 and 19 in that year than if the 15–19 group is utilized. Consequently, wives under 18 were omitted.

NOTE 4. *Pretests*

The actual field survey was preceded by two tests to determine whether any unusual difficulties would be encountered. One consisted of asking 1,100 adults two questions about "expected" and "ideal" family size, as part of a national sample survey on economic problems by the Economic Program of the Survey Research Center. No problems developed in connection with these questions; the results are closely comparable with those obtained later in our main survey.

A more intensive and crucial trial was a pretest of a preliminary version of the questionnaire with 100 interviews in four very different areas: a prosperous Iowa farm community, a low-income farm county in Georgia, an Irish-Catholic neighborhood in Brooklyn, and a Polish-Catholic area in Detroit. No problems were encountered. This bolstered the confidence of the field staff in the feasibility of the study.

NOTE 5. *Interval between pregnancies if contraception is not practiced*

After examining data from several studies in England and the United States, Dr. Alan F. Guttmacher concluded that "the following model timetable of the average interval between pregnancies can be constructed for nonlactating and lactating women who do not practice contraception" and (presumably) who cohabit at "normal" marital frequency.

	Nonlactating (months)	Lactating (months)
Postpartum amenorrhea	2	6
Anovulatory cycles	2	3
Time required for conception after ovulation is established	6	6
Pregnancy	9	9
Total	19	24

SOURCE: Alan F. Guttmacher, "Fertility of Man," *Fertility and Sterility*, vol. 3, no. 4, pp. 288–289, 1952.

NOTE 6. *Average number of births per married woman when fertility is not controlled*

Accurate statistics about the average number of births per married woman living through the childbearing period are not available for any country in which fertility is completely uncontrolled. There are, however, fairly accurate data for some countries in which very little use has been made of contraception and the fertility of the women now aged 50 (or more) has been relatively uncontrolled. Examples are given below. In each country the data were collected by interviewers in a census or a special study. Some of the children borne by the women interviewed undoubtedly were not reported; this is especially true for children who died soon after birth. It is believed, however, that the net deficit does not exceed 10 per cent in most of these countries, nor 20 per cent in any of them.

Country	Year	Age of women	Average number of births per woman		
			All women	Ever-married women	Women who had at least one birth
Brazil[a]	1940	45–49	6.2	N.A.	7.3
Ceylon[b]	1953	(See Note)	N.A.	6.6	N.A.
India[c]	1951	42–46	N.A.	5.9	N.A.
Mexico[d]	1950	45–49	5.1	N.A.	6.5
Peru[a]	1940	45–49	5.6	N.A.	6.5
Puerto Rico[e]	1950	45 or more	5.8	6.3	6.7

N.A. = not ascertained.

[a] *The Determinants and Consequences of Population Trends*, Population Studies, no. 17, United Nations, New York, 1953, p. 93.

[b] The Ceylonese women were first married in 1910–19 at an average age of about 20 and "remained in the married state (registered and customary marriages) until they passed the end of the fertility period which is usually regarded as 45 years." *Fertility Trends in Ceylon, 1953 Census*, Department of Census and Statistics, Monograph 8, Ceylon, 1956, pp. 13–14. Almost all the women were between 47 and 73 years of age in 1953; most were between 49 and 68.

[c] These Indian women were living with their husbands and had been married 27 years or more. *Couple Fertility*, National Sample Survey, no. 7, Indian Statistical Institute, Calcutta, 1956, p. 46.

[d] *Septimo Censo General de Población, 6 de Junio de 1950, Resumen General*, Dirección General de Estadística, Secretaria de Economía, Mexico, D.F., 1953.

[e] The average for ever-married Puerto Rican women may be slightly too high, because in computing it the assumption was made that the women who had married (91 per cent of the total) had had all the births and the single women had had none. *1950 Census of Population, Fertility by Social and Economic Status, for Puerto Rico: 1950*, U.S. Bureau of the Census, series PC-14, no. 21, June 24, 1954, pp. 1 and 11.

Note 7. *Fetal death rate according to official sources*

Annual reports published by the National Office of Vital Statistics since 1945 (and by the Bureau of the Census in prior years) show that the white population of the Birth Registration Area had a fetal death rate which declined from 35.1 per 1,000 births plus fetal deaths in 1922 to 15.3 in 1954. Since 1942 most states have tried to obtain the registration of all fetal deaths which occur after a pregnancy has lasted 20 weeks or 5 months, but many of these deaths have not been registered. Before 1942 several states required the registration of fetal deaths only if they occurred after the seventh month. For a recent report see *Vital Statistics of the United States, 1954,* U.S. Department of Health, Education and Welfare, 1956, vol. 1, p. xliv.

Note 8. John W. Riley and Matilda White, "The Use of Various Methods of Contraception," *American Sociological Review,* vol. 5, no. 6, pp. 890–903, December, 1940.

The information was collected in 1938–39 through personal interviews by regular field interviewers (women) of the Market Research Corporation of America. "The majority of the interviews (2,568) were made with upper class married women under 45 in 30 cities throughout the country." (In addition there were interviews with 457 young single women in the same cities and with 515 rural married women distributed throughout the United States, but the data for the single women are not included in this article.) The cities were "selected to represent different community characteristics." The upper middle class "was divided into 3 strata, labeled 'upper,' 'middle,' and 'lower,' respectively. Within these limitations, the sample was taken at random." The data on use represent "a cross section of customary action at a given time" and exclude couples who "had previously used some method of control" but no longer did so.

This concept regarding use corresponds fairly closely, but not exactly, to the concept "method used most recently" which is utilized in the present study.

Note 9. *Classifications of couples by fertility planning status based on pregnancies and on births*

The classification of couples according to their planning of fertility is based on their pregnancies and not on their births in both the overview and the more detailed classification in Chapter 3. That chapter focuses on the use of contraception in order to space pregnancies and limit their number, and on the success achieved. In Chapters 7 to 11, in contrast, the emphasis is on success in having the number of births desired.

For a large majority (about three-fourths) of the couples—those who had no fetal death—it makes no difference whether the criterion is pregnancies or births. For the other couples it is not appropriate that a classification by success in the use of contraception be influenced by fetal death. Let us consider a couple who wanted two children, stopped contraception in order to have two pregnancies, each of which produced a live birth, and then had an accidental and unwanted third pregnancy which was ended by a miscarriage or an illegal abortion. The couple would be classified as having Completely Planned fertility with respect to births and Excess Fertility with respect to pregnancies. The latter category is more correct from the standpoint of success in using contraception.

Basing a classification by fertility planning on pregnancies rather than on births has advantages when, as mentioned in Chapter 2, it is probable that a substantial number of illegal abortions were reported as miscarriages. Since such pregnancies would probably be reported as not wanted, a classification based on pregnancies would take this attitude into account. If births were the criteria, these failures to control conception would be disregarded.

For the three broad planning groups referred to in the overview of Chapter 3 (and in later chapters) the main differences between a distribution of couples by fertility planning status which is based on pregnancies and a distribution which is based on births are as follows:

1. A few couples classified as Partially Planned on the basis of pregnancies would be classified as Completely Planned on the basis of births. These are the couples who planned (by stopping contraception) each pregnancy resulting in a live birth, but who had one or more unplanned pregnancies which were ended by fetal death.

2. A larger number (but a small proportion) of couples classified as Excess Fertility on the basis of pregnancies would be classified as Completely Planned or Partially Planned on the basis of births. These are couples who planned or wanted, and had, a given number of children, but subsequently had one or more unwanted pregnancies which were ended by fetal death.

If the nine-group classification used later in Chapter 3 (and subsequently) were shifted from pregnancies to births, the main differences would be:

1. A few couples classified as Number Planned would be changed to Completely Planned and a few others to Quasi-planned.

2. A few couples classified as Quasi-planned would be shifted to Number Planned.

3. A somewhat larger number (but still a small proportion) of couples

classified as Excess Fertility would be changed to Completely Planned, Number Planned, or Quasi-planned.

Groups 1 and 2 would be restricted to Users; group 3 would include both Users and Nonusers.

NOTE 10. *The attitude of the Catholic Church regarding control of family size*

a. The idea of control. Official pronouncements state that upon couples living in "the married state" is imposed "the function of helping the conservation of the human race" by having children. However, "serious motives" may justify the avoidance of childbearing by a couple "for a long time, perhaps even the whole duration of the marriage." These ideas are contained in the following quotation from an address of Pope Pius XII to the Congress of the Italian Catholic Union of Midwives, Oct. 29, 1951, as published in *The Catholic Telegraph Register*, Nov. 9, 1951, p. 2.

The marriage contract, which confers upon husband and wife the right to satisfy the inclinations of nature, sets them up in a certain state of life, the married state. But upon couples who perform the act peculiar to their state, nature and the Creator impose the function of helping the conservation of the human race. The characteristic activity which gives their state its value is the *bonum prolis* [good of offspring]. The individual and society, the people and the state, the Church itself depend for their existence in the order established by God on fruitful marriage. To embrace the married state, therefore, continuously to make use of the faculty proper to it and lawful in it alone, and, on the other hand, to withdraw always and deliberately with no serious reason from its primary obligation, would be a sin against the very meaning of conjugal life.

There are serious motives, such as those often mentioned in the so-called medical, eugenic, economic, and social "indications," that can exempt for a long time, perhaps even the whole duration of the marriage, from the positive and obligatory carrying out of the act. From this it follows that observing the nonfertile periods alone can be lawful only under a moral aspect. Under the conditions mentioned it really is so. But if, according to a rational and just judgment, there are no similar grave reasons of a personal nature or deriving from external circumstances, then the determination to avoid habitually the fecundity of the union, while at the same time to continue fully satisfying their sensuality, can be derived only from a false appreciation of life and from reasons having nothing to do with proper ethical laws.

b. The number of children for a controlled family. The writers have been informed that no official pronouncements have been made regarding how many children a controlled family should have.

According to Rev. William J. Gibbons, S.J.:[1]

[1] William J. Gibbons, S.J., "The Catholic Value System in Relation to Human Fertility," in George F. Mair (ed.), *Studies in Population*, Princeton University Press, Princeton, N.J., 1949, p. 122.

Catholicism, as a value system, does not tell parents how many children they must have. Moral attitudes vary, spiritual motivation differs, economic and health considerations are not always the same. Unlike some advocates of planned parenthood, the Catholic Church has learned that ultimate decisions in this matter should be arrived at by the married people themselves. She does not tell them to what extent to use marriage, but declares to them what is morally acceptable and what is not. She counsels them as to the end and nature of marriage, and informs them of their responsibility toward children, and the advisability of moderation.

A similar statement was made by a representative of the Vatican at an international conference of Catholic intellectuals held in Venice in May, 1953, under the auspices of Pax Romana. He emphasized that the decision regarding the number of children for a couple to have should not be made by society, by the State, or even by the Church; instead, it should be made by the couple after considering carefully all the appropriate conditions affecting their situation.

c. The use of periodic continence as a method of control. Approval of periodic continence (rhythm) has been affirmed in various statements made during the last century, and even earlier. Three of them are quoted below.

(Reply of the Sacred Penitentiary: 2 March, 1853)

[Question] The Bishop of Amiens, France, humbly requests of the Eminent Father of the Sacred Penitentiary the solution of the following difficulty:

Certain married people among the faithful, relying on the opinion of learned physicians, are convinced that in each month there are some days on which conception cannot take place in a woman. Are those to be disturbed who do not use marriage except on these days, at least if they have legitimate reasons for refraining from the conjugal act?

[Reply] The Sacred Penitentiary, having pondered the proposed case, replies to the Venerable Father in Christ, the Bishop of Amiens, that those mentioned in the petition should not be disturbed, so long as they do nothing to prevent conception.[2]

(Reply of the Sacred Penitentiary: 16 June, 1880)

[Question] In the judgment of learned physicians and physiologists, women for the most part are not permanently able to conceive, but only periodically able, that is, from the time at which the menstrual flow begins to the fourth day after it has ceased; in the rest of the month they are usually sterile. They assert that this theory has been verified in 94 percent of the women observed.

Having learned of this, Doctor L. thought that a remedy might therein be found to prevent many serious sins, by persuading spouses who turn to

---

[2] H. Batzill (ed.), *Decisiones sanctae sedis de usu et abusu matrimonii*, no. 8, p. 16, Marietti, Turin, 1937. The authors wish to express their thanks to Rev. William J. Gibbons, S.J., who called their attention to the first two of these quotations.

onanism from fear of conception, to abstain from relations at that time at which conception is possible, and to have relations in the proper way at the time at which conception does not usually take place.

For as to abstaining at the time suitable for conception, he said that what is permissible always is permissible intermittently, that is, to abstain from the use of marriage so as to avoid too many children provided that there is no danger of incontinence and provided that there is mutual consent.

Moreover, as to having intercourse at the time of periodic sterility, he said that intercourse in this case is no more to be censured than in the case of the old or the permanently sterile.

Finally, the choice of such a way of acting to avoid children seemed to him harmless, if the spouses either remain neutral concerning the conception which may, perhaps, follow, or submit positively in this to divine Providence, or even desire, for a reasonable cause, that no children be conceived; furthermore, if there were no reasonable cause, the sin would be only venial.

Cardinal Gousset set forth an opinion similar to this one; periodicals worthy of credence have approved this same opinion: *Analecta Iuris Pontificii, Revue de science ecclésiastiques, Nouvelle revue théologique.*

But a certain Spanish theologian has condemned it in the periodical *Consultor de los parochos.*

Since this controversy has arisen, Doctor L. has asked of the Sacred Penitentiary: (1) Whether spouses can so act without mortal or venial sin; (2) Whether a confessor may urge this way of acting on a wife who detests the onanism of her husband but is unable to correct it, or on either spouse who wishes to avoid too many children; (3) Whether the danger of a reduction in the number of offspring must be provided against or whether this must be considered of secondary importance to the profit realized from avoidance of sin and peace of conscience.

[Reply] The Sacred Penitentiary, having earnestly pondered the question proposed, replies:

Spouses using marriage in the aforesaid way should not be disturbed, and a confessor may suggest, but cautiously, the opinion under discussion to those spouses whom he has vainly tried by another method to lead away from the detestable crime of onan.[3]

On July 20, 1932, to a new question: "Is that practice of spouses licit, whereby for good and serious reasons wishing to avoid offspring legitimately, by mutual consent and with proper intent they abstain from the use of marriage except on those days when according to the latest theories, conception is unlikely for natural reasons," the Sacred Penitentiary replied: The question has already been handled in the reply of June 16, 1880.[4]

d. The use of "artificial birth control" and coitus interruptus. According to Father Gibbons:[5]

[3] *Analecta Iuris Pontificii,* 22 (1883), p. 249; Batzill, *op. cit.,* no. 11, pp. 19–21.
[4] William J. Gibbons, S.J., "Fertility Control in the Light of Some Recent Catholic Statements," *Eugenics Quarterly,* vol. 3, no. 1, footnote p. 13, March, 1956.
[5] William J. Gibbons, S.J., "The Catholic Value System in Relation to Human Fertility," p. 119.

By artificial birth control the Church means the use of any mechanical or chemical contraceptives resorted to for the purpose of keeping the male seed from reaching the uterus and thus penetrating to the Fallopian tubes.

Artificial birth control and withdrawal were "branded with the guilt of grave sin" by Pius XI in Encyclical *Casti Connubii.*

But no reason, however grave, may be put forward by which anything intrinsically against nature may become conformable to nature and morally good. Since, therefore, the conjugal act is destined primarily by nature for the begetting of children, those who in exercising it deliberately frustrate its natural power and purpose, sin against nature and commit a deed which is shameful and intrinsically vicious . . . Any use whatsoever of matrimony exercised in such a way that the act is deliberately frustrated in its natural power to generate life is an offense against the law of God and of nature, and those who indulge in such are branded with guilt of grave sin.[6]

NOTE 11. *Unpublished tabulations of use of contraception by socioeconomic groups*

Table 4–1 shows in full detail the relation between religious preference and use of contraception (Past or Future, Motive or Action) for the couples without considering the age of the wife. Table 4–2 shows the relation of wife's religion to past Motive use for each age group. Unpublished tables are available showing the distribution of the data in Table 4–1 within each age group. They support the text statements in detail. In the remaining sections of this chapter the tables on use with age controls are limited to past Motive use in order to reduce the bulk of the data presented. In each case there are unpublished tables with age controls for Past and Future use on a Motive and Action basis for all couples and Fecund couples. Unfortunately, it is impossible to present the full statistical documentation for all the social characteristics considered. In some cases classifications are condensed for clarity as well as economy of space. The sections on religion and education are documented more fully than the other sections of this chapter. There are comparable unpublished tables with age controls for most of the other characteristics considered.

NOTE 12. *The relation between family income and the proportion of couples who are Users*

When family income is taken as a measure of economic status the results are essentially similar to those with husband's income, except that they are less regular and consistent in each age group. This is because the discrepancies between family income and husband's income are almost entirely a result of the income of working wives. Both

[6] *Ibid.,* pp. 132–133.

the fecundity status and the other characteristics of the couples with working wives are sufficiently distinctive to introduce dimensions other than income. There is also serious question whether the economic position of a family is improved proportionately to the income earned by a working wife, since the fact that she works usually adds some costs to the family budget and makes some kinds of economies more difficult.

NOTE 13. *The relation between income and the planning status of pregnancies*

The departures from the general pattern are especially marked in the younger ages. This may reflect a change between cohorts in the significance of income differentials, or it may reflect selective factors. The low-income families who begin to use contraception in the younger ages may include certain types of effective planners, for example, married college students. With advancing age the low-income Users include a large proportion of those beginning use late, who may be less effective planners.

NOTE 14. *The classification by place of present residence*

The 1950 census definition of metropolitan areas is used. The 12 largest cities are Baltimore, Boston, Chicago, Cleveland, Detroit, Los Angeles, New York, Philadelphia, Pittsburgh, St. Louis, San Francisco, and Washington, D.C. These central cities and their suburbs are all represented in the sample. "Other large cities" includes all other cities of 50,000 or more, whether or not they are central cities of metropolitan areas. "Suburbs of 12 largest cities," and "other suburbs" include all the metropolitan area around the cities in question, except another city of 50,000 or more and its "suburbs." "Small cities" are places with a population of 2,500 to 49,999, outside of metropolitan areas. Rural nonfarm refers to the population living in the open country or places of less than 2,500 but not on farms.

NOTE 15. *"Pure" community types*

The "large city" type in this classification includes only couples now living in a metropolitan area who had lived most of the time both before and after marriages in cities with 50,000 or more population. The "small city" type includes only couples now residing in a small city (less than 50,000 population) outside a metropolitan area and who lived in a small city most of the time both before and after marriage. Unfortunately, it is not possible to determine whether the earlier small-city residence was inside or outside a metropolitan area, although in most cases it is likely to have been outside. It is probable that some of the wives and husbands who were reported as having lived previously in a certain city actually had lived in the suburbs of that city.

NOTE 16. Christopher Tietze, Samuel R. Poliakoff, and John Rock, "Clinical Effectiveness of the Rhythm Method of Contraception," *Fertility and Sterility*, vol. 2, no. 5, pp. 444–450, September-October, 1951.

A contraceptive clinic prescribing periodic continence was established in 1936 at the Free Hospital for Women in Brookline, Mass. On the basis of records for 409 women during 7,267 months of exposure, plus follow-up information for a sample of the women who were pregnant when they withdrew from the study, the authors estimated that there were only 14.4 accidental pregnancies per 100 years of exposure while rhythm was being practiced.

. . . The rate of 14.4 is much higher than the rates reported for the most successful users of the diaphragm-and-jelly or of condoms (6 to 7 per 100 years of exposure), but it is in line with the results of several other clinics in urban and rural areas of the United States, prescribing mechanical and/or chemical contraception and serving a type of patient presumably comparable to those in our clinic in understanding and foresight and in their interest in family limitation. However, one should also note the fact that the computation of the "unsafe period" as done at the Rhythm Clinic includes a long 3-day extension on each end of the theoretical ovulation phase. Furthermore in most instances the actual determination of this period was made for the patient by a trained worker who also prescribed complete continence during the months when the patient's ovulatory rhythm was obviously upset.

NOTE 17. *"Percentage accidental" as a measure of the effectiveness of specific methods of regulating conception*

The best measure of the effectiveness of a given method of contraception which is possible with our data is the fraction whose denominator is the number of pregnancies after the first use of *any* method and whose numerator is the number of these pregnancies that are accidental. "Percentage accidental" understates the effectiveness of a specific method when all couples who used it at any time are being considered, because (by definition) some of these couples also used one or more other methods, and lack of information makes it necessary for us to charge *all* failures to *each* method. For example, if a couple had an accidental conception with the first method, changed to a second and had another failure, and then changed to a third method which they used successfully, our questionnaire shows merely that three methods were used and two accidental pregnancies occurred. Consequently, we are forced to count the two failures in computing "percentage accidental" for each of the three methods. The effect may be illustrated as follows:

Couples and methods	No. of pregnancies after first use of any method [a]		Percentage accidental
	Total	Accidental	
1. All Users, all methods	3,171	793	25
2. All Users of appliance methods	2,617	644 .	25
3. All Users of withdrawal	557	176	32
4. All Users of rhythm	1,134	364	32
5. Sum of lines 2, 3, and 4	4,308	1,184	27

[a] The 146 pregnancies after first use, among Users for whom planning status of *any* pregnancy was not ascertained, are excluded from this table.

The 1,755 Users who can be considered here had a total of 3,171 pregnancies after beginning contraception. Twenty-five per cent of these pregnancies were accidental (line 1). The experience of these 1,755 Users with each of the three types of methods is shown in lines 2, 3, and 4. Because the pregnancies of the Users who tried more than one type of method must appear on more than one line, the sum of lines 2, 3, and 4 is 4,308 pregnancies (instead of 3,171), of which 1,184 (instead of 793) are accidental. The result is an inflated "percentage accidental" of 27 instead of the 25 with which we began.

It might seem that "percentage accidental" would be satisfactory in comparisons of couples who used only one method. This is not the case because there is a tendency for couples who have accidents with one method to shift to another method which they hope will be more effective. In consequence, we have no way of knowing to what extent the experience of all couples with a given method is represented by the experience of the couples who have used only that method. Because the net tendency is to change from less effective to more effective methods, "percentage accidental" understates the relative difference in the effectiveness of the three types of methods shown in the table.

Lack of information also prevents us from making any distinction between the accidental conceptions occurring after a short delay and those occurring after a long delay. This undoubtedly works to the disadvantage of the more effective methods. A better measure of effectiveness would yield wider margins of superiority for these methods over others.

NOTE 18. E. Lewis-Faning, *Report on an Enquiry into Family Limitation and Its Influence on Human Fertility during the Past Fifty Years* (Papers of the Royal Commission on Population, vol. I), H.M. Stationery Office, London, 1949.

The universe selected for study consisted of wives under 45

whose first marriage had not been terminated and older women whose first marriage had lasted at least until age 45 (p. 3). The women interviewed were selected from hospital patients but did not constitute a probability sample of patients meeting the age and marital-status requirements, let alone a probability sample of all women in the universe. It was realized that the sampling design was not ideal from a scientific standpoint; nevertheless it was adopted for various reasons. One was a fear that efforts to obtain a really representative national sample might meet with much unfavorable publicity, which would jeopardize cooperation and quality of replies. Another was the fact that a probability sampling procedure would have required more time, and there was pressure to complete the study quickly. Wives in hospitals were found to be a biased sample of the population, having an overrepresentation of larger families and of working-class families. Both of these types of sampling bias are likely to exaggerate the proportion of Nonusers. On the other hand, the fact that in the British study the interviewing was done by medical personnel may have encouraged a more complete reporting of contraceptive practice than in our study. Also, the British sample was somewhat overweighted with urban couples and heavily overweighted with couples from London and Glasgow, who are more likely to be Users than are the couples in smaller cities or rural areas.

Despite these limitations it is likely that the sample gives a reasonably good picture of the British situation, especially with reference to the types of contraception used.

NOTE 19. *The difference between the fertility rates of all white women and of native white women*

During the first two or three decades of the present century the fertility rates of all white women in the United States were substantially higher than those of native white women. By the middle of the century, however, the difference had become negligible. This is shown by the age-specific birth rates per 1,000 women during 1918–21 and 1949–51 in the table on page 423.

The virtual disappearance of the differential has come about in two ways. First, the proportion of white women of childbearing age who are foreign born has declined substantially. Second, the differential between the fertility of native white women and foreign-born white women has decreased greatly.

NOTE 20. *Can women marrying in their 30s have as many children as they want?*

An affirmative answer is suggested by two of our findings.

Age	1918–21			1949–51		
	All white women	Native white women	Excess for all white women	All white women	Native white women	Excess for all white women
			Single and ever-married women			
15–19	53	52	1	71	71	0
20–24	168	160	8	193	193	0
25–29	169	157	12	165	164	1
30–34	131	121	10	102	102	0
35–39	90	83	7	51	51	0
40–44	36	33	3	14	14	0
			Ever-married women			
15–19	456	446	10	424	424	0
20–24	321	312	10	281	281	0
25–29	221	211	10	188	187	1
30–34	156	146	10	113	118	−5
35–39	101	95	6	56	56	0
40–44	42	38	4	16	16	0

SOURCE: Rates for 1918–21 are computed from those in P. K. Whelpton, "Corrected Birth Rate Tables by States 1918–21, 1929–31, by Race and Nativity for All Women and Married Women," *Population Statistics. 2. State Data*, National Resources Committee, Washington, D.C., 1937. Rates for 1949–51 are computed from registered births and enumerated women.

One is that such women do not ordinarily want many children; the average for those in our sample is 2.1. Another is that among couples with the wife in the early years of marriage the proportion Fecund is as high for wives marrying in their 30s as it is for wives marrying at younger ages. This is shown by the following:

Wife's age at marriage	*Percentage Fecund,* *for couples married* *less than 5 years*[a]
Under 18	89
18–19	93
20–21	92
22–24	88
25–29	85
30–39	93

[a] As has been stated elsewhere, duration of marriage is defined as the number of years since the wife's first marriage, not since the marriage of the couple. However, among the 649 couples with wife married less than 5 years, the group on which this table is based, there are only 7 (or 1.1 per cent) with wife married more than once.

The differences between these proportions are not statistically significant.

It is probable that among couples married less than 5 years there is somewhat more hidden subfecundity if the wife married in her 30s than if she married younger. However, we must remember that the onset of fecundity impairments is not due solely to rising age but is affected also by the number of children the wife has borne, as is shown in Chapter 2. Since the wives marrying in their 30s had borne relatively few children by the time of interview, the high proportion of them that are classified as Fecund is real and not merely a function of undiscovered fecundity impairments.

NOTE 21. *The effect of contraception and fecundity impairments on fertility*

In theory, this could be measured in several ways. We could ascertain the effect of contraception, assuming the observed incidence of fecundity impairments or assuming no fecundity impairments. Similarly, we could ascertain the effect of fecundity impairments, assuming the observed incidence of contraception or assuming the absence of contraception. In fact, however, the data gathered in the present study are not sufficiently detailed to permit all these procedures. Our chief obstacle is the impossibility of determining average family size under the conditions of no contraception and observed subfecundity. This will be made clear in the comparison of our data with similar material from the Indianapolis Study shown in Table A–1. In this comparison, the effect of subfecundity and contraception is estimated for couples with wife married 10–14 years in our sample and for the Indianapolis sample of couples married 12–15 years.

Before describing the results of the comparison, it should be made clear that the operational definition of fecundity is not the same for each sample. In the present study our definition of fecundity is oriented toward the future—the ability of couples to have children in coming years. In contrast, the definition used in the Indianapolis Study is oriented toward the past—the couple's ability to have children, or the actual number born, between marriage and interview. As a result, there are couples included among the "relatively fecund" in the Indianapolis Study who would be classified as Definitely Sterile, Probably Sterile, or Semifecund according to the criteria used in the present study. It is probable, however, that all couples classified as Fecund in the present study would also have been classified as "relatively fecund" in the Indianapolis Study. Because of the emphasis on past performance in the Indianapolis Study, all couples with high past fertility (four or more births) were classified as "relatively fecund." In the present study, however, a couple with eight children is classified as Definitely Sterile if the wife had her Fallopian tubes ligated. Hence, the present study includes among the Subfecund some couples who had normal or even relatively high past fertility.

The difference in definitions and classification tends to make the effect of subfecundity on fertility appear smaller in the present study than in the Indianapolis Study. This is shown in Table A–1. Assuming the observed incidence of contraception, the reduction in fertility due to fecundity impairments is estimated to be 15 per cent in the present study, but 18 to 21 per cent in the Indianapolis Study. Had we used the Indianapolis definitions in the present study, the effect of subfecundity would very probably have appeared to be greater, at comparable ages and durations of marriage, for our sample than for the Indianapolis sample. This conjecture is based on the association between high fertility and fecundity impairments and the fact that the couples in our sample had higher fertility than those in the Indianapolis sample.

Is the reduction in fertility due to contraception greater than that due to fecundity impairments? In the Indianapolis Study contraception appeared to have a decidedly greater effect. We cannot make a definite statement on the basis of the present study because we cannot discover what the effect of subfecundity would be if nobody used contraception; we can estimate only what it would be, assuming the observed incidence of contraception. It would be unrealistic to assume for our sample that fertility under the condition of no contraception would be the same as the fertility of Nonusers, because the Nonusers include such a high proportion of the Subfecund couples.

In the Indianapolis Study the number of children that would have been born to all couples if none of them had used contraception was estimated as follows: (1) it was assumed that the intervals between pregnancies, by order of pregnancy, would have been the same length as those of the more fecund when contraception was not used; and (2) an allowance was made for the fact that conditions associated with each additional pregnancy cause a small proportion of couples to be subfecund or sterile thereafter. A similar estimate was not possible for the present study because no information was collected on whether or how long contraception was used during the period preceding each pregnancy.

It seems probable that if such an estimate could be made for the present study it would show the reduction in fertility due to subfecundity to be about the same as that derived from the Indianapolis Study. This inference is based on the similarity of the other comparisons between the present study and the Indianapolis Study shown in Table A–1. The reduction due to contraception is somewhat greater for the

TABLE A–1. THE EFFECT OF SUBFECUNDITY AND CONTRACEPTION ON FERTILITY, IN PRESENT STUDY AND INDIANAPOLIS STUDY

Assumptions	Present study, marriages of 10–14 years' duration	Indianapolis Study, marriages of 12–15 years' duration
	Average no. of births per couple	
A. No contraception, no subfecundity	5.38–6.72[a]	6.33–7.77[b]
B. No contraception, observed subfecundity	c	4.59[d]
C. Observed contraception, no subfecundity	2.98[e]	2.07–2.16[f]
D. Observed contraception, observed subfecundity[g]	2.54	1.70
	Percentage reduction	
Reduction due to subfecundity:		
(1) With no contraception, $\dfrac{A-B}{A} \times 100$	c	27–41
(2) With observed contraception, $\dfrac{C-D}{C} \times 100$	15	18–21
Reduction due to contraception:		
(1) With no subfecundity, $\dfrac{A-C}{A} \times 100$	45–56	67–72
(2) With observed subfecundity, $\dfrac{B-D}{B} \times 100$	c	63
	Absolute reduction	
Reduction due to subfecundity:		
(1) With no contraception, $A-B$	c	1.74–3.18
(2) With observed contraception, $C-D$	0.44	0.37–0.46
Reduction due to contraception:		
(1) With no subfecundity, $A-C$	2.40–3.74	4.26–5.61
(2) With observed subfecundity, $B-D$	c	2.89
Total, $A-D$	2.84–4.18	4.63–6.07

[a] Assuming that Fecund couples not using contraception could have one pregnancy every 16 or 20 months and that the fetal death rate is 129 per 1,000, as observed in the present study. Sixteen months is taken as one extreme, because it is the estimate based on the most fecund 60 per cent of the couples in the Indianapolis Study (see footnote b). Twenty months is taken as the other extreme in order to have a wide range. It is 1 month longer than the interval for nonlactating women in Guttmacher's "model timetable" (Appendix A, Note 5) and 2 months longer than the estimated interval for all couples in the Indianapolis Study.

[b] Assuming that all couples could have births at the rate observed for "relatively fecund" couples when they were not using contraception. The lower figure is based on the most fecund 75 per cent and the higher figure on the most fecund 60 per cent. P. K. Whelpton and Clyde V. Kiser (eds.), *Social and Psychological Factors Affecting*

Indianapolis couples than for those in our sample. This is to be expected because the former wanted fewer children, consequently more of them used contraception intensively.

NOTE 22. *Method of estimating extent of bias in number of births wanted at interview*

As is pointed out in Chapter 8, the wives who thought that they were unable to have children in coming years and who did not want any were not asked how many children they had wanted. We know that some of these wives wanted fewer births than they had had, namely, those whose last pregnancy was not wanted ("no" to question 15), but ended with a birth. (They form part of the Excess Fertility group.) But because we do not know how many babies were born after the last pregnancy that was wanted, we have assumed for all the wives in question that the number of births wanted is the number that had occurred. Hence, our procedure overstates the number of births wanted by these wives.

In trying to estimate the extent of this bias, let us first compare the average numbers wanted, as defined in Chapter 8, by each fecundity group. These are shown in Table A–2 along with other data that will be referred to later. The outstanding feature of this comparison is the high number wanted by the Definitely Sterile—an average of 3.69 births. This is 20 per cent above the average wanted by all other groups combined (3.08). The number expected by the Probably Sterile, the other major group that includes wives who thought that they could not have more births, appears to be reasonable, however. Their average of 2.91 is not high, compared with those for the other fecundity groups. Consequently, we have assumed that the bias in our procedure does not affect significantly the number wanted for the Probably Sterile as a group. Attention will be confined, then, to overstatement among the Definitely Sterile.

We can make one estimate of the effect of the bias among the Definitely Sterile by assuming that their actual number wanted is the same as that for all other groups combined. This assumption yields the fol-

---

Fertility, Milbank Memorial Fund, New York, 1950, vol. 2, p. 319; or "VIII. The Comparative Influence on Fertility of Contraception and Impairments of Fecundity," *Milbank Memorial Fund Quarterly*, vol. 26, no. 2, p. 198, April, 1948.

c Cannot be determined from available data.

d Assuming that all couples could have births at the rate observed for all couples when they were not using contraception. Whelpton and Kiser, *op. cit.*

e The observed fertility of the couples classified as Fecund.

f The lower figure is the observed fertility of the most fecund 75 per cent of *all* couples; the higher figure is that of the most fecund 60 per cent.

g Observed fertility of all couples.

lowing estimates of the extent to which the number wanted, as defined, is overstated:

Group	Percentage by which number of births wanted is overstated
Definitely Sterile	20
Subfecund	6
All couples	2

However, these are probably maximum estimates of the effect of the bias. Wives in the Definitely Sterile group are likely to want more births than are those in the other fecundity groups, because the Definitely Sterile group contains higher proportions of couples from the socio-economic groups that want relatively many children (see Chapter 2). That the Definitely Sterile wives do want more children is suggested by their replies to the question regarding the number of children they would like to have if they could live their married lives over again (Appendix B, questions 19*j*, 20*h*, or 33). (We must shift from births wanted to children wanted because no allowance was made for child mortality in tabulating the replies to some of these questions.) As we see from Table A–2, the Definitely Sterile gave larger numbers in response to this question than did the wives in any other fecundity group.

How can we use this information to estimate a reasonable average number of children wanted at interview for the Definitely Sterile? First,

TABLE A–2. AVERAGE NUMBER OF BIRTHS AND CHILDREN WIVES WANTED AT INTERVIEW, AVERAGE NUMBER OF CHILDREN WIVES WOULD WANT IF MARRIED LIFE COULD BE RELIVED, AND PERCENTAGE BY WHICH CHILDREN WANTED AT INTERVIEW IS BELOW CHILDREN "WOULD WANT," FOR ALL WIVES, BY FECUNDITY OF COUPLE

Fecundity	Average no. wanted at interview		Average no. of children "would want" if married life could be relived	Percentage by which children wanted at interview is below children "would want"
	Births	Children		
Total	3.14	3.07	3.48	11.8
Fecund	3.12	3.05	3.45	11.6
Subfecund	3.18	3.12	3.54	11.9
Definitely Sterile	3.69	3.62	3.73	3.0
Probably Sterile	2.91	2.91	3.55	18.0
Semifecund	3.02	2.97	3.47	14.4
Indeterminate	2.79	2.71	3.26	16.9
Total excluding Definitely Sterile	3.08	3.01	3.45	12.8
Subfecund excluding Definitely Sterile	2.94	2.90	3.45	15.9

let us compare the number of children wanted at interview (as defined above) with the number the wives would want if they could relive their married lives. (For convenience, the latter number will be referred to as the number "would want.") For all fecundity groups the number of children wanted at interview is below the number "would want." However, the extent of the discrepancy is largest for the Probably Sterile, Semifecund, and Indeterminate (15.9 per cent for the three groups combined) and smallest for the Definitely Sterile (3.0 per cent), with the Fecund in an intermediate position (11.6 per cent). It appears more reasonable for the percentage difference for the Definitely Sterile to be larger than that for the Fecund (as is the case with the other three Subfecund groups) than for it to be so much smaller. If we assume that it is the same for the Definitely Sterile as for the other Subfecund groups (15.9 per cent), then the number of children wanted at interview is 3.14 for the Definitely Sterile. We can obtain the number of *births* wanted by the Definitely Sterile under these conditions by allowing for the children that die (0.07). This gives us 3.21, which is somewhat higher than the 3.08 obtained for our first estimate.

If the average number of births wanted by the Definitely Sterile is 3.21, rather than 3.69, then our procedure overstates the number wanted by the following proportions:

Group	*Percentage by which number of births wanted is overstated*
Definitely Sterile	15
Subfecund	5
All couples	2

On the basis of the analysis presented above, we think that our findings are useful, provided the bias in our procedure is taken into consideration.

In the subsection of Chapter 8 on "resulting family size" and in Table 8–11, two estimates of number of births wife wants are shown for Subfecund couples and for all couples. The higher estimate is the number wanted as defined earlier in Chapter 8. The lower estimate incorporates the allowance for overstatement by the Definitely Sterile described above, which gives them 3.21 births wanted.

Also shown in Chapter 8 and Table 8–11 are two estimates for number wanted for Subfecund couples and all couples in the 1916–20 cohorts. For these cohorts, the lower estimates were derived by the method described above for the whole sample. This procedure gave 3.14 births wanted by the wives of Definitely Sterile couples in the 1916–20 cohorts, which is almost one-fifth below the 3.72 obtained from the definition of number wanted described in Chapter 8. For the 1916–20 cohorts we estimate that our definition overstates the number wanted by the following proportions:

Group	Percentage by which number of births wanted is overstated
Definitely Sterile	18
Subfecund	8
All Couples	4

NOTE 23. *Comparability of prospective crude birth rates with official current rates*

Our prospective crude birth rates for 1955–60 and later periods are not precisely comparable with either of the two series of rates published by the National Office of Vital Statistics in *Vital Statistics of the United States, 1955*, 1957, vol. I, p. LXVIII. One of these series is based on registered births, and the other on births corrected for underregistration; both are based on population estimates that do not allow for underenumeration.

Our rates are based on numbers of births that are consistent with the NOVS series corrected for underregistration, but our figures for total population are not consistent with either NOVS series because we have corrected for underenumeration.

Our rates are slightly lower than the NOVS rates as the following comparison shows:

Source	Average annual crude birth rate, 1951–55
Published by NOVS:	
Registered births	24.7
Corrected births	25.1
Computed from corrected births and corrected population (consistent with projected births and population)	24.3

The actual rates cited in the text and in Table 11–2 for 1915–54 are the NOVS registered series. These are used because for recent years they are more consistent with the projected birth rates.

Appendix B

The Questionnaire

Shown below are questions 1 to 51 of the questionnaire used in this study. The replies to these questions by the 2,713 wives interviewed provide the information on such topics as fecundity, use of contraception, attitudes toward contraception, number of children already born, expectations about future childbearing, and attitudes toward family size. Later portions of the questionnaire sought information on the couple's socioeconomic background (e.g., religion, education, income, husband's occupation, whether the wife works, and other variables by which we have classified the couples) and on the wife's attitude toward various aspects of her way of life. We do not show this part of the questionnaire because it is rather long, because most of the questions on socioeconomic background are conventional, and because the questions on attitudes have not been used in the analysis in this book.

Questions 1 to 51 are presented so that interested readers may better understand how we obtained the information regarding the most important topics treated here. A crucial point in the interview came at question 19, which asked the wife whether she had reasons for believing that she and her husband could not have children in the future. Wives who gave different replies (yes, no, or uncertain) were asked different sets of questions up to question 41, which was asked of all wives. In reading this portion of the questionnaire, it may be helpful to refer to the following diagram, which describes the sequence of questions asked of the three groups:

I. Thinks cannot have children

(yes to 19)

↓

19a through 19j

↓

41

II. Uncertain as to whether can have children

(uncertain to 19)

↓

20 through 20g

yes to 20g	uncertain or no to 20g
↓	↓
20i through 20l	20h
↓	↓
36 through 41	38 through 41

III. Thinks can have children

$$\text{(no to 19)}$$
$$\downarrow$$
$$21$$

yes to 21	uncertain to 21	no to 21
$\downarrow$	$\downarrow$	$\downarrow$
29 through 41	25 through 28	22 through 24
	$\downarrow$	$\downarrow$
	36 through 41	36 through 41

1. Do you feel that it is easier or harder to raise a family these days than when you were a child?

   1*a*. Why do you feel that way?

2. What do you think is the ideal number of children for the *average* American family?

   (*If depends*) 2*a*. As things are now for the *average* American family how many children would you say is the ideal number?

3. How many children would there have to be in a family before you would call it large?

4. Now, thinking of the couple you feel closest to—either friends or relatives where the wife is about your age—how many children do you think they will have altogether when their family is completed?

   4*a*. How many do they have now?

5. Now about your own family—how many brothers and sisters did you have altogether while you were growing up?

   (*If any*) 5*a*. Do you feel that you had too few, about enough, or too many? Too few_____ About enough_____ Too many_____

   (*If none*) 5*b*. Have you been sorry that you didn't have any brothers or sisters? Yes_____ No_____

Now some questions about your own family:

6. What was the date of your marriage?

   —————————   —————————   —————————
   (Month)   (Day)   (Year)

7. Is this your first marriage? First Marriage_____ Married Before_____

   (*If R* married before*) 7*a*. When did your first marriage begin?

   —————————   —————————   —————————
   (Month)   (Day)   (Year)

   7*b*. When did it end?

   —————————   —————————
   (Month)   (Year)

* R means "respondent"—*Ed.*

7c. Did it end by death or divorce? Death_____ Divorce_____

(*Repeat 7a-7c for any other marriages*)

Second Marriage:	Began		Ended		How Ended
	(Month)	(Year)	(Month)	(Year)	Death_____ Divorce_____

(*All respondents*)

8. Is this your husband's first marriage? First Marriage_____ Married Before_____

    (*If husband married before*) 8a. Did he have any children before you were married? Yes_____ No_____

    (*If yes*) 8b. Are any of them living with you? Yes_____ No_____

    (*If yes*) 8c. How old are they?

(*All respondents*)

9. How many children have you had born alive altogether (including any children from your earlier marriage(s))? (*If none skip to question 14*)

10. I would like to know the birth dates of each of your children and whether each is a boy or a girl. Let's start with the oldest.

    (*Enter on birth record form*)

11. Are any of your children adopted? Yes_____ No_____

    (*If yes*) 11a. Which one(s)?

    11b. What is his (her, their) birth dates?

    11c. When did you adopt him (her, each of them)?

    (*Enter at bottom of birth record form*)

12. Have any of your children died after birth? Yes_____ No_____

    (*If yes*) 12a. Which child(ren) was that?

    12b. When did he (she) die?

    (*Enter on birth record form*)

13. Are any of your children not living with you here? Yes_____ No_____

    (*If yes*) 13a. How old are they?

(*All respondents*)

14. Have you had any (other) pregnancies that didn't result in a live birth? Yes_____ No_____ (*If never pregnant skip to question 17*)

    (*If ever had pregnancy not resulting in live birth*) 14a. In what month and year did that pregnancy end?

BIRTH RECORD FORM

Questions	Pregnancies											
	1st	2d	3d	4th	5th	6th	7th	8th	9th	10th	11th	12th
Q. 10 Birth dates of each child: day, month, year												
Check sex of each child	M F	M F	M F	M F	M F	M F	M F	M F	M F	M F	M F	M F
If twins enter here: MF, MM, or FF												
Q. 12 Enter date of death if child died after birth												
Q. 14a and b Enter if a miscarriage or stillbirth Date of end of pregnancy												
Length of pregnancy (in months)												
Q. 34b Enter date due if pregnant now												
Q. 49 Enter "Yes" if pregnancy begun when using some method												
Q. 50 Enter "Yes" if discontinued method to have child												

Question 11: enter adoptions below — do not count among pregnancies listed above.
Sex of child; Date of adoption (month, year); Date of birth (month, year)

(*Enter on birth record form*)

14*b*. How long had you been pregnant then?

(*Enter on birth record form*)

(*Repeat 14a and 14b, if more than one pregnancy that didn't result in a live birth*)

(*Correct numbering of pregnancies on birth record form*)

(*If you are not certain that entries on birth record form are correct, please check them over with respondent before proceeding.*)

(*If ever pregnant*)

15. Before your last pregnancy began did you really want another (a) child at some time in the future or would you just as soon not have had one?

    (*If wanted child*) 15*a*. How strongly did you feel about that?

    (*If child not wanted*) 15*b*. How did you feel about it when you learned you were going to have a child?

16. How about your husband—did he want another (a) child some time in the future, or would he just as soon not have had one?

(*All respondents*)

17. What do you feel have been (would be) some of the good things about having children?

18. What things do you feel have been (would be) not so good about having children?

19. Do you have any reason to believe that you and your husband couldn't have another (a) child, if you wanted to?

No_____ (*Skip to question 21*)
Uncertain_____ (*Skip to question 20*)
Yes_____ (*Continue with question 19a*)

If R believes they can't have another (a) child ("yes" to question 19)

19*a*. For how long a time have you thought you and your husband couldn't have another (a) child?

19*b*. Have you been told by a doctor that you couldn't have another (a) child? Yes_____ No_____

(*If yes*) 19*c*. What did he say were the reasons why you couldn't have one?

19*d*. Have you or your husband had an operation which makes pregnancy impossible?

> Wife: Yes_____ No_____
> Husband: Yes_____ No_____

(*If yes skip to question* 19*i*)

19*e*. Did the doctor think you could have a child if you or your husband took treatments or had an operation? Yes_____ Uncertain_____ No_____

(*If yes*) 19*f*. Do you think you will have the treatment (or operation)? Yes_____ Uncertain_____ No_____ (*Skip to question* 19*i*)

(*If no to question* 19*b*) 19*g*. What leads you to think you couldn't have one?

19*h*. Do you think you and your husband will see a doctor sometime to find out whether a child might be possible? Yes_____ Uncertain_____ No_____

19*i*. If you could have (more) children in coming years, how many children would you want to have altogether (counting those you have now)?

(*If married at least* 5 *years—see question* 6)

19*j*. Now if you could start your married life all over again and choose to have just the number of children you would want by the time you were 45, how many would that be? (*Skip to question* 41)

If R is uncertain whether they can have another (a) child ("uncertain" to q. 19)

20. For how long a time have you thought that you might not be able to have another (a) child?

20*a*. Have you had a doctor's opinion on whether you and your husband could have another child? Yes_____ No_____

(*If yes*) 20*b*. What did he say were the reasons why you may be unable to have another (a) child?

20*c*. Did the doctor think you could have a child if you or your husband took treatments or had an operation? Yes_____ Uncertain_____ No_____

(*If yes*) 20*d*. Do you think you will have the treatment (or operation)? Yes_____ Uncertain_____ No_____ (*Skip to question* 20*g*)

(*If no to question* 20*a*)

20*e*. What leads you to think you may be unable to have another (a) child?

20*f*. Do you think you and your husband will see a doctor some time to find out whether a child might be possible? Yes_____ Uncertain_____ No_____

20*g*. Do you expect to have another child? If it is possible for you to do so, would you say definitely yes, probably yes, probably no, or definitely no?

Definitely yes ⎫ (*Skip to question* 20*i*)
Probably yes ⎭

Uncertain ⎫
Probably no ⎬ (*Continue with question* 20*h*)
Definitely no ⎭

(*If uncertain, or probably, or definitely no*)

20*h*. If you could start your married life all over again and choose to have just the number of children you would want by the time you were 45, how many would that be? (*Skip to question* 38)

(*If definitely or probably yes to question* 20*g*)

20*i*. If you can have (more) children, how many (more) do you want to have?

20*j*. We are interested in why you would want to have_____ more? (no. given in Q. 20*i*)

20*k*. Can you also tell me why you wouldn't want to have more than _____ (more) children? (no. given in Q. 20*i*)

20*l*. We have been talking about the number of children you might have. Now, if you could start your married life over again and *choose* to have just the number of children you would want by the time you were 45, how many would that be? (*Skip to question* 36)

For respondent who believes they can have more children ("no" to q. 19)

21. Do you expect to have another (a) child? Would you say definitely yes, probably yes, probably no, or definitely no?

Definitely yes ⎫ (*Skip to question* 29)
Probably yes ⎭
Uncertain   (*Skip to question* 25)
Probably no ⎫ (*Continue with question* 22)
Definitely no ⎭

(*If probably or definitely no more children*)

22. Can you tell me why you don't expect to have another (a) child?

22*a*. Are there any other reasons why you don't *want* another (a) child?

23. Are there any things that might change so that you would have another
    (a) child? Yes_____ No_____

    (*If yes*) 23*a*. What are they?

    23*b*. How many (more) children would you have?

24. We have been talking about the number of children you expect to have
    altogether. Now, if you could start your married life over again and choose
    to have just the number you would want by the time you are 45, how
    many would that be? (*Skip to question* 36)

For respondents who are uncertain whether they expect to have (*more*) *children* ("*uncertain*" *to question* 21)

25. Can you tell me why you feel uncertain about whether you will have an-
    other child?

    25*a*. Are there any (other) reasons why you don't *want* to have another
    (a) child?

    25*b*. Are there any (other) reasons why you would *want* to have another
    (a) child?

26. If you do have another (a) child, about when do you think you are likely
    to have it?

27. If you do have (more) children, is it likely that you will have more than
    one? Yes_____ No_____

    (*If yes*) 27*a*. How many do you think you will have?

28. We have been talking about the number of children you expect to have.
    Now, if you could start your married life over again and have just the
    number of children you would want by the time you are 45, how many
    would that be? (*Skip to question* 36)

For respondent who expects to have more children ("*yes*" *to question* 21)

29. How many children do you think you will have altogether (counting those
    you have now)?

    (*If* "*in God's hands,*" "*up to fate,*" *etc.*) 29*a*. As you think things will
    turn out for your family, how many children do you think you are
    likely to have altogether? (*Skip to question* 30*a*)

30. How sure do you feel that is the number you actually will have? Would
    you say: Very sure_____ Fairly sure_____ Not sure_____

    (*If not sure or if question* 29*a asked*) 30*a*. What do you think is the
    smallest number you are likely to have?

    30*b*. What do you think is the largest number you are likely to have?

31. Altogether, then, you expect that you will most probably have _____ children when your family is completed. (This should be the total number of children expected in Question 29 or 29a.)

    We are interested in why you expect to have that number. Can you tell me why you don't expect to have more than _____ children?

    31a. Are there any other reasons why you don't *want* to have more than that number?

32. Can you also tell me why you don't *want* to have a family of less than _____ children?
    (no. given in Q. 29 or 29a)

    32a. Are there any other reasons why you don't *want* to have less than that number?

33. We have been talking about the number of children you expect to have. Now, if you could start your married life over again and choose to have just the number you would want by the time you are 45, how many would that be?

34. We are interested in when your children might come. Do you expect to have a child in the next 12 months? Yes_____ No_____

    (*If yes*) 34a. Are you pregnant now? Yes_____ No_____

    (*If yes*) 34b. When is the baby due? (*Enter on birth record form*) (*Skip to question 35a*)

35. About when do you expect to have your next (a) child?

    35a. And about how many years will there be between that child and the next?

(*Repeat question until account for all children expected* (*Q. 29 or 29a*)

                    Next child _____
                    Next child _____, *etc.*

    (*If can't give timing above*) 35b. Well, we'd just like to have your general idea of when your children might come.

36. Have you and your husband ever talked about how many children each of you want? Yes_____ No_____

    (*If yes*) 36a. About how recently have you talked this over?

37. How many children does your husband want to have altogether?

38. We are interested in how many children you wanted at earlier times in your life. Just before you were married how many children did you think you would want during your married life?

(*If has had a child*)

39. A year after your first child was born, how many children did you want to have altogether?

(*If answer to question 39 different from answer in question 38*)

39a. Why did you change your mind?

40. Have you changed your mind since then? Yes_____ No_____

    (*If yes*) 40a. When was the last time you changed your mind?

    40b. How many did you want just before that change?

    40c. How many did you want just after that change?

    40d. Why did you change your mind then?

41. Many married couples do something to limit the size of their families and to control when their children come. How do you feel about that?

    41a. Why do you feel that way?

    (*If opposed*) 41b. Are there any conditions under which you think it is all right for a married couple to limit family size or control when children come? Yes_____ No_____

    (*If yes*) 41c. Under what conditions would it be all right?

42. How does your husband feel about married couples limiting family size and controlling when children come?

43. Now in your own case, have you or your husband ever done anything to limit the number of your children or to keep from having them at certain times?

    Yes_____ (*Skip to question 45*)
    No_____ (*Continue with question 44*)

If answer to question 43 is "no"

(*Show card 2*)

44. Some things couples do may not be considered birth control. Doctors and public health workers are interested in learning how many people use these methods. Have you ever made use of either of the methods on this card? You can tell me by the numbers on the card.

    No—used neither _____ (*Skip to question 44b*)
    Yes—used rhythm (no. 1) _____ (*Skip to question 46*)
    Yes—used both rhythm and douche (nos. 1 & 2) _____ (*Skip to question 46*)
    Yes—used douche only (no. 2) _____ (*Continue with question 44a*)

Card 2

1. Safe period—rhythm
   (Avoiding those days of monthly cycle when conception is likely to occur)

2. Douche—for cleanliness
   (Soon after intercourse)

(*If used douche for cleanliness only*) 44a. When did you first begin to use that method? (*Continue with question* 44b)

(*If "no" to q.* 44 *or if douche only*) 44b. Do you expect to make use of any method to delay or avoid pregnancy at some later time in your married life? Yes_____ Uncertain_____ No_____ (*Skip to question* 52)

For respondents who have used some method

(*Show card* 1)

45. Doctors and public health workers are interested in knowing what methods people are using over the country as a whole. What methods have you used?

(You can tell me by the numbers on the card, if you wish.)

(*If more than one method*) 45a. What is the last method you used?

Card 1

1. Safe period—rhythm
   (Avoiding those days of monthly cycle when conception is likely to occur)

2. Douche
   (Soon after intercourse)

3. Withdrawal
   (By husband before completion)

4. Abstinence
   (Abstaining for more than a month)

5. Rubber condom
   (Prophylactic)

6. Diaphragm

7. Jelly

8. Vaginal suppository

9. Foam tablet

10. Tampon, vaginal cap, or stem pessary

11. Lactation
    (Continuing to nurse a baby because you wanted to postpone pregnancy)

---

46. Have you used some method almost always except when you wanted to have a child? Yes_____ No_____

(If pregnant now skip to question 47d)

47. Have you used a method in recent months? Yes_____ No_____

    (If no) 47a. About when did you stop using it?

    47b. Did you stop using it in order to have a child or for some other reason? To have a child_____ For other reason_____

    47c. Do you intend to use some method in the future? Yes_____ No_____

    (If pregnant now) 47d. Do you plan to use some method after your present pregnancy? Yes_____ No_____

(If respondent has never been pregnant, skip to question 51)

(If respondent has ever been pregnant, continue with question 48)

48. Did you use some method before your first pregnancy? Yes_____ No_____

    (If no) 48a. After which pregnancy did you first begin to use some method?

    48b. Did you want your pregnancies up to that one as soon as possible after marriage or not? Wanted as soon as possible_____ Not as soon as possible_____

49. Did any of your pregnancies begin when you were using some method to prevent pregnancy? Yes_____ No_____

    (If yes) 49a. Which pregnancy(ies) was that? *(Enter on birth record form)*

50. Did any of your pregnancies begin at a time when you purposely (stopped using some) (changed the rhythm) method because you wanted to have a child? Yes_____ No_____

    (If yes) 50a. Which ones? *(Enter on birth record form)*

(If married at least 4 years—see question 6)

(If never pregnant)

51. Has there ever been a period of 2 or more years when you did not use any method to prevent pregnancy? Yes_____ No_____

(If ever pregnant)

51. Has there ever been a period of 3 or more years when you weren't pregnant and nothing was done to prevent pregnancy and you didn't become pregnant? Yes＿＿＿ No＿

Here there followed 46 additional questions dealing with the respondent's attitudes toward her economic situation and the social and economic characteristics of the wife and husband.

Appendix C

Sampling Methods and Sampling Errors[1]

The individuals interviewed for this study are a representative cross section of a selected universe of white women living in private households in the United States. The selected universe consists of:

1. Married white women 18–39 years of age, inclusive, living in private households
   a. With husband present
   b. With husband absent because of military service
2. Single white women 18–24 years of age, inclusive

Age, in each case, refers to age at last birthday. Married women residing in military establishments, hospitals, religious and educational institutions, penal institutions, YWCAs, hotels, and larger rooming houses were excluded from the study. Single women living in some of these places were included, as is explained in the next section.

The Sample

The sample was selected by the Survey Research Center of the University of Michigan, using the method known as area probability sampling. By this method every member of the universe considered had an equal chance of being selected. The basic procedure was: (1) Select a sample of the primary sampling units (counties or groups of counties). (2) Within each of the selected primary sampling units choose a probability sample of places or areas (towns, communities or segments). (3) Within each of these places or areas choose a probability sample of private households, many of which will contain an eligible respondent.[2]

[1] Written with the collaboration of Dr. Leslie Kish and Miss Irene Hess of the Sampling Section of the Survey Research Center of the University of Michigan.
[2] The 1950 census shows that 96.5 per cent of the white women aged 18–39 were living in private households on the census date. It is estimated that a still higher percentage (perhaps 99.5) of the group considered in this book, namely, the white wives aged 18–39 living with husband or separated because husband was serving in the armed forces, were in private households on that date. Consequently, any errors which may result from excluding wives not living in private households are

The Survey Research Center has divided the United States into about 2,500 primary sampling units (each one a county or a group of counties) and sorted these units into 66 strata. Each of the 12 largest metropolitan areas composes one stratum; each contains only one primary sampling unit. Each of the other 54 strata contains from 3 to 200 primary sampling units, and each had a population of roughly 2 million in 1950. From each of these 54 strata one primary sampling unit was chosen with probability proportional to population. Within each of the 66 primary sampling units thus obtained about five places on the average were selected by probability methods. These places were cities, towns, villages, and open country areas. The distribution of the 66 primary sampling units is shown in Figure C–1. The geographic distribution of these units corresponds to that of the total population which is shown in Figure C–2.

Within each sample city or town a random selection of blocks was made. For cities with populations of 50,000 or more, census statistics showing average rental and property values are available for each block; this information was used as a basis for stratification of the blocks.[3] The clustering of sample households within sample blocks is about twice the degree of clustering usually used in national surveys conducted by the Survey Research Center; however, since less than half of the sample dwelling units contained an eligible respondent, the effective clustering of respondents is about the same as in other national studies by the Center.

In smaller cities and towns the map was divided into blocks and numbered systematically so as to yield a rough geographical stratification. The dwelling units found in the selected blocks were listed sys-

---

probably small compared to other errors. Sampling the wives outside of private households would have been expensive and did not seem justified.

Later reports on the study will refer to the other group of women interviewed, namely, single white women aged 18–24. The 1950 census shows that 93.2 per cent of all white women aged 18–24 were living in private households on the census date. For single women the percentage is smaller, perhaps 85 or less. Accordingly, the probability sample of single women in private households was supplemented by a "purposive" quota sample of single women not living in such households. This small addition to the probability sample was widely spread and carefully allocated into several college dormitories and into several YWCAs and rooming houses in large cities. The addition of these single women does not affect in any way the nature of the probability sample of married women on which this book is based.

[3] On the basis of census figures, a sampling rate was applied so as to yield an average of four expected dwelling units in each block. Each block was chosen with a probability directly proportional to its number of dwelling units reported in the 1950 census, and all dwelling units had the same chance of being included in the sample. It should be noted that if there were any major changes in population since the 1950 census, these changes affect area sampling by increasing or decreasing the yield of interviews from the areas affected.

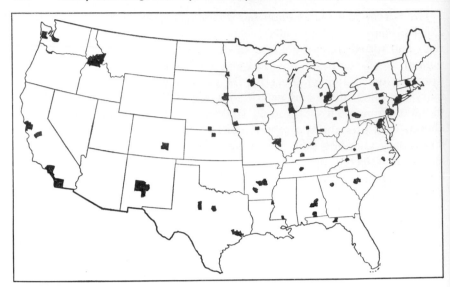

Fig. C–1. Location of the primary sampling units of the Survey Research Center in 1955.

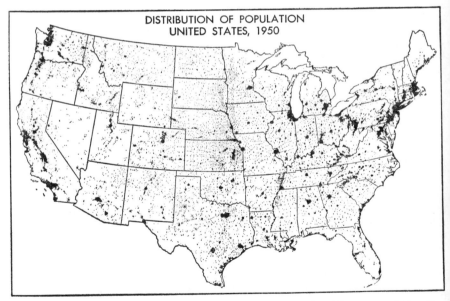

Fig. C–2. Distribution of population, United States, 1950. (*Courtesy of the Bureau of the Census.*)

tematically and a random subsample of them was taken, usually in clusters of about three dwelling units.

Rural areas were divided into small segments containing on the average about eight dwelling units, and a random selection was made from these segments. All the dwellings in the selected segments were included in the sample.

Each sample block or segment was marked on a map or aerial photograph. These mapping materials and detailed instructions guided the interviewers in carrying through an exact sampling procedure.

In this way a basic national sample of 8,305 occupied dwelling units was selected. Interviewers visited each of these dwelling units and obtained a list of the occupants together with those characteristics required to determine whether any of the occupants were eligible respondents. We had estimated in advance that 38 per cent of the dwelling units would contain an eligible wife. The percentage we found was 38.5. In the 28 dwelling units which contained two or more eligible respondents, only one was interviewed.[4]

If an individual to be interviewed was not at home on the first call, from 3 to 10 additional calls were made in an attempt to reach her. However, even after repeated calls, a small number of these persons were not found at home. A few refused to be interviewed.

Some information on sample size, and on eligible respondents interviewed and not interviewed, by marital status, is summarized below:

Item	Number	Per cent
Occupied dwelling units in sample:		
Total	8,305	100.0
With eligible respondent	3,198	38.5
No eligible respondent	5,092	61.3
Eligibility of respondent not ascertained	15	0.2
Dwelling units with eligible respondent:		
Total eligible respondents	3,198	100.0
Interviewed	2,913	91.1
Not interviewed	285	8.9
Refused	153	4.8
Other	132	4.1
Married respondents	2,978	100.0
Interviewed	2,713	91.1
Not interviewed	265	8.9
Refused	142	4.8
Other	123	4.1
Single respondents	220	100.0
Interviewed	200	90.9
Not interviewed	20	9.1
Refused	11	5.0
Other	9	4.1

[4] Taking at random only one respondent in households containing more than one eligible respondent introduced no significant bias. It resulted in dropping from the sample 11 married women and 20 single women who would have been included in a rigid execution of the sample design. It was not considered worthwhile to "weight up" the 28 households.

Although the study includes both married and single white women in specific age groups, the analysis reported in this book deals with married women only. The remaining sections of this appendix on sampling errors exclude any reference to the single women. It is anticipated that the data for these women will be discussed in a later report.

In Table C we present detailed estimates of the number of women aged 18–39 in various groups included in and excluded from the universe of study. The 2,713 married women for whom schedules were completed are a probability sample representative of approximately

TABLE C. GROUPS OF WOMEN AGED 18–39 INCLUDED IN OR EXCLUDED FROM STUDY, ABSOLUTE NUMBERS AND AS PERCENTAGES OF ALL WOMEN AND ALL WHITE WOMEN OF THESE AGES, UNITED STATES, APRIL, 1955[a]

Groups	Number (in thousands)	Percentage of:	
		All women aged 18–39	All white women aged 18–39
White women, aged 18–39			
Included:			
Total	19,729	77	86
Married and living with husband in private household	16,762	66	74
Married, husband away in armed forces	316	1	1
Single, aged 18–24[b]	2,651	10	11
Excluded:			
Total	3,024	11	14
Married and living with husband, but not in private household	20	—	—
Married, but not living with husband[c]	815	3	4
Widowed or divorced	813	3	4
Single, aged 25–39	1,376	5	6
Total	22,753	88	100
Nonwhite women, aged 18–39, all excluded	2,929	12	
Total women, aged 18–39	25,682	100	

The dash indicates a percentage below 0.5 in all tables.

[a] Estimates based on *Current Population Reports*, U.S. Bureau of the Census, especially series P-20, no. 62, Oct. 31, 1955, and P-25, no. 121, Sept. 27, 1955, and on unpublished tabulations of the Bureau's Current Population Survey.

[b] See footnote 2 of Appendix C for an explanation of the sample of single women.

[c] Excluding those separated because husband is in armed forces.

17 million white married women living with their husbands or temporarily separated from them by reason of their service in the armed forces. The married population represented by our sample constitutes approximately 67 per cent of all women, 75 per cent of all white women,

and 91 per cent of all white ever-married women among those aged 18–39.

Comparison of the Sample with Independent Estimates

It is desirable to compare some of the characteristics of the sample with independent estimates, describing as of April, 1955, the population of married women represented by our sample. Unfortunately, the data needed for a precise comparison are not available. It is possible, however, to make a rough check on the representativeness of the sample with respect to certain characteristics by comparisons with independently prepared estimates or the most recent data available from official sources.

For example, we have prepared on the basis of vital statistics and 1950 census data an estimate of the expected parity distribution for the population in April, 1955, which is shown in Table C–1, along with

TABLE C–1. PER CENT DISTRIBUTION BY NUMBER OF BIRTHS FOR WIVES IN SAMPLE AND IN INDEPENDENT ESTIMATE BASED ON CENSUS DATA AND VITAL STATISTICS

Number of births	Sample	Independent estimate
Total	100	100
0	16	15
1	22	24
2	31	30
3	17	17
4	7	8
5 or more	7	6

the actual distribution of the sample. The two distributions correspond quite closely. The minor discrepancies may result from errors in the independent estimates, response errors in the sample survey, or both. They are small enough to have arisen just from sampling variability in our survey. Furthermore, the differences between the two distributions are not significant for an investigation of this type.

In Table C–2 we present the age distribution as found among the wives in our sample and as estimated from the April, 1955, *Current Population Survey* of the Bureau of the Census. (The data from the *Current Population Survey* were adjusted to fit the special characteristics of the study group, e.g., elimination of the nonwhite women.) The expected and actual distributions correspond closely.

A special effort was made to check the labor-force participation rate

TABLE C–2. PER CENT DISTRIBUTION BY AGE FOR WIVES IN SAMPLE AND IN INDEPENDENT ESTIMATE BASED ON CENSUS REPORT

Wife's age	Sample	Independent estimate
Total	100	100
18–19	3	3
20–24	17	18
25–29	26	26
30–34	28	27
35–39	26	26

of the wives in the sample, since it was feared that "working" wives might be more difficult to locate for interviewing, and that if they were underrepresented the sample might be biased in a number of ways. Actually, the labor-force participation rate of the wives in our sample corresponds closely to an independent estimate for the population they represent: the percentage of wives who were in the labor force is 25 for our sample and 26 for an independent estimate for the comparable population in April, 1955, based on sample data from the *Current Population Survey.*

Our sample also is adequate with respect to the distribution by religious preference of white married women in the United States, as is indicated by the comparison shown in Table C–3. The independent estimate for white women in this table is based on the data for all women obtained in the *Current Population Survey* of March, 1957.

For a number of other characteristics, it is necessary to go back to 1950 census data in order to test our sample. Since many of our wives first married after 1950, these data can give only a rough check. Women

TABLE C–3. PER CENT DISTRIBUTION BY RELIGION FOR WIVES 20–39 YEARS OLD IN SAMPLE AND IN INDEPENDENT ESTIMATE FOR MARCH, 1957, BASED ON CENSUS REPORT

Wife's religion	Sample	Independent estimate, 1957[a]
Total	100	100
Protestant	66	66
Catholic	30	29
Other	4	5

[a] Based on data in "Religion Reported by the Civilian Population of the United States: March 1957," *Current Population Reports,* U.S. Bureau of the Census, series P-20, no. 79, Feb. 2, 1958.

whose first marriage occurred between the 1950 census and our 1955 interviews obviously should not have been enumerated as married in the 1950 census and may have distinctive characteristics. Furthermore, some women married prior to the 1950 census died between 1950 and 1955, and some of the characteristics of the surviving women changed during the 5-year period. The 1950 census results are not strictly comparable with our universe from another standpoint, since they are not based on wives with husband present or in the armed forces (as is our sample) but on all ever-married women, women married once with husband present, or other groups which differ from ours. Nevertheless, it is reassuring that our sample does not differ markedly from the roughly comparable 1950 population with respect to certain basic characteristics, as noted below.

Tables C–4 to C–6 show the distribution of our sample and the most comparable 1950 census population with respect to rural-urban residence, region of residence, and occupation of husband. In general, the distributions are closely similar. The somewhat greater concentration of our sample in rural-nonfarm areas is consistent with the continuing marked migration to suburbs from 1950 to 1955.

TABLE C–4. PER CENT DISTRIBUTION BY PLACE OF RESIDENCE, FOR WIVES IN SAMPLE AND IN 1950 CENSUS

Place of residence	Sample	1950 census[a]
Total	100	100
Urban	64	66
Rural nonfarm	25	22
Farm	11	12

[a] For white women, 18–39 years old, married and husband present.

TABLE C–5. PER CENT DISTRIBUTION BY REGION OF RESIDENCE, FOR WIVES IN SAMPLE AND IN 1950 CENSUS

Region of residence	Sample	1950 census[a]
Total	100	100
Northeast	25	26
North Central	31	31
South	28	29
West	16	14

[a] White women, 18–39 years old, married and husband present.

TABLE C–6. PER CENT DISTRIBUTION BY HUSBAND'S OCCUPATION, FOR WIVES IN SAMPLE AND IN 1950 CENSUS

Husband's occupation	Sample	1950 census[a]
Total	100	100
Professional, technical, and kindred workers	10	8
Farmers and farm managers	8	9
Managers, officials, and proprietors, except farm	13	10
Clerical, sales, and kindred workers	10	13
Craftsmen, foremen, and kindred workers	24	20
Operatives and kindred workers	21	22
Service workers	3	3
Farm laborers and foremen	1	2
Laborers, except farm and mine	4	6
All others	6	7

[a] White women, 18–39 years old, married once and husband present.

The regional distribution of the sample approximates closely the comparable 1950 distribution. In part this is a result of some regional stratification in the design of the sample. However, since the distribution of respondents by region is subject to a higher sampling error than the comparable distribution of all sample dwelling units, there was a possibility that the sample distribution by region might deviate more from the 1950 distribution.[5]

The two occupational distributions are reasonably similar, but the proportion of the husbands in our sample who are in some of the higher-status occupations may be slightly too high. At this time, however, it seems more likely that the differences are not due mainly to bias in the sample, but to real changes in occupation and marriage patterns between 1950 and 1955, to differences in occupational coding procedures, and to response errors.

The only characteristic checked in which the sample shows a significant variation from an outside estimate is wife's education. The most recent outside criterion is 1950 census data; consequently, it was necessary to obtain an estimate as of 1950 from our sample. For this purpose we took the wives who were 25–39 in 1955 and had married before 1950, i.e., who were 20–34 in 1950 and had married by then. The most closely comparable 1950 census groups of white women aged 20–34 are those ever married and those married once and living with husband. The group from our sample is intermediate between these two with respect to marital status. This difference appears unimportant in view of the close similarity of the educational status of the two census groups.

Our sample apparently includes too few wives with a grade school

[5] See the following section for a discussion of sampling variability.

Table C–7. Per Cent Distribution by Education, for Married Women Aged 20–34 in 1950, in Sample and in 1950 Census

Wife's education	Sample[a]	1950 census	
		Married once, husband present	All ever-married
Total	100	100	100
College	15	14	14
High school, 4	44	42	40
High school, 1–3	25	23	24
Grade school	16	21	22

[a] These sample data are for wives who in 1955 were living with husband (or were separated because husband was in the armed forces) and whose first marriage occurred prior to 1950.

education and too many with a high school education (Table C–7). In part this may result from the fact that the sample group and the two census groups differ somewhat as to marital status. It may also represent sampling variation. A third partial explanation may be response bias—a tendency for some grade school wives to report high school education. That there is such a bias in our data is suggested by the number of women who reported grade school education for their husbands but high school education for themselves. To affect the comparison in question, however, the bias would have to be larger for our study than for the 1950 census, and there is little basis for believing that this is the case.

Sampling Variability

Percentages. Properly conducted sample interview surveys yield useful estimates, but they do not yield exact values. Errors arise from several sources: sampling, nonresponse, reporting, and processing. Each type of error may affect in important degree the accuracy of information. The present discussion is limited to sampling errors.

Sample statistics reflect the random variations arising from interviewing only a fraction of the population. The distribution of individuals selected for a sample usually differs by an unknown amount from that of the population from which the sample is drawn. The value which would be obtained if interviews with the entire population were sought by the same survey procedures will be referred to as the population value. If different samples were used under the same survey conditions, some of the estimates would be larger than the population value and some would be smaller. The sampling error is a measure of the chance deviation of a sample statistic from the corresponding population value. The sampling error does not measure the actual error of a particular sample estimate; rather, it leads to statements in terms of confidence intervals that are correct in a specified proportion of cases in the long run. Each statement declares that the range of the sampling error on either side of the sample estimate includes the population value.

"Sampling error" as used here is to be interpreted as two standard errors; it is the range, on either side of the sample estimate, chosen frequently in social research in order to obtain the 95 per cent "level of confidence." If one requires a greater degree of confidence than this, a wider range than two standard errors should be used. On the other hand, most of the time the actual error of sampling will be less than the sampling error defined above; in about 68 cases of every 100, the population value can be expected to lie within a range of one-half the sampling error (one standard error) of the sample estimates.

For example, the survey estimate that 70 per cent of the married couples had already used a family limitation method at some time (Table 4–1) is subject to a sampling error of about 2 percentage points. Thus the statement that the population value is within the range 68 to 72 per cent would be true for at least 95 of every 100 samples drawn like the one in this study. The chances are that in 5 of each 100 samples the population value would lie outside that range; however, the chances are that in 68 of each 100 samples it would lie within the range 69 to 71 per cent (i.e., plus or minus one standard error).

The sampling error of the proportion of respondents having a certain characteristic depends on the size of the sample and also on the size of the proportion being estimated. Approximately, the sampling error is inversely proportional to the square root of the sample size. Thus, the sampling error of an estimate based on 400 cases is about one-half as large as that of an estimate based on 100 cases.

Sampling errors (standard errors) also vary with the proportion being estimated and reach a maximum, for samples of a given size, when the proportion is 50 per cent. (However, the relative size of the error decreases as the size of the percentage increases.) The relation of sampling error to sample size and proportion being estimated is evident in the formula for the computation of sampling errors for simple random samples. The sampling error of such a sample is equal to $2\sqrt{[p(1-p)]/n}$, where p is the proportion under consideration and n is the sample size. Although the survey uses a complex rather than a simple random sample, the relationship of sampling error to the sample size and the proportion being estimated is somewhat similar to that of the above formula.

There are other important factors that influence the size of the sampling error of any characteristic based on the interviews from the entire sample or from some specific subgroup. (See the first section of this Appendix for a discussion of the procedures used in the sample selection.) The effect of such factors varies for every type of estimate and for every subgroup of the population. For example, percentages based on only a subset of all the sampling units tend to have larger sampling errors than proportions of the same magnitude based on all sampling units. Among such subsets are regions, cities of specific size, and urban or rural areas. The fact that the sampling errors in this study are likely to be somewhat higher than simple random-sampling errors arises from the fact that the sample selection involved clusters of dwelling units, which may increase sampling error if the characteristic being sampled is "clustered." [6]

The sampling errors themselves are products of the sampling processes and are subject to the effect of random fluctuations, as well as the effect of the sample design. Therefore a range, rather than a single value, has been used in presenting sampling errors for proportions based on samples of a given size. These estimates, based on data from this study, are presented in Table C–8; they are not averages but rather two limits to the ranges of values which we found. The larger values are on the high or conservative side; only a small proportion of the computations yielded estimates larger than these. The smaller estimates were computed by use of the formula $2\sqrt{[p(1-p)]/n}$, which can be viewed as the lower limit to the survey's sampling errors. In our computations most survey statistics were found to have sampling errors between these high and low estimates. Whether the sampling error of an estimate tends toward the upper or lower limit depends on the type of data involved and the basis of classification.

TABLE C–8. APPROXIMATE SAMPLING ERROR[a] OF PERCENTAGES

Estimated percentages	No. of interviews							
	2,000	1,000	700	500	400	300	200	100
50	2.2–3.0	3.2–4.0	3.8–4.8	4.5–5.6	5.0–6.0	5.8–7.0	7.1–8.5	10–12
30 or 70	2.1–2.8	2.9–3.6	3.5–4.4	4.1–5.1	4.6–5.5	5.3–6.4	6.5–7.8	9.2–11
20 or 80	1.8–2.4	2.5–3.1	3.0–3.8	3.6–4.5	4.0–4.8	4.6–5.5	5.7–6.8	8.0–9.6
10 or 90	1.3–1.8	1.9–2.4	2.3–2.9	2.7–3.4	3.0–3.6	3.5–4.2	4.2–5.0	6.0–7.2
5 or 95	1.0–1.4	1.4–1.8	1.6–2.0	1.9–2.4	2.2–2.6	2.5–3.0	3.1–3.7	

[a] The figures in this table represent *two* standard errors. Hence, for most items the chances are 95 in 100 that the population value lies within a range equal to the estimated percentage plus or minus the sampling error.

[6] For a more detailed exposition see Leslie Kish, "Confidence Intervals for Clustered Samples," *American Sociological Review*, vol. 22, no. 2, pp. 154–165, April, 1957.

Two estimates of the sampling error are presented for each cell. The lower values are based on the standard-error formula for simple random samples. The higher values are based on the computations of individual sampling errors for study data and allow for the departures, such as stratification and clustering, from simple random sampling in the survey design.

Differences. Differences between survey estimates are often of even greater interest than the levels of the estimates. These differences reflect the random fluctuations of the sampling process as well as differences in population values. The sampling errors of differences indicate the range in which the "true" differences between the population values of the two compared classes can be expected to fall in a given proportion of trials, usually 95 out of 100 times. As with the sampling errors of single percentages, greater or lesser degrees of confidence in the statement are associated with larger or smaller multiples of the standard error.

Table C–9, which is a table of sampling errors of differences, also contains two estimates. These numbers, too, are based on the computations carried out on actual survey data. The larger numbers are on the "safe" side—they exceed most of the sampling errors actually computed. A lower limit is set by the smaller numbers of the table, which are based on an approximation to the standard formula for differences between estimates obtained from simple random samples.[7] Most of the sampling errors computed lie between these limits.

To illustrate the use of Table C–9, let us consider the proportion that had adopted a family limitation method among couples with Protestant wives, classified by place of present residence. Contraception had been practiced by 66 per cent of the 242 rural farm couples, by 70 per cent of the 344 rural-nonfarm couples living outside of metropolitan areas, and by 89 per cent of the 186 couples living in the suburbs of the 12 largest cities. (The percentages are given in Table 4–30.) The difference between the rural-farm and rural-nonfarm couples is not statistically significant, but each of these groups is significantly different in this respect from the couples in the suburbs of the 12 largest cities. (The sampling errors of differences between proportions near 80 per cent for $n = 200$, $n = 300$ are between 7.3 and 9.1 according to Table C–9.)

Numbers of Children per Couple. Besides percentages there are two other types of estimates which are of particular interest in this study. These are the average number of births and number of children ex-

---

[7] The approximation used is $2\sqrt{p(1-p)(1/n_1 + 1/n_2)}$, where p is a proportion approximating those being compared and n_1 and n_2 are the number of cases in the two samples.

TABLE C–9. APPROXIMATE SAMPLING ERROR[a] OF DIFFERENCES BETWEEN PERCENTAGES

No. of inter-views	No. of interviews							
	2,000	1,000	700	500	400	300	200	100
For percentages from 35 to 65								
2,000	3.2–4.0	3.9–4.9	4.4–5.5	5.0–6.2	5.5–6.9	6.2–7.8	7.4–9.2	10–12
1,000		4.5–5.6	4.9–6.1	5.5–6.9	5.9–7.4	6.6–8.3	7.7–9.6	10–13
700			5.3–6.6	5.9–7.4	6.3–7.9	6.9–8.6	8.0–10	11–13
500				6.3–7.9	6.7–8.4	7.3–9.1	8.4–10	11–13
400					7.1–8.9	7.6–9.5	8.7–11	11–14
300						8.2–10	9.1–11	12–14
200							10–12	12–15
100								14–17
For percentages around 20 and 80								
2,000	2.5–3.1	3.1–3.9	3.5–4.4	4.0–5.0	4.4–5.5	5.0–6.2	5.9–7.4	8.2–9.8
1,000		3.6–4.5	3.9–4.9	4.4–5.5	4.7–5.9	5.3–6.6	6.2–7.8	8.4–10
700			4.3–5.4	4.7–5.9	5.0–6.2	5.5–6.9	6.4–8.0	8.6–10
500				5.1–6.4	5.4–6.8	5.8–7.2	6.7–8.4	8.8–11
400					5.7–7.1	6.1–7.6	6.9–8.6	9.0–11
300						6.5–8.1	7.3–9.1	9.2–11
200							8.0–10	9.8–12
100								11–14
For percentages around 10 and 90								
2,000	1.9–2.4	2.3–2.9	2.6–3.2	3.0–3.8	3.3–4.1	3.7–4.6	4.4–5.5	
1,000		2.7–3.4	3.0–3.8	3.3–4.1	3.6–4.5	4.0–5.0	4.6–5.8	
700			3.2–4.0	3.5–4.4	3.8–4.8	4.1–5.1	4.8–6.0	
500				3.8–4.8	4.0–5.0	4.4–5.5	5.0–6.2	
400					4.2–5.2	4.6–5.8	5.2–6.9	
300						4.9–6.1	5.5–6.9	
200							6.0–7.5	
For percentages around 5 and 95								
2,000	1.4–1.8	1.7–2.1	1.9–2.4	2.2–2.8	2.4–3.0	2.7–3.4		
1,000		1.9–2.4	2.1–2.6	2.4–3.0	2.6–3.2	2.9–3.6		
700			2.3–2.9	2.6–3.2	2.7–3.4	3.0–3.8		
500				2.8–3.5	2.9–3.6	3.2–4.0		
400					3.1–3.9	3.3–4.1		
300						3.6–4.5		

[a] The values shown are the differences required for significance (two standard errors) in comparisons of percentages derived from *two different subgroups* of the survey. Two values—low and high—are given for each cell. (See note *a* to Table C–8.)

pected for couples classified in various ways, e.g., by age or income. As in the case of percentages, these averages are subject to random fluctuations because they are computed from data collected from a sample of individuals composing the universe for this study. The magnitude of the sampling error varies with the characteristic and the number of interviews on which the average is based and is influenced by the many complex factors in the sampling procedures.

TABLE C–10. APPROXIMATE SAMPLING ERRORS OF AVERAGES AND OF DIFFERENCES BETWEEN TWO AVERAGES, FOR NUMBER OF BIRTHS TO DATE AND TOTAL NUMBER EXPECTED[a] (IN THE SAME UNITS AS THE AVERAGE)

No. of interviews	No. of interviews							
	2,700	2,000	1,000	700	500	300	200	100
	Sampling error of averages[b]							
	0.08	0.08	0.10	0.12	0.16	0.21	0.27	0.37
	Sampling error of differences between two averages[c]							
2,000		0.12	0.13	0.14	0.18	0.23	0.28	0.38
1,000			0.14	0.15	0.19	0.23	0.29	0.38
700				0.16	0.20	0.24	0.30	0.39
500					0.22	0.26	0.31	0.40
300						0.30	0.34	0.43
200							0.38	0.46
100								0.52

[a] The figures in the table represent two standard errors. These are also conservative sampling errors for averages for ideal family size and number of children wanted at various stages of married life.

[b] For most items, the chances are 95 in 100 that the "true" average lies within a range equal to the estimated average plus or minus the sampling error.

[c] The values shown are the differences required for significance (.05 level) in comparisons of averages derived from *two different subgroups* of the survey.

In Table C–10 we present approximate sampling errors of these averages and of the differences between them. These sampling errors are conservative or high and are based on actual computations of the sampling errors (two standard errors) of the differences between averages for selected characteristics of subgroups and of the entire study population. Few differences between averages would be expected to have sampling errors exceeding those shown in the table. The sampling error of a difference between averages may be used to establish the range within which the "true" difference between population values of the compared averages may be expected to lie in at least 95 cases out of

100. Differences greater than the sampling error may be expected in less than 5 cases out of 100. Greater or lesser degree of confidence in the statement is associated with larger or smaller multiples of the standard error. For example, on the average the 787 Catholic women in the sample expected to have 3.40 children. From the data in Table C–10 we may say that this estimate is subject to an error of approximately 0.12. Thus the statement that the population value is within the range of 3.28 to 3.52 has at least 95 chances in 100 of being correct. The chances are less than 5 in 100 that the population value is outside this range. However, the chances are at least 68 in 100 that it lies within the smaller range of 3.34 to 3.46.

Many of the subgroups dealt with in the body of the report are so small that the sampling error for statistics based on them is considerable. Little significance can be attached to the differences between pairs of such statistics. However, where the pattern of differences or the trend of such individual statistics can be shown to follow a consistent over-all pattern, the pattern may be significant even when individual pairs of differences are not. In view of the uniqueness of much of the data in this study and the suggestive value of comparisons between these small subgroups, numerous comparisons of such groups are made in this study, even though substantial sampling error may be involved. We have tried to warn the reader of such instances. He may also make his own judgments on the basis of the tables of sampling errors we present.

Appendix D

The Classification of Couples by Fecundity

Some of the problems encountered in classifying couples by fecundity were mentioned briefly in Chapter 2. In this appendix the classification procedure and related problems are discussed in more detail.

To assign couples to the correct position along a fecundity-sterility continuum is obviously so important in this study of family growth that we felt it necessary to make the best possible efforts to estimate the extent and distribution of fecundity impairments despite the complexity of the problem and the crudeness of the available data. Our results have been sufficiently useful in understanding family growth patterns to encourage us in the belief that they have some validity and will serve as a useful benchmark for more exact studies of this topic.

The Fecundity Classes

The couples in our sample have been classified by fecundity as follows:

Group	No. of couples	Per cent
Total	2,713	100
Fecund	1,794	66
Subfecund	919	34
Definitely Sterile	283	10
Probably Sterile	187	7
Semifecund	328	12
Indeterminate	121	5

The terms are defined in Chapter 2, pages 21 to 26.

How was the information needed for this classification obtained? The first relevant question asked of each wife was:

19. "Do you have any reason to believe that you and your husband couldn't have another child (a child) if you wanted to?"

A woman who answered "yes" or "uncertain" to this question was asked additional questions to obtain reasons for her belief. For wives answering "yes" to 19, the additional questions are 19a, 19b, and one or more of 19c to 19h (see schedule in Appendix B). Wives answering "uncertain" were asked 20, 20a, and one or more of 20b to 20f.

One of these questions was whether the wife or her husband had consulted a doctor. No couple was classified as Definitely Sterile, and few were classified as Probably Sterile, unless there had been such consultation. (For only 16 per cent of the Probably Sterile was no consultation reported.) It is not always possible, however, for us to determine to what extent a wife's description of her physical condition (or that of her husband) reflects her own judgment, her doctor's judgment, or some combination of the two. In a large number of cases the comments are so definite that there is little room for ambiguity (e.g., a woman who reported a hysterectomy). A few wives who said they thought they could not have a child gave a reason which was insufficient to meet our criteria (e.g., "I am too nervous"). Such couples were not classified as Probably Sterile, but as Fecund, Semifecund, or Indeterminate, depending on the other information about them.

Definitely Sterile

A large majority (245) of the 283 Definitely Sterile couples had had an operation which made conception impossible. As indicated in Chapter 2, the high incidence of such operations led us to reread all interviews in which they were reported. We found no evidence that the question about operations (19d) was misunderstood. Although there were no specific follow-up questions on this matter, 133 wives volunteered information about the kind of operation they had:

Respondent's description of operation making pregnancy impossible	Number	Per cent
Total	133	100
Uterus removed (hysterectomy)[a]	58	44
Operation on ovaries	11	8
Operation on ovaries and tubes	3	2
Operation on "female organs"	8	6
Operation for tubular pregnancy	4	3
Operation for "female trouble"	5	4
Tubes cut and tied	8	6
Tubes removed	12	9
Tubes tied	21	16
Sterilization	3	2

[a] Includes such reports as "had my insides taken out."

An operation on the husband was reported by 25 wives. The remaining 88 wives reporting an operation did not volunteer information about what had been done, but their answers to other questions make it reasonably clear that the question about operations was not misunderstood. For example, some wives said that contraception was discontinued after the operation.

These supplementary reports lead us to the view that our data do not exaggerate the incidence of operations making conception impossible. On the contrary, the actual incidence may be even higher than is indicated by our figures, since there may have been some underreporting of such operations by Catholic respondents.

Thirty-eight couples were classified as Definitely Sterile because the wife quoted a doctor as reporting that the reproductive organs of herself or her husband had been damaged or were inadequate. The specific situations varied widely, including, for example, war injury to the husband and infantile uterus of the wife.

The 66 wives who believed that having a child was impossible but who gave no reason except failure to conceive for a long time were classified as Semifecund or Indeterminate rather than as Definitely Sterile or Probably Sterile.

The Definitely Sterile category is thought to be reasonably reliable because of the operations reported by over 86 per cent of the couples assigned to it.

Probably Sterile

As indicated in Chapter 2, the evidence used for classifying 187 couples as Probably Sterile leaves much to be desired from a medical point of view, but few couples were assigned to this group unless (1) the wife believed that she and her husband were unable to have another child, and in most cases gave a reasonable explanation for this belief; and (2) her reproductive history was consistent with her explanation.

For 48 per cent of the 187 Probably Sterile couples conception was believed to be improbable on the basis of the respondent's report of some physical limitations. For an additional 12 per cent not only was conception improbable but there was evidence that if it did occur the pregnancy would be unlikely to continue to term, might endanger the mother's health, or both (Table D–1).

For 40 per cent of the Probably Sterile conception was believed to be possible, but there was evidence that the fetus probably could not be born alive, that the mother's health would be seriously endangered, or that both of these conditions were present.

The reasons the wives gave for believing that they could not have another child are listed in Table D–2. This classification is crude, but

TABLE D–1. PER CENT DISTRIBUTION BY TYPE OF IMPAIRMENT, FOR PROBABLY
STERILE COUPLES

Possibility of conception and probable results	Number	Per cent
Total	187	100
Conception improbable, no other complications	89	48
Conception improbable *and* other complications	23	12
Seriously dangerous to mother's health	10	5
Live birth improbable[a]	8	4
Both dangerous and live birth improbable	5	3
Conception possible	75	40
Seriously dangerous to mother's health	15	8
Live birth improbable[a]	42	22
Both dangerous and live birth improbable	18	10

[a] Includes cases based on Rh factor and on repeated fetal deaths.

it indicates why the wives felt as they did. Some women gave more
than one reason. If Rh incompatibility or the necessity for a Caesarean
delivery was reported, the couple was not classified as Probably Sterile
unless there was supporting evidence. It was not possible to apply a uniform criterion which did not depend on a respondent's report of the
seriousness of her condition. However, it seems unlikely that the errors in
some of these smaller categories affect substantially the over-all distribution by fecundity.

TABLE D–2. PERCENTAGE REPORTING SPECIFIED REASONS WHY THEY ARE
UNLIKELY TO HAVE MORE CHILDREN, FOR WIVES OF PROBABLY STERILE
COUPLES

Reason	No. of reports	Percentage of wives reporting reason
Total [a]	236	126
Rh incompatibility	20	11
Necessity for dangerous Caesarean delivery	9	5
History of repeated fetal deaths	21	11
Other defects of wife's reproductive organs	92	49
Other defects of husband's reproductive organs	16	9
Other illness or health factor of wife	36	19
Failure to conceive for a long period [b]	21	11
Miscellaneous	9	5
No reason given	12	6

[a] The number of reasons tabulated (236) exceeds the number of Probably Sterile
couples (187), and the percentages add to more than 100 because several wives mentioned two or more reasons.

[b] Included here only when mentioned in combination with another of the listed
reasons.

It might be well to repeat that while we relied on the wife's report on the physical condition of herself and her husband we eliminated cases in which the reason given for probable sterility seemed insufficient. Nevertheless, our classification obviously would have been different if physician's records had been available or (better yet) if medical examinations and clinical tests could have been made. It represents the respondents' reports with the possibilities of error that they involve.

The Semifecund

Two criteria were used in defining this group: (1) a relatively long period since marriage when a couple cohabited and did not practice contraception (and the wife did not douche for cleanliness soon after intercourse) but conception did not occur, and (2) a relatively long average interval between births (i.e., a large quotient obtained by dividing years married by number of births). A "relatively long" period without a conception was defined as 2 or more years for never-pregnant women and 3 or more years for women pregnant at least once. (This definition is the same as that used in the Indianapolis Study, described briefly in Appendix A, Note 2.)

If the wife reported *never* using a family limitation method, her pregnancy record was examined to see whether there was a long period between the end of one pregnancy and the next conception (or between marriage and first conception). Time between marriages, and separations of 6 months or more (reported on the schedule under personal data items 24 and 24*a*), were subtracted in computing the length of these periods. If the wife reported the use of a family limitation method and had been married at least 4 years, she was asked question 51:

(If never pregnant): "Has there ever been a period of 2 or more years when you did not use any method to prevent pregnancy?"

(If ever pregnant): "Has there ever been a period of 3 or more years when you weren't pregnant and nothing was done to prevent pregnancy and you didn't become pregnant?"

If the foregoing information indicated that the couple might be classified as Semifecund, the second criterion was applied. Here, a relatively long average interval between births was defined as more than 35 months. This criterion was developed so that a couple who had children relatively frequently would not be classified as Semifecund merely because they had *one* long period without a conception. For example, one couple with 11 births had one long period and would have been classified as Semifecund if the second criterion had not been applied. It resulted in our classifying 49 couples as Fecund rather than Semifecund.

As was stated in Chapter 2, the validity of the Semifecund group depends in part on the accuracy of the wives' statements about contraception and abortion. It is possible that some respondents who were unwilling to report that they had tried to avoid conception, or had had an illegal abortion, were classified as Semifecund incorrectly, because a long period without conception was in reality the result of some type of preventive effort. It is difficult to assess how frequently this may have occurred, but we do not believe it was often. There is little question regarding half of the Semifecund couples, for they reported practicing contraception part of the time, and also long periods without either contraception or conception.

We read the questionnaires of the 165 couples classified as Semifecund and reporting no use of family limitation methods, looking for evidence which would confirm or conflict with the reported lack of use. In 87 of these cases the interviewer noted that the wife said at some time during the interview that she had difficulty in conceiving, although she was not questioned specifically about this if her answer to question 19 indicated she had no reason to believe that she and her husband could not have a child in the future. For only 5 of the 165 couples did it seem rather likely (but by no means certain) that contraception had been used but the wife failed to report it. These couples were not reclassified, since we felt we had insufficient evidence to alter the respondent's own report. The problem of the reliability of reporting efforts to avoid conception is discussed further in Appendix E.

One hypothesis developed in Chapter 2 is that there is a selective interrelationship between nonuse of contraception and subfecundity; namely, couples who find that they do not conceive easily are more likely to remain Nonusers than those who find that conceiving is easy. If this is true, and if the Nonusers have given genuine reports of their use of family limitation methods, we should expect that Nonusers would constitute not only a high proportion of Semifecund couples but also of Definitely Sterile and Probably Sterile couples. This is indeed the case, as the tables in Chapter 2 indicate.

These considerations lead us to the view that relatively few couples are misclassified as Semifecund because of misstatements about family limitation practices. They probably are more than balanced by the couples who are Semifecund but do not know it because they are using contraception regularly. Semifecundity is obviously a relative matter; our choice of criteria is arbitrary, but is believed to be reasonable.

Indeterminate

This group consists of 121 couples who would have been classified as Semifecund on the basis of having at least one long period with no conception, and few births in relation to years married, but instead were classified as Indeterminate because the wife said in answers to questions 43 and 44 that nothing had ever been done to avoid conception but that she used a douche for cleanliness soon after intercourse.

Does douching merely for cleanliness soon after intercourse reduce the likelihood of conceiving? We have been able to find usable data on this topic in the Indianapolis Study but not elsewhere. They show that DFCO did postpone conception in important degree. For example, among the 434 "relatively fecund" couples who had one or more pregnancies and reported that no attempt was made to delay the first, the average time from marriage to first conception was about 26 months for the 61 wives who douched for cleanliness only and 7 months for the 373 who did not do so. Similarly, among the 136 "relatively fecund" couples who had a second pregnancy which they did not try to delay, the interval from end of first to beginning of second averaged 22 months for the 28 DFCO wives and 12 months for the 115 others.[1]

On the basis of the Indianapolis Study results, it is quite certain that for some of the 121 DFCO couples in our study the long intervals with no conception were due to douching rather than inability to conceive; consequently these couples really belong in the Fecund group. In contrast, the extra notes made by the interviewer on the schedules for some of the other DFCO wives indicate that douching was an occasional rather than a regular event and probably did not delay conception significantly. Such couples really belong in the Semifecund group. Unfortunately, for most of the 121 couples in question the information on the schedules does not permit their being classified either as Fecund or Semifecund; consequently all are classified Indeterminate.

Among the 121 couples classified as Indeterminate are 21 wives who said in answer to question 19 that they believed they could not have another child because they had failed to conceive over long periods of time. In addition, 20 other wives indicated in unsolicited comments elsewhere in the interview that they had experienced difficulty in conceiving or that it "took a long time" to become pregnant. These statements may merely be additional evidence of the ignorance of some women regarding certain aspects of the reproductive process—specifically of the effect which douching soon after intercourse may have on the likelihood of conception.

If the wife's report of DFCO was intended to mask actual contraceptive practice, it would be expected that relatively more Catholics than Protestants would have made such a report. Actually, the proportions are 14 per cent for Catholic wives and 11 per cent for Protestants; the difference is not statistically significant with our small sample.

[1] See Appendix A, Note 2f.

Indeterminate, like Semifecund, is defined more or less arbitrarily along a time continuum. Many of the Indeterminate couples will have additional children, but as a group they are below "normal" in fecundity and have less than "normal" birth rates, since at least some of them are really Semifecund.

The Fecund

The Fecund couples are those for whom there is no reason to doubt fecundity. This is a residual group and includes all couples who do not meet the criteria for one of the four fecundity categories already discussed. It undoubtedly includes some couples whose family limitation practice has concealed impaired fecundity. It also includes couples who will qualify for one of the four Subfecund categories as time passes, and well before the wife reaches what is usually considered to be the end of the childbearing period. In short, all couples whose reproductive histories to date give us no reason to suspect that fecundity impairments limit reproduction are classified as Fecund.

The Fecund-Subfecund Dichotomy

In some of the discussion and tables, Indeterminate couples are treated as a separate group. When it is not feasible to use the detailed (five-group) classification these couples are considered as Subfecund rather than Fecund.

It might be argued that Indeterminate couples should be combined with the Fecund rather than with the Probably Sterile, Definitely Sterile, and Semifecund, because the Fecund group is much larger and would be less affected by the addition of these unclassifiable couples. This was not done for two main reasons. First, there is good evidence that the Definitely Sterile, Probably Sterile, and Semifecund couples have fecundity impairments and belong in the group where they have been placed. In contrast, for many of the couples classified as Fecund we do not have direct evidence that fecundity impairments are absent. On the contrary, as mentioned in Chapter 2, we are quite sure that some of the couples in the Fecund group actually are Subfecund but do not know it because the effective use of contraception has concealed subfecundity. In short, the Fecund group is already biased to some extent because we cannot identify and exclude all the couples with fecundity impairments. Combining the Indeterminate with the Fecund couples when a two-group classification is necessary would increase this bias, but combining them with the Definitely Sterile, Probably Sterile, and Semifecund couples tends to compensate for it.

Another reason for classifying the Indeterminate as Subfecund is the desirability of having the Fecund group as "pure" as feasible when studying the effect of contraception. It is among Fecund couples that contraception has the greatest influence on number of births. Changes in family size and in population growth occur primarily as a result of changes in the number of children wanted and the success of the efforts of Fecund couples to stop with this number. In consequence, it is especially important in analyzing the impact of contraception on fertility to concentrate attention on those couples who seem most likely to be Fecund.

Appendix E

The Accuracy of Reporting
on Use of Contraception

Of the couples in our sample 70 per cent are classified as Users, 11 per cent as DFCO (because the wife said that no attempt to delay or prevent pregnancy was made but that she douched for cleanliness only soon after intercourse), and 19 per cent as Nonusers. Since the distinction between Users and Nonusers is so important for many aspects of this study, the reliability of the responses in this area deserves discussion. In particular, how many respondents may have failed to report the use of contraception[1] because they thought the questions about it were "too personal," because they were not willing to admit adopting methods prohibited by their Church, or for some other reason? Only 10 wives refused point-blank to answer the questions about the couple's family limitation practices, but of course this gives no indication of the number who were unwilling to admit that contraception had been used. We have no reason to believe that any significant number of women reported that a method had been adopted although in fact it had not been.

Basis of Classification

Whether a couple had or had not practiced contraception was determined from the wife's answers to two questions. The first is:

43: "Now in your own case, have you or your husband ever done anything to limit the number of your children or to keep from having them at certain times?"

If the wife answered "yes," she was shown Card 1 (on which 11 methods were listed) and asked what methods had been used. If she answered "no," she was asked:

[1] As stated at various places in the text we are utilizing interchangeably, and without moral connotation, such terms as "contraception," "family limitation," and "conception control" in referring to certain methods which married couples adopt in order to try to regulate conception, namely, the various chemical and appliance contraceptives, withdrawal (coitus interruptus), rhythm (periodic continence), and abstinence. These terms do not include sterilization or illegal abortion.

44: "Some things couples do may not be considered birth control. Doctors and public health workers are interested in learning how many people use these methods. Have you ever made use of either of the methods on this card? You can tell me by the numbers on the card."

The card listed two methods: (1) safe period—rhythm (avoiding those days of monthly cycle when conception is likely to occur) and (2) douche —for cleanliness (soon after intercourse).[2] Question 44 was asked because experience in other studies and in our pretest showed that some of the wives using these practices thought that they were not meant to be included in the answer to a question like 43.

A significant number of wives—especially the Catholic wives—who answered question 43 in the negative did report rhythm in response to question 44. Apparently, they were more willing to say they used it when the wording of the question indicated that they need not accept the label of birth control. It is possible that a few wives who replied "no" to question 43 would have reported withdrawal or condom in response to question 44 if these methods had been listed on the card under a general heading such as "husband takes care."

A different type of problem is posed by the 306 wives who answered questions 43 and 44 by saying that nothing had ever been done to prevent conception but that they douched merely for cleanliness soon after intercourse. Should these couples be classified as Users or Nonusers? As was pointed out in Appendix D, some of these wives undoubtedly douched for cleanliness so irregularly or so long after intercourse that this practice had little effect on the conception rate. Such couples may well be considered as Nonusers from a practical standpoint. In contrast, other wives undoubtedly douched so regularly and so promptly that the likelihood of conceiving was reduced greatly.[3] These couples certainly were Users of contraception from the standpoint of their actions, if not of their motives.

It is probable that some of the DFCO wives were reporting honestly— they really believed that the practice did not affect conception. It is also probable that others were unwilling to admit to an interviewer (and perhaps even to themselves) that they were doing something which would delay or prevent pregnancy. With the information at hand we cannot tell in which of these groups a given DFCO couple belongs. If there had been enough DFCO couples in our sample, we would have treated them as a separate group in many of our tables about contraception. But because there are only 306 DFCO couples we show them separately in only a few tables, and in a few others show them with Users on an action basis and with Nonusers on a motive basis, as was done in

[2] See Appendix B.
[3] See Appendix A, Note 2f.

the Indianapolis Study. Fortunately, most results are approximately the same on one basis as on the other.

Most of the analysis is made on a motive basis because the DFCO couples tend to resemble the Nonusers more closely than the Users with respect to several demographic and social characteristics. For example, if we consider only women married at least 5 years and compare those with similar marriage durations (5–9 years, 10–14 years, and 15 or more years) the DFCOs are more like Nonusers than Users with respect to average number of pregnancies, average number of births, expected number of children, and number of pregnancies or births per months married. The DFCOs also resemble the Nonusers with respect to husband's income and wife's education. Finally, the DFCOs resemble the Nonusers very closely in their over-all fecundity distribution.

The main reason for combining the DFCOs with Nonusers is our desire to keep the User group "pure." When the proportions of couples definitely trying to limit family size, and partially or completely successful in their efforts, are as large as they are in the United States, the changes in the number of births per couple depend chiefly on the changes in the number of children wanted. In consequence, when studying past and expected future trends in fertility it seems advisable to focus attention on the couples who state unequivocally that they have used some method of contraception.

Comparisons with Other Studies

Since no prior study has ever obtained data on family limitation practices for a probability sample of the total population, there are no adequate outside data for comparisons. In the study conducted in Indianapolis in 1941 it was found that approximately 89.2 per cent of the couples had practiced contraception on a motive basis and 91.5 on an action basis compared with 70 and 81 per cent in the present study.[4] It should be remembered, however, that the Indianapolis Study was restricted to native white Protestant couples with at least an eighth-grade education, married 12 to 15 years, and residents of a large city most of their lives, in part because it was desired to focus attention on groups making relatively much use of contraception. In consequence, the proportion of couples practicing contraception would be expected to exceed the figure for a sample like ours. A more accurate comparison may be made by considering only the 86 couples in our sample with characteristics similar to those of the couples qualifying for the Indianapolis sample. The percentage of Users among these 86 couples is 87.2

[4] See Appendix A, Note 2, and especially section *c*, for information about the Indianapolis Study.

on a motive basis and 94.2 on an action basis—close to the percentages for Indianapolis. When only the "relatively fecund" couples in the Indianapolis Study and our comparable subsample are considered, the percentage of Users is virtually identical—98.4 and 98.3, respectively, on a motive basis and 99.6 and 100, respectively, on an action basis.

A sample which resembles ours more closely was interviewed in 1938–39 by the Market Research Corporation of America.[5] This MRCA study included married women under 45 of all religious beliefs, living in 30 cities and selected rural areas in various parts of the United States. Unfortunately, the results are not exactly comparable with those from our study because of two differences in procedures. First, the urban wives were chosen from those in "the upper middle class of the population," which would tend to have relatively more Users than the entire urban population which was sampled in the present study. Second, use of contraception relates to "customary action at a given time," which presumably is a period (of undefined length) preceding the interview, while in the present study it relates to all of married life. Because the incidence of recognized subfecundity increases with duration of marriage, the proportion of couples practicing contraception is smaller for a recent period than for the entire period since marriage. Riley and White do not state how DFCO couples were classified.

The proportion of upper middle class urban couples reported by Riley and White as currently practicing contraception is 83 per cent, which is somewhat larger than the 71 per cent for all the urban couples in the present study. Such a difference probably would be expected in view of the "upper middle class" limitation of the MRCA urban sample. What may be surprising is that the difference between the two studies is substantially larger for Catholics than for Protestants:

Religion	Percentage using contraception	
	MRCA study, 1940 (upper-middle-class urban couples)	Present study, 1955 (all urban couples)
Total	83	71
Protestant	83	78
Catholic	77	59
Other	88	82

For certain largely urban groups in the present study the proportion who are Users is about as high as for the upper-middle-class couples in

[5] John W. Riley and Matilda White, "The Use of Various Methods of Contraception," *American Sociological Review*, vol. 5, no. 6, pp. 890–903, December, 1940. More information about this study is given in Appendix A, Note 8.

the earlier study, namely: (1) couples with husbands having upper-white-collar occupations—81 per cent, and (2) couples with husband's income $6,000 or more in 1954—79 per cent.

The proportion of rural couples reported as Users is 71 per cent in the MRCA study and 68 per cent in the present study.

These comparisons do not provide a basis for firm conclusions about completeness of reporting family limitation practices. The somewhat lower percentage of Users for the urban couples in the present sample than for those in the 1938–39 sample may be due to differences in the universes that were studied or to the sampling procedures utilized. However, the large difference for urban Catholics supports the statement made at various places in the text that there may have been some tendency for Catholics who had attempted to regulate conception to refrain from telling our interviewers that they had done so.

Internal Evidence on Accuracy of Reporting Contraception

Internal criteria are helpful in evaluating the adequacy of our data on the proportion of couples adopting contraception. It is to be expected that a substantial minority of the couples in our sample would not have tried to limit family size and that they would be concentrated in certain groups. It seemed helpful to classify the 802 Nonusers as follows:

Nonusers who intend to use	233
Nonusers who do not intend to use	569
Fecund	163
Definitely Sterile	144
Probably Sterile	55
Semifecund	130
Indeterminate	77

There is probably little misreporting among the 233 Nonusers who said they intend to begin contraception at some future time. It does not seem likely that any wife who reported intended future use would have motivation for concealing current or past use. Most of the misreporting, then, appears to be concentrated among the 569 Nonusers who do not intend to use contraception.

When we classify by fecundity the Nonusers who do not intend to use, we find three groups that are unlikely to have concealed past use. First, let us consider the 163 Fecund couples. Our chief reason for believing that these couples are Nonusers is that their fertility is very high. This is especially true of those married 5 or more years, the group we would ordinarily expect to use contraception. If some of them had done so, it probably was for only a short time or was quite ineffective.

Next there are the 144 Definitely Sterile and the 55 Probably Sterile couples. Some of these couples never were physiologically able to have a child and never needed contraception. Others had a few children, but not as many as they wanted, and then became unable to have more; they, too, had no great need to adopt contraception. Still others (among the Definitely Sterile) had "sterilizing" operations to prevent further child-bearing, instead of resorting to contraception. Among all these subgroups of the Definitely and Probably Sterile, there is little reason to suspect any concealment of the use of contraception.

In contrast to the couples in the Definitely and Probably Sterile group who never needed to use contraception are those who did use it early in married life when they could have had a child and later became unable to reproduce. In some of these cases, the wife may have repressed the memory of early use of contraception in order to throw all the blame for childlessness on a physiological condition and avoid a feeling of personal responsibility. In general, however, we have little reason to doubt the nonuse of contraception reported by most of the 199 Definitely and Probably Sterile couples.

Having eliminated most of the 163 Fecund couples and the 199 Definitely and Probably Sterile couples from the Nonusers suspected of trying to conceal contraception, we can focus our attention on the 130 Nonusers classified as Semifecund and the 77 classified as Indeterminate. Both groups experienced long periods during which they did not conceive in spite of their reported nonuse. It seems quite possible that some of these couples failed to state their motives or actions correctly. This is especially true for those placed in the Indeterminate group because the wife reported that soon after coitus she douched for cleanliness only. It seems probable that some of these women either misreported their motivation or were actually confused about it themselves. They may have come to think that they were using douche merely for cleanliness, although at one time they may have suspected, or been aware, that douching might tend to prevent conception.

Since there seemed to be good reasons for being suspicious of the nonuse reported by some of the 130 Semifecund and 77 Indeterminate couples, their schedules were carefully read to look for evidence bearing on this question. In 97 of the 207 cases the respondent specifically mentioned difficulty in conceiving. Furthermore, among both the 97 and the remaining 110 there were frequent references to the beliefs that having children is not subject to human control, children should come naturally or in response to God's will, conception is up to fate, birth control is wrong, we must take what comes, etc. There were only 5 cases in which it seemed likely (but by no means certain) from other evidence that the wife might be concealing the couple's use of contraception, or misstating the reason for having douched soon after intercourse. These schedules were not changed, however, since we felt we had insufficient evidence to alter the respondent's report.

We realize that some of the other schedules which appear to be internally consistent may not be correct. Some of the wives may have subconsciously distorted or repressed their recollection of certain events to such an extent that they had no difficulty in answering our questions consistently but incorrectly. Some others may have had the ability to misrepresent intentionally without being detected by our check questions. All we claim is that there probably were relatively few of either type. The results of rereading the interviews substantiated the initial impression that most of the 207 couples in question did have genuine fecundity problems and had not been classified as Semifecund or Indeterminate simply because of false reporting on the use of contraception.

The interrelationship between fecundity and use is of such a character that the percentage of Users among Fecund couples in the study would not be seriously in error even if many of the 406 Subfecund couples who never expect to adopt contraception were Users who failed to report use. Eighty-two per cent of all the Fecund couples in the sample (and 83 per cent of those who reported on use) are now classified as Users. If 100 of these 406 Subfecund Nonusers are really Fecund Users, the correct percentage is 88 or 89 instead of 83. It is quite unlikely that as many as 100 Subfecund Nonusers need to be reclassified.

The Effect of Catholic Background on Reported Nonuse

Nonuse is especially frequent among Catholic couples. Catholic wives constitute 29 per cent of the total sample, but 42 per cent of the Nonusers. Only 57 per cent of the couples with Catholic wives are classified as Users, compared with 75 per cent of those with Protestant wives. Catholic religious ideology provides a motivation for not adopting most methods of conception control and might also encourage some Catholic Users to say nothing about resort to these methods.

If significant numbers of Catholics were failing to report having adopted contraception, a high proportion of Catholic Nonusers would be classified as Semifecund or Indeterminate according to our classification outline. (The logic here is the same as that presented in the preceding section.) Actually, the proportion Semifecund and Indeterminate is somewhat smaller for Protestants (15 per cent) than for Catholics (21 per cent) (Table 2–12). Part of this difference probably does reflect failure to report efforts to prevent conception. But part of it undoubtedly reflects the fact that Catholic Users adopt a method later than Protestant Users; i.e., they have more pregnancies before beginning preventive efforts (Table 4–4). This means that relatively more Catholics test their fecundity, find that it takes a long time to conceive, and never resort to contraception. Among couples who report the use of some method, Catholics are more likely than Protestants to be classified as Semifecund since they usually have a longer period of fecundity testing before use begins. This factor, rather than a higher proportion of Catholics than of Protestants concealing their use of contraception, probably accounts for the higher proportion of couples classified as Semifecund and Indeterminate among Catholics.

If more Catholics than Protestants do not use contraception, even when there is no evidence of impaired fecundity, the proportion of Catholics who are Nonusers should be relatively high among Fecund couples. This is, in fact, the case. Among Fecund Catholics 30 per cent are Nonusers as compared with only 12 per cent among Fecund Protestants. Of course, a Catholic couple who used a method and failed to report it might be classified as a Fecund Nonuser, if use did not prevent conception for a long period.

Among Nonusers the proportion Fecund should be relatively low and the proportion Subfecund relatively high for Catholics if they are more likely than Protestants to fail to report use of a method during substantial periods of time. In fact, however, the proportion of Nonusers who are in the Semifecund and Indeterminate categories is almost the same for Catholics and Protestants (37 per cent for Catholics and 35 per cent for Protestants) and the proportion in the Fecund category is considerably higher for Catholics. This means that by the test of their fertility performance, Catholic Nonusers apparently are no more likely than Protestants to have concealed their use of a method.

A final qualitative consideration is that the overwhelming majority of the interviews with Nonusers ring true when read as a whole. In very few cases did the interviewers or supervisors feel that a respondent was misrepresenting or avoiding an answer to the questions regarding attempts to regulate conception.

An Over-all View

The preceding discussion is not intended to deny that some couples who used contraception failed to report it. Those who made infrequent use or whose use occurred long ago are particularly unlikely to be found in the kind of checks described in the preceding paragraphs. On the other hand, their use is also unlikely to have had much effect on their reproductive histories. Our data show a smaller percentage ever using a method among the older women in the sample and those married a long time than among those in the mid-groups on age or duration of marriage.

It is not possible now to determine whether this represents a historical change in resort to contraception, or a selective "forgetting" by older women of use of a method a long time ago—particularly if such use was infrequent or unsuccessful.

It is probable that some of the wives did not understand the meaning of our questions on family limitation, and that some deliberately misrepresented the facts in this part of the interview. Some Users who failed to report their resort to preventive measures in response to our battery of questions might have done so if more detailed questions had been asked. While we are unable to estimate the extent to which the couples practicing contraception are underreported, we believe it is small. The considerations discussed in this Appendix lead us to conclude that a nonuse rate near 30 per cent on a motive basis and 19 per cent on an action basis is not unreasonable in a population of the type our sample represents.

Appendix F

Method of Determining Most Likely, Minimum, and Maximum Numbers of Births Expected

The numbers of expected births assigned to the couples in our study are based on the wife's responses to several questions. First of all, an attempt was made to classify each couple as to ability to have additional children. This resulted in the fecundity classification described in Chapter 2 and Appendix D. For the purpose of assigning expectation values, three fecundity groups were selected for separate treatment:

1. The Definitely Sterile
2. The Probably Sterile
3. All other (Semifecund, Indeterminate, and Fecund)

The method of determining the total number of births expected for each of these groups is described below.

1. *The Definitely Sterile.* For this group, the total number of births (most likely, minimum, and maximum) is equal to the total number of births that had occurred by the time of the interview.

2. *The Probably Sterile.* Some of the wives in this group thought that they might be able to have additional children in spite of substantial evidence to the contrary. It was found convenient to subdivide them into two groups as follows:

a. *Wouldn't have a child in future even if it were possible.* For this group, the total number of births expected (most likely, minimum, and maximum) is equal to the total that had occurred by interview.

b. *Will have a child if can.* These couples were further subdivided into two groups:

(1) *Conception neither dangerous to mother's health nor likely to result in fetal death.* It was considered that if any of the Probably Sterile would bear a child in the future, such couples were most likely to do so. For the purpose of establishing their most likely expectations, it was assumed (somewhat arbitrarily) that 30 per cent would be able to have a child in the future and that 70 per cent

478

would be unable to do so. In effect, this means that the *most likely* expected number of births for each couple in this subgroup is equal to births by the time of the interview plus 0.3. The *maximum* number of births expected is equal to children already born plus *all* the additional births these women said they would have if they could. Naturally, it seems highly unlikely that this number will be attained. *Minimum* expectations were established by assuming that these couples would have no births in the future and therefore are the numbers of children born by the time of the interview.

(2) *Conception dangerous to mother's health and/or likely to result in fetal death.* It seems less probable that births will occur under these conditions than when there is little health risk and little likelihood of pregnancy wastage. Hence, both the *minimum* and *most likely* expectations for these couples were assumed to be the number of children already born. The *maximum* number of births expected, however, was assumed to be equal to children already born plus all the additional births these women said they would have if they could.

3. *All other (Semifecund, Indeterminate, and Fecund).* Most of these couples are capable of having children in the future, although there are doubts about some classified as Semifecund and Indeterminate. All the wives were asked if they expected to bear another child. On the basis of their replies to this question the couples were subdivided into three groups, each of which was treated separately, as described below:

a. *Definitely or probably expect more children.* These wives were asked in question 29 how many children they thought they would have and in question 30 how sure they were of their expectations. If they were sure or fairly sure of their expectations and if they gave a single number in reply to question 29, this number was regarded as the couple's most likely, minimum, and maximum expected number of births. However, if they gave a range in reply to question 29, such as three or four births, the *most likely* expectation was assumed to be the average of the highest and lowest numbers, and the *maximum* and *minimum* expectations were assumed to be the highest and lowest numbers, respectively. The wives who were not sure of their reply to question 29 were asked in questions 30a and 30b, respectively, for the smallest and largest number of births they thought they would have. The *most likely* expectations for the women not sure of their reply to question 29 were assumed to be the number stated in reply to this question, if a single number was given, or to the average of the highest and lowest numbers if a range was given. The *maximum* and *minimum* expectations for the women not sure of their reply to question 29 were assumed to be the highest and lowest numbers given, respectively, whether in response to question 29, 30*a*, or 30*b*.

Some (16) of the women who were sure they would have more children declined to say how many they expected, but said the number was "in God's hands," "up to fate," or otherwise indeterminate. No expectation values were assigned to such couples.

b. *Uncertain if will have more.* The *minimum* expected number of births for such a couple was assumed to be equal to the number of children already born. The *maximum* expectation was taken as the wife's reply to the question asking how many more children they would have if they had any more. The *most likely* expectation was taken as the average of the minimum and maximum expectations, as determined above. In some cases, however, the wife declined to speculate about how many children she would have in the future if she had any; in such instances, the *most likely* expectation was assumed to be the number of children already born plus 0.5.

c. *Definitely or probably will not have more.* Most likely, minimum, and maximum expectations were assumed to be the number of children born by the time of the interview.

The large majority (over 90 per cent) of all the future births expected will occur to the couples with wives who definitely or probably expect another child. The adjustment of 0.3 for each couple in category 2*b*(1) above contributes less than 1 per cent to the most likely number of additional births expected. The remaining future births will occur to the "uncertain" wives in group 3*b* above.

In many instances, a couple's most likely expectation is a fractional number. Obviously, it is meaningless to state that any particular couple expects, for example, 2.5 or 4.3 births. This device is used so that the expectations of any group of couples would reflect the replies of the wives in couples with the characteristics represented by the group. We have assumed, for example, that half of the women who say they expect "4 or 5" births will have 4 and that half will have 5. We cannot, however, determine which particular couple will have 4 and which 5, so we simply assign 4.5 as the most likely number of births expected by each couple. When these couples are grouped with others and their expectations are summed, the result we obtain is the same as the result we would have obtained if we had assigned 4 to one-half of the couples and 5 to the other half.

Appendix G

Procedures Relating to
Forecasts of Births and Population

NOTE 1. *Projected birth rates for white women in the cohorts of 1916–20 to 1931–35, based chiefly on data from present study*

The study is limited to wives with husband present, or with husband temporarily absent because of military service. In projecting fertility rates for future years we want to use the expectations of these wives regarding additional births in conjunction with the information about past childbearing which is available from cohort fertility tables. These tables relate to all members of a cohort, or to all who have married by a given age; the study relates to those currently married and living with husband. In order to make the two series comparable, we must supplement our study data. Specifically, we must allow for the past births to the cohort members who had married by 1955, but were not included in our sample because they were widowed, divorced, or not living with husband because of other reasons than his military service. In addition, we must estimate the expected future birth rates of these women and of the single women who will marry by the end of the childbearing period (which is assumed to be ages 45–49).

The cohort fertility tables to which we refer were prepared by the Scripps Foundation for Research in Population Problems and will be published shortly.[1] The cohorts relate to 12-month periods from July 1 through June 30 and are identified by the year in which the latter date occurs. Thus, the girl babies of July 1, 1915, through June 30, 1916, constitute the initial members of the female cohort of 1916.[2] Those who survive to January 1, 1946, for example, are from 29½ to 30½ years old on that date. In some types of actuarial analysis it is customary to consider them as exactly 30 years old. We shall refer to exact ages in this note,

---

[1] Pascal K. Whelpton and Arthur A. Campbell, *Fertility Tables for Birth Cohorts of American Women*, to be published by the National Office of Vital Statistics.

[2] The reasons for this procedure are given in P. K. Whelpton, *Cohort Fertility: Native White Women in the United States*, Princeton University Press, Princeton, N.J., 1954, chap. 2; and Wilson H. Grabill, Clyde V. Kiser, and P. K. Whelpton, *Fertility of American Women*, Wiley & Sons, Inc., New York, 1958, Appendix B.

except when quoting census data. In general terms, the girls born between July 1 of year $y - 1$ and June 30 of year y constitute cohort y. On January 1 of year $y + x$ their age is between $x - \frac{1}{2}$ and $x + \frac{1}{2}$, and as a group they can be considered to be at exact age x.

There are four steps in the procedure followed to supplement the data from our study so as to obtain birth rates which will be comparable with those from cohort fertility tables. The fertility of the women who were single in 1955 but will marry later is considered in steps a and b; that of the women who had married by 1955 but were not included in our sample is considered in steps c and d. For the women who were single in 1955 we must estimate marriage rates and birth rates during the age intervals shown below:

Cohorts	*Intervals between exact ages*			
1916–20				35–39 and 45–49
1921–25			30–34 and 35–39,	35–39 and 45–49
1926–30		25–29 and 30–34,	30–34 and 35–39,	35–39 and 45–49
1931–35	20–24 and 25–29,	25–29 and 30–34,	30–34 and 35–39,	35–39 and 45–49

a. What proportion of the women in the cohorts of 1916–20 to 1931–35 who were single on January 1, 1955, will marry by ages 45–49? For the United States, unlike many of the other Western countries, there is comparatively little exact information on the changes in marital status which occur year by year to the women in a cohort. Using the Census Bureau's data on the number of women who are single or have married previously and the annual marriage data collected by the National Office of Vital

TABLE G–1. CUMULATIVE FIRST MARRIAGE RATE PER 1,000 WOMEN, FOR WHITE OR NATIVE WHITE WOMEN IN GROUPS OF COHORTS, BY AGE[a]

Cohorts	Exact ages						
	15–19	20–24	25–29	30–34	35–39	40–44	45–49
1931–35	128	658	882	929	943	948	950
1926–30	89	635	873	934	948	953	955
1921–25	85	562	860	924	942	950	955
1916–20	81	476	810	906	931	942	948
1911–15	91	467	753	870	916	931	940
1906–10	93	483	742	844	894	916	928
1901–05	89	490	755	844	883	892	918

[a] The numbers below the horizontal lines are estimates for native white women prepared by Scripps Foundation for Research in Population Problems, based chiefly on census data and annual numbers of marriages; those above the horizontal lines are forecasts for all white women. The first figure below a horizontal line refers to January 1, 1955, the second to January 1, 1950, etc.; similarly, the first figure above a horizontal line refers to January 1, 1960, the second to January 1, 1965, etc.

Statistics, the Scripps Foundation has estimated cumulative marriage rates of cohorts of women up to various ages[3] (Table G–1). The difference between the cumulative rates for successive dates and ages is the number of marriages per 1,000 women in the cohort during the time interval or age period in question. For example, among the native white women in the cohorts of 1921–25, who live to the ages specified, 85 of each 1,000 had married by exact ages 15–19 (by January 1, 1940), 562 by exact ages 20–24 (by January 1, 1945), 860 by exact ages 25–29 (by January 1, 1950), and 924 by exact ages 30–34 (by January 1, 1955). The differences between these cumulative rates are the current or period marriage rates for the cohorts of 1921–25, namely, 477 during 1940–44, 298 during 1945–49, and 64 during 1950–54 (Table G–2).

TABLE G–2. INCREASE IN CUMULATIVE FIRST MARRIAGE RATES, FOR WHITE OR NATIVE WHITE WOMEN IN GROUPS OF COHORTS, BY AGE INTERVALS[a]

Cohorts	Interval between exact ages					
	15–19 and 20–24	20–24 and 25–29	25–29 and 30–34	30–34 and 35–39	35–39 and 40–44	40–44 and 45–49
1931–35	530	224	47	14	5	2
1926–30	546	238	61	14	5	2
1921–25	477	298	64	18	8	5
1916–20	395	334	96	25	11	6
1911–15	376	286	117	46	15	9
1906–10	390	259	102	50	22	12
1901–05	401	265	89	39	9	26

[a] See Table G–1, footnote a.

For present purposes we need forecasts of the proportion of cohort members who will marry between 1955 and the year when they reach ages 45–49, and the ages at which they will marry. A medium series for white women (exact ages) is given above the horizontal lines in Tables G–1 and G–2; medium, high, and low series for all women (current ages) are shown in Table 10–6. The assumptions used in preparing these forecasts are discussed in Chapter 10. Here we shall merely summarize them as follows: (1) in the medium series the tendency to marry by various ages from 15–19 to 45–49 will reach a peak in the cohorts of 1926–30 or 1931–35, and then decline slightly; (2) in the low series there will be an early reversal of the tendency to marry younger, a partial return to

[3] If, for the women living at a given age, the number who have married prior to that age is divided by the total number and the product is multiplied by 1,000, the result is the cumulative marriage rate per 1,000.

the prewar marriage pattern, and a rate of 930 for the cohorts of 1931–35 by ages 45–49; and (3) in the high series the proportion married at each age will continue to rise and will reach 970 at ages 45–49 for the cohorts of 1931–35. The differences between the high and low series are relatively small (4 per cent) for the cohorts under consideration. According to the medium series there will be 17 first marriages between ages 35–39 and 45–49 per 1,000 women in the cohorts of 1916–20 (Table G–2, fourth line). Forecasts of marriage rates at successive ages for later groups of cohorts are shown on lines 1 to 3 of Table G–2.

b. What will be the future birth rates of the single women who will marry? The next problem is how to use the study information about number of births expected, together with other relevant information about fertility, in estimating the childbearing of the women who were single in 1955 but will have married by ages 45–49. Let us start by considering the single women aged 35–39 in the cohorts of 1916–20. One clue as to their probable future fertility is the actual fertility in this age interval of corresponding women in the cohorts of 1900–05. Census data show that the birth rate of the members of these cohorts who married after ages 35–39 was 690 by ages 45–49 (Table G–3). However, the rates by ages 35–39 for women married 0–4 or 5–9 years are substantially larger for the cohorts of 1916–20 according to study data than for the cohorts of 1900–05 according to census data. Moreover, the additional children that the married women in the later group expect to have after ages 35–39 will make the increase in their birth rate after these ages substantially larger

TABLE G–3. CUMULATIVE BIRTH RATES BY AGES 35–39 AND 45–49 AND INCREASE BETWEEN THESE AGES, FOR WHITE OR NATIVE WHITE WIVES IN COHORTS OF 1900–05 AND 1916–20, BY DURATION OF MARRIAGE

Years married by ages		Cohorts of 1900–05[a]			Cohorts of 1916–20[b]		
		Actual			Actual rate by 35–39	Expected	
35–39	45–49	Rate by 35–39	Increase	Rate by 45–49		Increase	Rate by 45–49
10 or more	20 or more	2,711	75	2,786	2,699	299	2,998
5–9	15–19	1,066	572	1,638	1,723	500	2,223
0–4	10–14	486	561	1,047	944	1,084	2,028
	0–9			690			1,000[c]

[a] For wives married once, husband present. The rates by ages 45–49 are for white wives, from *United States Census of Population: 1950*, vol. IV, *Special Reports*, pt. 5, chap. C, "Fertility," p. 56. The rates by ages 35–39 are for native white wives from *Population, Differential Fertility 1940 and 1910, Fertility by Duration of Marriage*, U.S. Bureau of the Census, 1947, p. 17.

[b] From present study.

[c] Estimated, as explained in text.

than the corresponding increase which actually occurred for the earlier group according to census data.

Do these intercohort differences result from differences in the way the data were collected? If not, do they mean that the wives in the cohorts of 1916–20 tend to exaggerate their future childbearing, or that they really will bear more children and finish with substantially larger families? Only time will tell. It is probable that these wives will not have as many births as they said they would, but we are not yet ready to estimate the reduction that seems called for. (This is done in the fifth section of Chapter 10.) In consequence, their reports are used unchanged in making the estimates discussed here.

Because the wives in the 1916–20 cohorts who married before exact ages 35–39 expect to have larger families than the corresponding wives in the earlier group, a final rate of 1,000 births per 1,000 women appears to be a reasonable medium estimate for the members of the cohorts of 1916–20 who will marry between 35–39 and 45–49. Corresponding high and low estimates are 1,300 and 700.

We now have for the cohorts of 1916–20 the actual birth rates by exact ages 35–39 and the expected final rates (1) reported by the women who in 1955 were married and living with husband, and (2) estimated for the single women who will marry. These are shown on lines 2 through 9 in the top deck of Table G–4.

We shall estimate next the future birth rates for the brides-to-be in the cohorts of 1921–25, 1926–30, and 1931–35. For the comparatively few who will marry between ages 35–39 and 45–49, we shall use the birth rate estimated above for the corresponding women in the 1916–20 cohorts. This would not be acceptable if there were evidence of an upward or downward trend in the fertility of the cohorts in question. No significant change is under way, however, judging from the following comparisons of the average number of births expected by the wives in the four groups of cohorts who married at given younger ages:

| Cohorts | Average no. of births expected ("most likely") by wives married | | | |
| | Before exact ages 15–19 | | Between exact ages 15–19 and 20–24 | |
	No. of wives	Births per 1,000 wives	No. of wives	Births per 1,000 wives
1916–20	98	3,701	370	2,985
1921–25	82	3,153	391	3,166
1926–30	99	3,440	493	3,114
1931–35	123	3,361	491	3,149

TABLE G–4. PAST, EXPECTED, AND ESTIMATED FUTURE BIRTH RATES BY SPECIFIED EXACT AGES, AND INCREASES BETWEEN THESE AGES, FOR WHITE WOMEN IN GROUPS OF COHORTS WHO MARRY BY AGES 45–49, BY MARITAL STATUS AND AGE AT MARRIAGE

Marital status in 1955 and age at marriage	Proportion of total women in cohorts in 1955[a] (A)	15–19 rate (B)	Increase (C)	20–24 rate (D)	Increase (E)	25–29 rate (F)	Increase (G)	30–34 rate (H)	Increase (I)	35–39 rate (J)	Most likely Increase (K)	Most likely 45–49 rate (L)	Min. 45–49 rate (M)	Max. 45–49 rate (N)
					Actual rates and increases[b]						Expected or est. rates and increases[b]			
Cohorts of 1916–20														
1. Total marrying by 45–49[c]	948	454	384	838	574	1,412	645	2,057	454	2,511	305	2,816	2,619	2,995
2. Wives interviewed, marrying:	842	459	383	842	589	1,431	676	2,107	453	2,560	338	2,898	2,700	3,077
3. Before 15–19	98	459	1,235	1,694	859	2,553	612	3,165	353	3,518	183	3,701	3,459	3,800[d]
4. 15–19 to 19–23	370		617	617	1,022	1,639	676	2,315	402	2,717	268	2,985	2,819	3,130[d]
5. 20–24 to 24–28	270				740	740	1,060	1,800	579	2,379	383	2,762	2,591	2,952
6. 25–29 to 29–33	83						931	931	792	1,723	500	2,223	1,929	2,515
7. 30–34 to 34–38	21								944	944	1,084	2,028	1,500	2,588
8. Single, will marry:	17										1,000	1,000	700	1,300
9. 35–39 to 44–48	17										1,000	1,000	700	1,300
10. Weighted average[e]		459	383	842	589	1,431	676	2,107	453	2,560	296	2,856	2,656	3,038
11. Other already married[f]	89	404	371	775	384	1,159	421	1,580	468	2,048	551	2,599	2,417	2,765
Cohorts of 1921–25														
1. Total marrying by 45–49[c]	955	281	606	887	686	1,573	686	2,259	563	2,822	65	2,887	2,636	3,175
2. Wives interviewed, marrying:	837	284	608	892	702	1,594	719	2,313	617	2,930	52	2,982	2,737	3,267
3. Before 15–19	82	284	1,189	1,473	865	2,338	514	2,852	254	3,106	47	3,153	2,986	3,315
4. 15–19 to 19–23	391		770	770	1,168	1,938	744	2,682	448	3,130	36	3,166	2,952	3,389
5. 20–24 to 24–28	312				968	968	989	1,957	784	2,741	46	2,787	2,488	3,149
6. 25–29 to 29–33	52						830	830	1,459	2,289	218	2,507	2,217	2,978
7. 30–34 to 34–38	18								950	950	721	1,671	1,211	2,131
8. Single, will marry:	31								950	950	1,100	1,000	700	2,600
9. 35–39 to 44–48	13										1,000	1,000	700	1,300
10. Weighted average[e]		284	608	892	702	1,594	719	2,313	564	2,877	51	2,928	2,674	3,220
11. Other already married[f]	87	250	571	821	470	1,291	444	1,735	567	2,302	362	2,664	2,433	2,930

Line														
1. Total marrying by ages 45–49 [c]	955	484	458	942	913	1,855	2,750	895	2,941	191	30	2,971	2,644	3,263
2. Wives interviewed, marrying:	812	489	458	947	933	1,880	2,953	1,073	3,088	135	8	3,096	2,778	3,376
3. Before 15–19	99	489	1,273	1,762	920	2,682	3,379	697	3,379	61		3,440	3,216	3,581
4. 15–19 to 19–23	493		783	783	1,320	2,103	2,999	896	3,103	104	11	3,114	2,824	3,351
5. 20–24 to 24–28	220				1,020	1,020	2,658	1,638	2,897	239	5	2,902	2,480	3,340
6. Single, will marry:	82						900	900	2,033	1,133	206	2,239	1,790	2,687
7. 25–29 to 29–33	61						900	900	2,350	1,450	200	2,550	2,100	3,000
8. 30–34 to 34–38	14								950	950	1,100	2,050	1,500	2,600
9. 35–39 to 44–48	7										1,000	1,000	700	1,300
10. Weighted average [e]		489	458	947	933	1,880	2,816	936	2,999	183	14	3,013	2,682	3,309
11. Other already married [f]	61	430	441	871	652	1,523	2,112	589	2,399	287	343	2,742	2,441	3,011

Line														
1. Total marrying by ages 45–49 [c]	955	478	633	1,111	1,183	2,294	2,856	562	2,988	132	13	3,001	2,612	3,337
2. Wives interviewed, marrying:	614	483	634	1,117	1,655	2,772	3,178	406	3,191	13		3,191	2,838	3,462
3. Before 15–19	123	1,621	1,621	2,104	1,077	3,181	3,361	180	3,361			3,361	3,140	3,628
4. 15–19 to 19–23	491		871	871	1,799	2,670	3,132	462	3,149	17	9	3,149	2,763	3,420
5. 20–24 to 24–28	292				1,050	1,050	2,344	1,294	2,732	388		2,741	2,257	3,225
6. Single, will marry:	224					1,050	2,700	1,650	2,950	250	200	2,950	2,450	3,450
7. 25–29 to 29–33	47						900	900	2,350	1,450	1,100	2,550	2,100	3,000
8. 30–34 to 34–38	14								950	950	1,000	2,050	1,500	2,600
9. 35–39 to 44–48	7											1,000	700	1,300
10. Weighted average [e]		483	634	1,117	1,208	2,325	2,925	600	3,046	121		3,046	2,649	3,385
11. Other already married [f]	44	425	603	1,028	855	1,883	2,194	311	2,437	243	333	2,770	2,411	3,080

[a] The estimated proportion "marrying by ages 45–49" (line 1) is taken from the column for ages 45–49 in Table G–1.

The proportion "wives interviewed" (line 2) is obtained for each group of cohorts by multiplying the percentage of the ever-married women who had married by 1955 (from Table G–1) by the percentage of the ever-married women who in 1955 were currently married with husband present or in armed forces (from Table G–5). For example, for women in the cohorts of 1916–20 (who were 35–39 years old at the time of the study) Table G–1 shows that 931 per 1000 had married, and Table G–5 shows that among those who had married, 904 per 1,000 were currently married with husband present or in armed forces. The product is 842 per 1,000.

The proportion of wives interviewed who married at various ages (on lines 3 to 7 for the cohorts of 1916–20 and lines 3 and 4 for the cohorts of 1931–35) is obtained by subdividing the number on line 2 according to the distribution of the wives interviewed.

The proportions on the lines "single, will marry," are taken from Table G–2.

The proportion "other already married" (line 11) is obtained by multiplying the percentage who had married by 1955 (from Table G–1) by the percentage "other ever married" (from Table G–5).

The sum of the proportions "wives interviewed" (line 2), "single, will marry" (line 7 in the top deck, line 7 in the second deck, etc.), and "other already married" (line 8 in the top deck, line 11) equals the proportion "marrying by 45–49" (line 1).

[b] The rates for "wives interviewed" are actual if to the left of the vertical double lines, and expected or estimated if to the right. Rates for other women are partially or wholly estimated.

[c] The rates for all women who marry by 45–49 are a weighted average of those on lines 10 and 11. At each age the rates on line 10 are weighted according to the 1955 proportion of ever-married women with husband present or in armed forces shown in Table G–5, and the rates on line 11 are weighted according to the proportion of ever-married women in the other groups in Table G–5.

[d] Adjusted to allow for the failure of a few highly fertile women to state maximum expectations.

[e] Average of the lines for "wives interviewed" and for "single, will marry," by the age in question, weighted in columns B to N by the proportions in column A.

[f] Includes women who are widowed, divorced, or separated from husband for other reasons than his serving in armed forces. The rates are obtained by multiplying the rates on line 10 by the indexes in Table G–6, lower deck, line 3.

The final birth rates expected by the wives in our sample who married before 15–19 fluctuate irregularly, in part because they are based on small numbers of women; hence sampling variability is large. The final rate expected by wives marrying at ages from 15–19 up to 20–24 (the ages at which a majority of women have been marrying recently) does rise 6 per cent from the cohorts of 1916–20 to 1921–25, but is practically the same for the next two groups.

In estimating the fertility of women marrying at ages from 30–34 up to 35–39 in the three groups of cohorts, the experience and opinions of the corresponding women in the cohorts of 1916–20 are used, for the reasons just mentioned. These women had a cumulative birth rate of 944 by exact ages 35–39; the most likely rate on the basis of their expectations regarding subsequent childbearing is 2,028, with 1,500 and 2,588 as lower and upper limits (Table G–4, top deck, line 7). For the three groups of cohorts in question it is assumed that the rate by ages 35–39 will be 950 and the rate by ages 45–49 between 1,500 and 2,600, with 2,050 as a medium estimate (Table G–4, decks 2, 3, and 4, line 8).

Estimates of the birth rates of the women in the cohorts of 1926–30 and 1931–35 who will first marry between exact ages 25–29 and 30–34 are based on the actual and expected rates of corresponding women in the cohorts of 1921–25. Because of the greater uncertainty connected with the longer future period, the range between the medium and the high or low rate is widened somewhat. The results are shown in Table G–4 (decks 3 and 4, line 7).

Finally, the rates for women in the cohorts of 1931–35 who will marry between exact ages 20–24 and 25–29 are estimated from the actual rate and reported expectations of corresponding women in the cohorts of 1926–30. They appear in Table G–4, bottom deck, line 6.

Because the estimated final birth rates of the women who were single in 1955 but will marry before ages 45–49 are based on the actual rates and expectations of the wives in our study, it is appropriate to average the rates for the two groups. The weights used are the proportions as of 1955 shown in column A of Table G–4, which come from Table G–2 and the actual numbers of wives interviewed. The resulting birth rates are shown in Table G–4 on line 10 of each deck.

c. What proportion of the women in the cohorts of 1916–20 to 1931–35 had married before 1955 but were not represented in our sample? Next we shall consider the other women in the cohorts who marry before ages 45–49, namely, those who at the time of our field work had married previously but were currently widowed, divorced, legally separated from husband, or married but not living with husband because of other reasons than his serving in the armed forces. Among the white women in each group under 45–49, nearly all who have married at younger ages are currently married and living with husband rather than separated, widowed, or divorced. Estimates based on the Bureau's Current Population Survey show that in 1955 more than 90 per cent of the white ever-married women under 40, and nearly as many of those in their early 40s, were living with husband or were separated because of his military service (Table G–5). The situation was similar in 1950. This may seem surprising in view of all that is said about the high divorce rate in the United States. It should be remembered, however, that a large proportion of divorced persons remarry fairly soon. In former decades higher death rates meant a larger proportion of widows in the population, even though many who were widowed married again. In recent decades death rates have been so low that comparatively few marriages have been broken by death while the wife was under 40.

d. *What is the birth rate of widows, divorcees, and other women not living with spouse?* The cumulative effect of broken marriage on fertility

TABLE G–5. PER CENT DISTRIBUTION BY CURRENT MARITAL STATUS, FOR WHITE WOMEN WHO HAVE MARRIED PREVIOUSLY, BY AGE, 1955 AND 1950[a]

Year and marital status	Current ages						
	15–19	20–24	25–29	30–34	35–39	40–44	45–49
1955							
Total	100.0	100.0	100.0	100.0	100.0	100.0	100.0
Married (sampled in study)	91.4	93.3	93.0	90.6	90.4	87.9	84.4
Husband present	85.5	90.1	92.0	89.9	90.1	87.6	84.3
Husband in armed forces	5.9	3.2	1.0	0.7	0.3	0.3	0.1
Other ever married	8.6	6.7	7.0	9.4	9.6	12.1	15.6
Husband absent (other)	3.0	1.3	1.5	2.0	1.4	1.5	1.8
Separated	2.8	3.4	2.3	3.2	2.3	2.4	2.3
Widowed	0.2	0.3	0.6	1.1	2.5	4.3	8.2
Divorced	2.6	1.7	2.6	3.1	3.4	3.9	3.3
1950							
Total	100.0	100.0	100.0	100.0	100.0	100.0	100.0
Married, husband present	90.5	93.1	93.3	92.7	91.4	89.1	85.7
Married once	86.2	86.3	83.6	81.6	78.5	75.2	72.3
Married more than once	4.3	6.8	9.7	11.1	12.9	13.9	13.4
Other ever married	9.5	6.9	6.7	7.3	8.6	10.9	14.3
Married, husband absent	4.6	2.1	1.5	1.3	1.3	1.4	1.3
Separated	2.7	2.0	1.6	1.6	1.7	1.7	1.8
Widowed	0.3	0.5	0.8	1.4	2.3	4.0	7.6
Divorced	1.9	2.3	2.8	3.0	3.3	3.8	3.6

[a] The 1950 data are from *United States Census of Population: 1950*, vol. IV, *Special Reports*, pt. 5, chap. C, "Fertility," p. 45. The 1955 data are estimated from those for all women in *Current Population Reports: Population Characteristics*, U.S. Bureau of the Census, series P-20, no. 62, p. 8.

is not as large as might be expected. Among all ever-married white women aged 45–49 in 1950, census data show the following numbers of births per 1,000 women during prior years: 2,456 for all women, 2,487 for wives with husband present, 2,464 for widows, 1,801 for divorcees, and 2,345 for other women with husband absent (Table G–6). A generally similar pattern of relationships at younger ages is shown by the indexes in the bottom deck of the table. Census data for 1940 and 1910 give similar pictures. The important fact for the present discussion is that at each age the cumulative birth rate for all ever-married women differs from that for married women husband present—the group that makes up nearly all our sample—by less than 3 per cent. This is partly because a large majority of all ever-married women under 40 are currently living with husband (as brought out in *c*), partly because some of the married women currently living with husband had remarried after one or more marriages was dissolved in the past, and partly because the differences between the childbearing of the various marital-status groups are small to medium in size.

The average of (1) the past and expected future birth rates reported by the wives interviewed and (2) the estimated future rates for the single

TABLE G–6. NUMBER OF CHILDREN EVER BORN PER 1,000 EVER-MARRIED WHITE WOMEN, BY AGE, BY CURRENT MARITAL STATUS, 1950 CENSUS[a]

Marital status	Current ages						
	15–19	20–24	25–29	30–34	35–39	40–44	45–49
	Rates						
Total	548	1,028	1,620	2,034	2,218	2,329	2,456
Married, husband present	554	1,034	1,640	2,073	2,257	2,374	2,487
Other ever married	489	949	1,333	1,548	1,804	1,963	2,272
Husband absent	465	971	1,435	1,623	1,927	2,039	2,345
Widowed	–	1,269	1,519	1,860	2,057	2,213	2,464
Divorced	473	845	1,167	1,326	1,514	1,633	1,801
	Index[b]						
Total	99	99	99	98	98	98	99
Married, husband present	100	100	100	100	100	100	100
Other ever married	88	92	81	75	80	83	91
Husband absent	84	94	88	78	85	86	94
Widowed	–	123	93	90	91	93	99
Divorced	85	82	71	64	67	69	72

[a] *United States Census of Population: 1950*, vol. IV, *Special Reports*, pt. 5, chap. C, "Fertility," p. 45.
[b] Based on the rate for married women, husband present.

women marrying after 1955 (obtained in *b*) are assumed to represent the rates for the women who will be currently married at those ages. This assumption seems reasonable because, with few exceptions, the wives reported their expected childbearing during future years on the basis of the continuation of their present marriage. Only a very small number were seriously expecting that it would be broken by separation, divorce, or death before they reached 45–49. These rates are shown on line 10 of Table G–4. Rates for the other ever-married women are computed by multiplying these rates by the indexes shown in the bottom deck of Table G–6. The results are shown on line 11 of Table G–4.

The final step is to average the rates on lines 10 and 11 in order to obtain estimated birth rates for all the women in the cohorts who married by specified ages. In selecting the weights to be used consideration was given to these facts. First, at each age the proportion of the ever-married women who are currently married with husband present is high (84 to 93 per cent in Table G–5). Second, birth rates of other ever-married women, as a group, differ from those of women currently married with husband present by between 8 and 25 per cent (Table G–6). Third, because of the foregoing relationships, the various weighting systems which might be devised would give similar results. Fourth, the scanty information available regarding the distribution of ever-married women by marital subgroups suggests that it has been fairly stable. Fifth, there is little basis for estimating the changes that may occur. The final choice was to use as weights the proportions shown for 1955 in Table G–5, which are based on sample data collected by the Bureau of the Census.

The estimated birth rates for all women in the cohorts who will marry before ages 45–49 are shown on line 1 of each deck of Table G–4.

The next step is to use these estimated rates by exact ages as a basis for estimating rates by current ages (i.e., 6 months older), which are used in Chapter 10. This was done by means of relationships shown in cohort fertility tables. The results are shown in Tables 10–2 and 10–3.

NOTE 2. *Meaning of "increase" in the birth rate of ever-married women from one age period to another*

In Tables 10–2, 10–5, and G–4 cumulative birth rates of ever-married women up to specified current or exact ages are shown in alternate columns, and the "increases" between cumulative rates by successive ages are shown in the intervening columns. For example, in the lower deck of Table 10–2 the cumulative birth rate of native white women in the cohorts of 1931–35 who have married by ages 15–19 is 601, the rate for those who have married by ages 20–24 is 1,280, and the "increase" is 679. In the accompanying discussion the latter figure and others like it are used in evaluating the current fertility of ever-married women during the age intervals in question. These "increases" should be referred to as indexes of current fertility, but at times (to simplify terminology) they are referred to as birth "rates."

To understand their meaning let us use the following example based on 10,000 native white women in the cohorts of 1931–35. The proportions married by ages 15–19 and 20–24 are from unpublished tables; the cumulative birth rates are from Table 10–2; the cumulative numbers of births are obtained by multiplying the numbers of ever-married women by the cumulative birth rates; and the influence of mortality is ignored, because death rates during the childbearing ages are too low to affect the results significantly.

Current ages	No. ever married	Cumulative	
		Birth rate	No. of births
15–19	1,670	601	1,004
20–24	7,070	1,280	9,050
Increase	5,400	679	8,046

The "increase" in the cumulative birth rate (679) is not a birth rate, because there is no logical number of women which, when multiplied by a rate of 679 per 1,000, will yield the 8,046 births that occurred. What is needed is two birth rates, one for the 1,670 women who married before ages 15–19 and another for the 7,070 who married between ages 15–19 and 20–24. Unfortunately, it has not been feasible to include such rates in cohort fertility tables, because birth certificates lack information about duration of marriage. For the cohorts included in our study, however, we can estimate them by drawing on the experience of the wives interviewed. The results for our example are shown below:

Age at marriage	No. of women	Birth rate between ages 15–19 and 20–24[a]	No. of births
Under 15–19	1,670	1,760	2,939
Between 15–19 and 20–24	5,400	946	5,107
Total	7,070		8,046

[a]The birth rates are for a 5-year period.

The period birth rate for the ever-married women is obtained by dividing the number of births (8,046) by the average of the numbers of these women at the beginning and end of the age interval (1,670 and 7,070); it is 1,841. It should be noted that the increase of 679 in the cumulative rate is much smaller than this period rate and substantially smaller than the lower of the rates for the two subgroups shown above.

At older age intervals the number of women married before the beginning of the interval is substantially larger than the number married before the beginning of the 15–19 to 20–24 interval, and the number becoming brides during the interval is substantially smaller. For the cohorts of 1931–35 in our example, 7,070 women had married by ages 20–24, and about 1,780 will marry between ages 20–24 and 25–29. In consequence, as age rises the current birth rate for the group married before the beginning of the age interval determines in rapidly increasing degree the number of births to members of the cohort during the age interval and approaches closely the "increase" in the cumulative rates. This is shown below for the cohorts of 1916–20 during the age interval from 30–34 to 35–39, using cumulative birth rates from Table 10–2, cumulative marriage rates from unpublished tables, and the experience of the wives in our sample who were members of the 1916–20 cohorts:

Current ages	No. ever married	Cumulative	
		Birth rate	No. of births
30–34	9,060	2,105	19,071
35–39	9,310	2,478	23,070
Increase	250	373	3,999

Age at marriage	No. of women	Period	
		Birth rate	No. of births
Under 30–34	9,060	417	3,780
Between 30–34 and 35–39	250	876	219
Total	9,310		3,999

For this age interval the increase in the cumulative birth rate (373) is much closer to the period rate (435 based on the average number of ever-married women at the beginning and end of the age interval) than is the case for ages 15–19 to 20–24.

At still older age intervals (e.g., 40–44 to 45–49) some cohorts may have a small negative "increase" in the cumulative birth rate of ever-married women; i.e., the cumulative rate is smaller at ages 45–49 than at 40–44. This occurs when the increase in the proportion marrying during the age interval (which usually is somewhat less than 1 per cent) exceeds the increase in the cumulative birth rate of *all* members of the cohort (which usually is a smaller fraction of 1 per cent).

In Tables 10–2 and 10–5 it is useful to have columns showing for different groups of cohorts how the cumulative birth rate of ever-married women rises from younger to older ages. Once the "increases" in these rates are shown in the tables, it is convenient to use them as indexes in discussing intercohort changes in fertility during age intervals. The "increases" are, in fact, a type of index, appropriate for intercohort comparisons for a given age period. They should not be used, however, in comparing fertility during one age period with that during another age period.

NOTE 3. *Numbers of first marriages and births during 1955–60, estimated in July, 1958*

The projections of the first marriage rates of all women and the birth rates of ever-married women in various cohorts were made early in July, 1958. It was believed that the projected rates for the 5 years beginning July 1, 1955, when applied to the appropriate numbers of women in the cohorts concerned, should give numbers of marriages and births in line with the numbers that had already occurred since July 1, 1955, plus forecasts of the numbers during the remainder of the period.

The National Office of Vital Statistics had reported the number of marriages and births registered during 1955 and 1956 and issued provisional figures for 1957 and January–March, 1958. Estimates for April–June, 1958, were prepared on the basis of ratios between January–June and January–March, 1955–57. This gave highly accurate data for three of the five years in the 1955–60 period. Forecasts were made for the two years from July 1, 1958, to June 30, 1960, and added to the foregoing.

First marriages. The number of first marriages during 1955–56, 1956–57, and 1957–58 was estimated from the reported numbers of all marriages by assuming that 74.2 per cent of all marriages are first marriages. (This is the 1950–55 proportion for the states tabulating this information.) In the medium series we assumed that the number of marriages will drop 7 per cent from 1957–58 to 1958–59 (as it did from 1956–57 to 1957–58) and remain the same in 1959–60. The low series is based on the assumption that the number will drop 10 per cent from 1957–58 to 1958–59 and another 10 per cent from 1958–59 to 1959–60. The high assumption is that there will be as many marriages in 1958–59 and 1959–60 as in 1957–58. The resulting numbers (in thousands) are:

Year (July 1 to June 30)	All marriages	First marriages		
		Medium	Low	High
1955–56	1,551	1,151	1,151	1,151
1956–57	1,559	1,156	1,156	1,156
1957–58	1,445	1,072	1,072	1,072
1958–59		997	965	1,072
1959–60		997	868	1,072
1955–60		5,373	5,212	5,523

Births. The reported number of births during 1955–58 was increased by 1.4 per cent to allow for births not registered. (This is the adjustment factor for 1955.)

In the medium forecasts for the next two years we assumed that the number of births would decrease 5 per cent from 1957–58 to 1958–59 and another 5 per cent in the next year. The low series is based on successive decreases of 15 per cent, and the high on successive increases of 5 per cent.

The resulting numbers of births (in thousands) are:

Year (July 1 to June 30)	Births		
	Medium	Low	High
1955–56	4,149	4,149	4,149
1956–57	4,291	4,291	4,291
1957–58	4,295	4,295	4,295
1958–59	4,080	3,651	4,510
1959–60	3,876	3,103	4,736
1955–60	20,691	19,489	21,981

Later, it appeared that the low and medium needed slight upward revisions. During July–November, 1958, the number of marriages was 2.6 per cent below, and the number of births 2.0 per cent below the corresponding figures for 1957.

GLOSSARY

Symbols and Abbreviations Used in Tables

*   Average or proportion not computed because less than 20 cases in base. Sampling variability would be very large for smaller numbers. (See Appendix C, Sampling Methods and Sampling Errors.)

−   The category described by the column and line headings is possible, but it contains fewer than 0.5 per cent of the cases (if the statistic described is a proportion) or has an average that rounds to zero (if the statistic described is an average).

··   The category described by the column and line headings is not possible.

0   Occurs only in tables showing absolute numbers and means that the category is possible but contains no cases.

N.A. Not ascertained.

abortion. Unless otherwise indicated, abortion is used in the colloquial sense and denotes the illegal termination of a pregnancy. (Technically, abortion denotes the expulsion of a dead fetus during the early or middle stages of gestation, commonly defined as before 28 weeks have elapsed.)

—**induced.** *See* intentional.

—**intentional.** Performed for health or eugenic reasons or to avoid an unwanted child.

—**spontaneous.** Not induced intentionally.

Action. *See* Users, Action.

appliance method. Any method of contraception that makes use of a chemical product or a mechanical device.

artificial birth control. A term used (mostly by Catholics) in referring to chemical and appliance methods of preventing conception, which are forbidden by the Catholic Church.

birth. Synonymous with a baby born alive. (Technically it refers to the delivery of a fetus which is alive when delivery is completed.) In this study all births to the wives interviewed are included, but not the births during the previous marriages of their husbands.

birth cohort. A group of persons born in a given 12-month period. In this book the period is July 1 to June 30, and the cohort is identified by the second half year. Most of the discussion relates to cohorts of women.

birth parity. *See* parity.

497

cohort. In this report "cohort" refers to "birth cohort." *See* birth cohort.

completed family. Refers to the number of children a woman has borne by the time she has reached the end of the childbearing period (usually assumed to be between ages 45 and 50).

Completely Planned fertility. One of the fertility planning status categories used in this study. It includes couples who used contraception and (1) had no pregnancies, or (2) had all their pregnancies when contraception was stopped in order to conceive.

contraception. Denotes any or all methods of avoiding conception, except celibacy and sterilization. These methods include periodic continence (rhythm), abstinence for long periods, withdrawal (coitus interruptus), as well as such appliance or chemical methods as condom, diaphragm, jelly, and douche. This term is used with no moral connotation and as synonymous with such terms as birth control, conception control, family limitation, family planning, preventive measures, and regulating conception.

cumulative birth rate. The number of births that have occurred by a given age per 1,000 women in a cohort who live to that age. The rate may be based on all women or on the women who have married.

cumulative marriage rate. The number of first marriages occurring by a given age per 1,000 women in a cohort who live to that age.

Definitely Sterile. One of the fecundity status categories used in this study. It includes couples who cannot have children in the future, regardless of the number they have had in the past.

DFCO. *See* douche for cleanliness only.

douche for cleanliness only. Denotes (1) the use of a douche soon after intercourse, for cleanliness but not to prevent conception, and (2) the couples who have never tried to prevent conception, but the wife has used this practice.

exact age. Relates to ages which vary from 6 months less than to 6 months more than the age indicated. A group of exact ages, e.g., 20–24, includes all ages from 19.5 up to but excluding 24.5. In contrast, a group of current ages, e.g., 20–24, includes all ages from 20.0 up to but excluding 25.0.

Excess Fertility. One of the fertility planning status categories used in this study. It includes couples whose most recent pregnancy was unwanted then or later by the husband, the wife, or both.

Fecund. When capitalized, denotes couples for whom there is no evidence of impaired fecundity according to the criteria used in this study. When not capitalized, it is used as defined by the Population Association of America, i.e., "having the physiological capacity to participate in reproduction." [1]

fecundity. "The physiological capacity to participate in reproduction." [1]

fecundity categories. The two main categories used in this study are Fecund and Subfecund. Subfecund is subdivided into Definitely Sterile, Probably

[1] "Organization for Research in Population," *Human Biology,* vol. 6, no. 1, p. 238, February, 1934.

Sterile, Semifecund, and Indeterminate. For brief explanations, see each term in glossary. For more details see Chapter 2 and Appendix D.

Fecundity Indeterminate. *See* Indeterminate.

fertility. Refers to the number of children actually born, in contrast to "fecundity"—the physiological capacity for bearing children.[2]

fertility planning status categories. Three categories are used in the condensed classification, namely (1) Completely Planned, (2) Partially Planned, and (3) Excess Fertility. Nine categories are used in the detailed classification, namely (1) Completely Planned with one or more pregnancies, (2) Completely Planned, never pregnant, (3) Number Planned, (4) Quasi-planned Users, (5) Excess Fertility Users, (6) Quasi-planned Future Users, (7) Quasi-planned Nonusers, (8) Excess Fertility Future Users, and (9) Excess Fertility Nonusers. *See* Figure 3–8.

fetal death. The death of a product of conception (fetus) prior to its complete expulsion or separation from the mother.

fetal death rate. The number of known fetal deaths per 1,000 known fetuses (the sum of babies born alive and known fetal deaths). Many fetal deaths occur too early in pregnancy to be recognized and reported.

final birth rate. The cumulative rate by the end of the childbearing period, usually assumed to be between ages 45 and 50.

Indeterminate. One of the fecundity status categories used in this study. It includes the couples who cannot be classified as to fecundity because the wife douched for cleanliness only soon after intercourse. Not all DFCO couples are Fecundity Indeterminate, but only those who never did anything to prevent conception, who had no conception during one or more long periods (3 years for wives who have been pregnant and 2 years for those who have not), and whose average interval between births (if any occurred) was 3 years or longer.

Indianapolis Study. The study "Social and Psychological Factors Affecting Fertility," conducted in Indianapolis in 1941. *See* Appendix A, Note 2, for details.

marriage duration. Usually refers in this report to the length of time from a wife's first marriage to the day she was interviewed.

miscarriage. The lay term for what is technically called a "spontaneous" or "unintentional" abortion. It usually refers to a spontaneous abortion occurring before the end of the seventh or eighth month of gestation; one occurring later is usually called a "stillbirth."

Motive. *See* Users, Motive.

Nonusers. Couples who have never tried to prevent conception, i.e., who have never used any method of contraception. In this analysis douching for cleanliness only soon after intercourse is considered a method of contraception on an Action basis but not on a Motive basis.

Number and Spacing Planned. *See* Completely Planned fertility.

Number Planned. One of the fertility planning status categories used in this study. It includes couples whose last conception occurred when contra-

[2] *Ibid.*

ception was stopped in order to have a child but who had one or more previous conceptions under other conditions.

occupational categories. Those used for husbands in this study are: upper white collar—proprietors, managers, officials, and professional workers; lower white collar—salesmen, clerical, and kindred workers; upper blue collar—craftsmen, foremen, and kindred workers; lower blue collar—operatives and kindred workers, service workers, and laborers (nonfarm); farm—farmers, farm managers, and farm laborers. The foregoing categories exclude husbands who were in the armed forces, who were not in the labor force, or whose occupation was not ascertained.

parity. Denotes the number of children a woman has borne; i.e., a zero-parity woman has not borne a child, a one-parity (or first-parity) woman has borne one child, etc.

Partially Planned fertility. One of the fertility planning status categories used in this study. It includes (1) couples who wanted their last pregnancy but did not plan it by stopping contraception in order to conceive; and (2) couples who have had no pregnancy and have not used contraception.

period rates. Rates that relate to events (births, deaths, or marriages in this book) that occur in a specified time interval (usually a calendar year or group of years) as distinguished from those that occur during the lifetime of a cohort.

periodic continence. Refraining from intercourse during the fecund period of the wife's menstrual cycle in an effort to avoid conception.

pregnancy. Refers to all pregnancies of the wives interviewed, including those occurring during previous marriages.

—accidental. Conception occurred in spite of preventive efforts.

—completed. One which had terminated with a birth or a fetal death.

—other unplanned. Conception occurred while contraception was stopped for other reasons than the desire for a child.

—planned. Conception occurred after contraception was discontinued because a (another) child was wanted by wife, husband, or both.

—uncompleted. One in progress when the wife was interviewed.

—unplanned. Conception occurred while contraception was being practiced or was stopped for other reasons than to have a child. It includes accidental and "other unplanned" pregnancies.

—unwanted. Before conception occurred the wife, the husband, or both did not want a child at any future time.

pregnancy wastage. The termination of pregnancy in fetal death rather than birth.

probability sample. A sample selected in such a way that every member of the whole group under study has an equal chance of being included.

Probably Sterile. One of the fecundity status categories used in this study. It includes couples for whom a future birth is considered to be improbable (rather than impossible) on the basis of the specific physical limitations that were reported. For most of these couples conception is improbable. Conception is not improbable for the other couples, but pregnancy would be (1) unlikely to result in a birth (e.g., because of a history of repeated fetal deaths), or (2) a serious threat to the wife's health.

pure community type. A classification of couples by size of place of present residence, which is limited to couples who lived in a place of this size most of their lives (both before and after marriage). Four types of places are distinguished: (1) large city (above 50,000), (2) small city (below 50,000), (3) rural nonfarm, (4) farm. See Appendix A, Note 15, for details.

Quasi-planned fertility. One of the fertility planning status categories used in this study. It includes (1) couples whose last pregnancy was wanted when it occurred or later, but was not planned by stopping contraception in order to conceive; and (2) couples who have never had a pregnancy but have not used contraception.

rhythm. *See* periodic continence.

sampling error. The deviation of a statistical value for a sample from the value for the whole group from which the sample was selected.

Semifecund. One of the fecundity status groups used in this study. It includes couples who had no conception during one or more long periods when contraception was not used and the wife did not douche for cleanliness only soon after intercourse. (A long period is defined as 3 years for wives who have ever been pregnant and 2 years for those who have not.) An additional requirement for couples who had had births is that the average interval between births must be 3 years or longer.

Sterile, Definitely. *See* Definitely Sterile.

Sterile, Probably. *See* Probably Sterile.

sterilizing operation. An operation on wife or husband which makes conception impossible. Some of these operations are contraceptive in intent; others are performed to safeguard a wife's health or for eugenic reasons even though the couple may want a (another) child.

stillbirth. Lay term for the delivery of a dead fetus, usually after the seventh or eighth month of pregnancy. *See also* miscarriage.

Subfecund. One of the fecundity status categories used in this study. It includes all couples not classified as Fecund. *See* Fecund, fecundity categories.

Users. Couples who at some time have tried to prevent conception, i.e., have used some method of contraception. Unless otherwise specified in this report the group does not include couples who did not use any method of contraception but the wife douched for cleanliness only soon after intercourse. *See also* Users, Action, and Users, Motive.

—Action. Couples who have used some method to prevent conception *and* those whose wives have douched for cleanliness only soon after intercourse.

—Future. Nonusers who expect to use later some method of preventing conception.

—**Motive.** Couples who have deliberately attempted to prevent conception. Excludes DFCO couples, who may be unwittingly practicing contraception.

—**Never.** Couples who expect to remain Nonusers.

—**Past.** Couples who have already practiced contraception.

INDEX